Fix Your Own PC

7th Edition

Corey Sandler

Wiley Publishing, Inc.

Fix Your Own PC, 7th Edition

Wiley Publishing, Inc.
909 Third Avenue
New York, NY 10022

Library of Congress Control Number: 2002107904

ISBN: 0-7645-4944-8

Printed in the United States of America

10 9 8 7 6 5 4 3 2 1

7O/RZ/QW/QS/IN

Distributed in the United States by Wiley Publishing, Inc.

Distributed by CDG Books Canada Inc. for Canada; by Transworld Publishers Limited in the United Kingdom; by IDG Norge Books for Norway; by IDG Sweden Books for Sweden; by IDG Books Australia Publishing Corporation Pty. Ltd. for Australia and New Zealand; by TransQuest Publishers Pte Ltd. for Singapore, Malaysia, Thailand, Indonesia, and Hong Kong; by Gotop Information Inc. for Taiwan; by ICG Muse, Inc. for Japan; by Intersoft for South Africa; by Eyrolles for France; by International Thomson Publishing for Germany, Austria, and Switzerland; by Distribuidora Cuspide for Argentina; by LR International for Brazil; by Galileo Libros for Chile; by Ediciones ZETA S.C.R. Ltda. for Peru; by WS Computer Publishing Corporation, Inc., for the Philippines; by Contemporanea de Ediciones for Venezuela; by Express Computer Distributors for the Caribbean and West Indies; by Micronesia Media Distributor, Inc. for Micronesia; by Chips Computadoras S.A. de C.V. for Mexico; by Editorial Norma de Panama S.A. for Panama; by American Bookshops for Finland.

For general information on Wiley products and services please contact our Customer Care department within the U.S. at 800-762-2974, outside the U.S. at 317-572-3993 or fax 317-572-4002.

For sales inquiries and reseller information, including discounts, premium and bulk quantity sales, and foreign-language translations, please contact our Customer Care department at 800-434-3422, fax 317-572-4002 or write to Wiley Publishing, Inc., Attn: Customer Care Department, 10475 Crosspoint Boulevard, Indianapolis, IN 46256.

For information on licensing foreign or domestic rights, please contact our Sub-Rights Customer Care department at 212-884-5000.

For information on using Wiley products and services in the classroom or for ordering examination copies, please contact our Educational Sales department at 800-434-2086 or fax 317-572-4005.

For press review copies, author interviews, or other publicity information, please contact our Public Relations department at 317-572-3168 or fax 317-572-4168.

For authorization to photocopy items for corporate, personal, or educational use, please contact Copyright Clearance Center, 222 Rosewood Drive, Danvers, MA 01923, or fax 978-750-4470.

Wiley Publishing, Inc.

Fix Your Own PC

7th Edition

About the Author

Corey Sandler is one of the pioneers of computer journalism. After covering IBM for Gannett Newspapers and the Associated Press, he became the first executive editor of *PC Magazine*. He was later the founding editor of *Digital News*. Sandler has written more than 180 books on computer, business, video game, and travel topics. Recent bestsellers include *Fix Your Own PC*, 6th Edition (IDG Books Worldwide, Inc., 2000), *Buy More Pay Less* (Prentice Hall Press, 1998), and the Econoguide Travel Book series (Contemporary Books).

Credits

Acquisitions Director
Andy Cummings

Acquisitions Editor
Gregory Croy

Project Editors
Rebekah Mancilla, Kevin Kent, Pat O'Brien

Technical Editor
Tom Badgett

Editorial Assistant
Amanda Foxworth

Editorial Manager
Ami Frank Sullivan

Vice President and Executive Group Publisher
Richard Swadley

Proofreaders
John Greenough, Susan Moritz, Carl Pierce,
Christine Pingleton, Linda Quiqley

Indexer
Steve Rath

Project Coordinator
Nancee Reeves

To my father, who showed me the way things work.
Ask me how to drive to the post office,
and I explain how a carburetor works.

Acknowledgments

Let's take a look behind the scenes of this book:

At the Word Association offices, Janice Keefe managed operations and the author with good cheer and professionalism. Tom Badgett, regular squadron leader of my high-tech flying circus, worried the bits and bytes as technical editor for this edition.

Thanks to Pat O'Brien, Kevin Kent, and Greg Croy of Wiley Publishing, Inc. for their capable stewardship of the manuscript.

They follow in the capable footsteps of old friends Tracy Brown, Sharon Eames, Ed Adams, Martine Edwards, Juliana Aldous, Terry Somerson, Brenda McLaughlin, Paul Farrell, Jono Hardjowirigo, and Michael Sprague, champions of the book in its earlier editions.

Thanks, too, to copy editor Rebekah Mancilla as well as the entire production and art team at Wiley Publishing, Inc.

Photographer Jack Weinhold once again worked his magic in the photo studio. Nearly all the pictures in this book were created without benefit of film with a high-resolution digital camera.

Preface

What? You want me to take off the covers of my PC and poke around inside?

Yes, actually. That's the reason you bought this book, right?

But wait: I'll be very gentle. And all the work will be very basic. We are *not* going to be building a PC from nuts and bolts; there will be no wiring and soldering involved.

This is the seventh time that we have come together in these pages, and the pace of change from edition to edition continues to increase. Computers are faster and more capable than ever. However, as underlying technology of personal computers becomes more and more complex, the process of making repairs and upgrades becomes more and more simple.

More so than ever, computers are a mix-and-match product. Think about it: You don't throw away your car when the battery fails or a tire goes flat; you can even consider major changes, such as replacing an engine with a more powerful or updated model. So, too, you can update your computer and its memory, drives, and adapters.

And as computers and software become smarter, they are capable of assisting you in their own upkeep. Modern motherboards, controller chips, and adapters can report on the health of a system, working closely with software enhancements, including Plug-and-Play extensions to the Windows operating systems.

All that said, I will be the first to admit that I once trembled at the thought of applying a screwdriver to a brand-spanking-new PC. But I can assure you that after you add more memory, plug in the first video card, and install the first hard drive, you'll find yourself prowling the corridors of your office or the streets of your town in search of more challenging electronic territory to conquer.

Why Fix Your Own PC?

First of all, you should consider fixing your own PC *because you can.*

PCs are constructed with a modular design — a sort of high-tech Lcgo set — that lets even nontechnical types unplug one module and replace it with another quite easily. The biggest challenge is not the actual repair or upgrade process but figuring out which modules to change.

And although computers have become incredibly more complex over their short history, the number of modules within them has actually decreased. Memory is now installed in huge blocks instead of bit by bit, and motherboards are now highly integrated, meaning that they include many functions that used to be handled by accessories.

Fix Your Own PC will help you do it yourself so that you can save time and money, customize your system in every way, and give yourself the sense of pride that comes with accomplishing work on your own.

This book is your personal guide to diagnosing, fixing, and understanding your PC. I direct you in words, with tons of photos and illustrations, as well as troubleshooting flowcharts through all the nooks and crannies of your personal computer.

Who Should Read This Book?

Repairing a PC is much less physically challenging than fixing a toaster, a bicycle, or an automobile. It does, though, require quite a bit more expenditure of logical energy. In other words, this is a job that exercises the muscle between your ears.

This book is not for the PC technician, the microelectronics designer, or the neighborhood propeller-head who wants to build a PC from a box of resistors, transistors, copper wire, and chewing gum. Not that there's anything wrong with that. . . .

Instead, this book is for the intelligent, adventurous, nontechnical PC user. You are someone who's not afraid to take a screwdriver to a PC (or if you are, you soon won't be anymore), and you want to know how to change a hard drive, fix balky memory, or figure out why your monitor has gone black.

This book presents news that you can use. Just like you don't have to know how a carburetor works in order to drive to the post office, you don't have to know the coercivity levels of the read-write head in order to install a hard drive.

The Tools You Need

Repair jobs on PCs require few specialized tools. You can purchase a simple computer tool kit from mail-order houses or computer superstores. Here's a basic kit for all the projects in this book:

1. **A set of good-quality Phillips-head screwdrivers.** These are the screwdrivers with the X-shaped head. You want small-, medium-, and large-diameter heads.

2. **A set of standard flat-blade screwdrivers.** You should have screwdrivers in small, medium, and large sizes.

3. **An antistatic strap or grounding pad.** These inexpensive devices are available at most computer stores or through mail-order outfits.

Other inexpensive niceties include an IC extraction tool, an IC pin straightener, and a claw part holder to grab onto tiny screws and start them into a hole.

I also suggest that you have at hand a vacuum cleaner with a soft bristle brush end and also a strong pinpoint light source. You also need a clean and sturdy work surface; I recommend a desk or table with a white or light-colored surface.

That's all you need to make nearly any repair or upgrade to a PC. If you choose to get into some advanced projects, you'll want to beg, steal, or borrow a multifunction voltmeter.

What's in This Book?

This is the seventh edition of *Fix Your Own PC*. Through the years, this book has helped hundreds of thousands of readers understand how their PCs work — and to solve the knotty modern-day problems that sooner or later afflict your electronic desktop companion.

These pages cover PCs from the first IBM right through to the latest Intel Pentium 4, Intel Celeron, Intel Itanium, AMD Athlon, and AMD Duron screamers. This book's newest edition has been completely updated and expanded, and it includes details on new technologies, the latest accelerated graphics port (AGP) in 2X and 4X forms; the Universal Serial Bus (USB), including version 2.0; Ultra and Wide SCSI; enhanced IDE controllers and hard drives; new memory technologies, including RDRAM and EDO; CD-Rs and CD-RWs, DVDs; and much more.

How This Book Is Organized

This book consists of 24 chapters, 7 appendixes, a glossary, and a special section of troubleshooting flowcharts that guide you to the sections of the book that will best help you diagnose and fix your PC's problems.

I begin with an exploration of the modular design of the computer, move on to a discussion of the family tree of CPUs (the microprocessor brain of the PC), delve into BIOS chips (the set of basic instructions for the hardware), and then look at the bus (the superhighway that interconnects the parts).

Next, I discuss some basic hardware skills, including a tour of the motherboard. And then I take apart a brand-new machine.

From there, it's on to detailed chapters covering major components of the machine — from memory to floppy and hard drives, monitors, serial and parallel ports, modems, printers, mice, and scanners.

A synopsis of each chapter

Chapter 1: Looking Under the Hood. Start with this chapter to take a look under the hoods of personal computers — whether dinosaurs, senior citizens, or modern machines.

Chapter 2: The Microprocessor. Here you perform a bit of PC psychiatry, examining the brain of your computer's CPU.

Chapter 3: BIOS. Here you learn how to determine which BIOS you have, and how and why to update it.

Chapter 4: The Computer Bus. This chapter explores the current PCI bus and its new extensions, as well as the older industry standard architecture (ISA) or AT-bus, PC cards, and senior citizen and dinosaur buses.

Chapter 5: Basic Hardware Skills. You learn the tools of the trade while investigating the basic components of the computer in detail, from the case and cover to the motherboard and expansion cards, the CPU and BIOS, system memory, and more.

Chapter 6: Step-by-Step through a Modern Machine. In the service of the reader, I take apart a brand-new Pentium 4 PC to show all its parts and prepare the way for repairs and upgrades to any machine.

Chapter 7: Shopping for PC Parts. This chapter explores the minimum configuration for current versions of Windows including XP, 2000, and Me, as well as older editions including Windows 95/98 and the senior-citizen Windows 3.1 operating system.

Chapter 8: Memory. Computer memory is the essential thinking space for your machine. In this chapter, you learn about types of memory and as much technical background as you need to understand how they work.

Chapter 9: Floppy Drives. This chapter introduces you to storage technologies as well as troubleshooting and repair strategies for floppy disk drives and controllers.

Chapter 10: Hard Drives. Faster, larger, cheaper . . . what more could you want? How about a user's guide to understanding and troubleshooting hard drive types, interfaces, and cabling.

Chapter 11: Removable Hard Drives. Here I discuss removable storage devices, from high-capacity floppies, such as the Zip drive and the SuperDisk, to the gigabyte-sized cartridge systems. I also introduce the CD-recordable device.

Chapter 12: CD and DVD Drives. This chapter is where you learn about the hardware side of CD-ROMs, CD-Rs, CD-RWs, and DVD drives.

Chapter 13: Video Display Adapters and Standards. In this chapter, you learn about the history and technology of video adapters, from dinosaur CGA, MDA, EGA, and other ancient systems to modern VGA and SVGA controllers.

Chapter 14: Monitors and LCDs. And, of course, you need to have a screen to view your computer's work in progress. Here I explore the types of monitors available for your PC and then explain the essential components of a high-quality display.

Chapter 15: Serial, USB, and FireWire Connections. How a serial port works and how to troubleshoot it when it doesn't — that's what you learn in this chapter. You also learn about Universal

Serial Bus (USB) technology and about the FireWire protocol for high-speed serial communication.

Chapter 16: Modems. Without a modem, you'd have no Internet, no America Online, and no easy way to play Super Space Creature Massacre with your cousin in Columbus. In this chapter, you learn about how to choose and troubleshoot a modem.

Chapter 17: The Parallel Interface. This chapter delves into the original parallel port (sometimes referred to as unidirectional), as well as more recent bidirectional, enhanced parallel port, and enhanced capabilities port designs.

Chapter 18: Hard Copy. Put your words and pictures on paper with a printer. This is the place to learn about types of printers, from dinosaur daisywheels to state-of-the-art ink jet and laser devices.

Chapter 19: Your Computer's Hands, Eyes, and Ears. Reach in and control your PC through the keyboard or with a mouse or give it a view with a scanner or a digital camera. And lend an ear to a guide to sound cards and game ports. You learn about the hardware and the repair strategies for each within these pages.

Chapter 20: Networks, Gateways, and Routers. Get connected: setting up a small office or home network to share computers, printers, and modems.

Chapter 21: Living the Good Life: Backing Up Regularly. Before you have to deal with the hardware side of a system failure, read this chapter to learn about strategies and methods for making back-up copies of your work in a safe place — on a removable disk, on another PC, or in other ways.

Chapter 22: Diagnostic and Reporting Programs. Utilities are power tools for savvy PC users; they extend the operating system and your applications in ways that make your machine adapt to you instead of the other way around. One specialized, essential utility is a capable diagnostic program to give your PC a health check. And I begin with a discussion of a must for any computer user: an antivirus program.

Chapter 23: Troubleshooting Windows. Current versions of the Microsoft operating system offer some powerful utilities for configuring and troubleshooting your PC, including Device Manager, the Maintenance Wizard, and the System Information Utility.

Chapter 24: Commonsense Solutions to Common Problems. You are not alone: Here are some sensible solutions to knotty problems that the gurus of hardware and software have revealed.

Appendixes

The appendixes contain references to some of the essential — and arcane — communications that you receive from a PC in distress, a listing of hardware and software suppliers and manufacturers, and an encyclopedia of cable connectors.

Also, let your fingers do the walking though 11 flowcharts that help you figure out the source of problems in your system.

The charts begin with diagnosing a dead machine and move on to specific problems with floppy disks, hard disk drives, parallel ports, serial ports, multimedia devices, and video quality. And finally, there's a guide to decision-making after an electrical disaster.

Each of the charts includes a cross-reference to the appropriate chapter of this book for details on troubleshooting, repair, and replacement.

Glossary

PCs are covered here from A (accelerated graphics port) to Z (ZIF socket) and everything in between, with nearly 500 definitions of terms used in this book and in the instruction manuals for your system and software.

Icons

To help you identify important points, I use several icons throughout the book.

CROSS-REFERENCE

Follow the link to more details elsewhere in the book.

WARNING

Here be dragons — don't say you weren't warned.

NOTE

Here's more than you may want to know about the subject.

Modern Machines, Senior Citizens, and Dinosaurs

Throughout this book, I make an important distinction between what I call modern machines, senior citizens, and dinosaurs.

- **Modern machines** are those that can work with current operating systems (Windows XP, Windows Me, Windows 2000, Windows 98, Windows 95, and Windows NT) and can use current hardware peripherals. With this seventh edition, modern machines begin with Intel's Pentium II chips, moving onto Intel Celeron, Pentium III, and Pentium 4 CPUs. Also included are the AMD Athlon and K6 microprocessors. In this edition, the Pentium II processor moves to the endangered species list.
- **Senior citizens** include machines that are still capable of productive work and deserving of our respect, even though they have lost more than a few steps to the new chips on the block. This group includes the original Intel Pentium series as well as the Intel 486 family, in DX, DX-2, and DX-4 versions. The decision whether to perform life-prolonging surgery on these machines or to pull the plug is a close call.
- **Dinosaurs** are based on the obsolete 8088, 8086, 80286, 386, and 486SX microprocessors — including IBM PCs, PC-XTs,

and PC-ATs, as well as dozens of clone machines using the same chips. They're interesting to historians and collectors, but not well adapted to the modern era. But if you want to keep one alive or if it is essential to resuscitate a dinosaur in order to retrieve data, I instruct you on how to make repairs to these devices, too.

Modern machines generally use advanced bus designs, including PCI and PCI/ISA mixes, while senior citizens usually employ ISA, EISA, or VL designs. Dinosaurs generally limp along with a poky PC or AT bus.

Don't let your eyes glaze over with this sudden introduction to the alphabet soup of the PC world. I translate most technical terms as I introduce them; you can also turn to the Glossary at the end of this book for more help.

If you're truly starting from scratch, I also help you figure out exactly what type of machine lies beneath the covers.

And don't feel that all is lost if you happen to be the somewhat proud owner of a senior citizen. It is still possible to get a reasonable amount of work from an older machine, and it is also possible in some cases to upgrade a senior citizen to near-modern capabilities in a cost-effective manner. I discuss your options in this book.

How to Reach Me

You can contact the author at the following address. Please enclose a stamped, self-addressed envelope if you want a written reply. No phone calls, please.

Corey Sandler
Word Association, Inc.
P.O. Box 2779
Nantucket, MA 02584
USA

My Web page is at www.econoguide.com.
You can also send me e-mail at csandler@econoguide.com.

Contents at a Glance

Contents

CHAPTER 14   MONITORS AND LCDs   380

Chapter 17 The Parallel Interface   440

Chapter 18 Hard Copy   450

Chapter 21 Living the Good Life: Backing Up Regularly — 514

Fix Your Own PC

7th Edition

Chapter 1

Tools Needed:

- Phillips screwdriver
- Antistatic strip, wrist strap, or grounding pad

Looking Under the Hood

Welcome to anatomy class. It's time to prepare for open-case surgery on your computer.

This chapter takes a look under the hood of your machine. Along the way, I tell you what you can expect to see inside a range of modern machines, as well as some older, still-useful senior citizens of PC society. Later on in the book, I explore individual components in much greater detail. But the first step in understanding the way your machine works is to expose the innards of your computer.

Before you remove the cover, turn off the computer and unplug it. Why do both? This is a great habit to get into in order to protect yourself from mental lapses — sort of a belt-and-suspenders kind of thing.

NOTE

Some advice-givers suggest that you turn off the computer but leave it plugged into the wall outlet. In that way, they reason, the computer is grounded and there's less chance of damage from static electricity. This reasoning is true enough, but I don't like that procedure. For example, although the power switch may be off, the switch itself and in some instances the power supply may contain line voltage and a dropped screw

or tool can cause major damage. Additionally, the power cord from the computer to the wall socket is an attractive nuisance; sooner or later you're going to trip over it and crash the machine to the floor. Instead of taking chances, invest in a grounding strap and use it religiously.

No electricity circulates in the computer when it's off and unplugged. Actually, very little shock hazard exists when the computer is on — as long as you never disassemble the sealed power supply or the monitor. The computer bus runs on the 3.3-, 5-, or 12-volt DC current that comes out of a properly functioning power supply.

However, you face the potential danger of short-circuiting components of an electrified system if you touch a screwdriver across the traces of the motherboard or drop a bracket into the works. Also, plugging a card into the powered-up bus or plugging a cable into a connector can momentarily short some of the electrical lines and destroy the motherboard or a peripheral.

And so, *Fix Your Own PC* **basic repair rule number one** is this: Avoid touching the interior of a powered-on computer with any metallic tool, adapter card, screw, or cable.

One more note about electricity: You can very easily damage the microprocessor, memory chips, and other components if you stroll across the carpeted floor of your office or den and deliver from your fingertips a static electricity shock of a few thousand volts.

Therefore, *Fix Your Own PC* **basic repair rule number two** is this: Ground yourself before you lay hands on the innards of a PC, an adapter, a memory module, or any other exposed electronic device.

> **NOTE**
>
> One easy way to ground yourself is to touch the unpainted center screw that holds the plastic cover over the nearest electric outlet. Don't stick your finger in the outlet; just touch the screw. (If the screw is painted, scrape off a spot to make a better electrical contact.) This technique works well for most buildings and wiring schemes. Remember, however, that older buildings may not fully adhere to modern electrical codes and outlet boxes may be floating without a good ground connection. For purposes of discharging any static electricity in your body, this metallic contact may still be sufficient; however, don't depend on older house or office wiring to offer a real ground through the outlet box.

If you're going to be doing repair work regularly, you should make the worthwhile investment of a few dollars in an antistatic strip, wrist strap, or grounding pad with a wire that is connected to an electrical ground. The straps cost just a few dollars and are an inexpensive solution to a potentially dangerous and costly problem. Figure 1-1 shows an example of an antistatic strap in use.

Next, prepare your operating room. You don't want to add to your troubles by crashing your system to the floor. That leads to *Fix Your Own PC* **basic repair rule number three**: Place the computer on a sturdy surface under a strong light.

You have to remove screws and most or all of the cables that attach to the computer in order to remove the cover. Therefore, *Fix Your Own PC* **basic repair rule number four** is this: Remember, you've got to put this thing back together.

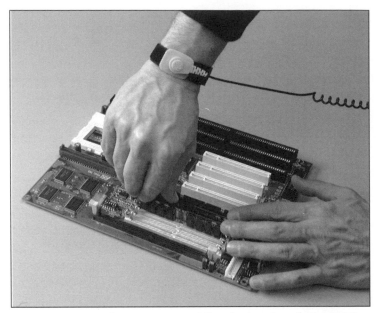

FIGURE 1-1: *A good way to protect the electronics of your PC from static electricity is to wear an antistatic wrist strap that attaches to an electrical ground, such as a cold water pipe or the center screw on a power outlet.*

Keep a small, compartmentalized box at hand to hold screws and other parts; an empty egg carton around the house or office will work well. You should also have a notepad, a roll of masking tape, and a marker pen. Keep notes on any unusual steps in disassembling the case and use the tape and pen to mark cables with their intended destination. (You could even color-code parts that go together.)

The Case for Computer Cases

The computer case has two important purposes:

- To hold the contents in a safe, cool, and relatively clean environment
- To keep radio frequency radiation within

A properly designed case supports the motherboard mechanically and electrically and gives you all the room that you need for internal hard drives, floppy drives, and adapter cards, along with providing easily accessible input-output ports for keyboards, a mouse, and external peripherals, such as a monitor and printer.

NOTE

Electromagnetic shielding is increasingly important as modern machines move data at faster and faster speeds. In order to pass Federal Communications Commission (FCC) regulations, when the PC is sold, the case must present an essentially unbroken wall with all openings filled to keep electromagnetic waves generated by the computer inside the chassis.

Radio station PC

PC cases are available in dozens of types, but nearly all follow the same basic design: a heavy metal shell that slides tightly into place over a metal frame that holds the computer's motherboard and all the internal devices attached to it.

Why all this heavy metal? Blame it on or credit it to the government — the Federal Communications Commission to be exact. All electronic devices, including microprocessors, generate electrical signals that can become interference; they become, in effect, tiny local radio transmitters. As long as the signals are bouncing around within a closed metal box, that's where they will stay.

The problems of radio frequency (RF) interference became worse as PCs began to operate faster and faster. Currently, the fastest microcomputing chips commercially available have reached 2 GHz, with plans for 3.5 GHz and more.

Consider for a moment that the clock speed of the original IBM PC was an anemic 4.77 MHz (MHz stands for megahertz, meaning one million cycles per second), and you can gain some perspective on just how fast processors are running today. A 2 GHz CPU operates about 450 times faster than an original 4.77 MHz microprocessor; advances in bus speeds and memory

technologies push the differential to the equivalent of thousands of times faster.

Therefore, to avoid interference with your neighbor's garage door opener, your kids' television set, or the PC in the next cubicle, the FCC requires that all computers be tested for RF leakage. The solution to passing the test generally involves heavy metal cases, internal shielding, and less obvious solutions, including little copper fingers that help extend an electronic girdle around your interfering PC. Figure 1-2 shows an example of a basic desktop PC that includes a copper protective shield.

FIGURE 1-2: *Slide the cover back away from the flange at the front of the case and then lift the cover up and away. On some machines, you find copper fingers that are part of the system's defense against release of RF radiation.*

CROSS-REFERENCE

You can find more detail on current microprocessors in Chapter 2.

WARNING

When the computer is in your hands, however, nothing prevents you from leaving slot covers off or even running the PC without its cover. Neither is a good idea because you end up endangering the life of your PC and the quality of radio signals in your home or office. In addition to permitting broadcast of stray radio signals, operating the computer without covers may introduce dirt into the disk drives and onto the electrical contacts, and allow metal objects like paper clips or staples or a cup of coffee to fall in and short the wires, and interfere with the cooling air flow of the PC's fan.

Though stray electromagnetic radiation won't harm the computer or cause it to malfunction, it may cause interference with televisions, FM radios, portable and cellular telephones, and other devices whenever the computer is on. And although prevailing wisdom is that electromagnetic radiation is not a threat to human beings — at least at the levels present in a PC — it is good practice to stay an arm's length away from your computer and the video monitor and to keep slot covers and cases on.

NOTE

Lightweight laptop or portable computers have electromagnetic shielding, too — even those with plastic cases. Some portables, for example, have aluminum plates embedded in the plastic. Another solution that laptops employ is to apply a layer of aluminum paint over the plastic parts.

PCs by the case

Cases are available in either desktop (full, low-profile, or baby sizes) or tower (full and mid-size) models.

A *baby case* is a tightly packed, slimmed-down box with limited options for expansion. A *low-profile* case, just as the name implies, is designed to squeeze the equivalent of ten pounds of computer into a five-pound case.

My strong preference is for *tower cases*, in either full-size or mid-size designs, like the one shown in Figure 1-3 and, undressed, in Figure 1-4. Towers usually offer considerably more room for additional internal hard drives, CD-ROM and DVD drives, Zip drives, SuperDisks, and the like. And they usually include larger power supplies to support those extra devices. In general, a larger power supply is a good thing to have because it allows a healthy margin for those times when the CD-ROM drive is loading to the hard drive while the network card is pumping data across the Ethernet and the high-end video card is displaying a complex graphic; modern switching power supplies adjust their output to the need.

FIGURE 1-3: *Vertical or tower cases offer maximum expandability. This sturdy case has a pair of drive cages that can hold three 5.25-inch devices and four 3.5-inch drives.*

FIGURE 1-4: *The cover of this tower case lifts up and away to expose both sides of the internal frame within. A new motherboard is shown here connected to electrical and data cables before installation in the case.*

Another advantage of a tower unit is that it is designed to sit on the floor, so it does not take up precious desk space. However, almost any computer can be mounted on its side; just take care to support it properly so that it does not tip over. One way to add this support is with a snap-on support that adds a wider base to the desktop case. Such units are available from office supply stores and computer stores.

Note that some older CD-ROM drives, especially those that use a caddy to carry the disc, may not work in any position other than horizontal.

Opening the case

Consult your instruction manual to see whether your computer's case uses any unusual fasteners or means of closing.

Begin by unplugging the power cord. It is a good practice to also unplug all cables leading into the PC — video, printer, modem, keyboard, and mouse. If the connectors on the PC are not labeled, tape small paper tags on the back panel to identify the ports; add corresponding identification labels to the cables.

A standard Phillips screwdriver will remove the screws on a PC case; you may also be able to use a socket wrench or nut driver. Some older computers used special screws that required a hex driver for removal; when I find a machine like that, one of the first things I do is rummage through my toolbox for a set of standard replacement screws. The same applies to some older Compaq models that use Torx screws; you need to obtain a star-shaped Torx screwdriver to remove the fasteners.

NOTE

Many systems have a few smaller screws around the air exhaust from the power supply fan; you don't want to remove them to get to the innards of the case. Consult the instruction manual for your PC if you have any doubts about the location of the screws.

Some manufacturers have introduced screwless cases that substitute simple latches or thumbscrews. You can also purchase large plastic screws and substitute them for the original metal screws to make it a bit easier to remove a standard cover. Figure 1-5 shows an example of a state-of-the-art case opening with the push of a pair of latches at each end, like a clamshell, to reveal an easy-to-work-on interior.

Remove the cover screws and then pull the cover forward and up, or backward and up, depending on the design. The tower case sometimes has a full-length plastic faceplate with lights and cutouts for the floppy drives. Some older models won't let you remove the floppy or hard disk drives until you snap this plastic cover off. Other tower models mount this faceplate semipermanently with screws and let you slip the drives out from the back. Examine your computer's manual and use your own judgment.

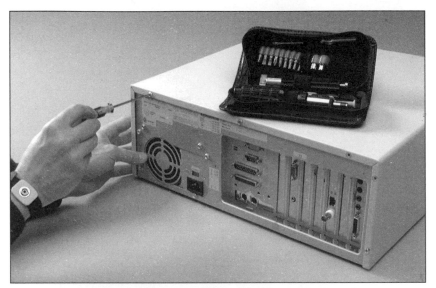

FIGURE 1-5: *This ultramodern case opens with the push of two buttons. In this photo, the motherboard sits on the desktop while the upright half of the case holds the drive cage with a CD-R, hard drive, and floppy disk drive.*

A desktop computer case, like the one shown in Figure 1-6, usually has four or five screws on the back panel to hold its cover in place. A tower case may have four to six screws.

Another case design has panels on each of the vertical sides of the tower case. Each panel is held in place with just two screws, and after you remove them, you'll find very easy access to the motherboard and devices within. This design is represented in a bare-bones system examined in more detail in Chapter 7.

Now comes the time to slide off the cover on a standard case. Some cases pull back toward the rear of the PC, others lift straight up, and with some designs, you must pull them back slightly before lifting them straight up. Additionally, some cases include plastic or metal compression fittings that you must hold to keep them unlatched while you pull off the cover; consult your instruction manual for the details of your particular system. The cover may be a bit sticky until it breaks loose, but once it starts sliding, it should move smoothly.

Remove the case slowly and evenly. You want to avoid pinching or cutting any misbehaving wires that may have crept up near the top of the case, and you want to avoid tumbling the whole assemblage onto the floor with a misguided yank.

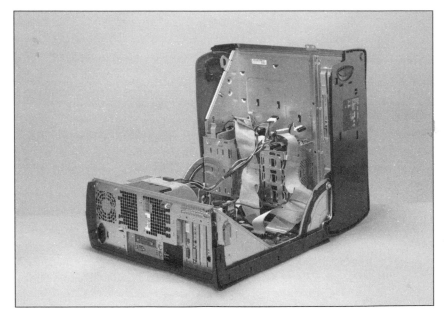

FIGURE 1-6: *To remove the cover from most desktop and tower cases, remove the screws around the perimeter of the back panel. On some ultra-compact desktop cases, the screws may attach along the sides. Be careful not to remove the group of screws that surround the power supply and hold it in place.*

Some cases include decorative front panels (sometimes referred to as *bezels*) that hide some of the access points; an example is shown in Figure 1-7. This sort of design adds a touch of class to an office or home installation, but the panels can also stand in the way of a power user with a wide range of devices. The best compromise is a case that allows you to remove or reposition the front panel cover to match your needs. In Figure 1-8, you can see the interior construction of this sort of case.

FIGURE 1-8: *To open the side panels on this case, pop off the front bezel and then slide the panels off.*

FIGURE 1-7: *The panel on this modern case sits in front of four device bays. The panel includes an opening for a CD-ROM. If you install another 5.25-inch device, such as a DVD-ROM or tape backup system, you have to open the panel for access.*

 WARNING

It's easy to catch the power supply wires or the floppy drive ribbon cable on the sharp edges of the case cover. Be gentle and use good sense when removing or reinstalling the cover. Ripping these wires loose increases the diagnostic challenge.

 WARNING

It's easy to catch the power supply wires or the floppy drive ribbon cable on the sharp edges of the case cover. Be gentle and use good sense when removing or reinstalling the cover. Ripping these wires loose increases the diagnostic challenge.

Here's another reason to do your work in a well-lit and comfortable environment: If the case seems to catch on something in removal or reinstallation, examine the situation with a powerful lamp or flashlight before you force the cover on or off.

Taking a good look

Now it's time to look at the innards of the computer. In a typical modern machine, you see the main motherboard with a large vertical or horizontal microprocessor topped by a fan or heat sink, one or more rows of memory modules, several plug-in circuit boards, a spaghetti bowl of gray ribbon cables, a metal box holding the power supply, a hard drive, a CD-ROM, and a floppy drive.

Hundreds of thousands of combinations of add-in cards, drives, memory modules, and other devices are possible; even an office full of the same brand of PCs is likely to have very different combinations of parts under the hood. Users may have had different requirements when the machines were purchased, technologies may have changed over the course of a series of orders, or the manufacturer may have had a mix-and-match assembly line where Brand X disk drives were installed on Mondays and Wednesdays, Brand Y on Tuesdays and Thursdays, and whatever was on sale was stuck in boxes put together on Fridays.

All that said, however, most computers — from the very first IBM PC to the latest state-of-the-art Pentium 4 or AMD Athlon — are more alike than they are different.

By the way, if the inside of the case looks like the back of your shoe closet — full of dust balls, cat hair, and spider webs — go get your vacuum cleaner. Working very carefully, hover the suction hose an inch or so above the electronics and let it suck out the dirt. Pay special attention to the air holes on the front or back of the machine; if these holes are clogged, the PC's fan will be much less effective in bringing cooling air through the case.

The Modular Design of a PC

One of the most important features of the PC is its modular design. Nearly every PC is made up of the same basic building blocks: motherboard, expansion cards, power supply, drives connected by cables to internal controllers, and external keyboard and monitor. These pieces can be inserted or removed with relative ease, thus enabling you to make many types of repairs and to upgrade your system.

The biggest circuit board in your computer is the *motherboard*, sometimes called the *mainboard*. The motherboard is

the home of the *CPU* (central processing unit), also called the *microprocessor*. The CPU is the brain of the computer, where the bulk of the actual manipulation of data and instructions takes place. In modern machines (as defined in this book), the CPU uses one of the younger members of the Pentium family, including the Pentium 4 and Pentium III, or equivalent chips, including AMD's Athlon and Duron and K6 chips. Senior citizen machines use an original Pentium or one of the later 486 chips. And dinosaurs were based on early 486s and older 386, 80286, 8088, or similar CPUs.

Expansion cards or *adapters* are smaller, special-purpose circuit boards that plug into sockets on the motherboard. These sockets are called *bus slots* or *expansion slots*. The computer bus is functionally an extension of the address lines of the microprocessor. The particular kind of bus slot on your motherboard tells a lot about the motherboard and your computer's capabilities. A modern variant of the bus slot is the *accelerated graphics port* (AGP), a special pathway to the microprocessor intended for use by a particular class of high-speed graphics adapters.

Your computer also has a *power supply*, a transformer that converts AC current into low-voltage DC current to run the computer. The power supply is easy to identify on the inside of the case; it's usually a large shiny or black metal box, sprouting many wires and connectors that spread out like spaghetti to all corners of the case. You can also spot the power supply from the back panel of the case; look for the AC power cord from a wall outlet.

Floppy drives and hard drives are electromechanical boxes usually connected to the rest of the computer with gray, flat-ribbon cables and four-wire power connectors from the power supply box. Floppy disk drives need to have an opening for the insertion of disks; hard drives may be mounted just behind the front panel of the computer, but can also be hung anywhere there is space and connecting cables.

NOTE

Some older IBM PS/2 machines and a handful of current machines, including many portables, use fixed plug-in connectors for power and data, thus allowing easy swap of devices; the downside is that standard drives can't be used in such systems without adaptation. Consult your PC's instruction manual for details.

Most modern machines also include a CD-ROM or CD-RW or an even more capable DVD-ROM. You also find advanced storage devices, such as Zip drives, SuperDisks, tape backups, and the like. Each of these devices connects to your computer in two ways: with a data cable (usually to the internal IDE connector on the motherboard) and with a cable from the power supply. Each of these devices needs an access slot on the outside of the machine for insertion of disks or tapes.

Some thin wires lead to the drive indicator light, the speaker, the power-on indicator, and other lamps and switches on the front panel. Other wires can include connectors from the CD-ROM or DVD-ROM to a sound card, from the motherboard to front-panel displays, and specialized environment-friendly (or *green*) functions, including sleep mode, temperature monitors, and variable fan-speed controls.

If your PC is a dinosaur, the memory chips—marked with identifying numbers—are probably arranged in rows of nine and reside in a segregated section of the motherboard.

Whether your computer is a modern machine or senior citizen, it uses one or another variant of a memory module that holds a large block of RAM that plugs into a location close to the CPU.

Single in-line memory modules (SIMMs) or *dual in-line memory modules* (DIMMs) are strips of circuit board—typically about two to three inches long—that plug into special connectors on the motherboard or occasionally into a plug-in board that attaches to the motherboard. Depending on the design and the type and capacity of memory chip used, the SIMMs or DIMMs may have

just a few or as many as 16 or 18 RAM (random access memory) chips installed. SIMM boards have 72 pins or edge connectors that attach them to the motherboard, while DIMMs use a 168-pin circuit board configuration. Notebook and laptop computers frequently use a variation of the DIMM, the SODIMM (small outline DIMM) in a 144-pin circuit board configuration.

SIMMs typically hold from 1MB to 64MB of memory and DIMMs from 8MB to 256MB of RAM. SODIMMs range from 4MB to 128MB.

The highest-capacity, fastest chips usually sell at a premium. When you examine a price list for memory, after you pass the entry-level sizes of 16MB, you should see a logical progression: A 64MB DIMM should be about twice the price of a 32MB module, a 128MB DIMM about double the cost of a 64MB, and so on. When one price is way out of whack as compared to others, it usually means that the product is new technology or an unusual size or configuration. Unless you absolutely need the latest and greatest, you're always better off waiting for prices to fall more into line. In general, laptop memory modules cost more than those for a desktop machine because, in many cases, they are specialty devices designed for that manufacturer's computer.

As I wrote this edition of *Fix Your Own PC*, 1GB DIMMs were available; over the course of a year they had dropped from a scary price of about $1,800 to about $200. At the same time, 512MB DIMMs sold for as little as $115, while the sweet spot of the most memory for your money was at the 256MB level, with modules priced as low as $16.

Memory makers are currently working on a single chip that holds 1GB of RAM, targeted for commercial availability sometime in 2002. This technology will enable more reasonably priced large-capacity DIMM modules.

In 2001, motherboard makers offered advanced systems using RIMM (Rambus in-line memory module) sockets. Similar in appearance to DIMMs, the first iteration of direct Rambus DRAMs was capable of transferring data at speeds up to 800 MHz over a narrow Rambus channel. RIMMs use a 184-pin connector. Another advanced memory design, double data-rate DIMMs (DDR DIMMs) use similar but incompatible 184-pin sockets.

A near-cousin to the SIMM and DIMM memory configuration is the *single in-line package* (SIP), an earlier version that uses tiny pins instead of edge connectors to connect to the motherboard. SIPs were used only for a short period and were supplanted by SIMMs, but you may still see SIP devices that do other things inside your computer, such as hold terminating resistors or other components.

 CROSS-REFERENCE

Chapter 8 examines memory types and configuration in much greater detail.

After you've grounded yourself, it is okay to press down on the chips and strips to make sure that they're seated firmly, but don't blindly poke around inside the computer with a screwdriver. Take special care not to scratch or push down on any of the metal traces of the circuit board that serve as the wiring between elements of the computer; it is relatively easy to introduce a tiny crack across the traces, thus disrupting the flow of power or data.

Notice the expansion cards lined up in neat rows and plugged into a set of plastic and metal slots on the motherboard. In most designs, the cards are held in place by the clamping action of the metal fingers within the slot and are locked down with a single screw that connects through a bracket into a support frame of the computer case. (Some modern case designs use a plastic lockdown lever that holds expansion cards in place without the need for screws.)

To remove a card, you need to disconnect any external cables attached to the card, unscrew the bracket screw, and carefully work the card out of the slot in the motherboard. Installing a card

is just as simple; just be careful to ensure that the card is fully inserted into the slot.

 NOTE

Some baby and other mini- and low-profile case designs use a riser card that installs into a single slot on the small motherboard; add-on cards plug into slots on the riser.

And finally, take a look at the motherboard. In most designs, the board floats above the bottom or side of the case on plastic standoffs with a handful of screws holding it in place. Somewhere near the center you should be able to spot the CPU; it's usually the largest chip on the board and generally installed in an oversized holder with a heat sink, fan, or both. On dinosaurs and most senior citizens, you should be able to read the inscription on the chip; on most modern machines, the high-speed CPU is usually covered with a heat sink or fan and stands up vertically like a black monolith.

Located at the back of the machine are ports for serial and parallel cables to external devices, a video port to connect to the monitor, and connectors for a keyboard and mouse, as shown in Figure 1-9. On some systems, you may find other connectors, including ports for SCSI devices, joysticks, speakers, microphones, and more. The newest machines include two or four universal serial bus (USB) ports, and the most modern of multimedia devices may include a FireWire port for connecting digital camcorders and other devices.

Most modern machines use motherboards that follow a specification called ATX or microATX, which places most input-output connectors directly on the board, matching up with an opening in the case. You can see an example of an ATX motherboard, with a Pentium II CPU in place, in Figure 1-10.

Microsoft and Intel helped to simplify the process of connecting cables to adapters on a modern PC with the introduction of the PC99 specification. Most motherboard and adapter makers have subscribed to the specification's recommendations for color-coding connectors and the ends of appropriate cables. Table 1-1 lists the major connectors.

FIGURE 1-9: *The back panel of a modern basic Pentium machine has serial, parallel, video, mouse, keyboard, and Ethernet connections.*

TABLE 1-1: PC99 Recommended Colors	
Connector	**Color**
Analog VGA	Blue
Audio line in	Light blue
Audio line out	Lime
Digital monitor	White
IEEE 1394 FireWire	Gray
Microphone	Pink
MIDI/Gameport	Gold
Parallel	Burgundy
PS/2-compatible keyboard	Purple
PS/2-compatible mouse	Green
Serial	Teal or turquoise
Speaker out/subwoofer	Orange
Right-to-left speaker	Brown
USB	Black
Video out	Yellow

FIGURE 1-10: *The ATX form factor motherboard brings together a bank of connectors directly on the motherboard, thus eliminating most cable connections. And most ATX-design systems also include a pair of USB ports (shown next to the keyboard and mouse ports in this design).*

PCs by Numbers: Basic Parts

Just how modular is a PC? The following are the basic parts for most systems; I've indicated where you can find more details about each particular part in this book:

▪ **Case.** The box that holds the internal parts of the computer and, almost as important, serves as a critical element of the cooling system for the electronic parts within. See Chapter 1.

- **Motherboard.** This is the heart of the computer and is home to the CPU, its supporting logic chips, and system memory. See Chapter 5.
- **CPU.** The microprocessor brain of the computer. See Chapter 2.
- **BIOS.** The basic set of instructions used by the computer to bring itself to life and to control input and output of data. See Chapter 3.
- **RAM.** The thinking space for the computer, used to hold programs and data under the control of the CPU. See Chapter 8.
- **Video adapter.** Responsible for converting the 0s and 1s of a computer's digital data into an image that can be displayed on a television-like screen. See Chapter 13.
- **Keyboard.** The primary means of communication between a human user and the machine. See Chapter 5.
- **Monitor.** The video display device that provides a window into the operations and results of a computer's work. See Chapter 13.
- **Power supply.** The source of carefully regulated voltage for all of the computer's internal parts. See Chapter 5.
- **Floppy and hard drive controllers.** The taskmasters for a computer's primary storage devices. See Chapters 9 and 10.
- **Floppy disk drive.** A simple, removable mechanism for storing data and programs. See Chapter 9.
- **Hard disk drive.** A high-capacity, high-speed storage system usually mounted within the case of the computer. See Chapter 10.
- **High-capacity removable drive.** A variant of the hard drive used for archiving data and for transporting large amounts of data or large programs from one machine to another. See Chapter 11.
- **Serial port.** A basic means of communication from your computer to external devices such as modems, certain printers, and other peripherals. See Chapter 15.

- **Parallel port.** A communication route generally used for printers. See Chapter 17.
- **Internal or external modem.** A hardware device that converts a computer's digital signals into an analog equivalent, used to transmit data over a telephone connection. See Chapter 16.
- **Printer.** A hard-copy output device. See Chapter 18.

Multimedia-capable systems include a few additional modular parts:

- **Sound card.** A device that gives your computer a voice and an orchestra. See Chapter 12.
- **Internal or external CD-ROM drive.** A form of removable storage primarily used to install programs or as a source of video or audio. See Chapter 12.
- **CD Recordable, CD Read/Write, or DVD drive.** A variant of the CD-ROM that can be used to both play and record discs. DVD is a developing protocol that packs huge amounts of data onto a disc and can be used to hold entire movies or other large multimedia files. See Chapter 12.
- **Game controller.** A hardware interface for joysticks and other devices used with games. See Chapter 12.

Even more adventuresome users build up their systems with devices such as scanners, video capture cards, and video-editing cards.

You can tuck almost anything else into the obliging slots of a PC. For example, many computers in offices, and even those in some small home offices, have a network card like the one shown in Figure 1-11. Setting up a small network in your office is relatively easy by using the built-in facilities of Windows 95/98 and later versions.

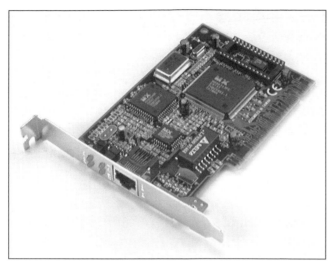

FIGURE 1-11: *A basic PCI Ethernet card. All current versions of Windows include basic networking software for setting up a small office or home installation.*

What Kind of PC Do You Have?

The first step in analyzing a PC is to understand what type of system it is: Is it a modern machine, a senior citizen, or a dinosaur? Does it have an ISA or EISA or VL or PCI bus? Does it possess a poky 8 MHz or a zippy 300 MHz processor? Is the hard disk an old ST506, an obsolete ESDI, a modern IDE, or a high-performance EIDE or SCSI model?

NOTE

Don't worry about the jargon yet. I define the terms later in the explanations of repairs and upgrades. If you need an immediate explanation, however, check the glossary at the back of this book.

The first place to look in order to learn about many systems is on the front *bezel* — the plastic faceplate where the computer manufacturer may proudly hang an advertising sign. In many cases, the model name for the computer gives you a great deal of information about what lies within.

For example, the following sections give a few sample names from machines I have used.

Intel processors

The collection of machines in my office includes PCs from a variety of makers, including Dell, Gateway, Hewlett Packard, IBM, and from defunct makers including Austin and CompuAdd, as well as units put together using parts from Dalco Electronics and TigerDirect. A quick survey of model names turned up the following alphanumeric soup for PCs built around processors from Intel and AMD:

- **P4-1800.** Close to the state-of-the-art, this machine mates a 1.8 GHz Pentium 4 CPU with 256MB of high-speed RDRAM, an ATA/100 40GB hard drive, a 4X AGP video slot, and four USB ports.

- **PIII-800.** A Pentium III running at 800 MHz makes for a pretty speedy computer, especially when you couple it with 128MB or so of RAM and a high-speed, 20GB hard drive. This stuff gets cheaper and better all the time. Standard equipment on this level of machine includes AGP video and USB ports.

- **PII-300.** PII indicates a Pentium II CPU, running in this example at a brisk 300 MHz. Virtually all modern Pentium-based computers use a combination of PCI and ISA buses to interconnect various elements. Later model Pentium II machines based on ATX form motherboards introduced AGP video and USB ports.

- **P6-200.** P6 was an unofficial industry label for Intel's Pentium Pro, in this case running at a more-than-respectable 200 MHz clock speed. The Pentium Pro had its short moment in the sun and was primarily used in servers and very demanding business applications. It quickly gave way to the more capable Pentium II processor, which was eventually supplanted by the Pentium III.

- **P5-100-PCI.** A P or P5 in a product name generally indicates that the computer uses a Pentium processor, in this case running at 100 MHz. The letters after the number indicate that the motherboard includes a PCI bus, which was introduced about the same time as the arrival of the Pentium.

- **P5-200 with MMX.** This Intel 200 MHz Pentium processor uses MMX technology; a set of extensions that delivers improved graphics and multimedia functions. This particular model includes 512K of pipeline burst SRAM cache, 32MB of SDRAM DIMM memory, and a PCI local-bus 3-D graphics accelerator with 2MB SGRAM video memory.

- **Pentium 100ES.** The Pentium part is easy, and the 100 indicates a 100 MHz chip. The meaning of ES, however, is less obvious but is an important distinction. This model, intended for use as a high-performance file server, uses an EISA bus, a relatively uncommon design that was also supplanted by PCI. If you have one of these, your upgrade and repair path is sharply limited.

- **4DX2-66V.** The processor in this venerable senior citizen is a 486DX2 running at 66 MHz. The V at the end means that this particular motherboard uses a VL or local bus, a popular design of several years ago that PCI bus models pushed aside.

- **486DX4-100.** Are you getting the clues here? A top-end 486 system in the senior citizen class, this system uses an Intel DX4 chip that, despite its enumeration, is actually clock-tripled rather than quadrupled. It runs at 100 MHz internally.

- **4SX-33.** This is a 486SX model running at 33 MHz. With this edition of *Fix Your Own PC*, this class of machines marks the line between senior citizen and dinosaur. You have to poke around under the covers or in the instruction manual to determine the type of bus it uses. This somewhat underpowered chip came out near the end of the VL bus era and the dawn of the PCI age; some motherboards included slots to serve both designs.

- **216.** Another dinosaur, this is an 80286 running at an anemic 16 MHz. The motherboard almost certainly uses a very basic AT (also called ISA) 16-bit bus. I keep this one around as a museum piece; it's like a sled without wheels among racing cars.

- **IBM Personal Computer.** Even deeper in the closet is an original IBM PC, the classic dinosaur that started the PC revolution. It uses an 8088 processor running at 4.77 MHz, a pair of gigantic (in size, not capacity) 5.25-inch 360K floppy drives, 64K of memory chips on the motherboard, and a crude CGA video adapter. I haven't fired it up in years, but I can't quite bring myself to deliver it to the dump. It cost almost $5,000 when I bought it.

Modern machines using non-Intel CPUs

What remains is the rest of the world: machines that use CPUs other than Intel chips. I have worked with machines built around AMD, Cyrix, SGS, and NexGen microprocessors. The following is a tour of some of these models:

- **AMD Athlon, Athlon XP.** Athlon is AMD's answer to Intel's Pentium 4. At the time of this writing, AMD had reached the 1.4 GHz mark for its Athlons, and a bit faster for the Athlon XP version. Athlon CPUs use a proprietary mounting socket that's mechanically compatible with Intel's Slot 1 (SC242), but with different electrical signals. This is a very important distinction; an AMD Athlon can't be substituted in a motherboard designed for an Intel Pentium 4, or the other way around.

- **AMD K6-III 450.** Systems based on AMD's K6-III offer similar, or even better, performance compared with similarly equipped Intel PIII systems, at a lower initial cost.

- **AMD K6-266 MMX.** AMD's K6 modern machine processor delivers full compatibility with — and some superiority over — similar Pentium CPUs from Intel at a significant cost saving.
- **Cyrix 6x86-P166+, IBM 6x86-P200+, Cyrix 6x86-P200+.** The Cyrix series of modern machine processors are functionally equivalent to Intel Pentium designs. The company used some special tricks to eke more speed out of their designs while maintaining near-perfect compatibility with Intel equivalents. They do make things a bit difficult with their naming scheme, however. The Cyrix 6x86-P166+ actually runs at 133 MHz, but claims to outperform an Intel Pentium 166 MHz chip. Isn't marketing fun? Now, one more issue: IBM manufactured chips for Cyrix for some time, and some machines may have chips with the IBM name instead of Cyrix. An IBM 6x86-P200+ runs at 166 MHz, acts like a 200 MHz Intel CPU, and is the same as a Cyrix 6x86-P200+. Similarly, SGS-Thomson also made chips for Cyrix, and some systems may have an SGS logo.
- **AMD K5 PR100 MHz.** AMD's K5 is roughly equivalent to a Pentium P5.
- **Nx586 P100.** This system uses the NexGen Nx586 processor, a now-discontinued competitor to Intel's Pentium chip. The Nx586 was not pin-compatible with the Pentium and therefore required special motherboards and chip sets. It also lacked an on-chip floating point unit (FPU). The chip model here is the P100, which actually runs at 93 MHz but claimed to rival a Pentium at 100 MHz. NexGen was bought out by AMD, and although that company may be able to support the chip, serious problems with a NexGen-based machine may require a change of motherboard and CPU.

The next place to look is the instruction manual that comes with the system. If you don't have the manual, there's a quick and easy way to check most of the elements of a PC if you have a copy of MSD (Microsoft Diagnostics), a capable utility that is supplied as part of MS-DOS 6.*x* and Windows 3.1. Boot up the system and go to the DOS prompt. Microsoft warns that not all of MSD's readings are accurate if you run it from within Windows or from a DOS window opened under Windows, so exit Windows if it's running and execute MSD from the DOS prompt.

If you are running Windows XP, Windows Me, Windows 2000, Windows 98, or Windows 95, a built-in system information screen is available from within Microsoft applications, such as Word, Excel, and other Office programs. Just click Help, and then About Microsoft Word (or the name of the application running), and then click System Info. You receive a full report like the one shown in Figure 1-12. In Windows 98 and later operating systems, you can display this information directly by choosing System Information in the System Tools dialog box (Start ➪ Programs ➪ Accessories ➪ System Tools).

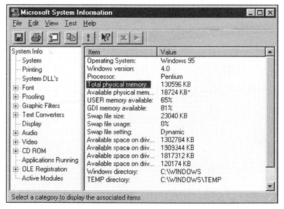

FIGURE 1-12: *A System Information report from within Microsoft Word about one of the machines in the Word Association office. Similar displays are available under Windows 98, Windows Me, Windows 2000, and Windows XP.*

The final way to determine the nature of your machine is to look for yourself. Locate the CPU chip on the motherboard. The processor's manufacturer and number are printed on the chip. Although some computers tuck the CPU chip and part of the motherboard under the drives to save space, the CPU itself is still pretty easy to find. It is usually the largest chip on the motherboard, and on modern machines it is usually covered with a cooling fan or heat sink, or both.

Most Pentium II and early Pentium III and AMD Athlon chips reside in carriers that stand up vertically from the motherboard. Later versions of Pentium III and Athlon CPUs, and current Pentium 4 microprocessors, have returned to a horizontal surface socket on the motherboard.

The 8088 CPUs of a dinosaur are rectangular, about two inches long and half an inch wide. The 80286 chip is roughly one inch square. Senior citizen 80386, 486, and Pentium CPUs are big square chips that are hard to miss. Some 486 and Pentium chips are mounted in large chip carriers that make them easy to remove for upgrades; you may also see aluminum heat sinks atop some of the advanced chips.

The CPU may be labeled 8088, 80286, 80386, 80486, Pentium, or Pentium Pro; some dinosaur XT-style clones used an NEC V20 or V30 chip, and some modern machines use chips from manufacturers including AMD, NexGen, and Cyrix. And TI (Texas Instruments) and IBM also have variants of the Intel CPU with their names on them.

CROSS-REFERENCE

See Chapter 2 for a more thorough discussion of the CPU march of time from the dawn of computer dinosaurs to the arrival of the modern machine.

Reinstalling the Cover

After you've looked around inside the machine, put the cover back on the computer, tucking in the cables.

Before you reinstall the cover, look down inside it and check to see whether there are any pegs or other protrusions on the inside front surface. If there aren't any pegs, simply tip the cover up extra high in front as you slide it onto the chassis, and then slide it straight back into place. Tighten the machine screws gently; force is neither necessary nor helpful. If there is a peg or two on the inside of the cover, installing the cover is a bit trickier; you must wiggle the cover up and down a bit to make it slide that last half-inch into position. If you have one of the newer cover designs, simply reverse the process that you used to take the cover off in the first place. You may have a wraparound cover that takes a little adjustment to get in place, or you may have just one side to snap back on. As with any repair procedure, try to observe carefully — and remember — how you removed the cover so that you can replace it easily when the time comes.

After you get the cover in place, install the screws, reattach the power cable, and flip on the power switch.

If the computer doesn't boot up, don't panic. If the machine worked before you took off the cover, the problem almost certainly is an accidentally dislodged, misconnected, or pinched cable. You did plug it back into the power outlet, right?

SUMMARY

Now that you've completed a basic tour of the PC, you can move on to a more detailed examination of the brain of the computer — its microprocessor. The information in the next chapter prepares you to learn about the CPU inside your own machine and also prepares you for fixing and upgrading your machine to some of the latest technology.

Notes

Chapter 2

In This Chapter:

- Exploring CPUs
- Measuring CPUs
- Exploring Chipsets
- Modern Intel and Clone CPUs
- Senior Citizen and Dinosaur CPUs
- Pentium OverDrive Processors
- Upgrading Senior Citizen CPUs
- Math Coprocessors
- Troubleshooting Intel OverDrives

Tools Needed:

- Phillips Screwdriver
- Antistatic Strip, Wrist Strap, or Grounding Pad

The Microprocessor

Intel has owned the heart of the PC market from its birth, when IBM chose Intel's 8088 microprocessor as the brains of the first PC. Today, Intel is still inside most PCs, although Advanced Micro Devices (AMD) has mounted a serious challenge for a small but significant slice of the market. Throughout the history of the PC, other makers, including Cyrix and IBM, have picked up some of the pieces of the pie. Intel processors (also known as *CPUs*, for *central processing units*) are used in about 80 percent of business and home computers. The second largest maker is AMD. Another large manufacturer is Motorola, which makes processors for Apple's Macintosh computers and those embedded in specialized systems like cell phones, industrial controllers, and other devices.

When the IBM PC was born in 1981, Intel's 8088 was not the fastest processor available, but designers felt that the chip offered the best combination of speed, price, and availability of peripherals; and perhaps most important, the 8088 did not seem to present much of a threat to "real" computers, such as the massive mainframes and minicomputer that were IBM's bread and butter.

IBM's choice actually hobbled the expansion capabilities of PCs for many years and is still a factor in today's backward-compatible hardware and operating systems. Backward compatibility is an essential part of high-tech; it means that the latest, greatest hardware is still able to work with software developed for machines that thrived in the days of the dinosaurs. This is mostly true, assuming that everyone — from software designers to hardware makers — follows the rules at every step.

It is important to note that, in general, you can't change your computer's CPU from one family to another because they involve different supporting chipsets, sockets, bus designs, and electrical voltages. In most cases, however, you can replace a slower processor with a faster version within the same family.

In this book, you'll learn that I segregate computers into modern machines, senior citizens, and dinosaurs. Modern PCs will work with nearly all current software and hardware; senior citizens may be a few steps behind the younger competition but are still capable, and dinosaurs are mostly valuable for curiosity's sake. If you're working with a dinosaur system, you can sometimes substitute a more capable CPU from a clone maker. Additionally, some dinosaur and senior citizen motherboard designs can work with Intel's OverDrive CPUs or with upgrade processors that use AMD, Cyrix, or other chips.

This chapter examines all of the major chips used in PCs, working backward from the current state-of-the-art for desktops, the Pentium 4 and AMD's Athlon.

At the time of this writing, Pentium 4 CPUs are available in two forms: the first series of microprocessors, from 1.4 to 1.7 GHz, were offered in a large carrier that used a Socket 423 on the flat surface of the motherboard. Most CPUs from 1.7 GHz and faster were produced on a smaller die, plugging into a smaller Socket 478 with pins placed much closer together. An example of a current Intel Pentium 4 is shown in Figure 2-1.

FIGURE 2-1: *An Intel Pentium 4 in its small Socket 487 form. (Photo courtesy of Intel Corporation.)*

 NOTE

Before this discussion of CPUs begins in earnest, here's an interesting perspective on the speed of today's CPUs. Intel's first microprocessor, the 4004, ran at 108 KHz (108,000 cycles per second), compared to the Pentium 4 processor's initial speed of 1.5 GHz (1.5 billion Hz). If automobile speed had increased similarly over the same period, you could now drive from San Francisco to New York in about 13 seconds. By the end of 2002, Pentium 4s are expected to operate at as much as 3.5 GHz; that would equate to a trip across the United States in about 5 seconds.

Moore's Law

An interesting perspective on computer history comes from Moore's Law, one of the underlying unofficial basic tenets of microprocessor development. Gordon Moore, one of the founders of Intel, predicted in 1965 that the number of transistors per integrated circuit would double every 18 months. Moore's original horizon was just ten years, but his forecast has proven to be uncannily accurate.

Intel's first commercially used microprocessor, predating the personal computer, was the 4004, which had 2,250 transistors when it was introduced in 1971. By 2000, the Pentium 4 crammed 42 million transistors onto its tiny surface. The details of the most important members of the Intel family and their relation to Moore's Law are shown in Table 2-1. The same information is presented as a graph in Figure 2-2.

TABLE 2-1: The Numbers behind Moore's Law

Processor	Year of Introduction	Transistors
4004	1971	2,250
8008	1972	2,500
8080	1974	5,000
8086	1978	29,000
286	1982	120,000
386	1985	275,000
486 DX	1989	1,180,000
Pentium	1993	3,100,000
Pentium II	1997	7,500,000
Pentium III	1999	24,000,000
Pentium 4	2000	42,000,000

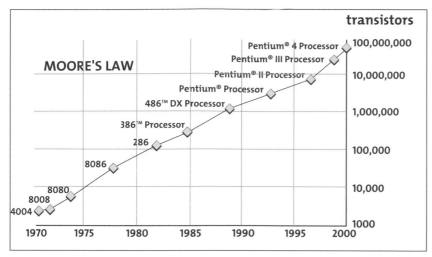

FIGURE 2-2: *Moore's Law*

How a CPU Works

The tiny CPU microprocessor — ranging in size from a sugar cube to a cell phone — is the locomotive of the computer and is often its single most expensive internal component. The basic assignment of the CPU is to read data from storage, manipulate that information, and then move the data back to storage or output it to external devices, such as monitors or printers.

CPUs are measured by the number of cycles per second used by the processor; think of cycles as clicks on the ratchet wheel of a machine pushing something forward. The cycles are measured in megahertz, meaning 1 million cycles per second.

The CPU's megahertz speed, however, is not the only determinant of the ultimate speed of the computer. The processor must be wedded to a fast bus — an electronic superhighway — for the interchange of information and memory and peripherals that can keep up with its speed. In general, speed is limited by the slowest element in the data stream.

The heart of the CPU is a dime-sized piece of silicon. Etched onto the silicon are millions of tiny transistors that operate as voltage-controlled switches, turning current flow off and on. CPUs are manufactured in high-tech clean rooms; depending on the maker and technology, the transistors are etched by chemicals or by exposure to intense light (photolithographic processes).

A computer is a binary device, meaning that all information is stored and manipulated as a series of 0s or 1s, or Offs and Ons. The transistors are grouped to create computer words that represent letters or numbers that are then used to cause the screen to display an image or a block of type, or to prepare a digital representation of an image for output to a printer. The data in the CPU can also be moved to permanent storage on a hard drive or other storage device that is capable of retaining information after the power is turned off.

Another type of information manipulated by the CPU is an *instruction*, a code that tells the system what to do with a particular piece or group of data: move it from one location to another or apply a mathematical operation to it. Think of instructions as verbs. Some of the transistors of the CPU hold *instruction pointers* that tell the CPU the location in memory for an instruction. *Registers* hold data waiting to be processed, or data that has been processed and is waiting to be moved or stored. A specialized section of the CPU is the *arithmetic logic unit (ALU)*, which acts as a calculator to perform math and logic functions.

Here's an example of a sequence that may take place in a CPU:

1. The CPU comes to an instruction pointer; this triggers an *instruction fetch* to bring the instruction from memory within the CPU, in RAM, or elsewhere in the system. (The further the fetch has to go to retrieve the instruction, the slower the process.)
2. Then the *instruction decoder* accepts the instruction from the fetch and translates it for the use of the CPU.
3. The entire operation is coordinated by the *control unit*. This specialized area issues the commands for action by the fetch and decoder.
4. Once the ALU performs the instruction or series of instructions, the control unit moves on to the next fetch.

Sometimes what seems like a very simple instruction can actually involve dozens, hundreds, or thousands of steps. In fact, most computers are capable of just one operation: addition. Through manipulation, addition can be used to solve multiplication, division, and subtraction problems.

This points up the basic truth of computers: They are very stupid but extremely fast. Though a human may intuitively know that 25×25 equals 625, a computer has to work it out step by step, starting with summing 00011001 25 times to come up with the binary answer of 00000010 01110001.

Some instructions take more time than others to execute, and some data or instructions are closer at hand than others. And so, to keep everything moving along in a coordinated fashion, the microprocessor creates a regularly beating heartbeat. The system's clock or clock generator sends out precisely spaced pulses that push along instructions and data.

The original IBM PC used the Intel 8088 as its CPU; that microprocessor had a clock speed of 4.77 MHz or just under 5 million cycles per second. Today, modern machines have moved into gigahertz territory; as this book goes to press, Intel Pentium 4 or AMD Athlon CPUs are approaching 2 billion cycles per second.

But as has been mentioned, the number of cycles per second is just one element of a CPU's speed. Another is the architecture of the chip and the system itself. One important improvement in recent years has been the addition of *cache* memory within the CPU or located nearby on the CPU carrier. Either design allows the microprocessor to store instructions or data close at hand; sophisticated algorithms anticipate the need for information before the CPU calls for it and pre-fetches it. When the information is needed, the CPU doesn't have to waste cycles waiting for a fetch instruction to be issued, move across the system bus to memory, and then return across the bus. Advanced processors, including nearly all modern CPUs, add a second level of high-speed memory called *L2 cache* (level 2 cache) between the CPU's cache and the system RAM.

Key to getting the most out of cache is a sophisticated algorithm to manage its use. *Branch prediction* makes an intelligent guess at the next direction for the processor to fetch the instruction before it is called. *Speculative execution* goes one step beyond to execute the predicted branch before the CPU even asks for it. And *out-of-order completion* works on instructions in an illogical but more efficient manner.

Other improvements on the hardware side in recent years include *multiple ALUs* to allow subdivision of complex mathematical problems into multiple concurrent processes. A specialized *floating point arithmetic unit* offloads some of the ALU's work, concentrating on very large and small numbers with many integers on either side of the decimal point. And *pipelining* works with the CPU to divide instructions into small pieces that can piggyback one on the other, moving along on nearly parallel tracks.

Taking the Measure of a CPU

Microprocessors have three important measures of their speed and capability: the data bus, the address bus, and the processor clock speed. The following is an essential guide to these key measures:

- **Data bus.** The more bits of information that can be moved in and out of the chip at a time, the better the flow of data. The computer moves information in the form of bytes, which are made up of eight bits (individual 0s or 1s) of the binary code. Depending on the capabilities of the microprocessor to manipulate and store blocks of data, computer words can be made up of 8, 16, 32, or more bits, or one, two, three, or more bytes.

NOTE

All information within the computer is represented by numbers, and for simplicity's sake, the PC uses binary math—just 0s and 1s, on and off, yes or no. And so the letter *W* is represented by the ASCII code 87, which is represented in binary math as 1 0 1 0 1 1 1 (from right to left, one 1, one 2, one 4, no 8s, one 16, no 32s, one 64—for a grand total of 87 in decimal notation).

The original PC could work on just one computer word at a time. Modern machines can chomp on four or eight words with each cycle. Put another way, an eight-word machine is a 64-bit processor.

Think of the data bus as the highway the CPU uses to move information: A two-lane (16-bit) highway is twice as good as a one-lane (8-bit) road, and a four- or eight-lane super-highway is that much better. The original 8088 CPU has an 8-bit data bus. The 286 and 386SX microprocessors have a 16-bit data bus. The 386DX CPUs, as well as the 486 series, have 32-bit data buses, while Pentium chips pump data through a 64-bit external data bus.

▪ **Address bus.** These are the wires the CPU uses to describe the location in memory where data is retrieved or sent. The more bits in the address bus, the more memory locations are possible. Remember that the computer calculates numbers using a binary system: A 4-bit number, for example, can hold values from 0 to 15.

The original 8088 and 8086 processors had a 20-bit address bus, meaning they could work with up to 1,048,576 bytes of memory, which translates in computer shorthand to 1,024K or 1MB. The 286 and 386SX families used a 24-bit bus, which expanded the memory capacity of the system to 16MB. The 386DX, 486, Pentium, and Pentium Pro chips offered a 32-bit address bus, which zoomed memory capacity to 4,096MB, or 4GB. And the Pentium II chip went up a notch to a 36-bit

bus, permitting memory addresses corresponding to 64GB of memory. (Some of the last models in the Pentium Pro series also used a 36-bit bus.) The next generation of chips, the Pentium 4 and AMD Athlon, have 64-bit address buses and support tens of gigabytes of memory (1.84×10^{19} bytes, theoretically).

NOTE

Semiconductor makers have begun a shift to produce chips with copper, rather than aluminum, wires. Copper conducts electricity better than aluminum, increasing speed and reducing the creation of heat. The changeover is considered essential to the next breakthrough in chip speed; by 2002, for example, Intel plans to produce Pentium 4s that operate at 2.2 GHz, with 3.5 GHz microprocessors envisioned within a year after that. Future CPUs may use more exotic metals to conduct electricity.

▪ **Processor clock speed.** The clock is the CPU's metronome. Each beat of the clock—actually a crystal oscillator or an electronic equivalent that vibrates a fixed number of times per second when electricity is applied—is a signal to the CPU to perform an action or move data. The clock speed is measured in cycles per second, which are reported in hertz. A 700 MHz (megahertz) clock operates at 700 million cycles per second; a 1.7 GHz clock pulses at 1.7 billion cycles per second. (A hertz is a measurement named after German physicist Heinrich Hertz, who made important discoveries about electro-magnetic theory in the 1880s.)

Obviously, the faster the clock speed, the faster the CPU can move data. However, each CPU has its own speed limit, based on such issues as heat buildup caused by high-frequency operations and the electrical characteristics of each actual product. Furthermore, a CPU's performance depends not only on its clock speed but also on its processing capability (including the number of internal cycles necessary for an instruction to be executed), how fast the bus can move data to and from the chip, and other factors, such as internal and external cache sizes, pipelining, and superscalar architecture.

The 8088 and 8086 processors needed about 12 cycles to complete a basic instruction. Improvements in the internal instructions enabled a drop to about five cycles for the 286 and 386 class, and two cycles for a 486 chip. The Pentium chip can generally operate at one cycle per instruction.

And then there are wait cycles, which are wasted clock ticks while the CPU pauses until the rest of the system catches up with it. Old, slow 8086 systems needed four cycles plus several wait cycles to transfer data to and from memory. Finally, just to make things more difficult, modern CPUs are capable of running at multiples of the motherboard's speed. The original Pentiums, running at 60 and 66 MHz, matched the speed of the motherboard at a 1:1 ratio. But every Pentium-class microprocessor since then runs faster than the motherboard.

In recent years, chip makers have changed the fabrication process to allow transistors to be even tinier and closer together. As this book goes to press, nearly all processors use 0.18 micron or 0.13 micron fabrication, an improvement over the 0.25 micron process.

The smaller fabrication process allows CPUs to operate faster at the same time because they give off less heat.

The Intel Family Tree

The Intel family of processors has gone through eight major generations. The first four generations used the number 8 as a first name, beginning with the *8088/8086/80186* family and running through the *80286*, *80386*, and *80486* series. Over the years, Intel dropped the 80 prefix from the names of the chips for marketing purposes, calling them 386 and 486 processors. Within the 80386 and 80486 family line, some chips were subdivided into SX and DX, DX2, and DX4 groups.

The fifth family was the *Pentium*. With its introduction, Intel changed its naming convention by inventing a name that has a connection to the Greek word *pente*, meaning five, and no doubt Intel changed the name so it could make the name a trademark (numbers can't be registered as trademarks). Some technical types maintain a link to the family by calling the Pentium the P5, a reference to its once-intended 80586 name. Next came the Pentium Pro (the P6 to some), used almost exclusively in servers and other special-purpose machines. Intel later added the MMX multimedia extensions to the Pentium family, creating a subgroup of CPUs.

The sixth generation was the *Pentium II*, a completely new chip architecture. These chips were initially expensive, physically huge by existing standards, and required relatively high power. Within a relatively short time, however, the PII became a popular, high-speed alternative for the Pentium and Pentium Pro.

Seventh in line was the *Pentium III*, an enhanced and expanded Pentium II architecture. The Pentium III was the last in Intel's line of 32-bit processors, available in a wide range of speeds and socket arrangements.

The *Celeron* chip was originally introduced as a subset of the Pentium II, a slower and less-expensive cousin intended for use in low-priced but still-capable new systems. Modern versions of the Celeron are based on the Pentium III design.

And Intel also brought to market the Pentium Xeon II processors for high-end servers and workstations. The Xeon and the 350 MHz and 400 MHz Pentium IIs were the first Intel chips to run on a system bus of 100 MHz, offering up to a 50-percent increase in bus performance over the common 66 MHz speed of most machines current at the time. Later, Intel introduced the Pentium III Xeon chip, a natural follow-on to the Pentium III in much the same way as the PII Xeon followed the Pentium II chip.

The Xeon chip family began at 400 MHz and included as much as 2MB of high-speed cache memory to increase chip performance. Xeon chips are more expensive to manufacture because the processors come in a Slot 2 (SC330) package, which is larger (330 pins as opposed to 242 pins) than the current Slot 1 (SC242) package used for desktops. The custom-made cache memory also adds to the price.

The eighth family from Intel is the *Pentium 4*, a 64-bit microprocessor introduced in 2000 at 1.4 GHz; as this book goes to press, that chip has zoomed past 2.0 GHz headed toward 3.5 GHz or more.

Table 2-2 shows the progression of CPUs from Intel.

TABLE 2-2: Intel CPUs by Family

Pentium 4

Pentium 4. 2.2 GHz and faster.	Processor package: PGA478. System Bus Speed: 400 MHz. Introduced early 2002. 42 million transistors. 0.18 micron process technology. Integrated 512K L2 advanced transfer cache.
Pentium 4. 2.0, 1.9, 1.8, 1.7, 1.6 GHz.	Processor package: PGA423 and PGA478. System Bus Speed: 400 MHz. Introduced July and August 2001. 42 million transistors. 0.18 micron process technology. Integrated 256K L2 advanced transfer cache.
Pentium 4. 1.4 and 1.5 GHz.	Processor package: PGA423. System bus speed: 400 MHz. Introduced: November 2000. Intel's advanced processor includes many features aimed at multimedia applications, including the ability to create movies, deliver TV-like video over the Internet, render 3-D graphics in real time, and simultaneously run several multimedia applications while connected to the Internet. 0.18 micron process. 256K L2 integrated advanced transfer cache.

Celeron

Intel Celeron. 1.2 MHz.	Processor package: Flip-Chip Pin Grid Array (FC-PGA). System bus speed: 100 MHz. 256K cache on-die. 0.13 micron technology. Used in value PCs.
Intel Celeron. 1.0–1.1 MHz.	Processor package: Flip-Chip Pin Grid Array (FC-PGA). System bus speed: 100 MHz. 128K cache on-die. 0.18 micron process. Used in value PCs.
Intel Celeron. 800–950 MHz.	Processor package: Flip-Chip Pin Grid Array (FC-PGA). System bus speed: 100 MHz. Introduced: July 2001. 128K cache on-die. 0.18 micron process. Used in value PCs.
Intel Celeron. 850 MHz.	Processor package: Flip-Chip Pin Grid Array (FC-PGA). System bus speed: 100 MHz. Introduced: May 2001. 0.18 micron process. Designed for value PCs.

Continued

Ch 2

TABLE 2-2: *Continued*	
Celeron	
Intel Celeron. 800 MHz.	Processor package: Flip-Chip Pin Grid Array (FC-PGA). System bus speed: 100 MHz. Introduced: January 2001. 128K on-die L2 cache. 0.18 micron process. Designed for value PCs.
Intel Celeron. 733 and 766 MHz.	Processor package: Flip-Chip Pin Grid Array (FC-PGA). System bus speed: 66 MHz. Introduced: November 2000. 128K on-die L2 cache. 0.18 micron process. Designed for value PCs.
Intel Celeron. 633, 667, and 700 MHz.	Processor package: Flip-Chip Pin Grid Array (FC-PGA). System bus speed: 66 MHz. Introduced: June 2000. 128K on-die L2 cache. 0.18 micron process. Designed for value PCs.
Intel Celeron. 566 and 600 MHz.	Processor package: Flip-Chip Pin Grid Array (FC-PGA). System bus speed: 66 MHz. Introduced: March 2000. 128K on-die cache. 0.18 micron process. Designed for value PCs.
Intel Celeron. 533 MHz.	Processor package: Plastic Pin Grid Array (PPGA), 370 pins. System bus speed: 66 MHz. Introduced: January 2000. 19 million transistors. 0.25 micron process. 128K on-die cache. Designed for value PCs.
Intel Celeron. 466 and 500 MHz.	Processor package: Plastic Pin Grid Array (PPGA), 370 pins. System bus speed: 66 MHz. Introduced: April 1999 and August 1999. 19 million transistors. 0.25 micron process. 128K on-die cache.
Intel Celeron. 433 MHz.	Processor package: Single Edge Processor Package (SEPP), 242 pins. System bus speed: 66 MHz. Introduced: March 1999. 19 million transistors. 0.25 micron process. 128K on-die cache.
Intel Celeron. 400, 366 MHz.	Processor package: Single Edge Processor Package (SEPP), 242 pins; or Plastic Pin Grid Array (PPGA), 370 pins. System bus speed: 66 MHz. Introduced: January 1999. 19 million transistors. 0.25 micron process. Designed for value PCs.
Intel Celeron. 333 MHz.	Processor package: Single Edge Processor Package (SEPP), 242 pins. System bus speed: 66 MHz. Introduced: August 1998. 19 million transistors. 0.25 micron process. Designed for value PCs.
Intel Celeron. 300 MHz.	Processor package: Single Edge Processor Package (SEPP), 242 pins. System bus speed: 66 MHz. Introduced: August 1998. The Intel Celeron processor was designed for use in economy PCs, optimized for uses including gaming and educational software. 19 million transistors. 0.25 micron process.

Celeron

Intel Celeron. 300 MHz.	Processor package: Single Edge Processor Package (SEPP), 242 pins. System bus speed: 66 MHz. Introduced: June 1998. 7.5 million transistors. 0.25 micron process. Designed for value PCs.
Intel Celeron. 266 MHz.	Processor package: Single Edge Processor Package (SEPP), 242 pins. System bus speed: 66 MHz. Introduced: 7.5 million transistors. 0.25 micron process. Designed for value PCs.

Xeon

Intel Xeon. 2.0, 1.7, 1.5, and 1.4 GHz.	Processor package: Organic Lan Grid Array 603 (OLGA 603). System bus speed: 400 MHz. Introduced: September 25, 2001 (2.0 processor), May 2001. 256K integrated L2 advanced transfer cache. 0.18 micron process. Designed for high-performance and mid-range dual processor workstations.

Pentium III

Pentium III Xeon. 933 MHz.	Processor package: SC330. System bus speed: 133 MHz. Addressable memory: 64GB. Introduced: May 2001. Integrated 2MB advanced transfer cache. System bus width 64 bits; addressable memory 64GB. 0.18 micron process. Designed for high-end servers and multiprocessing systems.
Pentium III Xeon. 900 MHz.	Processor package: SC330. System bus speed: 100 MHz. Addressable memory: 64GB. Introduced: March 2001. Integrated 2MB advanced transfer cache. System bus width 64 bits; addressable memory 64GB. 0.18 micron process. Designed for high-end servers and multiprocessing systems.
Pentium III and Pentium III Xeon. 933 MHz.	Processor package: Single Edge Contact Cartridge (SECC2), Flip-Chip Pin Grid Array (FC-PGA), and SC330. System bus speed: 133 MHz. Addressable memory: 64GB. Introduced: May 2000. 256K L2 integrated advanced transfer cache. 0.18 micron process. Designed for servers and workstations.
Pentium III. 700 MHz.	Processor package: SC330. System bus speed: 100 MHz. Addressable memory: 64GB. Introduced: May 2000. 1MB and 2MB integrated L2 advanced transfer cache. 0.18 micron process. Designed for four- and eight-way servers.
Pentium III Xeon. 866 MHz.	Processor package: Single Edge Contact Cartridge (SECC2). System bus speed: 133 MHz. Addressable memory: 64GB. Introduced: April 2000. 28 million transistors. 0.18 micron process. 256K integrated L2 advanced transfer cache. Designed for servers and workstations.

Continued

Ch 2

TABLE 2-2: *Continued*	
Pentium III	
Pentium III. 850 and 866 MHz, 1.0 GHz.	Processor package: Single Edge Contact Cartridge (SECC and SECC2). System bus speed: 100 and 133 MHz. Addressable memory: 64GB. Introduced: March 2000. 0.18 micron process. 256K integrated L2 advanced transfer cache.
Pentium III Xeon. 800 MHz.	Processor package: Single Edge Contact Cartridge (SECC2). System bus speed: 133 MHz. Addressable memory: 64GB. Introduced: January 2000. 256K integrated L2 advanced transfer cache. 0.18 micron process. Designed for servers and workstations.
Pentium III Xeon. 600, 667, and 733 MHz.	Processor package: Single Edge Contact Cartridge (SECC2). System bus speed: 133 MHz. Addressable memory: 64GB. Introduced: October 1999. 28 million transistors. 0.18 micron process. 256K integrated L2 advanced transfer cache. Designed for servers and workstations.
Pentium III. 500, 533, 550, 600, 650, 667, 700, and 733MHz.	Processor package: Single Edge Contact Cartridge (SECC2) and Flip-Chip Pin Grid Array (FC-PGA). System bus speed: 100 and 133 MHz. Introduced: October 1999. 28 million transistors. 0.18 micron process. 256K integrated L2 advanced transfer cache.
Pentium III Xeon. 500 and 550 MHz.	Processor package: Single Edge Contact Cartridge (SECC2). System bus speed: 100 MHz. Addressable memory: 64GB. Introduced: March 1999. The Pentium III Xeon extended the Pentium III's instruction set to add advanced cache technology. It was designed for systems with multiprocessor configurations. 9.5 million transistors. 0.25 micron process. L2 cache: 512K, 1MB, or 2 MB. Designed for servers and workstations.
Pentium III. 450, 500, 550, and 600 MHz.	Processor package: Single Edge Contact Cartridge (SECC2). System bus speed: 100 MHz. Addressable memory: 64GB. Introduced: February, May, and August 1999. The Pentium III processor featured 70 new instructions including many aimed at use with Internet applications including streaming audio, video, and speech recognition. 9.5 million transistors. 0.25 micron process. 512K L2 cache.
Pentium II	
Pentium II Xeon. 450 MHz.	Processor package: Single Edge Contact Cartridge (SECC). System bus speed: 100 MHz. Addressable memory: 64GB. Introduced: January 1999. L2 cache: 512K, 1MB, or 2MB. 7.5 million transistors. Designed for servers and workstations.
Pentium II Xeon. 450 MHz.	Processor package: Single Edge Contact Cartridge (SECC). System bus speed: 100 MHz. Addressable memory: 64GB. Introduced: October 1998. 512K L2 cache. 7.5 million transistors. Designed for dual-processor workstations and servers.

Pentium II

Pentium II	
Pentium II. 450 MHz.	Processor package: Single Edge Contact Cartridge (SECC), 242 pins. System bus speed: 100 MHz. Addressable memory: 64GB. Introduced: August 1998. 7.5 million transistors. 0.25 micron process.
Pentium II Xeon. 400 MHz.	Processor package: Single Edge Contact Cartridge (SECC). System bus speed: 100 MHz. Addressable memory: 64GB. Introduced: June 1998. The Pentium II Xeon was intended for mid-range and high-end servers and workstations and included facilities that make it easier to perform advanced data warehousing, digital content creation, and electronic and mechanical design automation. Systems can be configured to scale to four or eight Xeon processors, with extensions for even larger banks of CPUS. L2 cache 512K or 1MB. 7.5 million transistors. 0.25 micron process.
Pentium II. 350 and 400 MHz.	Processor package: Single Edge Contact Cartridge (SECC), 242 pins. System bus speed: 100 MHz. Addressable memory: 64GB. Introduced: April 1998. 7.5 million transistors. 0.25 micron process. 512K L2 cache.
Pentium II. 333 MHz.	Processor package: Single Edge Contact Cartridge (SECC), 242 pins. System bus speed: 66 MHz. Addressable memory: 64GB. Introduced: 7.5 million transistors. 0.25 micron process. 512K L2 cache.
Pentium II. 300, 266, 233 MHz.	Processor package: Single Edge Contact Cartridge (SECC), 242 pins. System bus speed: 66 MHz. Bus width: 64 bits. Addressable memory: 64GB. Introduced: May 1997. The Pentium II processor added Intel MMX technology, designed to process video, audio, and graphics data efficiently. It was introduced in the upright Single Edge Contact (SEC) cartridge that also incorporated a high-speed cache memory chip. 7.5 million transistors. 0.35 micron process. 512K L2 cache.

Pentium Pro

Pentium Pro	
Pentium Pro. 200 MHz.	Processor package: Dual Cavity Pin Grid Array Package, 387 pins. System bus speed: 66 MHz. Addressable memory: 4GB. Introduced: August 1997. 5.5 million transistors. 0.35 micron process. 1MB integrated L2 cache. Internal bus width 300 bits. Designed for workstations and servers.

Continued

**Ch
2**

TABLE 2-2: *Continued*

Pentium Pro

Pentium Pro. 200, 180, 166, 150 MHz.	Processor package: Dual Cavity Pin Grid Array Package, 387 pins. System bus speed: 66 and 60 MHz. Addressable memory: 4GB. Introduced: November 1995. The Pentium Pro was intended as the engine for 32-bit server and workstation applications, and was used widely for computer-aided design, mechanical engineering, and scientific computation. The CPU included a cache memory chip. 5.5 million transistors. 0.35 micron. 256K or 512K L2 cache.

Pentium

Pentium with MMX. 233 MHz.	Processor package: Plastic Pin Grid Array Package, 296 pins. System bus speed: 66 MHz. Addressable memory: 4GB. Introduced: June 1997. 4.5 million transistors. 0.35 micron CMOS. 32-bit microprocessor with 64-bit external bus.
Pentium with MMX. 200, 166 MHz.	Processor package: Plastic Pin Grid Array Package, 296 pins. System bus speed: 66 MHz. Addressable memory: 4GB. Introduced: January 1997. 4.5 million transistors. 0.35 micron CMOS. 32-bit microprocessor with 64-bit external bus.
Pentium. 200 MHz.	Processor package: Plastic Pin Grid Array Package, 296 pins. System bus speed: 66 MHz. Addressable memory: 4GB. Introduced: June 1996. 3.3 million transistors. 0.35 micron BiCMOS. 32-bit microprocessor with 64-bit external data bus.
Pentium. 166, 150 MHz.	Processor package: Pin Grid Array Package, 296 pins. System bus speed: 66, 60, and 50 MHz. Addressable memory: 4GB. Introduced: January 1996. 3.3 million transistors. 0.35 micron BiCMOS. 32-bit microprocessor with 64-bit external data bus.
Pentium. 133 MHz.	Processor package: Pin Grid Array Package, 296 pins. System bus speed: 66 MHz. Addressable memory: 4GB. Introduced: June 1995. 3.3 million transistors. 0.35 micron BiCMOS. 32-bit microprocessor with 64-bit external bus.
Pentium. 120 MHz.	Processor package: Pin Grid Array Package, 296 pins. System bus speed: 66 MHz. Addressable memory: 4GB. Introduced: March 1995. 3.2 million transistors (0.6 and .35 micron processes). BiCMOS. 32-bit microprocessor with 64-bit external bus.
Pentium. 75 MHz.	Processor package: Lead Tape Carrier Package (TCP), 320 pins; or Staggered Pin Grid Array (SPGA), 296 pins. System bus speed: 50 MHz. Addressable memory: 4GB. Introduced: October 1994. 3.2 million transistors. 0.6 micron, BiCMOS. 32-bit microprocessor with 64-bit external bus.
Pentium. 90, 100 MHz.	Processor package: Pin Grid Array Package, 296 pins. System bus speed: 60 and 66 MHz. Addressable memory: 4GB. Introduced: March 1994. 3.2 million transistors. 0.6 micron, BiCMOS. 32-bit microprocessor with 64-bit external bus.

Pentium

Pentium. 60, 66 MHz.	Processor package: Pin Grid Array Package, 273 pins. System bus speed: 60 or 66 MHz. Addressable memory: 4GB. Introduced: March 1993. The advanced Pentium, the fifth major generation of Intel processors, included features that permitted multimedia audio and video. 3.1 million transistors. 0.8 micron, BiCMOS. 32-bit microprocessor with 64-bit external bus.

Intel 486

IntelDX4. 75 MHz.	Processor package: Pin Grid Array Package, 168 pins; or SQFP Package, 208 pins. System bus speed: 50 MHz. Addressable memory: 4GB. Introduced: March 1994. 1.6 million transistors. 0.6 micron.
Intel486 SL. 20, 25, 33 MHz.	System bus speed: 33 or 55 MHz. Addressable memory: 4GB. Introduced: November 1992. 1.5 million transistors. 0.8 micron. First CPU specifically designed for notebook PCs.
IntelDX2. 50, 66 MHz.	System bus speed: 33 or 50 MHz. Addressable memory: 4GB. Introduced: March 1992. 1.2 million transistors. 0.8 micron. Introduced speed-doubling technology permitting microprocessor to run at twice the speed of the bus.
Intel486 SX. 16, 20, 25, 33 MHz.	System bus speed: 33 or 50 MHz. Addressable memory: 4GB. Bus width: 32 bits. Addressable memory: 4GB. Introduced: April 1991 and September 1991. 1.2 million transistors at 1 micron process or 0.9 million at 0.8 process. Same as Intel486 DX without a math coprocessor on chip. Upgradeable with the Intel OverDrive processor.
Intel486. 25, 33, 60 MHz.	System bus speed: 33 or 50 MHz. Addressable memory: 4GB. Bus width: 32 bits. Addressable memory: 4GB. Introduced: April 1989. The first Intel processor to include a built-in math coprocessor, which sped computing by offloading complex math functions from the central processor. 1.2 million transistors at 0.8 micron.

Intel 386

Intel386 SL. 20, 25 MHz.	System bus speed: 25 or 33 MHz. Addressable memory: 4GB. Introduced: October 1990, September 1991. 885,000 transistors at 1 micron process. 32-bit microprocessor with 16-bit external bus. First CPU made specifically for portable PCs.
Intel386 SX. 16, 20, 25, 33 MHz.	System bus speed: 25 or 33 MHz. Bus width: 16 bits. Addressable memory: 16MB. Introduced: June 1988. 275,000 transistors. Originally 1.5 micron process, then 1 micron. 32-bit microprocessor with 16-bit external bus.

Continued

TABLE 2-2: *Continued*

Intel 386

Intel386 DX. 20, 25, 33 MHz.	System bus speed: 25 or 33 MHz. Bus width: 32 bits. Addressable memory: 4GB. Possessing more than 100 times as many transistors as the original 4004, the 32-bit chip was capable of *multitasking,* meaning it could run multiple programs at the same time. October 1985, February 1987, April 1988, April 1989. 275,000 transistors. Originally 1.5 micron process, then 1 micron.

Intel 80286

80286. 6, 10, 12 MHz.	System bus speed: 6, 8, 8.33 MHz. Bus width: 16 bits. Addressable memory: 16MB. Introduced: February 1982. The first new generation of processor from Intel, it launched the PC AT clone industry and introduced the concept of downward compatibility with all of its predecessors, allowing nearly all earlier software to run on later chips. Within six years of its release, there were an estimated 15 million personal computers based on the 80286. 134,000 transistors. 1.5 micron process.

Intel 808X family

8088. 4.77, 8 MHz.	System bus speed: 4.77 MHz. Bus width: 8 bits. Addressable memory: 1MB. Introduced: June 1979. The original chip for the IBM PC, identical to the 8086 except for its 8-bit external bus. 29,000 transistors. 3 micron process. 16-bit internal, 8-bit external.
8086. 8, 10 MHz.	Bus width: 16 bits. Addressable memory: 1MB. Introduced: June 1978. 29,000 transistors. 3 micron process. Used in early portables.
8085. 5 MHz.	Introduced: March 1976. 6,500 transistors. 3 micron process. Used in scales and simple calculators.
8080. 2 MHz.	Bus width: 8 bits. Addressable memory: 64K. Introduced: April 1974. Used as the brains of one of the first personal computers offered to the public, the Altair (named after one of the worlds visited by the Starship *Enterprise* in the original *Star Trek* television show). 6,000 transistors. 6 micron process.
8008. 200 KHz.	Bus width: 8 bits. Addressable memory: 16K. Introduced: April 1972. Twice as powerful as the 4004, it was used in homemade and hobbyist computers, including the Mark-8, and in dumb terminals and simple calculators. 3,500 transistors. 10 micron process.

Intel 808X family

4004. 108 KHz.	Bus width: 4 bits. Addressable memory: 640 bytes. Introduced: November 1971. Intel's first microprocessor was the engine behind the Busicom calculator. 2,300 transistors. 10 micron process.

Mobile CPUs

Mobile Intel Celeron. 450–850 MHz.	Processor packages: Ball Grid Array (BGA2) and Pin Grid Array (PGA2). System bus speed: 100 MHz. Addressable memory: 64GB. Introduced: July 2001. 0.18 micron process. 128K on-die L2 Cache.
Ultra Low Voltage Mobile Pentium III. 600 MHz.	Processor package: Ball Grid Array (BGA). System bus speed: 100 MHz front side bus. Addressable memory: 64GB. Introduced: May 2001. 256K integrated advanced transfer cache. Designed for business and computer mobile PCs.
Low Voltage Mobile Pentium III. 750 MHz.	Processor package: Ball Grid Array (BGA2). System bus speed: 100 MHz. Addressable memory: 64GB. Introduced: May 2001. Intel SpeedStep technology to adjust clock speed based on demand, saving power. 256K integrated advanced transfer cache. 0.18 micron process.
Ultra Low Voltage Mobile Celeron. 600 MHz.	Processor package: Ball Grid Array (BGA). System bus speed: 100 MHz front side bus. Addressable memory: 64GB. Introduced: May 2001. 128K on-die L2 cache.
Low Voltage Mobile Celeron. 600 MHz.	Processor package: Ball Grid Array (BGA). System bus speed: 100 MHz Addressable memory: 64GB. Introduced: May 2001. 256K advanced transfer cache. 0.18 micron process. Designed for value mobile PCs.
Mobile Intel Celeron. 800 MHz.	Processor package: Ball Grid Array (BGA2) and Pin Grid Array (PGA2). System bus speed: 100 MHz. Addressable memory: 64GB. Introduced: May 2001. 128K on-die L2 cache. 0.18 micron process.
Mobile Pentium III. 900 MHz, 1.0 GHz.	Processor package: Ball Grid Array (BGA2) and Micro Pin Grid Array (Micro-PGA2). System bus speed: 100 MHz. Addressable memory: 64GB. Introduced: March 2001. Intel SpeedStep Technology. Integrated 256K L2 advanced transfer cache. Designed for use in high-end business and consumer portables.
Mobile Intel Celeron. 750 MHz.	Processor package: Ball Grid Array (BGA2) and Pin Grid Array (PGA2). System bus speed: 100 MHz. Addressable memory: 64GB. Introduced: March 2001. 128K on-die L2 cache. Designed for value portables.
Low Voltage Mobile Pentium III. 600 and 700 MHz.	Processor package: Ball Grid Array (BGA2). System bus speed: 100 MHz. Addressable memory: 64GB. Introduced: February 2001 and June 2000. Intel SpeedStep technology. 256K integrated L2 advanced transfer cache.

Continued

TABLE 2-2: *Continued*

Mobile CPUs

Ultra Low Voltage Mobile Pentium III. 500 MHz; 300 MHz in battery optimized mode.	Processor package: Ball Grid Array (BGA). System bus speed: 100 MHz front side bus. Addressable memory: 64GB. Introduced: January 2001. Intel SpeedStep technology. 256K integrated advanced transfer cache.
Ultra Low Voltage Mobile Celeron. 500 MHz.	Processor package: Ball Grid Array (BGA). System bus speed: 100 MHz front side bus. Addressable memory: 64GB. Introduced: January 2001. 128K on-die L2 cache.
Mobile Pentium III. 800 and 850 MHz.	Processor package: Ball Grid Array (BGA2) or Micro Pin Grid Array (Micro-PGA2). System bus speed: 100 MHz. Addressable memory: 64GB. Introduced: September 2000. Intel SpeedStep Technology. 0.18 micron process. 256K L2 integrated advanced transfer cache.
Mobile Intel Celeron. 700 MHz.	Processor package: Ball Grid Array (BGA2) and Pin Grid Array (PGA2). System bus speed: 100 MHz. Addressable memory: 64GB. Introduced: September 2000. 128K on-die L2 cache. Designed for value portables.
Low Voltage Mobile Pentium III. 600 MHz.	Processor package: Ball Grid Array (BGA2). System bus speed: 100 MHz. Addressable memory: 64GB. Introduced: June 2000. 256K integrated L2 advanced transfer cache. Uses Intel SpeedStep Technology.
Low Voltage Mobile Intel Celeron. 500 MHz.	Processor package: Ball Grid Array (BGA2). System bus speed: 100 MHz. Addressable memory: 64GB. Introduced: June 2000. 128K integrated L2 advanced transfer cache.
Mobile Pentium III. 750 MHz.	Processor package: Ball Grid Array (BGA2) or Micro Pin Grid Array (Micro-PGA2). System bus speed: 100 MHz. Addressable memory: 64GB. Introduced: June 2000. Intel SpeedStep Technology. 0.18 micron process. 256K L2 integrated advanced transfer cache.
Mobile Intel Celeron. 600 and 650 MHz.	Processor package: Ball Grid Array (BGA2) and Pin Grid Array (PGA2). System bus speed: 100 MHz. Addressable memory: 64GB. Introduced: June 2000. 128K on-die L2 cache. 0.18 micron process. Designed for value portables.
Mobile Pentium III. 700 MHz.	Processor package: Ball Grid Array (BGA2) or Micro Pin Grid Array (Micro-PGA2). System bus speed: 100 MHz. Addressable memory: 64GB. Introduced: April 2000. Intel SpeedStep Technology. 0.18 micron process. 256K integrated L2 advanced transfer cache.
Mobile Intel Celeron. 550 MHz.	Processor package: Ball Grid Array (BGA2) and Pin Grid Array (PGA2). System bus speed: 100 MHz. Addressable memory: 64GB. Introduced: April 2000. 128K on-die L2 cache. 0.18 micron process. Designed for value portables.

Ch 2

Mobile CPUs

Mobile Intel Celeron. 500, 450 MHz.	Processor package: Ball Grid Array (BGA2) and Pin Grid Array (PGA2). System bus speed: 100 MHz. Addressable memory: 64GB. Introduced: February 2000. 128K on-die L2 Cache.
Mobile Pentium III. 650, 600 MHz.	Processor package: Ball Grid Array (BGA2) or Micro Pin Grid Array (micro PGA). System bus speed: 100 MHz. Addressable memory: 64GB. Introduced: January 2000. Intel SpeedStep Technology. 256K integrated L2 advanced transfer cache.
Mobile Pentium III. 500, 450, and 400 MHz.	Processor package: Mobile Module, Ball Grid Array (BGA) or Micro Pin Grid Array (micro PGA). System bus speed: 100 MHz. Addressable memory: 64GB. Introduced: October 1999. 28 million transistors. 0.18 micron process. 256K integrated L2 advanced transfer cache.
Mobile Intel Celeron. 466 and 433 MHz.	Processor package: Ball Grid Array (BGA). System bus speed: 66 MHz. Addressable memory: 64GB. Introduced: September 1999. 18.9 million transistors. 0.25 micron process. 128K on-die L2 cache. Designed for value mobile PCs.
Mobile Pentium II. 400 MHz.	Processor package: Ball Grid Array (BGA). System bus speed: 66 MHz. Addressable memory: 64GB. Introduced: June 1999. 27.4 million transistors. 0.18 micron process. 256K on-die L2 cache.
Mobile Pentium II. 400 MHz.	Processor package: Mini-Cartridge and MMC1, MMC2. System bus speed: 66 MHz. Addressable memory: 64GB. Introduced: June 1999. 27.4 million transistors. 0.25 micron process. 256K on-die L2 cache.
Mobile Intel Celeron. 400 MHz.	Processor package: Ball Grid Array (BGA), 615 balls. System bus speed: 66 MHz. Addressable memory: 64GB. Introduced: June 1999. 18.9 million transistors. 0.25 micron process. 128K on-die L2 cache.
Mobile Intel Celeron. 366 MHz.	Processor package: Ball Grid Array (BGA), 615 balls. System bus speed: 66 MHz. Addressable memory: 64GB. Introduced: May 1999. 18.9 million transistors. 0.25 micron process. 128K on-die L2 cache.
Mobile Intel Celeron. 333 MHz.	Processor package: Ball Grid Array (BGA), 615 balls. System bus speed: 66 MHz. Addressable memory: 64GB. Introduced: April 1999. 18.9 million transistors. 0.25 micron process. 128K on-die L2 cache.
Mobile Pentium II. 266, 300, 333, and 366 MHz.	Processor package: Ball Grid Array (BGA). System bus speed: 66 MHz. Addressable memory: 64GB. Introduced: January 1999. 27.4 million transistors. 0.25 micron process. 256K on-die L2 cache.

Continued

TABLE 2-2: *Continued*

Mobile Intel Celeron. 266 and 300 MHz.	Processor package: Ball Grid Array (BGA), 615 balls. System bus speed: 66 MHz. Addressable memory: 64GB. Introduced: January 1999. 18.9 million transistors. 0.25 micron process. 128K on-die L2 cache.
Mobile Pentium with MMX. 300 MHz.	Processor package: Tape Carrier Package (TCP), 320-pin. System bus speed: 66 MHz. Addressable memory: 64GB. Introduced: January 1999. 4.5 million transistors. 0.25 micron process. 32-bit microprocessor works with 64-bit bus width.
Mobile Pentium II. 300 MHz.	Processor package: Mobile mini-cartridge, 240 pins. System bus speed: 66 MHz. Addressable memory: 64GB. Introduced: September 1998. 7.5 million transistors. 0.25 micron process. 512K L2 cache.
Mobile Pentium II. 233 and 266 MHz.	Processor package: Mobile mini-cartridge, 240 pins. System bus speed: 66 MHz. Addressable memory: 64GB. Introduced: April 1998. 7.5 million transistors. 0.25 micron process. 512K L2 cache.
Mobile Pentium with MMX. 266 MHz.	Processor package: Tape Carrier Package (TCP), 320-pin. System bus speed: 66MHz. Addressable memory: 64GB. Introduced: January 1998. 4.5 million transistors. 0.25 micron process. 32-bit microprocessor with 64-bit bus width.
Mobile Pentium with MMX. 200, 233 MHz.	Processor package: Tape Carrier Package (TCP), 320-pin. System bus speed: 66 MHz. Addressable memory: 64GB. Introduced: September 1997. 4.5 million transistors. 0.25 micron process. 32-bit microprocessor with 64-bit bus width.

Table 2-3 examines in greater detail the capabilities of Intel processors, from the dinosaur 8086 to the modern Pentium 4 and Itanium.

TABLE 2-3: Intel Processors

	8086	8088	80286
Address bus	16 bit	16 bit	24 bit
Data bus	16 bit	8 bit	16 bit
FPU?	No	No	No
Memory management?	No	No	No
Internal cache?	No	No	No
Clock speed (MHz)	5, 8, 10	5, 8, 10	6, 8, 10, 12
Average cycles/ instruction	12	12	4.9
Frequency of FPU	=CPU	=CPU	2/3 CPU

	8086	8088	80286
Upgradeable?	No	No	No
Address range	1MB	1MB	16MB
Frequency scalability?	No	No	No
Voltage	5 volts	5 volts	5 volts
Number of transistors	29,000	29,000	134,000
Date of introduction	June 1978	June 1979	February 1982

	i386 SX	i386 DX	i386 SL
Address bus	24 bit	32 bit	24 bit
Data bus	16 bit	32 bit	16 bit
FPU?	n/a	n/a	n/a
Memory management?	Yes	Yes	Yes
Internal cache?	No	No	Control
Clock speed (MHz)	16, 20, 25, 33	16, 20, 25, 33	16, 20, 25
Average cycles/ instruction	4.9	4.9	<4.9
Frequency of FPU	=CPU	=CPU	=CPU
Upgradeable?	No	No	No
Address range	16MB	4GB	16MB
Voltage	5 volts	5 volts	3 or 5 volts
Number of transistors	275,000	275,000	855,000
Date of introduction	June 1988	October 1985	October 1990

	i486 SX	i486 DX	i486 SL	i486 DX2	i486DX4
Internal bus	32 bits	32 bits	32 bits	32 bits	32 bits
External bus	32 bits	32 bits	32 bits	32 bits	32 bits
Virtual address space	64TB	64TB	64TB	64TB	64TB
Physical address space	4GB	4GB	4GB	4GB	4GB
Clock speed (MHz)	16, 20, 25, 33	25, 33, 50	25, 33	50, 66	75, 100
Math coprocessor	Available	Built in	Built in	Built in	Built in
Cache control	Built in	Built in	Built in	Built in	Built in
Level 1 cache	Built in	Built in	Built in	Built in	Built in
OverDrive support?	Yes	Yes	No	Yes	Yes

Continued

TABLE 2-3: *Continued*

	i486 SX	i486 DX	i486 SL	i486 DX2	i486DX4
Number of transistors	1.2 million	1.2 million	1.4 million	1.2 million	1.6 million
Date of introduction	April 1991	April 1989	November 1992	March 1992	March 1994

	Pentium	Pentium with MMX	Pentium Pro	Pentium II
Internal bus	32 bits	32 bits	32 bits	32 bits
External bus	64 bits	64 bits	64 bits to front, 64 bits to L2 cache	64 bits
Virtual address space	64TB	64TB	64TB	64TB
Physical address space	4GB	4GB	64GB	64GB
Clock speed (MHz)	60–165	150–200	150–200	233–400
Math coprocessor	Built in	Built in	Built in	Built in
Cache control	Built in	Built in	Built in	Built in
Level 1 cache	Built in	Built in	Built in	Built in
OverDrive support?	Yes	Yes	Yes	Yes
Number of transistors	3.1–3.3 million	4.5 million	5.5 million	7.5 million
Date of introduction	March 1993	January 1997	November 1995	January 1997

	Celeron	Pentium III	Pentium 4	Itanium
Internal bus	32 bits	32 bits	32 bits	64 bits
External bus	64 bits	64 bits	64 bits	64 bits
Virtual address space	64TB	64TB	64TB	64TB
Physical address space	64GB	64GB	64GB	64GB to 1TB
Clock speed (MHz)	400–1100	450–1300	1300–2200	800 and greater
Math coprocessor	Built in	Built in	Built in	Built in
Cache control	Built in	Built in	Built in	Built in
1st-level cache	Built in	Built in	Built in	Built in
OverDrive support?	No	No	No	No
Number of transistors	19 million (includes L2 cache)	9.5 million	42 million	25 million
Date of introduction	August 1998	February 1999	November 2000	Mid-2001

Chipsets

No matter how capable a modern CPU is, it still needs to be surrounded by the appropriate supporting cast. The most important such element is the motherboard's chipset, which interfaces among the CPU, the BIOS, the data bus, and the memory bus.

Most Intel CPUs are mated to a particular Intel-manufactured chipset, although you'll also see some supporting chips from Taiwanese manufacturers such as the ALI Aladdin products (Acer Laboratories, Inc.), SiS, and VIA. In general, the Intel chipsets offer the most stable support for Intel CPUs. The clone systems are generally marketed to manufacturers on the basis of price rather than features. In most cases, the bus, system clock, BIOS, and motherboard are optimized for a particular chipset, and the support chips are likely to be soldered into place and not changeable.

The state-of-the-art in chipsets for standard systems in 2001 was Intel's 850 chipset, which mates the Pentium 4's 3.2-giga-bytes-per-second bus to 3.2-gigabytes-per-second of memory bandwidth using high-speed Dual RDRAM memory. Intel also offered the 845 chipset, which allows use of the Pentium 4 with slightly slower but less-expensive SDRAM memory. (Table 2-4 contains information about current Intel chipsets. You can also find this chipset comparison information online at Intel's Web site at `developer.intel.com/design/chipsets/linecard.htm`.) Industry analysts expect major PC manufacturers to use Intel 845 and 850 chipsets or derivatives of them through the end of 2002.

An earlier high-end chipset was Intel's 840, which supports dual Pentium III or Pentium III Xeon CPUs, dual RDRAM channels, up to 8GB of RAM with combined transfer speeds up to 3.2 gigabytes per second (GBps), and AGP graphics with up to 1 GBps data transfer speeds. It also enables bridging multiple PCI buses to expand the number of PCI slots available to the system and supports 100 or 133 MHz system buses.

A notch below the 840 is the 820 chipset, which supports two CPUs and 1GB of RAM. The 820 also supports the Universal Serial Bus, bus-mastering, IDE, AGP, and more. The 820 chipset was the first Intel chipset to support RDRAM and the first to support a 133 MHz system bus.

CROSS-REFERENCE

For more information on RDRAM, see Chapter 8.

AC'97 (Audio Codec 97) components are part of all current chipsets. AC'97 allows the processor to emulate an audio card or modem in software. In a way, this is both a step forward and backward at the same time. The idea is to make use of the system's CPU and memory instead of more expensive specialized controllers and RAM on a modem or audio card; the high-speed and abundant memory of modern machines make this possible and lower the overall cost of the system. You still get better performance by using a dedicated modem or sound card, but many users will not notice the difference.

Ch 2

TABLE 2-4: Current Intel Chipsets

Host	860 Chipset	850 Chipset	845 Chipset	840 Chipset	820/820E Chipset	815E Chipset	440GX AGPset	440BX AGPset
Target Segment	Workstation	Entry-level workstation, Performance PC, Mainstream PC	Performance PC, Mainstream PC	Workstation	Mainstream PC	Mainstream PC, Value PC	Workstation	Workstation
Host Processor	Intel Xeon processor for DP workstations	Pentium 4 processor	Pentium 4 processor	Pentium III processor, Pentium III Xeon processor	Pentium III processor, Pentium II processor	Celeron or Pentium III processor (.13 and .18)	Pentium III Xeon processor, Pentium II Xeon processor	Celeron processor, Pentium III processor, Pentium II processor
Number of Processors	1–2	1	1	1–2	1–2	1	2–4	1–2
System Bus Memory Modules	400MHz (data) 4 RIMMs, up to 8 RIMMS with MRH-R	400MHz (data) 4 RIMMs	400MHz (data) 3 double-sided DIMMs	133/100 MHz 2 RIMMs, up to 4 RIMMs with MRH-R	133/100 MHz 2 RIMMs	133/100/66 MHz 3 DIMMs	100/66 MHz 4 double-sided DIMMs	100/66 MHz 4 double-sided DIMMs
Memory Type	PC800/600 RDRAM	PC800/600 RDRAM	PC133 SDRAM	PC800/600 RDRAM	PC800/700/ 600 RDRAM	PC133/100 SDRAM	PC100 SDRAM	PC100 SDRAM
Max Memory	4GB (w/ 2 repeaters)	2 GB	3GB	4GB (with 2 repeaters)	1GB	512MB	2GB	1GB
Number of Rows/Devices	32 RDRAM/ channel	32 RDRAM/ channel (64 total)	6 rows	32 RDRAM/ channel	32 RDRAM devices	6 rows	8 rows	8 rows
Mbit Support	256/128 Mbit	256/128 Mbit	512/256/128/ 64 Mbit	256/128/ 64 Mbit	256/128/ 64 Mbit	256/128/64/ 16 Mbit	256/128/ 64 Mbit	128/64/ 16 Mbit
ECC/Parity	Yes	Yes	Yes	Yes	Yes	N/A	Yes	ECC/Parity
Memory Controller Hub Type	82860 MCH	82850 MCH	82845 MCH	82840 MCH	82820 MCH		82443GX	82443BX

Host	860 Chipset	850 Chipset	845 Chipset	840 Chipset	820/820E Chipset	815E Chipset	440GX AGPset	440BX AGPset
Package	1024 OLGA	615 OLGA	FC-BGA 593	544 BGA	324 BGA	544 BGA	492 BGA	492 BGA
I/O Controller Hub Type	ICH2	ICH2	ICH2	ICH	ICH2		PIIX4E	PIIX4E
ICH Package	360 EBGA	360 EBGA	360 EBGA	241 BGA	360 EBGA	360 EBGA	PIIX4 324 BGA	PIIX4 324 BGA
PCI Support	PCI 2.2	PCI 2.2	PCI 2.2	PCI 2.2	PCI 2.2	PCI 2.2	PCI 2.1	PCI 2.1
PCI Masters	6	6	6	6	6	6	6	6
IDE	ATA/100	ATA/100	ATA/100	ATA/66	820E: ATA/100. 820: ATA/66	815E: ATA/100. 815: ATA/66	ATA/33	ATA/33
Graphics	AGP 4X/2X (1.5V)	AGP 4X/2X (1.5V)	AGP 4X/2X (1.5V)	AGP 4X/2X	AGP 4X/2X/1X	AGP 4X/2X/1X,	AGP 4X/2X/1X,	AGP 2X/1X
AC'97 Digital Circuits	Audio/Modem	Audio/Modem	Audio/Modem	Audio/Modem	Audio/Modem	Audio/Modem	Audio/Modem	Audio/Modem
LAN MAC/ PNA	Yes	Yes	Yes	No	Yes	815E: Yes. 815: No	No	No
USB Ports/ Controllers	2 controllers, 4 ports	2 controllers, 4 ports	2 controllers, 4 ports	1 controller, 2 ports	820E: 2 controllers, 4 ports. 820: 1 controller, 2 ports	815E: 2 controllers, 4 ports. 815: 1 controller, 2 ports	1 controller, 2 ports	1 controller, 2 ports

Intel 860 chipset

The 860 chipset was designed for high-performance multiprocessor systems, generally those using Intel Xeon processors, and includes the following features:

- The 82860 Memory Controller Hub (MCH) is the main interface to the processor host bus, the memory, and graphics interfaces. The chip offers a 400 MHz system bus and the capability to add as many as two additional high-performance 64-bit 66 MHz PCI segments. And the set supports 1.5V AGP4X technology for graphics, allowing 1 GBps of graphics bandwidth.

- The dual RDRAM memory channels can together deliver 3.2 GBps of memory bandwidth to the processor.
- The enhanced 82801BA I/O Controller Hub (ICH2) delivers twice the I/O bandwidth over traditional bridge architecture. Included is a direct connection from the graphics and memory for faster access to peripherals, including support for 32-bit PCI, Ultra ATA/100, and an integrated LAN controller. Dual USB controllers can be used to configure four full-bandwidth USB ports.
- The set supports six channels of digital audio.
- The 82806AA 64-bit PCI Controller Hub (P64H) supports 64-bit PCI slots at 33 MHz or 66 MHz.

Intel 850 chipset

The Intel 850 chipset was designed in tandem with the Intel Pentium 4 processor and the Intel NetBurst micro-architecture, which doubles the length of the pipeline between the processor and the chipset for higher performance. Some of this chipset's key features include the following:

- The 82850 Memory Controller Hub (MCH) delivers dual RDRAM memory channels, a 400 MHz system bus, and 1.5V AGP4X technology for graphics.
- The 400 MHz system bus is balanced with dual RDRAM channels at 3.2 GBps, triple the potential bandwidth of systems based on Intel Pentium III processors.
- Included in the set is an 82801BA I/O Controller Hub (ICH2), like the Intel 860, providing a direct connection from the graphics and memory for faster access to peripherals.
- Two USB controllers double the bandwidth available for USB peripherals to 24 MBps over four ports.
- AC'97 audio delivers six channels of digital audio, including full surround-sound capability.
- The LAN Connect Interface (LCI) includes networking facilities such as home phone line and 10/100 MBps Ethernet.
- Dual Ultra ATA/100 controllers support the fastest IDE interface for transfers to storage devices.
- The set supports use of a Communication and Networking Riser (CNR), allowing the upgrade to include an integrated audio card, modem card, or network card.

Intel 845 chipset

Intel introduced the Pentium 4 processor with the high-performance Intel 850 support chipset, based around RDRAM memory. The Intel 845 chipset offers most of the same facilities, but works instead with less-expensive PC133 SDRAM memory. Key qualities of the 845 chipset are as follows:

- The 845 chipset consists of two controller hubs. The 82845 Memory Controller Hub (MCH) supports a 400 MHz system bus, PC133 SDRAM memory, and the latest graphics devices through the 1.5V AGP4X interface. The 82801BA I/O Controller Hub (ICH2) makes a direct connection to the graphics and memory for faster access to peripherals; this is the same hub used in the 850 chipset.
- The 400 MHz system bus delivers a high-bandwidth connection between the Pentium 4 processor and the platform, providing three times the bandwidth over platforms based on Intel Pentium III processors.
- Two USB controllers provide high-performance peripherals with 24 MBps of bandwidth, while enabling support for up to four USB ports, a doubling of bandwidth and ports over earlier systems.
- The chipset also includes dual Ultra ATA/100 controllers.

Intel 840 chipset

The 840 chipset was designed for use with high-performance multiprocessor systems and introduced as a companion to Intel Pentium III or Intel Pentium III Xeon processors. Its features include the following:

- The 82840 Memory Controller Hub (MCH) provides graphics support for AGP 2X/4X, dual RDRAM memory channels, and multiple PCI segments for high performance I/O. The set can be paired with an 82803 RDRAM-based memory repeater hub (MRH-R), which converts each memory channel into two memory channels for expanded memory capacity.
- The 82806 64-bit PCI Controller Hub (P64H) supports 64-bit PCI slots at speeds of either 33 or 66 MHz.

Intel 440GX AGPset

The 440GX AGPset was designed for midrange workstations and enterprise servers, released to support Pentium II Xeon and Intel Pentium III Xeon processors. Based around a 100 MHz system bus, the chipset builds on the Intel 440BX AGPset with support for up to 2GB of SDRAM memory.

Intel 440BX AGPset

The 440BX AGPset was intended to optimize the Pentium III processor for 3-D and video applications with 100 MHz system bus SDRAM and ATA/66 hard drive interface in UDMA mode 2. The chipset allows motherboard designs with either a 66 MHz or 100 MHz system bus. It is also commonly used in advanced mobile systems.

AMD-760

Designed for the AMD Athlon processor, the set includes two chips: the AMD-761 system bus controller, or northbridge, and the AMD-766 peripheral bus controller, or southbridge. The chipset's principal advance is the facility to use PC2100 DDR memory and PC1600 DDR memory. The AMD-760 chipset supports up to a 266 MHz front side bus and 266 MHz high-performance Double Data Rate (DDR) memory as well as AGP-4X graphics adapters.

AMD-760 MP

A multiprocessing chipset aimed at use with AMD Athlon MP processors, the AMD-760 MP consists of the AMD-762 system bus controller, or northbridge, and the AMD-766 peripheral bus controller, or southbridge. The chipset can work with one or two AMD Athlon MP processors, a 266 MHz front side bus, PC2100 DDR memory, and AGP-4X graphics, and incorporates 33 MHz/32-bit/64-bit PCI support.

Identifying an Intel CPU

If you're not sure about the type and speed of CPU within your machine, you can, of course, take off the cover and examine the microprocessor installed on the motherboard. You can also try to read the text on your monitor as the system BIOS goes through its bootup tests.

One easier way — and the only way to be absolutely certain that the 1.4 GHz chip you purchased really delivers that speed — is to use a utility program that queries the internal identification of the CPU and tests its operation.

One such program is Intel's Frequency ID program, offered for free on the company's Web site. To download the utility, go to `support.intel.com/support/processors/tools/frequency id/index.htm` or conduct a search at the main Web site, `www.intel.com`, and look for Frequency ID.

Intel's Frequency ID utility queries the microprocessor on your system and comes back with one or two status reports, depending on the age of your system. The program, of course, works only with Intel brand microprocessors.

The utility will display a dialog box with the Frequency Test tab and the CPU ID data tab for the following processors: Pentium 4, Intel Xeon, Pentium III, Pentium III Xeon, and Intel Celerons with a 0.18 micron core. You'll see only the CPU ID data tab for Pentium II, Intel Celerons with a 0.25 micron core, Pentium Pro, Pentium, and Pentium MMX processors.

The CPU ID data tab reports the Intel processor name, family, type, and the *stepping* of the processor — the usually minor revisions to an existing product over the course of its life. Also on the page is information about the L1 and L2 memory caches in the

Ch
2

processor, and the cartridge or packaging type for the CPU. Some of the information you find on this tab includes the following:

- The CPU Type number indicates whether the Intel processor was intended for installation by a consumer (indicated by a 1) or by a professional PC system manufacturer (0).
- The CPU Family number indicates the Intel processor generation and brand; for example, a Pentium III processor is considered a sixth-generation processor.
- The CPU Model number identifies to Intel the processor's manufacturing technology and design generation within the family.

An example of a CPU ID data tab is shown in Figure 2-3.

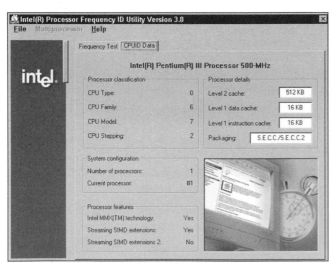

FIGURE 2-3: *A CPU ID report for an Intel Pentium III*

The Frequency Test Tab provides information on the expected and actual operating status of the tested processor and system bus. If all is well, both sets of numbers will be the same. You can see an example of one report in Figure 2-4.

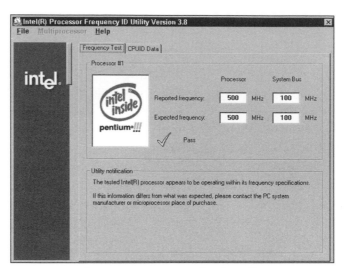

FIGURE 2-4: *The Frequency Test tab of Intel's Frequency ID utility reports on the expected and actual speed of your processor and the system bus of your PC.*

Benchmark Index of Intel Processors

Over the years, Intel has introduced, updated, and then abandoned a number of different suites of benchmark tests to compare the relative speed of microprocessors; the benchmarks have changed as new microprocessors were optimized for new tasks, including graphics, video, and the Internet. In Table 2-5, I've listed seven different scales used by Intel over the years, but enough of an overlap exists to show the steady onward march of speed and capability.

The first suite was the *Intel Comparative Microprocessor Performance* (iCOMP) index, which tracked the relative performance of various Intel chips from early 386 chips through the Pentium III. It was primarily based on the PCBench 7.0 test, with lesser weight going to SPECint92, and a small component of the total score based on SPECfp92 and Whetstone tests.

In 1996, Intel updated and recalculated the iCOMP index to better reflect modern 32-bit software and multimedia applications, releasing the iCOMP Index 2.0. This result is a weighted average based on five industry-standard benchmarks: CPUmark32, Norton SI-32, SPECint95, SPECfp95, and the Intel Media Benchmark. The base processor for the iCOMP 2.0 was a Pentium 120 MHz processor, rated at 100 on the scale.

iCOMP 3.0 compares the performance of later CPUs in the Intel family. As with previous iCOMP comparisons, Index 3.0 is not a benchmark; rather, it is a collection of benchmarks that attempts to produce a meaningful index of relative performance based on a variety of criteria. For example, Index 3.0 takes into account the increasing importance of multimedia, 3-D technologies, and the Internet.

It's not easy to directly compare the various iCOMP benchmarks, or iCOMP and other tests, because each index compares different criteria. Within a given index, however, different numbers can help you evaluate relative CPU performance.

*SPECint_base*2000* is part of SPEC CPU*2000, a software benchmark produced by the Standard Performance Evaluation Corporation (SPEC), a group of computer vendors and researchers. Elements of the benchmark are SPECint_base*2000, which measures computer-intensive integer performance, and SPECfp_base*2000, which measures floating-point performance. SPEC benchmarks are selected from existing application and benchmark source code running across multiple platforms.

SYSmark2001 is a suite of software tests and benchmarks developed by the Business Applications Performance Corporation (BAPCO), a consortium of computer industry publications, independent testing labs, and manufacturers. It measures system performance on popular business-oriented applications in the Windows operating environment. Among the elements of the test are Microsoft Excel, Microsoft PowerPoint, Microsoft Word, Adobe Photoshop, Adobe Premiere, Macromedia Dreamweaver, and Macromedia Flash. *SYSmark 2000* was an earlier suite of tests based on older applications.

Although later indexes do not exactly track backward into older Intel processors, it is fair to say that an Intel Pentium 120 MHz operates about 30 times faster than an i386 SX-20 CPU, and about three times as fast as a 486DX-22 66 MHz workhorse. By a rough conversion of one index into another, a current Pentium 4 2 GHz (2000 MHz) could be considered as much as 12,000 times faster than an original 8088 chip at 4.77 MHz.

In Table 2-5, MIPS stands for millions of instructions per second and is a measure of a chip's raw horsepower; it doesn't take into account actual work performed by a machine and input-output logjams. By the way, the original Cray 1 supercomputer, once considered the *sine qua non* of big iron machines, ran at 125 MIPS. Today's Pentium 4 machines are capable of speeds approaching 2,000 MIPS.

The real value of Table 2-5 is that it can help buyers evaluate the relative bang for the buck they will receive by specifying a particular CPU speed. Going from a Pentium 4 1.4 GHz to a 2.0 GHz model brings a theoretical processing increase of 30 percent; compare that increase to the price difference to help you decide which chip to buy.

Table 2-5 has information for nearly every microprocessor produced by Intel, from the dawn of the dinosaur through a 2.0 GHz Intel Pentium 4. The higher the rating, the higher the relative performance of the microprocessor.

Ch 2

TABLE 2-5: Benchmark Index of Intel Processors

Processor Type and Speed in MHz	Intel iCOMP	Intel iCOMP 2.0	MIPS	Intel iCOMP 3.0	SPECint base2000 Windows 2000	SYSmark 2000 under Windows 2000	Sysmark 2001 under Windows 2000	Sysmark 2001 under Windows Me
8088 4.77			0.33					
8088 8			0.75					
80286 8			1.2					
80286 10			1.5					
80286 12			2.66					
i386 DX-16			5.0–6.0					
i386 DX-20			6.0–7.0					
i386 SX-16			2.5					
i386 SX-20	32		4.2					
i386 SL-20			4.21					
i386 SL-25	41		5.3					
i386 SX-25	39							
i386 DX-25	49		8.5					
i386 SX-33	56							
i386 DX-33	68		11.4					
i486 SX-16	67		13.0					
i486 SX-20	78		16.5					
i486 SX-25	100		25.0					
i486 SL-25	122							
486 DX-25	122		20.0					
i486 SX-33	136		27.0					
i486 DX-33	166		27.0					
i486 SL-33	166							
i486 DX2-40	182							
i486 DX2-50	231		41.0					
i486 DX-50	249		41.0					
i486 DX2-66	297		54.0					
i486 DX4-75	319		53.0					
i486 DX4-100	435		70.7					

Processor Type and Speed in MHz	Intel iCOMP	Intel iCOMP 2.0	MIPS	Intel iCOMP 3.0	SPECint base2000 Windows 2000	SYSmark 2000 under Windows 2000	Sysmark 2001 under Windows 2000	Sysmark 2001 under Windows Me
Pentium 60	510		100.0					
Pentium 66	567		112.0					
Pentium 75	610	67	126.5					
Pentium 90	735		149.8					
Pentium 100	870	90	166.3					
Pentium 120	1000	100	203.0					
Pentium 133	1110	111	218.9					
Pentium 150		114						
Pentium 166		127						
Pentium 166 with MMX		160						
Pentium 200		142						
Pentium 200 with MMX		182						
Pentium 233 with MMX		203						
Pentium Pro 150		168						
Pentium Pro 180		197						
Pentium Pro 200		220						
Pentium II 233		267						
Pentium II 266		303						
Pentium II 300		332		860				
Pentium II 333		366		940				
Pentium II 350		386		1000				
Pentium II 400		440		1130				
Pentium II 450				1240				
Pentium III 450		510		1500				
Pentium III 500				1650				
Pentium III 550				1780				

Continued

TABLE 2-5: *Continued*

Processor Type and Speed in MHz	Intel iCOMP	Intel iCOMP 2.0	MIPS	Intel iCOMP 3.0	SPECint base2000 Windows 2000	SYSmark 2000 under Windows 2000	Sysmark 2001 under Windows 2000	Sysmark 2001 under Windows Me
Pentium III 600				1930				
Celeron 566						96		
Celeron 600						100		
Celeron 633						106		
Celeron 667						109		
Celeron 700						111		55
Celeron 733						114		57
Celeron 766						115		58
Celeron 800						126		66
Celeron 850						130		68
Celeron 900								71
Celeron 950								73
Celeron 1000 (1 GHz)								75
Celeron 1100 (1.1 GHz)								79
Pentium III 600E				2110		139		
Pentium III 600EB						146		
Pentium III 650				2270		147		
Pentium III 667				2320		158		
Pentium III 700				2420		154		
Pentium III 733				2510		168		
Pentium III 750				2540		161		
Pentium III 800				2690		167		
Pentium III 800EB						178	96	
Pentium III 850						173		
Pentium III 866				2890	411	183		
Pentium III 933				3100	421	190		
Pentium III 1000 (1 GHz)				3280	402	200		
Pentium III 1300 (1.3 GHz)					421	212		

Processor Type and Speed in MHz	Intel iCOMP	Intel iCOMP 2.0	MIPS	Intel iCOMP 3.0	SPECint base2000 Windows 2000	SYSmark 2000 under Windows 2000	Sysmark 2001 under Windows 2000	Sysmark 2001 under Windows Me
Pentium 4 1300 (1.3 GHz)	1,700				475		134	
Pentium 4 1400 (1.4 GHz)					498		143	
Pentium 4 1500 (1.5 GHz)					526		151	
Pentium 4 1600 (1.6 GHz)					551		160	
Pentium 4 1700 (1.7 GHz)					573		166	
Pentium 4 1800 (1.8 GHz)					598		174	
Pentium 4 1900 (1.9 GHz)					619		180	
Pentium 4 2000 (2 GHz)					640		187	

NOTE

For more information on Intel products, consult the company's Web page at www.intel.com.

CPU Sockets and Slots

As chips have become more and more complex, they have made increasingly greater demands on the motherboard circuitry — more data lines, more power, and faster interconnections with the computer's various elements.

Since the arrival of the 486 CPU, Intel has produced its microprocessors with connectors for 15 different sockets or slots; one other socket was announced but never used in commercial products. Most of the sockets held the processor flat on the motherboard. Intel changed over to an upright package for the CPU with the arrival of the Pentium II; that design continued through most of the lifetime of the Pentium III. The upright slot allowed for better cooling of the increasingly hot CPU and took up a bit less space on the motherboard. Modern Pentium 4 chips — more densely integrated and thus smaller — have returned to a horizontal socket on the motherboard. Early AMD chips used industry-standard sockets, changing over to a proprietary slot with the arrival of the first Athlons and then back to a socket.

Why the change back to sockets? High-speed CPUs require shorter electrical connections, called *traces*; sockets sit directly on the motherboard, while cards plugged into slots sit relatively farther away. Another reason for a return to sockets is the integration of cache memory directly into the CPU carrier itself instead of on an attached circuit board.

Table 2-6 is a roadmap to the motherboard-microprocessor connection.

TABLE 2-6: Modern Machine CPU Sockets and Slots

Socket Name	Carrier Design	Voltage	Typical Bus Speeds	Processors
486 Socket	168-pin LIF	5v	20, 25, 33 MHz	486 DX, DX2, DX4. Am5x86. Cyrix 5x86.
Socket 1	169-pin LIF or ZIF	5v	16, 20, 25, 33 MHz	486 SX/SX2, DX/DX2, DX4 with adapter, DX4 OverDrive, Cyrix 5x86.
Socket 2	238-pin LIF or ZIF	5v	25, 33, 40, 50 MHz	486 SX/SX2, DX/DX2, DX4 with adapter, DX4 OverDrive, Pentium OverDrive, Am5x86, Cyrix 5x86.
Socket 3	237-pin PGA LIF or ZIF	5v/3.3v	25, 33, 40, 50 MHz	SX/SX2, DX/DX2, DX4 with adapter, DX4 OverDrive, 486 Pentium OverDrive, Pentium 60/66, Pentium 60/66 OverDrive.
Socket 4	273-pin PGA LIF or ZIF	5v	60, 66 MHz	Pentium 60/66, Pentium 60/66 OverDrive.
Socket 5	296-pin LIF or ZIF, or 320-pin SPGA LIF or ZIF	STD 3.3v, VR 3.3–3.465, VRE 3.5–3.6v	50, 60, 66 MHz	Pentium 75 through Pentium 133, Pentium 75+ OverDrive. AMD K5, AMD 6x86L. WinChip.
Socket 6	235-pin PGA ZIF	3.3v	25, 33, 40 MHz	Designed for 486DX4, but not used in commercial products.
Socket 7/ Super 7	296-pin LIF or 321-pin SPGA ZIF	STD 3.3v, VR 3.3–3.465, VRE 3.5–3.6v	40, 50, 55, 60, 62, 66, 68, 75, 83, 90, 95, 100, 102, 112, 124 MHz	Pentium 75 through Pentium 200, Pentium 75+ OverDrive, AMD K5, AMD K6, Cyrix 6x86, Cyris 6x86MX, Cyrix M II, IDT WinChip 180-240. Super 7 supports AMD K6-2, AMD K6-3.
Socket 8	387-pin SPGA LIF or ZIF	VID VRM 3.1–3.3v	60, 66, 75 MHz	Pentium Pro, Pentium II OverDrives.
Socket 9/ Socket 370	370-pin PPGA ZIF	VID VRM 1.05–2.1v	66, 100, 133 MHz	Celeron in PPGA, Pentium III, VIA C3.
Slot 1 (SC242)	242-pin SEPP A/B blocks, 121 pins each, or 242-pin SEPP	VID VRM 2.8–3.3v	60, 66, 68, 75, 83, 100, 102, 112, 124, 133 MHz	Pentium II, Pentium III, Celeron Slot 1.
Slot 2 (SC330)	330-pin SECC A/B blocks, 165 pins each	VID VRM 2.8–3.3v	100, 133 MHz	Pentium II Xeon, Pentium III Xeon.
Slot A	242-pin SECC	VID VRM 1.3–2.05v	100 MHz (x2), 133 MHz (x2)	AMD Athlon, AMD Thunderbird 750 MHz–1 GHz.

Socket Name	Carrier Design	Voltage	Typical Bus Speeds	Processors
Socket A	462-pin ZIF	VID VRM 1.1–2.05v	100 MHz (x2), 133 MHz (x2)	AMD Duron, AMD Thunderbird.
Socket 423	423-pin ZIF	VID VRM 1.0–1.85v	100 MHz (x4)	Pentium 4 1.3–2.0 GHz.
Socket 478	478-pin ZIF	VID VRM 1.0–1.85v	100 MHz (x4), 133 (x4)	Pentium 4 1.8 GHz and faster.
Socket 603	603-pin ZIF	VID VRM 1.1–1.85v	100 MHz (x4)	Pentium Xeon 1.4 and faster.
PAC 418	418-pin VLIF	VID VRM 1.25–1.6v	133 MHz (x2), 100 MHz (x4)	Itanium.

Key to Carrier Design and Voltage classes:
Carriers — LIF: Low-Insertion Force, without handle; PGA: Pin Grid Array; PPGA: Plastic Pin Grid Array; SECC: Single Edge Contact Cartridge; SEPP: Single Edge Processor Package; SPGA: Staggered Pin Grid Array; VLIF: Very Low Insertion Force socket; ZIF: Zero-Insertion Force, with handle
Voltage — STD: 3.3v (3.135v to 3.465v). Standard voltage; VR: 3.38v (3.300v to 3.465v). Voltage regulated; VRE: 3.52v (3.450v to 3.600v) (B-step). Voltage regulated extended; VRE: 3.5v (3.400v to 3.600v) (C2 step and later). Voltage regulated extended; VID VRM: Voltage ID Voltage Regulator Module. CPU programs module to proper voltage.

Modern Intel CPUs

A modern machine requires a modern CPU, defined in this seventh edition as beginning with late-model Pentium IIs and continuing on to Pentium IIIs, advanced Celerons, the Pentium 4, and the advanced Intel Itanium.

CROSS-REFERENCE

In "Modern Clone CPUs," later in this chapter, I discuss modern CPUs from competitors, including AMD and VIA.

Pentium 4

The Pentium 4 processor arrived in November of 2000, delivering new levels of performance for processing video and audio, 3D graphics, and advanced Internet technologies. The CPU is based on a new generation of technologies under the banner of the Intel NetBurst micro-architecture.

Acceptance of the Pentium 4 was held back somewhat by economic conditions and by the reluctance of some buyers to change to the more expensive Rambus memory architecture. Early shipments of Rambus motherboards ran into some technical difficulties, although that problem was quickly remedied. Rambus offers increased memory speed, although overall system performance boosts using current motherboards is generally in the range of about 5 to 15 percent. As this book goes to press, Rambus modules were priced significantly higher than SDRAM, although the overall price of memory fell dramatically during 2001.

Intel considers NetBurst technology to be the company's first completely new desktop processor design since the Pentium Pro in 1995. Highlights include Hyper Pipelined Technology, which enables the Pentium 4 processor to execute software instructions in a 20-stage pipeline, as compared to the 10-stage pipeline of the Pentium III processor. For higher performance, the Rapid Execution Engine allows frequently used Arithmetic Logic Unit instructions to be executed at double the core clock.

A 400 MHz system bus speeds the transfer of data between the processor and main memory. In addition, 144 new instructions have been added to further speed the processing of video, audio, and 3-D applications.

The Pentium 4 was first introduced with a companion chipset, the Intel 850, which is designed to use RDRAM. In 2001, the company delivered the Intel 845 chipset, which mates the Pentium 4 to conventional and less-expensive SDRAM. First introduced at 1.3 GHz, the clock speed of the Pentium 4 reached the 2.0 GHz milestone in August of 2001, and Intel said it had prototypes for microprocessors in the family running as fast as 3.5 GHz.

Intel planned to introduce a 2.2 GHz Pentium 4 in early 2002, based on a revised prototype code-named Northwood. The later version of the Pentium 4 includes a performance-enhancing secondary cache with 512KB of memory, double the size of the first chips in the series. In addition to a boost in speed and throughput, the smaller size of the Northwood design should result in a continuation of the downward trend in prices because of reduced manufacturing costs.

According to Intel, systems based on the Pentium 4 processor at 2.0 GHz can create and share digital media up to 81 percent faster than a computer with a Pentium III processor at 1.0 GHz. Intel studies also say that a Pentium 4 processor at 2.0 GHz allows business users a 50-percent boost in efficiency over a 1.0 GHz Pentium III in multitasking environments where background tasks like virus checking, encryption, and file compression increase the processor workload.

CROSS-REFERENCE

See Chapter 8 for more detail on Rambus and other memory technologies.

Itanium

Itanium, Intel's successor to the 32-bit Pentium processor, arrived in mid-2001, about a year behind its promised debut date. The much-awaited CPU is a 64-bit processor that is initially aimed at use in high-speed, high-demand network servers, database engines, and other large-scale applications that require fast CPU performance and large memory and storage support. Early machines were based around motherboards that could accommodate four or eight Itanium processors and massive amounts of memory.

As with previous chip designs, Intel promises backwards compatibility as well as forward-looking improvements. The Itanium is designed to run existing IA-32 (32-bit Pentium) software, as well as new IA-64 (64-bit Itanium) software that is being designed by a whole host of developers as of this book's writing.

The Itanium isn't the first workstation or desktop-class 64-bit CPU architecture. Hewlett-Packard, IBM, Sun, and others have had RISC (Reduced Instruction Set Computer) chips with 64-bit internal addressing for some time. However, Intel claims Itanium is different because it is more than just a 64-bit chip; it is an architecture that includes support for Internet server tasks, higher-end multimedia, and other jobs that users are demanding now and likely will demand in the near future. New and powerful multimedia instructions—similar to and compatible with MMX—help Itanium provide support for these future tasks.

One facet of Intel's IA-64 architecture is Explicitly Parallel Instruction Computing (EPIC), a technique that helps maximize CPU performance, throughput, and efficiency by supporting instruction level parallelism (ILP) as well as a high level of synergy between the compiler and the processor. Itanium's ILP supports multiple independent instruction bundles (three instructions per bundle). In addition to this parallel processing, Itanium is designed with sophisticated speculative or predictive features. Like a data cache in a hard disk controller that guesses what data will be required next based on previous data access, Itanium's speculative features help the processor look ahead to future instructions based on what has gone before. Properly executed, speculation obviously can improve CPU throughput because applications don't have to wait for an instruction fetch and execution. In other words, processing latency is reduced.

There's another part of the Intel IA-64 architecture design that may have significant impact on users and the computer industry as a whole. With the exception of Sun Microsystems, other major computer manufacturers, even those with their own 64-bit CPUs, have promised to support Intel's hardware when it is available.

Pentium III

Pentium III was widely used in business and home machines from its introduction in 1999 through mid-2001. The CPU uses a 32-bit internal architecture with a 64-bit data bus like previous members of the Pentium family. The microprocessors include MMX multimedia features that extend the original enhancements to the previous Pentium II designs. Figure 2-5 shows a 500 MHz Pentium III for Slot 1.

Depending on version, the PIII is based on 0.25 or 0.18 micron technology, a measure of the fineness of the etched connectors and gates that make up the processor's logic. All Pentium IIs used 0.25 micron designs.

Pentium III chips were available in speeds beginning at 450 MHz and topping out at 1.3 GHz. The microprocessor supports a 512K byte Level 2, or L2, cache, mounted outside of the CPU but in the same processor cartridge.

NOTE

A Level 1, or L1, cache is a special block of internal memory within the processor. It is used by the CPU to store instructions or data that the machine believes it will have to access again soon. Writing to or reading from that L1 cache is much faster than going out of the CPU and down the bus to the memory SIMMs or DIMMs. A Level 2, or L2, cache is a secondary external cache. If the CPU cannot find the data or instructions it wants in the internal cache, it looks in the Level 2 cache. If it still cannot find what it is looking for, the cache controller finds the data or instruction in system memory and copies it into one of the caches.

FIGURE 2-5: *A 500 MHz Pentium III CPU in a SECC2 carrier for installation in Slot 1. Packaged CPUs from Intel include an attached heat sink and fan, as well as a three-year warranty. Less-expensive white-box CPUs available from some computer supply houses have the same Intel processor but lack the necessary fan and heat sink and have a shorter warranty.*

As you read Pentium III chip descriptions and price lists, notice chips that include a B at the end of the CPU speed (for example, 600B), which means the chip supports a 133 MHz system bus. The B designation differentiates chips of the same speed that use different system bus speeds. The chip needs to be matched to the speed of the bus on the motherboard.

Later versions of the Pentium III use Advanced Transfer Cache (ATC), a design that places L2 cache entirely within the CPU package instead of outside the CPU case (discrete cache). This later

Pentium III release was code-named Coppermine during chip development. Communication between the CPU and this internal L2 cache is 256 bits wide, enabling faster data transfer than with the external design.

Chips with an E after the CPU speed designation use this internal L2 cache. The Pentium III 600EB, for example, supports both the 133 MHz system bus and ATC. Chips that carry the E designator also use Advanced System Buffering, a series of enhancements in the system bus buffer and bus queue. Advanced System Buffering helps achieve an increase in the use of available bandwidth in both 100 and 133 MHz system buses. Intel E chips have 256K of L2 cache, whereas chips without ATC support 512K of L2 cache. Even with the reduced cache size, E chips are potentially faster than earlier chips because of the fast data transfer possible between the CPU and the L2 cache. Coppermine, or E, chips with the onboard L2 cache are available in speeds up to 800 MHz.

All PIII processors include 70 new instructions beyond those recognized by the Pentium II. These instructions are designed primarily to enhance multimedia and Internet functionality, including better manipulation of high-resolution and high-quality images; better processing of high-quality audio, MPEG2 video, and simultaneous MPEG2 encoding and decoding; and reduced CPU use for speech recognition.

The original series of Pentium III chips use the same Slot 1 (SC242) motherboard socket and SEC chip mounting design as the Pentium II. See Figure 2-6. Later versions of the CPU were also offered in a flat package that installs on the motherboard in a Socket 9/Socket 370.

A non-performance-related feature that may appeal to network managers and others charged with tracking PC hardware is the fact that each Pentium III has an internal serial number. With the appropriate polling software to extract this number, managers can track which computers are connected to managed networks, locations of hardware, and so on.

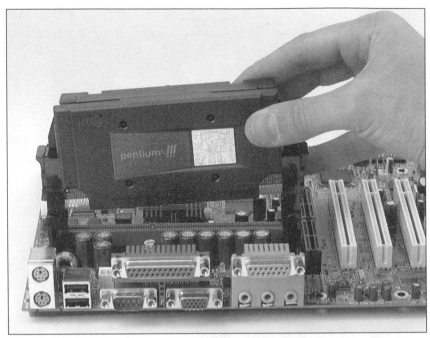

FIGURE 2-6: *A Pentium III installs in Slot 1 much like an adapter plugs into the bus; the Pentium II uses the same type of slot.*

Pentium III Xeon chips — aimed at multiprocessor server systems — use the Slot 2 (SC330) mount, the same as the Pentium II Xeon. An alternative socket arrangement also is available, the FC-PGA370, a 370-pin, low-profile socket, which is designed for high performance and a high level of mechanical stability and reliability. The FC in this designation stands for *flip-chip*, and the PGA stands for *pin grid array*. This is a *zero insertion force* (ZIF) socket and is the same 370-pin arrangement used in the Celeron processor. All FC-PGA370 Pentiums are E chips, which means they support Advanced Transfer Cache and Advanced System Buffering and operate with 100 MHz system buses.

As with all high-speed processors, it is important to draw away the damaging heat generated by the Pentium III. Figure 2-7 shows three types of add-on fans.

Ch
2

FIGURE 2-7: *High-speed CPUs require a fan and heat sink to remove some of the heat they generate. From top left, clockwise, are add-on fans for a Celeron, Pentium III, and Pentium II or upright Celeron processor.*

Celeron

The Celeron processor is Intel's line of "value" CPUs, allowing manufacturers to use lower-price motherboards, chipsets, and components while still delivering systems that by most measures are quite capable for many users. When these processors were first introduced, they offered a way for users to buy a capable system for several hundred dollars in savings compared to a Pentium II or Pentium III system. Today, though, the drop in the cost of memory and other components has resulted in a small differential between Celerons and full-featured Pentium III and Pentium 4 systems.

The first generation of Celerons, based on the Pentium II and using a 66 MHz system bus, were introduced in 1998 in 333, 366, 400, 433, 466, 500, and 533 versions. The second generation, based on the Pentium III, included processors from 533 through 766 MHz, still wedded to a 66 MHz system bus. In 2000 and 2001,

the Celeron gained access to a 100 MHz system bus as it was extended from 800 MHz to 1.2 GHz.

In October of 2001, Intel introduced a 1.2 GHz processor based on 0.13 micron process technology and including additional design features such as 256K of on-chip, L2 cache. Earlier Celerons offered just 128K of L2 cache.

Early Celeron systems used the Intel 440BX chipset; current Celeron systems use the Intel 810E2 chipset that includes an advanced I/O controller, support for ATA-100 Ultra DMA hard drives, and a USB controller that supports four ports.

The Celeron processor was introduced to provide Pentium II–level performance for most business applications at a lower cost than the full-featured Pentium II on which it was originally based. In fact, the original Celeron, for all practical purposes, was a Pentium II with a smaller amount of Level 2 cache, 128K compared to the PII's 512K.

Depending on your motherboard and the socket design, you may be able to install a Celeron in a board designed for use with a Pentium II or III. This is one way for some users to ease into a Pentium III system. Some boards include both a Socket 370 and a Slot 1; another way to accomplish this is to use an adapter, like the one shown in Figure 2-8.

WHEN A CELERON SEEMS NOT A CELERON

Under Windows 98, when you look at the computer information on the General tab of the System Properties dialog box, you may find that the operating system reports the presence of a Pentium II when you perfectly well know that you have an Intel Celeron inside. This is an error without any consequence. The original series of Celeron chips was derived from a Pentium II base, and some of the code may fool system utilities.

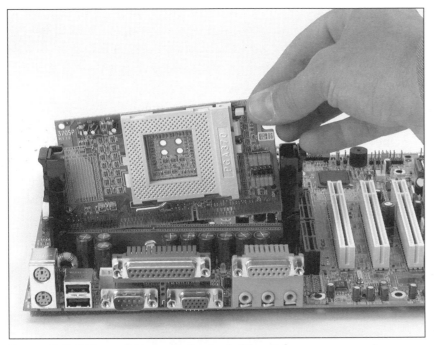

FIGURE 2-8: *This workaround adapter holds a Celeron processor in a socket that installs into Slot 1 on a modern motherboard.*

Pentium II

The Pentium II was a major step forward when Intel introduced it in ancient times, way back in 1997, that is. Originally aimed at high-end business and home users, today the Pentium II is on the endangered species list of *Fix Your Own PC*, on its way from modern machine to senior citizen status. A PII with a reasonable amount of memory — at least 64MB and preferably 96MB or more — is capable of running Windows 98, Internet Explorer 5.5, and Microsoft Office 2000 at an acceptable speed. I would not recommend attempting to run a more demanding operating system like Windows 2000 or Windows XP, or more complex software such as video editing or intensive illustration of CAD-CAM programs.

The PII is built on the processing power of the Pentium Pro and adds MMX support. The heart of the Pentium II market was

for chips running at 233, 266, 300, 333, 350, 400, and 450 MHz. Figure 2-9 shows a PII processor installed on a motherboard.

The Pentium II was the first Intel microprocessor since the birth of the PC to move away from a design that placed the CPU flat on the motherboard. Instead, Intel introduced the single edge contact cartridge (SECC), a daughter card that fits into a motherboard slot. Originally designated a Slot 1 interface, Intel also refers to it as an SC242 connector for the 242 pin connectors on the socket. The SECC stands upright on the motherboard, with a cooling fan, heat sink, or both to draw away the considerable heat generated by the high number of electrical cycles of the chip.

Later Pentium IIs and Pentium III chips use an improved version of this design, the SECC 2 — basically the same package technology but without an extended thermal plate (a separate heat sink, in plain language). Instead, the heat sink is attached directly to the back of the processor. This design change reduces thermal resistance, according to Intel, which simply means that the directly attached heat sink dissipates heat better than an add-on heat sink.

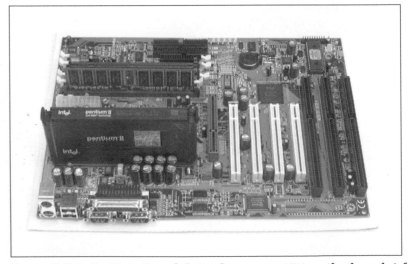

FIGURE 2-9: *A Pentium II module in place on an ATX motherboard. A fan, heat sink, and supporting bracket are not yet installed.*

A key component of the SC242 infrastructure is Intel's dual independent bus (DIB) architecture, which supports two independent buses (a system bus and a backside L2 bus) as opposed to Socket 7's single-bus architecture. The DIB architecture in the SC242 card is a repackaged version of the Pentium Pro/Socket 8 infrastructure introduced in late 1995.

Along with the change in socket and bus design comes improved graphics performance with systems that include AGP (accelerated graphics port) technology.

As I have noted, the Pentium II is many orders of magnitude faster than its predecessors. However, it still deals with the outside world — the memory and devices plugged into the computer's interconnecting bus — at 60 MHz or 66 MHz, the same speed used in a senior citizen 486 machine.

Mobile processors

In addition to the standard Pentium processors I've already discussed, Intel has offered mobile versions of its Pentium III, Pentium II, and Celeron CPUs. As this book went to press, a low-power version of the Pentium 4 was expected.

Mobile versions are designed to provide high-speed performance in a small physical package and to draw less power from the limited resources of batteries as opposed to AC current from a wall socket. In general, the technical specifications of the mobile versions are similar to their desktop counterparts. However, there are fewer speed choices, the packaging is smaller, and the mobile processors include some interesting power- and resource-management features that may not be available on the full-sized versions.

NOTE

I'm not going to discuss fixing problematic laptop and portable computers in this book. There simply aren't that many user-repairable parts inside these things. Spacing is tight, and in most cases, components are soldered in place. Consider this section as educational background to help you make an intelligent purchase of a portable, or to compare its facilities to a desktop PC.

As you might expect, mobile CPUs need to get the most power and the longest life out of the batteries in your laptop or notebook PC. Intel's mobile PIIIs include a technology called Quick Start that enables the processor to power down and use minimal power during operational downtime, such as when you are thinking about what to type next or while you are reading the contents of a Web page.

One of Silicon Valley's deepest secrets finally saw the light of day in 2000: the Crusoe processor, the first product of Transmeta Corporation (www.transmeta.com). The key features of this chip are its ability to offload a great deal of its instructions to software instead of silicon and to operate with very low power demands and heat production.

The Crusoe, named in a light-hearted nod toward the famed literary traveler Robinson Crusoe, is targeted at the burgeoning mobile computer hardware market — Internet machines, wireless computers, and intelligent personal assistants. According to the company, the processor is designed to consume very small amounts of power — in the one-watt range, using Transmeta's own LongRun power management technology — and it is capable, through software emulation, of running software written for x086 CPUs such as the mobile Pentium III.

The Crusoe converts Pentium-class instructions to its own native code, a Very Long Instruction Word (VLIW) design. By using software in this way to actually interpret CPU instructions for mainstream chips, Transmeta hopes to keep the Crusoe up-to-date through software transfusions in the field as needed.

Transmeta's initial chips were the TM5400 and the similar TM5500, ranging in speed from 500 to 800 MHz and including a 256K L2 cache, and the TM5600/TM5800, with the same range of speeds and a 512K L2 cache.

Transmeta is quick to point out that processor speed alone is not a complete measure of a mobile CPU's capabilities. One way Crusoe saves power, for example, is to adjust CPU speed to the task at hand, using only the amount of power required. While current mobile CPU benchmarks focus on how fast a system can

Ch
2

complete specific tasks, Transmeta adds to its benchmark tests a throughput (measured both as the amount of work completed and the rate at which the work is done) versus battery consumption component.

In addition, Crusoe is designed to work with the applications likely to be most popular in the future, including multimedia and Internet communications. Transmeta says that Crusoe can adapt to individual application and user patterns, teaching itself how to do best what you call upon your individual Crusoe-powered device to do. One way is through instruction translation caching. When Crusoe translates an x086 instruction into its own VLIW instruction once, it stores the translation so that next time the instruction is submitted, no translation is required.

Not surprisingly, Intel had its own new technology aimed at the same market. At about the same time as the Crusoe announcement, Intel revealed the SpeedStep technology for selected mobile CPUs. Microprocessors using this technology will automatically drop their speed when operating under battery power and step back up to their rated speed when plugged into the wall. Slower CPUs produce less heat and consume less power. According to Intel, in a typical use this scheme allows the mobile CPU to operate at 80 percent of its processing power while using 40 to 50 percent less battery power. A manual override lets users turn the CPU back to full speed, even during battery operation, when more power is needed.

Modern Clone CPUs

Although Intel is inside most PCs, it is not completely alone. In 2001, Intel had about an 80 percent market share for PC microprocessors; most of the remaining 20 percent was owned by Advanced Micro Devices, better known as AMD. (Over the years, other companies have chipped away at corners of the market, offering devices that were less expensive or slightly faster than Intel originals. In addition to AMD, microprocessors have also come from IBM, Cyrix [now part of Via Technologies], IDT, and a few others.)

The Athlon processor, introduced in 1999, is a near-equivalent to the Intel Pentium 4, offering some enhancements including a 200 MHz system bus, compared to the 100 or 133 MHz bus used on most Intel systems.

In 2001, AMD introduced the Athlon XP, a not-very-well veiled attempt to latch onto the marketing juggernaut of Microsoft for its Windows XP operating system. Officially, the XP stands for "Xtra Performance," but the company doesn't mind if customers think that in some way the Athlon XP is the specific processor for the new operating system.

Both CPUs will run Microsoft Windows in all of its flavors, and nearly every current application will work without problem. The only oddity some users may find are unusual or erroneous reports generated by some troubleshooting utilities expecting to find Intel ID codes in the processor.

IBM quietly became one of Intel's major competitors by devoting part of its vast manufacturing capability to chip fabrication. In 1998, IBM released the 6x86MX processors, based on a Cyrix design, at performance ratings of 300 and 333. According to IBM, the performance rating roughly corresponds to a megahertz speed rating of an Intel chip, although the actual speed of the chip is lower.

Over the years, IBM also fabricated chips for Cyrix, IDT, and Advanced Micro Devices to sell under IBM's name. By early 2000, IBM's microprocessor products were primarily based on the PowerPC chip, not a mainstream product but one used as an embedded controller in a wide range of devices. In 2001, the Taiwanese chip foundry Via introduced its C3 processor, an outgrowth of its purchase of Cyrix in 1999. Along the way, most of Intel's competitors have contributed to the complexity of chipnaming schemes. The problem arose out of the success that companies had in optimizing the speed of their clones.

In 1996, chip designers Cyrix and AMD, together with contract chipmakers IBM and SGS-Thomson, came up with something they called the P-Rating Specification, which was intended to relate the performance of their CPUs to an Intel equivalent. Under that scheme, a P166+ was supposed to indicate that the chip performed at a speed comparable to an Intel Pentium at 166 MHz. For example, a Cyrix 6x86 ran at an actual clock speed of 133 MHz, but benchmarks showed it performing at a level equivalent to a 166 MHz Pentium.

By 2000, the advanced designs of the AMD K6-III and the Athlon were more than able to stand on their own merits, and AMD quietly dispensed with the P-Rating scheme, with an Athlon 800 running at 800 MHz, just as the name suggests.

But in late 2001, AMD brought back a version of the scheme. With the introduction of AMD's Athlon XP, the company assigned model names to its CPUs based on their claimed equivalency to an Intel processor. For example, the Athlon XP 1800+ operates at a frequency of 1.53 GHz but gains its name because AMD claims this model will outperform an Intel Pentium 4 processor operating at 1.8 GHz on a broad array of end user applications.

 NOTE

As successful as AMD has been in building a business in the shadows of Intel, it still concentrates on business opportunities at the margins — finding customers who are looking to save money or gain a short-term technological advantage. AMD has also been able to take advantage of occasional delays in the shipment of Intel processors.

As this book goes to press, though, Compaq and Hewlett-Packard were the only major makers selling current machines based on AMD processors. Gateway and IBM, which offered AMD processors at various times in their history, turned back once again to an all-Intel world in 2001.

Athlon XP

At the time of its introduction in late 2001, AMD's new Athlon XP processor claimed to be the world's highest-performance processor for desktop PCs. The company also put forth a marketing and industry-standard proposal to develop a reliable measurement of processor performance that goes beyond mere measurement of a CPU's clock speed.

"For most of the PC's first 20 years, megahertz was a reliable indicator of PC processor performance because the major players used the same architecture for product design, and clock speed was a good proxy for performance. This is no longer true," said W. "Jerry" Sanders III, AMD chairman and chief executive officer. "The performance of our seventh-generation AMD Athlon processor architecture demonstrates that clock speed is only half of the performance equation."

AMD's True Performance Initiative will stress the company's position that the true indicator of performance is how fast applications run, not the megahertz of their processor. Megahertz measures only how many cycles per second the engine spins, not how much torque it delivers, the company says.

The Athlon XP processor contains about 37.5 million transistors and 384K of on-chip, full-speed cache while reducing power consumption by 20 percent over previous generations of the Athlon. The CPU, built with 0.18 micron technology and installed in a Pin Grid Array carrier, is compatible with AMD's Socket A infrastructure. The CPU supports an advanced 266 MHz front-side bus. The chip is intended for use with DDR memory.

The AMD Athlon XP processor features a new architecture called QuantiSpeed, which the company says delivers up to a 25-percent performance advantage versus competitive processors, including the original AMD Athlon, on a broad array of real-world applications, in such categories as digital media, office productivity, and 3-D gaming.

AMD compares its Athlon XP to the Pentium 4, and claims superiority. According to the company, the XP conducts nine operations per clock cycle, compared to six for the Pentium 4. The XP has 384K of on-chip cache (128K of L1 and 256K of L2) versus 264K for the Pentium 4 (8K of L1 and 256K of L2). The new processor also includes 3DNow! Professional technology, which adds 52 new instructions, accelerating 3-D performance for digital media applications such as photo, video, and audio editing.

AMD identifies the AMD Athlon XP processor using model numbers, as opposed to clock speed in megahertz. The numbers are supposed to indicate AMD's comparison to an Intel Pentium 4 CPU. The AMD Athlon XP processor 1800+ operates at a frequency of 1.53 GHz; AMD claims this model will outperform an Intel Pentium 4 processor operating at 1.8 GHz on a broad array of end user applications. Table 2-7 lists the model names and actual clock speeds for the initial Athlon XP processors.

TABLE 2-7: Initial Athlon XP Processors

AMD Processor	Clock Speed
Athlon XP 1800+	1.53 GHz
Athlon XP 1700+	1.47 GHz
Athlon XP 1600+	1.40 GHz
Athlon XP 1500+	1.33 GHz

Although the Athlon XP processor is physically compatible with older Socket A motherboards intended for the original Athlon CPU, most systems will require an update to the BIOS to properly identify the processor and take advantage of the enhanced performance features. New motherboards will be certified by AMD to indicate their appropriateness for use with the Athlon XP.

AMD Athlon

AMD made its first serious foray against Intel at the low end with its K6 series. Intel countered with the Celeron chips, designed for medium- to low-priced personal and business systems. Then late in 1999, the two companies raised the stakes and started competing at the high end of the scale. AMD's Athlon chip series, designed to compete with the high end of Intel's Pentium III series and the full range of Pentium 4s, was first with a CPU that ran at 750 MHz, barely besting Intel's 733 MHz PIII.

The Athlon series performed well, and AMD priced it at a significant discount from Intel's price; at various times in 2000, AMD also took advantage of production difficulties at Intel to increase its market share. Many mainstream computer manufacturers promoted Athlon chips over Pentium 4s in that year. By 2001, though, aggressive cuts in prices by Intel and great leaps in technology began to push AMD aside.

AMD's Athlon series uses 0.18 micron technology, the same as the later series of Intel's Pentium III and most Pentium 4s, and the 200 MHz Athlon system bus is designed for scalable multiprocessing, using Digital Equipment Corporation's high-performance Alpha EV6 bus technology. Later Athlons advanced to use a 266 MHz system bus.

As with the Athlon XP, AMD compares its Athlon XP to the Pentium 4. According to the company, the XP conducts nine operations per clock cycle, compared to six for the Pentium 4. The later versions of the Athlon have 384K of on-chip cache (128K of L1 and 256K of L2) versus 264K for the Pentium 4 (8K of L1 and 256K of L2).

And just like Intel, AMD promotes the multimedia power of the Athlon design. The company says that Athlon, with its enhanced 3DNow! technology, includes 24 new instructions; of those, 19 are designed to improve MMX integer math calculations and enhance data movement for Internet streaming applications and 5 provide digital signal processing (DSP) extensions for soft modem, soft ADSL, Dolby Digital, and MP3 applications.

Another strong point of the Athlon is its cache design: the most current Athlons (as fast as 1.4 GHz) offer a total of 384K of cache (128K of L1 and 256K of on-chip L2), significantly more than the 264K on a Pentium 4. Early Athlons did not include L2 cache on the chip.

The original Athlons linked to the motherboard through AMD's Slot A. Intel kept some of the design elements of its Slot 1 (SC242) as a trade secret, blocking use of the connector by its competitors — principally AMD. Slot A, AMD's equivalent connector, is mechanically all but identical to Intel's design, but its electrical design is based on the bus for the Alpha microprocessor originally developed by Digital Equipment Corporation. You cannot use an AMD Athlon in an Intel Slot 1, or a Pentium III in a Slot A. Just like Intel, though, AMD changed back to a motherboard-mounted receptacle (Socket A) a few models into the production of the Athlon. You'll find Slot A versions of the Athlon from 600 MHz through 950 MHz. Socket A versions arrived with the 700 MHz version and continued through 1.4 GHz.

You may find adaptors that allow the use of a Socket A CPU in a Slot A, or the other way around. Although these may work, AMD does not support their use because of concerns about heat dissipation and possible electrical irregularities.

As you work to repair or upgrade your computer, remember that AMD does not sell directly to consumers. You have to go through an authorized reseller who, in most cases, will supply a total solution: motherboard, CPU, and support chips.

AMD made a midcourse change in the construction of Athlon chips in 2000, introducing an advanced version based on a project known as "Thunderbird." (Outsiders had at first expected Thunderbird to be released as a new product line.)

The main difference between the two chips is the location of L2 cache. The original Athlon had 512K of cache external to the processor, mounted within a cartridge that plugged into AMD's Slot A and communicating at 33, 40, or 50 percent of the core clock speed. Newer Athlons have 256K of L2 cache on the microprocessor die itself and communicating at 100 percent of the core clock speed; these CPUs are mostly offered in a version that plugs into a small Socket A on the motherboard, although some versions sold to system manufacturers were packaged in a Slot A

carrier. Table 2-8 displays a comparison of the original and updated Athlon CPUs.

TABLE 2-8: Original and New Athlons

	Original Athlon	"Thunderbird" Athlon
Manufacturing process	0.25 or 0.18 micron, Aluminum traces	0.18 micron, Aluminum or copper traces
Number of transistors	22 million	37 million
Voltage	1.6–1.8 v	1.7 v
Maximum current at 1 GHz	37 A	33.6 A
L2 cache	External, 512K	On-die, 256K
L2 cache clock	33, 40, 50 percent of core clock	100 percent of core clock
L2-Cache organization	2-way set associative	16-way set associative
Package	Slot A cartridge	Socket A or Slot A cartridge (OEM version)

AMD Athlon MP

The AMD Athlon MP is a derivative of the Athlon designed for use in high-performance multiprocessing servers and workstations. A key element of the chip is Smart MP technology, which greatly enhances overall platform performance by increasing data movement between two or more CPUs, the chipset, and the memory system.

Smart MP technology features dual point-to-point, high-speed 266 MHz system buses with error correcting code support designed to provide up to 2.1 GBps per CPU of bus bandwidth in a dual-processor system.

Like other Athlons, the MP attaches through Socket A and supports DDR memory technology. Other features include a high-performance, full-speed cache with hardware data pre-fetch, a fully pipelined superscalar floating point engine, and an L2 Translation Look-aside Buffer (TLB). The MP also incorporates 3DNow! Professional technology, which has 52 instructions that extend AMD's 3DNow! technology; the company claims this results in smoother, richer, and more lifelike images, more precise digital audio, and an enriched Internet experience.

AMD Duron

AMD's Duron is a scaled-down derivative of the AMD Athlon, a low-cost alternative to Intel's Celeron processor, aimed at every-day computing for business and home users. Initial releases of the 25.2-million-transistor chip in 2001 were at 950 MHz, 1 GHz, and 1.1 GHz speeds.

The AMD Duron processor consumes less power than the AMD Athlon processor, enabling lower cost systems. Duron-based PCs are likely to employ lower cost memory and graphics solutions, including Unified Memory Architecture (UMA) graphics designs that use some of the system memory for video purposes. The AMD Duron processor features 128K of on-chip level one (L1) cache memory and 64K of full-speed, on-chip level two (L2) cache memory, a superscalar floating point unit, and connection to a high-speed 200 MHz front-side bus. The processor is manufactured using AMD's 0.18 micron aluminum process technology and uses a Socket A connector.

According to AMD, an AMD Duron processor with UMA outperforms an equivalent Intel Celeron processor with UMA by up to 25 percent on a variety of real-world software applications. As an example, AMD compared a 1.1 GHz AMD Duron processor with 128MB of PC133 memory using the KM-133 chipset against a 1.1 GHz Celeron processor with 128MB of PC133 memory using the Intel 810 chipset.

AMD compares the Duron to the Celeron, noting its product includes a total of 192K of on-chip L1 and L2 cache, compared to 160K in the Intel CPU. And the Duron works with a 200 MHz system bus, while the Celeron uses a 100 or 133 MHz bus.

VIA C3

Introduced in 2001, the VIA C3 was the first commercially available processor to be manufactured using leading-edge 0.13 and 0.15 micron manufacturing processes, resulting in the tiniest x86 processor at the time.

The chip delivers ultra-low power consumption and produces little heat, and is intended for use in value-priced computers, portables, and PC appliances. The first chips in the family were available at speeds of 800 and 866 MHz. The processors are compatible with the industry standard Socket 370 and support 100 and 133 MHz system buses; they include 128K of Level 1 and 64K of Level 2 cache. See Figure 2-10.

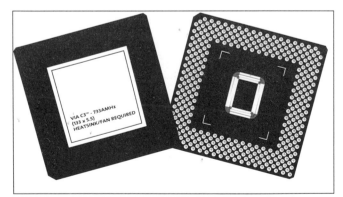

FIGURE 2-10: *An early VIA C3 microprocessor, a low-cost, low-power Socket 370 device*

Cyrix, which began as an independent chip maker, became part of National Semiconductor and in 1999 was sold to VIA Technologies, a Taiwanese chip designer with products that include the Apollo chipset used in many clone motherboards. For information on the company's products, consult `www.viatech.com`.

AMD K6

The K6 chip from AMD established itself as a strong contender for the low- to mid-priced computer market during 1999. Later releases of the K6 went head to head with Intel products, including the Pentium III, and gained considerable ground with a variety of system manufacturers that wanted to be able to offer competitively priced systems with industry-acceptable performance characteristics.

AMD (`www.amd.com`) signed a cross-licensing deal with Intel for the rights to the MMX technology and its instruction set, and added MMX to its K6 chip. In addition to their use in new systems, AMD chips are widely used as the basis of upgrades for older Pentium computers, as in the Kingston Turbochip series in Figure 2-11.

The reason the K6 uses the older Socket 7 motherboard mount instead of Intel's Slot 1 mount used in the Pentium II is that Intel claims Slot 1 technology is proprietary. AMD chose to use Socket 7 connectors, an open industry standard that enjoys broad support from a variety of manufacturers. AMD was one of the leaders of the Super Socket 7 Platform Initiative, which sought to keep alive that connection for its K6 chips and other designs. Super 7 mounting adds a 100 MHz bus and AGP support to the basic Socket 7 design. Figure 2-12 shows the K6.

FIGURE 2-11: *Based on the AMD K6-2 processor, the Turbochip 366 from Kingston Technology upgrades systems with either Socket 5 or Socket 7 pin layouts. Kingston claims the 366 MHz chip runs faster than a 400 MHz Intel Pentium II.*

For more information on AMD products, consult the company's Web page at `www.amd.com`.

FIGURE 2-12: *The AMD K6 233 MMX CPU, a Pentium clone, sits in a socket flush on this Tiger Direct K6 motherboard; a fan sits atop the chip to draw away heat. This bare-bones system awaits installation of drives, memory, and adapter cards.*

Cyrix MII

The Cyrix MII chip, introduced in 1998, offered competition for the Pentium II at speeds from 300 to 433 MHz. Built on the 6x86MX, the Cyrix MII includes MMX instructions, an enhanced memory management unit, and 64K L1 cache. According to Cyrix, the design is optimized to provide high performance with Windows 9*x* and other operating systems running 16- and 32-bit applications.

NOTE

For more information on Cyrix products, consult Via Technology's Web page at www.viatech.com.

In Table 2-9, I've brought together a selection of many of the more important clone chips.

TABLE 2-9: A Selection of Clones				
Processor	Intel Family or Equivalent	Clock Speed (MHz)	Bus Speed (MHz)	Mother-board Mounting
Athlon XP	Pentium 4	1,333 to 1,530	266	Socket A
AMD Athlon	Pentium 4	550 to 1,400	200	Slot A or Socket A
AMD Duron	Celeron	950 to 1,100	200	Socket A
VIA C3	Celeron	800 to 866	100/133	Socket 370
AMD K6-III	Pentium III	400 to 450	100	Socket 7
AMD K6-2	Pentium II	400 to 533	66/100	Socket 7
AMD K6	Pentium II	166 to 300	66	Socket 7
AMD K5	Pentium	90 to 166	60	Socket 7
AMD K5	Pentium	75	50	Socket 7
Cyrix 6x86-P200+	Pentium	150	75	Socket 7
Cyrix 6x86-P166+	Pentium	133	66	Socket 7

Processor	Intel Family or Equivalent	Clock Speed (MHz)	Bus Speed (MHz)	Mother-board Mounting
Cyrix 6x86-P150+	Pentium	120	60	Socket 7
Cyrix 6x86-P133+	Pentium	110	55	Socket 7
Cyrix 6x86-P120+	Pentium	100	50	Socket 7
Cyrix 6x86MX-PR166	Pentium MMX	150/166	60/66	Socket 7
Cyrix 6x86MX-PR200	Pentium MMX	160/150	66/75	Socket 7
Cyrix 6x86MX-PR233	Pentium MMX	188	75	Socket 7
Cyrix MII	Pentium II	300 to 433	66	Socket 7

Senior Citizen CPUs

Some of my best friends and parents are senior citizens; someday I hope to be one, too. Senior citizens have put in a long lifetime of hard and effective work, and they are able to look back to the past and have a perspective on the future. And best of all, they are still capable of performing meaningful work. But, alas, that doesn't mean that they can do things as fast as today's youngsters, and they sure can't wear the same accessories.

That said: If you have a senior citizen computer in your home or office that still performs a useful function, I'd suggest you keep it around as an extra machine or donate it to a school or charity. The tough question is: Does it make sense to upgrade a senior citizen to near-modern status? With the plunge in prices for new

computers, I would be very careful here. It might make sense to add more memory or replace a too-small or malfunctioning hard drive; it might not be worthwhile to change processors or motherboards.

Pentium MMX

The last implementation of the Pentium microprocessor was a family of chips that included "MMX" multimedia extensions for higher quality and greater speed in the processing and presentation of graphics, video, and audio.

Specifically, MMX opened the door to video conferencing, full-motion video, more advanced technologies, and, oh yes, mind-boggling games, too. MMX was first introduced as an extension to the Pentium chip in 1997.

NOTE

Beginning with the Pentium II, MMX technology was built into the basic set of instructions for the microprocessor. With Pentium III chips and beyond, MMX is not explicitly mentioned as part of the design, although many facets of the original MMX are incorporated in the new designs.

MMX extensions can provide speed boosts of 10 to 20 percent over Pentiums of the same clock speed, but software makers had to specifically write code to take advantage of the new instructions. Software makers responded to this new CPU capability with a variety of MMX-enabled products, including software playback of MPEG2 video without the need for costly hardware accelerators, a feature that meshed nicely with the arrival of MPEG2-capable DVD-ROM drives.

In addition to tweaks to the hardware, Intel added 57 powerful new instructions to its architecture — the first significant change to the x086 instruction set since the introduction of the 80386 — to speed up certain computer-intensive loops in multimedia and communications applications. While the loops typically occupy 10 percent or less of the overall application code, they can account for up to 90 percent of the execution time.

The 57 new instructions are specifically aimed at media- and signal-processing tasks, including video playback, graphics, and advanced audio functions. MMX-enabled programs are able to call for a single operation of the CPU instead of requesting a series of complex operations.

Shoehorning MMX into the existing Pentium chip resulted in a few compromises, principal among them the fact that Pentium MMX CPUs cannot execute MMX and floating point instructions at the same time, a rather rare circumstance in any case. Pentium II and later chips did not have this problem.

MMX instructions process multiple data elements in parallel using a technique called Single Instruction Multiple Data (SIMD). Intel claims performance benefits ranging from 50 to 400 percent, depending on the application.

At the same time as the Pentium was adapted to add the MMX instruction, Intel also made some significant changes on the hardware side, including a larger L1 cache with 16K instruction and 16K data — double the size of the cache used on earlier Pentiums. Of course, the value of the cache depends upon how well the CPU's cache management algorithm (a snippet of computer code) is written. And only a limited amount of real estate exists on the CPU for the cache. The first Intel CPU with an L1 cache was the 486, which had an 8K memory.

NOTE

Faster chips, beginning with the Pentium III family and continuing with Pentium 4 chips, add a second block of cache, called L2 or Level 2 cache memory, which can be as large as 2MB on Pentium Xeon chips. The L2 cache can be located in a slot on the motherboard; some Pentium III chips (B model chips) and some clones include the L2 within the oversized CPU carrier itself. Pentium III and Pentium 4 chips are discussed more extensively earlier in the chapter.

The Pentium processor with MMX technology is a dual-voltage chip, operating at 3.3 volts for I/O operations and 2.8 volts at the core of the chip itself. The lower voltage requirement, as you might expect, helped to lower the electrical load and heat production in desktop machines. A special version of the chip, with a 2.5-volt demand, is intended for notebook applications.

Because of the change in voltage level, the first group of MMX CPUs could not be plugged into most of the existing Pentium motherboards. (Later motherboards for MMX CPUs added a voltage regulator to accommodate the new voltage levels.) The first Intel chipset to support the dual voltage was the 430HX. Additionally, some earlier versions of the system BIOS will not work with MMX chips and will need to be updated or replaced.

Another issue with MMX CPUs involves the use of the proper CPU socket on motherboards designed before the introduction of the Pentium with MMX extensions. Socket 5 is the basic plug-in socket for Pentium CPUs. The specification calls for certain voltage support, a specific pin configuration, socket height above the motherboard, and so on. Socket 7 expands this basic CPU mounting specification to support chips that require more power and may produce more heat than original Pentium CPUs. This would include a Pentium OverDrive processor with MMX support, for example. In technical terms, Socket 7 is a superset of the Socket 5 standard, meaning that it builds upon the existing socket. Intel says using an OverDrive or other chip requiring the facilities of Socket 5 in a Socket 7 system could result in reduced performance or possible damage to the system.

A motherboard specifically designed for use with the Pentium MMX will likely offer a Socket 7. An older system may offer a Socket 5 design that meets the electrical and physical demands of Socket 7. The Socket 7 specification defines a system that includes a motherboard with a voltage regulator that can supply at least 5 amps to the processor socket, that has at least 1.75 inches of clearance above the socket, and that includes enough ventilation to dissipate 17 watts of processor power. So if you install a high-end

OverDrive chip in a non-Socket 7-compliant socket, you are likely to see reduced performance and run the risk of damaging the system.

WARNING

Be sure to question your system maker or supplier of a Pentium MMX chip to make certain your motherboard supports a new CPU.

Finally, you may need to update your version of Windows 95 to make an MMX chip work properly with an EIDE CD-ROM.

Pentium Pro

Intended as Intel's mid-range processor, the Pentium Pro arrived near the end of 1995 in high-end servers and special-purpose machines. In 1996, the CPU became the chip of choice in most high-demand applications; increasing numbers of business and home users adopted the chip for use in workstation applications.

This chip frequently found a home in server designs that accommodate multiple chips. The Pentium Pro can work in four-chip units for high-end applications. The Pentium Pro chip began at the middle of the Pentium speed range, with a 150 MHz model, and topped out at 200 MHz. In between are 166 MHz and 180 MHz models. Intel's Pentium Pro uses the Socket 8 pinout designed for a ZIF socket on the motherboard.

A Pentium Pro-based system should work with any software intended for a Pentium machine, but it will be at its best when it is paired with a 32-bit operating system, such as Windows 98, Windows 2000, Windows NT, or OS/2 Warp.

The Pentium Pro is superpipelined (its pipelines are deep and multistaged), and it uses what Intel calls dynamic execution (a speculative, out-of-order design) to enhance performance over the Pentium chip.

NOTE

A computer pipeline is a scheme that enables a processor to fetch the next instruction while it is executing the current one. In this way, it keeps the pipeline full and doesn't waste time asking for an instruction after it has dealt with the one at hand.

The Pentium Pro contains 8K of instruction and 8K of data L1 cache, the same as the Pentium. However, it moved beyond that to add the L2 cache in the same chip-carrying package. Models of the Pentium Pro are available with 256K, 512K, or 1MB of four-way, set-associative L2 cache. Because the cache is essentially on the CPU chip itself, it runs at the CPU speed, and performance is therefore much faster than in a system using an L2 cache on the motherboard.

The Pentium Pro is actually two chips—the CPU and a memory chip for caching—mounted within what Intel calls a Multi-Chip Module. The Pentium Pro with 256K of L2 cache integrates about 15.5 million transistors on the chip, compared to approximately 3.1 million transistors on the Pentium processor. Add cache memory, and the number of transistors goes up: 31 million for the 512K cache model and 64 million transistors on chips with 1MB of L2 cache. The Pentium Pro operates at a low 3.3 volts, except for the 150 MHz model, which is rated at 3.1 volts.

The Pentium Pro introduced a number of important dynamic execution technologies that are now part of more advanced processors. Among the technologies are *multiple branch prediction*, in which the processor is able to look multiple steps ahead in the software and predict which branches, or groups of instructions, are likely to be processed next; *dataflow analysis*, which assigns the processor to decide which instructions are dependent on each other's results and then to create an optimized schedule of instructions; and *speculative execution*, which calls upon the processor to carry out instructions on a speculative basis. In theory, the Pentium Pro guesses right more often than wrong, and keeps the chip's superscalar processing power busy while boosting over-all software performance.

Today, however, compared to a Pentium 4, Pentium III, or even a Pentium II, the Pro series is a slacker. If you're using a Pentium Pro box and it is working satisfactorily for you in the applications you use most frequently, stick with it. If you find yourself trying to wring more and more performance out of a machine that just won't seem to keep up, consider a motherboard transplant or, at the very least, an OverDrive upgrade.

Optimizing a Pentium Pro processor is a bit more complex than it was for earlier, simpler CPUs. First, you should think about your intended uses for the machine and then consider the particular Pentium Pro chip you use and the associated chipset on the motherboard. In some instances, for example, a 166 MHz Pentium Pro CPU with a 512K cache can offer better performance than a 200 MHz Pentium Pro chip with more raw speed potential but with a 256K cache.

Intel engineers initially said that most workstation users would be well served by the Pentium Pro with a 256K cache, while machines used as application servers or for Web sites would most likely benefit from the larger 512K cache. That was not widely accepted by the marketplace or by makers; the bulk of Pentium Pro sales were made with chips including the larger 512K cache.

Intel Pentium

Intel's Pentium chip is a microprocessor with power greater than that of many room-sized minicomputers of only a decade ago, with a 32-bit internal register and a 64-bit data bus. Under development as the 80586, Intel made a name change just before it was formally introduced in 1993 in order to have a product name that could be trademarked. The CPU fits into a flat socket on the motherboard, as shown in Figure 2-13.

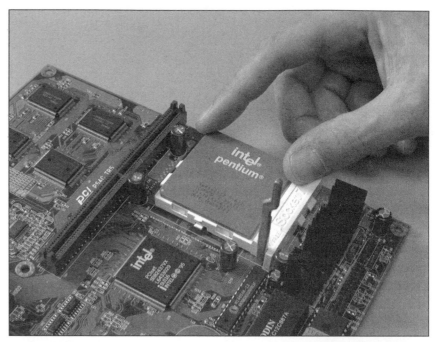

FIGURE 2-13: *A 133 MHz Pentium chip slips into a waiting socket on a motherboard.*

Pentium characteristics

The Pentium chips at the low end of the spectrum — 60 and 75 MHz clock speed — were certainly speedy, but they were not necessarily markedly faster than a well-designed machine based on a 486DX4/100 chip. The end of the run for the Pentium family saw chips reach 200 MHz, resulting in significant boosts in processing speeds.

The main improvement offered by the Pentium over earlier chips was its speed in processing floating-point math calculations. Now, before you try to say that the only math going on in your house occurs on a pocket calculator next to your checkbook, consider the fact that graphics programs are very math intensive. And graphics programs include your basic Intergalactic Monster Ping Pong game as well as Windows itself, which is a graphical user interface.

The chip communicates with the bus across an interface that is 64 bits wide; internally, the Pentium is essentially a pair of 32-bit chips that can be chained together to perform a task split between them. The Pentium's standard 16K internal cache can handle program instructions and also can buffer some of the data coming in and out of the chip.

The processor is fully compatible with earlier Intel PC chips. True speed comes with the use of Pentium-optimized software; the split-processor design is not as efficient at running DOS applications as it is with Windows and OS/2 programs.

One concern with Pentium chips was their propensity for building up heat. Nearly all early Pentium systems included vaned heat sinks intended to draw away heat. Figure 2-14 shows an example. Many later designs included tiny fans atop the chips, and there have even been a few models that included tiny electronic cooling systems. Intel reduced much of the heat problem with its later versions of the chip, which were made with super-efficient technology that permits them to run at 3.3 or 3.1 volts instead of the original 5-volt draw.

FIGURE 2-14: *A Pentium 100 MHz CPU with a heat sink in place. This passive cooling device is very dependent on a proper flow of air through the PC drawn by the fan on the power supply and often by a supplementary cooling fan at the front or back of the case.*

Inside the Pentium

The Pentium, like other Intel CPUs, is built upon the base of previous x086 chips, but added more significant enhancements than any processor before it, including new architectural features such as superscalar architecture, a totally redesigned floating point unit, branch prediction, and separate code and data caches. Other enhancements to the architecture included speedy hardwired instructions for common operations, enhanced microcode, increased page size, pipelining, and a 64-bit data bus.

A good deal of the raw speed gain for the Pentium came from the shrinking size and tighter integration of the chip. Individual elements of the chips are created at less than a micron (one-millionth of a meter) in size, with 3.1 million transistors on a single chip. The integration of elements such as math coprocessors and caches onto the CPU chip dramatically decreased the time required to access them. The Pentium processor is a superscalar device, built around two instruction pipelines that are each capable of performing independently. The pipelines permit the Pentium to execute two integer instructions in a single clock cycle, nearly double the performance of a 486 chip operating at the same frequency.

In certain circumstances, the Pentium processor can issue two instructions at once, one to each of the pipelines, in a process known as *instruction pairing*. Each pipeline is like an individual computer itself, with its own *arithmetic logic unit* (ALU), address generation circuitry, and interface to the data cache.

While the 486 processor offered a dual-purpose 8K cache, the original Pentium processor featured separate 8K caches, one for instructions and one for data. The caches serve as temporary storage places for instructions and data obtained from the slower main memory; the theory is that data and instructions are often used multiple times, and it is much faster to retrieve information from an on-chip cache than from main memory.

The chip manages the use of the caches through the use of a *least recently used (LRU) algorithm* that discards the oldest copies of instructions. *Dynamic branch prediction* is a technology that enables the processor to preload into cache an instruction it expects to execute soon. Together, these two features speed operations considerably. According to Intel, for example, a single iteration of the sieve of Eratosthenes benchmark requires only two clock cycles on a Pentium processor, compared to six clock cycles on a 486 chip. (Eratosthenes was a great scholar and director of the famed library of Alexandria, about 275-195 B.C. Among his mathematical musings was a way to calculate prime numbers; that ancient formula is used to test modern computers.)

The Pentium also introduced a completely redesigned *floating-point unit (FPU) processor*. (Alas, in the process, a math flaw was introduced in some early models of the chip; see the nearby sidebar for more details about it.) The FPU includes an eight-stage pipeline capable of executing one floating point operation every clock cycle; in certain circumstances, it can perform two operations per cycle.

The Pentium processor uses a 32-bit bus for its internal processing, the same as the 486DX and 386DX chips. However, Pentiums communicate to the external data bus across a 64-bit-wide highway, doubling the amount of data that can be transferred in a single bus cycle. In addition, a Pentium processor burst mode can load 256-bit chunks of data into the data cache in a single bus cycle. The 64-bit data bus enables a Pentium processor to transfer data to and from memory at rates up to 528 MBps. This is more than triple the peak transfer rate of a 50 MHz 486 chip.

In the CPU itself, Intel designers took several of the most commonly used instructions — including MOV and ALU — and hardwired them into the processor instead of the microcode library of instructions. The Pentium processor includes a number of built-in features for testing the chip's reliability. These include a built-in self test that tests 70 percent of the Pentium processor's components upon resetting the chip.

In addition to speed boosts, Intel made a basic change to the packaging of the chip itself, going away from the ceramic container it had used more or less since the birth of the microprocessor. Newer high-speed Pentiums use a plastic pin grid array (PPGA) that includes a copper/nickel alloy heat sink directly above the chip to help draw away heat. In addition, the traces (tiny strips of metal that interconnect elements) of the chip itself use copper instead of tungsten to improve conductivity and reduce heat.

FLOATING-POINT UNIT FLAW IN THE PENTIUM PROCESSOR

Early models of the Pentium had their 15 minutes of fame on the national news, late-night talk shows, and the Internet flame circuit. The cause of the upset was a misbehaving floating-point unit processor that would occasionally insist that $1 + 1 = 3$ or something like that. In Intel's defense, the error was likely to come up only in extremely rare circumstances among technical and scientific users and almost never for home and office users. According to Intel, the mistake was likely to occur about once in 9 billion possible independent divides, and the largest group of PC users had the least chance of running into the problem.

But Intel made some very serious public relations errors in dealing with the problem. It took several weeks to decide that it would replace the chip from any user who wanted to remove a suspect processor. In theory, Intel will still replace a flawed Pentium processor with an updated chip anytime during the life of the user's computer.

The affected chips were the slowest Pentium models, running at 60, 66, 75, 90, or 100 MHz. If your machine was delivered before January 1, 1995, it is very likely that your processor has the floating-point unit flaw. Pentium systems sold after that date should have been fixed, although it is still possible that the machine you purchased was sitting in the retail channel long enough to have been built before the problem was identified.

A more precise way to determine whether your Pentium is an old version is to run one of several identification programs. Use the Frequency ID utility available from Intel at its Web site, www.intel.com.

Should you replace your flawed dinosaur Pentium? Intel says you don't need to, and it is probably correct, unless you are using your PC to redesign the space shuttle or to control your personal artificial heart. For most of the rest of us, the chances of seeing the flaw are very remote, and the effect of the error if it occurred would probably be very evident.

But a lot of PC users can't stand the thought of their machines being less than perfect. After all, that's why people have computers on their desks — so they won't make the sort of dumb mistakes that people constantly commit. Perhaps more rationally, the consideration also exists that it's next to impossible to predict what sort of software is coming in future years. Intel's chip-swap is ancient history; if you want to update your machine, consider purchasing a faster OverDrive or replacement CPU.

If you bought your machine from a major manufacturer and it is still under some level of support or warranty, you can call technical support to find out about repair programs; be sure to have your system's serial number and date of purchase available.

Intel 486

Intel's 486 microprocessors were the first real workhorses of the microcomputer, and many millions of them are still in productive use today. A carefully maintained 486-based PC, enhanced with a fast hard drive and at least 16MB of RAM, is capable of working with Windows 95 and even Windows 98 for tasks that do not require a tremendous amount of calculation, such as word processing. Think of the 486 family as a good, solid old Chevy. It's not the fastest, it can't carry the greatest amount of cargo, and let's face it, it's no longer very sexy. But 486 machines — especially those in the DX2 and DX4 family (discussed later) — still get the job done.

This generation brought together in one chip the brains of the 386, the formerly external math coprocessor and cache controller, and other enhancements that permitted increased processing speed. The 486 was pushed as fast as 120 MHz clock speed in doubled and quadrupled versions.

The 486 was different from the 286/386 line in some important ways. In fact, it was only pretending to be an 80x86 chip. Inside, it was talking RISC, or Reduced Instruction Set Computer. RISC devices do only a few things, very fast. Workstations such as those from Sun, Hewlett-Packard, and others are RISC machines.

The 486 was available in DX and SX versions, but the distinction was different from the 386 models. Both 486 DX and SX chips operate at 32 bits internally and externally, but the SX lacks the internal math coprocessor. (Actually, it's still there, but disabled.)

In my discussion, I have split the 486 family to include 486, 486DX2, and 486DX4 chips in the senior citizen class, relegating the SX and SL versions to the dinosaur bin.

Intel DX2 and DX4

The DX2 and DX4 designs, introduced from 1992 to 1995, are very powerful speed-ups to the 486 chip family, able to run internally at twice (DX2) or three times (DX4) the external bus speed. The most popular versions of the chips are the 486DX2-66, which runs at 66 MHz, and the 486DX4-100, which reaches just short of 100 MHz. Systems based around the DX4-100 rival the processing power of the low- to mid-range Pentium processors at a lower price.

Why did Intel name the fastest 486 chip DX4 instead of the more accurate DX3? The answer lies in an arcane argument between engineering and marketing about whether the name relates to tripling the speed of a 33 MHz bus or quadrupling the speed of a less common 25 MHz bus; either way a DX4 tops out at about 99 MHz.

The Intel DX4 processor is functionally identical to and 100-percent binary compatible with the original Intel 486DX microprocessor, including the same RISC technology CPU, a floating point unit, and a memory management unit.

The 16K Intel DX4 processor cache has twice the capacity of the cache in the DX2 microprocessor. Based on advanced 0.6 micron fabrication for its 1.5 million transistors, the DX4 runs at 3.3 volts. The Intel DX4 processor includes all the SL technology features including static design, stop clock, auto halt power down, auto idle power down, I/O restart, and Intel's System Management Mode. Static design enables the processor to operate at 0 MHz while maintaining its state and consuming minimal power. The auto idle feature lets the Intel DX4 processor hibernate when it is idle during a memory cycle, waiting for I/O or memory to respond. According to Intel, the auto idle power down feature saves at least 10 percent on processor power consumption with no impact on performance.

For years, one of the workhorse machines in my office was a Gateway 486DX2 running at 66 MHz. When it was first installed, it was a speed demon, capable of running any current software. Today, it is a turtle; in certain operations — such as loading a massive program or executing complex graphics — it is painfully slow, minutes slower than the Pentium 4 1.8 GHz machine I am using to write these words. But it is capable of loading Windows 95 and

Office 97 and is an acceptable machine for standard office operations like preparation of letters. I considered performing a brain transplant — adding an OverDrive chip or a new motherboard and CPU — but rejected the idea on a cost-benefit basis. Instead, I maximized the system's memory to 32MB.

Dinosaur CPUs

Dinosaurs are fascinating. Dinosaurs are sometimes quaint. Dinosaurs (at least the computer version) can live long and productive lives. But dinosaurs cannot be expected to interact with modern needs and facilities.

In this book, a dinosaur is a machine that cannot run a modern operating system (Windows 98, Windows Me, Windows 2000, Windows XP, or Linux), cannot work with current software, and cannot interface with modern hardware including high-speed and high-capacity memory modules, advanced video display adapters, and other devices.

That doesn't mean that you can't find a use for a dinosaur. To begin with, a dinosaur machine should be able to perform adequately on basic office tasks including word processing and spreadsheets and as a backup storage system on a network. (To use a network in conjunction with modern machines, a dinosaur has to be at least able to run Windows for Workgroups or Windows 95.)

In my office, I have a dinosaur in the corner, a creaking 486 machine that is still able to work with an outdated but still-useful label printer. There are no drivers available to allow the printer to work on my modern Windows network, but it still happily confers with its dinosaur buddy.

486 SL

The SL versions of the 486 CPU, introduced between 1992 and 1994 and designed for use with portable systems, were able to work at 3.3 volts instead of 5 volts and offered shutdown monitoring capabilities. Lower voltage means better suitability for battery-operated portable PCs and less heat production inside the case of a desktop machine. IBM's SLC2 design, produced under license from Intel, included the energy-saving features of the SL, plus a 16K cache and clock-doubling circuitry, which I discuss later.

In later chips, Intel incorporated the low-power-draw design into standard 486DX chips as a matter of course. In desktop systems, going to low-voltage versions has the benefit of reducing the damaging effects of heat generated by high-speed CPUs.

Cyrix chips are clones of the Intel original, with their own microcode. The Cyrix 486SLC was actually more like a 386SX than a 486, and plugged directly into a 386SX socket without any modification. It offered 32-bit internal registers and 16-bit communication with a standard bus. It included a small 1K cache but lacked the math coprocessor circuit.

The Cyrix 486DLC added 32-bit communication with the data bus but still lacked the coprocessor. In some systems, designers paired the DLC chip with an external coprocessor, but the result was still below that of an Intel original, although the net price was usually lower.

386 SL

The SL and SLC variants of the 386, introduced by Intel and IBM in 1990 and 1991, were special low-power versions of the 386DX designed with an eye on the developing portable computer market. In addition to low demands on battery power, the chips included special circuitry that could manage the shutdown of other elements of the system. SL CPUs could also work with flash memory.

IBM took the SL concept one step further with its SLC design, which added an 8K cache and other enhancements that in certain situations could nearly double the performance of a plain 386.

386, 386SX

The 386 family, introduced in 1985, brought the first 32-bit processor for personal computers, able to crunch twice as much data with each clock cycle internally and able to communicate with 32-bit peripherals and address as much as 4GB of real memory and 64MB of virtual memory. The 386 could also work with a separate math coprocessor chip, called the 80387, which was valuable in certain types of applications, including graphics and very large spreadsheets.

The standard AT/386 hardware design limited physical memory to 16MB. The last 15MB of this memory is extended memory, which can be used either as extended or as expanded memory in 386 or 486 computers if you run a memory manager such as the EMM386 program that is a part of the later versions of DOS or QEMM386, a third-party utility.

Virtual memory gets its name because computer programs think this memory exists even though it isn't really there. For the ordinary DOS user, the most important difference between 386 and earlier chips was the virtual 8088 mode, which made the 386 computer look like several 8088 computers running simultaneously on the same machine. During much of the useful life of the 386, however, few peripherals and chips were able to operate on a full 32-bit-wide highway, and not that many users truly needed that much speed then.

Intel's reduced version of the CPU, the 386SX, processed 32 bits internally but communicated to the rest of the system over 16-bit data lines. The SX chip enabled manufacturers to produce lower-cost computers, albeit with lesser capabilities. 386 clock speeds ran from 12.5 MHz to 33 MHz. The chip also introduced the first small processor cache (a mere 16 bytes), which permitted the storage of some program instructions before they were needed.

Ch 2

Intel 80286

The 80286, introduced in 1982, was a true 16-bit chip able to address as much as 16MB of memory and able to work with virtual memory, a scheme that uses disk-based storage to simulate up to 1GB of memory.

The 286 also brought the first baby steps toward multitasking and introduced the concept of real mode (an emulation of the 8086) and protected mode (the ability to multitask with multiple programs running in their own separate world; DOS was unable to take advantage of that ability, but future operating system enhancements—including Windows—would). IBM built its Advanced Technology PC AT around the chip. When introduced, the 286 ran at 6 MHz, but IBM soon raised it to 8 MHz; clone makers found ways to boost it to as much as 20 MHz.

In addition to the doubled external data bus, the AT introduced an improved set of internal instructions that could execute commands much more efficiently than the 8088 CPU, using about 4.5 cycles per instruction instead of 12.

Other companies, including Harris, manufactured some versions of the 80286 chip under license. Figure 2-15 shows an example of a Harris chip.

Intel 8088

Introduced in 1979, the chip that launched the PC revolution was a hybrid device that processed information internally in 16-bit chunks but communicated externally to the bus in 8-bit words. Used as the brain of the original IBM PC and its clones, as well as in the PC XT and the PCjr, the chip ran at a poky 4.77 MHz clock speed and could address only up to 1MB of memory—an upper limit of 640K of RAM, with the top 384K set aside for memory addresses for the video card, the hard disk, and the read-only memory basic input/output system (ROM BIOS). Some early XT clones managed to boost the clock speed a bit, but machines based on the original PC CPU are today glacially slow compared to modern machines.

FIGURE 2-15: *A Harris version of an 80286 chip on a dinosaur motherboard*

Intel 8086

A true 16-bit chip, the 8086 processed information internally 16 bits at a time and communicated externally with the PC's bus across a 16-wire data connection. Introduced in 1978, it was bypassed for the original PC because the 16-bit bus added more expense than fit IBM's business plan. It was later used in a few relatively unimportant versions.

Dinosaur clones

In the early days of the personal computer there was a time when Intel's dominance was not taken for granted. A number of manufacturers came up with their own microprocessors, or cloned Intel devices. Some of the devices were worth consideration, but like Microsoft, Intel was a champion at marketing its devices and striking deals with computer makers. Of the would-be competitors, only AMD is still much of a factor.

IDT WinChips

One line of clones that tried—and failed—to slow the Intel juggernaut were the WinChips from IDT, introduced in 1997. These Pentium II clones were offered in a 296-pin ceramic pin grid array for Socket 7 motherboards.

A relatively small number of these chips were sold; IDT ended the line in 1998, returning to the manufacture of more specialized chips. Although the chips performed adequately, there is no ongoing support for WinChips, and owners of machines using this processor should consider a motherboard and CPU transplant if they run into any difficulties.

Cyrix 6x86

The Cyrix 6x86 processor, offered in 1996, was pin-compatible with the Pentium. In magazine lab tests, the 6x86 generally outperformed equivalent Intel processors, turning in results just short of Pentium Pro processors.

There were reports of heat-related failures on some 6x86 systems; Cyrix says its chips should not overheat if system vendors follow their recommendations for heat sinks and high-volume fans, and install sufficient airflow ducts in cases. If you have a 6x86-based system, you should make certain the cooling system is appropriate and take care to avoid blocking air vents.

AMD5K86

The AMD5K86, introduced in 1995, received good marks for compatibility and speed; its main advantage came in its price break compared to Intel's Pentium chip. The chip's advanced features included out-of-order speculative execution, an 8K data cache, and a 16K instruction cache (twice that of the standard Pentium).

Nx586 P100

The Next Generation Nx586 P100 model actually ran at 93 MHz, but was claimed to rival a Pentium at 100 MHz when it was introduced in 1995. It had the disadvantage of not being pin-compatible with a Pentium chip, and therefore required a special motherboard and support chips. In 1996, AMD purchased Next Generation and incorporated its research and development labs.

NEC V20, NEC V30

Functional equivalents of the 8088 and the 8086, respectively, these chips made by Japanese maker NEC could boost processing speed by as much as 30 percent over original PC designs. They were first offered in 1981.

NOTE

MS-DOS, the operating system designed for the 8088 microprocessor, is limited to the capabilities of the least common denominator—the original 8088 microprocessor. Consequently, programs operating under MS-DOS cannot use memory over 1MB without a special program to open up that RAM. To get around the memory limit of DOS, many programs are able to use what is called expanded memory. Expanded memory cards can be added to dinosaur XTs and ATs, although there is no cost justification for doing so today. The issue of memory management for DOS pretty much ended with the arrival of Windows 95 for modern machines. Many modern machines use 64MB, 128MB, or more RAM for complex graphics or database work.

Pentium OverDrive Processors

Until the development of the Pentium III (which drove down the cost of the Pentium II) and Celeron chips, Intel's OverDrive technology was a cost-effective bridge between an underpowered older machine and new technology. Intel delivered OverDrive processors for 486SX- and DX-based machines and for Pentium processors from

60 MHz to 100 MHz in speed, eventually extending the family to include MMX-based systems and chips that allowed the migration of compatible Pentium Pro systems to the Pentium II architecture.

The OverDrive days are over, however. Intel announced in 1999 that it would no longer manufacture and support Pentium II OverDrive chips for Pentium processors. In today's market, it doesn't make sense to gild an outdated lily—a better idea is to change motherboards and processors, or consider a cross-species upgrade to a clone processor.

As part of the OverDrive design process, Intel introduced a series of standardized sockets intended to handle not only the original chip but also future OverDrives, which often require additional pins. Figure 2-16 shows an example of an OverDrive, and Table 2-10 lists iCOMP index data for various OverDrive microprocessors.

TABLE 2-10: Intel iCOMP Index for Microprocessors with Intel OverDrive Processors			
CPU	iCOMP Index before OverDrive	iCOMP Index with OverDrive	Equivalent CPU after Upgrade
i486 SX-20	78	182	i486 DX2-40
i486 SX-25	100	231	i486 DX2-50
i486 DX-25	122	231	i486 DX2-50
i486 SX-33	136	297	i486 DX2-66
i486 DX-33	166	297	i486 DX2-66
Pentium 60	51	75	Pentium 83
Pentium 66	57	84	Pentium 90
Pentium 75	67	92	Pentium 105
Pentium 90	81	114	Pentium 150
Pentium 100	90	127	Pentium 166
Pentium 133	111	127	Pentium 166
Pentium 100	90	142	Pentium 200
Pentium 133	111	142	Pentium 200
Pentium 166	127	142	Pentium 200

Dollars and sense

Faster computer performance for a relatively small investment is an intriguing concept. However, don't expect an OverDrive chip to do the same thing as a new computer. An OverDrive chip can speed things up but not as much as a new computer and sometimes not as much as an infusion of extra RAM. A very few third-party manufacturers continue OverDrive production; still, if the machine you have isn't fast enough for the job, the best way to fix it may well be to replace it with another motherboard that contains a modern CPU.

FIGURE 2-16: *On some motherboards, an Intel OverDrive can be installed in place of the original 486 or Pentium chip in the processor socket, while some older designs have a separate OverDrive socket on the motherboard.*

CROSS-REFERENCE

See Chapter 8 for more information on your computer's memory.

Remember, too, that adding an OverDrive CPU doesn't change the performance of your hard drive, memory, or video adapter. So if you decide to install an OverDrive, consider improving these devices, too. But before you do so, calculate the total cost of the upgrade and compare it to a completely new system, or a bare-bones upgrade that will deliver a new CPU as well as an updated motherboard and supporting chips.

An OverDrive road map

Intel OverDrive chips have been available for processors from 486 through Pentium Pro processors. By mid-1998, Intel had discontinued offering the Pentium 63/83 MHz OverDrive processor for upgradeable 486 systems and the Pentium 120/133 MHz OverDrive processor for upgradeable Pentium 60/66 MHz processor–based systems. You may find some of these chips at stores or mail-order outfits, but owners of these senior citizens and early modern machines may need to shop for non-Intel upgrades.

The 486 Intel OverDrives worked with most models of SX2, DX2, DX, and SX CPUs with 237- or 238-pin sockets. Two versions of the Pentium OverDrive processors were available at the start of 1997: 63 MHz Pentium OverDrive processors for 25 or 50 MHz systems and 83 MHz Pentium OverDrive processors for 33 or 66 MHz systems. In early 1998, Intel announced new OverDrive chips to provide even higher speed upgrades for Pentium and Pentium Pro processors, including one chip that steps up some Pentium Pro CPUs to Pentium II.

The Overdrive CPU still interconnects with the external bus at its original clock rate, enabling it to work with the rest of the original system and any of its installed peripherals.

NOTE

Intel provides an online branded upgrade guide that provides useful information on Intel OverDrive products for specific computer brands and models. Point your browser to www.intel.com/overdrive/upgrade/index.htm to view the latest information there.

Table 2-11 provides a guide to OverDrive use.

TABLE 2-11: What Goes Where?		
OverDrive Processor	**Replaces**	**Socket**
486 Pentium OverDrive	486SX, DX, SX2, DX2	Socket 2/3
60/66 Pentium OverDrive	Pentium 60/66	Socket 4
Pentium OverDrive with MMX	Pentium 75/90/100	Socket 5/7

Pentium-level CPU upgrades from other makers

Intel is not the only game in town when it comes to upgrading older CPUs to more modern capabilities and performance. A number of companies offer replacement chips that bring a 386 to near-486 power, 486s to Pentium-like performance, and older Pentiums to faster models.

The chips, which generally work in either an OverDrive socket or the primary socket, use an AMD or Cyrix processor. You may find it difficult or impossible to find upgrades for 386 systems; 486 and Pentium chips were widely available at the start of 1998, but declined in popularity and availability during 1999. In 2002, these chips were available only on ancient motherboards pulled from seriously outdated systems. Check the catalogs of suppliers such as TigerDirect for the latest upgrade chip technologies.

One of the larger players in this market is Evergreen Technologies (www.evergreennow.com), which uses AMD and Intel Celeron processors. Among Evergreen's offerings are the following:

- 486/20, 25, DX2/50 to 586/80 or 100 MHz
- 486/33, 40, DX2/66 to 568/120 or 133 MHz
- Pentium 75 and higher to 180 or 200 MHz MMX
- Pentium II 233 to 350 MHz to 766 MHz or 1 GHz
- Pentium III 400 MHz and higher to 1 GHz

Another source is PowerLeap products (www.powerleap. com). The company offers AMD and Intel Pentium III and Celeron upgrades, including:

- Upgrade AMD K5 or K6 to AMD K6-III
- Classic Pentiums running at 75–200 MHz to 233 MHz with MMX
- Pentium II and Pentium III to 800 MHz to 1 GHz

Another supplier of upgrades is Kingston Technology Company (www.kingston.com), with its line of TurboChips. Kingston's offerings include the TurboChip 366, which uses the AMD K6-2 processor. Other TurboChips range from the TurboChip 133 to the TurboChip 233, designed to upgrade 486 through Pentium computers.

Installing a third-party upgrade to a dinosaur

For this example, I installed a TurboChip 100 and then a TurboChip 133 into a Gateway 2000 486SX-33 computer, a capable — but relatively slow — home computer. Installation is straightforward, without the need for alterations to the motherboard, switch settings, or device drivers on most systems. The only consideration for some users is the fact that the TurboChip, with its cooling fan, sits $^7/_8$-inch higher than the chip it replaces. A small number of PCs may have disk drives or other parts that sit close to the microprocessor socket and could cause a problem here.

The TurboChip replaces your existing processor or plugs into an Intel OverDrive socket if the original processor cannot be removed. If you use the OverDrive socket, you will probably have to set jumpers or switches to disable the existing CPU.

Many 486 computers use ZIF sockets with a lever or retaining screw to permit easy removal of the CPU. Kingston also provides a PGA socket extender to use with certain types of ZIF socket installations, which use an overhead locking bar that would not ordinarily close with the higher TurboChip in place.

WARNING

The most important step in installing a Kingston upgrade is to take the same precautions as you would when working with any chips on your system: Be sure to switch off and unplug the system before working under the covers, ground yourself before touching a chip, use even pressure to remove the existing CPU if necessary, take special care to align pin 1 of the TurboChip with pin 1 of the socket, and install the new chip with even pressure. Watch carefully to be certain you do not bend or misalign any pins as you install the new chip.

Before installing the chip, I ran the Landmark Speed 2.0 benchmark program on the Gateway machine. It reported that the 33 MHz SX chip was the functional equivalent of a 112.5 MHz PC-AT. Another way to state this comparison is to say that the unimproved Gateway machine was running about 14 times faster than an 8 MHz PC-AT. After I installed the TurboChip 100, the Landmark Speed 2.0 benchmark indicated the presence of a 100 MHz 486DX chip at the functional equivalent of a 334 MHz PC-AT. The Gateway's speed had tripled. Of course, the raw clock speed rating of the CPU is not a true measure of the power of the computer. More realistically, you can expect a near doubling of performance.

The installation took a total of 15 minutes, with 5 minutes of the time devoted to a careful check, double-check, and triple-check of the orientation of the chip in the ZIF socket of the Gateway machine. The only trick consists of carefully noting the notched corner of the original Intel chip and orienting the replacement Kingston chip's notch in the same place on the socket.

I checked the installation one more time before powering up the system. After replacing the covers, my final step consisted of pasting a Kingston TurboChip sticker over the outdated 486-33SX label.

Pentium Pro to Pentium II OverDrives

Again, Intel has discontinued production of its Pentium Pro OverDrive processors. If you can still find the chips—from an overstocked dealer or a friend with extras—upgradeable systems based on the 150 and 180 MHz Pentium Pro processors can be upgraded to processor speeds of 300 MHz, according to Intel, and systems with 166 and 200 MHz Pentium Pro processors can be upgraded to processor speeds of 333 MHz. This OverDrive also incorporates Intel's MMX media enhancement technology.

Before starting this OverDrive upgrade, you should find out whether you need a BIOS upgrade. Intel will help. Point your browser to `www.intel.com/overdrive/upgrade/bios/index.htm` and follow the instructions on the screen. You can download a free software utility that will check your current system BIOS and report its compatibility with a Pentium II upgrade.

Pentium MMX OverDrives

In the past, Intel offered a Pentium OverDrive processor with MMX technology to upgrade Pentium processor–based systems to the additional MMX technology. The MMX OverDrive is an interesting enhancement because the MMX chip, in most cases, uses a different voltage than the original Pentium CPU you are upgrading. The chip carrier converts the voltage automatically.

Table 2-12 lists estimated speed gains using an Intel OverDrive/MMX OverDrive chip.

TABLE 2-12: OverDrive Speed Gains

Standard Pentium Speed	Speed After OverDrive/ MMX Upgrade
166 MHz	200 MHz
100, 133 MHz	166 MHz or 200 MHz
90, 120, 150 MHz	180 MHz
75 MHz	150 MHz

NOTE

A small number of early Pentium systems were designed with instructions that incorrectly support the write-back mode of the Pentium OverDrive processor. To upgrade these systems to Pentium processors, you need to use a special interposer chip carrier that sits between the OverDrive and the CPU socket on the motherboard. The interposer disables the write-back mode. If your system manufacturer advises you that the interposer is required, the company may be able to supply the part, or you may need to deal directly with Intel, which supplies the part for free or very low cost.

Third-party vendors, such as PowerLeap, also offer MMX upgrades of slower Pentium systems. PowerLeap's upgrade (either an AMD K6 or Intel Pentium CPU), for example, offers what the company claims is a relatively painless enhancement (see Figure 2-17).

Figure 2-17: *PowerLeap's PL-ProMMX upgrades Pentium 75 to 200 systems with Socket 5 or 7 chips with a speedy 400 MHz AMD K6-III.*

Upgrading a 486 Senior Citizen

Intel's plans for OverDrive chips go back to the early days of 486 motherboards. As a result, there are three types of 486 systems:

- Motherboards that come equipped with a special OverDrive socket, which supplements your CPU
- Motherboards in which the user must remove the CPU and replace it with a new OverDrive CPU in a special 168-pin version of the DX2 OverDrive processor
- Motherboards that will not work with an OverDrive chip

If you have any doubts about the design of your system's motherboard, consult the instruction manual or contact the PC's manufacturer.

Intel publishes the *OverDrive Compatibility Guide* (still available at www.intel.com/overdrive/UPGRADE/Index.htm), which contains a list of systems that have been tested and confirmed as compatible with the OverDrive chip. Intel recommends against using the OverDrive in any system not on the list and will not honor warranty claims for chips damaged as a result of improper usage.

> **NOTE**
>
> Intel no longer offers for sale or supports Overdrive chips, according to information on the company's Web site. Upgrade hardware still is available from companies such as PowerLeap, but as I have said, if you need the power of an upgraded PC, your best bet today likely is a new machine. Remember, too, that "new to you" hardware may offer a significant upgrade in performance over what you currently have. Many local computer stores offer refurbished hardware that can provide you better performance at attractive prices without the trouble of finding and installing outdated Overdrive or other upgrade hardware.

Note also that Intel's certification applies to systems rather than motherboards because of variables including the types of peripheral components in a system and whether the system has sufficient airflow to properly cool the OverDrive processor. Because of Intel's position, many no-name 486 machines are not certified as compatible.

Some single- or two-socket systems may have a larger socket. These models are upgradeable with a 486 or Pentium OverDrive.

Getting a handle on 486 sockets

Two common types of sockets for OverDrive processors are those with a handle (also called ZIF sockets) and those without a handle (sometimes called low insertion force sockets).

WARNING

Always turn off your computer and remove the power plug before attempting any work inside the box. Ground yourself by touching a grounding strap.

To open a socket with a handle, push down and away on the handle to unhook it from the small catch that holds it in place. Lift the handle to a 90-degree upright position and then remove the processor or insert a new one. Place the old processor on a soft, nonconductive surface such as the piece of foam usually provided with the replacement chip. To close the socket, lower the socket handle and hook it under the catch.

If your system's processor socket does not have a handle, you should obtain a chip removal tool—basically a small nonconductive spatula-like device that slips under the chip and gives you a fulcrum point to push up on the chip from its underside. Work slowly and be careful not to bend or break the pins on the chip you are removing. When you've removed the chip, carefully align the replacement processor over the proper holes and push it into place evenly, again taking care to avoid bending or breaking pins.

There are several socket designs with different sizes on 486 processor systems. If your system has a socket with 17 pinholes per side (168- or 169-pinhole socket), you cannot upgrade with Intel's Pentium OverDrive processor (although a processor upgrade may be available from other makers, usually employing an AMD or Cyrix CPU).

To use an Intel OverDrive in a 486 system, the socket must have 19 pinholes per side (237- or 238-pinhole socket). An easy way to tell if you have such a socket is to examine the original 486 processor in place; look for an extra row of pinholes around the processor.

Some 486 systems offer a second, special socket intended for the OverDrive processor upgrade. In this design, all you have to

do is install the OverDrive processor in the empty socket; the system will automatically disable the 486 processor.

Installing an OverDrive in a single-socket 486 motherboard

Here's a step-by-step tour through the installation process of an OverDrive in a single-socket motherboard, a circuit design that requires the removal of the original CPU:

1. **Turn off the PC and unplug the power cord.** Remove the PC's covers. Before handling the internals of the computer, ground yourself by touching a grounding strap or the center screw of an electrical outlet cover.
2. **Locate the 486 CPU on the motherboard or on a removable CPU card.** On some systems, you may need to take apart much of the system to gain access to the chip, including removing cards and hard drives.
3. **Using an extraction tool, carefully remove the 486 CPU.** Remove the chip with a firm, even pull that does not bend the pins or damage the motherboard.
4. **Install the OverDrive processor into the socket.** Align pin 1 of the chip with the marked hole in the socket and press down firmly and evenly. Take care not to bend any of the pins of the chip under its body or outside of the socket.
5. **If necessary, set jumpers or switches on the motherboard so that it will recognize the presence of the OverDrive.** Consult your instruction manual or call the system manufacturer for further details. Some systems may require new BIOS chips or software updates to configuration programs.
6. **Reinstall any boards or cables you removed to make room for the installation of the OverDrive.** Plug the system into an electrical current and turn it on to test the processor.

Installing an OverDrive in a 486 motherboard with an upgrade socket

Putting an OverDrive into place on a motherboard with an upgrade socket is a slightly easier process because you may not need to remove the original CPU.

1. **Turn off the PC and unplug the power cord.** Remove the PC's covers. Before handling the internals of the computer, ground yourself by touching a grounding strap or by touching the center screw of an electrical outlet cover.

2. **Locate the empty OverDrive socket.** Some systems have standard sockets, while others have a low insertion force or zero insertion force socket.

3. **Orient the OverDrive processor correctly before installing it.** There are several designs for sockets. A keyed socket has four rows of pinholes and a key pinhole; match the key pin on the chip with the key pinhole on the socket. If the socket has fewer than three rows of pinholes or does not have a key pinhole, your computer may still be upgradeable with the OverDrive processor. Consult your computer system manufacturer for more information.

4. **Insert the OverDrive processor in the empty socket.** If the socket is a zero insertion force design, be sure to unlock or release the socket before inserting the chip and close the lock/unlock lever or turn the lock/unlock screw to the closed position after the chip is in place.

5. **If the system has a standard socket, you may have to press firmly to seat the pins in the socket.** Be sure to press evenly and watch that none of the pins bend underneath the chip or outside the socket. And do not press hard enough to bend the motherboard.

6. **If necessary, set jumpers or switches on the motherboard so that it will recognize the presence of the OverDrive.** Consult your instruction manual or call the system manufacturer for further details.

Installing an OverDrive in a Pentium motherboard

A Pentium motherboard may have a heat sink or fan atop the original processor, adding slightly to the job at hand:

1. **Turn off the PC and unplug the power cord.** Remove the PC's covers. Before handling the internals of the computer, ground yourself by touching a grounding strap or by touching the center screw of an electrical outlet cover.

2. **Locate the original Pentium processor.** If the original Pentium processor has a fan cooling system, unplug the cable; it will not be needed for the Pentium OverDrive processor. Unfasten any clips holding the processor and heat sink to the socket.

3. **If you have a 75, 90, or 100 MHz system, open the socket handle and remove the original Pentium processor.** Orient the Pentium OverDrive processor so that the side with the processor speed mark is next to the number in the socket label.

   If you have a 60 or 66 MHz system, open the socket handle and remove the original Pentium processor. Orient the Pentium OverDrive Processor so that the speed mark on the processor is next to the *S* in the socket label.

4. **Close the socket handle.** Put the cover back on your computer, plug it in, and test the system using your standard applications, a utility benchmark program, or the special diagnostic software that comes with the Pentium OverDrive processor.

Dinosaur Arithmetic: Math Coprocessors

A math coprocessor is a specialized form of microprocessor that is capable of performing certain types of floating point math calculations much faster than a general-purpose CPU. It works in cooperation with the CPU, taking charge of some jobs ordinarily performed by the microprocessor and adding speed to your system by doing the calculations faster than the main chip and by reducing some of the CPU's workload. Math coprocessors are an add-on to dinosaur 386 and 286 CPUs; a floating-point unit is included within 486DX and all current Pentium chips.

A floating-point number is a value in which the decimal point can move one way or the other as the result of mathematical manipulations. It's easier to define by saying what a floating-point number is not: whole numbers (integers) and predetermined values like dollars and cents in which there are always two numbers to the right of the decimal point.

A floating-point number has three parts: the *sign*, which indicates whether its value is greater than or less than zero; a *significant digit* (also called a *mantissa*), which includes all the mathematically meaningful digits; and an *exponent*, which expresses the order of magnitude of the significant, which would be the location to which the decimal point floats.

However, just because you are running a spreadsheet model of the economy of France from 1870 to 1999, don't automatically assume that your application makes much use of floating-point calculations. A computer magazine conducted some interesting tests a number of years back and found that a coprocessor delivered little or no benefit in most spreadsheet applications based on database sorts. It also found that most financial calculations involve mostly addition and subtraction, which yield no benefit. And even with most commercial applications that perform heavy-duty calculations, only a relatively small amount of their work is actually related to the math, with the rest devoted to overhead, including display and sorting.

The real boost came in custom software for very complex calculations, including manipulation of arrays of irrational numbers and trigonometric functions. (An *irrational number* is a value such as *pi*, which must be rounded off because it cannot be expressed with a finite number of digits.)

And one more interesting finding by the magazine was that no matter what combination of 386 chip and coprocessor it tried, a 486 chip with its built-in math coprocessor was always faster. This would apply in spades for Pentium chips.

Therefore, unless you are running some very strange and demanding software, it would seem that the most cost-efficient upgrade for owners of a 386 modern machine would be to install an OverDrive or similar replacement technology that would move your PC to the 486 or Pentium class. Not only will you pick up the floating-point math unit, but you'll also improve the overall capabilities of the CPU. This option is not available to owners of most dinosaurs, however.

How do you choose the proper math coprocessor?

The best-known maker of math coprocessors is Intel, the designer and prime manufacturer of nearly all the microprocessors used in PCs. Other makers of coprocessors over the years have included AMD, Cyrix Corporation, Integrated Information Technology, ULSI, and Weight.

Start by checking the instruction manual from your computer maker; you may need to call the manufacturer's technical support line. Intel's faxback service also contains compatibility listings for Intel math coprocessors for many widely used computers.

Here are some general guidelines:

- **Pentium, 486DX, 486DX/2, 486DX/4, 486SL.** These CPUs include a built-in math coprocessor and do not need an external chip.
- **486SX.** You can bring a 486SX near to the capability of a 486DX CPU by adding an i487 math coprocessor chip. In 486SX-based computers, the microprocessor and math coprocessor run at the same speed. A better solution, however, is to use an OverDrive processor instead of the i487; the OverDrive unit includes the

math coprocessor and will also boost overall system performance by up to 70 percent.

- **386DX, 386SX, 386SL.** None of the members of the 386 class of CPUs have an integral math coprocessor; the SX and SL versions of the chips differ in their compatibility with 16-bit data buses, unlike the 32-bit bus lines of the DX version. You will need to select the appropriate 387DX or 387SX math coprocessors. Note that the 387DX is not certified to operate with non-Intel microprocessors that operate faster than 33 MHz, and the 387SX is not certified to operate with non-Intel microprocessors that operate faster than the speed rating of the math coprocessor.

  Users with 386DX systems and CAD or scientific applications can also consider Intel's RapidCAD Engineering Coprocessor, which can boost math operations by up to 70 percent over the performance of a 386DX and 387DX combination. Systems based on the 386SX 16, 20, or 25 MHz microprocessor or the 386SL 16, 20, or 25 MHz microprocessor can use the 387SL math coprocessor.

- **80286-based computers.** Most computers based on the 286 processor drive the math coprocessor at two-thirds the microprocessor speed. The 287 math coprocessor is capable of running at speeds of up to 12.5 MHz. Some laptops, including the Compaq 286/LTE and the Tandy 2800, use a nonstandard design and can use a special small-form coprocessor, the 287XLT. In this realm of the dinosaurs, of course, the effort may not be worthwhile. In any case, consult your instruction guide and speak to the manufacturer before you attempt to upgrade such a system. Most of the software applications you might want to run on a computer won't work with machines in this class.

- **8088- and 8086-based computers.** In the original design for 8088 and 8086 computers, the microprocessor and math coprocessor usually run at the same speed. This class of computer started out with a clock speed of 4.77 MHz, and

subsequent models operated at 8 or 20 MHz. The math coprocessor must match the computer's fastest operating speed.

Installing a math coprocessor

Before you begin, be sure that you have the proper math coprocessor, rated at a speed equal to or greater than that of the microprocessor. Check your system's instruction manual and acquaint yourself with the location and orientation of the socket for the coprocessor. Finally, inspect the chip itself, looking for damage, including bent pins. You may not want to try to repair bent pins; return the chip to the vendor for a new one.

1. **Ground yourself.** Touch the metal back or side panel on your computer, or the center screw on an electrical outlet, to ground yourself and prevent static electricity from damaging your system or the math coprocessor.
2. **Switch off the power and unplug the computer.** After the system is disconnected from power, remove the covers.
3. **Locate the socket.** The empty socket for the coprocessor is almost always next to the CPU itself. It may be marked with a name or number; consult your instruction manual or call your computer company's technical support line if you have any doubts about its location.
4. **Orient the math coprocessor correctly.** Chips are marked with a dot for pin 1 (387 and 487 coprocessors), or they're marked with a dot and beveled edge (8087s and 80287s). The socket is marked with a similar dot or bevel, and both should match when installed.
5. **Insert the math coprocessor.** Align the chip with pin 1 above socket 1 and lightly press the chip into place. Watch to be sure that none of the pins becomes bent under the chip so that they will not make contact. Be sure that each pin is above its corresponding socket before you press down firmly.

Depending on the design of the particular chip and the socket, you may have to press down fairly hard to seat the chip; take care, however, not to make the motherboard bend as you insert the chip, or you could end up damaging the delicate circuitry beneath its surface.

6. **Set switches or jumpers on the motherboard.** On some systems, you need to set switches or jumpers or both on the motherboard to let the computer know you have added a math coprocessor. Consult the PC's instruction manual or contact the system manufacturer for more information. Information for some motherboards is available on Intel's faxback system.

   In most cases, if you have correctly inserted the math coprocessor, an incorrect jumper or switch setting will not damage the chip; it simply will not work properly.

   Some systems are capable of recognizing the presence of the coprocessor, while others will adjust based on a configuration program.

7. **Restart the computer.** Put the cover back on the computer, reconnect all the cables and cords, plug the power cord into the wall outlet, and turn the computer on.

8. **Run a reference or system configuration program.** Some computers have a system-installation, reference, or system-configuration program that must be run to enable the system to work with a math coprocessor. The program may be stored in ROM or on a disk. See your system manual for more information.

9. **Test the math coprocessor.** Use the diagnostics software program on the utilities diskette that came with your math coprocessor to test the chip. If the program shows that the math coprocessor isn't operating correctly, verify that you have set the switches or jumpers properly and installed the chip properly; if you are unable to proceed, contact the supplier of the chip.

Installing an Intel 387 math coprocessor in a Weitek socket

Some 386 motherboards were designed to work with coprocessors by Weitek, a manufacturer that created chips that were competitive to Intel's chip. Many of these systems have a square socket that will accommodate either a Weitek or Intel coprocessor.

This socket has three rows of holes on all four sides. In many such computers—including the Compaq 386—the inner two rows of pins are compatible with the Intel 387. To install, place the pins of the Intel 387 over the inner two rows of holes and align pin 1 with the key pin hole before pressing down.

Some computers, including the Tandy 4000, have the Weitek socket but do not support the Intel 387DX. Consult your computer manual or contact the manufacturer for further information on using the Weitek socket.

Troubleshooting Intel OverDrives

Problem: You have installed an Intel OverDrive, but the computer does not power up when you turn the switch on, or the operating system prompt does not appear on the screen.

Solution: Check that the power cord is attached to the system and is plugged into the wall socket. If that does not solve the problem, unplug the wire and check that the cables and connectors inside the computer are attached correctly and that any boards you may have removed are reinstalled correctly.

Check that the OverDrive processor is oriented correctly in the socket, especially if it is installed in an overlarge 238-pin socket. All chips should be fully inserted into the socket with only about a dime's width between the bottom of the chip and the top of the socket.

Be sure that you have installed the OverDrive in the upgrade socket and have not put it into the Weitek 4170 math coprocessor socket that is present on some motherboards.

Ch 2

IBM PS/2 computers require that you run the reference diskette to update the system information. Other systems may require setting jumpers and sockets.

Problem: The OverDrive processor fails the Intel Diagnostics program.
Solution: Is the OverDrive processor fully inserted in its socket? If you are using a ZIF socket, is the socket lever fully locked or the screw fully closed?

Does your computer require an update to its BIOS? Consult the manufacturer of your computer or Intel.

Check jumpers and switches to be sure they are set correctly.

You can remove the OverDrive processor and install it in another identical or similar PC to see if it performs properly. Be sure that you have the correct model of OverDrive for the second computer. If the chip works, there is a problem with the first computer; if the chip fails, it is probably defective.

If the OverDrive Processor still fails the diagnostic tests, remove it and return it to your dealer or Intel.

Problem: The PC does not run any faster with the OverDrive processor installed.
Solution: Are jumpers or switches on the motherboard set correctly, as described in your computer's manual? (Some systems require no changes to settings.)

Have you run any necessary setup programs, such as the reference diskette for IBM PS/2 systems?

Use the Intel Diagnostics to be sure the OverDrive is installed properly. Use a general system diagnostic program to check the entire computer as well.

Does the system have a second-level cache? Check the CMOS setup screen to ensure that it is turned on.

Check the integrity of your cache. With the OverDrive installed, go to the CMOS setup and switch off the cache. Using an application such as a spreadsheet, database, or word processor, run a specific number of commands on a lengthy file and time how long they take to execute. Then perform the identical test with the cache switched on. If there is no performance difference, you may have a problem with your second-level cache. Contact your computer manufacturer for more assistance.

Problem: The OverDrive feels hot to the touch.
Solution: The OverDrive processor (and many other high-speed chips) generate heat when operating. According to Intel, the heat sink that is part of the chip will draw away heat so that a chip fan is not necessary.

Be sure that your PC's fan is operating properly, that input air ports are not blocked with dust, and that exhaust ports are not blocked by being too close to a wall or other obstruction.

Problem: The computer boots up and runs normally for a while and then hangs up or shuts down.
Solution: Check that the OverDrive is fully inserted into the socket and properly oriented. Is the key pin aligned with the socket's key pin?

If you are using a ZIF socket, is the lever fully locked or the screw fully closed?

Are jumpers or system switches set correctly, if changes are necessary? Consult your computer manual or the manufacturer of the system.

Do you need to update your system's BIOS? Owners of IBM PS/2 Models 90 or 95 must run the latest reference diskette. Consult your computer manual or Intel's customer support.

Do you have to wait for the computer to cool off before it boots? Your computer may not be producing enough air flow to cool the OverDrive. Check with Intel's customer support for information about using an alternate OverDrive processor.

SUMMARY

In this chapter, you've looked at the grand march of processor history. In the next chapter, you examine the system BIOS, the most basic level of instructions for the PC.

Notes

Chapter 3

Tools Needed:

- Chip-removal tool

BIOS

The basic input/output system, or BIOS, is the lowest-level set of instructions for your computer, defining your PC's personality and handling essential tasks. The microprocessor uses the BIOS to bring the machine to life when you first turn the power on. The process is called "booting" the computer; the term comes from the old phrase "pulling yourself up by your bootstraps."

The BIOS also runs startup diagnostics on the system. After your PC is up and running, it oversees the basic functions of interpreting signals from the keyboard and the interchange of information through ports.

The BIOS exists as a ROM (read-only memory) chip or set of chips on your motherboard, together with additional ROM BIOS chips that may be present on some adapter cards, and the set of device drivers from various pieces of hardware in the system.

In logical terms, the BIOS sits between the hardware and the operating system. Most pieces of hardware come equipped with software device drivers that help a generic system to work with the specialized functions that they deliver; the drivers occupy a logical layer between the BIOS and the operating system.

The purpose of this layered structure is to permit the operating system to do its thing without dealing directly with the hardware; the BIOS and associated drivers interpret commands for the needs of the specific mix of hardware in your system.

At the lower half of this stack of layers, the operating system does not have to deal directly with the specific set of software applications (such as word processors, browsers, databases, and the like). Instead, the Application Program Interface (API) stands between the operating system and applications; therefore, applications don't need to know much about the structure of the operating system and can just send a command that says "print this" or "save this to disk."

Some elements of the BIOS need to be available at the time of bootup (for example, basic functionality for a video card, the keyboard, mouse, and a hard drive), whereas other elements (such as a sound card, a printer, or scanner) can wait for the operating system to be fully loaded before they become fully functional. That's why certain devices have their instructions resident in the BIOS on the motherboard or in ROMs on adapter cards; these are scanned and loaded first and are usually indicated on your monitor during bootup. Device drivers are stored on the hard drive and are loaded a bit later along with the operating system.

Because ROM chips are relatively slow to disgorge their information (typically with access times of 150 nanoseconds versus as little as 8 nanoseconds for modern RAM), most systems pick up a bit of speed by "shadowing" the contents of ROM to system RAM during bootup. The information is copied to memory and made available there for use after the system is up and running.

Shadowing is more useful in 16-bit operating systems including DOS and Windows 3.1; modern 32-bit operating systems generally use a different set of BIOS instructions after they are running, using the 16-bit code only for bootup. Consult the instruction manual for your motherboard and BIOS before making any changes to the shadowing settings.

Another important part of the BIOS is the POST (power-on self test) that checks for the presence and functionality of essential pieces of the system at bootup, and then gives a numeric or text report of any problems it has found.

As important as all of these functions are, most PC users don't know the maker and version of the BIOS in their machine, and few have ever explored the settings on the CMOS configuration screen that is a part of nearly every modern machine.

If you never add memory, drives, or other internal devices, have no interest in adjusting the personality of your machine to suit your needs, and never experience a problem with the basic functions of your PC, then you probably never need to visit the configuration settings of your BIOS. That is, of course, if you are satisfied that the manufacturer of your machine did the job correctly in the first place.

For the rest of us, it's important to know the identity and version of the BIOS in our PCs. We need to know how to display the configuration setup screen, how to make changes, and what broad range of available capabilities it offers.

Most users don't need to upgrade their PC's BIOS chips during the typical three-to-five years of usable life in a PC. Most modern machines can work with most current hardware or can be updated with device drivers; similarly, most existing BIOS chips can work with enhanced versions of operating systems.

In some situations, however, major alterations — usually improvements — lie beyond the predictions made by BIOS designers. In the early days of personal computers, the original PCs were quickly locked out of using higher-capacity floppy and hard disk drives and were unable to keep pace with advances in video standards. In more modern machines, some early BIOS chips had difficulties working with SCSI controllers and CD-ROMs. In fact, some BIOS chips are unable to keep pace with change as new operating systems are introduced.

The good news is that in most cases, BIOS chips can be upgraded or replaced. Nearly all modern machines use a form of chip called a *Programmable ROM* (PROM), sometimes referred to as an *EPROM* (erasable programmable ROM) or *flash memory*.

Elements of a Modern BIOS

What should you expect from a thoroughly modern BIOS? To begin with, you want a system that is capable of working with all of the most current hardware options, including high-speed hard drive interfaces, USB 2.0, FireWire, and more. These are the obvious needs. But one step beyond them are many niceties that have been added to BIOS systems in recent years.

In 2002, advanced features of a typical BIOS — as delivered or as upgraded after installation — included the following features:

- Full support for Windows XP, 2000, Me, and earlier operating systems including Windows 95/98
- Full support for current CPUs including the Intel Pentium 4 and AMD Athlon and Athlon XP
- Support for current chipsets. (I've included details of most modern chipsets in chapter 2.)
- The ability to choose to boot from any drive, from labels A to L, as well as from CD-ROM, Zip, and LS 120 (Superdisk) drives
- The ability to boot from a specified SCSI drive ahead of an IDE device
- USB 2.0 support, even before operating systems offered drivers for devices
- Support for hard drives up to 137GB (and with provisions for larger drives to come), and drives with more than 1,024 cylinders

- EIDE/LBA translation for large hard drives
- Ultra DMA 33/66 and Fast-ATA Mode 4 data transfer
- HDD S.M.A.R.T. support for drive monitoring
- Facilities to assign IRQs to devices
- Support for Plug and Play 2.1
- AGP/128-bit 3-D graphics support
- Boot sector antivirus protection
- Three modes of password security
- Flash BIOS upgrades

Table 3-1 contains an example of the contents of a modern machine, based on a Pentium 4 1.8 GHz CPU and RDRAM memory.

TABLE 3-1: A Modern BIOS Screen in a Dell Dimension 8200

Intel Pentium 4 Processor:	1.80 GHz
BIOS Version:	A01
Level 2 Cache:	256K Integrated
Service Tag:	*xxx*
System Time	00:00:00
System Date	DY/MO/DATE/YR
Diskette Drive A:	3.5 inch, 1.44MB
Primary Drive 0:	Hard Drive
Primary Drive 1:	Off
Secondary Drive 0:	CD-R
Secondary Drive 1:	Off
Boot Sequence	\<Enter\>
System Memory	256 SDRAM
AGP Aperture	128MB
CPU Information	\<Enter\>

Integrated Devices (Legacy Select Options)	\<Enter\>
PCI IRQ Assignments	\<Enter\>
IRQ Reservations	\<Enter\>
System Security	\<Enter\>
Keyboard Numlock	On
Report Keyboard Errors	Report
Auto Power On	Disabled
Remote Wake Up	Off
AC Power Recovery	Last
Fast Boot	On
Suspend Mode	S3
System Event Log	\<Enter\>
Asset Tag	*Xxxxxxxx*

Legacy Select Options

Option	Function
Sound	Turns integrated sound (if present on the motherboard) off and on. The default is On.
Mouse Port	Turns the mouse port off and on. The default is On.
USB Emulation	Turns USB emulation off and on. The default is On.
USB Controller	Turns the USB controller off and on. The default is On.
Serial Port 1	Sets serial port options and turns the port off and on. The default is Auto.
Parallel Port	Displays parallel port settings when \<Enter\> is pressed. The default mode is PS/2 and the I/O address default is 378h.

Continued

TABLE 3-1: *Continued*	
Option	**Function**
IDE Drive Interface	Sets the IDE drive interface options. The default is Auto.
Diskette Interface	Sets diskette interface options. The default is Auto.
PC Speaker	Turns the PC speaker off and on. The default is On.
Primary Video Controller	Sets the primary video controller. The default is AGP.
Video DAC Snoop	Turns the video DAC Snoop off and on. The default is Off.

Boot options

In ordinary operation, you want to boot your PC from its primary hard drive. In case of trouble or certain types of maintenance operations, however, a flexible BIOS should allow you to choose another source for bootup files.

A capable modern BIOS should permit you to specify several startup devices and permit you to choose the order in which the system searches for a bootup disk. Typical options include the floppy disk drive, a CD-ROM, a ZIP or other removable disk, and other hard disks in the system.

NOTE

It's a good idea to set your BIOS so that it searches first on the hard drive, rather than looking to the floppy disk. This action decreases the risk of loading a virus from a floppy disk inadvertently left in the drive and speeds up booting. If you need to boot from the floppy, go to the BIOS screen and change the order of boot devices.

Most modern BIOS chips can boot from an alternate hard drive, either a secondary IDE or a SCSI drive. You can use this feature to choose from different hard drives loaded with different operating systems, for example.

NOTE

If you change the boot order for hard drives, the system will change the drive letters for the bootup and secondary drives each time, which can confuse some applications.

Multiple video cards

Windows 98 and later versions of operating systems allow you to install two graphics cards to power multiple displays; this feature is especially valuable to graphic artists and other users working with very complex applications. On one of my systems, for example, I have a large monitor that displays photographs and drawings for page production; a second, smaller monitor keeps all of the menus and directories out of the way.

Any current BIOS will permit the use of two graphic cards with a current version of Windows. Until recently, however, most BIOS chips worked against the best use of your cards. With these BIOS setups, if the system detected two graphics cards, the adapter in a PCI slot was recognized as the main card and a card in an AGP slot was secondary—despite the fact that, in most cases, AGP is faster and more capable than PCI.

If you expect to use a second graphic card, look for a BIOS that allows you to specify which card will be treated as the primary card, regardless of how it attaches to the bus.

Disabling ports

The arrival of new high-speed means of input and output—including USB and FireWire—as well as new uses for serial, parallel, and PS/2 ports, has greatly expanded the types of tasks that can be performed by a PC. At the same time, though, modern machines must still deal with a limited number of IRQs for all of these devices. The arrival of the PCI bus alleviated some of these problems by permitting some sharing of IRQs. The developing world of USB also allows multiple devices to use a single port.

However, a very valuable feature for modern BIOS systems is a facility to disable ports that are not in use and reclaim IRQ and DMA resources that the system would otherwise demand.

For example, if you are working with a machine on a network, you may not need to use your parallel port to connect with a printer. Similarly, many systems use Ethernet cards to attach to networks and cable or DSL modems and therefore don't need serial ports; many current mouse or trackball devices connect to a USB port rather than to a serial port or PS/2 port.

Be aware that merely freeing up an IRQ or DMA resource does not necessarily mean that another device will automatically use the facility; you may have to make manual reassignments for resources.

BIOS Failure

BIOS chips are fairly reliable. Nevertheless, because of the importance of the bootup information included within them, the first task that the BIOS chip performs when it is turned on is to check its own validity by examining every single bit. In some designs, this can amount to a million bits or more.

The chip calculates a checksum — a mathematical summation of the value of the bits — and compares it with the official checksum stored in the BIOS ROM. If the numbers don't agree, the BIOS stops the boot and displays a BIOS Checksum Error message. If you receive this message, try turning off the machine and then starting over again. If the error does not recur, you can (nervously) hope that the problem was a once-in-a-very-blue-moon occurrence.

If you get past the BIOS self-check, chances are very strong that any problems you encounter don't lie within the BIOS. If you don't get past the BIOS self-check, the only cure for a failed BIOS chip or chips is replacement.

Sources for BIOS chips

To replace a BIOS chip, begin by contacting a distributor that works with the existing code within your system. Although it is theoretically possible to upgrade a Phoenix BIOS with a set of new AMI or Award chips, you may run into compatibility problems with some custom chipsets on the motherboard.

NOTE

Although you will continue to see motherboards that use Phoenix and Award BIOS chips, these former competitors merged in 1998. You can learn more about the Award side of the deal at www.award.com, but for real product information and corporate data, point your browser to www.phoenix.com.

A number of sources provide replacement and upgrade chips. You may have to go no further than the original supplier of your PC or the motherboard, or you may need to go to a specialized supplier. A set of chips typically sells for about $50 to $100, plus the cost of shipping.

One particularly good reference and supply source for replacement BIOS chips is Unicore Software, Inc. (www.unicore.com). This company supplies a number of software utilities to help with BIOS problem diagnosis and sells upgrade BIOS chips. You can find out a lot about your system's BIOS with its online utilities, but some manufacturers may not display standard BIOS messages, which means you may need to call Unicore and discuss your particular BIOS issues.

A BIOS Update

An important BIOS improvement was introduced in 1994 when new codes permitted the use of hard disk drives larger than 500MB. If your BIOS was manufactured prior to 1994, your system may only be able to work with the first 500MB of a drive, even if it has a listed capacity much larger than that.

This is a problem that has not completely gone away. In the past few years, the price of large-capacity hard drives entered into a near freefall while capacities began to increase substantially. At the time of this writing, you can purchase a quality 40GB hard drive for as little as $99. That's a price drop of two-thirds in the two years between editions of this book.

If your machine is two or three years old, for example, you may be limited to 18GB as your largest drive. So even though your local computer store or online retailer will gladly sell you a 40GB hard drive, your older machine will limit you to the first 18GB of these really large drives. For many users of older machines, an update to a new BIOS is worthwhile for that feature alone.

A number of hard drive manufacturers, however, have come up with workarounds that let you create a logical hard drive on a physical device. For example, a 9GB hard drive can be logically divided into three 3GB drives as far as the BIOS is concerned.

The lesson for PC owners is this: Investigate the capabilities of your PC's BIOS chipset and ask hard drive makers about any software workarounds that they offer to buyers who have hard drives ahead of their BIOS systems.

Determining your BIOS needs

The first step is to determine the type of BIOS in your system, the number of chips, and their sizes. Modern machines typically use one or more 256K, 512K, or 1MB chips; BIOS systems for a state-of-the-art Pentium 4 system may have chips as large as 4MB.

Nearly every modern machine uses a form of flash memory, or electrically erasable programmable read-only memory (EEPROM). These chips allow the user or technician to load a new set of instructions from a CD-ROM, diskette, or over the Internet. Check your machine's instruction manual for details.

On the other hand, dinosaurs and many senior citizens may use one or more BIOS chips that may have to be physically removed in order to be replaced or reprogrammed. Some of these chips are EPROMs (erasable programmable read-only memory) that can accept new instructions, which are burned into place by intensive ultraviolet light in a special device; they are recognizable because they have a clear window above the code on the chip.

Modern machines generally use just a single high-capacity chip. In the oldest of machines, the 128K BIOS may have been made up of eight 16K chips. Figure 3-1 shows an example of a modern machine's BIOS chip; Figure 3-2 shows an older version.

Your computer's instruction manual may not be all that helpful in disclosing the exact BIOS model in your system; manufacturers may change or update the BIOS over the course of the lift of a particular model.

One way to be certain of the identity of your BIOS is to take off the covers and do some exploration. Follow the standard precautions, please: Turn off and unplug the system before removing the covers and ground yourself before touching the motherboard.

Ch
3

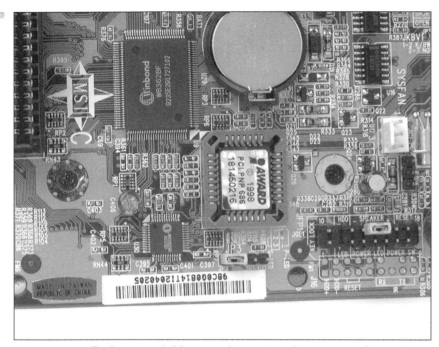

FIGURE 3-1: *A flash-upgradable Award BIOS in a chip carrier of a modern motherboard*

The chips may be clearly labeled on top, or you may need to carefully peel away a covering label. The chips are usually labeled with the name of the BIOS maker; the most common are AMI, Award, IBM, or Phoenix. Look for a number marked on the chip, usually located on the end opposite the notch. On many machines, chips labeled with a number beginning with 27 are standard EPROMs, while those labeled with a number beginning with 28 or 29 are flash chips that you can upgrade in place. As noted earlier, an EPROM is an electrically programmable read-only memory chip, a device that can accept and hold on to new instructions sent to it from a program loaded onto the computer or received over a network or the Internet.

Depending on how your motherboard manufacturer has configured its particular form of BIOS (most manufacturers don't produce their own BIOS code; they use BIOS from one of several manufacturers, including AMI, Phoenix, or Award), you may be able to learn a lot about what's inside your machine by reading BIOS messages during bootup. Look for the BIOS manufacturer, BIOS revision number, date, and other information. On some systems, you can pause the bootup process by pressing the Pause button on the keyboard.

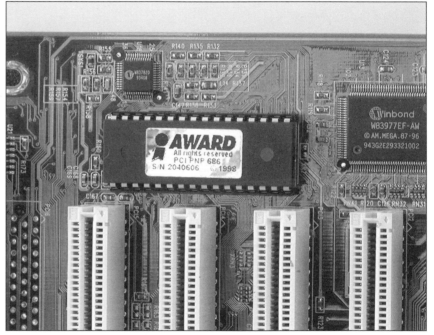

FIGURE 3-2: *An older-style BIOS chip on a modern motherboard*

The Unicore Software Web site offers a free BIOS wizard that may be able to display key information from your system BIOS. Go to the Web site at `www.unicore.com` to download a small program that queries the BIOS in your system and produces a report that you can use to shop for an upgrade on your own, or submit directly to Unicore for a quote. An example of one of the reports from the program is shown in Figure 3-3.

Ch 3

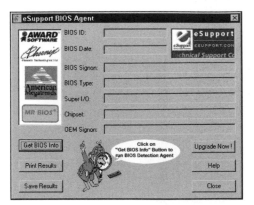

FIGURE 3-3: *The Unicore Software BIOS wizard*

Installing a New BIOS

If necessary, it's relatively easy to upgrade the BIOS chips on your motherboard to add new capabilities. You can upgrade your BIOS by using one of the following two methods:

- Most modern machines use a special type of ROM chip called *flash memory* that you can upgrade by running a software program from a CD, a diskette, or from a file downloaded from the Internet. The contents of the new BIOS are recorded electrically into the nonvolatile memory of the chips.
- The other way to upgrade BIOS chips involves a bit of careful work with a chip-extraction tool.

Both of these methods are explored in the next two sections.

Flash updates for BIOS chips

Nearly all current modern machines and many late-model senior citizens use a form of BIOS chip that can be upgraded in place by reading a new set of instructions from a floppy disk, a CD, or from your hard drive after you've downloaded the upgrade over the Internet. Point your browser to the Web site of your motherboard's

manufacturer and follow support or download links to get the upgrade software.

Contact the maker of your system or a distributor of BIOS upgrades for instructions. Be sure to correctly identify the brand and model number of the BIOS in your present system. Follow the instructions provided for the flash upgrade carefully; in most instances, the upgrade is done from the DOS prompt or from a special boot disk that takes control of the system independent of the BIOS.

I would never install a new BIOS without having in hand a full set of detailed instructions about the various settings or having a knowledgeable technician available by telephone.

Before you update any BIOS chips, make a copy of all of the entries on your system's CMOS Setup screen; in most cases, you'll have to resort to a pen and notepad, although a handful of BIOS designs allow you to print their settings or save them to a file.

In addition to upgrading your BIOS chip, you can install system bus cards that expand or extend your motherboard BIOS. Some cards are BIOS upgrade-specific; in other cases, BIOS extensions may be part of a card designed for another purpose. For example, I recently tried to install a 27GB hard drive in a machine that was a couple of years old. Even after downloading and installing a flash BIOS upgrade from the manufacturer, the system's motherboard BIOS recognized only 18GB of the 27GB hard drive.

Therefore, I turned to an upgrade adapter—an UltraATA 66 PCI controller card that contains two high-speed IDE controllers and BIOS extensions to support drives up to 128GB. The card is a Plug-and-Play device and enhances the computer BIOS for extended drive support, operating faster than the built-in IDE controller on the motherboard. If you install such a device, in most cases, you want to disable the motherboard's IDE controller. On most modern machines, simply reboot your machine, enter the BIOS setup, and disable the built-in IDE controller. Then make sure that all of your IDE drives use the new controller by moving the cables from the motherboard to the PCI card.

Changing the chips

If you have to physically remove and replace BIOS chips, make a copy of all of the entries on your system's CMOS Setup screen. Manufacturers of BIOS chips have come up with various different ways to call for the display of the CMOS Setup screen. On many systems, you have to press the Delete or F2 key at a particular moment during the bootup process; other systems use a Ctrl + Alt + Esc keyboard combination. Check the instruction manual that came with your computer or read the onscreen messages that appear during the bootup process.

To install the chips, turn off your machine and remove the power cord. Ground yourself before touching the innards of the PC. You may need to remove hard drives and adapter cards that block access to the BIOS chips. Use a chip-removal tool to gently and evenly pry the chips from their sockets.

 NOTE

Most dinosaur BIOS sets consist of one or more pairs of chips, referred to as the *odd* and *even* chips. You must replace both at the same time and install them in the proper sockets.

The BIOS vendor may supply a simple tweezer-like device with U-shaped hooks on the ends — or you can purchase fancier and better models from a tool catalog or store — that you can use to carefully remove the chips one at a time. Be sure to work the chips out of their sockets evenly; try to avoid bending the pins so that you can reinstall the chips if necessary. Install the new chips in their place. Follow any special instructions from the maker for setup routines.

As with most other electronic circuit and memory devices, the chips are marked at one end with a dot or a notch to indicate the end that matches a corresponding dot or notch on the socket. Spend a few moments making certain that you have the chips oriented properly and that they are intended for the specific socket.

On some new chips, the pins are set a bit wider than the corresponding holes on the socket. Before installation, gently rock the chips on a firm surface to push the pins inward a tiny amount. Be sure that you don't twist any of the pins.

Gently insert the chips into the sockets; be sure to apply pressure evenly so the pins are not bent or misaligned. When the chip is about halfway into the socket, stop your work and examine the socket from all four sides. Look for any pin that may be bent under or outside its intended hole. If you find any wrongly positioned pins, use your extractor and remove the chip and carefully straighten the pin or pins. Be careful not to bend a pin back and forth too much or it will break off. If a pin breaks, the chip is ruined.

After the new BIOS chips are in place, reinstall any components that you removed and power up the system. You will have to run a new setup program and inform the system of memory, drives, and other elements of your PC.

SUMMARY

You've now explored the BIOS instructions. The next chapter moves along to the system bus, which is the superhighway that interconnects most of the elements of the computer.

Chapter 4

In This Chapter:

- Modern Bus Designs
- Dinosaur Peripheral Buses
- Exploring IRQs and DMA

Driving the Computer Bus

The electrical bus that interconnects the micro-processor, system memory, and peripherals is a high-speed superhighway. But, as any commuter knows, even an expressway can suffer from slowdowns and bottlenecks.

Throughout the history of the PCs covered in this book, the user has had six routes to choose from; in other words, six standard bus designs have been available: PC, ISA, EISA, MCA, VL, and PCI. Today, nearly all new motherboards use a PCI bus, sometimes in conjunction with an ISA bus, to support older "legacy" add-in devices.

In addition to the superhighways, a few outrigger buses hang onto the main road like high-speed rush-hour lanes: AGP for video adapters, SCSI for high-bandwidth storage devices and scanners, and USB for an almost limitless array of fast and easy-to-configure devices. Portables and a small number of desktop machines also have ports for PC Cards for communication and storage.

In this chapter, I look at the various buses for modern machines and give a backwards glance at older buses. I also explore the black art of IRQs (interrupt requests) and DMA (direct memory access). These two features of all PCs are the doorbells (IRQs) and back alleys (DMA) of the bus; one rings the CPU's chimes to tell it that a piece of hardware is seeking its attention, and the other opens a channel for quick delivery of a message between a device and system memory without involving the CPU.

Modern Machine Bus Designs

A modern motherboard uses a hierarchy of several buses to connect the microprocessor to the system and memory and to interlink various devices. The *processor bus* is at the top of the hierarchy; below the processor bus is a typical motherboard that includes several subsidiary buses, such as an *I/O* or *peripheral bus* and a *memory bus*.

A *bus*, in electrical terms, is a set of parallel conductors that connects one element of the system to another. Within a computer, a bus includes the following three principal lines of communication:

- **Control lines.** These wires or traces allow the microprocessor to direct devices to perform particular operations.
- **Address lines.** The microprocessor connects to specific memory locations within attached devices using this pathway.
- **Data lines.** Data that is transmitted or retrieved from a device travels on these lines.

Processor bus (front-side bus)

The processor bus (also known as the *front-side bus* or FSB) is the main highway of the computer, and, in most cases, the highest-speed route. It runs at the full motherboard speed, originally 66 MHz and reaching to 400 MHz as this edition goes to press.

Essential elements of modern chipsets are the north and south bridges — Intel refers to them as the GMCH (Graphics and Memory Controller Hub) and the ICH (I/O Controller Hub), respectively.

In a modern system, the processor bus is used by the CPU to communicate through the north bridge of the chipset to close-in cache memory and main memory. From there, the processor connects to the peripheral bus (including PCI on a modern machine) and special-purpose buses, such as AGP for a modern class of graphics cards. Some north bridge chipsets also include some integrated functions, such as video and audio controllers. On the most modern of Intel chipsets, the north bridge is part of a multifunction circuit called the Memory Controller Hub.

The processor bus also connects through the PCI bus to a slower south bridge, which controls the IDE bus that transports data to and from storage devices. Other elements of the south bridge include the USB serial subsystem; a bridge from PCI to the older ISA bus still used by some devices; the keyboard/mouse controller; power management; and various other features, including support for Plug-and-Play technology.

CROSS-REFERENCE

I discuss CPUs that support these high-speed system buses in Chapter 2.

In addition to the raw speed of the processor bus, two other elements determine the actual potential throughput of data in the system: the bus width and the number of data cycles per clock tick. All modern processor buses in consumer-level PCs work with 64-bit (8 byte) computer words; most also move data once in each clock cycle. However, the latest designs, embraced by Intel for its Pentium 4 CPU and by AMD for its Athlon family of microprocessors, move more than one block of data per clock cycle, thus greatly increasing throughput. A listing of common modern processor bus designs is shown in Table 4-1.

TABLE 4-1: Processor (Front-Side) Bus Designs

Processor Design	Bus Speed (MHz)	Bus Width (bits)	Data Cycles per Clock	Throughput (MB/second)
33 MHz 486 FSB	33	32	1	133
66 MHz FSB	66	64	1	533
100 MHz FSB	100	64	1	800
133 MHz FSB	133	64	1	1066
200 MHz FSB	100	64	2	1600
266 MHz FSB	133	64	2	2133
400 MHz FSB	100	64	4	3200

The move to 100 MHz was not a huge one for motherboard makers. In many cases, existing 66 MHz board designs were easily adapted to a 100 MHz bus. The move to a 133 MHz system bus, however, required a redesign of the motherboard and supporting chips. The step to 266 was based on the 133 MHz design.

One final note: The electrical frequency of these high-speed buses is right in the middle of the FM radio band. You have to be especially careful to select and maintain the integrity of your computer case to prevent the speedy bus from shutting down a good portion of your radio and television reception with its own signal.

I/O or peripheral bus

One of the reasons behind the runaway success story of the PC has been the ability of owners to customize their machines in almost infinite ways through the use of devices that plug into the machine — under the covers by plugging into an internal bus connector or outside by attaching to a port. The computer communicates with add-on or peripheral devices through one of its I/O (input/output) buses.

The most common I/O bus for modern machines and many senior citizens is the *PCI bus*; in its basic version, PCI is a 32-bit bus that operates at 33 MHz. A typical modern machine will offer four to six PCI slots.

Many modern machines also include an *ISA bus* — an enhancement of the original PC bus — with several slots to accommodate older "legacy" devices. At the time of this writing, though, motherboards with an independent ISA bus are trundling off to dinosaur-land. Instead, the motherboard's chipset includes ISA circuitry for specialized functions.

Most modern machines also have a single *AGP bus* slot, specialized for the needs of a video adapter.

In addition to ISA, older buses include *MCA*, an IBM advancement that never moved beyond that company's brand of machines. Also outdated is *EISA*, an extension to ISA with its own incompatible design.

Because ISA, MCA, and EISA came out of the original PC bus design, they all share some significant limitations on speed. The original I/O bus for the PC was essentially a direct expansion of the processor bus and devices communicated at the same speed as the processor bus. As new designs permitted the processor bus to operate faster and faster, the original I/O bus designs had to hold to their older, slower speeds to maintain compatibility with devices already on the market.

MIGRATING OLDER DEVICES TO A NEW MOTHERBOARD

You can't change the design of a bus already in place on your motherboard. Your alternative is a major construction project: installation of a new motherboard.

Many modern-machine motherboards are combinations of more than one type of bus, allowing a mix and match of expansion cards. The most common combo is a PCI motherboard that includes one or more ISA slots to allow use of older legacy cards.

If you are working with a combination board, the issue often comes down to making decisions about which cards are worth holding on to, and which ones you should discard and replace with more modern versions. No method exists for converting an ISA card to plug into a PCI slot or vice versa; when you run out of parking spaces for cards, you have to go outside the box to external devices. In the early days of PCs, one large, cumbersome, and expensive solution was to purchase an *expansion chassis*, which was a PC-sized box with a whole set of PC slots and a connecting cable that hooked the box into a slot on the original PC.

Today, ISA cards are becoming increasingly difficult to find; those that are still available typically offer only basic features, such as serial, parallel, or networking communications.

The good news is that most modern machines offer USB ports, and a wide variety of devices are now available using that means of entry to the computer. And many older modern and some senior citizen machines can be upgraded to offer USB if they don't already provide that facility.

The need for speed

Many PC system devices don't require blazing speed — for example, the keyboard and mouse demand very little from the system. However, in the modern era, the increasing demands from devices such as advanced video cards, sound cards, and network interfaces required the design of faster buses.

One of the downsides of the standard bus design, however, is that fast devices can become jammed behind slower ones. For example, think of a superhighway where speedy sports cars get stuck behind lumbering trucks. The solution was to take the higher-speed devices off the original I/O buses and give them an express lane—their own set of communication lines to the processor. This design was called a *local bus*.

The first such extension was the VESA Local Bus or VL Bus, which added a second set of slots that sat at the back end of the 16-bit ISA slots. This allowed older devices to plug into the front slots, and newer VL Bus devices to attach to both the ISA and the extended VL Bus slots. The VL Bus was a simple set of wires that ran directly to the microprocessor; the scheme was designed specifically to work with Intel's 486 microprocessor and few motherboards were developed that worked with other CPUs.

The successor to the VL Bus was the PCI bus, introduced in 1992 and still in wide use a decade later. PCI sits between the processor and the original I/O bus—still present on nearly all modern machines either as a legacy ISA bus or as part of an integrated set of I/O devices on the motherboard. Note that PCI does not directly connect to the microprocessor as the VL Bus did; instead, it works through a specialized set of controller chips.

Table 4-2 lists major peripheral buses from the time of the original IBM PC through modern machines.

TABLE 4-2: Peripheral Bus

Bus	Bus Speed (MHz)	Bus Width (bits)	Data Cycles per Clock	Throughput (MB/second)
PC/XT	4.77	8	1/2	2.39
ISA (8-bit)	6, 8, 8.33*	8	1/2	4.17
ISA (16-bit)	8.33	16	1/2	8.33
EISA	8.33	32	1	33
MCA-16	5	16	1	10
MCA-32	5	32	1	20
VESA VL	33	32	1	133

Bus	Bus Speed (MHz)	Bus Width (bits)	Data Cycles per Clock	Throughput (MB/second)
PCI	33	32	1	133
PCI (66 MHz)	66	32	1	266
PCI (64-bit)	33	64	1	266
PCI (66 MHz, 64-bit)	66	64	1	533
PCI-X	133	64	1	1066

The ISA bus, which grew out of the original PC bus, was initially introduced with a 6 MHz bus speed and later improved to 8 MHz. At the time of the introduction of the 16-bit AT bus, the clock speed was set at 8.33 MHz.

PCI bus

Nearly all modern machines use the PCI (peripheral component interconnect) bus to link adapters that add function to the system, including video cards, network interfaces, sound cards, and other devices. The PCI can also be the gateway to yet another group of subsidiary buses, such as SCSI.

The original PCI bus is a 32-bit path that operates at 33 MHz. Workstations, servers, and other advanced machines may use extensions of PCI that run at 66 MHz, use a 64-bit bus width, or both. Designers have also created a specification for a PCI bus that can run at a blazing 133 MHz.

In addition to its speed, PCI has the advantage of being able to operate, more or less, independent of the CPU; devices plugged into the PCI bus can move data and instructions back and forth over the bus while the microprocessor is otherwise engaged.

PCI devices must use a PCI slot, which has a different physical and electrical design from ISA, EISA, and AGP. The slots are white, making them a visual contrast from the black ISA slots.

The 64-bit version of PCI uses an extended connector to handle the additional 32 bits of data. Figure 4-1 shows an example of standard 32-bit PCI slots on a motherboard that also offers ISA connectors.

FIGURE 4-1: *On the right side of this crowded ATX motherboard are seven bus slots (four white PCI connectors and three black ISA connectors). Where they come together, there's room for only one adapter, either a PCI or ISA device, but not both.*

mind a couple of caveats, however; first, PCI devices can share IRQs with each other, but not with an ISA device that may already be plugged into the system. Second, some PCI devices are better behaved than others, occasionally putting the lie to the shared IRQ theory. My best advice is to conduct a trial-and-error testing process if you choose to share an IRQ among PCI cards. If the system works, be happy; if it grinds to a halt, undo the last IRQ assignment that you made and try something else.

Under current versions of Windows (beginning with the B revision of Windows 95), PCs can use IRQ steering, which gives the operating system the task of dynamically assigning (or steering) IRQs to PCI devices, making use of the Plug-and-Play definitions of newer cards whenever possible.

Typically running at a clock speed of 33 MHz (with some specialized systems at 66, 100, or 133 MHz), the PCI local bus employs a 32-bit data bus that supports multiple peripheral components and add-in cards at a peak bandwidth of 133 MBps (megabytes per second) — a substantial improvement over the 5 MBps peak transfer rate of the standard ISA bus. The actual throughput over a fully loaded, 133 MBps PCI bus is about 90 MBps because of system overhead. This increased bandwidth allows the PCI local bus to provide more than four times the graphics performance of the ISA bus.

Later PCI bus designs include 39 additional signal pins to permit the bus to support 64-bit data transfers. This enhancement increases addressable memory from about 4GB to more than 17GB and improves data transfer speed over the bus. A 64-bit PCI bus ships data among system components 64 bits at a time — not 32 bits — which potentially doubles bus throughput (at least to memory and other devices that can handle 64-bit-wide information). Until implementation of Intel's Itanium 64-bit CPU, Intel CPUs support only 32-bit internal architecture. Other CPU makers, though, have CPUs with internal 64-bit architecture and 64-bit PCI buses.

The PCI local bus, however, offers much more than high bandwidth. It enables peripherals to take full advantage of available

The bus, developed by Intel, includes *arbitrated bus mastering* — which is the ability for devices on the bus to operate semi-independent of the microprocessor. PCI also permits *parity checking*, which is the ability to set system configuration without jumpers or switches for all devices in the system, and support for the Plug-and-Play specification that allows the computer to recognize most devices as they are attached to the system.

PCI, in its early versions, was capable of working with no more than three peripheral devices plugged directly into it. Relatively few motherboards were produced using that design. With the introduction of PCI 2.0, the standard took full flight.

For some users, a major advantage of a PCI bus is its ability to share IRQs (interrupt requests), a feature that can make installation of a wide range of adapters much easier to manage. Keep in processing power without being dependent on processor speed or architecture. It also supports autoconfiguration of Plug-and-Play enabled add-in cards and offers system designers a standardized design path. PCI devices can be either *targets* (devices that accept commands) or *masters* (devices that can perform some processing independent of the CPU and the bus). Finally, PCI provides built-in upgradability to accommodate future technical advances.

AGP bus

The AGP (accelerated graphics port) bus is a high-speed 32-bit bus designed specifically for use with video cards. AGP runs at 66 MHz. The original specification called for one data transfer per clock cycle; subsequent versions transfer two, four, and eight times with each cycle and are referred to as AGP2X, AGP4X, and AGP8X, respectively.

The initial AGP specification and AGP2X provided 3.3 volts to the adapter card; later versions support lower-demand 1.5-volt cards. Later versions of the slot are backward compatible, meaning they will work with cards designed for older AGP specifications, running at the original speed. However, some motherboards may demand particular AGP speeds or may be optimized to an individual specification. Figure 4-2 shows an AGP slot.

High-end graphics workstations may employ an extension to the AGP specification called AGP Pro; this design is intended for cards that have a higher power demand, as much as 110 watts. AGP Pro adds another section of connectors to the front and back end of the slot; adapters designed for the AGP standard need to be carefully positioned in the middle of the overlong AGP Pro slot.

AGP operates independent of the PCI bus, and mostly independent of the microprocessor, thus offloading the heavy demands of a graphics card. As such, a graphics card can have a direct connection to RAM, allowing it to share the large resources there instead of the relatively small allocation of memory on the card; on the other hand, high-performance graphics cards are designed with memory close at hand for maximum speed.

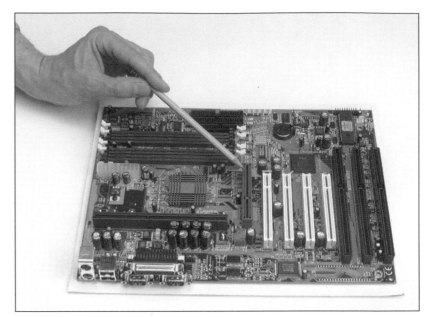

FIGURE 4-2: *The AGP slot sits alongside a set of PCI and ISA slots in this Pentium III motherboard.*

Some of the specifics of the various versions of AGP are shown in Table 4-3.

TABLE 4-3: AGP Standards				
Version	**Bus Speed (MHz)**	**Bus Width (bits)**	**Data Cycles per Clock**	**Throughput (MB/second)**
AGP	66	32	1	266
AGP2X	66	32	2	533
AGP4X	66	32	4	1066
AGP8X	66	32	8	2133

Information presented in three dimensions can be particularly memory-and transfer bus-intensive. With today's games, artificial reality, and artificial intelligence applications, 3-D data is becoming more common. Traditionally, the main system CPU has used the computer's bus to move graphical information from your computer's memory to where it belongs on a display adapter. This means that the transfer was limited to a maximum data rate of 66 MHz or less in slower systems. Not only is this bus speed relatively slow by today's computer standards, it's also crowded. Graphical information going to and from your video adapter must share this highway with other data going to and from memory and other peripherals.

AGP technology opens a high-speed pathway between a PC's graphics controller and system memory so that the graphics controller can execute texture maps directly from system memory, rather than caching them in its limited local video memory. It also helps speed the flow of decoded video from the CPU to the graphics controller. AGP is separate from the main PCI bus, so other computer data isn't competing with graphics data for bandwidth. The PCI bus can transfer data at speeds up to 132 MBps. AGP, on the other hand, handles graphical data directly from system memory to the video display adapter at speeds up to 533 MBps (peak; 1 GBps with new support chips) — a significant improvement.

In some systems, AGP exists as integrated circuitry directly on the motherboard rather than as a plug-in card. This form of AGP, introduced with Intel's 810 chipset, has some of the same operating characteristics, although it uses a segment of system RAM for its purposes. The downside is that if you ever choose to upgrade the video circuitry on the board, you have to use a slower PCI card because there is no AGP slot.

PC Cards

The Personal Computer Memory Card International Association standard defines a removable credit-card-size device that can be used in a wide range of portable computers and desktops. When it was first introduced, users were forced to memorize its tongue-twisting acronym of a name: PCMCIA. Luckily, more sensible heads prevailed and the working title for cards that use the PCMCIA standard was dubbed PC Card in 1995.

The PC Card bus branches off a PCI bus. Plug-in cards can be used for memory, tiny hard drives, modems, network adapters, sound cards, SCSI adapters, 1394 FireWire I/O cards, and more. Future versions of PC Card specifications may permit video adapter and even processor upgrades. Some of the details of PC Cards are shown in Table 4-4.

TABLE 4-4: PC Card Standards

Bus	Bus Speed (MHz)	Bus Width (bits)	Data Cycles per Clock	Throughput (MB/second)
PC Card	10	16	1	20
CardBus	33	32	1	133

PC Cards are not in common use on desktop PCs, but are ubiquitous on laptops where they are used for modems, network interfaces, and storage. On laptops, PC Cards face challenges from the burgeoning USB interface.

The original PC Card standard was limited by its 16-bit data interface standard. A newer standard, called CardBus, supports 32-bit interfaces and the ability to take advantage of internal bus speeds that can be four to six times faster than 16-bit PC Cards. In 2001, the association adopted the CardBay standard, which allows the same connector to bring USB 2.0 functionality to the PC Card format.

CardBus slots can accept 16-bit PC Card devices, but only 32-bit cards can take advantage of the wider format and faster data transfer supported by CardBus. In addition, CardBus devices operate at 3.3 volts (the PC Card uses 5 volts), resulting in lower power consumption and reduced heat.

Both PC Card and CardBus devices use a 68-pin interface that connects the card to the motherboard or to the system's expansion bus. However, a special tab on CardBus devices prevents you from plugging a CardBus card into a 16-bit PC Card interface.

PC Card slots are available in four types, measured by the thickness of the card that they will accept. The same standard for slot size is supported by the CardBus, as well. (Be sure to check the capability of your PC Card reader before making a purchase. A properly designed Type III socket will work with Types I and II, as well; a Type II socket also should accept Type I cards.)

- **Type I.** A 3.3 mm-thick slot, commonly used for RAM, flash memory, electronically erasable programmable read-only memory, and other such devices. Type I slots are most often used in personal digital assistants and handheld devices.
- **Type II.** A 5 mm-thick slot, fully I/O capable, used for memory enhancements or for I/O devices, such as modems and network connections.
- **Type III.** A 10.5 mm-thick slot, designed primarily for removable hard drive devices.
- **Type IV.** Now available from some manufacturers, Type IV slots can run two PC Card peripherals simultaneously and can be Plug-and-Play certified.

One of the advanced features of a PC Card and CardBus interface is *hot swap*. In theory, hot swap enables you to insert and remove cards while PC power is on without losing data or damaging the card or system. Not all applications or versions of operating systems, though, can recognize when you have inserted or removed cards, so save your data before trying this feature for the first time.

If you need to read a PC Card directly in a desktop, a number of adapters are available. Perhaps the easiest is a USB to PC Card reader; you'll also find devices that link a parallel port to a PC Card reader. A more permanent solution involves installation of a PC Card reader that attaches to the internal bus of your system. Figure 4-3 shows one such solution.

ISA bus

Prior to the arrival of PCI, the predominant design for internal connections to adapters was the ISA (industry standard architecture) bus, which was developed from the original PC bus. Its first incarnation used 8-bit computer words moving at a poky 4.77 MHz; it was subsequently improved to 16 bits and 8.33 MHz with

the introduction of the PC-AT in 1984. The arrival of the new machine came just as the clone industry exploded, and the bus was widely imitated. Clone makers dubbed the bus the *industry standard architecture* (ISA).

FIGURE 4-3: *This PC Card/floppy disk combination drive from SCM Microsystems occupies a single drive bay.*

ISA slots build on the original PC bus slots, adding a second block of connectors for the additional 8 bits of information.

Modern machines are no longer built around the limited ISA bus. However, the bus is still present in one way or another: either as a "legacy" bus that branches off the PCI bus to allow users to continue using older adapter cards designed for the ISA, or as a hidden bus that communicates with basic components of the PC that have remained essentially unchanged throughout the history of the device, such as the keyboard and mouse.

In Figure 4-4, you can see the larger ISA slots on a mixed PCI/ISA motherboard.

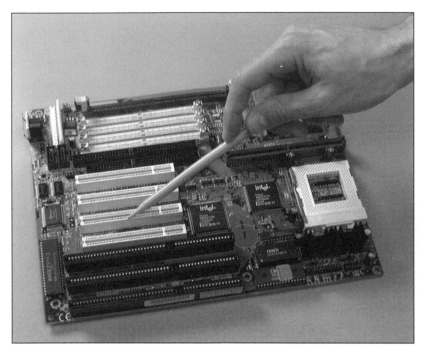

FIGURE 4-4: *The black ISA slots, below the pencil toward the front of the motherboard, are available for compatibility with older adapter cards and adapter cards that don't need the high speed of the white PCI bus slots.*

NOTE

Some manufacturers have begun offering "legacy-free" designs, which is marketing shorthand for PCs that make no attempt to be backward compatible with outdated older technologies. A legacy-free machine may dispense with serial, parallel, and PS/2 ports in favor of advanced USB and FireWire ports. And motherboards may offer only PCI and AGP slots, thus eliminating holdover ISA slots. If you are buying a new machine, a legacy-free design may make sense because modern ports — especially USB — have been linked to nearly every type of peripheral, including keyboards, mice, monitors, printers, and scanners. And nearly every type of adapter card is now available in a PCI version.

Memory bus

The microprocessor communicates with RAM using the memory bus. In modern machines, this bus branches off the north bridge or memory controller hub. The speed of the bus is related to the design of the chipset and the type of memory in use.

When memory runs at the same speed as the processor bus (as is the case with many modern machines), there is no need for cache memory on the motherboard, which allows the CPU manufacturer to move L2 cache onto the processor cartridge (in the case of Pentium II and early Pentium III CPUs) or onto the processor die itself.

Table 4-5 shows some of the important specifications of commonly used memory designs.

TABLE 4-5: Memory Bus Designs				
Memory Design	Bus Speed (MHz)	Bus Width (bits)	Data Cycles per Clock	Throughput (MB/second)
FPM DRAM	22	64	1	177
EDO DRAM	33	64	1	266
PC66 SDRAM	66	64	1	533
PC100 SDRAM	100	64	1	800
PC133 SDRAM	133	64	1	1066
PC600 RDRAM	300	16	2	1200
PC700 RDRAM	350	16	2	1400
PC800 RDRAM	400	16	2	1600
PC800 RDRAM Dual Channel	400	32	2	3200
PC1600 DDR SDRAM	100	64	2	1600
PC2100 DDR SDRAM	133	64	2	2133

CROSS-REFERENCE

For more details on RAM, see Chapter 8.

I/O subsystems: Serial, Parallel, SCSI, FireWire, and USB

Thousands of valuable devices exist on the side streets off the computer's superhighway: the I/O subsystems that are used by modems, printers, scanners, and external storage units. Table 4-6 includes some of the specifications for these subsystems. Additionally, I discuss the most commonly used subsystems elsewhere in this book, as follows:

- **Serial.** Chapter 15
- **Parallel.** Chapter 17
- **USB.** Chapter 15

- **FireWire.** Chapter 15
- **SCSI.** Chapter 10

Dinosaur Peripheral Buses

Most senior citizens use the ISA bus, with later models adding the VESA local bus as the first step toward high-speed, special-purpose interconnects. Toward the end of the senior-citizen era of computers, the PCI bus was added to many motherboards.

One class of machines has been pretty much left in the dust: Micro Channel Architecture PCs. The MCA standard, developed by IBM, had some sophisticated advantages over the ISA/AT bus,

TABLE 4-6: I/O Subsystems

I/O Subsystem	Bus Speed (MHz)	Bus Width (bits)	Data Cycles per Clock	Throughput (MB/second)
RS-232 Serial	0.1152	1	1/10	0.01152
IEEE-1284 Parallel	8.33	8	1/6	1.38
IEEE-1284 EPP/ECP Parallel	8.33	8	1/3	2.77
USB 1.1	12	1	1	1.5
USB 2.0	480	1	1	60
IEEE-1394 FireWire	100, 200, 400, 800, 1600	1	1	12.4, 25, 50, 100, 200
SCSI	5	8	1	5
SCSI Wide	5	16	1	10
SCSI Fast	10	8	1	10
SCSI Fast/Wide	10	16	1	20
SCSI Ultra	20	8	1	20
SCSI Ultra/Wide	20	16	1	40
SCSI Ultra 2	40	8	1	40
SCSI Ultra 2/Wide	40	16	1	80
SCSI Ultra 3 (SCSI Ultra 160)	40	16	2	160
SCSI Ultra 4 (SCSI Ultra 320)	80	16	2	320

but it never really caught on outside of IBM's corporate accounts. Although these machines are still capable, today their repair and upgrade paths are limited.

VESA VL bus

The VESA local (VL) bus was created to connect video adapters directly to processors and to help computers avoid traveling relatively slow buses. Established by the Video Electronics Standards Association (VESA), a group of manufacturers of video adapters, the VL bus is actually a secondary, faster bus that is used together with the principal data bus of a computer.

The most common implementation of VL buses is an enhancement to ISA bus systems. Some VL bus systems have their video circuitry mounted directly on the motherboard, which saves some of the expense of a separate adapter but may limit the ability to enhance or repair the adapter. Subsequent designs added as many as two additional VL bus slots (the specification recommends a limit of three VL slots) that can be used for other devices. Nearly every VL design also extended the expansion capability of the system with a set of standard ISA slots.

Because the VL bus design is tied to the processor's speed and processor family (386, 486, and so on), not every VL bus card is compatible with every VL bus-based system.

The VL bus was widely adopted in many advanced 486 systems. But in 1995, it was mostly pushed aside by the widespread adoption of PCI bus designs for Pentium systems.

Micro Channel Architecture

Micro Channel was IBM's proprietary 32-bit bus with bus mastering. Unlike EISA, Micro Channel Architecture (MCA) is not compatible with ISA devices. Special features include the ability of the bus to reach out and identify any adapter plugged into it, thus permitting automatic configuration. The bus is also smart enough to shut off a misbehaving adapter. Finally, MCA adapters generate less electrical interference, which reduces the chance for errors on high-speed buses.

Many of IBM's PS/2 machines used the MCA bus, and a handful of clones were built with the same design. However, the MCA bus did not become a predominant design and has been mostly supplanted by VESA and PCI designs.

The Micro Channel design departs in several significant and interesting ways from the ISA used by most other modern machines. However, the basics of the processors (power supply, video adapter, memory, and data storage) are similar. In this section, I concentrate on the differences that you need to understand to troubleshoot problems that may arise with a Micro Channel machine.

Micro Channel computers can have a combination of 16- and 32-bit connectors on the motherboard. You can install an 8-bit or 16-bit adapter in a 16-bit slot; a 32-bit slot can accommodate 8-, 16-, and 32-bit adapters.

IBM's bus has 32 signal paths for data, which enables 32 bits of data to be sent simultaneously through the channel, but (as with most other designs) only one device at a time can use the bus to send or receive data. The bus has three functions:

- **Expansion bus.** The channel provides paths for transferring data to and from adapters, and for controlling the flow of information to and from adapters.
- **Address bus.** Every memory location and I/O device attached to the Micro Channel bus is assigned a unique number, known as an *address*. A device wanting to transfer data begins by sending out the address of the device or memory location that is its target.
- **Data bus.** The Micro Channel's data bus is capable of supporting data-bus widths of 8, 16, or 32 bits, depending on the capabilities of the sending and receiving devices. A 32-bit adapter sending data to an 8-bit device effectively works as an 8-bit unit, sending four consecutive 8-bit transfers instead of a single 32-bit burst.

Of course, you receive benefits only from using 32-bit devices within a Micro Channel system. A 32-bit bus is capable of addressing as much as 4GB of memory.

Some advanced PS/2 machines have a dual bus that provides both a data bus from the microprocessor to the memory controller and another data bus from the Micro Channel devices to the memory controller. A dual-bus design enables a microprocessor to read and write to system memory while a bus master simultaneously controls the Micro Channel bus.

Arbitration

When more than one device wants to use the Micro Channel bus at the same time, the computer uses a system called *arbitration*. Every device is assigned a unique arbitration level; the listing of priorities for each device is held in a software file called an *adapter description file*.

The Micro Channel includes a fairness feature intended to make sure that every device gets a turn to use the bus, even if it has a much lower arbitration level than another active device. The Micro Channel configuration process allows the user to turn off the fairness feature for one or more devices. Do so only with caution, however, because a busy or ill-behaved device can lock out all other adapters.

Masters and slaves

The Micro Channel bus categorizes the two ends of a data-transfer process as either *master* or *slave*. When a master has control of the bus, it can send or receive data from a slave without demanding the direct involvement of the CPU.

The following are the three types of masters:

- **System master.** A device that assigns system resources and issues the commands of the primary operating system.
- **Bus master.** A device that takes control of the bus in order to transfer data directly to and from I/O devices and memory without using the CPU or the DMA controller. A bus master

can have its own microprocessor, instruction cache, and memory. A Micro Channel computer can have as many as 15 bus masters, thus permitting some level of multiprocessing.

- **DMA controller.** Circuitry that manages data transfer between DMA slaves and memory slaves.

A slave is a device that is selected by a master as the source or target of a transfer. The Micro Channel system has the following three types of slaves:

- **Memory slave.** A device that provides a block of system memory. A memory slave responds by putting requested data on the bus or by writing data from the bus to RAM. The system master, bus master, or DMA controller can select a memory slave.
- **I/O slave.** A device that communicates with or controls a peripheral, including printers and modems. The system master or bus master can select an I/O slave.
- **DMA slave.** A device that requires the DMA controller to manage data transfers. This is the only type of slave that can initiate arbitration. The DMA controller or bus master can select a DMA slave.

PC Bus

The original design for the IBM PC offered a handful of slots capable of accepting cards that dealt with 8 bits of information at a time. The bus itself extended 62 wires from the processor; 20 of the lines were available as address lines that helped direct information to and from locations in memory, and 8 lines were dedicated to the transmission of data. The remainder of the lines were given over to electrical needs, interrupts, and control circuits.

The PC Bus was used for the very first machines from IBM and the early PC clones. The IBM PC-XT, which brought the first internal hard drive to the family, used a slightly modified version.

No modern machines use the PC Bus. However, you may be able to use an old 8-bit adapter card in a 16-bit ISA slot, which is actually made up of an 8-bit connector and a second, extended bus line connector. However, an 8-bit card will fit in a 16-bit slot only if it has a high skirt. Before you get too excited about that concept, here's what it means: The original design for an 8-bit card had the gold-plated electrical contact fingers stick down from the body of the card, leaving about half an inch of vertical clearance—the skirt—on each side of the contacts. Some card designers, though, tried to cram electronics onto every available square inch of space and integrated the fingers into a solid expanse of card from front to back. This sort of card would fit properly in an 8-bit slot, but would end up butting into the slot for the extended bus lines on a 16-bit slot.

NOTE

On the original PC-XT and some of its clones, you should know one special consideration on the use of the slots: IBM, which once considered PCs as slaves to its huge mainframes, reserved Slot 8, the one nearest to the power supply, for special-purpose adapters—including mainframe emulation cards. This slot is electrically isolated from the rest of the bus; many ordinary cards won't work in this slot. Check the instruction manuals (if you still have them) or the maker of your old cards (if they are still in business) if you have any questions.

IRQs: Irksome Essentials

The various pieces of hardware attached to a CPU through a system bus need the attention of the microprocessor in order to perform services or to supervise the movement of information from place to place. Luckily, not all of the devices need the CPU's attention all of the time. Even if they did, the computer would not be able to deal with more than one thing at a time.

Some devices, such as keyboards, are in heavy use, while other pieces of hardware, such as sound cards or floppy disk drives, may be operated only for a few seconds at a time over the course of a day's work. The computer solution is *interrupts*, which do exactly what their name suggests: They are electronic flag-wavers that grab the CPU's attention when necessary.

Interrupts are signals that run along the wires of the bus. They are carried out in the order of their importance to the system, determined by a pecking order set by interrupt numbers. In computer terminology, these are called *IRQs (interrupt requests)*.

The original PCs had a single Intel 8259A PIC (programmable interrupt controller) that was capable of arbitrating among eight requests for attention. The requests were numbered IRQ 0 through 7. The essential system timer was assigned IRQ 0 with the highest priority, and the keyboard used IRQ 1.

As PCs became more capable and complex, it became obvious that additional interrupts were needed to service new devices, including network adapters, sound cards, and more. The PC-AT and all modern machines, therefore, have a second interrupt controller with eight more lines, numbered IRQ 8 through 15. To maintain compatibility with older hardware and operating systems, the eight new interrupts are cascaded to the first controller over the IRQ 2 line. This results in a total of 15 IRQs, rather than 16.

Because the eight additional IRQs enter into the system between IRQ 1 and 3, interrupts 8 through 15 have a higher priority than IRQs 3 through 7. On a modern machine, the system claims permanent ownership of IRQs 0, 1, 8, and 13. The remaining 11 are open to assignment.

It is important to understand that, on a standard PC, no two devices can simultaneously use the same IRQ without causing serious problems, including a system lockup. In theory, two devices can have the same assignment if they are never used together; this is a dangerous practice, though.

PCI, MCA, and EISA systems are capable of allowing multiple hardware devices to share a single IRQ. On a PCI bus, this sharing is achieved through IRQ or interrupt steering. Multiple devices can be assigned the same IRQ, but an interim process decides which of these devices gets to use the interrupt at any given time.

Most devices come preset to use a particular IRQ; their instruction manuals should inform you which other interrupts they can be set to and how to make the reassignment. Older devices use connector blocks or DIP switches to change interrupts; on some modern devices, you can change their settings with a software command.

In theory, IRQ 7 is assigned to the first parallel port (LPT 1), and IRQ 5 to the second possible parallel port (LPT 2). But for most users and in most situations, the parallel port does not use any interrupts. Therefore, it is common for other devices to lay claim to these two interrupts.

Table 4-7 contains some typical assignments for IRQs on a modern machine.

Ch 4

TABLE 4-7: Typical IRQ Assignments on a Modern Machine

Interrupt	Function	Physical Type
IRQ0	System timer	Motherboard
IRQ1	Keyboard controller	Motherboard
IRQ2	Cascade from second 8259A PIC	Motherboard
IRQ3	Serial port COM2 or internal modem	8/16-bit slot or motherboard resource
IRQ4	Serial port COM1	8/16-bit slot or motherboard resource
IRQ5	Sound card or LPT2 (parallel port 2)	8/16-bit slot
IRQ6	Floppy disk controller	8/16-bit slot or motherboard resource
IRQ7	Parallel port LPT1	8/16-bit slot or motherboard resource
IRQ8	CMOS real-time clock	Motherboard
IRQ9	Available as IRQ9 or redirected to IRQ2	8/16-bit slot or motherboard resource. Recommended for network interface.

Interrupt	Function	Physical Type
IRQ10	Available for use	16-bit slot or motherboard resource. Typically used for USB.
IRQ11	Available for use	16-bit slot or motherboard resource. Often used for SCSI.
IRQ12	Available for use	16-bit slot or motherboard resource. Often used for mouse port.
IRQ13	Math coprocessor	Motherboard resource
IRQ14	Hard disk controller	16-bit slot or motherboard resource. Used for primary IDE.
IRQ15	Disk controller	16-bit slot or motherboard resource. Used for secondary IDE.

For the record, Table 4-8 contains the typical assignments for IRQs on a dinosaur.

TABLE 4-8: Typical IRQ Assignments on a Dinosaur Machine

Interrupt	Function	Physical Type
IRQ0	System timer	Motherboard resource
IRQ1	Keyboard controller	Motherboard resource
IRQ2	Available for use	8-bit slot
IRQ3	Serial port COM2	8-bit slot
IRQ4	Serial port COM1	8-bit slot
IRQ5	Hard disk controller	8-bit slot
IRQ6	Floppy disk controller	8-bit slot
IRQ7	Parallel port LPT1	8-bit slot

Two devices are not supposed to share the same IRQ; however, in modern machines, this is possible. You will find, however, that although your computer and operating system may support shared IRQs, individual hardware products may not. Read your documentation carefully or call the product vendor to determine whether this sharing is possible. If you try to expand a modern machine with multimedia capabilities, you'll quickly discover that you can soon end up with only a few options to avoid conflicts.

First of all, realize that some IRQs are permanently assigned; the interrupts for system timer, keyboard, COM ports, and disk controllers are immutable.

Modern machines with current BIOS, in concert with modern operating systems beginning with Windows 95B (OSR 2) with Plug-and-Play facilities, can use a facility called *interrupt steering*, also known as *IRQ steering*. Under this scheme, Windows takes over from the BIOS the task of assigning IRQs, seeking to avoid conflicts. And, depending on the nature of the devices, the operating system will allow two or more to share a single interrupt.

If you have any ISA slots and devices, though, these pieces of hardware must be manually assigned to a non-shareable interrupt among the original eight IRQs of the dinosaur PC.

NOTE

Under Windows 95B, Windows 98, and later versions of the Windows operating system, interrupt steering can be turned on or off from the Device Manager. Double-click the System Devices branch, and double-click PCI Bus. Choose the IRQ Steering tab to enable or disable the feature. In most instances, you'll want to keep the facility enabled; this is a feature ordinarily related to the facilities of the BIOS.

After the fact, you can use a diagnostic program to check IRQ settings, although the reports are not 100 percent accurate because not all devices may be active when you run the test.

The easiest way to track the assignment of IRQs in your system is to consult the Device Manager that is part of the Systems tab of Control Panel in Windows. Under the View menu, check to see the display of Resources by Connection and examine the Interrupts report.

CROSS-REFERENCE

Appendix D lists IRQ assignments. Chapter 3 discusses a BIOS that allows users to reclaim IRQs.

DMA: Mind Transfers Made Easy

The other half of the communication process for many hardware devices, including some disk controllers, sound cards, and other I/O cards, is *direct memory access (DMA)*. DMA is a facility that allows transfer of data directly, without intervention by the microprocessor. This allows for greater speed in data transfer and avoids bogging down the CPU in unnecessary tasks.

The dinosaur PC had a single Intel 8237A, four-channel DMA controller capable of 8-bit data transfers. DMA line 0 was reserved by the system for dynamic RAM refresh, DMA 2 was assigned to floppy disk transfers, and DMA 3 was to be used for hard disk transfers.

With the arrival of the PC-AT and other modern machines capable of 16-bit operations, a second DMA controller was added. The output of the first controller is routed to the first input of the second chip.

Therefore, a modern machine has seven DMA lines, numbered 0 through 3 and 5 through 7. The lower lines still are used only for transfers between 8-bit devices and 8- or 16-bit memory; DMA lines 5 through 7 are available for full 16-bit transfers in either direction.

Because of the improved speed of CPUs beginning with the 80286, DMA is no longer needed for RAM refresh operations, and DMA 0 is therefore available for reassignment on modern machines. Similarly, DMA 3 is not used for hard disk transfers on 16-bit machines.

Depending on the type of adapter, some DMA channels can be shared. For example, a network adapter and an I/O device can coexist although the I/O unit wouldn't be available when the network was in use.

Table 4-9 contains some typical assignments for DMA channels on a modern system.

TABLE 4-9: Typical DMA Channel Assignments

DMA Channel	Assignment
0	(16-bit slot) Available. Typically used by sound card.
1	(8/16-bit slot) Available. Typically used by sound card.
2	(8/16-bit slot or motherboard resource) Floppy controller.
3	(8/16-bit slot or motherboard resource) Available. Typically used for LPT1.
4	Cascade channels 0–3.
5	(16-bit slot) Available.
6	(16-bit slot) Available.
7	(16-bit slot) Available.

CROSS-REFERENCE

Appendix D deals with DMA in more detail.

SUMMARY

The first four chapters of this book have explored the basic foundations of the computer. With that initial exploration complete, I move on to discuss the hardware of the PC in the next chapter.

Notes

Chapter 5

Tools Needed:

- Phillips or flat-blade screwdriver
- Antistatic strip, wrist strap, or grounding pad
- Needle-nose pliers
- Tweezers
- Nut drivers
- Chip insertion and extraction tools

Basic Hardware Skills

At this point in the book, you're approaching the time when you'll lay hands on a computer to take it apart. Before you do, though, explore with me the basic components of the computer in more detail, including the case, the motherboard, cooling fans, expansion cards, system configuration switches or memory, and the power supply.

Tools of the Trade

Before you do any repair work on your PC — in fact, before you even think about taking off the cover of your computer — start by assembling the appropriate computer toolkit. I'm not talking about hundreds of dollars here: You can obtain all you need for less than $50 from a computer dealer, mail-order house, or well-equipped hardware store.

Your computer toolkit should include a set of good quality needle-nose pliers, a small-blade straightedge, and several Phillips-head screwdrivers. The next step up is a collection of nut drivers, one or more tweezers, and a set of chip insertion and extraction tools.

If you are working on some very old equipment, or specialized devices, you may need a set of Torx blades, which work with special screws used by some manufacturers in hopes that you won't try to open their magic boxes by yourself.

You can assemble the pieces yourself or pick up a package from a computer supply house. Prepackaged kits range from as low as $10 for basic tools to electronic kitchen sinks topping out at more than $300.

My favorite portable kit includes a set of appropriate flat-blade and Phillips screwdrivers, a set of torque bits and nut drivers, an IC inserter and extractor, tweezers, and parts holders. I'm especially fond of a little spring-loaded tweezer device that I can attach to a screw and guide deep into the innards of a computer to mate with its intended hole.

To clean the connectors of adapter cards, keep a small bottle of rubbing alcohol and a set of cotton swabs. Some people clean connectors with a fresh pencil eraser; take care to guard against dropping bits of rubber into the slots.

A low-tech nicety is a small, compartmentalized plastic or wooden box, such as a sewing kit. Mark the compartments with letters or numbers, and keep a notepad and pen in the box. As you remove screws and parts, put them into individual sections and note where they go. Use stickers or labels with corresponding numbers or letters on the computer components.

Want to go even lower-tech? Use an egg carton; it comes all set up with 12 small compartments and you can write notes directly on the cardboard or foam as you store screws and parts.

You should have a way to ground yourself before touching the static-sensitive chips under the covers of the PC. The official way to do this is with a *grounding strap*, which attaches to your wrist or ankle and connects to an electrical ground. You can purchase a grounding strap for less than $10 from a computer store. Another useful and even less expensive device is a static touchpad (see Figure 5-1) or touch strip that you can anchor on the desktop and connect to a ground.

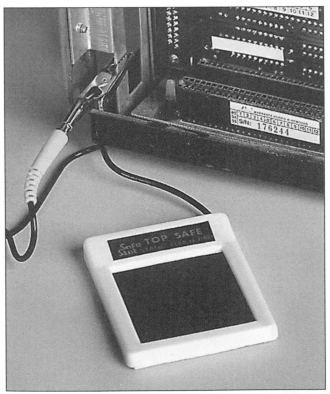

Figure 5-1: *A good practice is to install an antistatic device, such as this touchpad, on your desktop. You can also purchase a keyboard mat or touch strip. Get in the habit of grounding yourself before you touch any part of your computer.*

You can also make your own antistatic device. Run a wire from the center screw of a grounded electrical outlet plate — be careful not to insert the wire into the slots of the outlet itself — and tape the other end to your desktop. Touch the bare end of the wire to discharge any static in your body before touching any electronic parts.

In any case, it is also useful to check all the outlets in your office or home to ensure that they are properly grounded. Simple plug-in ground fault detectors are available at Radio Shack or other suppliers for as little as $10. They indicate open grounds, open neutral, hot/ground reverse, hot/neutral reverse, and check the integrity of a ground fault circuit interrupter if present. If they indicate a problem, contact a professional electrician to work on your wiring.

Advanced Tools

A useful tool for advanced troubleshooters is a simple multimeter that can check DC and AC voltage and DC current; older designs use a meter with a needle, while more modern (and sturdier) devices have digital readouts. Use the meter to check for proper output from a power supply and to check voltage levels on connectors. Some devices also enable you to check the continuity of cables, which can tell you if a wire is broken or shorted. Meters sell for about $20 to $100 for consumer-grade devices. Be sure to study and understand the instruction manual before you use a multimeter. As you use the meter, be especially careful not to short across connectors or traces on the motherboard.

More sophisticated testers exist for serial and network cables. An RS232 breakout box, for example, includes a set of jumper wires to reconfigure cables, DIP switches to cross over connections, and LEDs to monitor signals on a live cable, and sells for about $30. A similar breakout box is available for the eight lines of an RJ45 connector used in Ethernet cable.

A multi-purpose cable tester, which sells for about $125, has connectors and circuitry to test a range of wiring devices, including serial, parallel, network, USB, and FireWire cables.

If you are going to make your own cables, you should invest in a fine-point soldering iron, a set of wire strippers, some needle-nose pliers, and cable crimpers. You also need raw cable and a set of connectors for the cables you want to make. All are available from the same sources already mentioned. Having stated that, I haven't built a cable from scratch in years. Cables are more standardized than they used to be, and most cables are available at reasonable prices from mail-order houses or computer retailers.

CROSS-REFERENCE

Appendix F presents an encyclopedia of cables and connectors for the PC.

Testing the System Unit Case and Cover

In general, if the case looks all right, it works all right. Not always, though: it is possible for the case itself to cause system troubles.

A poorly designed case with misshapen pieces of metal in the wrong places can cause intermittent electrical shorts. I have come across cases where the bottom (or the side on a tower unit) sat perilously close to soldered component leads on the underside of the motherboard. Sometimes the motherboard actually touched the case. If such a motherboard boots at all, sooner or later the vibration of the disk drives and fans will bring the electrically active motherboard in contact with the metal case. At best, this will cause intermittent shorts or hang-ups. At worst, something may fry.

In another instance, the high-tech and expensive case on a modern machine included a row of small metal (often, copper) fingers that were part of the protection against RF (radio frequency) leakage. Unfortunately, a few of the fingers broke loose in the process of removing and reinstalling the cover, with the result that a few of these pieces of metal were rattling around on the motherboard, just waiting to short out the machine. If your case uses this design, proceed with caution.

RF radiation usually does not present any problems for the user, although it may interfere with other electronic devices in your home or office. You can usually detect RF leakage by bringing a television set or FM radio near the PC. If you see a pattern that changes as the PC performs various assignments, or if the reception on the FM radio is affected by a whine or pulsing beat that changes as the PC responds to keyboard commands, you have an RF radiation problem.

Should you fix it? RF radiation is in most cases just an annoyance. In the most severe instances, though — when it interferes with television reception in the home, changes the channel on the office stereo system, or opens and closes your neighbor's garage door — you're going to want to seal up all the openings in the PC case properly. (Be sure not to block air intakes and vents, of course.) Figure 5-2 shows a properly shielded new computer case awaiting installation of internal parts.

Ch
5

Tower systems place the motherboard on its end along one side of the box with add-in cards mounted horizontally.

In another type of design, a riser card stands up on a slot on the motherboard like a Christmas tree, with slots branching off one or both sides for add-ins. Riser card systems are often used in low-profile desktop machines. The riser card makes for a compact box but a sometimes difficult repair and upgrade assignment.

It's worth your time to examine the design of a PC case to determine how difficult it will be to install peripherals and to access the motherboard itself for the memory and CPU sockets or slots. Figure 5-3 shows an example of a case that requires some additional disassembly before you can work on it.

FIGURE 5-2: *An untouched mid-tower case. Note the RF shielding that occupies the future homes of hard, floppy, and CD-ROM drives. The metal plates can be removed, and plastic faceplates are supplied to finish off the appearance of the front.*

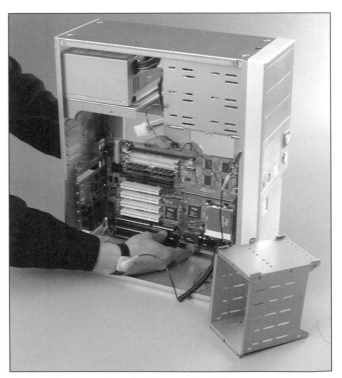

FIGURE 5-3: *You may find it worthwhile to remove drive cages on some cases to make it easier to remove or install a motherboard. Within some compact cases, you have to remove the power supply that overhangs the motherboard.*

The Mother of All Boards

The motherboard holds together all of the essential internal parts of the computer and provides connections to external devices and the power supply. (Some manufacturers and technical types refer to the motherboard as the *system board* or the *mainboard*.)

In a desktop machine, the motherboard lies beneath the add-in cards and internal peripherals of the PC. In most systems, several add-in cards stand upright in slots on the motherboard.

The components of the motherboard

All PC motherboards include the following in one form or another:

- **CPU (central processing unit, or microprocessor).** This is the brains of the outfit.
- **System ROM BIOS (Read-Only Memory Basic Input/Output System).** The set of instructions that tells the CPU how to control the simplest, basic functions of the hardware.
- **Chipset.** A group of circuits on the motherboard that allow the CPU to control the hardware; CPUs and chipsets must be properly matched and fully supported by the other components of the motherboard.
- **RAM (random access memory).** The active thinking space for the computer. Modern machines have slots that accept memory modules — usually DIMMs or RIMMs. Older modern machines and some senior citizens may require lower-capacity SIMMs. And dinosaurs may have sockets on the motherboard to accept individual memory chips.
- **Expansion bus.** The interconnecting superhighway that enables you to add devices to the system. Modern machines generally use a 32-bit PCI bus; some motherboards offer a few holdover 16-bit ISA bus slots for use with "legacy" devices. Modern motherboards generally add an AGP (Accelerated Graphics Port) slot that is a separate bus used to connect a special video card directly to the memory bus.
- **IRQ (interrupt request) lines.** A set of electrical lines used by the hardware in the bus to seek the attention of the CPU.
- **DMA (direct memory access) channels.** A set of channels that can transfer information between devices without the help of the CPU.
- **Memory or local bus.** The private highway between the CPU and memory. It also has bridges to connect it to other, usually slower buses. It has allowed other devices in the past (see VESA bus), and some have a special *bridge* that can connect devices without slowing them down (though devices on such a bridge are often referred to as directly connected, or *local*).
- **Input ports.** Connections between the motherboard and input devices, such as a keyboard, a mouse, a scanner, a camera, and other devices.
- **Output ports.** Connections between the motherboard and output devices, such as a printer, an external storage device such as a hard drive, a modem, and other devices.
- **Display adapter.** Circuitry that converts computer information into letters or pictures presented on a monitor. The display adapter can be on an expansion card that plugs into the bus or be part of the motherboard itself.
- **Connection to storage devices.** On many modern machines, the motherboard includes an integrated IDE or SCSI I/O controller with connectors to devices from floppy disk drives, hard drives, CD-ROM drives, and other such systems. On older machines, and some modern machines with special needs, a storage controller plugs into the expansion bus.
- **Setup system.** A means to customize the way the PC operates through switches, jumpers, or software settings held in battery-backed memory.
- **Clock.** The heartbeat of the system, the clock chip or clock crystal sets the pulse with which information moves along the bus.
- **Real-time clock/CMOS battery.** The calendar for the system, keeping track of the date and time as well as system configuration settings used by the PC at bootup. The small rechargeable or lithium battery keeps the information unaltered even with the power off.

Senior citizens and dinosaurs may have the following:

- **A VESA local (VL) bus.** An extension to the memory bus used primarily for graphics adapters that could run faster than adapters in the expansion bus.

Ch
5

- **A math coprocessor.** Or an empty socket for such a chip that, when asked, performs complex math faster than the CPU, freeing the CPU to go on to other chores.
- **OverDrive socket.** On some senior citizens and early modern machines, a means of upgrading the CPU with later models.

CPU

The CPU, also referred to as the microprocessor, is the engine of the computer, the place where data is actually processed. I explore the lineage of CPU chips in Chapter 2; a review appears here in Tables 5-1, 5-2, and 5-3.

TABLE 5-1: Modern Machine CPUs

CPU Chip	Commonly Used with Systems of This Type
Intel Pentium 4	ISA/PCI combo with AGP, and PCI with AGP
AMD Athlon	ISA/PCI combo with AGP, and PCI with AGP
Intel Pentium III	ISA, PCI, ISA/PCI combo with AGP, and PCI with AGP
Intel Pentium III Xeon	ISA/PCI combo with AGP
Intel Celeron	ISA, PCI with AGP, ISA/PCI combo with AGP
Intel Pentium II	ISA, PCI, ISA/PCI combo, and PCI with AGP
Intel Pentium II Xeon	ISA, PCI, ISA/PCI combo, and PCI with AGP
AMD K6/2, AMD K6/3	ISA/PCI combo with AGP

TABLE 5-2: Senior Citizen CPUs

CPU Chip	Commonly Used with Systems of This Type
Intel Pentium with MMX	ISA, PCI, ISA/PCI combo
Intel Pentium Pro	ISA, PCI, ISA/PCI combo
Intel Pentium	ISA, EISA, VL, PCI
Cyrix 6x86, AMD K5	ISA, PCI
Intel 486DX	ISA, EISA, PS/2, VL, PCI
Cyrix 486SLC	ISA, VL, PCICyrix 486DLC, AMD Am486DX4-100
Intel 486DX2, Intel 486DX4	ISA, VL, PCI

TABLE 5-3: Dinosaur CPUs

CPU Chip	Used with Systems of This Type
Intel 486SX	ISA, EISA, PS/2, VL, PCI
Intel 386SL, IBM 386SLC	Portables using proprietary buses
Intel 386, 386SX	ISA machines, EISA, PS/2s
Intel 286	PC-AT bus
NEC V20, NEC V30	PC bus
Intel 8086	PC bus
Intel 8088	PC bus

Throughout the history of the PC, the CPU has almost always been located in a socket on the motherboard or on a carrier that plugged into a special slot on the board. A few senior citizen designs moved the microprocessor to a system board card that attached to a backplane bus; this short-lived design was intended to enable easy upgrades of the processor.

With the arrival of the Intel 386, motherboards accepted CPUs mounted in zero insertion force (ZIF) sockets or additional OverDrive sockets intended for use with upgrade chips.

With the introduction of the Pentium II, Pentium II Xeon, and Pentium III, the processors were housed inside a sealed rectangular single edge contact cartridge (SECC) containing the CPU, secondary cache, and support chips; the cartridge plugged into a slot connector (see Figures 5-4 and 5-5). Intel Celerons, some late-model Pentium IIIs, and the Pentium 4 returned to surface-mount sockets on the motherboard, in two versions: a 423-pin OLGA PGA package and a 478-pin micro flip-chip PGA package.

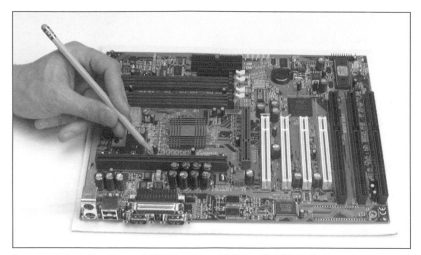

FIGURE 5-4: *A Pentium II Slot 1 on an ATX motherboard. A supporting frame to hold a heat sink and fan attaches to pins that rise from the board.*

Similarly, AMD K6 processors plugged into a horizontal Socket 7 on the motherboard; the advanced AMD Athlon processor stands upright in a Slot A mount, mechanically the same as Intel's Slot 1 (SC242) but electrically incompatible.

FIGURE 5-5: *A Pentium II module includes locking clips on each end; it inserts into Slot 1 like an add-in card. Some Pentium III and AMD modules used a similar cartridge.*

Chipsets

The CPU is supported by a group of special integrated circuits on the motherboard called a *chipset*. These chips (most manufactured by Intel; other makers include AMD and VIA) interface among the CPU, BIOS, and buses.

In most cases, the motherboard is optimized for a particular chipset, and the support chips are likely to be soldered into place and not changeable.

The state-of-the-art in chipsets for standard systems in 2001 was Intel's 850 chipset, which mates the Pentium 4's 3.2-gigabytes-per-second bus to 3.2-gigabytes-per-second of memory bandwidth using high-speed Dual RDRAM memory. Intel also offered the 845 chipset, which allows use of the Pentium 4 with slightly slower but less expensive SDRAM memory.

CROSS-REFERENCE

For more details on motherboard chipsets, see Chapter 2.

ROM BIOS

The ROM (read-only memory) BIOS (basic input/output system) provides the most basic level of hardware control while the computer is running. As I have already discussed, computers in the PC family are equipped with a read-only memory, basic input/output system, (ROM BIOS) chip. The BIOS chip contains the nitty-gritty directions your computer needs to connect to a floppy drive, video card, or another device.

On a modern machine, the system's CMOS setup screen and memory are associated with the ROM BIOS.

When your computer is first powered up, it gives itself a quick diagnostic exam; it's called a power-on self-test (POST) and then it executes a set of basic instructions to start, or boot, the motherboard and CPU.

Your computer needs to know what pieces of hardware are installed in it. Modern systems are able to use the facilities of Plug-and-Play (more about this later in this chapter) to detect the presence of many devices attached to the system; in some cases, you will have to manually instruct the system about some devices by using a setup or configuration program or by making selections on the CMOS setup screen.

Dinosaurs may need to be instructed about the specifications for every last piece of equipment, from keyboard, floppy disks, and hard drives to video cards, parallel ports, and serial ports. On an XT and some early AT machines, you have to set switches or notify the system in some other mechanical way.

In the day of the dinosaur, BIOS chips were rarely replaced except if they had failed. Then came a period when computer users were regularly offered upgrades to the BIOS chips, which required that they be pried out of their sockets and replaced.

Today, BIOS chips rarely need to be replaced but they can easily be upgraded in place. Flash BIOS chips can accept a new set of instructions loaded into their memory from a disk or over the Internet; these BIOS chips retain the new instructions when power is turned off.

CROSS-REFERENCE

I explore BIOS replacement and other BIOS issues in detail in Chapter 3.

The ROM BIOS in the original IBM PC computer was a true dinosaur. IBM didn't bother to include directions to enable it to work with a hard disk, because nobody thought users would ever want or could ever afford hard disks. In fact, the original IBM PC came with a cassette port so that users could save data on an ordinary audio cassette recorder, a painfully slow process. If anyone ever actually made regular use of that port, that fact has been lost in the mists of history; however, to maintain compatibility, support for the cassette port continued to be part of the ROM BIOS for many years to follow.

IBM XTs and their clones were a bit smarter. These computers were instructed to search for additional ROMs located on cards plugged into the bus—for example, ROMs on a hard disk controller card or on a video card.

The BIOS chips in ATs and AT clones were even smarter. They knew about hard disks and actually had directions built in for the most popular hard disks then available. The AT computers (ISAs) kept the search-for-other-ROMs feature, too.

EISA computers are smarter yet. They include the full instructions of ISA computers and add to them accommodations for special EISA adapter cards, which transfer data at extraordinarily high speeds. But you, the installer, must tell the EISA computer which EISA cards are installed.

MCA computers, like EISA computers, demand that you run a Micro Channel setup program from the reference disk shipped with your computer whenever you install a new card.

PCI and VL bus systems have setup screens that are part of their ROM BIOS code.

Random access memory

Random access memory (RAM), also called *system memory*, provides a temporary storage area for the operating system, programs, and data.

Nearly all of today's modern machines work with high-speed, high-density memory mounted on modules that plug into special slots on the motherboard. The most common design is a DIMM (Dual In-Line Memory Module). Some of the latest Pentium 4-based systems use a similar module called a RIMM (Rambus In-line Memory Module) for high-speed Rambus memory. Older modern machines and many senior citizens used lower-capacity SIMMs (Single In-Line Memory Modules).

A modern machine running Windows XP should have at least 64MB of RAM, with 128MB or 256MB common on machines working with graphics-intensive applications. Earlier versions of Windows can work with smaller amounts of memory, although they would benefit from at least 64MB.

The IBM PC, the original dinosaur of dinosaurs, came equipped with as little as 16K or 64K of memory, installed in individual memory chips on the motherboard. Later improvements allowed these first machines to work with as much as 640K of memory — considered a massive amount, and priced as such when it was first offered — you will still not be able to run Microsoft Windows or any modern software. It is not economically feasible to upgrade such an outdated system; it's cheaper to buy a new motherboard capable of accepting high-capacity memory chips or even better, a new system with modern supporting peripherals.

That original PC limit of 640K of system memory went on to become the basic building block for every subsequent operating system. Over the years various schemes for expanded or extended memory have permitted machines to work with memory that lies above that base or system memory. Such memory is essential for use with Windows and many DOS multimedia programs.

On all machines, the first 64K of memory is filled with housekeeping information (data the computer needs to operate itself). Consider the example of the interrupt vector table, an element of the operating system that tells the microprocessor what to do if a particular piece of hardware requires its attention. The table must be correct and in the proper place for the computer to do any work. (Because of this, most memory-test diagnostic programs can't read from or write to the first 64K of memory without crashing the computer.)

CROSS-REFERENCE

I discuss memory in more detail in Chapter 8.

Direct memory access

Direct memory access (DMA) channels enable direct information transfer from peripherals to system memory without the involvement of the microprocessor; this change both speeds up the transfer and removes some of the workload from the CPU.

Some dinosaur clones did without DMA, but virtually every member of the PC family has used them for modern machines. Older machines required users to become directly involved in assigning specific DMA channels to devices, but modern Plug-and-Play motherboards have mostly automated the process.

DMA is routinely used for most of the peripherals of the PC, with the exception of floppy disk drives; some backup programs, though, are capable of rerouting floppy disk transfer to the DMA channels to pick up speed in making massive archival backups.

On modern machines, DMA is part of the integrated motherboard chipset; on older machines DMA was managed by discrete chips soldered into place on the motherboard, making it nearly impossible to replace them if they fail. Such failures, though, are relatively rare in modern machines. If the DMA chips or the integrated chipset fail, you are probably due for a motherboard replacement.

Bus

The bus is a main information path inside the computer. On older machines, it connects the microprocessor, memory, ROM, and all expansion cards. On more modern machines, it is an interconnection between the microprocessor and a number of special-purpose high-speed buses that bring together all the pieces of the machine. PC buses have gone through an ever-improving progression from 8-bit PC to 16-bit AT to ISA, EISA, MCA, VL, and 32- and 64-bit PCI designs. They are all, though, essentially the same: a series of thin wires, called *traces,* that run from connectors on the motherboard to control chips and the CPU itself. High-performance buses are wider (capable of handling more parallel pathways) and faster; advanced systems also include intelligence that can arbitrate among multiple demands for access to the bus at the same moment.

CROSS-REFERENCE

I discuss the design essentials of computer buses in Chapter 4.

On a typical modern machine, you'll find two important buses. The first is the system bus, also known as a *local bus*; this connects the microprocessor and system memory. The motherboard connects the system bus through a bridge to peripheral interconnects such as the ISA and PCI buses. The bridge is managed by the motherboard's chipset.

With the arrival of high-speed CPUs and RAM, designers sought to isolate the path between the processor and memory and then make it more direct. Current machines use a Dual Independent Bus (DIB), which replaces the single system bus with a frontside bus and a backside bus. The frontside bus connects the system memory to the processor, under the management of the memory controller, and other subsidiary buses to the CPU and system memory. The backside bus serves one purpose: to provide a direct, fast channel between the CPU and Level 2 cache.

Bus connectors for expansion cards

Modern machines are based around motherboards that use the flexible PCI bus; some boards include a few older and slower ISA sockets to work with "legacy" adapters.

Modern buses

The PCI (peripheral component interconnect) bus was originally implemented as a 32-bit bus running at clock speeds of 33 or 66 MHz; modern machines can work with PCI devices at a system bus speed of 100 or 133 MHz. Among its many advanced features is *bus mastering,* which allows certain PCI devices to take control of the bus and operate independently of the CPU.

Standard 32-bit cards have 120 active connections, with 4 additional pin locations used for "keying" the card into proper position, giving a total of 124 pin locations.

A 64-bit version of the PCI bus is used in high-end servers and workstations; the second 32 bits of information are transported across an extension to the standard card and to the bus on the motherboard — the extension adds another 60 pins for a total of 184.

At the time of this writing, many computer manufacturers have begun to use motherboards that use only the PCI bus (along with two or four USB ports); if you have any "legacy" adapters that require an ISA bus, you'll have to upgrade the hardware.

However, you will still find many modern machines that also offer a secondary bus to work with older "legacy" devices. The most common is a combination of PCI and ISA.

You'll also find some older systems that put PCI alongside an EISA or VL bus.

The ISA (industry standard architecture) bus was developed for the PC-AT computer and its clones. The 16-bit bus, with two connector sockets for each expansion card, uses a 62-pin socket that is mechanically identical to the sockets of the original IBM PC and XT, which was an 8-bit design. This allows most older 8-bit cards to work in a 286, 386, 486, or Pentium ISA bus computer. More importantly for modern computer users, most cards that work with an ISA bus can work in a combination motherboard that shares the faster PCI bus.

Dinosaur buses

PC and PC/XT used the PC bus, an 8-bit bus with a single 62-pin connector for each expansion card.

EISA motherboards use a versatile bus connector socket that can accept ordinary 8-bit cards, ordinary 16-bit ISA-style cards, or EISA cards.

MCA buses include 16-bit and 32-bit socket designs. Cards for 16-bit devices have 58 fingers, with signals available on each side of the card for a total of 116 connections. Cards for 32-bit devices have 93 fingers, again with connections on both sides of the card for a total of 186 wires. MCA cards generate less electrical interference than other adapters, which enhances system reliability and the integrity of data.

VL, or VESA local, bus systems are extensions to an ISA or EISA motherboard that connect directly to the CPU. Some early designs for local buses used proprietary cards and connectors, but standardization was eventually achieved. VL motherboards place an MCA connector in line with a standard ISA connector; VL cards include pins that plug into both.

WARNING

Avoid touching the gold-plated connectors at the bottom of expansion cards. First of all, you could end up sending a surge of static electricity through the delicate electronic components. And the oil on your hands could speed the corrosion process on the contacts of both the card and the connectors. Handle the card by its nonconductive sides or by the bracket.

System setup: DIP switches, jumpers, or CMOS memory

From the early days of personal computing up to the era of the modern machines, users had to instruct the system about the various installed parts. As machines have progressed, though, the process of doing so has become simpler; put another way, the machines have become smarter.

Modern machine configuration

Nearly all current machines use a setup or configuration program to write system hardware information to CMOS memory in the clock/calendar chip. Here, the system records the amount of memory, the type of floppy and hard drives installed, the video adapter type, and whether a math coprocessor is installed. CMOS also keeps track of the date and time. CMOS memory chips hold onto their information with the assistance of a small, rechargeable or long-lived lithium battery so that configuration information is not lost while the power is shut down overnight.

Plug-and-Play

The arrival of Windows 95 heralded an important feature of the motherboard and BIOS called Plug-and-Play that enables the system to identify the presence of a new card or other device, install new drivers, adjust other settings if possible, or request that the human operator make the requisite adjustments. Plug-and-Play continued under later versions of Windows, including 98, 2000, NT, and XP.

In theory, anytime you attach a compatible device into the system bus, the USB, a bi-directional parallel port, a serial port, or just about any I/O port, the operating system will recognize the piece of hardware and work with you to install proper drivers and make system settings. Similarly, the operating system is able to detect the removal of a card or device that had previously been recognized.

Ch
5

Plug-and-Play is not infallible; you'll need to pay attention to the settings of your system anytime you make a change or run into a problem.

CROSS-REFERENCE

You can find more details about Plug-and-Play later in this chapter and, from another angle, in Chapter 23 when I discuss using Windows for troubleshooting.

Dinosaur DIPs

PC, PC/XT, AT, and some later machines used tiny controls called *DIP switches* to tell the ROM BIOS what hardware was installed on the machine. Technicians or users set the switches to reflect the amount of memory and number of floppy drives installed, the video type, and the presence or absence of a numeric coprocessor.

Another way to inform the system of the nature of its components was to make changes to *jumpers,* small pins with plastic and metal devices that you can move into place to open or close the electrical connection between the pins. In this way, they work just like switches although they are more trouble for users. Be sure to save any of the connectors if you are asked to remove them. (I sometimes tape extra jumpers to the sides of the case for potential future use; just be sure to secure them safely so that they do not fall into the electrical connectors or moving parts of the drives.)

Each motherboard manufacturer uses jumpers and switches slightly differently. You must have the motherboard manual to know which function a particular jumper controls.

Clock crystal

The computer's CPU beats to an internal clock that is based on a quartz crystal that vibrates at a known frequency when electricity is applied. With each beat of the clock, the CPU moves a block of information through its set of microscopic switches. The tempo of the internal clock is measured in MHz; a megahertz represents one million cycles per second.

Although the design of a Pentium 4 alone makes it faster than a Pentium III or a dinosaur chip, it is the clock crystal that sets the throttle for the processor.

The original IBM PC had a clock crystal that beat at a somnolent 4.77 MHz, just under five million beats per second. As I'm writing this book, the fastest CPUs sold to consumers have gone past 2 GHz (two billion beats per second) and Intel, AMD, and other makers are still pushing the speed limit.

Faster is better, although high speed also brings with it heat buildup and RF radiation. As I've already discussed, for these reasons a properly designed case and ventilation system are essential; do not modify a PC case or block its air holes.

Clock crystals are usually soldered onto the motherboard. Some early dinosaurs had crystals in sockets, and some early upgrade kits gave a CPU a quick boost by offering a faster, replacement crystal. On the most modern of machines, the crystal is a component of the chipset.

On modern machines, the crystal is more flexible. It beats at a high speed that is adjusted by instructing the microprocessor to change its "clock multiplier." This adjustment can be made from the setup or configuration screen of most current devices.

Crystals on modern machines rarely fail. If you do have a problem with the clock, the motherboard will likely have to be replaced or professionally repaired.

Battery power for real-time clock/CMOS memory

Modern machines have three interrelated clocks:

- The real-time clock, located on the motherboard and powered by the same battery that maintains the memory of the CMOS setup, is continually updated whether the system is turned on and receiving AC power or turned off.
- The CMOS clock is a logical clock stored in the BIOS chip on the system board; when the system is turned off, the CMOS

records the most recent date and time but that information is not updated while the machine is turned off.

- The operating system is another logical clock that exists in system memory while the computer is operating; the information is not maintained when power is off.

When the computer boots up, the CMOS clock obtains the latest time and date from the real-time clock. After Windows loads, it reads the current time from the CMOS clock and starts its own operating system clock.

Now here's a tricky situation: the operating system clock runs independently of the CMOS. If your system is loaded down with some very computation-intensive tasks, it is possible for the operating system clock to slip a few tenths of a second or more behind the CMOS clock. In some very unusual situations, this can result in some odd system messages or information in saved files.

Diagnosing CMOS battery issues

Batteries that back up the settings for the BIOS in a modern PC last a long time — but not forever. Among symptoms of a failing or dead battery: the system clock loses time or startup settings are not held in memory when the machine is turned off.

Consult the instruction manual for your PC to find out what type of battery is used on the motherboard. Throughout the history of PCs, a number of different designs have been used, including a holder for ordinary AA and 9-volt batteries, small button batteries, specialized longlife rechargeable power sources, and small lithium batteries.

Some motherboards were designed with batteries wired into place, an eventually cruel form of built-in obsolescence. Depending on the design of the motherboard, though, it may be possible to wire a replacement battery in place, attached to the top of the original connectors. Seek the advice of the system manufacturer or a competent repair shop; be sure to weigh the cost of such a repair against the value of the system.

The most obvious indication that your computer's backup battery is dead or dying is its inability to keep time. Another clue: the CMOS doesn't hold onto settings when the machine is turned off.

If it has been several years since you first put your PC into use, or since the last time you changed its battery, chances are the battery has reached the end of its life. You can test the voltage of the battery using a simple voltmeter. Consult the instruction manual, or the battery itself, to determine the expected full voltage; modern machines typically use batteries in the range from 3 to 6 volts.

You can attempt, however, to determine the source of the problem before you take off the covers; you goal is to see if the system is losing time from a slow real-time clock, which usually indicates a battery problem, or from the operating system clock, which is a sign that you have a software or operating system problem, or that the system's microprocessor is overburdened.

Here is a simple test:

1. At the end of your day, reboot your system and go to the BIOS setup screen. (There are several different ways to go to the setup screen, depending on the manufacturer of your BIOS. Most display an instruction as the system starts; you can also consult the owner's manual.) Locate the section of the settings that allows you to manually enter the date and time.
2. Determine the current time from a reliable source outside of the computer — use a digital watch or clock that displays hours, minutes, and seconds, or try to coincide your work to a radio station's chime on the hour. Set the system clock on the BIOS screen to the exact time as your source, and make note of the time you have entered.
3. Now turn off your machine and leave it unpowered for at least the overnight period; leaving it dormant for the weekend is even better.
4. When you return, power up your computer and once again go directly to the BIOS setup screen. Check the time listed on the BIOS screen against your original reliable source.

If you experienced a significant loss of time between power-off and power-on, your CMOS battery is probably not providing enough voltage to keep the clock current.

On the other hand, if the clock has kept good time, any problem you note with the system time—inaccurate time and date stamping on saved files, or an inaccurate time display on your taskbar—is most likely with the operating system clock. Here's a way to gain an indication of that sort of problem:

1. Set the correct time in the Windows clock by opening Time/Date Properties by double-clicking on the time in the Windows taskbar, or click the Start button, point to Settings, click Control Panel and then double-click on the Date/Time icon. Type the correct time in the digital display.
2. Wait until the system time displayed on your taskbar has dropped significantly out of sync with actual time.
3. Shut down your computer and wait two minutes before you restart it.

If the system clock corrects itself to the current time, the problem is likely with the operating system clock, possibly because of a problem with the operating system itself, a driver, or a piece of software. You can attempt to troubleshoot the problem by performing a *clean boot* of Windows. For details, go to `www.microsoft.com` and search Microsoft's knowledge base for "clean boot" and select the document related to the particular version of Windows in use on your machine.

Replacing a CMOS battery

The most modern machines use a long-life battery—sometimes using high-tech lithium dioxide or magnesium dioxide formulations. Some machines use a specialized real-time clock that comes with an integrated battery and claims of a useful life of 10 years or more.

In my experience, batteries can be counted on for three to six years of life.

On some motherboards, the battery is installed in a battery socket and can be replaced. You'll find circular watch-type batteries and the occasional AA, AAA, or other consumer alkaline battery.

Important note: Before you remove any battery, make a record of any settings in your CMOS setup screen. Depending on the design of your system, you may lose all configuration data when the battery is out of the system.

On other boards—mostly senior citizens—the clock and battery are soldered into place on the motherboard; the maker is gambling (with your money, no less) that the life of the battery will be longer than the useful life of the motherboard. Not only does this configuration make replacement of the battery very difficult, it also opens the system to the possibility of serious and sometimes fatal damage from a leaking battery. If you have such a system, you should keep a close eye on the health of the battery and consider bringing the system to a technician to see if the technician can surgically remove the battery and install a socketed replacement.

If your system uses an integrated real time clock-battery, the device is usually a rectangular chip similar in shape to a BIOS chip. The most common such devices have markings including "DALLAS" and "REAL TIME" and may even have a picture of a clock. They are installed in a socket near the CPU. To remove one of these units, you'll need to use a chip puller; insert the lifting prongs under both ends and gently rock it out of place. To install a new integrated device take care not to bend one of the pins and make sure all pins are properly seated in the socket.

Modern machines with removable batteries typically use one of several designs:

- A small holder that accepts a round coin-shaped battery, such as those used in some clocks and cameras, as shown in Figure 5-6.
- A larger battery pack that can hold either a set of rechargeable cells or, in some designs, a group of AA or AAA alkaline batteries.

- A connector cap that attaches to the top of a special rechargeable cell, shaped somewhat like a standard 9V battery.

An aging senior citizen may have a large computer clock battery such as the one shown in Figure 5-7.

The battery pack or connector cap design sometimes places the battery on a clip that attaches to the drive cage of your PC case, while the small coin-shaped batteries are often directly on the motherboard. If you have any doubt as to the location of the battery, consult the instruction manual for your system or call the manufacturer.

FIGURE 5-7: *Computer clock battery for a senior citizen*

FIGURE 5-6: *A button battery for CMOS backup in a holder that enables easy replacement*

When you purchase a PC or a replacement battery, it should include specifications from the battery maker describing the typical life of the cells. A good practice is to replace the battery a few months ahead of the recommended life.

In most cases, when you remove the old battery to replace it with a new one, the contents of your CMOS setup will be lost. That's why I strongly urge you to maintain a current copy of your settings. Write them down in a notebook or use the facility of some setup screens that allow you to print a hard copy of your settings.

Dinosaur PCs and PC-XTs did not have a clock on the motherboard; instead, some of the first multifunction cards developed for those systems added a clock along with communications ports.

Dinosaur: Math coprocessor socket

This socket can accommodate an optional mathematics chip for heavy number crunching. Math coprocessors are a benefit in complex graphics and some spreadsheet work; only a relatively small proportion of PC owners, though, actually install the chip. Beginning with the 486DX chip and including all Pentium CPUs, a math coprocessor is built into the microprocessor. The 486SX chip has the math coprocessor section disabled or removed.

Nearly all pre-486DX PC motherboards have an available socket for a coprocessor. Some 486DX motherboards have a socket that can accommodate a Weitek coprocessor, which operates even faster than the math coprocessor built into the 486 chip.

Senior citizen: OverDrive sockets

Modern machines, beginning with late-model 486 motherboards and continuing into Pentium-based PCs, may include a specialized socket near the CPU intended to accommodate an Intel OverDrive chip. These chips are capable of upgrading the processor to faster and more efficient speeds as they are developed. Other versions of OverDrive chips are intended to physically replace older CPUs. Later Pentium machines don't include provisions for OverDrive expansion, and Intel quit manufacturing OverDrive chips for the Pentium family in late 1999.

In addition, some third-party makers, such as Kingston and Evergreen, offer their own CPU upgrade chips that may work in the OverDrive socket or in the original CPU socket.

CROSS-REFERENCE

I discuss OverDrive and CPU upgrade chips in more detail in Chapter 2.

Integrated I/O and display adapter circuitry on the motherboard

Serial and parallel ports were originally adaptations to the PC, installed as single-purpose adapter cards or as elements of multi-function cards such as a display adapter and printer port, or a combination game port, clock, and serial port. Modern machines now typically have most or all of these functions as part of the motherboard.

So, too, hard and floppy drive controllers began life as separate adapter cards that plugged into the bus. Although many modern machines still put high-performance drive controllers on add-in cards, other current machines make use of IDE and EIDE circuitry that is integrated onto the motherboard.

Display adapters began as separate cards that plugged into the bus, although some integrated designs of modern machines placed the display circuitry on the motherboard itself. Current machines generally pick up some speed with display adapter cards that plug into special, local bus slots or into VL, PCI, or AGP bus slots.

You will, however, also see some modern machines that use highly integrated motherboards that include graphics adapter circuitry on the motherboard with its own hard-wired equivalent of an AGP slot.

One advantage of integrating many functions on the motherboard is the capability of the manufacturer to fine-tune and test all the components together and guarantee the complete product—no more worries about subtle incompatibilities between your floppy drive controller and your motherboard.

Integration can also reduce the overall price of a system because no need exists for redundant electronics on the adapter cards, plus you won't need to buy the cards or pay for their installation. And another advantage lies in the fact that integrated functions do not demand use of any of the limited slots on the motherboard. An older AT form factor motherboard with onboard I/O is shown in Figure 5-8. On this design, a cable runs from the I/O header on the motherboard to a bracket that mounts in an available slot at the rear of the system.

On more modern ATX motherboards, the serial and parallel ports (as well as USB) are attached directly to the board and line up with openings in the rear of the case. This saves real estate at the slots, reduces the chance for cables to come loose, and adds to the useful standardization of motherboards and PC cases.

A possible disadvantage to an integrated subsystem is that a problem could make the board fail. Modern motherboards, though, usually include jumpers or switches that allow you to manually disable components; the most advanced boards will automatically detect a replacement adapter card in the bus and shut off integrated circuitry.

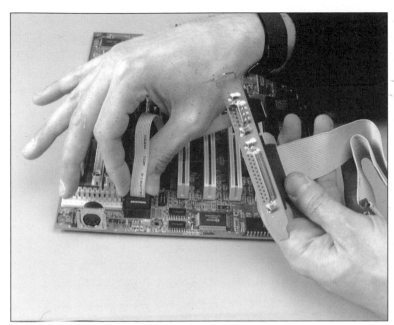

FIGURE 5-8: *On this AT form factor motherboard, a cable leads to a bracket with ports that poke through the rear panel of the case with serial and parallel connectors.*

How the motherboard works

The mother of all boards in your PC is the home of the CPU and its supporting chips, including the ROM BIOS. As I've already discussed, system memory may lie on the motherboard or on an add-in card; other elements that may be integrated onto the motherboard include serial and parallel ports, the video adapter, and floppy and hard drive adapters. The motherboard is also connected to a power supply that provides low-voltage DC power and a fan that helps keep the closed box cool.

To understand how the motherboard components interact, consider what happens when you turn on the power. What follows is a generic description of a modern machine coming to life.

The computer's first steps are hard-wired into the circuitry. When you flick on the power switch, the power supply takes a few fractions of a second to get ready to transform the voltage and spin its fan; when it is ready, it sends a power-good signal to the clock reset chip on the motherboard. The clock reset chip in turn sends a reset message to the microprocessor. The CPU resets and initializes itself with its ordinary startup instructions; the early steps include the running of a self-test.

The final, hard-wired step as the computer comes to life is an instruction to look in a specific, very high address for further instructions. There, the microprocessor finds a pointer that sends it to the place in memory where the ROM BIOS is located.

At this point, the computer marches according to the instructions programmed into the ROM. It is important to remember that ROMs can be changed; you can upgrade or replace them to provide different instructions to the microcomputer. Over the course of PC history, some major computer manufacturers (IBM among them) were large enough to produce their own ROM BIOS, while most others used off-the-shelf or custom-modified versions of BIOS chips from makers including IBM, Phoenix, Award, and American Megatrends (AMI). There are also more than a few Asian sources.

The various BIOS chips all use some form of power-on self-test (POST), but the details may vary from machine to machine. The error messages or informational messages displayed onscreen may differ slightly too.

The POST usually begins by writing the BIOS name, date, and copyright information on the screen; then it checks the keyboard (on many systems, you can see the Caps Lock and Num Lock lights flash on and off). The test usually extends to the controller chip inside the keyboard itself. Next, it reads the DIP switches on a dinosaur PC or consults the CMOS settings on a modern machine to learn what equipment it should expect. On EISA and MCA machines, the BIOS may be able to interrogate devices plugged into the bus to determine their capabilities.

On many a ROM BIOS, the next step is to conduct an inventory and test of system memory; you may see a countdown onscreen as it checks the RAM chips.

Ch
5

The POST also checks many of the other parts of the system, including the CPU itself, the DMA chips, and other critical elements of the system.

The POST checks the floppy drives (the floppy drive light flashes, and the drive spins as it's doing this). If a printer is attached to the parallel port and turned on at bootup, the POST initializes the printer, clearing its memory and preparing it to accept output.

When the POST is done, the ROM BIOS checks for BIOS extensions — those extra ROMs installed on a hard disk controller or an EGA or VGA video card — and follows the initialization instructions in each of these ROM extensions in turn.

NOTE

Many computer manufacturers suppress the onscreen display that tracks the progress of this POST test, displaying instead a company logo, machine name, or other vendor-specific information. Check your computer's documentation. You can probably disable this vendor splash screen in favor of the native bootup reporting. This usually involves making a simple change to the CMOS settings. Especially if you are having trouble with a machine, viewing the boot process on screen as it progresses may help you understand where problems lie.

The ROM BIOS next tries to boot a disk in drive A:, looking at track 0, sector 1 — the DOS boot sector. If no disk is present, it tries drive C:, the hard disk, again checking only track 0, sector 1. It is possible to change the order and drive names for bootup on many systems through switches or changes to the CMOS setup.

Windows 3.1 is loaded on top of DOS. Windows 95/98 and ME are more of an operating system by themselves; DOS is still there, somewhere, but it basically comes into play only when you launch a DOS window or instruct the system to restart as a DOS machine instead of a Windows 95/98 machine. Windows XP, based on Windows 2000, has its own underlying operating system and takes full control of the computer by itself.

When the selected drive spins to life, the drive heads look to the boot sector to load two hidden operating system files. Through Windows 95/98, these were called IO.SYS and MSDOS.SYS; later versions of the operating system use new files with similar functions.

These boot sector files are dedicated to low-level hardware control. IO.SYS contains resident device drivers, the software instructions for operating standard hardware devices, such as the keyboard, the disk drives, the printer, and the serial ports.

Under operating systems through Windows 95/98, the boot sector then looks for a CONFIG.SYS file. This file contains directions to the operating system about specific keyboards, device drivers, and other important settings for the system. Typical device drivers cover mice, sound cards, CD-ROM drives, scanners, and certain unusual data storage devices.

As a final step, the computer loads a command-line processor or a shell (the interface between the keyboard/mouse and the DOS commands). Most systems use COMMAND.COM, part of DOS or the underlying structure of Windows, but shells from sources other than Microsoft can be used.

Motherboard form factors

Though literally hundreds of different motherboards are on the market from dozens of manufacturers large and small, it is by no means a world of anarchy.

Here's why: It all has to do with the modular nature of modern machines. It's a mix-and-match world where a computer maker — Dell, Gateway, IBM, or you — can assemble a machine from off-the-shelf parts. But everything has to work together.

First of all, every motherboard has to be compatible with a particular set of BIOS chips, memory, and the CPU. Second, the connectors on the bus have to be standardized so that they will work properly with any adapter card meant to be plugged into the bus. Next, the motherboard has to match up with the power supply connectors and voltage.

And finally, the motherboard has to be mechanically standardized so that adapter sockets on the board line up with openings on computer cases and so that serial, parallel, USB, and other ports can be accessed from outside the case. And the motherboard has to line up with attachment points in the case. Boards generally use nonconducting standoffs from the metal case, as shown in Figure 5-9.

Think of the automobile industry: General Motors or Ford can come up with a very fancy car with all sorts of special features and spectacular design, but it still must work with the gasoline sold at every service station. Your neighborhood mechanic has to be able to change the oil with the tools in his kit. The wheels have to work with tires available at Goodyear as well as Sears. And the vehicle must fit on Interstate 95 as well as in your garage. Get the idea?

Table 5-4 lists the most commonly used form factors for modern machines. Table 5-5 describes older form factors used in senior citizens and dinosaurs.

TABLE 5-4: Modern Machine Form Factors

Form Factor	Maximum Width	Maximum Depth
ATX	12 inches	9.6 inches
FlexATX	9 inches	7.5 inches
MicroATX	9.6 inches	9.6 inches
Mini ATX	11.2 inches	8.2 inches
NLX	8 to 9 inches	10 to 11 inches

TABLE 5-5: Senior Citizen and Dinosaur Form Factors

Form Factor	Maximum Width	Maximum Depth
LPX	9 inches	11 to 13 inches
Mini LPX	8 to 9 inches	10 to 11 inches
Baby AT	8.5 inches	10 to 13 inches
AT	12 inches	11 to 13 inches

FIGURE 5-9: *One support system for motherboards is nonconducting plastic standoffs installed from the underside to support the board and keep it from touching the metal case. Some designs use metal posts and screws that attach to specially isolated attachment points on the board. A replacement motherboard should come with an appropriate set of new standoffs; for unusual cases you can order specialized supports from computer supply houses.*

The computer industry's solution is something the engineers call motherboard form factors. Today, nearly all PCs use one of several variants of the ATX motherboard design. Here are the most common in use for modern machines:

- **ATX.** As this book goes to press, the ATX is the most common and most flexible motherboard design, offering a high degree of integration of devices and ports on the motherboard. Figure 5-10 shows an example.

Ch 5

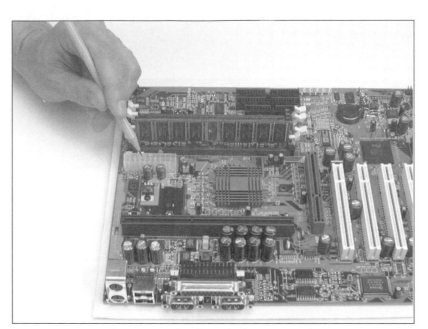

FIGURE 5-10: *On this ATX motherboard, the main power connection sits between the Pentium II module's Slot 1 and the memory DIMM slots.*

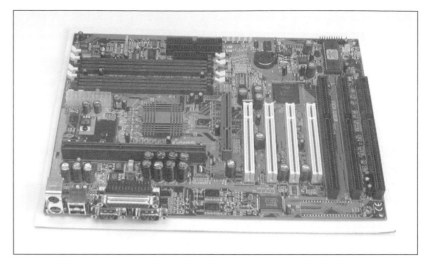

FIGURE 5-11: *This close-up of the back of a Micro-Star MS-6111 motherboard shows the I/O connectors. The bank of I/O connectors on this ATX motherboard neatly brings together, from left to right, mouse and keyboard connectors, a pair of stacked USB ports, two DB-9 serial ports, and above them a DB-25 enhanced parallel port.*

Among the features of the ATX is a stacked I/O connector panel that typically includes serial, parallel, keyboard, mouse, and USB connectors; all of these ports are directly attached to the motherboard, eliminating cables and extra hardware. The CPU was moved to a central location to enable the upright Pentium II or Pentium III to install in its own slot without interfering with adapter cards. The I/O layout on an ATX board is shown in Figure 5-11.

- **MicroATX.** A reduced-size version of the ATX specification, permitting smaller desktop and tower systems and less-expensive motherboards.

- **FlexATX.** Developed by Intel as an extension to the microATX specification, FlexATX motherboards are intended as the basis for small closed-box PCs. Among the first uses: the Barbie PC and the Hot Wheels PC.

  Some closed-box designs rely on external expansion and feature no PCI slots, instead relying on USB ports at the front and back panels for simple plug-and-play expandability. Some FlexATX desktop boards have eliminated legacy connectors including PS/2, and MIDI/game, serial, and parallel ports.

Before the arrival of the micro and flex version of the ATX, manufacturers also produced systems based on a pair of low-profile or slimline designs. Some of the early desktop versions of machines based on the LPX were called pizza boxes because of their shape.

- **NLX.** A more recent version of the slimline or low-profile design, this design shrank the size of the motherboard at the same time as it added more space for connectors at the rear of the chassis and allowed for the placement of connectors at the front through the use of a riser card. The internal connector for the riser card was given greater functionality, including electric connections for the PCI bus, ISA bus, power, floppy, serial bus, and other I/O signals.
- **LPX.** Introduced for use in low-profile cases, the LPX is now relatively rare because of limitations in expandability. Expansion cards plug sideways into a single bus riser card that plugs into a single slot on the motherboard. The LPX added standard locations for serial, parallel, video, mouse, and keyboard connectors; the serial ports used smaller DB9 connectors, and the mouse and keyboard used mini-DIN PS/2 connectors.

Through the first half of the history of the PC, nearly all machines used an AT motherboard, which was the successor to the original IBM PC design.

- **AT.** The full-size AT motherboard was introduced with IBM's PC-AT machine and was the largest motherboard offered for PCs. Serial and parallel ports and connectors for video output and the keyboard were generally located on adapter cards that plugged into the bus. An AT motherboard fits only into AT desktop or AT tower cases. Figure 5-12 shows a basic AT motherboard.
- **Baby AT.** Widely used for senior citizens and modern machines, the baby AT keyboard port — usually a large 5-pin DIN connector — was part of the motherboard and matched up with an opening in the case. This board fits in AT and baby AT desktop and tower units.

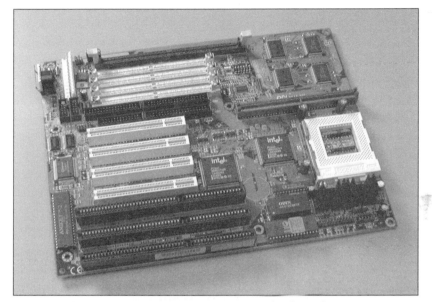

FIGURE 5-12: *Bare Micro-Star Pentium AT motherboard.*

Testing the motherboard

Very few motherboard components are individually serviceable. Here's a list of the pieces you can work with:

CPU

- Most dinosaur CPU chips are installed in sockets and you can remove them for replacement or upgrade, although some machines, including a family of relatively inexpensive 386SX machines produced in the early 1990s, had the CPU soldered into place.
- Modern machines have their CPU in sockets or in a large slot that holds a CPU cartridge like an adapter card.

Control chipset

- On most motherboards, the clock generator and timer chips, the clock crystal and clock reset chip, DIP switches, the CMOS chip, the bus controller chip, the DMA controller chip (for direct disk drive to RAM information transfer), and all the chip sockets are soldered into place and can't be easily replaced.

Memory

- RAM chips on dinosaurs can be replaced if they are not soldered into place.
- Memory chips of modern machines are held on SIMMs, SIPPs, DIMMS, RDRAMs, and other designs of carriers that plug into sockets; the entire module can be easily changed, but individual chips can't be replaced.

ROM BIOS

- On dinosaurs and senior citizens, BIOS chips are usually held in sockets and can be replaced if they fail or for upgrading.
- On modern machines, BIOS chips may be in a socket or soldered into place. Most hold instructions in flash memory that can be changed in place by reading in new code from a floppy disk or other source.

CMOS battery

- The clock/CMOS battery is a simple slip-out/slip-in replacement on most motherboards, but some poorly designed dinosaurs had the battery soldered into place. Some modern machines have switched over to an integrated battery and real-time clock that plugs into a socket; a handful of these integrated devices were soldered in place on the board, presumably in expectation that the device will last longer than the useful life of the motherboard.

One indicator of a serious problem with a motherboard, an NMI (nonmaskable interrupt) error, is often the signal that something has gone seriously wrong with your PC's motherboard. An interrupt is a signal from a particular device that it wants the attention of the microprocessor.

A nonmaskable interrupt is one that the hardware is not permitted to mask, or ignore, while processing another task. When an NMI occurs, the NMI error message goes up on the screen, and everything is deadlocked until you address the NMI error—no matter what else is going on. If you're lucky, the NMI may be indicating a memory parity error, which would require only the replacement of a memory module.

The board itself is a maze of printed circuits, none of which is readily repairable. That's the bad news; the good news is that replacement motherboards—almost certainly even more advanced than the original—sell for about $80 to $200. The solution to the failure of anything more significant than a RAM module, a dead CMOS battery, or an adapter card is the replacement of the entire motherboard.

Removing a motherboard

To get to the motherboard, start by turning off the computer and unplugging it from the wall. Remove the system cover and be sure to ground yourself before reaching into the case.

Unplug all external cables from connectors on the rear of the case. In most systems you have to remove add-in cards and some or all of the hard drives, floppy drives, CD-ROM drives, and other internal devices.

On tower cases and some desktops, you may need to unbolt one or more drive cages that hold add-in drives; many of these cages overhang parts of the motherboard. In cramped designs, such as the low-profile cases, you may even have to remove the power supply that sometimes hangs over the motherboard or be very careful when slipping the motherboard out from underneath.

I suggest that you keep a notebook close at hand and make a sketch of the innards of the case to help you put things back where they were. Use sticky-tab papers to mark pieces or make notes on masking tape to identify the parts. Be especially careful to note the polarity of cables, that is, which connector pin is assigned to pin 1 of the connector. Some motherboard connectors include slots or tabs to prevent incorrect connection; others, however, can be inserted either way. I sometimes use a felt-tipped marker to place a mark on the cable and another on the mother-board or connector before disconnecting the cable. When it comes time to hook everything back up, simply line up the two marks and you have restored proper polarity.

A high-tech solution is to use a digital camera or a video camera to document the inside of the case before you take it apart.

Assign numbers to any cables you remove and place matching numbers on their connectors. Put screws into envelopes or containers marked with a description of their purpose. Trust me on this one: A few minutes spent organizing the parts you take out can save hours when it comes to putting them all back together again.

After everything is out of the way, unplug the power supply's electrical cable or cables from the motherboard.

Here's a step-by-step walk-through of a typical project; your case may be slightly different:

1. Remove the cover. Turn off the power and unplug the PC from the wall. Remove the screws that hold the cover in place and store them in a safe place. Slide the cover off. (Some case manufacturers have improved their designs considerably, making it even easier to get inside the box. These new cases may have a single thumbscrew at the rear of the case that, when released, enables you to slide a flat cover off of the case. Other designs use clips on each side of the case. Pressing them releases the connection and lets you lift or slide the cover right off. In Chapter 6, I'll explore a state-of-the-art system that uses a case that opens up like a clamshell to reveal the motherboard on one side and the drive cage on the other.)

2. Ground yourself. Touch a grounding strip or the center screw of an electrical outlet plate to release static electricity in your body. Even better, wear a properly grounded antistatic wrist strap.

3. Remove cards. Remove all the expansion cards, marking any cables or wires you must disconnect in the process.

4. Mark and remove wires. Attach labels to all wires connected to pins on the motherboard. Such wires typically include a pair of wires to the tiny internal speaker on PCs, a wire that powers the small in-use light on disk drives, and similar wires to other indicators on the face of the PC. Mark them well so that you can properly reinstall them. Finally, remove the wires that run from the power supply to the main electrical connections on the motherboard.

5. Remove power supply if necessary. A desktop computer case is pretty crowded. It may be necessary — or you may find it easier — to remove the power supply screws and slide the power supply out of the case so you have some working room.

6. Remove mounting screws and slide the motherboard out.
   - **Modern machines:** Many modern motherboards are mounted with as few as one or as many as half a dozen small screws, with the motherboard reinforced and electrically insulated at the screw holes. At other places, especially beneath the bus slots, are plastic standoff supports that pop through the board and slip into slots on the case beneath. Look for an insulating washer under the screw heads. Remove the screws, and then slide the motherboard half an inch sideways, moving it away from the power supply. It might make sense to remove the power supply and possibly the drive cage in a smaller case to make room to remove the board. Lift it up and wiggle it out of the chassis. Sometimes it's easier to squeeze the tops of the standoffs and lift the motherboard

out. Save the washers and standoffs to mount the new motherboard. You can also purchase new hardware from computer supply houses.

- **Dinosaurs:** Most PC/XT motherboards have nine standoffs (little metal or plastic legs) that attach the board to the bottom of the case. Look for screws on the bottom of the computer that correspond to the nine screws or nuts on the top of the motherboard. You can remove either the top nuts or the bottom screws. Other XT clones use two screws and a handful of insulated plastic pegs. After you remove the nuts or screws, slide the motherboard out of the chassis. Some older systems have paper or plastic insulating washers on both the top and bottom of the motherboard at each of the nine standoffs and/or screws. You may need to reuse these insulating washers, the standoffs, and the screws to mount a new motherboard.

Installing a new motherboard

In theory, installing a new motherboard is simply the reverse process of removing the old one. Unfortunately, only the loosest of standards apply to motherboard sizes, location of mounting holes, and electrical connection points. And board makers are (thankfully) constantly striving to improve their products, making them smaller and more tightly integrated. I have never seen a replacement go perfectly smoothly, but I have also never failed to complete the job sooner or later. This is an indoor job, no heavy lifting.

Make sure the motherboard you purchase comes with a detailed and understandable manual; you'll need instructions about electrical connectors, jumpers, DIP switches, and settings. I would turn down a hot new board at a great price but a sketchy instruction manual in favor of a capable motherboard with a good manual and even better, support from the technical desk of the seller.

In some cases, you can read the instruction manual and technical documents for a motherboard before you make a purchase by consulting the website for the manufacturer.

1. **Prepare the case and motherboard.** Gently place the new motherboard into the case so that the keyboard connector is lined up exactly with the keyboard hole at the back of the case. Lift up the motherboard slightly to determine where you must install plastic standoffs so that the new motherboard is secure and can't touch the metal case at any point. The more standoffs you install, the more stable the motherboard will be. Most cases have slotted grooves that accept the underside of the standoffs and lock them into place. In some places, you may have standoffs that merely sit atop the bare metal bottom of the case. Don't pass up a chance to add support to the motherboard anywhere you can.

   Find the location on the chassis itself of the one or two brass hexagonal studs that actually hold the motherboard in place. You may have to reposition this metal connector to match a different hole location on the new motherboard.

2. **Set switches or jumpers.** You may need to change the default settings of switches or jumpers on the motherboard to indicate the type or speed of the CPU; on modern motherboards all — or nearly all — adjustments can be made from the setup screen. Consult the instruction manual.

3. **Install the motherboard.** Once you have determined the proper location for all the standoffs, you can lay the motherboard in the case by sliding the plastic standoffs into the grooves of the case. Be careful not to warp the motherboard as you slide it into place; bending the motherboard can short it out or break its electrical traces. Attach the board with a screw into the brass stud, using a nonconductive paper or plastic washer between the screw and the motherboard.

4. Connect electrical cables to the motherboard. Locate the two white rectangular power leads that come from your power supply; on most motherboards they are usually (but not always) marked P8 and P9.

Stop, look, and think: A mistake here could fry your motherboard. The good news is that it is pretty difficult to make a mistake with these connectors. They are keyed so that they should only fit in the proper direction, and they are color coded for position. The most important color code is this: The two connectors line up alongside each other with black wires adjacent to each other. On most cables, the color order goes like this: orange, red, yellow, blue, black, black, black, black, white, red, red, and red. On most motherboards, these leads plug into a connector near the keyboard port at the back end of the board.

Some of the really good news associated with the introduction of ATX form factor motherboards is the use of a single power connector. It's a lot easier to power up the board, and you have no chance of erroneously swapping P8 and P9.

Next, connect the power indicator, turbo, reset, and hard drive light connectors to pins on the motherboard indicated in the manual that accompanies it. The pins are usually marked with numbers or labels printed directly on the motherboard. Pay special attention to the polarity of the plugs you install; the instruction manual usually indicates the color of wire for each pin or whether a particular pin is + or – voltage. In general, power supply wires are as follows: Red or yellow are positive, blue or white are negative, and black is ground.

5. Install the CPU and RAM. If the microprocessor and memory are not already on the motherboard, you need to install them now. If I have room to work inside the case, I prefer to perform this step at this stage of the installation; if your case is very crowded, you might want to put the CPU and memory in place before installing the motherboard. Either way, take care not to damage the somewhat delicate

pins on the CPU and be sure to take appropriate antistatic precautions.

Read the instruction manual for your motherboard carefully to determine memory options; some boards require banks to be filled in matched pairs, while others may not work with certain types of memory such as EDO. If you want to reuse memory SIMMs from the original motherboard, be sure they are appropriate for the new board.

 CROSS-REFERENCE

I discuss ways to adapt certain older-style memory carriers to some new boards in Chapter 8.

On most high-speed CPUs, beginning with late-model 486s and continuing through the Pentium, Celeron, and Athlon families, you need to connect a CPU fan to the power supply to help remove the heat produced by the microprocessor. In our state-of-the-art demonstration system in Chapter 6, the CPU sits within a wind tunnel-like enclosure that is cooled by a large fan mounted on the rear panel of the case.

6. Install add-in cards. Reinstall expansion cards into appropriate slots on the motherboard. If you are upgrading to a motherboard with a different slot design, make sure your old cards fit into the new board. Some full-size dinosaur-era PC cards are too large to fit in the 8/16-bit ISA slots on an AT motherboard. Some cards are wider than others, and you need to give some thought to which cards can safely sit next to each other. Cards that include a daughter card, for example, are considerably thicker than cards without this extra circuitry. A disk controller card may not be all that thick itself, but it requires that one or more ribbon cables connect to it. If you place two wide cards or two cards with side-mounting cables side by side it may be difficult to get everything to fit. Just look at the cards that need to reside next to each other and separate the ones that need more than normal space.

And just to make things interesting, most ISA 16-bit cards have their components on the opposite side of those on PCI cards. The place where ISA and PCI come together on the motherboard can be a very crowded neighborhood.

7. **Reinstall drive cages if you have removed them.** Reattach power connections to hard drives and floppy drives if you disconnected them.

8. **Attach data cables.** If your system's hard drive, floppy drive, and CD-ROM drive connect to an EIDE port on the motherboard, you need to attach those cables so that they can communicate with the bus. If the drives connect to an adapter card instead, you probably didn't remove the cables during the installation of the motherboard.

9. **Double-check everything.** Take a few moments to check the inside of the case once more. Look for any unattached cables. There are likely to be a few extra power leads from the power supply, but indicator lights, speakers, and other such elements of the motherboard should all be attached.

10. **Attach external components.** Plug in the keyboard, mouse, and video display.

    Turn on the system. Plug in the computer and turn it on. If you've done everything correctly, your system will display the new motherboard's CMOS setup screen where you can inform it about the elements of your computer. Consult the instruction manual for your motherboard to understand the specifics of your ROM BIOS.

11. **Check out the system under power.** Careful readers will notice that I haven't asked you to put the cover on yet. Shine a powerful light on your system and study the innards for a moment. Are all the fans spinning? Do you hear any unusual sounds, such as wires touching fans or components vibrating in place? Do you see curls of smoke? I hope not.

12. **Turn off the machine, remove the power cord, and connect cables to external devices once again.** Assuming that the system is running properly, replace the cover carefully. Although it is fine to run the machine for a short period of time without the cover on, you need to replace the cover once it is ready to run to avoid damage from dirt and improper cooling and to avoid radio frequency interference to radios, televisions, and other electronic devices.

What if the new motherboard doesn't run?

Stop, look, and listen: You don't want to see smoke or sparks, and you want to hear a power supply fan and the correct audio tones from the speaker. If anything looks or sounds wrong, turn off the computer.

There's not much else to do except to reverse all the installation steps and check and double-check everything you've done. Here are some common reasons why a new motherboard may not work:

- CPU not oriented properly in socket
- Improper settings on switches or jumpers
- Keyboard and mouse cables reversed
- Memory modules not properly seated in slots
- Power supply not properly connected to the board
- Traces on bottom of motherboard shorting out to case

Of course, it is also possible that you have received a bad motherboard, although dead-on-arrival boards are much less likely in these days of modern devices. Once again, though, this is a time when you will be very thankful to be dealing with a reputable vendor who offers technical assistance and/or replacement if necessary.

Working with Expansion Cards

In this section, you learn how to remove and install an expansion card.

CROSS-REFERENCE

I discuss how to remove the system cover in Chapter 1; review that section if you need to.

WARNING

Be sure to turn off the power and remove the power cord before going under the cover. And I recommend using a grounding strap or grounding pad.

Removing an expansion card

An expansion card becomes part of the computer through the bottom connector that plugs into the system-bus expansion slots on the motherboard. The connector picks up electrical power and ties into data and communication lines through the slot.

On most systems, the card is held firmly in its slot by a bracket that attaches to the back wall of the system unit chassis with a single screw. That same bracket may also hold serial, parallel, video, mouse, SCSI, telephone, or other ports. In dinosaurs and some modern machines, the other end of the card slips into a plastic groove that holds it in place laterally; high-density integration has enabled modern expansion cards to become smaller and smaller, and today few cards extend all the way across the length or width of a motherboard.

On some modern machines, like the state-of-the-art model I examine in Chapter 6, the entire group of cards is held in place by a single arm that closes over the top of the devices and locks into place.

To remove an expansion card, begin by disconnecting any external cables connected to the port at the back of the computer. Next, take out the screw that attaches the card to the system unit chassis and set it aside in a safe place. Some people like to work with magnetized screwdrivers to help hold onto the screw; this is a good idea in theory, so long as you take care not to lay the screwdriver down on a floppy or hard disk drive. The magnetic power of the screwdriver is relatively low, but magnetism is the enemy of data stored on a disk.

Removing these cards doesn't take much force, but watch your fingers—the card bristles with prickly solder blobs and little metal legs. Put your fingers in comfortable places before lifting.

It's also helpful to rock the card back and forth slightly from end to end—not side to side—to dislodge it from the slot.

Installing a new card to replace a bad card

Most of the time, the replacement card looks a lot like the card you take out of the system. Unless you are upgrading the machine with an adapter of greater functionality, you replace an 8-bit video card with another 8-bit video card, a 32-bit PCI card with another of the same standard, and so forth. Compare the bus connectors on the two cards. If they are the same, just slide the new card into the old card's expansion slot.

Carefully line up the card edge connector with the slot on the motherboard. If the card has external connectors for ports on the back, you may have to angle the card slightly to come under the lip of the PC chassis before you position it above the slots. Also, the bottom of the bracket may need to fit into a slot or past a metal lip that you can't see. Work gently. When the card is properly positioned over the slot, press down firmly, applying even pressure at front and back.

When the card is in place, the screw hole on the card lines up with the screw hole in the back of the chassis. Check the bottom of the card where it goes into the bus connector to make sure the card is fully inserted. Then reinstall the screw and test the machine. (If your machine uses a locking bracket, carefully lower it into place to hold the cards.)

If the bus connectors are not the same, consult the instruction manual or speak with the manufacturer to be certain the device is compatible with your system. SCSI host adapter cards, for example, are available in versions with 8-bit, 16-bit, EISA, and PCI edge connectors. Video cards, as another example, began as 8-bit ISA adapters, moved on to 16-bit PCI devices, and new adapters are mostly offered to fit the specialized AGP slot on modern motherboards.

Ch
5

Some computers have slots that can accommodate more than one kind of bus connector. ISA machines, for example, can usually handle 8-bit as well as 16-bit cards. Today's modern machines often support PCI, a few ISA, and a single AGP slot; some older modern motherboards augmented PCI slots with VL and less frequently, EISA slots. Consult your instruction manual or call the manufacturer if you have any doubts about the capabilities of specific slots.

Did you ever carry an air conditioner into the house, set it up carefully in the window, and then find out that the plug won't fit the electric outlet? Perhaps the air conditioner is looking for 220 volts, while the outlet is an ordinary 110-volt line.

PC expansion cards, like electric appliances, plug right in when the card edge connector matches the motherboard-bus connector. When the connectors don't match, no action takes place.

Here are some tips for choosing the slot for installing the new card:

Modern machines

- PCI cards will only work in the PCI bus.
- AGP adapters can only be installed in an AGP slot.
- If you have an ISA 16-bit expansion card, it will fit in either an AT-style ISA computer or an EISA computer.

Senior citizen and dinosaur machines

- VL and PCI bus designs are generally paired with a separate ISA bus. This enables you to use any ISA cards you want, reserving special high-speed adapters for the VL and PCI slots with their extra connectors.
- EISA cards fit only in EISA motherboards, though ordinary 8-bit and 16-bit cards will fit in EISA motherboard connectors.
- MCA cards fit in high-end PS/2 computers with the relatively obscure MCA bus. Use only MCA cards in MCA computers; nothing else fits.

- If you are installing an 8-bit card with the short, single bus connector, any bus expansion slot in any of the clones will do. These 8-bit cards fit in XT clones, in 286/386/486/Pentium ISA computers, and in EISA computers. Don't worry about long versus short slots; if the board physically fits into the slot, it will work.

To install your new card, follow these steps:

1. **Remove the slot cover at the back of the chassis that covers the exterior opening for an unused slot; on most machines this requires you to remove a screw, although some newer systems have slot covers that are held in place by friction and are merely pulled up and out.** The slot covers are slender metal strips (usually three-quarters of an inch wide) at the back of the chassis. (The slot covers are part of your PC's defense against the leakage of RF radiation that can interfere with radio, television, and other signals in your home or office.) You'll see one slot cover for each unused expansion slot; the bracket of the new card replaces the cover.

2. **Remove the cover for the slot you want to use and save the screw if your system uses one.** Put that cover away in your computer toolkit; you'll want to put it back into place if you ever remove a card from the bus and don't replace it.

3. **Line up the card with a motherboard expansion slot and the empty slot cover.** If the card has external connectors for ports on the back, you may have to angle the card slightly to come under the lip of the PC chassis before you position it above the slots. Also, the bottom of the bracket may need to fit into a slot or past a metal lip that you can't see. Work gently. When the card is properly positioned over the slot, press down firmly, applying even pressure at front and back. When it bottoms out and the screw hole on the card lines up with the screw hole on the chassis, reinstall the screw or replace the locking bracket used by some newer machines.

NOTE

Note that some slim-line PC designs call for adapter cards to be installed sideways into a riser card that comes up from the motherboard. The same principles apply to the use of a riser card, except that you will be pushing in toward the center of the riser card instead of down to the motherboard itself. Sometimes it is easier to remove the riser board and install the cards, and then reinstall the riser.

Similarly, PCs using tower cases have the motherboard mounted vertically. With a tower case, it may be easier to turn the PC on its side to remove and install adapter cards.

4. **The final step after installation is to attach any necessary external cables to the port on the back of any new card.**

Plug-and-Play

One of the most intriguing features of Windows 95/98 and later is the Plug-and-Play specification. In theory, Plug-and-Play enables Windows to reach out and interrogate every piece of hardware within and without the system to determine its presence and its need of interrupts, DMA channels, port settings, and other elements of the PC.

Plug-and-Play works through the use of BIOS chips on hardware and a huge list of devices maintained by Windows. In theory, when you turn on your PC, Windows knows everything it needs to know about your system and is able to manage devices so that they do not conflict with each other.

By the way, this is one feature that Apple's Macintosh has had for years. Before you let an Apple fan rant and rave about the supposed superiority of that system, remember that Apple was able to enforce its will because it was a closed architecture. Manufacturers were forced to comply with Apple's directives, which resulted in higher prices and limits on device availability. The open PC architecture, like most democracies, presented a wild, disorganized, and lively marketplace.

Sometime between now and forever, all the elements of your PC may conform to the Plug-and-Play specification, and all will be well with the world. In the meantime, you can expect to have a mix of Plug-and-Play and old-style devices in your machine and on the market for years to come. Users will still have to configure non-Plug-and-Play devices manually and may even run into some conflicts with automatically set devices.

Each branch of the PC family uses slightly different techniques to tell the computer what parts are installed.

PCI machines

Nearly every modern machine with a PCI bus uses a BIOS that allows the user to make system settings on a configuration screen.

On most machines, the bootup sequence displays a message to remind users how to load the Setup screen. Common choices include the Del key, F1, or a key combination such as Ctrl + Esc. If you are unsure of the necessary procedure, consult the instruction manual for your PC.

Most users will only make changes to the basic screen of Setup; be sure to read the instruction manual and consult help screens for assistance. I would suggest you make notes on any changes you make to the Setup so that you can undo them if they cause problems.

You also need to understand the method your particular style of Setup screen uses to record changes you have made. Some require you to press Esc and then a function key; others have a menu option to select to save changes. Be sure you understand the process or your changes may not be recorded.

ISA machines

Modern machines with an ISA bus may use a setup screen, a setup program run from a special floppy disk, DIP switches on the motherboard, or a combination of one or more of these means.

Ch
5

Early ATs and AT clones used a separate system setup disk. Running the system configuration software program (often called SETUP) let the user edit the list of drives, memory type, display type, and so on in the CMOS chip. Because the CMOS chip is backed up with batteries, it remembers what hardware is installed in the computer, even when the power is off.

Several problems occurred when putting the setup program on the floppy disk. First of all, the disk could become lost or damaged. Second, the disk was useless if the setting that enabled the computer to recognize the presence of a floppy disk drive was damaged. The next step in the development of PC systems, then, was to put the setup program right into the ROM BIOS.

Before you make any changes to the setup screen, make a copy of the settings and place it in the instruction manual for your computer. Some setup programs let you print the settings to a file that you can edit within a word processor, or print settings directly to an attached printer. If you can't obtain such an automatic copy, use a pen and piece of paper for the task.

Take care with the entries you make in the setup program; you shouldn't be able to damage your computer with a software setting, but some instructions could make things difficult. Pay special attention to the hard drive setting; enter the wrong hard disk type, and your hard disk and all its data will seem to disappear. It's still there somewhere, so don't panic — you have to correct the setting before the system can find the drive and its contents.

When in doubt, check your computer's instruction manual or call the manufacturer for more details on setup settings.

Running an EISA configuration utility

Because EISA computers are compatible with ISA computers, most EISA PCs require you to run the standard ISA setup routine that I've already described whenever you add hardware devices to your EISA computer. Once you do that, you must also run an EISA configuration utility.

EISA configuration utility (ECU) instructions come with all EISA computers. After installing a card, run the ECU, copy the EISA card configuration file for your new card into your computer, and then use the ECU to configure your computer. EISA computers use these card configuration files to manage the expansion cards in your computer.

ISA cards (the 8-bit and 16-bit AT-style cards) use jumpers and switches. An ISA computer doesn't manage the card for you — you have to do it yourself.

What do I mean by manage the card? Expansion cards use resources, much as automobiles in a parking lot take up space. If owners self-park their cars, each owner must cruise until he or she finds a free space. In a lot with valet parking, the owners can rely on attendants to arrange the cars efficiently. Think of EISA as valet parking. Once the EISA computer knows what resources (space) your expansion card requires, it shuffles the assigned spaces for the cards, parking them here or there, until it finds a free space for all of them. To do this, though, EISA must know each card's vital statistics. That's where the EISA configuration file comes in.

EISA cards come with an EISA configuration file disk. In addition, most EISA computer vendors provide a generic configuration file for ISA cards. On some EISA computers, you don't have to inform the system about the presence of ISA cards, and therefore won't have to use this generic ISA file. Other EISA computers make it mandatory. In either case, ISA cards are not as convenient as EISA cards because you may have to remove the computer cover and reset the jumpers on the ISA card if you want to change the resources it uses.

On the other hand, ISA cards are much cheaper than EISA cards. Network servers often need high-speed EISA network cards and hard disk adapter cards, but ordinary workstations often run just fine with the ISA versions.

Using the boot reference disk on a PS/2 computer with MCA

The Micro Channel Architecture (MCA) is off by itself, completely incompatible with ISA and EISA architecture. IBM developed the MCA and used it in many, but not all, IBM PS/2 computers.

PS/2 computers with the Micro Channel bus use a boot reference disk to load and edit the configuration information for your computer. The reference disk is self-booting. Simply put it in the A: drive and reboot the computer with Ctrl + Alt + Del (that means hold down the Ctrl and Alt keys, then press the Del key once, and then release all three keys). You should ask the boot disk to reconfigure the computer automatically whenever you add a new piece of hardware to an MCA computer. Some new expansion boards require a special configuration file, which is shipped on a disk with the new board. Just follow the instructions that come with the board.

In PS/2s, the configuration is backed up with a lithium battery. Because the chips forget this configuration information slowly, you can replace the lithium battery without losing the configuration information if you do it quickly. In an emergency, you may be able to cause the system to lose its configuration information, such as when you have installed a password and can't remember it. You can try to leave the lithium battery disconnected for at least 20 minutes and then reconfigure the computer with the reference disk.

Dinosaur XT and XT clones

XT-style computers are the least flexible. XTs look at the settings on switches on the motherboard for an inventory of hardware devices — elements such as floppy drives, memory, and video. The motherboard has a switch to set if you have installed an 8087 math coprocessor chip.

Set the switches according to the instructions shipped with the motherboard. If the maker of your machine is still in business, you may be able to obtain information from technical support.

Table 5-6 is a generic listing of switch settings based on the original IBM PC-XT. Remember, though, not all clone makers designed these same generic switch settings into their XT motherboards. The wrong settings won't blow up the computer, but it won't work right either.

TABLE 5-6: Typical XT Switch Settings

Switch	Typical Setting
Switch 1	Normally OFF
Switch 2	OFF = 8087 math coprocessor installed ON = No math coprocessor installed
Switches 3 and 4	Indicate the amount of memory installed on the motherboard. This is an area where one motherboard can differ greatly from another. Consult the motherboard maker. You may be able to obtain help from a memory chip vendor, although few companies still sell the antique 16K and 64K RAM chips that were used on early machines.
Switches 5 and 6	Indicate the video display. 5 ON, 6 ON = CGA color, with 80 characters per line 5 OFF, 6 ON = CGA color, with 40 characters per line 5 OFF, 6 OFF = Monochrome adapter
Switches 7 and 8	Indicate number of floppy drives installed. Note that XTs work only with double-density 5.25-inch floppy drives. 7 ON, 8 ON = 1 floppy 7 OFF, 8 ON = 2 floppies 7 ON, 8 OFF = 3 floppies (!) 7 OFF, 8 OFF = 4 floppies (!)

Ch 5

Look for a bank of eight switches in a row on the motherboard. They will be either rocker switches or slide switches. The switches may be marked ON and OFF, CLOSED and OPEN, or sometimes 1 and 0. ON, CLOSED, and 1 all mean that the switch is closed, which in electrical terms means it is on. OFF, OPEN, and 0 mean that the switch is open and therefore disabled.

You will need a ballpoint pen, a toothpick, or a tiny screwdriver to change the switches. Set rocker switches by pressing the rocker down on the side of the switch you want; for example, press down on the OFF side of switch 1 to turn the switch off.

Slide switches are moved laterally toward the setting you want to use.

Power Supplies

The power supply is a transformer that changes 115 volts of AC (alternating current) from the power line into 3.3, 5, and 12 volts of DC (direct current) for the components of the computer.

You have three important issues to consider when you buy a power supply: selecting the proper capacity, getting a good quality unit, and finding the proper shape and size for your case. Make sure to measure your power supply before ordering a replacement.

There are four styles in common use for current machines: MicroATX, AT, ATX, and SFX. Dinosaurs used a variety of large power supply designs; the most common dinosaur style is classified as the PC/XT design.

The power supply is inside the computer case and easy enough to find — just look for a big shiny or black box with a fan and a power plug coming out the back. To remove a power supply, start by unplugging it from the wall and then disconnect each of the power connectors from the supply to the motherboard and internal devices. You might want to label each connector as you remove it to help when you install a new power supply. In most computer designs, the power supply is attached to the case by four screws that come through the rear panel. On some PCs,

especially compact desktop units, you may need to remove some adapter cards or device cages to gain access to the power supply.

Modern PCs use an ATX design power supply, with a dual-row motherboard power connector. ATX supplies are turned on and off by a low-voltage signal from the motherboard that is connected to a button on the case.

Dinosaur PCs used a larger AT power supply which attached to the motherboard with two single-row power connectors. They include a line voltage cable that connects to a heavy-duty, on-off switch on the case or to a switch built into the power supply itself.

Nearly all PCs use off-the-shelf power supplies that can be replaced easily; a handful of models, though, use specially designed supplies that have to be ordered directly from the manufacturer or a parts warehouse.

The current crop of high-speed CPUs in the Intel Pentium 4 and AMD Athlon and Duron class require more power than ever before.

Both CPU manufacturers now require that power supplies deliver at least 18 to 20 amps on the 5V line.

If you are purchasing a replacement power supply for a high-end machine, make sure it is certified to work with the fastest CPUs.

Following is a description of the most common power supplies in use in modern machines. A small number of PCs use power supplies of an unusual design or specification; to replace them you will have to contact the PC's manufacturer or search for components from specialty suppliers. The following are current power supply designs:

- **AT:** full-size units, used from about 1991 to 1999. Power was delivered to the motherboard with two six-pin connectors. Dimension: 8.35 × 5.9 × 5.9 inches.
- **AT:** slim-size units, used from about 1994 to 1999. Power was delivered to the motherboard with two six-pin connectors. Dimensions: 5.9 × 5.5 × 3.4 inches.
- **ATX:** introduced in 1997. Power is delivered to the motherboard through a single 20-pin connector. Dimensions: 5.9 × 5.5 × 3.4 inches.

■ **SFX:** introduced in 1999 for some low-profile and all-in-one systems. Power is delivered to the motherboard through a single 20-pin connector. Versions include ones with AC receptacle on the short side (more common) as well as on the long side (used by manufacturers including Hewlett Packard and eMachines for some of their models.) Dimensions: 3.9 × 4.9 × 3.0 inches.

How the power supply works

The power supply has a very simple job: to provide clean, smooth power at +12 volts DC, –12 volts DC, +5 volts DC, –5 volts DC, and for some modern machines, a source of +3.3 volts DC.

It monitors its own power output on startup and sends a power-good signal to the motherboard when the voltages have stabilized at their required levels. The microprocessor resets, and bootup starts when the motherboard receives this signal.

The flow of electricity is measured in watts. Power supplies are rated by the wattage they support—the higher the wattage, the more peripherals the unit can support.

Modern machines typically have a power supply rated at least 200 watts, with 250- and 300- or even 400-watt units increasingly common. You may also come across some slimline computers that are seriously underpowered, not capable of supporting internal CD-ROMs and multiple hard drives.

WARNING

The electronics inside the power supply are not reparable by amateurs and are usually not worth the expense of a professional repair. A new power supply usually sells for $25 to $50. Do not open the power supply itself.

Modern machines can work with an astonishing variety of devices, and you may find that you have run out of power connectors running off the power supply. Assuming you have enough available power—add up the wattage demands of peripherals and be sure to leave an unclaimed overhead of about 30 watts to handle startup power for hard drives and CD-ROMs—you can use a power cable splitter that connects to a power lead at one end and branches into two available connectors.

Dinosaur PCs had power supplies as small as 65 watts. Modern machines have as much as 400 watts in a typical configuration.

The biggest power draw for a PC is almost always the monitor; a typical 17- or 19-inch screen draws about 100 to 150 watts, about the same as a lightbulb. The power for the display screen does not come from the power supply inside the computer case, however. Display monitors have their own, internal power supplies.

Within the PC itself, a typical CPU demands as little as 10 or 20 watts and as much as 45 or 50 watts, depending on its speed and design. A typical high-speed hard drive or CD-ROM uses 10 to 25 watts when it is in full operation, and less when it is powered-on but is not being accessed. Other plug-in devices, like internal modems and adapters, may ask for 5 to 10 watts apiece. A large bank of RAM may need about that much power as well. A sampling of the power demands of common PC components is in Table 5-7.

Depending on its components, a typical modern machine may draw a total of 150 to 200 watts; high-end machines with fast processors, 256 MB of memory, several drives, and other devices may draw as much as 400 watts.

Your electric company charges on the basis of kilowatt hours, a measurement equal to 1,000 watts over the course of an hour. Rates vary around the country, and bills include a number of components including generation, transmission, distribution, and taxes. To obtain a rough idea of your average cost per kilowatt, divide your total monthly bill by the number of kilowatt hours used that month.

In my office, electricity costs in early 2002 worked out to about 16 cents per kilowatt hour. That means it costs 16 cents to keep ten hundred-watt light bulbs lit for an hour, or about 8 cents to run one of my computers and a monitor for the same period.

Ch
5

That sounds like a great bargain, and it probably is, but the pennies can add up quickly. I figure my main computer draws just under a kilowatt hour each hour it is in use — for the PC, a large monitor, a laser printer, lighting, and necessary musical accompaniment. That's about 16 cents per hour. The machines are on at least ten hours a day, an average of six days a week: that's just under $10 per week, or about $500 per year for electricity. Consider that a high-end new PC sells for about $1,000 and you'll see you are spending a good portion of the cost of a PC for power.

Most modern PCs support Advanced Power Management (APM) or the Advanced Configuration and Power Interface (ACPI). Check the instruction manual for your PC to learn about settings that allow you to manage the power use of your machine.

The biggest possible savings is a setting that powers your monitor down after a reasonable period of inactivity; the monitor can come back to life in a few seconds but in the meantime you can save a few kilowatt hours each week during your coffee breaks, lunch, and meetings.

A "switching" power supply only draws what is needed. If your PC needs 250 watts, a 400-watt switching power supply will only deliver what is needed.

Be sure your system has a power supply with a reasonable amount of overhead beyond your expected needs. Not only is this insurance against power problems, but in general a larger power supply delivering less than its full potential will run cooler and more efficiently than a smaller power supply that is fully taxed.

TABLE 5-7: Power Demands of PC Parts

Component	Wattage	Lines Used
Motherboard (without CPU or RAM)	20 to 30	+3.3V and +5V
CPUs (higher speed generally are higher draw)	10 to 70	+5V or +12V
RAM	7 to 10 per 128 MB	+3.3V
Typical PCI adapter card	5	+5V
High-wattage AGP graphics card	20 to 50	+3.3V
SCSI controller PCI card with cache	20 to 25	+3.3V and +5V
Ethernet 10/100 NIC	4	+5V
Ultra2 SCSI PCI card	5	+3.3V and +5V
Floppy drive	5	+5V
IDE CD-ROM (higher speeds generally are higher draw)	10 to 25	+5V and +12V
SCSI CD-R/RW	10 to 17	+5V and +12V
SCSI CD-ROM	12	+5V and +12V
5200 rpm IDE hard drive	5 to 11	+5V and +12V
7200 rpm IDE hard drive	5 to 15	+5V and +12V
7200 rpm Ultra2 SCSI hard drive	24	+5V and +12V
10,000 rpm SCSI hard drive	10 to 40	+5V and +12V

Experts recommend a power supply capable of delivering 150 percent of your expected need.

Check the specifications for any device you have installed in your machine. Most list the number of watts they require. You may see some devices that tell you amperage and voltage requirements instead; to convert to watts, multiply the voltage by the amps.

ATX power supplies

Standard assignments for the various connectors of an ATX power supply are shown in Tables 5-8 through 5-12. Actual wire colors may vary slightly, but the pin assignments are fixed.

The ATX specification added 3.3-volt output to the demands on the power supply. The connection to the motherboard uses a single 20-pin connector. A typical power supply, like the one shown in Figure 5-13, also includes six peripheral power connectors, two floppy drive connectors, one auxiliary power connector, and one 12-volt connector.

TABLE 5-8: Connector to Motherboard Wire Assignments from ATX Power Supply

Pin	Wire Color	Function	Pin	Wire Color	Function
1	Orange	+3.3V DC	11	Orange	+3.3V DC
2	Orange	+3.3V DC	12	Brown	−12V DC
3	Black	Ground	13	Black	Ground
4	Red	+5V DC	14	Green	PS On for remote start
5	Black	Ground	15	Black	Ground
6	Red	+5V DC	16	Black	Ground
7	Black	Ground	17	Black	Ground
8	White	Power Good	18	Blue	−5V DC
9	Purple	+5VSB	19	Red	+5V DC
10	Yellow	+12V DC	20	Red	+5V DC

Note: Connector is MOLEX 39-01-2200 or equivalent.

TABLE 5-9: Peripheral Connectors from ATX Power Supply

Pin	Wire Color	Function
1	Yellow	+12V DC
2	Black	Ground
3	Black	Ground
4	Red	+5V DC

Note: Connector is AMP 1-480424-0 or equivalent.

TABLE 5-10: Floppy Drive Connectors from ATX Power Supply

Pin	Wire Color	Function
1	Red	+5V DC
2	Black	Ground
3	Black	Ground
4	Yellow	+12V DC

Note: Connector is AMP 171822-4 or equivalent.

TABLE 5-11: Auxiliary Power Connectors from ATX Power Supply

Pin	Wire Color	Function
1	Red	+5V DC
2	Black	Ground
3	Black	Ground
4	Yellow	+12V DC

Note: Connector is MOLEX 90331-0010 or equivalent.

TABLE 5-12: 12V Power Connector from ATX Power Supply

Pin	Wire Color	Function
1	Black	Ground
2	Black	Ground
3	Yellow	+12V DC
4	Yellow	+12V DC

Note: Connector is MOLEX 39-29-9042 or equivalent.

Ch 5

FIGURE 5-13: *An ATX form factor power supply.*

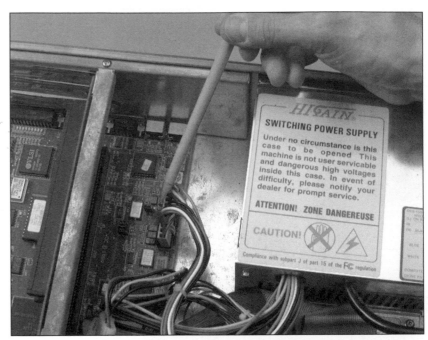

FIGURE 5-14: *On many motherboards, a pair of power supply connectors, marked P8 and P9, provide all the power for the CPU, logic chips, and devices plugged into the bus.*

AT power supplies

PC/XT and AT power supplies have two large six-pin power connectors marked P8 and P9, shown in Figure 5-14, that send voltage to the motherboard. On most such systems, the two connectors attach to a single attachment point, with the black wires on each connector next to each other. There are also five or six smaller connectors that are intended for internal devices such as floppy, hard, and CD-ROM drives. The larger power connectors (see Figures 5-15 and 5-16) are generally used by hard drives and CD-ROMs, and the miniplugs are used by 3.5-inch floppy drives. No matter what the size of the connector, the voltage level and type are the same.

If you find a mismatch between power connector and receptacle, you can purchase converter plugs that change a large connector to a small one, as shown in Figure 5-17.

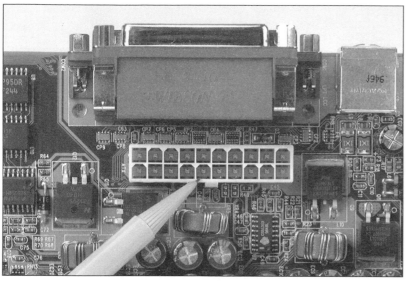

FIGURE 5-15: *On ATX form motherboards, a single ATX Power connector links the board to the power supply.*

FIGURE 5-16: *A four-wire power supply connector has beveled edges that keep it properly oriented. The yellow wire is +12 volts, the two black wires are ground, and the red wire is +5 volts.*

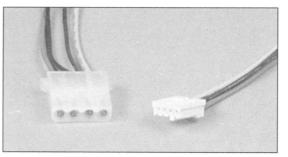

FIGURE 5-17: *Some dinosaurs and other machines may need an adapter to convert a standard power lead to work with a 3.5-inch floppy drive or other modern device that requires the new, miniaturized plug.*

Similarly, you can connect more than one device to a single power cable with the use of a Y-splitter, such as the one shown in Figure 5-18.

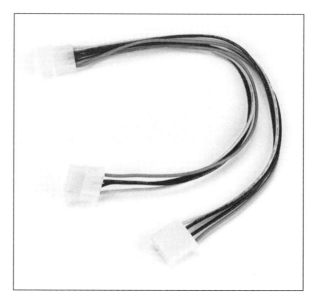

FIGURE 5-18: *A Y-splitter lets you send electricity to two devices using a single lead from the power supply.*

Ch 5

Another power-cable variant splits off a miniconnector to power a small device such as a CPU fan. An example is shown in Figure 5-19.

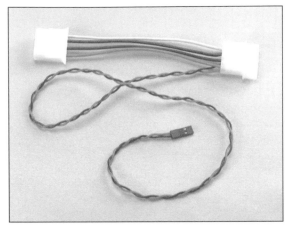

FIGURE 5-19: *This power cable includes a split-off to power a small electrical device such as a fan or power-on indicator light.*

Tables 5-13, 5-14, and 5-15 list the assignments for the wires from a standard AT power supply.

TABLE 5-13: Device Connector Wire Assignments for AT Power Supply

Pin	Wire Color	Function
1	Yellow	+12V DC
2	Black	Ground
3	Black	Ground
4	Red	+5V DC

TABLE 5-14: P8 Connector to Motherboard Wire Assignments for AT Power Supply

Pin	Wire Color	Function
1	Orange or White	Power good signal
2	Red	+5V DC
3	Yellow	+12V DC
4	Blue or Brown	−12V DC
5	Black	Ground
6	Black	Ground

TABLE 5-15: P9 Connector to Motherboard Wire Assignments for AT Power Supply

Pin	Wire Color	Function
1	Black	Ground
2	Black	Ground
3	Blue or White	−5V DC
4	Red	+5V DC
5	Red	+5V DC
6	Red	+5V DC

NOTE

An essential component of any PC system is a high-quality surge protector that stands between the computer and the wall outlet. The surge protector should meet Underwriters Laboratories' UL 1449 standard, with a rated response time of no more than 1 nanosecond. If you use an uninterruptible power supply, that unit should include surge protection as part of its design.

Testing the power supply

Loss of CMOS setup in modern machines is often caused by a bad power supply.

On a typical system, the CMOS chip requires at least 4.5 volts to hold the configuration setup information (date, time, and installed hardware) reliably. It is powered by batteries whenever the computer is turned off. When the 5-volt line climbs above 5 volts, or the power-good line to the motherboard is on, the CMOS battery backup disengages. If a defective power supply sends the power-good signal before the 5-volt line is high enough, the setup information is lost. Be sure to check the batteries first. They tend to wear out after a year of service. If you replace the batteries and run the CMOS setup routine, but the problem still remains, then you probably have a faulty power supply.

Power supplies are not serviceable in the field. Besides, replacements are cheap. If your power supply is not performing correctly, do not attempt to repair it—just throw it away. New power supplies range in price from about $25 to $50. Nearly all power supplies come from obscure Asian manufacturers; I'd pay more attention to the warranty claims of the store or mail-order house than to any brand name for the power supply.

You can easily test the voltages produced by your power supply with a handheld voltmeter. To do this, you must hook the power supply up to 115 volts and to a load of some kind—a disk drive or the motherboard will do. The four-wire connectors are identical, so you can use any one of them to test your power supply while it is hooked into the computer. This is probably the best way to test the power supply because it should perform properly when fully loaded with all add-on boards, drives, and other such devices. You're looking for +5, –5, +12, and –12 volts.

NOTE

If the DC voltages are low, consider the external circumstances before condemning the power supply. It's smart to test the AC line current. The minimum acceptable standard is 104 volts AC. If your power is marginal, I recommend you purchase an uninterruptible power supply or a power line conditioner.

Unfortunately, power supplies occasionally fail for only a microsecond, perhaps on bootup or during drive access. In addition, a defective unit may send the power-good signal prematurely, causing the microprocessor to reset while voltages are unstable. Premature reset can cause a problem in almost any part of the computer because random errors may be introduced any place in memory. If you turn the computer power switch off and on again, the same problem may recur, or a different one, or no problem at all, may occur. The ordinary voltmeter does not respond rapidly enough to catch a momentary dip or surge in power. In this case, substitute a known good power supply and retest the machine to confirm the bad power supply diagnosis.

Occasionally, one of the four-wire power connectors fails while the others remain functional. If you suspect a problem with one of the four-wire connectors—because disk drive B: doesn't function at all, for instance—you can try switching the suspect power connector with the known good one from the A: drive. If you establish a four-wire connector as the problem, you can try rewiring a new connector; don't go under the covers of the power supply, though.

Removing and replacing the power supply

Before you remove the power supply, unplug the 110-volt power cord and disconnect the four-wire power supply connectors from disk drives, tape drives, and other devices.

The motherboard receives power from a single long connector or from two multiwire connectors. Examine these connectors closely before removing them and place labels on them to help with reinstallation. They must be reinstalled properly. If you jam the connectors on backward and turn on the computer, you will damage the motherboard.

Typically, you remove four screws that hold the power supply to the back panel of the chassis. With some designs, you need to slide the power supply forward an inch or two to clear the lugs on the bottom of the case and lift it up out of the case.

To install a power supply, perform the steps in reverse order. Make sure you reinstall the power connectors on the motherboard correctly.

Cooling the System

It's a basic law of physics: The faster those electrons zip around within the microprocessor, the more heat they generate. The heat is caused by the friction between the electrical current and the pathways it travels.

The dinosaurs were poky enough so that the little heat they generated could be removed by the flow of air generated by a single fan at the back of the power supply. Air was drawn in through holes at the front of the case and exhausted at the rear.

That solution was good enough for CPUs running from the original 4.77 MHz through the approximate 66 MHz speed of the venerable 486DX2 senior citizen.

But with the arrival of microprocessors faster than 100 MHz, the buildup of heat threatened the life of the microprocessor and other components. There are three solutions to the heat buildup problem:

- Installation of a heat sink atop the CPU. This passive solution uses a vaned metallic device that draws heat up and away from the chip and into the air stream of the system's fan.

- Addition of a powered fan that sits atop the CPU. This fan draws heat away from the chip. In some cases, the fan is combined with a heat sink. Examples of CPU fans are shown in Figures 5-20, 5-21, and 5-22.

- Increased system cooling. Modern machine cases can include an additional fan at the front of the case as well as a rear-facing fan at the power supply and a chip-top fan.

FIGURE 5-20: *An external fan/heat sink attaches to the outside of the Pentium II/III SECC cartridge. On most motherboards, a supporting bracket is then connected from the cartridge to the motherboard to lock the CPU in place. An electrical connector powers the fan from a header on the motherboard.*

Your best defense against heat buildup is to select a properly designed case and to follow the chip manufacturer's recommendations on supplementary cooling.

FIGURE 5-21: *This Pentium 133 CPU uses a clip-on cooling fan.*

FIGURE 5-22: *On this modern Pentium 4 1.8GHz system, the CPU and its associated chipset sit beneath a massive heat sink that is in turn covered by a plastic sheath that leads to a fan that exhausts air out of the case.*

In one of the machines I built for my office, I added a SIIG DiskFan, shown in Figure 5-23. It installs in a 3.5-inch disk bay and exhausts air from the front midsection of the tower case.

Yet another type of cooling exhausts air through the rear of the computer. An example is SIIG's AirCooler Pro, a dual-exhaust slot fan shown in Figure 5-24. This device attaches to one of the brackets intended to hold an adapter card in the bus; a nonconductive plastic support holds the device in place while an electrical cable connects to the power supply within the case. The two fans on the AirCooler Pro can be extended a few inches into the case and their heads individually directed toward sources of heat; air is exhausted through holes in the bracket at the rear. (Of course, you do need to have an unused Industry Standard Architecture (ISA) or Peripheral Component Interconnect (PCI) slot to hold a fan like this.)

If you're a belt-and-suspenders type, you can add a third level of fan to most cases. Some designs come with brackets and vents on the front of the case enabling installation of a fan to supplement the device on the CPU itself and in the power supply. An example of a case of this design is shown in Figure 5-25.

Ch
5

FIGURE 5-23: *This fan installs in a 3.5-inch disk-drive bay to remove heat buildup from within the case; it receives power from a connector within. The manufacturer recommends installing the fan above the floppy and hard drives to draw off the rising heat from those devices.*

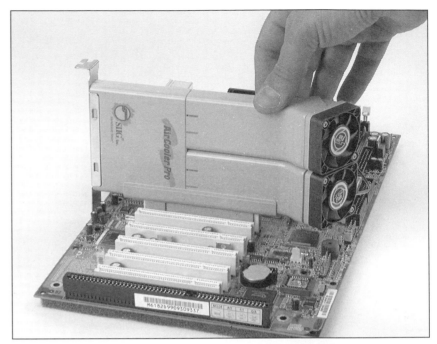

FIGURE 5-24: *The unusual AirCooler Pro's two fans can be aimed at sources of heat within the case; air is exhausted through the rear of the computer. The fan sits atop an ISA or PCI slot. You can also purchase simpler single-fan devices that also attach to slot brackets.*

If you choose to add another fan to the front of a case, be sure to purchase a quality device that won't add a lot of noise to the system. Any device at the front of the case is usually aimed at the user, and most PCs are already noisy enough. Figure 5-26 shows a lightweight and quiet brushless fan in a plastic housing.

Many current motherboards make use of the facilities of the latest Intel chipsets to monitor the condition of the hardware, including use of a thermistor to check internal temperature of the case and the microprocessor. The system can also control the speed of the chassis fan and other devices to increase cooling when necessary.

FIGURE 5-25: *The bare innards of a modern ATX mid-tower case. The thicket of power cords connects to the motherboard, drives, and other devices that will take up residence within. The capacious case includes bays for four 3.5-inch devices and three 5.25-inch devices. Note the opening for an additional cooling fan at the front of the case.*

FIGURE 5-26: *This exhaust fan mounts in available brackets at the front of some PC case designs. It draws power from any power connector.*

For older systems that lack such facilities, you can use separate temperature monitoring devices. One such device is PC Power and Cooling's 110 Alert, an inexpensive piece of equipment that sounds an alarm if the PC's internal temperature rises above 110 degrees Fahrenheit, or alerts you when your CPU fan falters. For information, consult `www.pcpowercooling.com`.

A Tale of Five Motherboards

Here's an up-close peak at five modern motherboards.

One is a modernized version of a relatively old standby, a fine replacement for a system built around a Pentium, AMD K5 or K6, or Cyrix 6x86MMX processor. It adds modern features including support for PC100, AGP video, and ATA/66 disk drives.

The second is a highly integrated modern motherboard for Pentium II/III and Celeron CPUs, with built-in AGP video, USB ports, and support for audio, modem, and multimedia daughter-boards that share system resources. It's a fine candidate for a low-cost speedy system.

The third is a state-of-the-art motherboard with a full range of customization options including an AGP slot, support for as many as eight IDE devices, and a menu-driven customization program for most of the settings of the board.

The fourth is a state-of-the-art Intel motherboard designed specifically for the Pentium 4 and RDRAM memory, along with AGP4X and USB 2.0 ports.

CROSS-REFERENCE

I discuss some of the features of a fifth motherboard in Chapter 6, as we take apart a modern machine to examine all of its critical parts.

Asus P5S-B Super7 motherboard for Pentium-class processors

The Asus P5S-B, shown in Figures 5-27 through 5-31, is a good candidate to replace an older and less advanced motherboard for Pentium-class CPUs and clones, including Intel Pentium, AMD K5, AMD K6, and IBM/Cyrix 6x86MMX processors. It brings AGP video, ATA/66 IDE connections, and PC100 memory support, all features that were not available when Pentium processors were first introduced.

FIGURE 5-27: *The Asus motherboard is a compact baby AT, about 9 by 10 inches in size. The zero insertion force Socket 7 includes a thermal sensor below the chip to monitor heat buildup. A flash upgradeable Award BIOS lies to the left of the PCI slots.*

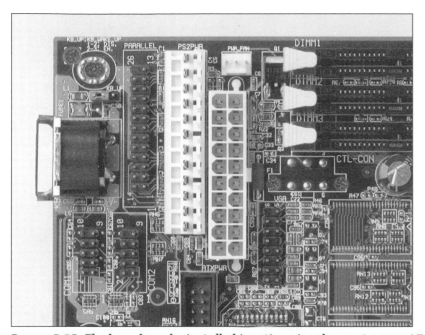

FIGURE 5-28: *The board can be installed in a tiny pizza box system, an AT case, or an ATX case. The AT and ATX cases use different specifications for power supplies and cables. The motherboard includes an old-form AT electrical connector alongside a newer ATX connector.*

FIGURE 5-29: *Beneath the heat sink on this board is an SiS AGPset, a chipset that includes an AGP 2X video adapter; it is set up to use shared system memory. An optional version of the motherboard includes 8MB of SDRAM as local graphics memory, freeing up system resources that would be taken by a shared memory video scheme.*

Ch
5

FIGURE 5-30: *There's a tight fit for cables to attach to the two IDE connectors that sit in the shadow to the right of the last two PCI slots.*

FIGURE 5-31: *To use a PS/2 mouse, USB, or infrared devices on the Asus P5S, you need to purchase and install an optional USB/MIR connector, which attaches to an 18-pin block on the motherboard.*

Micro-Star MS-6182 for Intel Pentium II/III and Celeron processors

The Micro-Star MS-6182, shown in Figures 5-32 through 5-37, is an example of a highly integrated motherboard based around Intel's 810 Integrated Graphics chipset, featuring a built-in graphics adapter and a sound chip with multimedia inputs and outputs. For many users, there's not much more to add to this board other than a CPU and memory.

FIGURE 5-32: *The Micro-Star MS-6182 includes most of the elements of a modern machine on the motherboard, including a graphics adapter and audio subsystem. The manager for the system is Intel's 810 chipset, visible in the top center under a large heat sink between Slot 1 for the CPU and the three DIMM slots for memory.*

FIGURE 5-33: *The MS-6182 motherboard includes a bank of four LEDs alongside the CPU that report the various startup phases of the motherboard in sequence. Each light can glow red or green, giving a total of 16 possible messages. If the system hangs up, you can examine lights to determine where the motherboard has run into trouble. This is a particularly valuable feature on a motherboard that is so highly integrated. If, for example, the onboard video subsystem fails, you should be able to install a plug-in card in the bus to work around the problem.*

The Intel 810 chipset includes three core components: the graphics and memory controller hub (GMCH), the I/O controller hub (ICHO/ICH), and the firmware hub (FWH).

The GMCH manages the system bus (66 or 100 MHz), a 100 MHz SDRAM controller, and a 2D/3D graphics accelerator.

The ICHO/ICH manages an Ultra ATA/33 and Ultra ATA/66 controller for disk drives, a USB host controller, and the PCI controller.

The FWH implements Intel's 82802 firmware hub for future security and management tasks.

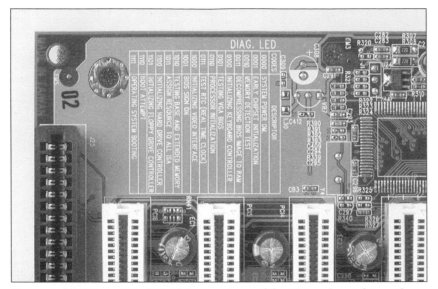

Figure 5-34: *Micro-Star lists the meanings of the LED codes right on the motherboard.*

Figure 5-35: *The 810 chipset on the MS-6182 supports Intel's definition for an audio/modem riser (AMR), intended to hold advanced audio daughterboards and modems that can link directly to the processor. The integrated Audio Codec '97 will enable developers to use the host processor for basic sound facilities. To the right of the AMR on Micro-Star's motherboard is another slot, the panel link/TV-out Interface designed to work with proprietary multimedia adapters. The Micro-Star motherboard is also available with a Creative Labs sound chip, which offers advanced features including wave-table audio; you can also plug a sound card into one of the PCI slots to expand beyond the basic facilities of the board as delivered.*

FIGURE 5-36: *The J2 overclocking jumper on the Micro-Star motherboard is set to detect automatically the proper bus frequency for the CPU. Changing the shorting blocks enables you to force the CPU to operate at 133 MHz, beyond the recommended speed. Many techies happily do so, but Intel and motherboard makers warn that overclocking could result in damage to the CPU and other components.*

FIGURE 5-37: *The ATX format motherboard includes a full suite of input and output ports. From the top to bottom, they include a stacked pair with a mouse connector above the keyboard port; two USB ports; a parallel port above a VGA video connector; and a multimedia panel with a midi/game port, line out, line in, and microphone connector. A set of pins on the opposite side of the board can be used to connect a cable that runs to a USB connector on the front of some PC cases.*

Ch
5

Abit BE6-II motherboard for Intel Pentium II, III, and Celeron processors

The Abit BE6-II, shown in Figures 5-38 through 5-43, is a high-end motherboard for users who want to customize their system. Built around Intel's 440BX chipset, it offers an AGP video slot, USB ports, five PCI and one ISA slot, and four IDE connectors.

Abit's BIOS includes CPU Soft Menu III, a technology that lets the user configure most of the board's settings from a menu instead of using pin blocks and switches on the motherboard. There are 120 different front-side bus settings for the CPU, for example, from 84 to 200 MHz. You can also ask the BIOS to make its own decisions on the best configuration.

FIGURE 5-39: *The Ultra ATA/66 chipset on the Abit BE6-II supports as many as eight IDE devices, four at ATA/66's 66.6 megabytes per second (MBps) speed and four at the previous ATA/33 standard. IDE3 and IDE4, the white connectors, use ATA/66; to their right are the black connectors for IDE1 and IDE2, which use the ATA/33 specification. Below IDE1 is the smaller connector for the floppy disk drive. The ATA/66 controller is designed for high-speed mass storage. In general, devices like CD-ROMs, Zip drives, and Superdrives should use the ATA/33 connectors. You need to add a driver for Ultra ATA/66 to Windows systems; the instruction manual gives details on how to update the hard disk driver.*

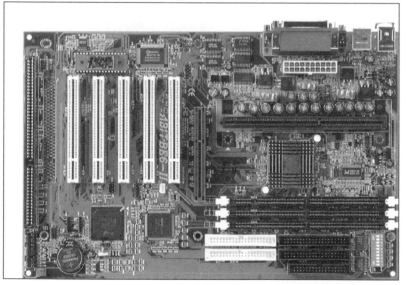

FIGURE 5-38: *The capable Abit BE6-II motherboard is neatly designed, offering more than the usual working space for installing cards and attaching cables. The 440BX chipset lies beneath a heat sink between the memory DIMM slots and Slot 1 for the CPU.*

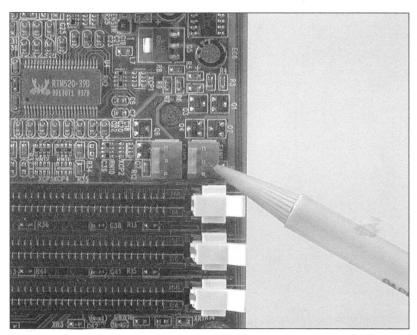

FIGURE 5-40: *Just above the memory DIMM slot on the Abit BE6-II is the header to provide power to the fan on the Pentium II/III or Celeron CPU. Alongside is a second fan header, and there is a third fan header at the front of the motherboard near the CMOS battery. High-speed processors and chipsets can benefit from additional cooling fans attached to components or on the case.*

FIGURE 5-41: *Advanced features on the Abit BE6-II include SB-LINK, Wake on Ring, and Wake on LAN; the headers for each are located, from left to right, below the PCI slots on this motherboard. SB-LINK, when used with a PCI audio adapter that supports this feature, serves as a bridge between the motherboard and the sound card to deliver high-end audio to real-mode DOS games. This solves one of the problems faced by the latest multimedia games that go around Windows to pick up the maximum speed directly from the hardware. If you have an internal modem adapter that supports Wake on Ring, attach a cable to the motherboard to enable the modem to wake up and start the computer when an incoming call arrives. Similarly, if you use a network adapter with a Wake on LAN feature, a cable attachment to the motherboard enables a message sent over the network to wake the computer. You also need a utility program like Intel LDCM.*

Ch
5

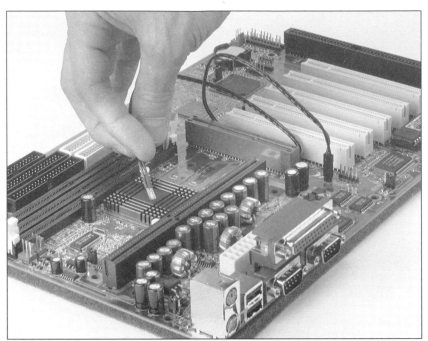

FIGURE 5-42: *The TSYS2 header, above the AGP slot to the right of the PCI slots on the Abit BE6-II, accepts a thermistor sensor cable that can be used to monitor the temperature at a particular location or device within the case.*

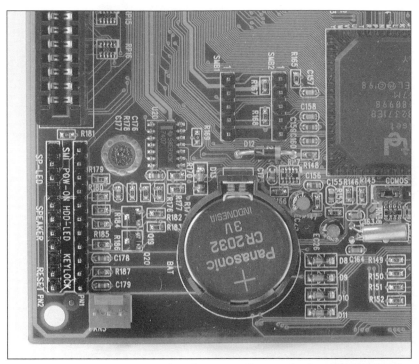

FIGURE 5-43: *The main interface between the motherboard and the front panel of the PC's case can be found at PN1 and PN2 at the front of the board, in this picture to the left of the backup battery. Note that the connectors lie at the end of the ISA slot; some older, extra-long ISA cards could make access to the pins difficult. In any case, you want to make attachments to the pins before installing any ISA or PCI cards on the board. PN1 makes connection to the three-wire power LED cable, plus two-wire cables for the keylock (if used on the case), the hard disk drive LED, power-on switch, and hardware-suspend switch. PN2 is the header for the two-wire hardware reset switch, the four-wire internal speaker cable, and a two-wire system suspend LED. Take care to install the cables with the proper orientation. The instruction manual shows + and – orientation for each wire.*

Ch 5

Intel D850MD motherboard for Pentium 4 with RDRAM memory

Intel's motherboards are, by definition, fully compatible with Intel's microprocessors. The D850MD board was designed as the third element of a matched set, along with the Pentium 4 processor and its supporting Intel 850 chipset.

This board is used by a number of PC manufacturers, including Dell Computer; you can read more about the board in the discussion of the Dell Pentium 4 1.8GHz system we examine in detail in Chapter 6.

The compact board, in the Micro ATX form factor, uses a 478 Pin Grid Array (PGA) socket for Pentium 4 CPUs running at 1.4GHz and faster. The AGP connector supports the 2X and 4X specifications for high-speed graphics cards. There are just three dedicated PCI connectors, each supporting bus-mastering. And there is one optional Communication and Networking Riser (CNR) connector.

Intel also offers a full-size ATX version of the board, with five PCI slots; in Dell's system, the company attaches a small daughterboard to the end of the mainboard to add two more PCI slots for a total of five.

The basic board, shown in Figure 5-44, is a neatly designed and tightly integrated device.

Intel's 850 chipset mates the Pentium 4's 3.2-gigabytes-per-second bus to 3.2-gigabytes-per-second of memory bandwidth using Dual RDRAM to eliminate memory bottlenecks that would have negatively impacted system efficiency. The two RDRAM channels support up to two RIMMs per channel, four RIMM sockets in total. The system can support memory configurations from a minimum of 128MB to a maximum of 2GB, utilizing 128 Mbit or 256 Mbit technology and PC600- and PC800-compliant RDRAM RIMMs.

FIGURE 5-44: *The Intel D850MD motherboard is a Micro ATX design. To the left of the three white PCI slots is a horizontal connector that can be used to extend to a daughterboard; in the Dimension 8200 computer we examine in Chapter 6, Dell adds two more PCI slots. The four RDRAM memory slots sit below the CPU socket; all four must be populated with RAM or with empty continuity modules.*

Other features include Intel Rapid BIOS Boot to accelerate the power on self test (POST), Ultra ATA/100 disk support, support for as many as seven USB ports, AC'97 integrated audio, and an optional Integrated Intel PRO/100 Network Connection. The 4MB flash Intel/AMI BIOS features Plug-and-Play, IDE drive auto-configuration, Advanced Power Management (APM) 1.2, ACPI 1.0, DMI 2.0, and Multilingual support.

The board sends signals to four diagnostic lights on the back of the computer; each light can be yellow, green, or off. The BIOS uses the lights to display ten diagnostic codes that report on the progress of the POST at bootup of the system.

Intel and other makers also produce similar boards based on the Intel 845 chipset, which works with conventional PC133 SDRAM. The 845 chipset, released in mid-2001, was a tacit acknowledgement by Intel that some buyers were resisting upgrading to the Pentium 4 because of its original linkage to RDRAM memory, which is more expensive than SDRAM and was somewhat problematic when it was first released.

Dinosaur Time: Clock Card

The original PC required the user to manually enter the time and date when the machine was first booted. That was succeeded by a system that used an adapter card called a clock card that provided the date and time of day to the system for use in the file management system. Single-purpose clock cards existed for only a short period; a bit later in the early days of the PC, clock functions were commonly part of multifunction cards that also included serial and parallel ports and game controllers.

Modern machines include a real-time clock function as part of the motherboard; consult your instruction manual for any information about batteries that may have to be changed every few years.

On a dinosaur, the clock card or multifunction card usually has a silver, disk-shaped battery about the size of a quarter. A few clock cards use a cylindrical battery about three-quarters of an inch long and half an inch in diameter. And a small number of cards used off-the-shelf AA or 9-volt batteries.

The battery on the clock card powers the clock/calendar chip whenever the computer is not receiving wall current. The batteries on the clock card must be replaced every few years; consult the instruction manual for details. You can also test the voltage on the battery using a simple voltmeter.

Because a number of possible clock card addresses and date/time formats are available, you must use the correct software with each clock card. Mismatched software looks for the clock at the wrong address and returns a no clock found message, even if a fully functional clock is present.

It is highly unlikely that you will be able to obtain a replacement clock card or multifunction card for an early PC anywhere but at a swap meet. The good news is that if the clock gives up the ghost, you can continue to use your elderly machine — you just have to manually set the time and date each time you boot up.

Matching Cables and Connectors

I can't begin to tell you how many times I have been faced with a mismatch of cable and connector — the wrong size or shape, an incorrect number of pins, the wrong gender (no offense intended, but a male plug and a male connector won't mate any better than a pair of females).

The first step is to analyze what you've got. Here's a step-by-step procedure:

1. Begin by counting the number of pins or holes.
2. Determine the gender you need for both ends of the cable; you need a male plug to mate with a female connector, for example.

3. Study the layout of the pins or holes — 5 over 4 or 34 over 34.
4. Examine the shape of the connector to choose the correct family of hardware from among tiny DIN or RJ plugs, mid-sized DB, and generally larger Centronics designs. (Other families exist.)

CROSS-REFERENCE

Somebody needs to write a book someday . . . an encyclopedia of computer cables and connectors. Until then, Appendix F is a partial collection selected from the hundreds of pieces of standard and nonstandard hardware out there.

SUMMARY

You've explored the basics of the computer. In the next chapter, I apply a screwdriver to a state-of-the-art PC and reveal its secrets in step-by-step detail.

Ch
5

Chapter 6

Step-by-Step through a Modern Machine

Throughout the history of the PC, the basic components of the machine have remained quite constant.

From the very first IBM PC, the building blocks have included a motherboard and microprocessor, a block of random access memory, a floppy disk, a hard drive, a video adapter, a power supply, and a case to hold all of the parts.

Today, the most modern machines include the same elements. The difference is the degree of integration — motherboards bring together many functions in a much smaller space — and the introduction of a designer's sense of style.

In this chapter, I take apart a state-of-the-art modern machine to identify the parts and show some common repair projects. I also delve into an older but still capable machine for a few essential upgrades.

A Tour of a Modern Machine

Our model for a state-of-the-art modern machine in this seventh edition is a Dell Dimension 8200, an elegant, full-featured midtower PC. Based around the Intel 850 chipset and a 1.8GHz Pentium 4 microprocessor, it uses high-speed RDRAM. Our test machine also includes a CD-RW, an advanced sound card, a network interface, and a 40GB ATA/100 hard drive.

For some users, those specifications are impressive enough. But for connoisseurs of technology, one of the most striking features of this PC is its elegant design. From its sleek charcoal case, which opens like a clamshell without the need for any tools, to its well-thought-out interior design, this PC is a work of art.

(Just for the record: I'm not endorsing Dell or any other particular PC manufacturer. Prices, engineering, and quality of manufacture and service can change from year to year and month to month in the computer industry. A savvy consumer shops carefully before committing to a system purchase. In my office, I run a mix of machines from Compaq, Dell, Gateway, and other systems that I have assembled myself by using industry-standard parts.)

Figure 6-1 shows the machine in its operating glory.

The rear panel of the PC neatly presents a wide range of input and output ports, as shown in Figure 6-2.

FIGURE 6-1: *Running Windows XP Professional, the system includes a 10/16/24 CD-RW and a floppy disk drive on the front panel; there is additional space for a second 5.25-inch drive such as a DVD or DVD recorder, and a second 3.5-inch drive such as a Zip. Behind a pop-out panel at the bottom-front of the system is a pair of USB ports and a headphone jack for multimedia equipment. In this setup, the system is topped by a 40GB external USB drive. Alongside are stereo speakers; a subwoofer speaker sits out of the way, on the floor. The PC, external drive, and monitor are plugged into an uninterruptible power supply that will support the system for enough time to allow an orderly shut down if there is a problem with electricity in the office or home.*

The power supply's cooling fan is located to the right of the electrical connection; below it is the air vent for a second fan that directly cools the Pentium 4 processor on the motherboard within.

Two-thirds of the way down on the right side of the rear panel is a steel hasp that can be used to lock the case closed.

FIGURE 6-2: *Below the electrical connection are the ports directly attached to the mini-ATX motherboard. From top left, moving clockwise, is a DB-15 serial port, a DB-25 parallel port, a PS/2 mouse connector, two USB ports, and a PS/2 keyboard connector. Some of the most current systems color-code the connectors on cables to make configuration easy.*

The bottom section of the rear panel shows the ports of devices that are plugged into the system bus. The top device is a video card plugged into the system's AGP 4X slot; the video card in the example system includes both a standard analog port for a computer monitor and a circular S-VHS port for use with a television screen.

The next device in the bus, plugged into a PCI slot, is a Creative Labs Sound Blaster Live! Card. In addition to audio input and output connectors, the card includes a larger joystick port.

The third device in the bus is an Ethernet network interface card.

Ch
6

The modern motherboard, made by Intel, makes use of the PC99 specification color-code connectors. The attached connectors, shown in Figure 6-3, are gathered in a tight cluster in a cutout on the rear panel of the case.

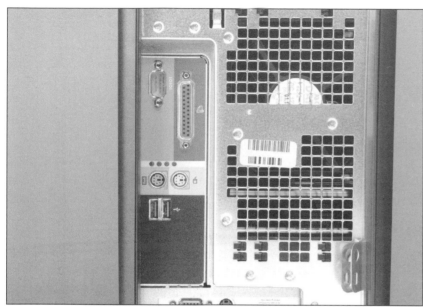

FIGURE 6-3: *The panel located to the left of the case-cooling fan holds the small DB-15 serial port, the larger DB-25 parallel port, the keyboard and mouse connectors, and a pair of USB ports. Two more USB ports are located on the front of the case.*

CROSS-REFERENCE

I list the assignments of the PC99 color scheme in Chapter 1.

The Intel motherboard used in the Dell Dimension 8200 includes a set of diagnostic lights on the rear panel, located between the serial and parallel ports and the keyboard and mouse ports. The four lights, labeled A, B, C, and D, can be yellow, green, or off. The codes indicate problems that may occur before the BIOS begins to run, the failure of the BIOS itself, and the most common hardware problems that the BIOS test may uncover, including problems with the memory, the PCI bus, the video controller, and the USB port.

This Intel motherboard includes an AGP slot and four PCI slots; the external access to the adapter cards is shown in Figure 6-4. I discuss the computer bus in its various forms in Chapter 4.

The first PCI card in the bus in this system is a Sound Blaster Live! Adapter that includes a MIDI or joystick controller, as well as a full set of ports for incoming line audio from an amplifier or a microphone, in addition to outputs to speakers and amplifiers. Within the case, the card has connectors to an internal CD-ROM for both analog and digital playback.

FIGURE 6-4: *The advanced I/O facilities of the Pentium 4 system include an ATI video card that includes both a standard SVGA output to a computer monitor and a small round S-VHS connector that can be used to drive a component television or videotape recorder; an adapter can be purchased to convert S-VHS to standard RCA plug outputs for consumer-grade televisions. The video card uses the AGP4X slot on the motherboard, sitting just above the bank of PCI slots.*

Ch
6

The third card shown is a network interface card, with an open RJ45 connector. This advanced machine also includes built-in USB ports.

CROSS-REFERENCE

You can learn more about USB technology in Chapter 15.

Later in this section, I add a USB 2.0 adapter for increased speed in use with external storage devices and an ATA/133 adapter that allows use of a Maxtor 160GB internal drive at its full capacity and speed.

Two of the USB ports are on the rear panel of the case; a second set, shown in Figure 6-5, is sheltered behind a decorative cover on the front.

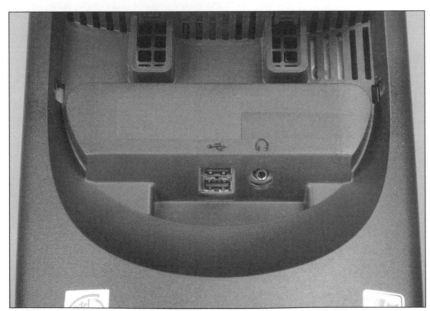

FIGURE 6-5: *Located behind a decorative cover on this modern machine is a second set of USB ports, best used for temporary attachments such as for downloading images from a digital camera, and a headphone connector for system audio.*

One of the design beauties of this modern machine is its elegant and simple case. The shell of the case is made of high-grade plastic, lined with metal panels that provide stiffness and shielding against RF leakage. Access to the interior of the case is completely tool-free; the case opens like a clamshell with the press of a pair of release buttons on the top and bottom of the case, as shown in Figure 6-6.

CROSS-REFERENCE

I discuss the function of the case in Chapter 5.

When fully opened, as shown in Figure 6-7, the case reveals the motherboard flat on the tabletop. The exterior plastic shell of the case covers a sturdy steel frame within. Each of the devices installed in a drive cage slides in and out on plastic rails; the case comes with extra rails for future upgrades to the system.

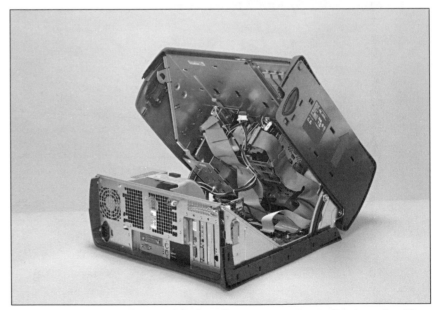

FIGURE 6-6: *To open this model of modern case, remove all external cables and place the unit on its side. Push buttons on the top and bottom release catches that hold the two halves of the case together.*

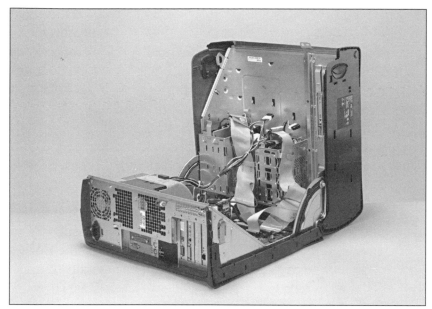

FIGURE 6-7: *Rising at a 90-degree angle are three drive cages. One holds devices that require external access through the case — the CD-R drive and an open slot that could hold a DVD drive, Zip drive, or other device. A second drive cage holds the floppy disk drive. A third drive cage has room for two internal hard drives. Each of the cages comes equipped with plastic rails that attach to drives before installation; this allows drives to slide in and out of the cages easily and permits precise positioning.*

FIGURE 6-8: *The power supply is shown at the upper-left. An extra-long wiring harness provides DC power to the drive cages at right and to the motherboard below. On this modern microATX motherboard, electrical power goes to the board at two locations.*

Turned on its side, as shown in Figure 6-8, other components of the system are visible. The interior is dominated by the metal case for the power supply located at the upper-left; below it is the plastic cowling that sits atop the CPU to create a wind tunnel effect.

The power supply changes 115 volts of AC (alternating current) from the power line into DC (direct current) for the components of the computer.

CROSS-REFERENCE

You can learn more about the power supply in Chapter 5.

Figure 6-9 shows the main wiring harness that supplies the bus, many onboard peripherals, and powered I/O chains, such as FireWire and USB. Figure 6-10 shows the secondary connection from the power supply to the motherboard, supplying the Intel Pentium 4 CPU, RDRAM memory, and associated chips.

Directly below the power supply is a large plastic cowling that sits atop the Pentium 4 CPU on the motherboard; the assembly extends to a fan that mounts at the back of the case, thus creating a wind tunnel to cool the 1.8GHz microprocessor.

The highly integrated Intel motherboard, as shown in Figure 6-11, makes it easy to install new adapters and memory modules. Intel is the single largest manufacturer of motherboards; its boards and CPUs power the machines offered for sale by many brand name resellers. Other makers, mostly in Asia, include Abit, Asus, Gigabyte, and MSI.

As Figure 6-12 shows, I've removed the fan cowling. The cowling allows system designers to use a larger fan on the rear panel of the case instead of a smaller unit clipped directly to the CPU. The result is a wind tunnel that isolates a stream of exhaust air from the larger and less-channeled interior of the case.

FIGURE 6-9: *The main power connection to the system on a microATX motherboard, marked as P1.*

Ch
6

FIGURE 6-11: *Four slots for memory modules sit above the cooling fan assembly for the microprocessor. This advanced motherboard uses RDRAM modules, called RIMMs; in this design, modules must be installed in pairs, and unused slots must be occupied by empty cards that complete the continuity of the circuit. Located to the right of the fan assembly are the five expansion slots. In this mostly tool-free design, the cards are held in place by a plastic lever that locks over the top of the installation brackets.*

FIGURE 6-10: *The secondary power connection on a microATX motherboard, used by the CPU, and marked as P2.*

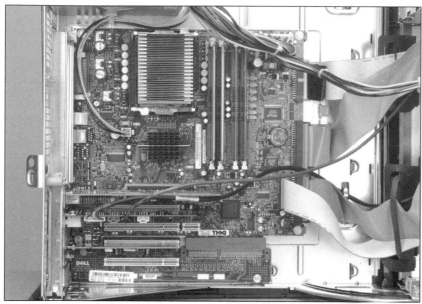

FIGURE 6-12: *Beneath the cooling fan assembly, the Pentium 4 sits beneath a massive heat sink that draws heat away from the microprocessor and into the stream of air moved by the case fan. The heat sink is held in place by clips at top and bottom.*

FIGURE 6-13: *A small and humble horizontal chip holds the brain of the system. The 1.8GHz Pentium 4 CPU installs in a zero-insertion force socket.*

Peeling away the heat sink, the final layer of protection, the Pentium 4 microprocessor is revealed in Figure 6-13. The Pentium 4 includes 42 million transistors.

CROSS-REFERENCE

I discuss microprocessors in more detail in Chapter 2.

To replace the CPU for repair or upgrade, the guillotine-like latch at the top of the socket is unhooked and lifted to release pressure on the pins of the microprocessor, as shown in Figure 6-14.

Ch 6

FIGURE 6-14: *Its latch open, the Pentium 4 can be removed. Most motherboards can only be upgraded within the same family of chips, although computer equipment manufacturers have proved ingenious over the years in coming up with adapters that permit use of CPUs that were not planned for when a particular motherboard was designed.*

FIGURE 6-15: *Memory modules, like this 128MB RIMM, plug into special sockets on the motherboard. The sockets for RIMMs and DIMMs are "keyed," requiring that modules be installed in the proper orientation; match the gaps or extra fingers on the module with the corresponding position on the socket.*

RIMM modules with RDRAM, like the one shown in Figure 6-15, are similar in shape to DIMM modules that hold SDRAM. RIMMs, however, are covered with a heat sink to keep them cool. RIMMs use Rambus memory based on CMOS DRAM that can provide sustainable system throughput ten times faster than standard SDRAM. RIMM modules use pipelining technology to send four 16-bit packets at a time to a 64-bit CPU.

CROSS-REFERENCE

I discuss memory technology in Chapter 8.

On a system based on RDRAM, unused memory sockets must be filled with continuity modules, like the one shown in Figure 6-16.

FIGURE 6-16: *Continuity modules complete the electrical circuit on a system based on RDRAM. Essential to the operation of the system, they hold no memory. On most systems based on RDRAM, the pair of sockets closest to the CPU—usually identified as Bank 0—must be populated first.*

FIGURE 6-17: *The retaining latch for adapter cards on this advanced case has been opened, allowing insertion or removal of cards held in place in the expansion slots. On most other systems, the brackets are held in place by screws that connect to the frame of the case. The cables connected to the second adapter card from the top link the sound card to the CD-R drive.*

To add a new adapter card or replace an existing one within this advanced case, you open the latch over the brackets, as shown in Figure 6-17. In this system, the only place you'll need to use a screwdriver is to install devices in the drive cages or to remove the power supply.

AGP (accelerated graphics port) video, common to most current modern machines, uses a special slot on the motherboard. The high-speed 32-bit bus was designed specifically for use with video cards. The original specification called for one data transfer per clock cycle; subsequent versions transfer two, four, and eight times with each cycle and are referred to as AGP2X, AGP4X, and AGP8X.

 CROSS-REFERENCE

I explore AGP in detail in Chapter 4.

The AGP 4X slot shown in Figure 6-18 has 172 pins. Some systems include AGP video in a chipset, electrically identical to an adapter in a slot but offering limited flexibility when it comes to upgrades or replacement.

FIGURE 6-18: *The AGP slot on Dell's Dimension system includes a plastic locking bracket that hooks into an L-shaped notch on the card to lock it in place and provide stability.*

FIGURE 6-19: *This AGP card includes 32MB of memory, soldered in place in four chips above and to the right of the nVidia processor. The card also offers a feature connector, located at the upper-left, for use with other video circuitry, such as a TV tuner or a hardware-based DVD decoder.*

The AGP card used in this system, as shown in Figure 6-19, is based on the nVidia GeForce2 chip, in wide use as the engine for a number of brand name and generic video cards.

CROSS-REFERENCE

You can learn more details about video cards in Chapter 13.

The sound card on this system, as shown in Figure 6-20, is a Sound Blaster Live! from Creative Labs, a capable device for most users; serious audiophiles and professional sound engineers will use cards with an even broader range of MIDI samples and signal processing circuitry.

CROSS-REFERENCE

I discuss sound cards in Chapter 19.

FIGURE 6-20: *The Sound Blaster Live! Card includes 13 connectors for various audio devices. Six are accessible from the outside of the case; the others require internal connections to devices such as a CD or DVD drive or a telephone answering device (sometimes part of the circuitry of a modem card).*

FIGURE 6-21: *The Intel motherboard used in this advanced system is adaptable for use in compact systems, including just two PCI slots on the main board itself. A small expansion board attaches to a connector shown at the bottom of this picture, adding two more PCI slots.*

With all of the adapter cards removed, the bus of this modern machine is fully revealed in Figure 6-21. The four white slots are for use with PCI cards (including one with extensions for a 64-bit universal PCI adapter, not commonly used in consumer machines). The black slot at top, with its plastic retaining hook, is for use with AGP video cards.

The machine includes a CD-R drive, installed in the upper drive cage, as shown in Figure 6-22. The cage includes space for two 5.25-inch drives; the second space can be used for a DVD or tape drive. With the use of special hardware, you can adapt it to hold a 3.5-inch device, such as a Zip drive or an additional hard drive.

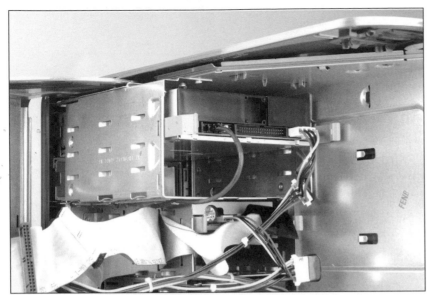

FIGURE 6-22: *CD and DVD drives of all designs include three groups of connectors. On this Matsushita CD-R, located from left to right are two plug-ins for audio output — digital and audio; a set of pins to accept a data cable that communicates with the bus, and a power input block.*

State-of-the Art Upgrades for a Modern Machine

Our test bed of a machine started life with just about everything an advanced user could want: a Pentium 4 processor running at a blazing 1.8GHz clock speed, 256MB of RDRAM memory, four USB ports, a 40GB ATA/100 hard drive, and a CD-R. However, things change.

CPU speeds advance every few months — zooming past 2GHz and heading toward 3GHz as this book goes to press. More memory is almost always better than less. Four USB ports is probably more than enough when attached to hubs that allow it to work with dozens of devices; however, nearly all machines sold before early 2002 don't support the 40-times-faster USB 2.0 standard.

Like memory, you can always find a use for more hard disk storage. And faster is always better when it comes to reading and writing huge files to that disk.

In my office, I regularly make use of large digital images (including the photos in this book) and audio files, so my priorities for upgrade are large storage devices — internal and external — and data controllers capable of reading and writing the files as quickly as possible. And so, off go the covers and into the bus and card cages for these projects:

- Installation of a USB 2.0 adapter to support a 40GB external hard drive and future high-speed devices
- Adding a FireWire adapter to allow direct high-speed connection to professional digital camcorders and cameras
- Installation of an ATA/133 hard drive adapter to support the transfer rate and capacity of a 160GB hard drive

CROSS-REFERENCE

I explore a USB 2.0 adapter in more detail in Chapter 15.

I used a card from Keyspan that offers four external and one internal high-speed USB ports that are capable of transferring data at as much as 480MB/second in combination with USB 2.0 drivers from Microsoft.

For devices to operate at the USB 2.0 speed, all the components in the chain must be compatible with the newer standard. If you use a USB hub to expand the number of ports and provide additional electrical power to the circuit, the hub must include USB 2.0 circuitry to operate at 480MB/second.

Older devices, including hubs, are compatible with USB 2.0 ports and drivers, but they will run at the original USB 1.1 speed of 12MB/second.

After the card and current software drivers were installed, I was able to attach and immediately use a Maxtor 40GB external USB hard drive for backup purposes. Within the box is a 5,400 RPM 3.5-inch IDE drive with a 2 MB cache buffer. Unlike many other USB devices, the drive requires its own power supply because of the needs of the drive motor.

The next enhancement to the system was the installation of a Belkin FireWire card that adds three 400MB/second ports for use with digital video devices, scanners, hard drives, and other peripherals. FireWire is an implementation of the IEEE 1394 standard.

The card, shown in Figure 6-23, is a Plug-and-Play device that installs in the PCI bus; I also installed a FireWire hub, as shown in Figure 6-24, to expand the number of available ports and amplify electrical current on the chain.

CROSS-REFERENCE

I cover FireWire technology in more detail in Chapter 15.

Like USB, FireWire can divide the available bandwidth *isochronously*, dedicating a particular slice of the spectrum to particular devices — useful in such applications as streaming video. FireWire can also operate *asynchronously,* a more flexible means of communication for devices that can accept information broken into packets and able to deal with sometimes-changing conditions along the shared cable as other devices request access to the stream of data.

FIGURE 6-23: *Belkin's FireWire PCI Card allows hot-swapping of devices. Just as with USB, a series of FireWire devices can be daisy-chained to each other. Unlike USB, though, the result is a peer-to-peer network between and among the devices on the node without active control by the PC; devices can even communicate with each other without management by the computer. The design also permits two computers to share a single peripheral.*

Ch
6

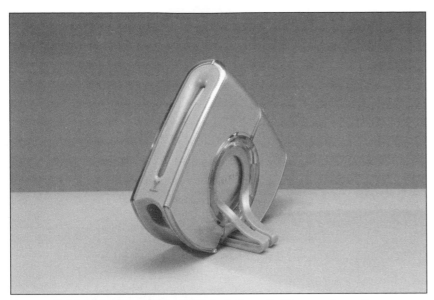

FIGURE 6-24: *This six-port FireWire hub from Belkin can draw its power from the bus or amplify available electrical current for devices through the use of a power block. The rear panel contains five ports; another port is hidden behind a panel on the front. A docking ring on the side mates the hub to additional hubs, routers, and other devices from the same manufacturer.*

The next project was to burst through a pair of barriers on hard drive capacity and speed of transfer.

CROSS-REFERENCE

I discuss hard drives in detail in Chapter 10.

I installed Maxtor's DiamondMax D540X, a 160GB hard drive that also introduced the Ultra ATA/133 standard (developed by Maxtor) that permits data transfer of as much as 133 MB/second to and from the interface. The drive, shown in Figure 6-25, slipped into place below the original 40GB hard drive in the system.

The chipset included as part of Ultra ATA/133 breaks through the 137GB barrier for ATA hard drives, allowing a new top end of 100,000 times more data: 48-bit addressing permits a single drive with more than 144 *petabytes* (144 million gigabytes) of storage.

The interface uses the same 80-conductor, 40-pin cable used for ATA/100 and provides backward compatibility with all parallel ATA devices, including Ultra ATA/33, ATA/66 and ATA/100. The interface includes a set of tightly controlled specifications for trace lengths and timing parameters, an essential element of any high-speed parallel interface.

Motherboards are expected to add support to ATA/133 (as well as the developing Serial ATA standard). In the meantime, Maxtor and licensed manufacturers will offer adapter cards, like the one shown in Figure 6-26, to update systems.

FIGURE 6-25: *In our demonstration system, the 160GB hard drive shares a drive cage with a 40GB drive; both devices are attached by cable to a new ATA/133 adapter card, although the smaller drive will be limited to its original 100MB/second transfer rate.*

Figure 6-26: *The ATA/133 adapter card includes new drivers to update Windows 98 and later operating systems to work with the new standard.*

Upgrading an Older Modern Machine

One of the foundations of this book is the fact that many older models still have a lot of mileage. Prime examples, as this book goes to press, are machines based on the Pentium II, Pentium III, and equivalent clones from manufacturers like AMD.

Don't expect an older machine to be able to support the latest microprocessors or be able to run the latest operating system at an acceptable speed.

However, you can consider several projects to upgrade a functional older modern machine to near-current capabilities:

- Memory is the easiest — and often the most cost-effective — upgrade to a computer. I suggest a boost to 128MB or 256MB of RAM. Though it may pain you to do so, you may have to remove older, smaller memory modules to make room for larger blocks of memory. As previously stated, prices for RAM have dropped sharply in recent years.

- You can easily install additional hard disk space to any machine by replacing the existing drive (and reinstalling the operating system, applications, and data), or by adding a second internal drive attached to the same drive controller. If your system can't accommodate another internal drive or if you'd rather add an external drive, you can purchase a USB, FireWire, or SCSI device that connects to a port on the PC.

- An older modern machine may lack some of the advanced current I/O facilities, such as USB, FireWire, and SCSI ports. Plug-and-Play PCI adapters are available that add ports to accommodate these devices.

- After you have compared the cost to purchasing a new machine, you may want to consider installing a new microprocessor within the same family or a processor upgrade that can convert some motherboards to accept a different, improved processor.

An example of a serviceable older modern machine worthy of upgrade is based on a Pentium II CPU running at 300MHz, installed in an Intel motherboard using the 440LX/EX chipset, a common combination for PCs sold from about 1997 through the arrival of the Pentium III in 1999.

NOTE

One way to learn most of the critical details of a motherboard and CPU is to use a system identification program. Some are included as part of utility programs, and you'll also find a basic version within the help screen of Microsoft Office programs, including Word and Excel. (From within the application, choose Help ⇨ About ⇨ System Information. A particularly useful version of a system information utility is posted on the Web site of Evergreen Technologies, maker of CPU upgrades. Go to www.evergreennow.com and go to the Support section and choose the Quick Prequalification link.

The Pentium II machine uses a conventional steel case with removable panels located above and below the motherboard. The panels are released by removing screws from the rear panel, as shown in Figure 6-27. The panels slide off and out of the way, as shown in Figure 6-28.

FIGURE 6-28: *A well-designed steel case leaves plenty of room for installation of adapter cards, memory modules, and internal storage devices. Be sure to keep openings in the exterior of the case covered by devices or metallic or shielded plastic plates to keep RF radiation from leaking out of the box, and to maintain the flow of air from cooling fans.*

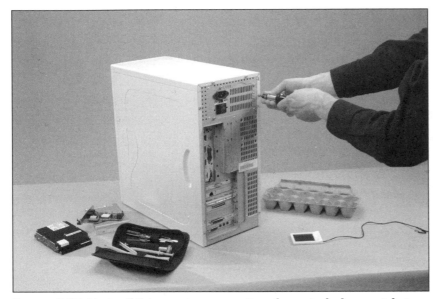

FIGURE 6-27: *My toolkit to open a conventional case includes a ratchet screwdriver, antistatic pad, and a low-tech holder for removed screws and connectors: an egg carton.*

With the upper panel removed, we can inspect the interior of the system, as shown in Figure 6-29. The motherboard in this system, manufactured by ASUS, includes four PCI slots, one ISA slot, and one shared ISA/PCI slot. The system includes an AGP slot for a graphics card, operating at the original speed rather than the 2X and 4X rates on current motherboards.

On many motherboards, it is necessary to unplug the main power harness, as shown in Figure 6-30, to gain access to the CPU, memory slots, and other elements.

FIGURE 6-29: *The Pentium II processor is held in an upright cartridge at upper left.*

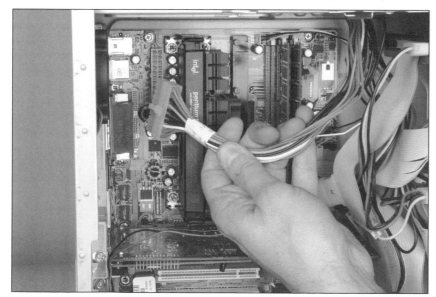

FIGURE 6-30: *The main power connection for an ATX motherboard is located alongside the CPU. Current motherboards for use with high-demand microprocessors, such as the Pentium 4, have two connections to the power supply.*

The simplest and most cost-effective performance boost for a PC is to add more memory. SDRAM, used in most modern PCs, can be installed one module at a time. In Figure 6-31, I'm adding a 128MB SIMM to the third of three sockets on the motherboard.

Most upgrades to modern I/O facilities require the use of a PCI slot. Nearly all modern machines can work with adapter cards that add FireWire or USB ports; the PC must be capable of running Windows 98SE or later operating systems, which can be modified by device drivers for that purpose.

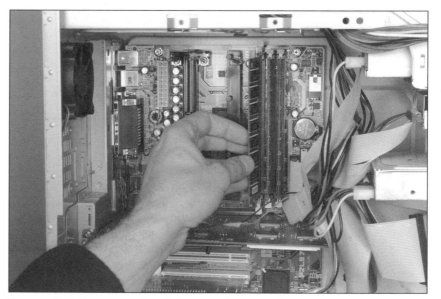

FIGURE 6-31: *Be sure to check the specifications for your motherboard in order to choose the proper type and speed of memory. If you install a mix of speeds, the system will operate at the slowest speed of the installed modules.*

Ch
6

In Figure 6-32, I'm installing the same Belkin FireWire PCI card I used with the state-of-the-art Pentium 4 machine previously in this chapter.

The last major reconstruction project on the older modern machine is a brain transplant. I begin with the removal of the Pentium II cartridge, as shown in Figure 6-33.

FIGURE 6-32: *To provide extra electrical power to devices attached to its ports, most FireWire adapter cards connect directly to the power supply as well as to the computer's PCI bus.*

FIGURE 6-33: *The upright Pentium II cartridge is held in place by clips at each end of Slot 1 on the motherboard; the CPU is cooled by a fan that requires its own power source.*

With the installation of a Performa processor upgrade from Evergreen Technologies, I boost the CPU power nearly three times from a Pentium II 300MHz to a Celeron 766MHz. The processor plugs into the vacated Slot 1, as shown in Figure 6-34. Be sure to carefully match the upgrade to your motherboard and its chipset; in some cases, it is necessary to adjust clock multiplier settings on the upgrade cartridge.

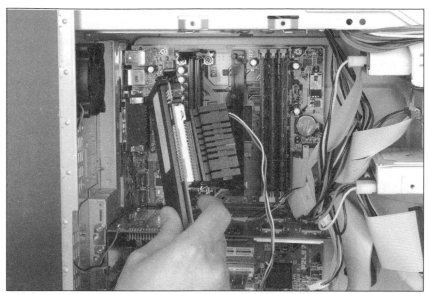

FIGURE 6-34: *This processor upgrade replaces the original Pentium II in Slot 1.*

SUMMARY

Now it's time to go shopping! In the next chapter, I look at shopping strategies and sources.

Chapter 7

Shopping for PC Parts

I've got some good news and some bad news. First the good news: Today's modern machines are, by some measures, probably 1,000 times faster than the original dinosaurs of twenty years ago and cost one-third to one-quarter as much. (If only other products followed the same pattern, we'd all be driving $29.95 Porsches.)

In recent years, CPUs have doubled in speed every one to two years. Hard disk drives have increased greatly in size and speed; today, you can purchase a 40GB hard drive for less than the price of a 1GB drive of just a few years ago. The price of memory has dropped so much that it is no longer much of a significant issue in calculating the cost of repairs and upgrades.

Now the bad news: With prices on almost every part of a modern machine plummeting so fast and so often, it is sometimes foolish to even bother to repair a dinosaur. On many senior citizens, it's a very close call. Only when you come to the world of modern machines is it sometimes worthwhile to perform major surgery.

This reality does not mean that you shouldn't replace or upgrade a hard drive, install a new video adapter with improved features, or add RAM or a new CPU to an underpowered senior citizen or modern machine. Just pay attention to the bottom line. This chapter helps you to calculate cost-benefit bottom lines for repair jobs and explore bare-bones computer recycling projects.

My Dream System

Every time this book goes through a major revision, I present a state-of-the-art system. And every time, the system is out of date before the ink dries on these pages. That's good news, of course. But just keep in mind that what is fresh and fast today is guaranteed to appear old and slow (and less expensive) in six months' time.

If I could design a system, it would include the latest *proven* technology and the best *consumer* hardware on the market. Later and greater toys will always come along, but I'm looking for a rocket I can ride right out of the box. Anyhow, here's the system I would put together today:

- Pentium 4 Processor at 2.0 GHz
- AGP4X graphics port
- 64MB DDR NVIDIA GeForce3 4X AGP graphics card
- USB 2.0 ports
- 256MB PC800 RDRAM
- 80GB Ultra ATA/100 hard drive
- 3.5-inch floppy disk drive
- 10/100 PCI Fast Ethernet NIC
- 16X/10X/40X CD-RW Drive
- 16X DVD ROM Drive with software decoding

- Sound Blaster Live! digital sound card
- 250MB Iomega Zip internal drive
- Programmable trackball
- Microsoft Windows XP Pro
- Microsoft Office XP Small Business suite

The retail price for this system in early 2002 was about $2,000.

Then I would add a 19-inch flat-screen Trinitron monitor for a desktop (about $450), or a 21-inch Trinitron monitor for graphics work (about $750). Bottom line: $2,450 for a desktop or $2,750 for a graphics workstation.

In the previous edition of this book, I specified a dream machine that was the available state-of-the-art in 2000. It included an 800 MHz Pentium III with a front-side bus of 133 MHz, a 27 GB hard drive, and a 21-inch monitor. This machine, arguably less than half as capable of today's dream machine, would have cost about $3,000.

Minimum Configuration Requirements

Like it or not, the vast majority of modern machines operate a version of Microsoft Windows. The needs of that operating system define the hardware configuration of machines offered for sale.

Those few machines that use an alternate system, such as Linux, use the same basic minimum configuration as used by Windows.

In late 2001, Microsoft introduced Windows XP, the most significant reworking of its Windows operating system for consumers since Windows 95. Windows XP (in its Home and Professional versions) has a lot to offer: It is notably more stable than earlier operating systems and if your PC has the horsepower to let it run at full throttle, it is a bit faster. You'll experience far fewer system crashes, and although the occasional application — including some from Microsoft — will still crash, Windows XP offers some

tools that allow you to save files in progress and even keep the rest of the operating system running if a program dies.

In this section, I go through the minimum requirements for current Windows operating systems. In every case, though, the minimum may be too little to deliver a satisfactory experience. I always recommend an extra dollop of RAM to enhance the speed and multitasking facilities of Windows.

Windows XP minimum configuration

Two versions of Windows XP are available: Home and Professional. The two versions are all but identical at their core, and most home and small business users will be happy with the Home edition.

The Pro edition adds support for machines with multiple processors and adds a suite of management tools and the ability to access your desktop remotely. Among the added tools are IntelliMirror, a desktop settings and software administration package for corporate networks, and security features, including file-level access control and file encryption.

Although the Home edition will work with no more than five computers in a peer-to-peer network, Windows XP Professional expands its reach to ten machines. Larger networks should work with server software.

Most benchmarks show that Windows XP is noticeably faster than Windows 95/98, but just a bit speedier than Windows 2000 Professional. For many users, the biggest improvement comes in a different area — reliability. Windows XP is much more stable than Windows 95 or 98; when applications do crash, they are not likely to halt the operating system. Windows XP and Office XP also work together to save data automatically in the event of a problem.

According to Microsoft, more than 90 percent of current applications written for Windows 2000/NT and Windows 9x will work on XP. This should include nearly all major programs; if you have any doubt about the compatibility of any program you have, you should consult the maker of the application before upgrading to Windows XP.

On my test machine, major Windows 98 applications, including Adobe PhotoShop, Adobe Illustrator, and Microsoft Money, installed and operated properly under the new operating system.

On the hardware side, Microsoft says Windows XP supports some 12,000 devices in its original release, including drivers for the top 1,000 best-selling devices. New devices will sport the XP logo on the box; if you have any doubt about other products, consult their manufacturers before upgrading to Windows XP. The Windows Upgrade Advisor should be able to identify problematic devices.

NOTE

Microsoft offers a free Windows XP "Upgrade Advisor" on its Web site (www.microsoft.com) that will check your system and determine its suitability for the new operating system. In addition to checking hardware requirements, the program will report on which — if any — of your hardware devices uses a driver not supported by Windows XP. If you receive such a report, consult the maker of your hardware for advice.

Here are the minimum requirements for installing XP:

- **CPU:** PC with 300 MHz or higher processor clock speed recommended; 233 MHz minimum required. Intel Pentium/Celeron family, AMD K6/Athlon/Duron family, or compatible processor recommended.
- **Memory:** 128MB of RAM or higher recommended. The operating system should work with as little as 64MB, but performance will be limited and some features may not work. For the best performance, a minimum of 256MB is suggested.
- **Storage:** 1.5GB of available hard disk space. CD-ROM or DVD drive.
- **Graphics:** Super VGA (800 × 600) or higher resolution video adapter and monitor.

- **I/O:** Keyboard and Microsoft Mouse or compatible pointing device.
- **Additional:** For instant messaging, voice and video conferencing, and application sharing, both parties need a Microsoft.NET Passport account and Internet access. For voice and video conferencing, both parties also need 33.6 Kbps or higher-speed modem, or a network connection, and a microphone and sound card with speakers or headset. For video conferencing, both parties also need a video-conferencing camera.

My personal recommendation: Stock your machine with at least 256MB of RAM.

One significant change introduced by Microsoft with Windows XP is an "activation" process for the operating system. When installed, you must turn on each copy of Windows XP by registering it with Microsoft by Internet or over the telephone.

Your copy of Windows XP is then uniquely associated with a particular computer, making it officially impossible to use the same disk to upgrade more than one machine. (It has always been against the license agreement to install and use one copy of the operating system on more than one machine, although the prohibition has been widely ignored.)

If you purchase a new machine with the operating system installed, it should come with the new version of Windows linked to the machine's BIOS, which should avoid the need for reactivation unless Windows XP needs to be installed on a new hard drive.

On older PCs upgraded to Windows XP, the operating system will be linked to a set of specific pieces of hardware, including a network adapter (if installed).

Under Microsoft's scheme, certain significant changes in hardware would result in the operating system requiring you to reactivate the installation by telephone or over the Internet.

Ch
7

Windows 2000 Professional minimum configuration

Windows 2000 was an important step in the history of Microsoft's operating system, although it was little used by consumers. It was built on the stable, 32-bit Windows NT technology but used the familiar Windows 98 user interface.

- **CPU:** 133 MHz or higher Pentium-compatible CPU
- **Memory:** 64MB of RAM recommended minimum; more memory generally improves responsiveness
- **Storage:** 2GB hard disk with a minimum of 650MB of free space, CD-ROM
- **Graphics:** Super VGA (800 × 600) or higher resolution video adapter and monitor
- **I/O:** Keyboard and Microsoft Mouse or compatible pointing device

Windows Me minimum configuration

Going the other direction, Windows Me (Millennium Edition) was an extension of the DOS-based Windows 9x series that used the desktop interface of Windows 2000 Professional. It was intended for use by consumers, adding a range of multimedia features but lacking the advanced security, reliability, and networking features of Windows 2000. It was not widely adopted for upgrades of Windows 98, but many new computers produced in 2000 and 2001 were offered with this operating system.

- **CPU:** 150 MHz or higher Pentium-compatible CPU
- **Memory:** 32MB of RAM recommended minimum; more memory generally improves responsiveness
- **Storage:** Hard disk with a minimum of 480 to 645MB of free space, CD-ROM
- **Graphics:** VGA or higher resolution video adapter and monitor

- **I/O:** Keyboard and Microsoft Mouse or compatible pointing device
- **DVD:** Decoder card or software (DVD option)

Windows 98 minimum configuration

Windows 98 brought full support of the Universal Serial Bus, infrared devices, multiple monitors, and a general pick-me-up in speed of loading and running many programs.

CROSS-REFERENCE

And as you learn in Chapter 23, Windows 98 and later editions, including Windows Me and Windows XP, also include some enhanced Plug-and-Play and troubleshooting features that make it easier to install and fix hardware.

Windows 98 also provided built-in support for WebTV for Windows, Intel MMX technology, and DirectX 5.0 for faster and higher resolution audio and video in programs that are written to take advantage of these facilities. Support for DVD means that users with a DVD drive can watch full-length feature movies on a PC monitor.

- A realistic starting point for CPU is a senior citizen Pentium. A Pentium II will perform adequately. But you won't find true happiness without a Pentium III, Celeron, Pentium 4, AMD K6, or AMD Athlon.
- The official minimum amount of RAM is 16MB, but I wouldn't recommend running the operating system without at least 32MB, and more reasonably, 64MB. More memory improves performance. (Note that some senior citizens may not be able to accommodate this much RAM, or may require a complete refitting of memory modules to reach this level.) With today's RAM prices, you should consider at least double the minimum for machines running graphics applications.

- A VGA color monitor is acceptable, but some software applications — especially graphics programs — demand SVGA. Any new monitor you purchase today will support SVGA.
- A VGA video card with at least 512K of RAM. An SVGA video card with 1 or 2MB reduces display delays with an SVGA monitor; go for 4MB or more if you are working with a lot of graphics.
- As far as hard disk storage, you'll need something in the range of 200MB just for the operating system and perhaps that much again for applications; this is before you begin to consider necessary space for storage of data and graphics files. With the tremendous drop in prices for hard drives, I recommend a minimum of 5GB; the best price-performance ratio for hard drives as this book goes to press is a 40GB device. (When using the FAT16 file system, a typical installation requires 225MB of free hard disk space, but may range from 165 to 300MB, depending on system configuration and options selected. When using the FAT32 file system, a typical installation requires 175MB of free hard disk space, but may range from 140 to 220MB, depending on system configuration and options selected.)
- A CD-ROM or DVD-ROM drive for installation of the program.
  - A mouse or other pointing device, officially optional but virtually a necessity.

Windows 95 minimum configuration

With this edition of *Fix Your Own PC*, I designate Windows 95 as the lowest acceptable Windows configuration for a modern machine. Microsoft no longer directly supports this operating system, although you should still be able to find drivers for hardware devices that were available at the time Windows 95 was in common use. Note that the original releases of Windows 95 (Windows 95 and Windows 95A) don't support USB drivers and devices; Windows 95B offers some support for USB, but not all devices will work with this outmoded operating system.

Here's what you need to work with Windows 95:

- A senior citizen 486DX2-66 CPU is the official starting point, although I have successfully run the operating system (a bit slowly) on 486SX-33 machines. Any modern machine (from Pentium or P6 clone to Pentium 4) is capable of working with Windows 95.
- Officially, 4MB of RAM is necessary, although I wouldn't bother to install Windows 95 on a machine with less than 8MB. With today's low prices for memory, I recommend you go up at least one notch to 16MB and even better to 32MB. That said, I have run Windows 95 on a 4MB, 486DX-33 laptop, but it wasn't a pleasant experience. I eventually upgraded that machine to 8MB, the maximum it would hold, and it became usable for another year or two as a backup mobile machine. The difference is speed. What you can do versus what is practical to do becomes vividly apparent when you start trying to get real work done with a minimal configuration.
- A VGA color monitor. Some software applications demand SVGA, and nearly all new monitors deliver at this standard.
- A VGA video card with at least 512K of RAM. An SVGA video card with 1 or 2MB reduces display delays with an SVGA monitor.
- A large, fast hard drive with 50 to 100MB of available space for the operating system. With the plummeting prices of hard drives, you have little reason to use a drive smaller than 5GB (a size you'll have trouble buying new today), and for just a relatively few dollars more you can have several gigabytes of extra space to play with.
- A mouse or other pointing device, officially optional but virtually a necessity.

Unless you have a very elderly machine and use some essential components that are not compatible with more advanced operating systems, you should consider upgrading to Windows 98 or later versions.

Ch
7

Windows 3.1 minimum configuration

Current users won't find many software applications that will support this older operating system, and many major hardware devices don't have drivers that permit use with Windows 3.1.

Windows for Workgroups is a variant of Windows 3.1, with some additional networking features.

NOTE

Microsoft no longer sells Windows 3.1 or Windows 95, and Windows 98 will soon join the list of discontinued products. You may find a dusty old copy on the shelves of a computer store, or you can legally transfer a licensed copy of the operating system if it is no longer being used on another PC.

If you are determined to run the older version of Windows or have a dinosaur machine not capable of running Windows 95/98, here are the minimum hardware elements for Windows 3.1:

- A 386SX-25 processor at a minimum, although a 486DX-33 is a more reasonable starting point.
- At least 4MB of RAM, although systems with less than 8MB will likely suffer slowdowns.
- A VGA video card with at least 512K of RAM, although an SVGA video card with 1 or 2MB reduces display delays.
- A high-resolution VGA color monitor, although SVGA is necessary for some software applications.
- A large, fast hard drive with 50 to 100MB of available space for the operating system and a few hundred megabytes of space for data.
- A mouse or other pointing device, officially optional but virtually a necessity.

The Obsolescence Factor

The hard fact of computer life is this: By the time you pick up a PC part at the back of the store and carry it to the checkout counter, it is already outdated and devalued. New products are constantly spilling out of the laboratories and factories and the very last place they appear is on the shelves or in the mail-order catalogs.

However, it is also true that if you keep waiting for the latest and greatest, you will always be waiting. Sooner or later you've got to jump in and make a purchase.

The way I see it, in most cases, we face three options when it comes to buying a new machine:

- Buy the hottest new technology as soon as it is offered to the public. You'll pay top dollar and likely have to put up with some troublesome bugs and incompatibilities until software catches up with hardware, but for a period of time — perhaps a month or two — you'll be as current as the magazine covers.
- Buy one step behind the state-of-the-art. You may end up with a slightly slower or smaller device, but you'll benefit from the inevitable price reduction when an item moves just a bit out of the spotlight. For example, as this book goes to press, the hottest Pentium 4 CPUs are 2 GHz speedsters; the best price/performance ratios are for systems based one or two notches behind, on 1.8 GHz chips. The older chips are potentially about 10 to 20 percent slower for a small number of particular types of operations, but are priced several hundred dollars below the top of the line.
- Buy the cheapest closeout products. You can find some incredible savings if you're willing to help a retailer or mail-order operator clear out back inventory. However, the truth is that saving money like this can become more expensive — both in time and money — down the road. Settling for an older Pentium III in the age of the Pentium 4 can mean that the latest and greatest operating systems or software will run noticeably slower than they would on a state-of-the-art machine. Buying an inexpensive smaller hard drive can be penny-wise and pound-foolish if you end up having to pull it out in six months because it is much too small for your applications. Also, you may end up with hardware that is no longer backed up with technical support by manufacturers.

The Rules of the Computer Shopping Game

You can pay $4,000 for a poorly designed, ill-configured, and otherwise inappropriate machine, or you can pay half that much — or less — for the perfect speedster. It's all related to your skills as a shopper.

Here are Sandler's Basic Rules for Computer Shopping:

1. Do your own research in this book, in computer magazines, and online before making a buying decision.
2. Ask lots of questions before you place your order.
3. Make the rapid pace of improvement work to your advantage: Buy the latest and greatest for the longest active life or buy one step behind the curve for the best price-performance.
4. Always pay with a credit card.

I explain the reasons behind the rules in the following sections.

A Bang-for-the-Buck Price Matrix

Is a machine that runs 10 percent faster on your desktop worth 50 percent more at the checkout counter? Is twice the storage space worth three times the price? Maybe yes — if you're running a very complex, mission-critical piece of software for your business. Maybe yes — if you're a maniacal game player and have money to burn. For the rest of us, sometimes it pays to search for the sweet spot — the combination of hardware that gives you the most bang for your bucks.

It is the very nature of technology's progress that yesterday's top of the line is today's most bang for the buck. As this book goes to press, the top of the line in consumer-level PCs is a Pentium 4 running at 2.0 GHz; the sweet spot, a savings of a few hundred dollars, is a still super-speedy Pentium 4 running at 1.8 GHz.

The prices presented in Table 7-1 are for an à-la-carte, build-it-yourself package, based on discount retail prices from several sources, including Web sites and catalogs.

You can, of course, save money by purchasing a preassembled package; computer manufacturers buy their parts at wholesale prices and in great volume. In my experience, however, after a maker adds in the cost of assembly, support, software (some of which you may not want), shipping, and marketing, the cost of a customized machine that you assemble from component parts is only about 10 to 15 percent higher than a package. And you'll have exactly the machine you want.

The price chart in this edition is just a snapshot in time. Throughout the history of the personal computer, prices have almost without exception headed down just as capabilities soared upward.

My wish list for a top-of-the-line system in this edition is a 2.0 GHz Pentium 4, outfitted with 256MB of high-speed Rambus memory, a fast 80GB hard drive, a CD-RW drive, a DVD drive, and a 250MB Zip drive.

The rock-bottom system has more than doubled in speed and dropped in price since the last edition, based on an AMD Thunderbird CPU running at 900 MHz, with 128MB of memory, and a 20GB hard drive.

In between these two ends of the spectrum lies one definition for a machine that gives the most bang for the buck. My advice calls for a selection of equipment that is just one step behind the state of the art. As this book goes to press, this class of machine would use a Pentium 4 at 1.8 GHz, a zippy processor that, in late 2001, was a few hundred dollars less than the 2.0 GHz version. I chose to outfit the model with 256MB of PC133 RAM, a fast 40GB hard drive, and a CD-RW drive just a bit slower than the top of the line. The difference in cost between the top of the line and the machine that delivers the most bang for the buck was about $666 — a lot of money when you pay the bill, but not a huge amount if you consider the expense spread over a typical three-year life for a modern machine.

Ch 7

TABLE 7-1: A Shopper's Guide to the Components of a Modern Machine

	Top of the Line	Most Bang for the Buck	Rock-Bottom
CPU	2.0 GHz Intel Pentium 4, Socket 423. About $400.	1.8 GHz Intel Pentium 4. About $225.	900 MHz AMD Thunderbird. About $73.
Motherboard	Socket 423 motherboard. Intel 850 chipset. 4x184-pin RIMM sockets. 400 MHz system bus. Ultra DMA/100. 5 PCI slots. AGP 4X. 3 USB. About $180.	Socket 478 motherboard. Intel 845 chipset. 3x168-pin DIMM sockets. 400 MHz system bus. Ultra DMA/100. 6 PCI slots. AGP 4X.1 About $135.	Socket A motherboard. VIA Apollo KT133A AGPset. 266/200 MHz system bus. 3x168-pin DIMM sockets. 6 PCI, 1 ISA slot. AGP 4X. About $90.
Computer Case	Full tower. 10 bays, 250-watt power supply. About $79.	Mid-tower. 7 bays, 250-watt power supply. About $50.	Mid-tower. 7 bays, 200-watt power supply. About $40.
Memory	256MB RDRAM PC800. About $135.	256MB PC133 SDRAM. About $30.	128MB DDR. $25.
Video Card	AGP 4X 64MB DDR. About $170.	AGP 64MB. About $90.	AGP 16MB. About $40.
Hard Drive	80GB ATA/100 7200 rpm. About $210.	40GB ATA/100. About $130.	20GB ATA/100. About $80.
Floppy Drive	120MB LS-120 SuperDisk, also reads and writes to 1.44MB floppy disks. About $50.	1.44MB floppy disk drive. About $18.	1.44MB floppy disk drive. About $18.
Backup	250MB internal Zip drive, about $100.	100MB internal Zip drive, about $50.	100MB internal Zip drive, about $50.
Keyboard, Mouse	Keyboard, about $20. Trackball or wireless wheel mouse, about $50.	Keyboard, about $15. Wheel mouse, about $30.	Basic keyboard, about $10. Basic mouse, about $5.
CD-ROM	CD-RW 24X10X40, about $150.	CD-RW 16X10X40, about $100.	CD-ROM 52X, about $30.
Sound Card	Sound Blaster Live, about $100.	Midrange Sound Blaster, about $60.	Basic Sound Blaster or clone, about $25.
Modem	Dual-mode 56K V.90/V.92 external, about $95.	56K V.90 external, about $60.	56K PCI internal, about $15.
Price Totals	About $1,719	About $1,053	About $496

Ch
7

You'll want to add a monitor. You can buy a stunning 21-inch monitor for about $700, a drop of several hundred dollars from the previous edition of this book. Or you may prefer a svelte 15-inch LCD screen, which has dropped below $300. A good-quality 17-inch monitor, appropriate for most applications, was priced at about $270 in late 2001. A basic but acceptable 15-inch screen for a rock-bottom system was priced as low as $150.

Just for giggles, here is this edition's recommendation along with the comparable systems I wrote about in the sixth edition in 2000, the fifth edition in 1998, and the fourth edition in 1997.

Top of the Line

- 2002 version: $1,719 for Pentium 4 2.0 GHz CPU, 256MB Rambus RAM, 80GB hard drive, high-speed CD-RW drive
- 2000 version: $2,480 for Pentium III 800 MHz CPU, 128MB RAM, 20GB hard drive, DVD and CD-R drives
- 1998 version: $2,900 for Pentium II 400 MHz CPU, 64MB RAM, 11GB SCSI hard drive, and a CD-R drive
- 1997 version: $2,200 for a Pentium MMX 233 MHz CPU, 32MB RAM, 3.1GB hard drive, 12X CD-ROM drive

Most Bang for the Buck

- 2002 version: $1,053 for Pentium 4 1.8 GHz CPU, 256MB RAM, 40GB hard drive, CD-RW drive.
- 2000 version: $1,335 for Pentium III 500 MHz CPU, 64MB RAM, 8GB hard drive, DVD/CD drive
- 1998 version: $1,100 for a Pentium II 266 MHz CPU, 32MB RAM, 6.4GB hard drive, and a 24X CD-ROM
- 1997 version: $1,350 for a Pentium 133 MHz CPU, 16MB RAM, 2.1GB hard drive, 8X CD-ROM

Rock-Bottom Minimum

- 2002 version: $496 for an AMD Athlon 900 MHz CPU, 128MB RAM, 20GB hard drive, 52X CD-ROM
- 2000 version: $685 for a Celeron 400 MHz CPU, 32MB RAM, 4GB hard drive, 48X CD-ROM.

- 1998 version: $650 for a Pentium MMX 233 MHz CPU, 16MB RAM, 3.2GB hard drive, and a 12X CD-ROM
- 1997 version: $925 for a 486DX4-100 MHz CPU, 16MB RAM, 1.2GB hard drive, 4X CD

Where to put your money down

Up to this point in the chapter, I've explored the necessary components of a build-your-own PC. The next step in understanding the financial side of repairs and upgrades is to consult a full-line mail-order catalog, a Web site, or a good retail outlet.

Every PC owner has his or her own comfort level. Speaking for myself, I am perfectly comfortable with ordering items over the telephone — from a set of screwdrivers to a complete PC system costing several thousand dollars. Even better is ordering over the Internet, which allows me to research products and easily compare one Web site's offerings and prices with another's. Here's a hint: Shop for parts and put them in the shopping cart feature of most Web pages. Then print the pages for comparison across Web sites.

For computer configurations, the Web is a fast and easy way to build a custom system, check the price and specs, add and remove components, and keep at it until you have just the system you want. You can use a spreadsheet program to help price and spec a new system this way; many computer manufacturers and parts supply houses have online configuration programs that allow you to mix and match parts and compare bottom lines.

Other folks, though, like to touch the hardware and squeeze the cellophane, preferring to make their purchases at a retail store.

Which is best for you? Table 7-2 presents the pluses and minuses of shopping in person or by phone or keyboard.

What about mail-order fraud? First of all, most mail-order operations are honest, and you can count on them to deliver. However, you can do one very important thing to increase your leverage: Always pay with a credit card and always monitor your credit card statements carefully. The bank that issues your credit card is required by law — and bound by good customer-service practices — to help you receive goods for payment. If you order a product and it does not arrive but a charge is posted to your account, contact the issuer of your credit card immediately and follow its procedures to protest the charge.

What about support? It has been my experience that you can obtain excellent — or lousy — technical support from any source, whether a mail-order outfit or a local retail store. Besides, most electronic equipment is extremely reliable. If it passes the infant-mortality stage of, say, the first six to eight weeks, it should last years. Almost all systems and components carry at least a 90-day warranty; many have one- and two-year buyer protection warranties. If a system or component fails during the warranty, the seller usually will simply replace it, so the issue of repair isn't all that serious. After the warranty period, you're on your own anyway, and that's why you're reading this book.

In addition, consider the packaged in-home or in-office repair service included with many systems from companies such as Dell and Gateway. If you buy a machine with this kind of warranty, a phone call usually brings a service person to your doorstep within 24 hours. If you bought from a local retail store, you will likely have to disconnect the machine and carry it into the store for service. What you decide to do depends on your personal level of comfort with doing some of your own work, or how well you know the company or person selling you the machine.

Note that in 2001, most major computer manufacturers began to offer different tiers of support. For example, Dell included a basic warranty of one year including onsite service and phone support. For an additional $50, the warranty and support were doubled to two years. And for $119, the warranty extended to three years and support was promised for the lifetime of the machine.

Be sure that you understand the terms of any warranty. Even though a company may promise onsite service, this may not extend to all parts of the machine or to all locations. You may be asked to ship products to a depot for service, which may cause a disruption in your office or home use.

I always ask lots of questions before I make a purchase. If I'm not satisfied with the answers, I take my business elsewhere. In other words, if company representatives are not very helpful before you make a purchase, what makes you think they'll be of assistance after they have your money?

TABLE 7-2: Internet, Telephone, and Mail Order versus Retail Stores

Internet, Telephone, Mail Order	Retail Store
+ Generally lower prices	− May be more expensive, although computer superstores approach mail-order prices
+ May have larger selection	− Sometimes more limited in selection
+/− The best mail-order houses have first-rate free technical support; some, though, are only order-takers	+/− The best retailers offer onsite technical experts or toll-free help
+/− The best outfits have liberal return and replacement policies	+/− The best outfits have liberal return and replacement policies
+ May not charge sales tax in some states	− Will charge sales tax if one is in place in local location
− Adds shipping charges	+ Take home your package
+/− Convenience factor: Overnight courier delivery to your home or office for extra charge	+/− Convenience factor: Immediate pickup if you drive to the store

The Upgrade Upset

You need to understand two basic facts about personal computers:

- Only a handful of true computer manufacturers exist — companies that build their own circuit boards, memory, and hard drives. Instead, nearly every computer company is more accurately called a *computer assembler*. Companies such as Gateway, Dell, and others, for example, buy cases and power supplies from one source, motherboards from another, memory and CPUs from a chipmaker, hard drives from other manufacturers, and so on.
- For an individual, the sum of the parts is more expensive than the whole. In other words, in most cases, assembling a complete computer from its component parts is more expensive than buying a complete package from a computer maker.

Why? Because when you buy your component parts, you are paying retail prices for each element, with a profit margin built into every piece by the dealer. When a major computer company builds its machines, it buys parts in large quantities and puts its profit margin on top of the total wholesale price. I estimate that a typical home-assembled machine will cost you 10 to 20 percent more than the price of a factory-built equivalent, and you will be pretty much on your own for technical support for the components. Consequently, I can't recommend that you build your own PC if your sole goal is to save some money.

However, here are some reasons why you may want to build your own:

- You want to construct a system that is highly customized to your needs or wants.
- You want to use some very high-quality parts not ordinarily offered by computer makers that sell to consumers — high-end redundant power supplies, for example.
- You want the satisfaction of doing it yourself, and you are willing to pay a bit more for the privilege.
- You want to recycle parts from an older or extra machine into an upgraded state-of-the-art system. (I explore ways to do this later in the chapter.)

NOTE

If you choose to build your own system, buy parts from a reputable dealer that has a technical support department willing to spend some time with you deciphering illiterate instruction sheets and unlabeled cables and circuit boards.

Fixing what's broken

A more logical task than building your own system is replacing the parts of a machine that have failed or become hopelessly outdated. A careful shopper can save hundreds or even thousands of dollars by reusing pieces of an older computer that are still working, substituting only what needs to be replaced.

A careful shopper can also replace a bad motherboard for a few hundred dollars and reinstall memory, hard drives, and adapter cards from the previous system. And while you're at it, you can often upgrade to near state of the art for just a few dollars more.

Worthwhile upgrades

When does an upgrade make sense? The bottom line is different for every user and every user's pocketbook, but in general, it is worth upgrading a PC when several major components are worth recycling. For example, if you have a current motherboard with a PCI bus and a capable BIOS, it probably makes sense to consider adding memory and possibly changing CPUs. Figure out the replacement cost for the components of your machine and subtract them from the price of a new system.

For the most modern machines, the most bang for your buck is to install additional RAM and possibly a new hard drive as a replacement or second storage device. If you already have a Pentium 4 CPU, you can consider purchasing a faster model of the microprocessor (and its cooling system) at the price of several hundred dollars; in my opinion, this is not the best use of your money.

For faster Pentiums with 16MB of RAM, the plummeting prices of memory argue for expansions to 64MB or more, even

Ch
7

though the actual increase in speed is relatively small. More memory, though, will make it easier to work with more than one program at a time under Windows 95/98, for example.

Installing an OverDrive chip or a third-party replacement CPU will always result in an improvement in processing speed, but be sure to weigh the price of the new chip alone against the cost of a new motherboard with a faster chipset and CPU.

For slower Pentiums (those with speeds below 100 MHz) with 8MB of RAM, the most cost-efficient upgrade is generally the addition of an extra block of memory. Get the system up to 16MB, or even better, up to 32MB. You can count on the memory transplant to improve performance by at least 25 percent — at a relatively low cost.

Figure 7-1 shows a new 1.8 GHz Pentium 4 at waiting socket; Intel's fastest consumer-level chip sits in a surface-mount socket on the motherboard.

Pentium 2 CPUs, like the one shown in Figure 7-2, were installed in large vertical cartridges that also contained cache memory. Some early Pentium 3 and AMD Athlon microprocessors used similar cartridges; later CPUs in those families returned to surface-mount sockets on the motherboard. In many cases, you can upgrade systems based on Pentium II or III CPUs by installing a faster microprocessor within the same family, or a compatible substitute. Figure 7-3 shows an Evergreen Performa upgrade that replaces an Intel Pentium II with a 766 MHz Intel Celeron CPU.

For 486 machines, the most bang for the buck generally comes from a combination of boosting RAM to 16MB or more and upgrading the CPU with a Pentium OverDrive or similar chip from a non-Intel source. In a lab test, a 486DX2-66 MHz machine was boosted by nearly 50 percent at a cost between $200 and $500, depending on whether older memory SIMMs could be reused. (The 8MB of additional RAM is probably worth about 25 percent of the boost just by itself.) Figure 7-4 shows the installation of a senior citizen Pentium.

FIGURE 7-1: *After the locking handle for this Pentium 4 CPU is put in place, a large heatsink is mounted over its top and a cowling is installed to create a wind tunnel to a fan on the rear of the computer.*

The motherboard trap

If you've read this far in this book, you are a good candidate for the most major of repair and upgrade tasks: changing the motherboard. The job is not all that difficult, but it does require a great deal of attention to detail. If you're the sort of person who can read a roadmap in a strange place, keep track of half a dozen different sets of screws, clips, and wires, and don't mind blazing a sometimes uncharted path from time to time, replacing the motherboard can be an entertaining electronic puzzle.

FIGURE 7-2: *A vertical Pentium II cartridge installs in a senior citizen PC.*

FIGURE 7-4: *A Pentium 133 MHz slips into place in a processor socket on a PCI/ISA motherboard.*

FIGURE 7-3: *Evergreen's Performa replaces a Pentium II with a faster, updated Celeron chip in a relatively simple brain transplant procedure.*

Before you buy and install a new motherboard, though, consider the hidden costs of the change. A new board may use a different bus — PCI instead of the ISA slots on an older machine, for example — which may limit your ability to reuse older components. Also, the type of memory configuration that your old motherboard uses may be different from the type that the new motherboard needs. Also, its CPU socket or slot may not work with a previous microprocessor.

A new board, like the ATX form factor design that includes I/O ports directly mounted on the motherboard, may require a new case as well.

And then you must consider the other costs of an upgrade: Will you want to upgrade to a graphics accelerator card, a larger hard drive, or a faster CD-ROM?

In any case, I suggest that you buy your motherboard and case from the same supplier; this way, you have a reasonable

Ch
7

expectation that the motherboard will actually fit and mount in the case, and you can have some hope that the seller's technical staff can assist you.

You can tell from this discussion that the overall cost of upgrading the motherboard may, in some cases, be higher than simply purchasing a packaged system complete with warranty and state-of-the-art everything. Again, do some online comparisons from packaged system houses and from the component shops before you decide on the next step toward upgrading. Although I am very comfortable upgrading machines from the motherboard up, I frequently decide to leave well enough alone and buy a new machine as my upgrade. All my computers are networked, so I usually leave the old machine on the network as a backup disk server or printer server, or use it to conduct other tasks that it can do very well in the background, even though it is slower and older than I personally want to use for my day-to-day work.

The bare-bones kit solution

One route to upgrading your system is to buy a bare-bones kit that includes a motherboard and CPU preinstalled in a case with power supply.

If you buy from a reliable source, you are relying on the expertise of the seller in matching the right CPU to the motherboard, the proper motherboard to the case, and mating the board to the half dozen power leads and connectors of the power supply and case. Figures 7-5 through 7-7 show good examples of current bare-bones systems.

It's up to you to install a floppy drive, hard drive, RAM, and video card. The drives and video cards should easily transfer from one modern machine to another. Memory may or may not be easy to move; new motherboards may use DIMMs instead of SIMMs or may demand faster chips than you have on your older machine.

Once again, it's time to sit down and add up the costs of new equipment and compare them with the price of a new system.

Don't overlook the fact that you also have to install an operating system and applications on the computer. You can transfer some from your old machine—most software licenses permit you to move the program from one system to another, as long as it does not end up running on both. If you have to pay for Windows 98 and a suite of applications, be sure to figure in that cost and compare it to the software package that is often included with new computers.

FIGURE 7-5: *This Tiger bare-bones case includes convenient side-panel access to the motherboard. The panel removes with just two screws.*

One of the systems I put together a few years ago was based around an AMD-K6 MMX processor running at 200 MHz—a clone of the Pentium MMX processor. The bare-bones package included an AT PCI motherboard with the AMD processor already installed in a Socket 7 carrier. The board included support for four 72-pin SIMMs or two 168-pin DIMMs, 512K of L2 cache, a dual-channel EIDE controller, two high-speed serial ports, and an ECP/EPP parallel port.

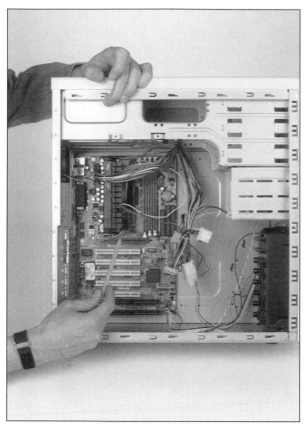

FIGURE 7-6: *A high-end bare-bones system, delivered with the motherboard and Pentium II processor in place. It's up to you to add memory, drives, and other internal peripherals and then bring it all to life with an operating system and application software.*

I added a floppy drive for installation of software and device drivers, a 6GB IDE hard drive, an SVGA video card, 32MB of RAM, a 24X CD-ROM, a basic sound card, a mouse, and a keyboard. The

cost of the system and parts would have been about $800 for all-new equipment, but I saved about half of that cost by recycling bits and pieces from other machines around the office.

FIGURE 7-7: *Under the side panel of a Tiger K6 bare-bones case.*

When you compare the $800 price tag to new prepackaged systems, you can see that this route does not represent much of a savings over buying a low-end package from a PC manufacturer.

But from the standpoint of a recycling project, such a project is a quick and easy way to upgrade a senior citizen or older modern machine to a zippy middle-of-the-road desktop.

SUMMARY

You've looked at the basics of upgrading systems in this chapter. The next chapter examines the essential area of computer memory: your PC's thinking room.

Chapter 8

Tools Needed:

- Phillips or flat-blade screwdriver
- Antistatic strip, wrist strap, or grounding pad

Memory

Memory is your computer's workspace. To a great extent, the effectiveness of your computer is related to the amount of random access memory it has. Given a choice between an adequate CPU with lots of RAM (random access memory), and a speedster CPU with insufficient RAM, I say, "Thanks for the memory."

System memory has been something of critical importance throughout the history of computers. More so than ever, today's high-speed, multitasking, graphics-rich machines demand huge amounts of memory. The first IBM PC, the dinosaur of dinosaurs, shipped with as little as 16KB of RAM. Today, a current machine should have a minimum of 64MB. That's an increase of about 4,000-fold.

I want to cover a critical distinction: Data or instructions stored in chips are said to be stored in *random access memory* (RAM). *Random access* means that the processor can jump directly to a particular bit of data. Think of RAM as the computer's desktop, where it temporarily gathers and works on the work of the moment.

Data or instructions located on a disk drive are said to be located in *storage*. Think of storage as the file cabinet crammed with all of your work transactions, as well as the instruction manuals for all the devices in your home or office. Sometimes you pull pieces out of the cabinet in order to work on them at your desk, but they always retain a relationship to their place in the file.

Storage is not quite as quickly accessible because a disk drive's read/write head must wait for the sector on the spinning disk to move into position.

CROSS-REFERENCE

I explore various forms of storage — from floppy disks to hard disks to removable disks to CD-ROMs and DVDs — in Chapters 9 through 12.

I need to add one more point to complete this analogy: At the end of the day, your computer desktop is swept clear and dumped into the trash, while the file cabinets are closed and locked away until they are needed next. In our computer analogy, RAM is a temporary workspace that goes away when power is turned off, while the disk drives are more or less permanent storage.

When I first began writing about personal computers in 1982, a 16K block of memory sold for about $100. A bit later, an add-in card with 256K of memory had dropped in price to $995, the equivalent of about $4,000 per megabyte.

At the time of this writing, you can purchase a 256MB SDRAM module for as little as $30, about 12 cents per megabyte or about two-tenths of a cent for 16KB. In other words, at today's prices, the memory on that early $995 quarter-of-a-megabyte expansion card would sell at retail for about 3 cents.

In the two years between the last edition of this book and this version, memory prices for common types of RAM modules dropped by nearly 90 percent. Though occasional bumps are inevitable on the downward-price slope because of production problems or errors in judging demand, there is no doubt that memory has become a relatively inexpensive commodity for PCs.

The bottom line: You have no reason to skimp on memory for a modern machine.

In this chapter, I introduce you to the various types of memory—an area of continuing improvements in size, speed, and cost—and give you a few hints for dealing with common memory problems.

A History of Memory

By one way of thinking, the first computer was the ancient abacus, which used beads on strings to represent its memory for stored numbers; the human brain managed the manipulation of this stored information.

The Aztecs used an abacus-like device, called the nepohualtzitzin, a millennia ago, about 900-1000 A.D. Counters were made from kernels of maize threaded through strings on a wooden frame. A Chinese device called suan-pan appeared about 1200. It later spread throughout Korea and Japan.

In England in the eighteenth century, Charles Babbage worked on his "difference engine"—a device that looked like a cross between a grasshopper and a knitting loom with cogs and wheels. Not coincidentally, about the same time, Joseph Marie

Jacquard developed a programmable knitting loom in France. The positions of those cogs and wheels, and the pins and stops of the loom, served as the programmable settings for the mechanical engines.

The first modern computers were still heavily mechanical, using similar wheels, cogs, and strange assemblages of magnets on wire that would flip one way or another to indicate a bit of information.

Today's computers are almost entirely electronic (with the exception of spinning disk drives), but the memory that they use is essentially an analog of those knitting looms or magnetic cores: RAM consists of electronic circuits that can electrically flip one way or another to indicate 0s or 1s used by the computer to store information.

The first dinosaur PCs—introduced in the 1980s—had rows of individual memory chips on their motherboards. They were small (each chip was 1K, and nine chips comprised a computer word plus an error-checking parity bit) and they were expensive.

Soon after the dawn of the dinosaur, designers began to run out of space on the motherboard for rows of chips. The next step in the evolutionary process was to move memory to expansion cards that plugged into the system's bus; the upright cards held rows of chips mounted in sockets.

Sometime around the arrival of these first senior-citizen computers, as designers began to pack more and more memory into a single chip, a new carrier was devised—the single in-line memory module (SIMM)—which was a miniature circuit board that could hold thousands, and later millions, of bytes of memory. Figure 8-1 shows an example of a SIMM.

At that time, memory moved back to the motherboard, with the addition of SIMM sockets that had a direct connection to the CPU.

Now in the era of the modern machine, nearly all current motherboards use dual in-line memory modules (DIMMs) that hold massive amounts of memory—as much as 1GB at the time of this writing—on a single circuit board that plugs into an ever-faster direct connection to the CPU. These DIMMs can hold various types of memory, including DRAM, EDO, SDRAM, and DDR.

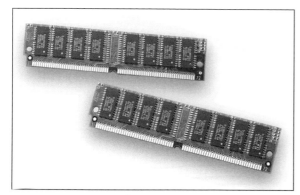

FIGURE 8-1: *A pair of 128MB 72-pin SIMMs, used in dinosaurs and some senior citizens. Note the positioning notch at the lower-left end of each SIMM, which corresponds to the number 1 pin. (Courtesy of PNY)*

Also at the time of this writing, the hot memory technology is RDRAM (Rambus memory), which uses a RIMM module, mechanically similar to a DIMM but with differing electrical properties. By the end of 2002 and into 2003, memory experts expect the emerging technology to be Double-Data Rate SDRAM (DDR SDRAM), a derivative of SDRAM.

I'll further explain each of these technologies later in this chapter.

Figure 8-2 shows a 168-pin DIMM.

FIGURE 8-2: *A 168-pin EDO DIMM. The module has an extra notch among the pins near the number 1 position. The notch is moved slightly on an SDRAM module to identify that type of memory. (Courtesy of PNY)*

How Much Memory Do You Need?

Hmmm . . . how much money do you need? Most of us would answer that we'd like a whole bunch of money, but we recognize that eventually we'd probably reach the point where we have enough to do everything that we need to do, in style.

The same holds true with memory:

- More memory is better than less memory.
- What seemed to be way too much memory a year or two ago seems like way too little today.
- Eventually, you'll reach a point where you have enough; adding more will waste money and could even slow down the machine.

The first IBM PC shipped with as little as 16K of RAM. A motherboard fully populated with individual memory chips totaling 64K was considered a high-end rocket. (Remember that 64K is

64 thousand bytes of RAM, not 64 million bytes, which today is a reasonable minimum amount for use under Windows.)

Today, you need more memory because current operating systems, such as Windows, need more working space than older systems for their own operations and additional memory to permit multiple applications to run. The price of user-friendly interfaces, graphics, sound, and even motion video and animation in standard office applications and games requires PCs with more memory.

In my opinion, the entry level for a Windows 95/98 machine is 32MB of RAM, with 64MB a more reasonable starting point. If you run graphics software or habitually keep multiple applications open simultaneously, step up to at least 128 MB. With today's low prices, it doesn't make sense to save a few dollars and sacrifice speed and functionality.

Windows XP officially requires a minimum of 64MB, but you should consider at least 256MB to be able to run multiple applications simultaneously.

It is important to note that motherboards and associated CPU chipsets have a limit on how much memory they can work with, and there is also a physical constraint on the number of SIMM or DIMM slots available to hold memory. Read the instruction manual that came with your machine or consult the manufacturer for details.

Some owners find themselves in the unpleasant situation of having to remove low-capacity SIMM or DIMM strips and replacing them with larger-capacity blocks of memory. If you have a lot of old memory, don't throw it away; consult the back pages of computer magazines to find brokers who will purchase used memory to recycle to less-demanding users. Or you may be able to donate the memory to community organizations that may have a need for older technology. Figure 8-3 pictures an older, small SIMM.

NOTE

In most cases, adding RAM to an underequipped system will improve performance. Depending on the type of motherboard, CPU, and chipset, boosts in memory will increase overall speed up to about 192MB to 256MB. (After that amount, additional memory will still benefit your system's ability to work with multiple open programs.)

In some relatively rare cases, though, adding RAM can slow down the system. The most common source of the problem is insufficient cache memory on the motherboard. You can also slow memory performance by mixing the speed of modules; in most instances, the system will move memory data no faster than the slowest module.

FIGURE 8-3: *An older 4MB SIMM*

How to Buy Memory

Modern operating systems, applications, and CPUs demand much more available memory; today's systems start at about 64MB, and consumer systems with 256MB and more are common. The good news is that although prices can fluctuate wildly because of international events and economic conditions, overall, the price of RAM has dropped precipitously in recent years.

You'll usually find the best prices on memory at places that treat it as a commodity: online stores, catalog marketers, and computer superstores.

Sometimes the pricing of modules doesn't seem to follow logic; for example, you may see situations where a 32MB DIMM is more expensive than a 64MB module. The reason is simple supply and demand. As prices of memory drop, lower-capacity modules are less in demand than higher-capacity ones. All modules, though, have some fixed costs: the printed circuit board, its connectors, packaging, shipping, and marketing.

As with hard drives, at any particular moment there is usually a "sweet spot" in the price curve. Compute the cost per megabyte for available modules and look for the point at which the cost goes up.

Remember, too, that all motherboards have a fixed number of memory slots. Look ahead and figure your memory needs in the future.

I used to think that it was safer not to put all my eggs in one basket. For example, if I wanted 32MB of memory in my machine, I would spread the risk a bit by installing two 16MB modules.

I have now changed my mind. Today's memory modules, purchased from a trusted source, are fully tested and considerably more reliable than previous hardware. The chips themselves are less likely to fail than the module that holds them, the socket on the motherboard, or the wiring to that socket. Therefore, one large module is generally more reliable than two or four smaller modules whose combined memory equals the memory of the large module.

Memory makers speak of infant-mortality failure modes for chips; this unpleasant term means that, like most other electronic elements of your system, memory that survives its first few weeks in your system is likely to last a long time. According to PNY Technologies, one of the leading memory resellers, the failure rate of memory once it has left the factory is less than 20 pieces per million; the risk lies in solder points, contacts, wiring, and sockets. The fewer of these involved, the better for the user.

And then there's a bonus in cost: As long as you are shopping in the middle of the market, among the sizes and types in the largest supply and ordinary demand — a larger module generally costs less per megabyte than a group of smaller ones because less hardware is involved.

An insider's view of memory

The good news is that memory is more or less Plug-and-Play; the bad news is that you have dozens of different types, sizes, and speeds of memory to choose from. And just to make the situation more complicated, some machines happily allow you to mix and match similar types, while other PCs choke and die if you give them anything but one specific type of memory.

Your best defense is to carefully read the instruction manual that comes with your computer or motherboard; call the PC manufacturer's support desk for assistance, as well.

It may be valuable to take off the covers of your PC and examine the layout of the motherboard. You need to know what types of memory are installed and whether there are any open chip sockets (dinosaurs), SIMM sockets (senior citizens and older modern machines), or DIMM (or RIMM) sockets in current modern machines.

Motherboards typically have four memory sockets, or slots. Some may have only two, while others may be hybrids with several DIMM and several SIMM slots. Sooner or later, though, you'll reach the limits of the board.

As much as it may pain you to do so, it may make sense to replace older, slower, and smaller memory modules with newer, faster, larger, and less-expensive replacements.

Several memory resellers have tips and technical information about memory on their Web sites. Check out:

- Crucial Technologies: `www.crucial.com`
- Kingston Technology: `www.kingston.com`
- PNY Technologies: `www.pny.com`

Counting the chips

For many users, the mathematics of memory is a black art best not examined too closely. Most of us in the industry can't disagree: this is an example of a situation where the technical types have taken over both the design and the nomenclature for a product. In this section, I try to clear up the muddle.

A *memory module* — a SIMM, DIMM, RIMM, or other such design — is a carrier for a group of chips. The size of the module is expressed as the sum of the capacities of all of the chips it holds. However, any memory that is used for other functions, such as error checking — including parity schemes — is subtracted from that sum.

The *capacity* of a modern memory module is expressed in megabytes, meaning millions of 8-bit bytes. Regarding the memory chips that make up the module: the *chip density* is measured in megabits, or millions of bits. Each memory chip is made up of hundreds of thousands or millions of cells that hold one bit of information. A 64 megabit chip has 64 million cells.

In some memory chip designs, the chip density is expressed as a description of the organization of the cells in width and depth; for example, this same 64 megabit chip may be called an 8M-by-8, or a 16M-by-4 device. A chip of larger capacity may be expressed as 16M-by-64 for 1,024 megabits.

To calculate the size of a module, determine the chip density in megabits and then multiply that result by the number of chips on the module. Then divide the total number of megabits by 8 to yield the module capacity in megabytes.

Checking memory from within Windows

You can watch the digit counter fly as your machine boots up, but detailed information about how much memory is present in your system and how it is allocated is a bit harder to come by.

If you are running Windows 95/98 and later versions, you can use two easy ways to take a reading of your system's memory capacity.

One way is to click Start ➪ Settings ➪ Control Panel and then to double-click the System icon. From there, choose the Performance tab. You see a report like the one shown in Figure 8-4 that tells you the total memory of your system, as well as the percentage of that memory that is free for use. If the percentage is low — below 25 percent — you're likely to run into performance problems as the system is forced to use the slower swap file on disk to store parts of its processes. If you are having memory problems, click the Virtual Memory button on the Performance tab and check who's controlling the virtual memory settings — you or Windows. If you've elected to control them yourself, check the Maximum and Minimum settings and the available space on the selected drive in the hard disk list box.

Another way to check system resources is to go to the Help pull-down menu of most current-version Microsoft applications and then choose the About (application name) item. For example, if you're running Microsoft Office under Windows 98: from within

Microsoft Word, choose About Microsoft Word from the Help menu and then click System Info for a detailed report about your system. Figure 8-5 shows a sample report from Microsoft's System Information utility.

FIGURE 8-4: *The memory performance report for a Pentium II 300 MHz machine, using a 128MB block of SDRAM. The report indicates that with Windows 95, Word for Windows 97, and various utilities running, 69 percent of memory resources are still available.*

Under current versions of Windows, the System Information utility is very useful, offering a view of memory usage and other elements of your system. Go to Start ➪ Programs ➪ Accessories ➪ System Tools.

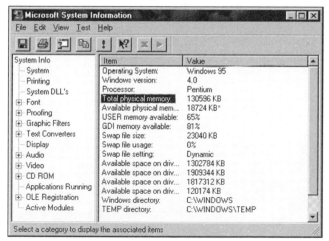

FIGURE 8-5: *Accessible from within Windows as well as many Microsoft brand applications, Microsoft System Information gives a report with information about the current operating system, as well as information about the processor, physical memory, hard drive space available, and other items.*

Where do you put your memory?

As previously noted, way back in the days of the dinosaurs, memory chips were mounted directly on the motherboard. Some early designs had them soldered into place, which made it very difficult to replace them if they failed. These were quickly supplanted by rows of small sockets to hold the memory.

Check the instruction manual for your motherboard to learn about specific needs for memory upgrades. Figures 8-6 and 8-7 show just one of many configurations for memory.

FIGURE 8-6: *On many boards, SIMMs need to be installed in pairs. This senior citizen Pentium board was designed so that the system won't operate with only a single SIMM in place. In this picture, a SIMM is being put in place in slot one of bank one; be sure to align pin 72 on the SIMM with pin 72 on the slot and push the assembly firmly into place. You may need to hold back the locking clip to enable the SIMM to slide into place properly.*

The capacities of the early memory chips were small, and they were expensive. And the motherboard of the original PC was only designed to hold 64K of RAM, which was considered more than any user had need for.

As operating systems and applications became more demanding and the hardware more accommodating, memory expansions

began to move to add-in cards that plugged into the PC's expansion bus.

FIGURE 8-7: *The second SIMM goes into place on the first bank of memory on the senior citizen Pentium motherboard. Note the antistatic strap.*

When machines became faster and faster, memory moved back to the motherboard, which enabled a speedier direct connection to the CPU. Memory in high-capacity modules was plugged into sockets on the motherboard. The first industry-standard carrier for a block of memory was a SIMM (Single In-Line Memory Module). This small printed circuit board was originally available with 30 electrical contacts and fit in a 30-pin connector, or slot.

The next step was the arrival of larger and faster 72-pin SIMM modules for 72-pin sockets.

Current motherboards ship with 168-pin DIMMs or 184-pin RIMMs or DDR modules, which put more memory in a smaller amount of real estate. They also provide better performance in today's high speed, wide-word machines because more information can be transferred in parallel from a single module.

Installation of a DIMM is shown in Figures 8-8, 8-9, and 8-10.

FIGURE 8-9: *The clips on the ends of the DIMM sockets on this ATX motherboard latch the memory modules into place.*

FIGURE 8-8: *A 64-megabyte DIMM being installed in the first memory slot of a motherboard. It is essential that you orient the DIMM in the right direction; pay attention to the notches in the DIMM and the matching protuberances on the slot.*

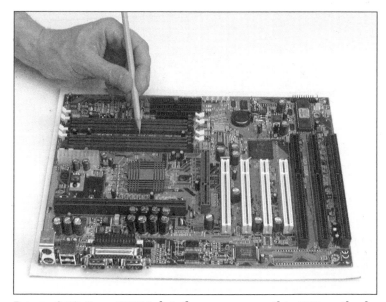

FIGURE 8-10: *Four DIMM slots for memory on this ATX motherboard represent eight banks of RAM.*

Ch 8

A Short Course in Memory Logic

If computers are so smart, how come they only understand two things: 0 and 1? The answer is that machines are not at all smart, but they are fast.

Computers do their work using an alphabet made up of just those two symbols: 0 and 1. And even the meaning of these symbols is different for the machine: 0 means that there is no value assigned, and 1 means that there is a value assigned. You can also think of 0 as "no" or "off," and 1 as "yes" or "on." (This explains, by the way, the cryptic marking on many computer power and setup switches: 0 means off and 1 means on.)

The machine uses the 0s and 1s to construct numbers using the binary mathematical system. It's not anywhere as complex as it seems. Each place in a binary number is a power of 2 (1, 2, 4, 8, 16, and so on). Each position is either on or off. Here's a quick and painless lesson.

In binary notation, the number 154 is represented as follows:

```
1 0 0 1 1 0 1 0
```

The way to translate that number in decimal terms is to read it from right to left this way:

```
No 1s, one 2, no 4s, one 8, one 16, no 32s, no 64s, and
one 128
```

or

```
0x1 + 1x2 + 0x4 + 1x8 + 1x16 + 0x32 + 0x64 + 1x128
```

As you can see, deciphering this value as 154 is a lot more work in binary math, but it is a lot simpler for the machine to manipulate values when they can only be on or off. A computer makes up for the relative awkwardness of its counting method with its blazing speed.

In a computer's binary system, numbers are divided into groups of eight binary digits called a byte. Each of the positions in the byte is called a bit, a term derived from the term binary digit.

As microcomputers have advanced from dinosaur to modern machine, the size of the collection of data bits that is processed as a unit (the CPU's register size) has increased. The original microcomputer CPUs only had the horsepower and bandwidth to deal with 8-bit data. Subsequent improvements have pushed register sizes to 16 bits (80286 CPUs), 32 bits (386, 486, and Pentium CPUs), and 64 bits for current CPUs.

The bigger the register size, the bigger the chunk of information processed by the CPU. At the same time, the memory in your PC must be fast enough to keep up with the demands of the CPU. So, along with the increase in register size, the size of the memory bus, which transfers data between the CPU registers (or in modern CPUs, the primary, or internal, cache) and memory, has also grown.

A 30-pin SIMM can move 8 bits at a time with each transaction between the CPU and its memory (each transaction is called a *bus cycle*). This rate is just fine for a dinosaur.

The next step up was a 32-bit CPU such as a 486 processor. The earliest devices in this class of senior citizens used four 30-pin SIMMs per bank to deliver 32 data bits at a time to the processor. Later motherboards moved to 72-pin SIMMs, permitting the 486 processor to simultaneously draw all 32 bits from a single SIMM bank.

With the arrival of the 64-bit Pentium, early motherboards continued with 32-bit SIMMs; they had to be installed in pairs, comprising a *memory bank*. The CPU communicated with a bank of memory as if it were a single logical unit.

Most current motherboard designs use 168-pin DIMMs that are 64 bits wide, so a single module delivers a full 64 bits to the memory bus. Advanced boards based on RDRAM use RIMMs with narrower 16-bit data paths that can transmit data very quickly using *pipelining technology* to send four packets at a time, thus allowing a 64-bit CPU to process the data as if a single 64-bit chunk had arrived.

NOTE

You need to buy memory upgrades in the correct configuration. The manual that came with your computer should be quite clear about what you need, but you may also need to contact the manufacturer. Or, consult with a memory reseller; most maintain databases of motherboards that can identify the specific needs of your machine.

Computer users live in a sort of netherworld beneath the decimal-based world of humans, where numbers are expressed in powers of 10, not coincidentally the number of fingers on two hands. You know that 1,000 is 10 times 10 times 10. And you also recognize that the Greek word *kilo*, abbreviated as K, stands for 1,000 when you refer to decimal numbers, and similarly that *mega* stands for 1 million and *giga* for 1 billion.

K, M, and G are used somewhat confusingly as adjectives in front of both decimal and binary numbers. When used to describe capacity for memory storage, K stands for 1,024. Table 8-1 is a cheat sheet to help you think of binary terms in decimal equivalents through Exabytes; beyond, lay Zettabytes and Yottabytes.

TABLE 8-1: Decimal Values of Binary Abbreviations

Abbreviation	Meaning	Value in a Binary Number
Kb	Kilobit	1,024 bits
KB	Kilobyte	1,024 bytes
Mb	Megabit	1,048,576 bits
MB	Megabyte	1,048,576 bytes
Gb	Gigabit	1,073,741,824 bits
GB	Gigabyte	1,073,741,824 bytes
Tb	Terabit	1,099,511,627,776 bits
TB	Terabyte	1,099,511,627,776 bytes
Pb	Petabit	1,125,899,906,842,624 bits
PB	Petabyte	1,125,899,906,842,624 bytes
Eb	Exabit	1,152,921,504,606,846,976 bits
EB	Exabyte	1,152,921,504,606,846,976 bytes

A NOTE ABOUT METALS

Some PC users search for gold on the contacts of memory modules. Most SIMMs have tin leads, while DIMMs and RIMMs usually have gold leads.

If you plug a tin-plated module into a socket with gold contacts, or the other way around, you face a slight risk that oxidation that occurs between the two metals could damage the socket or the module resulting in memory failures. It is possible for oxidation to cause problems in a period as short as a year, or it could take more years than your PC's useful life.

Don't ask for trouble here. Match the metal on the contacts to the metal in the socket: tin with tin, or gold with gold.

If you do end up with a mix, you may want to schedule semi-annual cleaning sessions with an electrical contact cleaning solution; never polish the contacts dry because this can generate damaging static electricity. Keep in mind that the memory modules themselves are designed for only a finite number of insertions and removals before the plating may be damaged — most modules can withstand just a few dozen ins and outs. It's a better bet to avoid the problem in the first place.

Current Memory Technologies

The race to come up with the fastest, largest, and (usually) least expensive memory technology continues. This race is all to the benefit of the user, but the result is a sometimes bewildering array of memory types.

Most experts look to the developing DDR SDRAM technology as the next great thing, comparable in bandwidth to dual-channel RDRAM despite apparent differences in bandwidth. RDRAM memory has a slightly greater latency than DDR or standard SDRAM; latency is the amount of time a system has to wait after a request for transfer of data from a new page of memory.

And, although RDRAM has extra bandwidth, it is only of value when the processor's bus is at least as large. For example, dual-channel RDRAM capable of 3.2GB/second of bandwidth could not reach its potential in a system with a 133MHz processor bus; RDRAM only approaches its capacity with a motherboard based on a high-speed Pentium 4 CPU and a 400 MHz bus.

In any case, a doubling of memory bandwidth does not usually result in anything near a doubling of system performance in the best cases because a well-designed modern system is drawing a high percentage of its data from L1 and L2 caches once an application is up and running.

When Intel first released the Pentium 4, its 850 chipsets were intended to support RDRAM. In late 2001, the 845 chipset was introduced permitting use of the Pentium 4 with SDRAM, and in early 2002 expanded its support to include DDR 200/266 memory.

Laboratory tests say that RDRAM offers a potential boost in performance of about 10 percent to 15 percent over SDRAM. As this book goes to press, though, a 256MB SDRAM module sold at retail for as little as $30, while an RDRAM module of the same size cost $135.

For graphics- and video-intensive users, the higher cost of an RDRAM system may be a worthwhile investment. If your work concentrates on standard office applications, you might want to invest the difference on a slightly faster CPU or a better video card.

Some industry analysts expect RDRAM and DDR to share the market for high-end systems through 2002, with DDR emerging as the leading technology in 2003.

However, Rambus designers plan to offer modules that will work with motherboards with 500 MHz buses in coming years. And the next improvement is expected to be Quad Rambus Signaling Level (QRSL) technology, which permits transmission of 4 bits per clock period per data line, doubling data-transfer rates to an effective speed of 4 GB/second for a single channel, and 8 GB/second for dual-channel modules.

The ultimate measure of the utility of a memory design is its bandwidth—the total capacity of the channel, determined by multiplying the speed of the memory bus by the number of data cycles per clock cycle and the width of the memory bus. You'll find a comparison for modern memory designs in Table 8-2.

TABLE 8-2: Bandwidth for Modern Memory Technologies

	Memory Bus Speed	Data Cycles per Clock Cycle	Effective Data Rate (Bus times data cycles)	Memory Bus Width	Bandwidth
PC66 SDRAM	66 MHz	1	66	8	533 MB/second
PC100 SDRAM	100 MHz	1	100	8 bytes	800 MB/second
PC133 SDRAM	133 MHz	1	133	8 bytes	1.1 GB/second
PC600 RDRAM	300 MHz	2	600	2 bytes	1.2 GB/second
PC700 RDRAM	350 MHz	2	700	2 bytes	1.4 GB/second
PC1600 DDR	100 MHz	2	200	8 bytes	1.6 GB/second
PC800 RDRAM	400 MHz	2	800	2 bytes	1.6 GB/second
PC2100 DDR	133 MHz	2	266	8 bytes	2.1 GB/second
PC2700 DDR	166 MHz	2	333	8 bytes	2.7 GB/second
PC800 Dual Channel RDRAM	400 MHz	2	800	4 bytes	3.2 GB/second

Synchronous DRAM

Most modern machines use synchronous DRAM (dynamic random access memory), a scheme that uses a clock coordinated with the CPU so that memory cycles are synchronized. The result is improved efficiency. The synchronous clock enables SDRAM to read and to write information with no wait states: one clock cycle per access up to 100 MHz.

If you're buying SDRAM for your system, make sure you buy memory fast enough for your CPU and system bus. Current SDRAM technology supports 7.5ns, 8ns, 10ns, and 12ns chips — nanosecond designations you are probably accustomed to seeing with asynchronous DRAMs. But with synchronous DRAM, you must be sure your chips can work with the system bus (sometimes referred to as the front-side bus) in your computer.

SDRAM DIMMs meant for 66MHz operation are usually rated at 10ns, DIMMs for a 100MHz bus are rated at 8ns, and those for a 133MHz bus are rated at 7.5ns. Memory manufacturers label their SDRAM with an indicator of their match to the front-side bus: PC66, PC100, and PC133.

SDRAM does not need to be installed in pairs. You can add any size of memory module, as long as you do not exceed the system specifications.

In most cases, you will get the best performance from your PC if you put the largest module (in megabytes) in the lowest-numbered slot on the motherboard — usually, but not always, the slot nearest the CPU socket. For example, if your computer has a 32MB module in place and you want to add 128MB, you should move the smaller module to slot 1 and place the 128MB module in slot 0.

Generally you can mix PC66, PC100, and PC133 memory in the same system. However, all of the memory in the PC will run at the slowest memory module's speed. Note, too, that some systems won't run properly with a mix of memory speeds; consult your instruction manual or system manufacturer for details.

You may come across "registered" SDRAM. This specialized type of memory process signals slightly differently from standard SDRAM; it contains a register that delays all information transferred to the module by one clock cycle. Registered SDRAM is intended primarily for use in servers that have huge banks of memory.

Most PCs will only accept unbuffered SDRAM. If your motherboard does support registered SDRAM and you choose to use that type, all of the modules in the PC must be registered; unbuffered and registered modules are not interchangeable.

Double data rate (DDR) SDRAM

The next generation of SDRAM was DDR (double data rate) memory. Like SDRAM, the operation of DDR is synchronous with the system clock. However, DDR reads data on both the rising and falling edges of the clock signal while SDRAM only carries information on the rising edge of a signal. This permits a DDR module to transfer data about twice as fast as SDRAM; on a PC133 bus, this permits an effective rate of 266MHz. This doesn't mean your system will run twice as fast, but your memory will, and that is bound to improve the overall performance of your PC.

DDR DIMMs are not compatible with systems designed for SDRAM or RDRAM; the modules have a different electrical layout and a different key notch so that they won't fit into the wrong socket. The modules have 184 pins, compared to 168 pins on an SDRAM DIMM. Less commonly used DDR SO-DIMMs have 200 pins, compared to 144 on an SDRAM SO-DIMM.

As a derivative of SDRAM, the DDR memory bus runs at standard rates of 100 MHz for PC1600, 133 MHz for PC2100, and 166 MHz for PC2700. But because the modules run at a double data rate, the industry convention is to refer to the effective data rates of 200, 266, and 333 MHz. Multiplying the data rate times the memory bus width of 8 bytes yields the naming conventions for DDR modules. For example, PC1600 operates a double data rate on a 100 MHz bus with 8 bytes: $100 \times 2 \times 8 = 1600$.

Rambus (RDRAM) memory

RDRAM, a proprietary memory technology developed by Rambus, Inc., is a CMOS DRAM that can provide sustainable system throughput three to four times faster than standard SDRAM, up 3.2 GBps using dual Rambus channels.

Rambus memory sends less information on the data bus (only 16 bits wide, as opposed to the 32 or 64 bits bus of a modern motherboard) but it sends data more frequently. Like DDR, Rambus memory also reads data on both the rising and falling edges of the clock signal, permitting transfer speeds of 800MHz and higher.

Rambus carriers are known as RIMMs (Rambus inline memory modules), which are mechanically similar to DIMMs, but they don't use the same electrical connections. An example of a 128MB RIMM is shown in Figure 8-11.

Memory modules must be installed in pairs of matched memory size. On an RDRAM motherboard, all of the memory slots are wired in series, meaning that each memory slot must be populated with a RIMM, or with a special continuity module that completes the circuit. Memory modules have a metal cover on one side to serve as a heat sink; continuity modules are bare circuit boards.

In theory, an 800 MHz data flow should be more than twice as fast as that of a DDR operating at 266MHz. However, Rambus modules take longer to start moving the first block of data than a DDR system; technically, Rambus memory has a higher latency. The reason for this is the serial wiring that connects the memory slots. The first bit of data must pass through each RIMM module before it reaches the bus.

The best use of the speed of a Rambus system is to transport lengthy streams of data — in a game or streaming video application, for example.

When Rambus was first introduced in 1999, motherboards with more than two RIMM modules ran into technical problems with Intel's original chipsets. Thousands of motherboards were built with three sockets and were ready to be shipped before Intel notified manufacturers of a two-RIMM limit. Some manufacturers scrapped the boards they had built and reissued new, two-RIMM boards. Others reworked the third RIMM socket to disable it.

Today, most modern motherboards intended for use with Rambus modules are based around the Intel 850 chipset and typically include four sockets for memory.

Manufacturers must pay a royalty to Rambus to produce RIMMS; that's one reason RIMMs are more expensive than SDRAM or DDR memory; another reason is that Rambus chips themselves are a bit more costly to make.

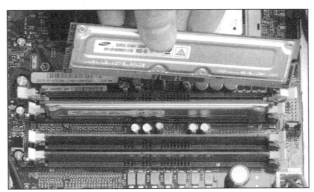

FIGURE 8-11: *A RIMM module installs in a Pentium 4 motherboard; in the foreground are two continuity modules to fill unused memory slots.*

EDO and burst-EDO RAM

Extended-data-out memory (EDO RAM) and burst-EDO memory are updates to the previous speed champion, fast page-mode (FPM) memory. FPM memory was more than adequate for 486 processors, but not quite up to the demands of the faster memory bus speeds of Pentium-based systems.

The difference comes down to a matter of persistence of memory: FPM loses data after it has been read, while EDO holds the last data request in a buffer while reading the next request. EDO's extended memory enables the bus speed to match the Pentium, which runs at 60 MHz or, more commonly, at 66 MHz, twice the realistic speed limit for FPM and 486-based systems. Newer 100 MHz bus systems with synchronous memory designs require even more performance out of their memory chips.

You need a motherboard and controller chipset that recognizes EDO memory; Intel introduced such facilities with its Triton chipset. In a real-world environment, EDO should offer a 10 to 15 percent speed advantage over comparable FPM chips.

EDO memory works with most current PC controllers, and you can mix it with FPM memory as long as the two types of memory reside in different banks. In my office, I upgraded an older machine by adding 8MB of new EDO RAM to 8MB of older FPM memory. Putting the EDO RAM in the first bank speeds loading of Windows 95 a tiny bit.

Another form of memory is burst extended-data-out (BEDO) DRAM, a form of EDO that uses pipelining to achieve better throughput performance. The throughput of BEDO and SDRAM is about the same, they just use different technologies to achieve the improvements. However, Intel chipsets don't support BEDO DRAM, so SDRAM has won out over BEDO DRAM with most system manufacturers.

Memory modules

As previously explored, machines dating from the late dinosaur era through modern times aggregate their memory on modules that plug into special sockets on the motherboard. The oldest of the dinosaurs accepted individual memory chips on the motherboard or on an adapter card that plugged into the bus.

If you are seeking to keep alive one of these ancient dinosaurs, you'll have to search the bins of used computer stores or the back bins of supply outlets.

The first widely-used memory module was a 30-pin SIMM, followed by more capacious and speedier 72-pin SIMMs. You should be able to find some types and sizes of this type of module from major memory suppliers such as Crucial, Kingston, or PNY.

184-pin DDR DIMMs and RDRAM RIMMs

The current co-owners of the position as state-of-the-art PC memory are DDR SDRAM and Rambus RDRAM. Each of these designs uses a memory module with 184 pins.

DDR DIMMs and RDRAM RIMMs are similar in mechanical construction but incompatible in electrical design and can't be interchanged, nor used in older machines designed for other memory technologies.

DDR can usually be installed one module at a time. RDRAM, though, must be installed in equal-size pairs and unused sockets must have a continuity module in place to complete the serial circuit required by the RDRAM specification.

168-pin DIMMs

Current modern machines use 168-pin DIMMs, high-capacity modules that are 64-bits wide. Because the memory matches the needs of the memory bus, you can install DIMMs one at a time in a Pentium-class machine.

NOTE

Some senior citizen motherboards bridged a technology gap by accepting both DIMMs and SIMMs. Some required you to use one or the other type. If the motherboard permitted you to mix memory types, you may need to set a jumper on the motherboard to indicate which socket to use as base memory.

Prior to the arrival of DIMMs, memory chips had almost always required 5 volts of power. Some early modern-machine motherboard designs continued with 5-volt modules, but most current motherboards are less demanding, requiring 3.3 volts. The position of a notch on the DIMM indicates the voltage demands of the module and should prevent users from using the wrong type of DIMM module.

It is possible to force a DIMM into place, probably ruining the motherboard in the process. Take care to buy the proper voltage

DIMM (you have to go out of your way to find the relatively rare 5-volt modules).

When 168-pin DIMMs first arrived, they were populated with DRAM. Today, nearly all use high-speed SDRAM. You will also find EDO and DDR memory; most motherboards do not permit a mix of memory types; be sure to consult the instruction manual to learn if there are any allowable combinations of SDRAM, EDO, or DDR.

One further distinction in current memory is buffered RAM, a relatively uncommon design. Most motherboard designs perform buffering themselves. Buffered RAM is indicated by another notch on the module, and again, you should take care not to try to force a module into the wrong type of socket.

72-pin SIMMs

The middle step in the evolution of memory modules — now relegated to dinosaur status — was the 72-pin SIMM, a 32-bit design that is the equivalent of four 30-pin SIMMs. As such, it takes only one SIMM to fulfill the needs of the 32-bit bus, and you can build the system up one SIMM at a time.

WARNING

Some machines require installation of the largest SIMM module in the first memory socket with lesser modules in successive sockets. Consult your instruction manual for advice.

Some 72-pin modules are considered double-sided, with one bank using one side of the card and its electrical connectors and the other bank making use of the other side. Some dinosaur motherboards, including many made by Micronics (and used in a range of antique Dell machines) would work only with certain sizes of modules — 1, 4, and 16MB modules are single-sided while 2, 8, and 32MB are double-sided. Again, check the instruction manual or consult the support desk.

Pentium machines required 64 bits of memory information; therefore, they require that modules be installed in pairs.

About the same time as the arrival of the Pentium came the first EDO memory systems, which ran about 15 to 20 percent faster than previous FPM systems.

EDO is only compatible with machines that specifically support this form of memory, but EDO PCs can also use standard FPM. You must have the same type of memory in a single bank, but most machines are able to work with one bank of EDO and one FPM. In such a system, you likely receive the best performance by putting EDO in bank 0 because the system addresses the first block of memory most often.

Some older memory modules were labeled in this format: 16X64, or 16X72. The first number represents the size of the individual chips on the module; the second number is the width of the data path in bits. Multiply the two numbers together, then divide by eight or nine, whichever results in an even number. This gives you the size of your module in megabytes (MB). (If the number is divisible only by eight, the module does not use parity or ECC.)

30-pin SIMMs

Further back in the dinosaur era, most 386SX PCs and some other outmoded motherboards used 30-pin SIMM modules. Each SIMM is 8 bits wide, and as a 16-bit processor, the 386SX required installation of pairs of modules.

Many of these machines are limited by their chipset and BIOS to working with smaller modules — 256K to 1MB — and can't handle large amounts of memory. Sometimes a BIOS upgrade helps.

There are two common designs for 30-pin SIMMs. The original format has nine chips and was the most universally compatible. A subsequent design used just three chips, two for data and one for the seventh and eighth data bits plus a single parity bit.

If you need to replace a module of the older design, you may have a hard time; check closeout suppliers and used-equipment vendors.

Motherboards based around 386DX, 486SX, and 486DX microprocessors use a 32-bit bus and require installation of 30-pin modules, four at a time. Each of the modules in a bank has to be the same size. To add 4MB to a bank, you must use four modules of 1MB each.

Although you can't mix sizes, many machines can work with modules of varying speed. However, the slowest memory in the machine becomes the fastest speed for the machine.

NOTE

Here's a golden rule of speed: You shouldn't install memory more than 10ns slower than the recommended speed for your particular motherboard.

If a manufacturer asks for 60ns RAM, you can install 70ns memory and expect good results. If you go to 80ns RAM, though, you may experience serious slowdowns or even a lockup. The higher the number, the slower the response, so 80ns is slower than 70ns memory.

Memory manufacturers mark chips with their slowest speeds. For example, a 70ns chip will typically run anywhere from 61 to 70ns.

Recycling 30-pin SIMMs

What do you do if you have a bunch of older 30-pin SIMMS with perfectly good memory chips, and a slightly less ancient motherboard with 72-pin slots? A careful shopper may be able to locate an interesting fixer-upper part that lets you plug two, four, or even eight 30-pin SIMMs into a small circuit card that in turn plugs into the 72-pin DIMM slot on the motherboard.

If you search the closeout bins, you may be able to find such a device with a name such as Simmstacker or Simm 4 Recycler. There was also the Simm Doubler, which allowed you to plug two 72-pin SIMMs into a single 72-pin slot. Though they accomplished

just what they promised, these are only stopgap solutions. For most modern applications, you're better off upgrading to a new motherboard and using faster and larger DIMMs. Figure 8-12 shows this sort of SIMM expansion device.

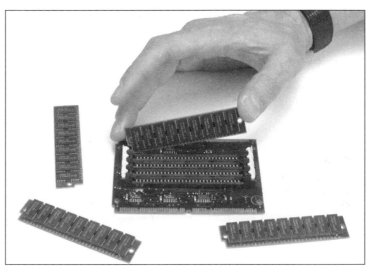

FIGURE 8-12: *One way to recycle older memory is to use a device like the SIMM Recycler. The unit pictured here converts four 30-pin SIMM modules into a single 72-pin module.*

Error detection and correction

When personal computers first came on the market, a great deal of attention focused on detecting errors in memory chips. There were two main reasons for this: First, early memory chips were somewhat prone to electronic hiccups. Second, the original computers were designed by engineers who were taught that it was better to stop a machine dead in its tracks than to allow it to make an error, no matter how minor the problem.

The following sections cover the two common methods used to examine the integrity of data: parity checking and error-correcting code.

Parity checking

Nearly every dinosaur, senior citizen, and most early modern machines used a parity scheme that added an extra bit of memory as an error-checking device. While 8 bits made up each byte, a ninth, associated bit recorded whether the sum of the other eight bits was odd or even. All circuitry had to accommodate this ninth bit of information, which added expense to the manufacture of the motherboard and required an extra memory chip with every eight on the motherboard.

Parity schemes were either even or odd, meaning that the parity bit (the ninth bit of each byte) was set to the value that would make the sum of nine bits even or odd, depending on the design of the system.

Parity was a rather primitive means for checking to see if the contents of any of the hundreds of thousands or millions of bits of information had failed. Think about this: If two bits with the same value in a particular byte fail, the errors cancel each other out and the parity check gives a false-positive report.

The easiest way to find out if a dinosaur machine has parity chips is to count the number of chips in the system. If the number is divisible by nine, then parity checking is in use.

Today, things are a bit different. First of all, memory chips are much more reliable than they were 20 years ago. The likelihood of a single bit going bad is not that great; more likely is the failure of an entire chip that the system would bring to the attention of the user. Second, engineers realized that for most users, a minor error in one bit was not likely to cause a major problem. It might make one character in a long document come out wrong (and the computer's spelling checker would likely find it), or it might cause a tiny problem with an onscreen graphic.

In today's way of thinking, only a relatively small number of users need to spend the extra money and effort to try to track down and correct every possible, rare error. If you are controlling the launch of the space shuttle or monitoring a heart-lung machine, you may want a redundant error-correcting computer.

Otherwise, it's more advantageous to let software programs perform their own internal error-checking processes and to remove error-checking processes from your hardware.

And so today, nearly all consumer and business modern machines (and a small group of dinosaurs) use non-parity memory. It's less expensive, a factor that takes on even greater importance in machines having 32MB of memory or even more.

You can't mix parity and non-parity modules on a motherboard.

NOTE

For a short period of time, some dinosaur machines used parity memory boards that didn't do parity checking. This so-called *fake-parity memory* has a chip in the right place for a parity chip, but it doesn't do any parity checking. This parity generator chip works by always sending the "OK" signal; it does not have the capacity to detect errors. Fake-parity memory came about as a lower-priced alternative to parity-checked memory and at a time when memory chips were in short supply. By removing one chip in each bank — the parity chip — manufacturers could produce more memory modules with fewer chips. Fake parity memory may work fine in your system, but it may not. It depends on your motherboard and memory slot design. You may be able to identify fake-parity boards by the BP, VT, GSM, or MPEC designations on the parity generator chip. Otherwise, you need a SIMM memory tester. Check with a service group or your computer's manufacturer.

Error-correcting code

Error-correcting code (ECC) is used in high-end machines used for banking and other real-time applications where the computer directly controls a process.

The difference between ECC and parity is that ECC can detect a 1-bit error and then fix it. Depending on the type of memory controller in the PC, ECC can also detect less-common 2-, 3-, or 4-bit memory errors, although in most such systems, it can't correct a multibit error.

ECC works by computing a value for data bits and comparing that value to decoded data retrieved from memory chips; a similar scheme is used in error-detection and correction systems used in telecommunications.

ECC memory on a modern machine may use a distinctive design of two x36 SIMMs in a bank; of the resulting 72 bits, 64 bits are allocated to data and 8 bits to ECC code. You may also see a motherboard with 72-pin SIMMs with an x39 or x40 width specification. Call a memory vendor and read the markings on the memory chips, check the instruction manual, or contact the manufacturer of a modern machine if you have any doubts about the type of memory.

About Memory Speed

Measuring the true speed of memory is a bit like nailing Jell-O to the wall; first, you must understand that RAM is very fast at what it does. In a modern machine, the real difference between one type of memory technology or another is the speed of the memory controller (part of the chipset) and the bus used to move data from one place to another.

Here's a brief review of a few of the basic building blocks of the PC. The CPU or microprocessor is the brains of the operation, where computing takes place. The CPU is supported by the chipset; among its functions is the memory controller, responsible for overseeing the flow of data between the memory and the CPU and back again.

The data highway on the motherboard is the bus, a set of parallel wires connecting the CPU, memory, and other devices, including those responsible for input and output. The motherboard also is home to the memory bus from the memory controller to the memory. The design for the memory bus on current modern machines includes a frontside bus (FSB) from the CPU to main memory and a backside bus (BSB) from the memory controller to L2 cache.

When the microprocessor requires data from memory, it issues a command to the memory controller, which fetches the information from memory and at the same time sends a message to the CPU to report when the data will be available.

The issuance of the command, its management by the controller, the report back to the CPU, and the actual movement of the data are all part of the memory system's overhead; the time for the retrieval of the data from memory is related to the speed of the processor, the chipset, and the memory bus that interconnects them all.

Older memory chips and modules were rated with access times ranging from 100ns to 50ns; the lower the rating, the faster the memory chips were in response to commands.

With the arrival of Synchronous DRAM (SDRAM) technology memory chips were fast enough to synchronize their cycles to the computer's system clock, the drumbeat that allows all of the disparate parts of the PC to work together. Each rise and fall of the clock signal is considered one clock cycle; a 133MHz clock generates 133 million clock cycles per second.

Some components of the computer are fast enough to perform their work on a single clock cycle, while others require multiple cycles. And modern CPUs typically run much faster than the bus, at what is called a clock multiplier.

The physical location of main memory also helps determine the speed of memory in a system. The faster the clock speed of the microprocessor and the memory bus it employs, the greater the effect on even tiny differences in distance.

Among the techniques used by engineers to speed the reaction of memory are *interleaving, pipelining,* and *bursting.*

When memory is *interleaved,* the processor alternates its attention between two or more memory banks or cell banks within a memory chip. Each time a block of memory is addressed by the CPU, it requires about one clock cycle to reset itself; by moving on to a different bank the CPU can work with that memory without pausing for the clock cycle.

SDRAM and some other memory chip designs include two independent cell banks that allow the same sort of process, permitting a continuous flow of data without pauses for resetting.

In a *pipelined* system, a task is divided into small overlapping tasks with pieces of the work completed at different stages.

Bursting is a technology in which the CPU makes an educated guess on what data or instructions it expects to need next; it grabs not only the block of information it needs but also other addresses that are contiguous to it because of the likelihood that additional data is located nearby.

Cache memory

In this section, I examine a most productive way in which a modern computer "cheats" to pick up speed. Cache memory is a small block of very fast memory that is physically located very close to the CPU. Because it is so close, and because the CPU does not have to go through the memory controller to get to it, the contents of cache memory are more quickly available. I'm talking about nanoseconds here (billionths of a second), but a few billionths here and a few billionths there quickly add up to some real time on a high-speed system.

Memory designers base their designs on what they call the "80/20" rule, which calculates that about 20 percent of the instructions, applications, and data on a typical computer is in use about 80 percent of the time. Among the most often-used bits of code: low-level instructions on saving or retrieving files, recognizing input from the keyboard, and, increasingly, Internet-related commands.

When the CPU makes an instruction, the memory controller saves a copy to cache; the most recently used bit of data is assigned the highest priority. When the cache is full, the oldest bit of data is overwritten.

Cache memory can be a part of the CPU itself, nearby on the module or cartridge that holds the processor, or in a socket on the motherboard. And modern designs often include more than one level of cache memory; the closest is called Level 1 or L1 cache, or primary cache.

Secondary cache, also called Level 2 or L2 cache, is another level of cache memory available to the CPU. In some systems without an L1 cache, the L2 cache functions as primary cache. L2 cache can be an integral part of the CPU or can reside on separate chips positioned close to the CPU. The fastest L2 cache is part of the CPU package because data transfer distance is reduced.

Cache memory is managed by a cache memory controller. When this specialized chip retrieves an instruction from main memory, it also grabs hold of the next few instructions and places them in memory, working under the logical assumption that adjacent instructions will also be called upon. The better the algorithm used to manage the cache controller, the more efficient the use of the cache and the better the speed for the CPU. Figure 8-13 shows an example of a cache memory module.

In my previous discussion of memory, I described RAM as the computer's desktop. Think of cache as a notepad for jotting reminders. If you keep your notepad right in front of you, when the phone rings, you can pick up previous topics and ask the caller the right questions without wasting time looking for a file. Likewise, when the CPU needs something and finds it in the cache, processing speeds can improve by at least 10 to 20 percent over the same machine without cache.

Cache memory also is a little different from conventional system memory. Whereas most system memory is dynamic (DRAM), meaning that the information it stores must be updated continuously, cache memory is usually static memory (SRAM), meaning that once the data is written into memory, it stays there until it is replaced or the system is powered down. This provides for fast performance and low overhead because neither the CPU nor the memory subsystem has to spend cycles keeping the memory refreshed. SRAM is more expensive than DRAM, and its benefit is only seen in relatively small amounts of memory, which explains why the entire system's memory is not constructed from static RAM.

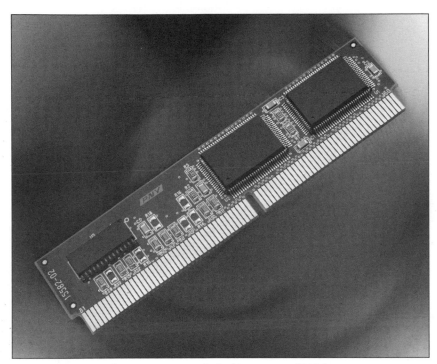

FIGURE 8-13: *A cache memory module (Courtesy of PNY)*

Unlike the system memory, in most cases, PC cache can't be easily upgraded. To upgrade your cache, you will probably need to upgrade your motherboard or purchase a new system. Consult your motherboard manual to determine if your system is one of a relatively small number of boards that can work with more than one specification for cache.

Memory Problems

Your best defense against memory problems is to purchase quality modules, test them after installation using a capable diagnostic program, and test them again with the diagnostics from time to time.

Nearly every PC from the birth of the species has included a memory check as part of the POST (power-on self-test) that occurs when a machine first boots up. Under the control of the BIOS, the system quickly counts all the memory it can find in the system. This process is not the same as a full test of the capabilities and accuracy of each chip that occurs when you run a diagnostic program.

The other type of memory error can be much more annoying—a fatal crash of your system in the middle of your work.

Errors at startup

If your computer fails to allow you to get past the POST, reboot immediately and see if the problem happens again.

If it does not, proceed to your operating system and run a full diagnostics check of the memory. If the diagnostic program reports no problem, you may have an intermittent problem with memory. As long as the problem occurs rarely and does not interfere with your work, you can continue to use the machine.

If the POST again reports a problem and refuses to let you continue into bootup, shut off the machine, let it cool off for about 15 minutes, and then try again. If the system performs without problem when it is cool, you may have a failing memory chip or a module that is not making good contact with its connectors. Heat causes parts of the system to expand, which can cause loss of connection.

If you suspect a mechanical problem with the system, turn off the machine and unplug the power cord. Remove the cover. Ground yourself before reaching into the system and then gently push down on memory chips or modules in the PC. Look for memory that may have worked its way out of the socket.

If your diagnostic program reports a failure of a block of memory, it's time to replace the RAM. There is no reasonable way to repair memory, and memory modules for current machines are very inexpensive.

Errors after bootup

You're typing along in your word processor and all of a sudden everything freezes. Or the screen suddenly clears and is replaced with the ominous Blue Screen of Death with a cryptic error message.

I won't burden you with unnecessary explanations about how operating systems handle memory or other memory matters that concern programmers; numerous books cover the technical side of memory. Instead, I focus only on fixing the suddenly forgetful machine.

First of all, if the problem occurs just once, or rarely, chalk it up to some unusual combination of software settings and memory usage, and proceed merrily on your way. (You should, though, make certain that you have instructed your word processor and other applications to save your work automatically on a regular basis — my very reliable machines are nevertheless set to save versions of work in progress every three minutes, meaning that the most I could lose is whatever I have accomplished in the last 179 seconds or so.)

If the problem recurs, try to identify a pattern: Does the system always freeze when you load a particular program or perform a particularly complex task? It may be that you are pushing your system to use more memory than it usually asks for, and there may be problems with that block that are not often exposed. A thorough test with a diagnostic program should help. There may be a conflict with other programs that reside in a particular block of memory not ordinarily used by your application.

If you can cause the problem to reoccur on command from within a particular piece of software, contact the technical support department for the application for advice on possible software memory settings that may cure the problem.

If the error seems related to Windows settings, you can reinstall the operating system to see if this will cure the problem. Windows 95 and Windows 98 will reinstall over a previous copy; consult the instruction manual or call technical support for assistance.

Dinosaur memory errors: NMI

On dinosaurs and senior citizens, one common announcement of memory problems is the following BIOS message:

```
NMI error at [address]
```

or

```
Memory parity interrupt at [address]
```

If you have a Phoenix BIOS, the message may continue as follows:

```
Type (S)hut off NMI, (R)eboot, (I)gnore
```

An NMI, or nonmaskable interrupt, is one condition that the hardware is not permitted to mask, or ignore, while processing another task. When an NMI occurs, the NMI error message goes up on the screen and everything deadlocks until you address the NMI error, no matter what else is going on.

The most important nonmaskable interrupt on dinosaurs and some senior citizens is a parity error — a report by the computer that it found something wrong with the contents of at least one byte in memory.

Parity is a system used by some computer systems to check each byte of data for errors. A special controller adds the values of the eight bits in a byte and determines if the total is odd or even; it then compares that result to the indicator in a ninth bit that accompanies each byte. If the comparison fails, the system declares an error.

As we have seen, the first dinosaur PCs all used parity memory systems. As systems began demanding more and more memory and the chips or modules became more reliable, system manufacturers began producing nonparity memory designs.

Today, most modern machines do not use parity.

In any case, a memory parity test is performed by the BIOS. The microprocessor and the operating system are not yet involved. So there is no point thinking about the possibilities of a bad CPU or defective software code when you're considering the causes of an NMI error.

What causes a parity error? Four possibilities exist:

- A bad RAM chip
- A drop in voltage that causes the chips to forget the stored data
- Malfunctioning address logic to the memory chips that causes one RAM chip to be mistaken for another
- A bad parity logic chip that reports a parity problem when none exists

The first two problems, a bad chip or low power, are the most likely to occur and the easiest to deal with. The last two are somewhat rarer symptoms of bad (and usually nonreplaceable) chips or circuits on the motherboard.

Here's how to troubleshoot a NMI error a little further. What can you determine from the address on the screen that's part of the NMI message? Unfortunately, the information does not explain where the problem is located, but instead points to the place in memory where the program was working when it got that error, even though the error could have come from any place in memory.

To correct the problem, try the following courses of action:

First, run a software memory test. If the test finds bad chips, consider yourself lucky and replace them. Note that memory test programs are generally unable to test the lowest 64K of RAM where the basic elements of the operating system reside. Check out www.tucows.com, a shareware Web site, a good source for memory testing and other diagnostic software. Especially strong on this site are utilities for optimizing system memory usage on the fly.

If you are lucky, the offending memory may only be loose in its socket. Turn off the PC and unplug it, open up the case, ground yourself, and press firmly on all of the SIMM or DIMM strips or, on a dinosaur, on the individual memory chips.

If you believe the chips are good, it's time to consider low power. For the memory to operate properly, it requires a reliable source of power. Do you have good incoming power? Most computers expect power from the wall outlet to be in the range of 104 to 120 volts. Do you have many added devices straining the power supply?

What time of the year is it? A summer heat wave could bring a brownout (a drop in voltage) in many parts of the country; you can call your power company to see if it is experiencing any problems. In some homes and offices, voltage will dip significantly when a major electrical motor is turned on. Are you sharing the line with a refrigerator or an elevator? If you have any doubts, test the current at the wall with a voltmeter. Basic units sell for less than $20 at Radio Shack; be sure to follow the manufacturer's instructions on working with live voltage.

In any case, it's a good idea to install an uninterruptible power supply that will condition your power line so that it falls within an acceptable range and that will also protect against power outages. UPS models start at about $100. Pick one with enough juice to enable you to perform an orderly shutdown of your system if the power fails completely.

One other possible cause of intermittent memory errors is a flaky power supply. You could try swapping memory from your machine to a known good machine, or try using a different power supply.

If you still have NMI errors, replace the power supply with a known good unit. Power supplies sell for about $30 to $100; it is a good idea to have a spare unit available, or at least to know of a retail outlet or mail-order service that can deliver a unit within a day. There is no way to test a power supply for those short-term voltage drops that produce intermittent NMI errors. If the problem doesn't go away after you replace the power supply, there are two other possible solutions, both expensive: Replace the motherboard or replace all the RAM chips. Neither solution is more likely than the other to be the correct choice, and you may end up doing both.

If this approach doesn't sound scientific, you won't get an argument from me. But there is really no other choice. Enormously expensive machines capable of analyzing the current flow on every wire in the motherboard could be built, but they would have to be redesigned every time a new motherboard is introduced. Nothing justifies that sort of an expense.

If you have a true dinosaur PC or PC/XT clone with memory chips soldered in place on the motherboard and a persistent memory error message, it's time to replace the whole machine, or at the least the motherboard and its memory. No cost-benefit scenario makes it worthwhile to try to bring a completely extinct creature back from the dead.

If you have a dinosaur XT with socketed memory chips on the motherboard, you can spend a reasonable amount of time checking that the chips are properly seated. If you have an extra known-good chip you can play a maddeningly slow game of swapping it in and out of the board in search of a failed chip; you'll have to boot up the machine each time you've plugged it in and run whatever tests you can. But, again, you'll still have an XT when you're through. And the memory you may be bringing to the new system may be old, slow, and too small.

The Relationship of Memory to the Operating System

One of the major tasks of the operating system—from dinosaur versions of DOS through current Windows (and the components of DOS that underlie it)—is the management of memory resources.

All things being equal, you should be running the most current version of Windows your system will support. On a truly ancient dinosaur, you should at the least be running the last stand-alone edition of DOS, labeled version 6.22.

(If you execute a VER (version) command from DOS in Windows 95, you are told that the DOS is Windows 95 plus a version number. Similarly, under Windows 98, the DOS is officially Windows 98 plus a version number, and Windows XP has its own underlaying equivalent to DOS.)

Current operating systems run in *protected memory*, which allows use of extended memory for programs and hardware drivers; only a small portion of the operating system has to stay within conventional memory, which reduces the chances of conflicts for precious memory resources.

PC-DOS and MS-DOS in versions preceding 5.0 can only address 1MB of RAM, and a good portion of that memory is already dedicated to the display adapter's RAM and BIOS, the hard disk's BIOS, and the PC's BIOS. Often, those BIOSes are copied (shadowed) into RAM, using even more of the 1MB. DOS 5.0 and later can trick 286 and later machines into using a large amount of memory. The all-but-forgotten DR-DOS 6.0 has the same capability.

Programs running under DOS 3.3 and earlier versions make use of expanded memory through a technique called bank switching. Blocks of 16K are switched in and out of a 64K window in RAM. Up to 8MB of extra RAM can be added in this manner. Expanded (bank-switched) memory cards still work, but modern machines make use of simpler facilities than are possible under current versions of DOS.

Organized Memory

The following list describes the organization of memory in a typical modern machine:

- **Conventional memory.** Also called base memory, this is the first 640K of memory, the original limit of user memory (for the operating system and applications) for dinosaurs and dino-DOS. The first several hundred bytes within conventional memory, used by the operating system and installable device drivers, are sometimes referred to as lower memory.
- **Upper memory.** This is the area between the top of conventional memory and 1MB. A total of 384K is available. (For the record, the exact amount is 393,216 bytes. Here's the math: A kilobyte is actually 1,024 bytes in size, making

640K equal to 655,360 bytes. 1MB equals $1,024 \times 1,024$, or 1,048,576 bytes. Therefore, 1MB minus 640K equals 393,216 bytes.)

Some sections of upper memory are usually taken over by parts of modern machine hardware, such as for video BIOS. You can (and should) use memory management software to stake your claim to unused sections of upper memory.

- **Extended memory.** Extended memory enables modern machines to use memory located above the upper-memory 1MB limit. Some programs can access this memory directly, while others must go through an extended memory manager or device driver.
- **High memory.** This first 64K of extended memory is generally controlled by HIMEM.SYS and used to hold DOS when the operating system is instructed to load DOS = HIGH.
- **Expanded memory.** A dinosaur-era work-around, not used in current machines. This scheme allowed memory above the 1MB ceiling to be bank-switched under the control of expanded memory manager software. Expanded memory divided memory into 16K pages. Blocks of four pages, called a page frame, were switched in and out of a 64K area in upper memory.

Memory Troubleshooter

Memory problems can have several sources: a physical failure of memory modules, incorrect settings in BIOS, Windows configuration problems, or improper settings within the application itself.

Here are some questions to ask:

Have you recently added memory? If so, there are several paths to follow: did you install the proper type, speed, and configuration of memory for your motherboard? Depending on its design, the motherboard may require you to install memory in banks of two modules, or populate the banks in a particular order. On modern RDRAM systems, modules must be installed in pairs and any unused sockets must be filled with continuity modules. Consult the instruction manual for your motherboard or seek the assistance of memory resellers who maintain databases of motherboard specifications.

Check, too, that the memory module is properly seated in the socket.

Has a BIOS setting been made to disable some portion of the RAM? Some BIOS screens include the ability to set a memory limit; some earlier BIOS screens required the user to specify the amount, type, and location of RAM.

Reboot your system and go to the BIOS configuration screen. (The route to the screen varies depending on the type of BIOS installed.) Look for RAM settings; they may be found on an Advanced tab of the CMOS.

Make note of any changes you make to the BIOS so that you can undo them in case you introduce a problem with your actions.

Have you chosen to manage the settings for virtual memory instead of leaving it to Windows? You may think you are smarter than the folks at Microsoft, but you may be setting yourself up for problems by choosing to take control of virtual memory settings instead of leaving it to Windows to automatically take control.

The default setting for Windows is to have the operating system control settings; you would have had to manually make a change here to take over. The recommended size is equivalent to 150 percent of the amount of RAM on your system.

To give control of virtual memory settings to Windows 95/98, click Start, then Settings, then Control Panel. Double-click System. Go to the System Properties dialog box, click the Performance tab, and then click Virtual Memory. Finally, click to select Let Windows manage my virtual memory settings (recommended), and then click OK.

Under Windows XP, the process is similar. The memory manager is located under the Advanced tab of System Properties.

Check to see if a virtual device driver is claiming some of your RAM without your knowledge. Some applications load special drivers at bootup that grab hold of a piece of memory.

This is more of an issue for operating systems through Windows 95/98 and Windows ME.

To check on use of these drivers, use the facilities of the MSCONFIG program to turn off the processing of the SYSTEM.INI file at bootup.

Here are the steps: Click on Start and then Run. In the Open box, type **MSCONFIG** and then click OK. The configuration utility will display. On the General tab, click on the box to enable Selective Startup. Click to clear (removing the check mark) the box called Process System.ini file. Click OK and then click Yes to restart your computer.

Watch the screen to see if your computer now reports the correct amount of RAM. If this does not solve the problem, the problem is probably not related to a virtual device driver; be sure to go back to MSCONFIG and return operations to Normal Startup.

If disabling the System.ini file seems to correct the problem, your next step is to try to identify the specific file included in System.ini that may be the source of the problem.

Go to the MSCONFIG utility. Click on Start and then Run. In the Open box, type **MSCONFIG** and then click OK. The configuration utility will display. On the System.ini tab, locate the listing for [386Enh] and click on the + sign to expand it.

Differentiate between the items in the [386Enh] listing that are preceded by the Windows logo and those that are not. Leave the components of Windows untouched.

Click on the check box to the left of the first non-Windows component to disable it. Then restart your computer.

If disabling the component does not fix the problem, go back to MSCONFIG and re-enable the component within the [386Enh] listing. Go on to the next non-Windows component, disable it and restart the system.

If you reach a point where the system responds properly, you can assume the disabled component was involved. At this point, your best bet is to attempt to identify the source of the component

and then contact the manufacturer of the product involved to see if there is an updated version or a known bug.

If the maker of the Virtual Device Driver is not obvious from its name, you can search a bit deeper in your system. Most such drivers can be found in the C:\Windows\System\VMM32 folder.

You can also click on Start then Find and then Files or Folders. Enter the name of the driver.

When you locate the driver, right click on its name and then click on Properties and then open the Version tab. You should be able to find the manufacturer of the driver on one or more of the panels displayed.

Check to see if a protected-mode driver is causing a memory mismatch. Some pieces of hardware use device drivers that are resident in the lower, or protected, mode of memory.

To investigate, click Start, then Settings and Control Panel. Then double-click System.

Distinguish between peripherals and System Devices. Start by making up a list of the most likely suspects; begin with any devices recently installed or updated.

Open the Device Manager tab and click on the + symbol to open one of the classes of devices in the list. Double click on one of the devices to open a dialog box; then click to select the Disable in this hardware profile check box.

Do *not* restart the computer.

Continue to open each of the devices, except for System Devices and the hard disk controller, and disable them.

When you have finished, restart the computer.

Check the available memory; one way within Windows is to click Start, then Control panel, and then double-click on System. From the System Properties dialog box, click the Performance tab and read the memory report there.

If your PC seems to be working properly, proceed under the assumption that one of the devices in the list is causing the problem. To isolate it, work backwards, enabling one device at a time and rebooting to see if the problem has come back. At this point, consult instruction manuals for the suspect device, check the manufacturer's website, or call the manufacturer for support on configuring the device so that it does not cause a memory conflict.

Do you receive an out-of-memory message when using a particular program? Check to see if the problem can be repeated — reboot and return to the program. If the problem recurs, check the instruction manuals for the program, the manufacturer's website, or call the company's support line for assistance.

Other reasons for running out of memory include having too many programs open at the same time; the best cure here is to add more RAM. Some programs allow you to make configuration settings that may allow them to demand less memory.

When you quit a program but do not restart the computer, some applications are not very good at freeing up all of the memory resources they had once required. It may be necessary to restart your computer to clear these demands.

SUMMARY

You've completed a tour of RAM, the temporary working space of the computer. From here, you move on to storage memory, including floppy and hard drives, removable media drives, and CD-ROMs.

Chapter 9

Tools Needed:

- Phillips or flat-blade screwdriver

Floppy Drives

The floppy disk drive has been part of the PC from the beginning, although its role has changed dramatically over the years. It's sometimes hard to remember that at one time, floppy disks were the primary means of data storage for the PC. Today, floppy disks serve a much different role — as emergency bootup devices and a means of transferring small amounts of data or simple programs.

The original IBM PC was shipped with one large, 3-inch-tall, single-sided, standard-density floppy disk drive, capable of holding a grand total of 160K of information on a fragile 5.25-inch floppy disk. The drives were quite slow at transferring data and — just to make things interesting — were prone to mechanical failure. Today, much smaller drives stand less than an inch tall, can hold nearly ten times more data on a 3.5-inch disk encased in a hard plastic protector, and are extremely reliable.

Floppy drives are so rarely used these days that some computer designs have dispensed with them altogether, relying instead upon CD-ROM, the Internet, and other external storage devices that attach via the increasingly common USB port. As Chapter 11 explains, technologies such as Iomega's Zip Drive or Imation's SuperDisk can squeeze 100MB, 120MB, 250MB, or more information on special 3.5-inch disks.

On some of the most primitive of the dinosaurs, a single 5.25-inch floppy disk drive was intended to hold the operating system, a simple application, such as a word processor or spreadsheet, and a small amount of data files. Soon, PC users moved on to a basic setup that consisted of a pair of double-density drives — one for the operating system and the application program, and a second for data storage.

With the arrival of the PC-XT came the first widespread use of hard disk drives for PCs. At that point, most of the previous assignments for the floppy disk drive were taken over by the hard drive, which stored the operating system, applications, and data. The floppy disk drive — by this time expanded in capacity but reduced in size — was relegated to a means to load new information and applications onto the hard drive and to easily transfer data from one machine to another (the sneaker net method), and as an emergency boot device in case the hard drive failed or its contents were damaged.

In the early days of PCs, a handful of applications attempted to prevent unauthorized copying by requiring that the floppy disk drive hold an official copy of the program, even if you were operating from the hard drive. That annoying feature is all but gone from modern machines, although you may still see some hardware-based security measures, such as software that will run only if you plug a cable or connector with security firmware into the serial or parallel port.

By the time that modern machines gained full acceptance, floppy disk drives were still the source of new programs and data. High-density designs took on a new role — that of a low-cost backup. Today, CD-ROMs and Internet downloads have taken over the role of loading huge programs and operating systems.

Today, the principal role of the floppy disk is to provide a secondary route for loading new programs or device drivers and to serve as an emergency boot drive when the hard drive is in trouble. Figure 9-1 shows a current floppy disk drive.

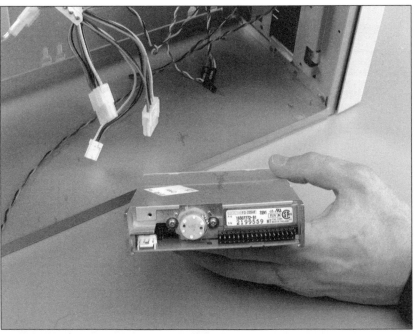

FIGURE 9-1: *A replacement floppy drive, showing connectors*

You can easily operate a PC without a floppy disk drive; in fact, Apple has dropped the drive from most of its models, and some desktop PC workstations have also dispensed with them. In either case, you can attach an external drive to a USB port. (Although it can be months or even years between occasions when I use the floppy drive on my systems, I like to know that I can easily boot a crashed machine to life to troubleshoot a problem with my hard drive.)

Understanding Storage Technologies

Before exploring floppy disk drives, I want to take a moment to distinguish the various disk storage technologies available for use on PCs:

- Removable and fixed media
- Magnetic and optical storage
- Random access and sequential storage

Removable versus fixed media

The distinction between fixed and removable media still makes sense from a troubleshooting perspective. Fixed media are sealed. If anything goes wrong with either the media or the media-access machinery, you have to replace the entire hard disk. If something is wrong with a floppy disk but the drive itself is okay, simply throw away the bad disk. Or, if the drive fails, throw away the mechanism and use the disk in a new drive.

The original IBM PC was capable of controlling one or two single-sided disk drives and a cassette tape drive. Both disk drives and the cassette drive used removable media — you could replace the disk in your disk drive with another or insert a different cassette in the tape recorder.

The cassette drive option was a joke from the moment of its release — it was painfully slow, of questionable reliability, and rarely used. IBM included the cassette drive interface because the first personal computers for hobbyists, including devices from Commodore and Radio Shack, used this means of loading and storing the simple BASIC language programs that users wrote for themselves. Soon after the cassette drive's release, though, IBM began to think beyond the hobbyist to the business user and the cassette port disappeared. Floppy disks became the basic vehicle for distributing PC software and were the first reliable means of data storage.

The first of the dinosaurs used a floppy disk capable of storing 160K of information under DOS 1.0. That was quickly upgraded to 180K with a revision of the operating system. The floppy disks themselves—5.25-inch-square, thin, black plastic envelopes over a fragile circle of plastic coated with metallic particles—were easily damaged and held too little data to satisfy either programmers or users.

About a year into the life of the PC came the first double-sided floppy disk drives with read/write heads that were capable of looking at both sides of the spinning disk. These drives doubled capacity to 360K, which seemed capacious at the time but is woefully inadequate in modern times.

In 1983, IBM introduced the XT, the first member of the PC family with a hard disk (or *fixed disk*, as IBM preferred to call it), which distinguished the new sealed medium from the removable floppy drive diskettes.

A few years later came the first 3.5-inch floppy disk drives, an improvement that had its genesis in the Apple Macintosh. Though they are called floppy disks, the circle of thin magnetized plastic is encased within a hard plastic shell, nicely protected by a sliding cover. The initial 3.5-inch disks doubled the capacity of removable floppies to 720K. In ensuing years, both 5.25-inch and 3.5-inch disks doubled again in capacity through the use of high-density magnetic material and new electronics.

In the early 1990s, IBM introduced super-high-capacity floppies capable of storage of 2.88MB; they were offered in IBM's own PS/2 series of machines and a handful of competitive machines, but the market did not embrace them.

TIP

Owners of machines with these high-capacity floppy drives may have to deal with IBM or search the backrooms of computer dealers to replace the devices and fresh media.

A current standard, widely embraced by many users, is the high-capacity Zip drive, developed by Iomega. Zip disks, slightly larger than a 3.5-inch floppy, can store from 100MB to 250MB of data, depending on the model you choose. Zip drives sell for about $70 for 100MB models and about $180 for a 250MB, USB drive. Disks are available for as little as $8 each in quantity for 100MB media; 250MB disks cost about $17 each.

The principal disadvantage of the Zip drive is that most machines are not able to boot from a Zip, which prevents their use as an emergency startup or antivirus repair device. However, the most modern BIOS systems now permit selection of an attached Zip drive as a boot device.

Another standard is the LS-120 SuperDisk, which can hold as much as 120MB of data. One advantage of this system is that SuperDisk drives can also read and write to standard 3.5-inch floppy drives of 1.44MB capacity, and can be used as a boot device. A number of computer makers offered SuperDisk drives in PCs in recent years, but the drive lags far behind Iomega's Zip drive in acceptance.

You can purchase an IDE internal SuperDisk drive for about $100, and external USB or parallel port devices for about $135. LS-120 disks sell for about $6–$8 apiece.

CROSS-REFERENCE

I discuss Zip and SuperDisk drives in more detail in Chapter 11.

Table 9-1 provides a history of the floppy standard.

Ch 9

TABLE 9-1: A PC Floppy Disk Chronology

Floppy Drive Type	Capacity	PC Usage
Single-sided 5.25 inch	160K	Original IBM PC
Single-sided 5.25-inch	180K	Original IBM PC, upgraded DOS
Double-sided 5.25-inch	360K	PC, PC-XT
Standard density 3.5-inch	720K	PC-AT
High-density 5.25-inch	1.2MB	PC-AT, modern machines
High-density 3.5-inch	1.44MB	Modern machines
Quad-density 3.5-inch	2.88MB	A relatively rare standard used in some modern machines

Magnetic versus optical media

As PCs have evolved, the bulk of all data storage has used a technology based on magnetism. An electronically controlled read/write head is instructed to record an indication of 1 or 0 across the length of a floppy or hard disk track, down the length of a tape, or on a removable platter of a hard drive cartridge.

Here's how magnetic recording works:

1. An intelligent controller instructs the storage device to vary an electrical current that is fed into an electromagnetic recording device.
2. The head produces a stream of plus or minus electrical signals that represent the 1s or 0s of digital information.
3. The information is written onto a medium that is coated with metallic particles that are able to hold onto a magnetic setting.
4. The medium moves under the head, either spinning (disks) or streaming past on rollers (tapes).
5. The controller reserves a special portion of the disk for itself for writing a special record to keep track of which files were recorded in particular places.

Later, the user can ask the drive to run the same section of the disk or tape under the head. As the changing magnetic field passes beneath the head, it induces a variable current flow, re-creating the original current flow used to write the data to the disk or tape.

Magnetic recording technology predates the dawn of the PC by many years. Audio tape recorders read and write the same way, and the ubiquitous VCR machines of our time use the same concept, differing principally in the pattern that the recording heads use to store information.

Over the past five years or so, the PC world has begun to make use of advanced optical media that use nonmagnetic means to write and read data. The leading optical device for PCs is the CD-ROM (compact disc read-only memory), a computer adaptation of the CDs produced for audio systems. These discs are increasingly used as a distribution method for operating systems and applications; the standard CD-ROM can hold about 660MB of information on a platter that costs less than a dollar to manufacture; slightly larger-capacity CD-ROMs are also available, although not all readers or writers will work properly with them. A variant of the CD-ROM is the DVD-ROM (digital versatile disc), which can pack as much as 17GB on a disc the same size as a CD-ROM disc.

 CROSS-REFERENCE

See Chapter 12 for more details about CD-ROM and DVD-ROM technology.

Floptical disk drives are a hybrid of optical and magnetic technologies, introduced in the mid-1990s. The drives use ordinary magnetic read/write techniques, but they cram more than 700 tracks into the space as opposed to high-density 3.5-inch diskettes that distribute only 80 tracks. Flopticals use optical technology to position the magnetic read/write head accurately over the correct track.

Another type of hybrid technology is the magneto-optical (MO) disk. These devices use a highly focused beam of laser light to illuminate and momentarily heat a tiny portion of a special magnetically coated disk. The burst of heat enables recording of a great deal of magnetic information; when not heated, the material is extremely stable magnetically, and so has a greater-than-normal retention rate. In other words, an MO disk is much less likely to lose its information by natural decay of magnetism or by accidental erasure.

The SuperDisk system, discussed previously in this chapter, uses yet another technology, a highly accurate magnetic read-write head that is controlled by a laser servomotor (hence the name LS-120 for the 120MB disk standard it uses).

Random access versus sequential media

Records and music CDs are random access media. This means that you can lift the needle on the record or move the laser on a CD directly to a particular song and then play it. Audio and video-cassette tapes, by comparison, are sequential. If you want to get from the first song to the tenth, or from the start of a movie to the end, you have to fast-forward through the length of the tape.

Floppy diskettes, hard drives, removable disk cartridges, CD-ROMs, DVD-ROMs, and Floptical disks are all random access media. Data is easy to find. It's easy to write new data to an empty portion of the disk. And the drive read/write mechanism can quickly move from one location on the disk to another. It's not quite instantaneous, though; all storage devices are measured in terms of their average seek and access speeds. The *seek speed* is the average amount of time, in milliseconds, it takes the read head to move to the location of the data. The *access time* includes the time it takes on average to transfer the located data.

Computer data tapes are sequential, similar to audio and videotapes. Most tapes use a storage design referred to as *serpentine*. They record several tracks on the tape, moving from one end to the other and then making a U-turn and continuing on the next track in the opposite direction. They are relatively inexpensive

and capable of storing huge amounts of data — as much as 200GB of information in some forms — but they are slow and difficult to use if you need to retrieve a particular piece of information.

Floppy Disks

Floppy disks — the material within the outside protective casing — are made of plastic (usually Mylar) coated with a ferric oxide capable of holding a magnetic charge. The plastic is flexible — hence the name *floppy*. Because of this, the plastic and coating are easily damaged. Although it is enclosed in a square protective jacket, the disk can still be damaged.

Ways to abuse your floppy disk

Here are some things you don't want to do with a floppy disk:

- Roll over it with your chair
- Use it as a coaster for a cup of coffee
- Spill a Coke over a stack of disks
- Bend a 5.25-inch floppy in half to fit it in an envelope
- Staple a 5.25-inch floppy disk to a file folder

Trust me, users have performed every one of those acts — and many more even stranger. The most infamous of all disk-destroying acts is attaching a floppy disk to the side of a file cabinet with a magnet; you probably won't lose the disk, but you'll almost certainly lose some or all of its contents. Also, be aware of less-than-obvious sources of magnetism, including some scissors, screwdrivers, and electric motors, such as those powering pencil sharpeners. Speaker systems and monitors also give off some magnetic radiation, although modern models have shields to reduce the chances of damage; still, it is not a good idea to place a floppy disk on a monitor or speaker.

Because they're enclosed in a stiff cover that prevents casual contamination, 3.5-inch floppy disks are sturdier and less sensitive to extraneous magnetic fields. Under their high-tech cover, standard 3.5-inch disks use the same read/write technology as 5.25-inch floppies.

The relatively rare, extra-high-density (2.88MB size) 3.5-inch floppy disks use a different coating—barium ferrite—plus a special perpendicular recording technology and twice as many sectors per track as high-density (1.44MB) floppy disks. The 2.88MB drive can read 1.44MB and 720K floppies as well because it has a separate recording head to maintain compatibility with the older 3.5-inch disk. You'll probably need a device driver to use the 2.88MB drives with older ROM BIOS chips.

How floppy disks work: Welcome to the Super Bowl

Imagine a circular stadium, with 40 or 80 concentric rows of seats; these are the tracks of a floppy disk. The stadium has 9, 12, or 18 aisles radiating out from the center, which split the stadium seats into sections (the disk's sectors). The stadium owner sells tickets only to groups, and only in multiple-sector, single-row blocks (clusters). If the group doesn't have enough spectators (bytes of data) to fill a complete block, that's tough; the rest of the seats in the cluster just have to go to waste and stay empty.

To help visitors or late arrivals find their group, the stadium owner keeps a master chart at the ticket office showing where each group has been seated. This chart also tells the stadium owner which clusters are still available and which clusters are unusable because some seats in the cluster are broken.

Here's the technical description:

When you insert a 3.5-inch floppy disk into the drive and close the door, the drive mechanism engages with a small slot on the bottom of the disk so that it will spin true. The process of inserting the disk pushes back a sliding cover over the media within the plastic case. At the same time, two read/write heads— one for the top surface of the floppy (side 0) and one for the bottom surface (side 1)—move into position, pressing lightly on the

disk. The heads are now prepared to read the magnetic marks on the disk or to write new ones.

NOTE

The read/write heads touch the disk media—this is very different from the design used by hard drives and most removable media storage devices, which float the heads above the surface. Floppy drives spin at only 300 RPM (for 3.5-inch disks) or 360 RPM (for 5.25-inch drives), and the media surface is coated with Teflon or similar compounds to reduce friction. However, over time, the surface of the disk does become degraded. No hard-and-fast rule exists for the expected lifetime of a floppy except this: They don't last forever.

The drive moves these read/write heads according to commands from the controller card. In turn, floppy disk drive controllers get their read or write instructions from DOS or the operating system. These instructions are quite explicit. For example, DOS may tell the floppy disk drive controller to instruct the floppy drive to move the read/write head to track 15, sector 5, and read the contents of that sector.

The floppy disk drive controller is not a particularly sophisticated device. It doesn't have to keep track of the contents of a disk; DOS does that. It doesn't have to know what parts of the disk are empty and available to store new data; DOS does that, too. Nor does it have to decide which read/write head on the drive it is going to activate. The floppy disk drive controller does, however, have to change the DOS-instruction move to track 15 into on/off signals that control the stepper motor that moves the heads from track to track. It also has to know what sector of the floppy disk is under the read/write head at any moment.

For 5.25-inch drives, the floppy disk drive controller locates sectors with the aid of an index hole punched in the floppy disk jacket and in the disk within. When the floppy disk spins, the two index holes line up once every revolution and an electric eye in the disk drive sends a signal to the floppy disk drive controller each time they line up. Knowing where the index mark is, the controller then counts the sector markers until the desired sector is under the read/write head. The controller reads the data in the sector, separating housekeeping bits from the actual data, and returns a clean stream of data to the microprocessor across the bus.

A 3.5-inch drive works in a similar fashion, except that the mechanism knows where it is on the spinning track because of a notch in the center metal spindle of the inner plastic disk. The rotor on the drive motor engages directly into the notch.

R.I.P. 5.25-inch drives

In this section, I discuss both 5.25-inch and 3.5-inch floppy disk drives. However, the 5.25-inch disk format is all but dead — all new machines have abandoned that older form in favor of advanced 3.5-inch drives.

The only reason to install a new 5.25-inch drive or replace an older one is if you have a large stack of 5.25-inch disks with important information recorded on them. If you have only a few such disks, perhaps you can find a friend or coworker who has a machine with both 5.25-inch and 3.5-inch drives installed and transfer the information to the smaller disks.

At one point in the evolution of the PC, some makers sold combo drives that included both 5.25-inch and 3.5-inch drives in a single slim body that occupy just a single bay in your PC. In any case, you'll find it very difficult to find replacement 5.25-inch drives now; your best bet is to search the bins of the used computer stores, online hobbyist sites, and the back closets of your office.

Tracks and sectors

The surface of the floppy is divided into circular tracks and then into sectors so that data can be stored in a particular location and easily found again. Imagine the floppy rotating in the floppy drive, like a record on a turntable. Hold an imaginary felt-tip marker half an inch from the outer edge of the record and gently lower it onto

the surface. The circle drawn on the surface of the record is track 0. If you could accurately move the marker just $\frac{1}{50}$ inch toward the center of the record, that new circle would be track 1, as shown in Figure 9-2.

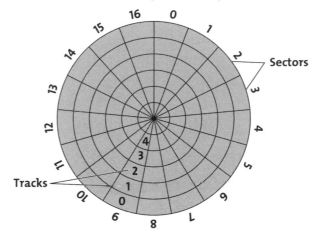

Constant Angular Velocity

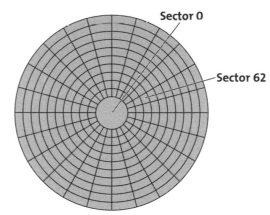

Constant Linear Velocity

FIGURE 9-2: *Bottom: The spiraling constant linear velocity (CLV) method used by CD-ROM drives. Top: A standard hard or floppy disk with sectors and tracks records data by using the constant angular velocity (CAV) method.*

You may imagine that information is written uniformly across the entire surface of a floppy disk, but that is not the case. A dinosaur 5.25-inch 360K floppy disk, for example, has all 40 tracks packed tightly together in a band less than an inch wide near the outer edge of the disk. This makes sense because the longest (most spacious) tracks are near the outer edge of the disk. At 48 tracks per inch (TPI), these 360K disks are called *double-density*. By comparison, 1.2MB floppy disks jam 80 tracks in the same band less than an inch wide. These high-density 1.2MB floppies have 96 TPI. Both the 720K and the 1.44MB versions of 3.5-inch disks have 80 tracks and are 96 TPI.

A track is a very large space. On a 360K floppy, for example, a single track holds more than 4,600 bytes of data. The track is divided into nine sectors. Each sector on a 360K disk holds 512 bytes of data—a more manageable size for the computer to deal with. A 1.2MB disk has 15 sectors, each with 512K of data. A 720K disk has nine sectors, each with 512 bytes of data per sector. A 1.44MB floppy records twice as much data per track, cramming 18 sectors onto each track.

Here's the calculation for the total amount of data storage available on a disk:

Tracks × Sectors × Bytes per sector × Number of sides = MB data

For example, for a 1.2MB floppy, 80 tracks × 15 sectors × 512 bytes per sector × two sides of the floppy = 1.2MB of data.

Table 9-2 compares the TPI and sectors per track in double-density versus high-density disks for both 5.25-inch and 3.5-inch disks.

Directory and FAT

When you format a disk, DOS creates a file allocation table (FAT) and a directory on track 0 so that stored data can be located on the disk. The directory contains the filename, size, date, time of last modification, file attributes, and physical location of the first part of the file. The FAT contains information about each cluster.

TABLE 9-2: Physical Disk Configuration for Standard Floppy Disk Types

Type	Size	Capacity	Tracks per Side	Sectors per Track	Bytes per Sector	Compatible OS
Double density	5.25-inch	360K	40	9	512	2.0 or later
High density	5.25-inch	1.2MB	80	15	512	3.0 or later
Double density	3.5-inch	720K	80	9	512	3.2 or later, all Windows
High density	3.5-inch	1.44MB	80	18	512	3.3 or later, all Windows
Extra high density	3.5-inch	2.88MB	80	36	512	5.0 or later, all Windows

A *cluster* is a conveniently sized group of sectors used to store information. There are typically one or two sectors per cluster for a floppy drive (one sector for 1.2 and 1.44MB disks, and two sectors for older 360 and 720K and the relatively rare 2.88MB disk) and four sectors per cluster for a hard drive. All reading and writing on disks is done in whole-cluster increments. If only half a cluster is filled with data from File A, the rest of the cluster is left blank.

As noted, the FAT stores information about the contents of each cluster. The FAT is a numeric list of all the clusters, with space for a coded entry for each cluster. A zero in an empty cluster's FAT indicates that the cluster is available for use. Physically defective areas on the disk are marked bad by locking out the appropriate clusters in the FAT. Clusters with a nonzero FAT entry contain data.

A file appears to DOS as a chain of clusters. The first cluster is entered in the directory, along with the filename and other directory information. The FAT entry for that first cluster shows the number of the next cluster in the chain. The last cluster containing data for File A is marked as the end.

The Brains of the Outfit: The Floppy Disk Controller

The floppy drive contains the motor and mechanism necessary to spin the disk and move the head to any desired track on the disk. It also has drive-door-closed (for 5.25-inch drives) or disk-present (for 3.5-inch drives) sensors, and write-protect sensors.

The brains of the disk reading-and-writing process are in the floppy drive controller, which is an interface (a connection point) between the computer bus and the floppy disk drives. The controller gets read/write instructions from the microprocessor and data from the bus and then sends both down a ribbon cable to the drives. Working the other way, the controller instructs the floppy drive to locate a particular block of data and then picks it up and sends it across the PC's bus.

Dinosaur PCs used separate floppy and hard drive controllers. Senior citizens often offered combination cards that featured both floppy and hard drive controllers. And nearly all modern machines include a FDD (floppy disk drive) and a pair of EIDE (Enhanced Integrated Drive Electronics) or HDD (hard disk drive) connectors on the motherboard. In any case, because the electronics for each subsystem are independent, one system may fail while the other continues to work properly.

Figure 9-3 shows the connectors on a current motherboard.

FIGURE 9-3: *A floppy disk connector is near the memory slots on this Micro-Star ATX motherboard. The port can drive two floppy drives on a single cable with a pair of connectors.*

Dinosaur PCs and advanced floppy disk drives

Early versions of DOS did not support 3.5-inch floppy drives. DOS 3.2 supports 720K drives, but not high-density 1.44MB drives.

DOS 3.3 and later versions can handle either 720K or 1.44MB drives. DOS 5.0 and later versions can handle 2.88MB floppy drives, plus all others. All versions of Windows will work with high-density floppy disk drives; some specialized drives may require installation of device drivers.

The BIOS chip in modern machines can operate either high- or low-density 3.5-inch floppy drives. Many dinosaur computers, on the other hand, were designed before the 3.5-inch drive became popular, or may support only low-density (720K) drives. These types of computers need a software device driver to tell DOS that the smaller, higher-capacity drives are in use. These drivers should be available from the maker of the 3.5-inch drive, although fewer calls for such assistance are being made as the dinosaurs go to their graveyards.

If you need to use a device driver, follow the manufacturer's instructions carefully; an automatic installation program may be included. If installation is manual, you'll likely have to copy the driver to your boot directory and change your CONFIG.SYS file to include a DEVICE = *xxxx* line.

In some cases, it may be necessary to change BIOS chips to support new floppy drive types, and dinosaur-era BIOS chips may be difficult to find.

Dinosaur compatibility

Many 5.25-inch high-density (1.2MB) drives have trouble working with disks formatted at double density because of the design of the read/write heads — the designs on the two technologies aren't compatible. Some quick calculation shows that a 1.2MB 5.25-inch disk can hold four times as much as a 360K disk. A high-capacity disk drive squeezes all of that information onto a disk by using a write head that has a magnetic gap only one-fourth the size of the equivalent magnetic gap on a 360K drive.

A 1.2MB disk drive should have no difficulty reading a 360K disk. If you use a 1.2MB disk drive to store information on a 360K disk, however, it writes a thin little track down the middle of a relatively wide space. Take that hybrid disk and try to read it on a dinosaur 360K drive, and the wider head will try to read the entire area, picking up all of the background information garbage as well as the data. For this reason, you should only use a 360K drive to format or write a 360K floppy.

Microfloppies — another and somewhat arcane name for 3.5-inch disks — are a bit more compatible. The heads for older 720K and 1.44MB disk drives are the same size, so you won't have any problems with writing or formatting disks across the two designs.

If 1.44MB and 720K disks have the same size heads, how does the 1.44MB disk manage to hold twice as much data? The difference lies in the magnetic capabilities of the disk itself; a high-density disk is capable of storing more bits per inch than a standard-density device.

In addition, just to make things fun, the write-protect scheme of a 3.5-inch drive is the opposite of the 5.25-inch write-protect notch. On 3.5-inch floppies, the disk is write-protected if the notch is open. When the notch is covered, recording is enabled.

Testing floppy drive components

A floppy drive subsystem has four basic components:

- Disk drive controller
- Disk drive
- Cable
- Disk

If you're having a problem with the drive, you need to test each component in turn to determine whether it is causing the problem. I'm going to turn the order of the preceding list on its head to make the troubleshooting process a bit easier.

The best way to test various pieces of equipment is with a combination of a capable diagnostic program and some old-fashioned logic.

CROSS-REFERENCE

I discuss diagnostic and troubleshooting programs in detail in Chapter 22.

Testing the disk

As with any other mechanical element of your computer, it is only a matter of time before a floppy disk or a floppy disk drive fails. It's not a case of *if*, but *when*. Obviously, you should never keep only a single copy of any critical data in one place. Back up any data held on a floppy disk to another floppy disk, to a hard drive, or to any other backup medium.

Here's how to conduct a simple test of a floppy disk: Format it and then copy a file to it. If you get a DOS error message — General failure reading, Data error, or Track 0 failure — try another disk, preferably a new one. Disks die over time; if two or more disks don't work, then the problem lies elsewhere.

Make sure that you're using the proper type of disk. If you try formatting a high-density disk in a dinosaur low-density drive, you sometimes get a Track 0 bad message, even though the disk is okay. It's just the wrong type of disk for the drive heads.

Many diagnostic programs are available that look at a floppy disk sector by sector, persistently reading and rereading the sector. They check the cyclic redundancy code (CRC), a mathematical algorithm that should show any data corruption in the sector. A CRC number can be calculated from the data read and then compared with the CRC recorded in the sector for when the data was originally written to disk. If the CRCs don't match, the data recovery program looks at the error correction code (ECC). The ECC algorithm points to the specific bad bit or bits in a corrupted sector. Norton Utilities and PC Tools also contain data recovery utilities to help the frustrated user recover accidentally deleted files or whole directories.

CROSS-REFERENCE

Chapter 21 covers floppy disk and hard disk data recovery options, particularly the many diagnostic programs that recover data from suspect floppies.

If you're not sure whether you have a damaged floppy, continue reading.

Check the suspect disk in a second floppy drive. Find a disk drive known to be good of the same type as the suspect drive. If you're having problems reading the disk in a 1.2MB drive, for example, try another 1.2MB drive. If the disk works fine in one drive but acts poorly in another, then the problems are probably caused by malfunctions in the system unit hardware — the floppy drive or the disk controller, for example — rather than by a bad disk.

CROSS-REFERENCE

See the troubleshooting charts in Appendix G for diagnostic assistance.

WARNING

On a dinosaur system, be careful not to mix versions of DOS on the same computer. For example, FORMAT.COM from DOS 5 does not work with DOS 6.2, and unraveling such a combination can be a complex mess.

Testing the cables

If the machine has recently been worked on, check to make sure that the floppy drive cable is properly installed. If it is correctly in place, check to make sure that the A: drive, and only the A: drive, has a terminator. If both the cable and the terminator are okay, then break out your diagnostic disk, such as OnTrack Data Advisor (www.ontrack.com), and see whether the drive works.

If the diagnostic disk program says that the drive is bad, replace the cable before junking the drive. Run the floppy drive test again. If it still says the drive is bad, replace the drive.

Testing the floppy drive

The proof of a floppy drive is in the reading. Start by placing a disk known to be good of the proper disk size and density in the suspect drive and see whether you can read a directory of the disk.

If the drive can't read a floppy that you know is good, go to the troubleshooting charts in Appendix G of this book. Begin at the START chart and work your way through until you locate the problem.

If your older machine has two drives — a 3.5- and a 5.25-inch drive, for example — and one of the two drives is working, the problem almost certainly does not lie in the disk controller but is instead due either to a cabling problem or to a dead drive.

If your system has two floppy disk drives — regardless of whether they are both 5.25-inch drives, both 3.5-inch drives, or one of each — one important test is to swap their data cabling. Start by turning off the power and removing the plug, and then take off the cover of the PC. Locate the floppy drives, their associated floppy disk controller, and the cables that interconnect them. Remove the data cable to Drive A: and mark it with a piece of tape or a soft marking pen; do the same with the data cable for Drive B:. Now reverse the assignments of the two drives, making the former Drive B: your first drive.

Power up the system and see if either of the floppy drives now works. If the formerly inoperative drive is still unresponsive and the other drive continues to work properly, you have a dead drive that must be replaced. If both drives now work, the problem may have been caused by improperly seated cables. Or, if you had just installed new drives before the failure, the problem may have been caused by improper termination settings on the drives.

Another potential source of the problem is an intentional or unintentional change made to the CMOS settings of your computer. Consult the instruction manual for your PC to learn how to get to the screen and check that the configuration screen properly indicates the type or capacity of floppy drive installed. CMOS settings can be damaged by static electricity, by failing batteries, and occasionally by ill-behaved software.

If the drive still reads and writes unreliably, the problem may be caused by a loose connection on cables or an intermittent failure of the drive electronics. Test utility programs read and write to a disk, repeatedly checking data accuracy at every point on the data storage surface.

Determining if a drive is out of alignment

If you are experiencing more and more data errors with a drive — especially with disks written on another machine or with older files that you recorded some time before — your floppy drive may be going out of alignment.

Alignment means that the heads of the drive are physically aligned with the tracks on the floppy disk, and the heads write information at the proper *level* (an electronics term roughly equivalent to volume on your stereo).

 WARNING

It is possible to have a brand-new disk drive that is out of alignment when you first start using it. You may not realize the problem until you swap disks with someone else or run a diagnostic program.

One way to test the alignment of your drive heads is to purchase a diagnostic program that comes with a preformatted test disk that is used as a reference point for tests. But before you do so, consider that realigning a floppy disk drive is not a job that you can do without some expensive tools and testing devices. And the cost of replacing an old floppy disk drive — less than $20 — is sure to be lower than the charge made by a PC repair shop to perform a realignment.

Testing the disk drive controller and power supply

If a new drive flunks tests and you have checked the cables, you may have a failed controller. The next step down the chain calls for replacement of the controller and retesting. If the drive is still bad, you should try installing a power supply that you know to be good. If the controller and drive are good, you have no choice but to replace the motherboard.

On nearly all modern machines, the controller for the floppy disk drive is a component of the motherboard; if you are running Windows, the first place to check is the System report of the Control Panel. Make certain that the controller is recognized by the system, and that Windows does not report any conflicts for the necessary system resources it requires.

You should also make sure that your BIOS is set up properly to recognize a floppy disk drive controller. Occasionally a power surge or a misbehaved piece of software can corrupt the settings in the CMOS memory for the BIOS.

In rare circumstances, a problem with the system's power supply can cause problems with floppy disk drives; this was more of an issue with dinosaur systems with small power supplies and inefficient motors on the drives. If your power supply is failing, you're likely to experience numerous concurrent problems, including errors on hard drives, memory errors, and system shutdowns. You can test the output of a power supply, or replace it with a unit known to be good to see if this is the cause of the problem.

NOTE

If you are trying to replace a dinosaur full-size drive, you may be out of luck in searching for a direct replacement. You can, though, find adapter hardware that enables you to install a tiny drive in a large space.

Testing the disk controller

Test the floppy disk drive controller the same way you test a floppy drive. First, make sure that the drive formats disks properly, and then use a diagnostic program to see whether the drive reads and writes properly for hours at a time. If the drive functions properly, then the drive controller must be working okay.

The controller is not likely to be at fault when one floppy drive works and the second one doesn't work. Conversely, if both drives are bad, it usually means a bad controller, not simultaneous drive failure. The same circuits are used to control both floppy drives, but the hard disk controller has separate circuitry. Therefore, a working hard disk tells you nothing about the state of the controller card, even if the same card controls both floppy and hard drives.

NOTE

Remember, dinosaur PCs used separate floppy disk controllers. Older senior citizens used combined hard- and floppy-disk controller cards.

Almost all of the machines in the current crop have the floppy controller integrated onto the motherboard; the floppy drive cable attaches directly to a connector on the motherboard. If those electronics fail, you should be able to disable the onboard controller with a jumper by plugging a new controller into the bus or by disabling the port from the configuration setup screen.

A low-end disk controller is now a commodity. No-name replacement controllers that combine Integrated Device Electronics (IDE) hard drives, floppy drives, and serial ports sold for as little as $14 from direct mail sources at the time of this writing. Prices for 3.5-inch disk drives in early 2002 were as low as $17.

If you have a dinosaur machine, you may not be able to use high-density floppy disk drives. Check with the manufacturer of your machine to see if the machine will accommodate more modern drives. You may need to update the ROM BIOS.

If you are looking for a replacement for a failed 5.25-inch drive for a dinosaur or senior citizen, you are not going to find them easily. Some specialty computer repair outlets may have some in stock, but your best bet may be to search for used parts.

Modern-machine and senior-citizen onboard controllers

On most modern machines and many senior citizens, the floppy disk drive controller resides on the motherboard and drives connect directly to it. If the controller fails, or if you want to use a special controller that plugs into the bus of the system, check your motherboard instruction manual to determine whether either of the following applies:

- A jumper or switch is present to disable the onboard FD controller.
- The configuration setup screen allows you to disable the onboard FD controller, a facility found in many current modern-machine BIOS chips.

Dinosaur controller cards

The ribbon cable coming off the back of the floppy drive runs to the floppy disk drive controller or to the floppy drive section of a combination hard/floppy controller. Follow the floppy drive ribbon cable carefully. It runs to other floppy drives installed in the system and then terminates at the floppy disk drive controller. Other ribbon cables in the machine may go to a hard drive or other device, but only the floppy drive cable plugs into the back of the floppy drive.

Installing a Floppy Disk Drive

The first step is to remove the old drive. It is often easier to remove the cables (a ribbon cable and a four-wire power cable) after the drive is loose. Examine the cables carefully before you disconnect them so that you will be able to reinstall them properly. Mark them with a piece of tape or a soft marker to help identify them for reinstallation later.

You also have to remove the four-wire power connector that comes from the power supply. Hold the connector (not the wires) and firmly pull it out of its attachment point on the drive.

On most dinosaurs, the floppy drives are mounted directly to the chassis. To remove the drive, you must remove the machine screws on the sides of the drive. Occasionally, the screws are installed from below. If that is the case, turn the computer on its side and look for holes in the bottom of the chassis to access these screws.

On most modern machines, floppy drives are installed with rails that slide into slots in the drive bays; however, designs vary. Some use a small metal clip that is screwed onto the front surface of the chassis next to the drive. Remove this clip to slide the drive out of the chassis — like a drawer sliding out of a cabinet. On other systems, the drives are held in place with screws on the side or bottom. After you remove these screws, the drive slides out on rails.

Within some PCs, especially those with slim-line or other low-profile designs, you may need to remove other parts of the system — the power supply, adapter cards, riser cards — in order to gain access to the cage holding the floppy disk drives.

Another issue, which is easily solved, involves installing a 3.5-inch floppy drive in a wider 5.25-inch drive bay. See Figure 9-4 for details.

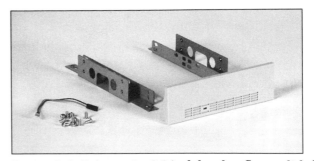

FIGURE 9-4: *To mount a 3.5-inch hard or floppy disk drive into a 5.25-inch drive bay, you need to install mounting rails. Some drive makers include them in installation kits. You can also purchase standard and specialized rails from computer supply companies, such as Dalco Electronics.*

Setting switches/jumpers on the new drive

Most floppy drives have jumpers or DIP switches to set the floppy's drive selector and terminating resistor options, as shown in Figure 9-5.

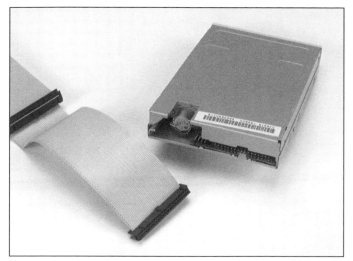

FIGURE 9-5: *Most modern drives don't need a jumper setting.*

However, on senior citizens through modern machines, you should not have to make any change to the floppy disk drive as delivered—the jumper block comes preset for use in PCs. In fact, to make things simple, the standard setup for current floppy drives is to leave the jumper block without any jumpers in place.

If you have two floppy drives connected to the controller in your system, the drive selector (DS) on both drive A: (the first drive recognized by the system) and drive B: (the second drive in the system) must be set to the second drive option. This may not seem to make sense, but the machine won't confuse the two drives when they're set to the same DS; the twist in the ribbon cable straightens everything out.

As I've previously noted, the floppy controller cable takes care of identifying each of the drives properly. The A: connector is at the end of the cable, nearest to the twist in the wires; the B: connector is in the middle of the cable.

NOTE

Consult the instruction manual that comes with your new floppy drive for the particular settings for that drive and for the location of the jumpers or switches.

The floppy drive data cable has three connectors: one for drive B: (which is straight-through), one for drive A: (which has part of the ribbon cable twisted at the end), and one for the floppy-drive controller. The cable, not the DS jumper, determines which drive the machine sees as drive A: and which as drive B:.

Checking terminating resistors

Older PCs and floppy drives—especially 5.25-inch drives—require a terminating resistor on the drive attached to the end of the data cable. The resistor helps set the proper electrical levels for the signal. Most (but not all) 5.25-inch drives come with the resistor in place; if you are installing a floppy drive as the first drive on the cable, you may need to remove the resistor.

NOTE

Consult the instruction manual that comes with your floppy drive or call the manufacturer to determine whether your drive has the resistor in place and whether it is necessary to remove it.

Most 3.5-inch drives have a built-in termination that does not have to be set by the user. Again, check the manual.

Sliding in the drive and connecting cables

After you configure the drive, you can install it. You should be able to reuse the rails and machine screws from the drive you are replacing, but not all floppy drives have the same physical dimensions or screw hole locations.

Screw the new drive down firmly but not too tightly, or you may strip the threads. After you secure the drive in the chassis, connect the ribbon cable. Most 5.25-inch drives use flat edge connectors to mate with a data cable; most 3.5-inch drives use pin connectors. Reconnect the four-wire power connector.

Most current 3.5-inch drives use small, half-inch connectors that click in place, held by a plastic clip. If you have an old-style floppy drive to mate to a modern power supply or the other way around, adapter cables are available to convert the older, large connectors.

Floppy disk drives require a data cable and juice from the power supply. The device that is intended as Drive A: takes the connector at the end of the data cable; if you have a Drive B:, it attaches to the connector in the middle of the cable. Modern disk drives generally use a 34-pin male connector that mates to a 34-pin female plug on the cable; older drives used a 34-pin edge connector. To deal with this occasional incompatibility, floppy disk drive cables are available with redundant female and edge connectors. Note that these connectors are not rectangular — two corners are cut off on a diagonal. Examine the socket on the floppy drive before installing the connector. It is difficult, but not impossible, to force the connector in improperly; the result will most likely be a destroyed disk drive and possibly a damaged power supply.

After you install the new drive, turn on the machine and test the drive rigorously. If it passes all the tests, you're finished. If it doesn't pass all the tests, recheck everything carefully, looking especially for incorrect switch settings and incorrect or loose cables.

Figure 9-6 shows a vertical case in which the 3.5-inch floppy slides into place in a snug lower-drive cage. On some machines, you may need to install mounting rails to convert a space intended for a 5.25-inch drive and a faceplate to fill the space around the front bezel of the case.

FIGURE 9-6: *The 3.5-inch floppy fits in the lower drive cage of this vertical case.*

Installing a Floppy Drive Controller

For dinosaurs and senior citizens, the first step in installing a new floppy drive controller is to remove the old controller card.

Fixing a problem with a controller on the motherboard

If you suspect a problem with the onboard floppy disk drive controller, you should begin by checking the BIOS setup screen for your system. Many modern machines use advanced BIOS code that lets you turn the FDD controller on or off from the keyboard. In some instances, power supply or battery backup problems can introduce errors to the CMOS memory of the machine.

Consult the motherboard instructional manual to determine whether you need to move a jumper, set a switch, or make a change to the configuration setup screen for the BIOS. A small number of older modern machines automatically disabled an onboard FDD controller if they detected the presence of a new controller installed in the bus.

If the FDD has been turned off, reset the option in the CMOS and reboot the system to see if this fixes the problem. Try a floppy disk drive known to be good with the controller, or move your floppy disk drive to a machine with a controller that's known to be good to isolate the problem.

If you decide that the FDD controller on the motherboard is bad, disable it from the BIOS setup screen. On some systems, you may have to disable it by moving a jumper on a switch block on the motherboard. On a few other systems, plugging a replacement FDD controller into one of the slots on the bus automatically disables the onboard controller.

Replacement disk controllers, usually combined with IDE hard drive circuitry (that you can disable to avoid conflicts if necessary) are available from parts suppliers. Simple add-in cards for IDE sell for about $20 from electronics suppliers; you'll also find controller cards that add multiple I/O functions including high-speed serial ports, SCSI ports, and game ports.

Removing the old controller card: Dinosaurs and senior citizens

Turn off the computer and unplug the power cord. Remove the system cover. The wide, flat gray cable running from the floppy disk controller to each floppy drive is called a *ribbon cable*. Examine the ribbon cable connections and routing before you remove any parts. Carefully examine the floppy drive ribbon cable; it's installed so that the red (or blue) stripe is toward pin 1 on the controller card's cable-connection pins.

Many controllers, especially those in modern machines, have the number 1 silk-screened on the controller next to the connector pins. Mark the cable that you are removing with a piece of tape or a soft marker. Plan now, before you take the cable off, to reinstall the cable so the colored stripe faces the end with the number 1.

Other controllers, especially those in dinosaur PCs, have a notch cut in the connector on the controller card. The end with this slot is pin 1, and again you will reinstall the cable with the colored edge toward pin 1. Notice that one section of the ribbon cable is split off at the connector and twisted. When you reinstall the cable, the section with the twist must be on the A: drive. The B: drive is hooked to the straight-through connector in the middle of the cable.

Remove the cables, and then unscrew and save the screw fastening the controller card to the system unit chassis. Finally, pull the card straight up out of the bus connector.

Replacing the controller card

Press the card down into the motherboard bus connector. Some controller cards are extra long and will only fit in a particular slot on your machine; other than such physical considerations, a disk controller card works in any ISA slot.

After you install the card, connect the ribbon cable and reattach the screw that holds the card to the system unit chassis. In some installations, it may be easier to attach the ribbon cable before you place the controller in the slot. Figure 9-7 shows the proper way to attach a floppy disk cable to the motherboard.

FIGURE 9-7: *An FDD connector and one of two HDD (EIDE circuitry for hard drives or CD-ROM drives) on an integrated motherboard. If you hold the drive connector end of the floppy disk drive cable in one hand (note twisted section of cable between the fingers of the left hand), you'll be sure to plug the proper end of the cable to the FDD connector.*

Test the machine. If it works, replace the cover and you're finished. If not, recheck the cable; the next chapter tells you how.

SUMMARY

In this chapter, I covered floppy drives, used primarily to load programs and occasionally to transfer small files from machine to machine. In the next chapter, I explore the huge capacity and high speed of hard disk drives.

Notes

Chapter 10

Tools Needed:

- Phillips or flat-blade screwdriver
- Antistatic strip, wrist strap, or grounding pad

Hard Drives

Hard disks were once an expensive, fragile luxury. In fact, the first PCs did without them. My first IBM PC came equipped with a pair of 160K floppy drives. One floppy held the operating system and a small word-processing program, and the other held the data files.

PC users couldn't help but cast a jealous eye at television-sized Winchester disk drives developed for room-sized mainframe computers. These early hard drives delivered what was considered a huge amount of storage at an acceptable price: A typical early hard drive offered 10MB of storage and only cost a few thousand dollars!

Over the life of the PC, hard disk storage has seen some of the most amazing changes in computer technology. Hard drives have become larger in capacity, smaller in size, faster in speed, and lower in price. Today, I consider the entry-level size for a hard drive to be 40GB, with prices tumbling on drives as large as 160GB.

In this chapter, I explore hard drive technology and organization. Then I tell you what you need to know about today's most common hard drive interfaces: ATA (also called IDE) and SCSI.

And I cast a backward glance at older standards, ST506 MFM and RLL drives and controller cards, as well as ESDI drives and controller cards.

And I also discuss the unpleasant facts of hard disk mortality. Here's a preview: If you're lucky, your hard drive will have a full, healthy, and productive life. And then it will die. Be prepared.

How a Hard Disk Works

All hard disks share the same basic construction. A small motor spins finely machined disks (usually made of aluminum or a high-tech glass and ceramic mix) at a precise speed. The disks — called *platters* — are coated with an oxide of magnesium, chromium, iron, or other metal particles capable of holding a magnetic charge. Because you can't remove the disks or bend them like the insubstantial media in a floppy disk, these devices are called *hard drives* or *fixed disks*.

Above and below each platter, a read/write head glides on a cushion of air very close to the surface of the platter. To write data, the heads magnetize tiny points on the tracks of the platter, using changes in polarity to encode data. To read data, the heads detect the changes in polarity on the disk as the 0s and 1s of binary information. In consumer hard drives, all the heads of the drive are mounted on the same assembly, and they move in and out — from the 0 or outer track to the inner track — on the same actuator mechanism.

If a modern drive has two platters, it usually has four read/write heads and four data surfaces; a three-platter drive would have six of each, and so on. Along with the data, an index to where data is stored is recorded on the disk. In technical terms, this is called an *embedded servo*, as shown in Figure 10-1.

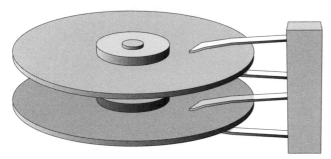

FIGURE 10-1: *A hard disk with two platters has four recording surfaces, so the hard disk needs four read/write heads. The heads move together, in and out across the platter surface.*

NOTE

An older scheme devoted one entire platter to the storage of servo information; it was called a dedicated servo. You can identify that sort of system when the specs indicate it has one less data surface than the number of platters multiplied by two. If your machine has such a system, it will almost certainly be necessary to replace your entire disk subsystem — controller and disk, and possibly the ROM BIOS — if your hard drive ever fails or becomes unreliable.

Some high-performance and high-capacity drives have several heads on a head assembly, with each head covering a smaller zone on the disk. The specs for this sort of drive might indicate something like 4 platters, 8 data surfaces, and 16 or more heads.

Early hard disks for PCs had motors that spun the disk at 3,600 rpm. Today, the most common speed for drives is 5,400 rpm, with high-performance drives spinning their platters at 7,200 rpm and a developing class of devices that operate at 10,000 rpm and even faster.

Under the covers of a disk drive

Modern hard disk drives usually have more than one platter, stacked one above another like dishes in the cupboard. There's

just enough room between the platters for a read/write head to float above (or below) the disks, kept aloft by a cushion of air generated by the spinning disk.

I've opened up the covers of a hard drive in Figure 10-2. (Remember what I said about the mortality of hard drives? This model gave up the magnetic ghost after three years of hard use.) Hard drives are shipped to consumers with sealed covers and high-tech air filters to exhaust heat; this is done to avoid tiny specks of dust that can sit like boulders on the platter as it spins just beneath the read/write head.

FIGURE 10-2: *The innards of this hard drive include three platters. Six read/write heads reside on the head assembly that moves in and out on a cushion of air above the platters.*

The main element of a standard read/write head is a tiny magnet. One common design is made of turns of copper wire on a ring of ferrite; there is a hairline gap on the side of the ferrite core facing the disk. When current is passed through the coil, the disk surface under the gap is magnetized.

To read information from the disk, the device's electronics sense the current caused by the passage of the magnetized sections of the disk as it spins beneath the gap. The electronics sense the transition from one polarity to another.

The signal pulses are amplified and converted from the analog waves detected by the read/write head, and then converted to precise digital pulses of 0 or 1. This is a potential point of failure on a disk drive: If the platter is unable to hold a strong, identifiable marking or if the write head is unable to put one in place, the decoding circuits may mistakenly identify a 0 as a 1.

The next step is to separate the data pulses from the clock pulses. A clock signal is a string of precisely spaced pulses that serve as timing references for other signals, including drive control and positioning.

The disk controller examines the sector address, and if it matches the address the computer is looking for, the processing continues. If not, the data is ignored.

If the sector is correct, most interfaces then perform some level of error detection. (Modern devices employ a scheme called *cyclic redundancy checking.*) The system computes an error-checking value that it compares to the value that was recorded along with the original value. If it finds an error, the controller tries again.

If the data is okay, the stream of data bits must be converted from serial form — one bit behind the other — to the parallel form in which it moves across the computer's bus. On IDE, EIDE, and SCSI drives, this conversion is performed by the drive's integrated electronics in a circuit called a data separator; on most other designs, the data moves from the drive to the controller as serial information and is converted by the controller.

Hundreds of hard disk and controller models are available, each with idiosyncratic switch settings and jumpers. It is absolutely essential to obtain a complete instruction manual from your disk drive manufacturer. Some massive books of settings and specifications are also for sale, but they become quickly outdated. If you are transferring a known-good disk drive from one machine to another and are missing the documentation, you may be able to obtain information from the drive manufacturer; many manufacturers also post pages of information on their Web sites and offer fax-on-demand services. Many of the Web pages from manufacturers also include downloadable device drivers and other software.

The BIOS included in most modern machines generally supports an autodetect mode that will help you set up a new drive easily. You can also get setup and other drive specifications from the CMOS settings in the original computer, assuming you check it out before you remove the drive. Simply enter the system BIOS and select the drive that you're moving. Write down the settings for capacity, number of platters, heads, and other data displayed there.

The true capacity of a hard drive

A hard drive advertised as a 1GB device (a very small drive by today's standards, but it serves this example well) may actually be a 1.1GB drive, or it may be capable of holding a mere 900MB of data. No hard-and-fast rule exists for stating data capacity, and in any case, the raw capacity of any drive is reduced by the formatting structure applied by the operating system.

All hard drives must be formatted to be used in a computer — the act of formatting adds control information and magnetic markings for the data structure. Also, in the process of formatting, the drive electronics may find that some sectors of the drive are unable to store data reliably and will list them in a table that the disk drive controller consults. Figure on an overhead of about 10 percent from the raw capacity of a drive. In other words, you can expect to be able to use only about 90 percent of the drive's stated capacity.

Some drive manufacturers list formatted capacity in their specifications, and this figure should provide a reasonably accurate means of comparing one drive to another.

The second problem involves the sometimes-loose way in which computer people use the kilo, mega, and giga prefixes;

those terms are commonly used for 1 thousand, 1 million, and 1 billion, respectively, but the math is incorrect if you use them for memory. And because the data in memory is what the computer writes to the hard disk, you'd think hard disk size would be measured the same way. But because computers use binary math, based on powers of 2, memory chips are made in quantities that are powers of 2. And the tenth power is 1,024, close enough to 1,000 for computer users to use the term kilo when referring to memory, as in 1 kilobyte. Thus, a megabyte is 2 to the 20th power, or $1,024 \times 1,024$ or 1,048,576 bytes; and a gigabyte is 2 to the 30th power, or $1,024 \times 1,024 \times 1,024$ or 1,073,741,824 bytes — at least, for memory.

But for hard disks, whose sizes have grown astronomically and are not constrained by the powers of two, marketing has prevailed over the meaning of megabyte and gigabyte. Hard disk sizes are almost always advertised with those terms meaning 1 million and 1 billion bytes. (After all, in all other cases except computer memory, the old Greek meanings prevail; kilo means one thousand, as in a 75K salary; mega means a million — a 700 megahertz CPU for example; and giga means a billion.) And if you're a manufacturer with a drive that holds 1,073,741,824 bytes, would you advertise it as a 1GB drive or a 1.07GB drive?

Today most drive manufacturers advertise capacity in digital terms — meaning a 40GB hard drive contains 40 billion bytes, which converted to binary accounting would equal about 37.25GB. Either way, it's a lot of space, but the only way to know whether a particular disk-drive manufacturer uses true binary accounting for determining the size of its drive is to ask the manufacturer or to study the drive's specs carefully.

And, ever mindful of the quest for the never-arriving horizon, technicians have already come up with labels for collections of huge amounts of data beyond mere gigabytes. A list of numbering terms is in Table 10-1.

TABLE 10-1: Data Numbering Scheme

Name	Number of Bytes
1 kilobyte	1,000 bytes
1 megabyte	1,000,000 bytes
1 gigabyte	1,000,000,000 bytes
1 terabyte	1,000,000,000,000 bytes
1 petabyte	1,000,000,000,000,000 bytes
1 exabyte	1,000,000,000,000,000,000 bytes
1 zettabyte	1,000,000,000,000,000,000,000 bytes
1 yottabyte	1,000,000,000,000,000,000,000,000 bytes

Hard Drives: Bigger . . .

The PC-XT was IBM's first PC with a hard drive. Introduced in 1982, it came equipped with a 10MB hard drive with an access time of 80 milliseconds (ms); the drive was considered huge and fast. Two years later, the capacity of the new PC-AT was doubled, and the access time cut in half.

In early 1996, a basic hard drive size for a Pentium machine was 540MB with a 13 ms access speed. A year later, when the fourth edition of this book was published, a serious Pentium user would expect a hard drive three to five times larger, nearly half again as fast, and half the price.

By the fall of 1998, the jump in available capacity — and in consumer expectations — had accelerated even as prices continued to drop. Then, few modern machines were sold with less than 4GB of storage, and it was easy and relatively inexpensive to add drives of 6, 9, or even 11GB to a computer. In 2000, as I prepared the sixth edition of this book, the basic hard drive for an upper-end machine was in the 10 to 12GB range, and the price for a 20GB drive was about $170, and 27GB drives cost a mere $250 or so.

In early 2002, as this seventh edition went to press, the cost of a 40GB drive had dropped below $100, and a state-of-the-art 160GB drive sold for about $320.

Let's look first at the march of disk drive capacity and speed over the years. Table 10-2, based on typical systems, includes ratios to compare capacity and access. The capacity ratio column shows that a typical 40GB hard drive, common on midrange machines as this book goes to press, is 4,000 times larger than the clunky device in the dinosaur PC-XT. The access speed for today's much larger drive is about nine times faster.

Notice what has happened to capacity and access times. Capacities for typical consumer hard drives have grown 10,000-fold from the PC-XT days of 1982, while access times are only about nine times better. That seems incongruous until you look at both figures together. Consider that the drive mechanics are sorting through 10,000 times more data.

It is also worth noting that since 1998, access times haven't improved appreciably. The industry has reached a mechanical plateau, of sorts, in how fast a mechanical device can move over a disk surface that is packed as densely as these drives are packed. Some of the new technologies that I talk about later in this chapter could get over that plateau within a few years.

...Faster...

Just what is hard drive speed? It all comes down to this: When you enter a command from the keyboard or when a program issues an instruction, how long does it take for the disk drive subsystem to deliver the information to the microprocessor or the video adapter?

One of the components of speed is the rotational speed of the drive. Older hard disks typically spin about ten times faster than a floppy disk drive, usually in the range from 2,400 to 3,600 rpm. That's about 40 to 60 times per second. Most mid-range, newer drives spin at about 5,400 rpm, although 7,200 rpm devices are now commonly available.

Ch 10

TABLE 10-2: A History of Typical PC Disk Drive Capacity and Speed

Model	Capacity	Access Speed (Lower is better)	Capacity Ratio (Higher is better)
IBM PC-XT (1982)	10MB	80 ms	1
IBM PC-AT (1984)	20MB	40 ms	2
IBM PS/2 (1987)	115MB	28 ms	11.5
486 Clone (1990)	320MB	15 ms	32
Pentium (1995)	540MB	13 ms	54
Pentium (1997)	2.5GB	12 ms	250
Pentium II (1998)	4GB	12 ms	400
Pentium II (1998)	6.5GB	8 ms	650
Pentium III (2000)	10GB	7.6 ms	1,000
Pentium III (2000)	17GB	8 ms	1,700
Pentium III (2000)	20GB	7.6 ms	2,000
Pentium III (2000)	28GB	8 ms	2,800
Pentium 4 (2002)	40GB	8.7 ms	4,000
Pentium 4 (2002)	100GB	8.7ms	10,000

All things being equal, 7,200 rpm drives increase overall system performance by about 5 percent over 5,400 rpm drives. If your machine is used to stream video or in graphics-intensive applications, you can expect even more benefit from a faster drive.

Currently, the speediest motors for consumer-grade drives spin at 15,000 rpm. One example is Seagate's Cheetah X15 SCSI and Fibre Channel family. At that speed, average drive latency is less than 3 ms, meaning that the drive not only sends data back to the system at a faster rate but also that the time for the drive to find requested information is improved.

Four factors are involved in the usable speed of a hard drive: physical seek time, latency, data buffer size, and transfer rate.

- **Physical seek time.** The average time required to position the read/write head of a drive over a specified track on the drive. The time varies based on the location of the track and the position of the head before it begins to move. In other words, moving from one track to the adjacent track is quicker than moving from the innermost track to the outside track.
- **Latency.** The average time it takes for the rotating drive to bring the data under the read/write head. Latency is related to the speed of the drive.
- **Data buffer size.** A data buffer is a specialized block of memory used to hold data being transferred from one device to another to help compensate for differences in transfer rates between devices.
- **Transfer rate.** The speed at which the collected information is pumped out of the drive to the computer bus or accepted from the bus.

A measure of the first two factors is *average access time*. The word average is an important component of that specification. Access time is supposed to mean the amount of time required for the read/write head mechanism to find the track or cylinder that holds the desired data (this is called *average seek time*), plus the time required for the head mechanism to become stable over the location of the data (called *settling time*), plus the average time

required for the proper data to spin under the read/write head (called *rotational latency*). Latency is directly related to the disk drive's speed of rotation.

Expressed as a formula, access time would be: average access = average seek + settling time + latency. Some manufacturers have dropped latency from their access time claims, and some ignore settling time. Be sure you are comparing fast apples to fast apples when you look at drive speed.

A drive manufacturer can fudge the numbers by calculating how fast the drive can get to a bit of information that is already directly under the read/write head. Such a number is all but useless as an indicator of true access time.

The final — and important — component of drive speed is data transfer. Data transfer is the rate at which a drive or controller dumps the information it has retrieved to the computer bus. This is an area that often has great mismatches — a slow data transfer system can cause quickly accessed data to back up on the hard drive side of the controller; a fast data transfer system can stand idle most of the time, waiting for a slow disk drive to find and pick up the requested data.

In general, data transfer speed depends on the rotational speed of the drive and the type of interface used to transfer the data. An Ultra-Wide SCSI connection, for example, can blast data to your computer at up to 80 MBps, but such high-performance interfaces are attached to fast spinning, fast accessing (8 ms or less) drives, usually of high capacity (4GB and greater). Newer Fibre Channel interfaces can obtain up to 200 MBps data transfer rates, while the speediest ATA/133 IDE permits bursts of up to 133 MBps.

Now that I've (sort of) cleared up the issue of speed on a drive, you should bear in mind one more issue: The stream of data that comes off a hard drive includes more than just the information you are looking for. The data includes formatting data and, on some drives, padding bits that mean nothing but are used to deal with speed variations at the narrow or wide parts of the disk. On an IDE or SCSI drive, the drive's integrated electronics take this information out of the data stream; on older designs, the drive controller card removes extra information. Either way, a full ten-pound gallon of data may contain only eight gallons or less of usable information.

...and Cheaper

Almost as amazing as has been the upward march of technological advances has been the downward plunge of hard disk drive prices.

I first began writing about IBM PCs and early clones in 1982, soon after the birth of the PC, when I was the first executive editor of *PC Magazine*. Here's a random selection of prices for hard drives from the October 1982 issue of *PC Magazine:* A 5MB (megabyte, not gigabyte!) Winchester in a box about the size of the PC it sat alongside, $1,899. A 19.2MB Winchester (actually a pair of 9.6MB drives) in a huge metal box, $2,799.

In 1996, a 1GB IDE hard drive seemed like a fantastic bargain at about $375. A year later, newer and improved versions of the same capacity drive were priced at about $170.

In early 2002, the best deal on hard drives was for devices 40 times larger and about half again as expensive: a 40GB drive for less than $100.

Here's one last exercise: I omit access speeds because it's simply too difficult to compare early PC buses, controller cards, and processors to modern-day systems. I can, though, compare the approximate cost per unformatted megabyte, as shown in Table 10-3 for IDE drives and Table 10-4 for SCSI drives. Taking the most extreme example, the cost of a megabyte of hard disk storage has declined from about $380 in 1982 to two cents in 1998, to less than one-third of a penny in 2001.

TABLE 10-3: A History of IDE Hard Disk Prices

Year	Capacity	Price	Cost per MB
1982	5MB	$1,899	$379.80
	19.2MB	$2,799	$145.78

Year	Capacity	Price	Cost per MB
1995	428MB	$183	$0.43
	722MB	$253	$0.35
	1GB	$375	$0.37
1997	540MB	$139	$0.26
	1GB	$170	$0.17
	2.7GB	$300	$0.09
1998	2.1GB	$129	$0.06
	6.4GB	$219	$0.03
	12GB	$280	$0.02
2000	6.4GB	$120	$0.02
	17GB	$170	$0.01
	20GB	$212	$0.01
	28GB	$270	$0.01
2002	10GB	$70	$0.007
	20GB	$80	$0.004
	40GB	$100	$0.003
	80GB	$175	$0.0025
	160GB	$320	$0.002

TABLE 10-4: A History of SCSI Hard Disk Prices

Year	Capacity	Price	Cost per MB
1995	9GB SCSI	$3,215	$0.35
1997	9GB SCSI	$1,650	$0.18
1998	9GB SCSI	$800	$0.09
2000	9GB SCSI	$340	$0.04
	18GB SCSI	$500	$0.03
	36GB SCSI	$980	$0.03
	50GB SCSI	$1,060	$0.02
2002	9GB SCSI	$154	$0.02
	18GB SCSI	$245	$0.01
	36GB SCSI	$330	$0.009
	73GB SCSI	$754	$0.01

Back in the early days of the PC, it hardly seemed necessary to have a hard disk. After all, word processors fit on a single floppy disk, and Pac-Man was considered the state of the art in multimedia.

Today, it is not uncommon for a suite of programs such as Microsoft Office XP to occupy from 210 to 245MB of disk space. Microsoft Windows 95 demanded as much as 65MB for a full installation. Upgrading to Windows 98 could take up to 300MB, if you choose to have the option to uninstall Windows 98 and return to your previous Windows 95 setup. And Windows XP demands as much as 1.5GB of space all by itself.

And all of this is before you put any data files on your disk; on my system, I commonly work with photo files as large as 15MB each.

Today, the best storage price-performance value seems to be IDE hard drives of about 40GB. Smaller drives are available, but their cost per GB is higher. Going the other direction, massive hard drives are much less expensive than they were in earlier times, but because of their special media or electronics, they have a higher cost per gigabyte. In Figure 10-3 is an example of a 20GB drive.

Although it may seem risky to put so many eggs in one basket — an entire business, your entire lifetime collection of photos or financial documents, or your great American novel on one hard drive — the fact is that modern drives are many times faster and much more reliable than the old behemoths. My preference is to use large, fast drives and to be absolutely religious about maintaining multiple backups on other disk drives or on removable storage media, such as Zip disks, SuperDisks, or CD-ROMs.

As this book went to press, the reigning champion in consumer hard drives was Maxtor's DiamondMax D540X, available in capacities up to 160GB. And, the drive was one of the first to work with the Ultra ATA/133 specification, allowing transfer of as much as 133 MBps to and from the interface. The drive includes a 2MB SDRAM cache.

FIGURE 10-3: *A 20GB ATA/66 drive, which sold in 2000 for about $212, was available in early 2002 for about $80.*

The drive includes four 40GB platters, running at 5400 RPM. The drive is downward compatible with earlier ATA technologies, including ATA/100 and ATA/66, but an ATA/133 upgrade is required to use the entire capacity of 160MB and to obtain the fastest speed.

Because ATA/133 capability is not common on motherboards, Maxtor shipped the new drive in a bundle that included an ATA/133 adapter card. The card and adapter are shown in Figure 10-4. Adapter cards from other manufacturers should be widely available by mid-2002, and motherboards with the capability to work with the drives at their full capacity should follow soon afterwards.

And all of this capacity and speed comes at an impressive price: The drive was available in early 2002 for about $320, which works out to about 5MB for a penny — the lowest cost for storage of any current drive.

Notebook computers usually use tiny 2.5-inch hard drives with increasing capacities and low power requirements. They are priced at a premium over full-size drives. There is no reason to install one of these drives in a typical desktop system, unless you happen to have an extra drive lying around on a shelf.

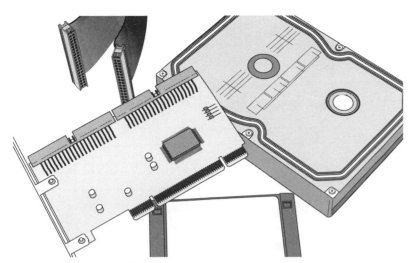

Figure 10-4: *Maxtor's DiamondMax 540X, a 160GB hard drive, introduced the company's ATA/133 interface. The drive was made available before motherboards directly supported the new interface; Maxtor included an ATA/133 PCI adapter with the hard drive to accommodate the new standard.*

Form Factor: What Fits Where?

Most desktop PCs have space for 5.25-inch or 3.5-inch devices in internal case bays; an unused bay for a floppy disk drive or CD-ROM can also be adapted to hold a hard drive.

As a point of reference: CD-ROM and DVD drives fit in a 5.25-inch-wide bay. Nearly all full-size and mid-size desktop or tower cases are about 6 inches tall or wide, respectively, and include at least a few 5.25-inch bays as well; most also offer a few internal 3.5-inch bays.

A hard drive does not need access from the outside of the case, and therefore it can easily be installed in one of the internal 3.5-inch bays. If you need to use a 5.25-inch bay for a smaller device, the bay can easily be adapted with rails and carriers. Some drives include the extra hardware, while in other cases, you have to pay a few dollars extra for a few pieces of sheet metal and screws. An installation into a 3.5-inch bay is shown in Figure 10-5.

Figure 10-5: *The 3.5-inch hard drive in the middle of this photo is installed in a drive cage of the same width; some systems may require the use of mounting rails to adapt the smaller device to a wider bay. Some technicians test the drive before screwing it into place in the drive cage. At the bottom of the photo is a floppy disk drive that will be installed in the same cage.*

Ch 10

The Hard Life of a Hard Disk

I want to start with a harsh fact of life: Hard disks do not last forever. They are electromechanical devices with a motor to spin a disk, an actuator to move the read/write head to various positions on the disk, bearings to support the spinning platter, and electronics to control the drive and communicate with the rest of the computer.

The good news is that as hard disk drives have become smaller, faster, more capacious, and considerably less expensive, they have also become more and more reliable. Some users make the mistake of looking at the older drives with their large cases and heavy motors and assume that bigger means sturdier; actually, the miniaturization of drives has brought simpler, less power-hungry circuitry and motors. This vast improvement in data density has been accompanied by improved platter surfaces and tiny, lightweight read/write assemblies that are much less likely to suffer a catastrophic crash.

A typical user who takes proper care of the system and provides the hard disk drive with a reliable source of electricity can expect a life of five to ten years or more from a hard disk. But looking at it from the other side, it is also true that you might suffer a catastrophic failure after a few weeks.

Either way, my recommendation is to always act as if your hard disk drive will fail at any moment, taking with it all of your work.

Hard disks are sealed boxes with high-tech filters designed to prevent particles of dust from clogging the heads or damaging the disks. They are not intended to be opened for service outside of a clean room. And, just as for floppy disk drives, the cost of repairing a hard disk drive is almost certainly more expensive than buying a new unit.

In any case, the value of your data is almost always much greater than the value of your computer. For example, this manuscript represents months of work, and you can bet that multiple copies of the files are stored away from the computer on which I'm writing it. My office procedure is to make backups of live files on the hard drive in another machine in the office network during the course of a day and then to burn a CD-ROM with the complete set of current files every other day.

What could possibly go wrong?

Hard disks are similar to floppy disks, but the technology is more advanced in every way. Hard disks spin faster, pack in more data per inch, move from track to track more quickly, and accommodate multiple platters in each drive unit.

As with other electronic items, from calculators to digital watches, each generation of hard disks is smaller, faster, and more powerful. Half-height models, which replaced the 3-inch-high hard disks of the 1980s, have now given way to mini-monsters less than an inch high. And laptop computers are being delivered with half-inch-tall hard drives with capacities of tens of gigabytes; a properly designed laptop computer uses specially cushioned drives that protect from the unusual insults a portable PC may have to endure. There are also tiny Microdrives, developed by IBM, that pack as much as 1GB in a 1-inch square that can be used in a CompactFlash slot or a PC Card Type II device.

The internal mechanical elements of the drives—always the Achilles heels of data storage devices—are improving.

More precise and reliable voice coil servo mechanisms have generally replaced cheap stepper motors in high-density, high-capacity hard drives. A voice coil mechanism uses servo track information to determine where to move the head in precise increments without the use of preset steps. A servo track is a marking on the drive platter itself; the voice coil moves relative distances from that servo track to find information.

Older drives used a stepper mechanism to move the read/write head in fixed increments, or steps, across the disk surface. The mechanical nature of a drive based on a stepper mechanism delivers precise positioning when the drive is new, but wear and tear can end up throwing the drives out of alignment.

Treat your hard disk gently. It is a delicate, precision-tooled mechanical device and is easily damaged. Dropping a hard disk might crash a read/write head into a platter. Even if the head is not damaged, the portion of the disk that made contact with the head could be injured and made unreadable.

WARNING

Hard disks and floppies survive X-rays well, but the magnetic field generated by a poorly shielded or malfunctioning airport metal detector can destroy the data. Your best bet is to ask for a visual examination of your portable computer and any disks that you carry with you. If the inspectors insist on putting your equipment through a machine, choose the X-ray machine over a hand-held metal detector.

Preparing for disaster

I recommend that you read this chapter before you need to be rescued. And then, when death is in the house, reread this chapter with the security of knowing you have put away safe backups of everything you should save.

Permit me to begin with a sermon. Call it "Sandler's Top Three Tips for Safe Computing:"

1. Back up your data regularly.
2. Perform Step 1 at least once a week, more often when you are in the middle of a critical assignment.
3. See Steps 1 and 2.

In addition to making backup copies of your data, I also recommend that you regularly run disk drive diagnostic and repair utilities. These programs analyze your drive, ensure that the surface is reliable, and lock out any questionable areas.

CROSS-REFERENCE

After you have read this chapter, read Chapter 21 to learn how to salvage useful data stored on an ailing hard disk.

SMART drives

Self-Monitoring, Analysis, and Reporting Technology (SMART) hard drives include technology that allow them to give themselves regular checkups throughout their lives, communicating any actual or impending problems to the user.

The system was introduced by IBM in 1992 and has since been adopted by most major drive manufacturers and supported by current versions of Windows. SMART software resides in the controller on the disk drive and on the host computer. Software on the drive monitors the internal performance of the motors, media, heads, and electronics of the drive; programming on the computer monitors the overall reliability status of the drive.

Manufacturers adjust the parameters of the software to reflect the projected life and performance of a particular drive. If the SMART system predicts the imminent failure of the drive, it issues a warning and offers advice on protecting existing data. Some advanced systems are able to notify network administrators of potential problems and even to automatically initiate relocation of critical files and backup of data to other storage devices.

Your machine's BIOS must support SMART diagnostics, or you must run application software that can interrogate the system. Appropriate software includes Norton Disk Doctor.

Buying a Hard Drive

Today's leading hard drive manufacturers include Fujitsu, IBM, Maxtor, Seagate, Toshiba, and Western Digital. Products from any one of these companies are all comparable, and because hard drives have been changing so much, it's hard to recommend a specific brand. I list the Web sites and phone numbers for major hard drive manufacturers in Table 10-5.

Ch 10

You can take steps, though, to try to ensure that you buy the most reliable and current technologies:

- Read the most recent reliability surveys and reviews in computer magazines.
- Include the support policy and the warranty period and terms in your buying decision. In general, a device with a generous technical support policy and warranty is of better quality; companies offer better after-the-sale support and warranties if they don't expect many of their customers to have to use them.
- Look at the specifications for machines offered for sale by major computer manufacturers, including Gateway, Dell, and Compaq, to see what brand of hard drives they are currently shipping with their systems. It is not in the interests of mass-market sellers to ship hard drives that have a high failure rate.
- Buy the hard disk drive that is one step down from the latest hot model. This strategy almost always saves you some money and keeps you away from any unproven technology. (This advice applies to any computer purchase.)
- Consider the price-performance ratio of whatever you buy. The easiest way to compute this for a hard drive is to calculate the cost per megabyte or gigabyte. If you look at a range of hard drive sizes, you'll usually see a sweet spot a few notches down from the largest or fastest device. As this book went to press, the best deals on a hard drive were for large drives from 40GB to 80GB.
- Buy from a reputable dealer who stands behind the sale. I never buy closeout or final-sale products unless I am absolutely certain of their quality. I'd rather spend a few dollars more and buy from a dealer or mail-order company that promises to buy back a faulty product or exchange it for a good one. The best retailers make an unconditional guarantee: If you're not happy with a product, they take it back. No ifs, ands, buts, or time limits (within reason).

TABLE 10-5: Support Telephone Numbers and Web Sites of Major Hard Drive Makers

Vendor	Contact Information
Compaq	(800) 282-6672 www.compaq.com/storage/desktops.html
Conner	Now part of Seagate Technologies (408) 438-8222 www.seagate.com
Fujitsu	(408) 894–3950 hdd.fujitsu.com/global
IBM	(800) 772-2227 www.storage.ibm.com/hdd
Maxtor	(800) 262–9867 www.maxtor.com
Quantum	Merged with Maxtor in 2001 (800) 826-8022 www.quantum.com
Seagate	(408) 438–8222 www.seagate.com
Toshiba	(805) 644-6350 www.toshiba.com/taecdpd
Western Digital	(800) 832–4778 www.wdc.com

Mean time between headaches

There are several supposed quantifications of the expected life span of a hard disk, although I don't recommend setting your watch by any of them. Instead, use them as a way to compare the relative sturdiness of various devices.

MTBF stands for *mean time between failures;* a similar measure is MTTF, which stands for *mean time to failure.* Both statistics are presented in terms of hours. In the 1990s, a typical disk drive might have a listing of 40,000 to 100,000 hours; as this book goes to press, many drives are accompanied by claims of an MTTF of 300,000 hours.

Think about what those numbers are supposed to specify: a mean (average) time to failure of about 30 years of continuous use.

Another measure is Start/stop, which estimates the expected lifetime of the drive in terms of the number of times it is turned on and off; engineers refer to this as "loading" and "unloading" the springs that position the read/write head. A high-end modern drive may promise a Start/stop life of 40,000.

Yet another measure of the quality of a disk drive is its reported Error Rate, an estimate of how often the drive will pass through a non-recoverable misread of stored data. A modern drive's specifications might claim an error rate of 1 in 10E13, which means once in every 100 trillion bits. On a typical 20GB hard drive, there might be something like 100 million bits when you take into account system files, indexes, and data checking bits. If you were to read the entire contents of a full drive 1,000 times, you could expect an error in a single bit — and further expect that your disk controller or one of your applications will catch the error and ask for a resend of the data, fix it, or alert you to the problem.

So, how in the world can a manufacturer rush to market with a hot new disk drive — at most a one- or two-year research and development project — and claim that a device should last 30 years? There is obviously no way for manufacturers to put a drive in a closet and run it for that long to see when or if it fails. Instead, drive manufacturers follow two testing tracks. One is to put drives through an intense simulation of heavy use that exercises all of their parts over a few weeks or months. The second testing regime uses a computer model that looks at every nut, bolt, chip, and platter and calculates expected lifetime based on supposedly known reliability of the parts.

You can consult the specifications for any current and most older hard drives on the Web sites of the major manufacturers. An example of the specifications for a modern drive, the Deskstar 75GXP, a 75GB speedster from IBM, is listed in Table 10-6.

If you are purchasing a new hard disk controller to go along with the drive, consult dealers, as well as the drive manufacturer, for their recommendations. This is less of an issue if you are attaching the drive to the built-in IDE controller that is part of the motherboard on many modern machines. You need a new controller only if that one is broken or if you need to step up to a higher performance design, such as a SCSI controller.

NOTE

As far as I'm concerned, the MTBF ratings are interesting if true, but much more important is how well the hard drive manufacturer stands behind the product. If a drive has a supposed MTBF of 100,000 hours but is under warranty for only 90 days (2,160 hours at most), I don't have reason to believe that the manufacturer has much faith in its own product. Look for drives with two- or three-year warranties, which are reasonable periods of use for a hard drive.

And when you receive your new drive, I recommend that you examine it carefully. Look at the date of manufacture, which is usually listed on a sticker on the drive; if it's more than a year old, you should be suspicious about the quality of the drive. The drive may be a white elephant that has been sitting on the shelf for an unusually long period of time. And, in some rare cases, disreputable repair shops or dealers have been known to try to pass off a remanufactured or returned drive as new.

Many drives are accompanied by a bad track table, which is generated at the factory. No drive is perfect, but low-level formatting locks out the bad tracks. The percentage of bad tracks should not exceed 5 percent of the total capacity of the drive.

Ch 10

TABLE 10-6: A Modern Hard Drive Specification Sheet

Configuration

Interface	ATA
Capacity	75GB
Sector size	512 bytes
Recording zones	15
User cylinders (physical)	27,724
Data heads (physical)	10
Data disks	5
Maximum areal density	11.0 Gbits/square inch
Maximum recording density	391,000 BPI
Track density	28,350 TPI

Performance

Data buffer	2MB
Rotational speed	7200 RPM
Latency	4.17 average ms
Media transfer rate	55.5 maximum MB/sec
Interface transfer rate	100 maximum MB/sec
Sustained data rate	37MB/sec
Average	8.5 ms
Track-to-track	1.2 ms
Full-track	15.0 ms

Reliability

Error rate (nonrecoverable)	1 in 10 trillion
Start/stop (load/unload at 40° C)	40,000

Power

Requirement	+5 VDC (+/−5%), +12 VDC (+10%/−8%)
Startup current	2.0 maximum A (12 V)
Idle	8.1 watts
Power consumption efficiency	0.11 watt/GB

Physical size

Height	25.4 mm
Width	101.6 mm
Depth	146.0 mm
Weight	670g

Environmental characteristics

Operating

Ambient temperature	5 to 55° C
Relative humidity (noncondensing)	8% to 90%
Maximum wet bulb (noncondensing)	29.4° C
Shock (half sine wave)	55 G/2 ms
Vibration (random [RMS])	0.67 G horizontal 0.56 G vertical
Acoustics (idle) Bels	3.6

Nonoperating

Ambient temperature	−40 to 65° C
Relative humidity (noncondensing)	5% to 95%
Maximum wet bulb (noncondensing)	35.0°
Shock (half sine wave)	225 G
Vibration (random [RMS])	1.04 G

CROSS-REFERENCE

See Chapter 21 for more information on safeguarding hard disk data.

The Data Structure of the Hard Disk

An operating system divides a hard disk into two sections: the system area and the data area.

The system area carries essential programs and directories that help the computer operate and keeps records of how information is stored on the disk.

The system area also includes a *boot sector* that holds a short program that gives the computer the basic instructions it needs to bring itself to life (the term boot comes from the phrase, "lifting yourself up by your own bootstraps," which is a colorful way to look at what DOS is performing when it first starts).

In this section, and throughout much of this book, I refer to DOS, which began as an operating system of its own and went on to underlay versions of Windows through Windows 98. Windows NT and Windows XP have their own rewritten basic operating system, but in action, that operating system mimics the functions of DOS.

Information in the boot sector includes how much, if any, of the disk belongs to the operating system (DOS or Windows understands that it may have to share the disk with another operating system) and where the system boot files are located.

Every disk has a boot sector on it, whether or not it is a system disk that is intended to fully start the operating system. System disks add a few other critical files that are necessary to initiate the operating system.

The boot sector is recorded on track 0, a fixed location on the disk. If that sector is in some way damaged or the files corrupted, you will have to find some other way to boot the system.

The next section of the disk holds the file attribute tables (FATs), the critical description of the organization of the disk. The tables are basically arrays of numbers that indicate, for example, that cluster X is linked to cluster Y, cluster Z is unusable, and cluster W is free. The system offers some measure of protection by maintaining a pair of identical FATs.

If the boot cluster is damaged, the operating system will not be able to recognize the disk and will display a message such as Non-System Disk, if it can give any message at all. Usually the machine just locks up. If the FAT is slightly damaged, the DOS command CHKDSK, the improved DOS program SCANDISK, or a data-recovery program may be able to reconstruct the pointers (the directions to the next cluster in the chain). If the FAT is unreadable, the pointer information and whatever is on the disk are lost. Even though the information is actually still on the disk, there is no way to access it in any meaningful form.

CHKDSK, which dates back to the very early versions of DOS, has been in place in the underlying system for Windows from the very start. Under Windows 95/98, Microsoft recommended the use of the enhanced SCANDISK program. With the arrival of Windows XP, Microsoft updated CHKDSK, including facilities that make repairs and display information about partitions that use the NTFS system. For more information on CHKDSK, see Chapter 22.

Some utility programs try to protect you from the irretrievable loss of the FAT by making a copy of the file elsewhere on the hard disk or on an emergency recovery disk.

The last part of the system area is the root directory, which begins at cluster 2. It contains the names of the root directory's files and subdirectories and indicates the pointer in the FAT that is the marker for the first cluster of each file. If the root directory is badly damaged, data on the disk cannot be retrieved.

Subdirectories are just lists of filenames, file sizes, file creation dates, file attributes, and first cluster numbers. In other words, a subdirectory is structured just like the root directory but is itself a file.

And here's a secret of most current operating systems: When you erase a file, the first letter of the filename is changed to the hexadecimal value E5 (E5H in computerspeak), and the FAT pointer is zeroed out, but the data is not actually erased from the disk. That is how undelete programs like the Windows Recycle Bin perform their magic: So long as no new file has written over the same space, the program can change E5 back to an alphabetic character, figure out what the first cluster number should be, and the file will once again appear in the disk directory and be available.

What goes where: The logical structure

Equally important, though, is an understanding of the logical structure of a hard disk. Hard disks are made up of cylinders and sectors.

Data on a hard disk is stored in concentric circles, called *tracks*. Across each track, the data is subdivided into small units of storage called *sectors;* the standard PC format packs 512 bytes per sector.

A *cylinder* is defined as the same track on each platter. (If you were to cut the hard disk along the thin edge of all platters with a circular cookie cutter, you would end up with a set of cylinders spread across more than one platter.) Each bit of data is located in a particular sector (pie slice), on a particular track (concentric data storage ring), on the top or bottom of a particular platter. The outermost track on every platter is cylinder 0. The next track is cylinder 1, and so on (see Figure 10-6).

There are two popular ways to package information: modified frequency modulation (MFM) and run length limited (RLL) encoding. Standard PC floppy disk drives from dinosaurs to modern machines use MFM. Today, nearly all modern hard drives use RLL; storage devices for senior citizens and dinosaurs may use the older, less efficient design.

One of the first schemes for computer storage was FM (frequency modulation). With the arrival of the first PCs, engineers developed a modified frequency modulation system that could store twice as much information in the same space; when MFM was introduced as the design behind floppy disks, it was called double density.

MFM encoding stores 17 sectors per track.

RLL encoding uses 26 sectors per track and packs more information — as much as twice as much — into the same area. RLL records groups of data as a block.

When it was first introduced, RLL required a higher quality surface, now adopted for all drives and encoding techniques. Either way, the data-coding scheme is built into the controller hardware, not the hard disk. An MFM controller with an RLL-certified hard drive produces MFM data encoding on an over-qualified recording surface.

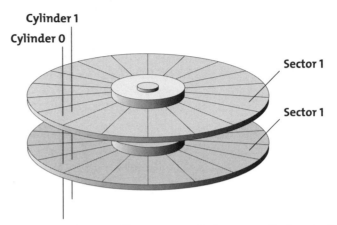

FIGURE 10-6: *Large files are recorded across cylinders instead of across tracks to minimize the amount of movement the read/write heads have to make to retrieve data.*

You don't need to delve any deeper into the highly technical differences between the two means of recording. It's more important to know the capacity of the drive and the type of interface — IDE, EIDE, SCSI, and so on — that it requires.

To the operating system, the data recorded across sectors, platters, and cylinders appears as a continuous stream of information. In other words, what you see as two platters, the operating system sees as a long length of tape.

DOS sees the data as a continuous stream, like the music on a cassette tape. Tracks 0 and 1 are the outermost tracks on a platter: Track 0 is on the top surface, and track 1 is on the bottom surface. Tracks 2 and 3 are also the outermost tracks but lie on the second platter of this hard drive. This makes sense because the read/write heads move together. Moving head 0 into position to read track 0 also moves the other heads into position to read the outermost tracks on the other platters (see Figure 10-7).

To the operating system, the disk is a large string of clusters. Data is read from and written to the disk in sector increments, and the operating system allocates space by the cluster, not by the individual sector.

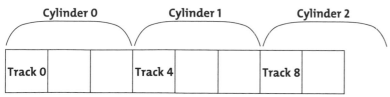

Ch
10

FIGURE 10-7: *A depiction of the recording pattern under DOS, which lies beneath most current versions of Windows.*

This is not a minor matter. The larger the capacity of a physical or logical drive, the larger the cluster size it uses. As an example, on a 1GB drive or logical volume, the cluster would ordinarily be 32K.

That's fine if you are storing files that are 32K, or 64K, or some other exact multiple of the cluster size. But if you store a batch file that is 10 bytes in length, it will still be placed into a box that is 32K in size; similarly, a file that is 33K will occupy two clusters, or 64K.

For this reason, it is quite possible to run out of storage space on a 1GB drive with just 700 or 800MB of data. Therefore, if your drive is filled with a large number of short files, your usable space is going to be less than the full capacity. One way to reduce the cluster size is to reduce the partition size — in other words, to subdivide the drive into smaller logical drives. For example, typing **FDISK** and using the resulting menu screens to partition a 1GB hard drive into two logical drives of 512MB each reduces the cluster size to 8K. Hard drive makers provide recommendations on partition settings with new drives and their accompanying installation software.

Formatting a Disk

In its raw form, a hard disk platter is merely a disk with a magnetizable coating; think of it as a gigantic blank piece of paper without rules or any other way to organize the information that will be recorded on it and no way to easily retrieve a particular bit of data.

The key to the kingdom here is *formatting* the disk to apply a structure.

A hard drive requires two separate types of formatting; between the two steps, the disk must also be subdivided. In this section, we explore these three steps:

- Low-level formatting
- Partitioning
- High-level formatting.

When you first turn on your PC, what you have is an extremely capable group of electronic components without a clue as to what to do.

As a convention that dates back to the birth of the personal computer, though, manufacturers tell the processor to always look to a particular place in memory — the address is FFFF0h — for its basic instructions.

Similarly, every startup hard disk has a consistent place where the processor can consult to find out essential information such as the number and type of partitions, as well as the bootup instructions that begin the process of loading the operating system. This startup location is called the master boot record or the boot sector.

The master boot record is always located at cylinder 0, head 0, and sector 1.

The elements of the master boot record include the master partition table, a tiny table that describes the partitions of the hard disk. There is room for only four physical partitions, also called primary partitions. Any additional partitions on the drive are logical partitions that are managed by the operating system and linked to a primary partition.

The computer looks to one of the primary partitions for bootup information and the operating system code; this is called the active primary partition.

The other critical element of the master boot record is the master boot code, which holds the small initial boot program that is loaded by the BIOS to start the boot process.

Low-level formatting

Low-level formatting applies magnetic signposts to divide the platter's tracks into sectors, setting the spacing between the sectors and tracks and applying codes to indicate the beginning and end of each sector (the sector header and trailer).

Current ATA/IDE and SCSI drives can be set up with 17 to 1,000 or more sectors on each track. Dinosaur drives using original ST-506 MFM controllers had 17 sectors per track; as early drives moved on to RLL encoding, they were set up with 25 or 26 sectors per track.

In the original scheme of things, each track on a drive had the same number of sectors. Although this offered the elegance of simplicity, it was also wasteful of valuable real estate. This is because the outer tracks of the hard drive have a lot more space than the inner ones.

Modern drives therefore use *zoned-bit recording,* which varies the number of sectors per track, packing more of them in the outer tracks. The scheme assigns *data zones* of varying size to the drive. Maxtor's high-capacity DiamondMax D540X, for example, has 16 data zones per surface for its 160MB of storage.

The fact that there is more data recorded on the outer tracks while the drive spins the platter at a constant speed means that the data transfer rate is significantly faster when the heads are positioned at the outside edge of the platter. Hard drive specifications usually indicate a maximum and minimum transfer rate for this reason; depending on the speed of rotation, the outer tracks can transfer data nearly twice as fast as inner tracks.

ATA/IDE and SCSI drives receive their low-level formatting at the factory, and for the purposes of this book, I'll leave the complexities of that job to the hard drive makers.

Partitioning the disk

The next step in preparing a disk is to assign logical units and file systems. If we were talking about real estate here, we'd be discussing the plot plan that divides up a piece of property into coordinates that can be mapped.

A partition is the basic container for data; each exists in a specified physical location on the drive and functions almost as if it were a single hard drive.

Each hard disk must have at least one partition; under Windows, it can have as many as four primary partitions with the same or differing file systems. A *primary partition* can be designated as an *extended partition* that can be further subdivided into *logical partitions*.

A PC must include one bootable partition for startup. Under DOS and Windows, only primary partitions are bootable. By default, the boot drive is assigned C: as its drive letter.

NOTE

See Chapter 22 for third-party partition software programs that go beyond Microsoft's standard specifications and that permit you to perform tasks, such as repartitioning a drive without losing the data in place.

Partitioning lays out a road map of the subdivisions of the disk. Depending on the capacity of the disk and the capability of the BIOS on your motherboard, you can have just a single partition or many. If you create more than one partition on a disk, partitions added after the first one are "logical" volumes, each with its own drive letter and name, even though they exist on a single physical drive.

After a disk has been partitioned, it must be formatted, which applies an index that the hard disk controller will use to store and retrieve information.

Windows 95 and 98 and the MS-DOS operating system that underlies them permit a system to have a total of 24 partitions. All

24 can be on the same drive, or they can be spread across many drives. (Why 24? It's a matter of alphabet logic: Physical and logical drives are identified by letters. A and B are reserved for floppy disk drives, which leaves 24 for hard drives.)

Some third-party partitioning software programs permit the use of more than 24 partitions, and Microsoft may extend the operating system's capabilities in future releases. Only one partition can be *active*, meaning it is the part of the drive where the operating system will look for the elements it needs to boot the system to life.

Windows XP and Windows 2000 assign drive letters differently from the design for Windows 98, Windows Me, and Windows NT 4.0. Basic drives, which are located on physical drives within your local computer, are subject to the same 24-volume limit (plus the A and B floppy drive reservations).

But the latest Windows versions also permit mounted drives, which are volumes attached to an empty folder on an NTFS volume. Mounted drives function like any other volume, but they are identified by a label or name instead of a drive letter. They are not subject to the volume limit, and include other advanced administrative and networking features that are beyond the scope of this book.

Microsoft's utility under DOS and Windows versions through Windows Me is called FDISK, and you find it in the system utilities folder of a Windows installation. You can also obtain a copy from the Microsoft Web site; if you have created an emergency boot disk for a Windows system, you will find a copy of the file there.

Under Windows XP, the partitioning utility is called DISKPART. On an already-partitioned drive, DISKPART is only available when you are using the Recovery Console. You can also access the Computer Management utility from within Windows; from the Control Panel, choose Performance and Maintenance and the Administrative Tools (you must be signed in as the administrator to make changes). Now select the Computer Management shortcut, highlight Storage, and then choose Disk Management. From the screen shown in Figure 10-8, you can choose a drive and, from the Action menu, add or delete a partition.

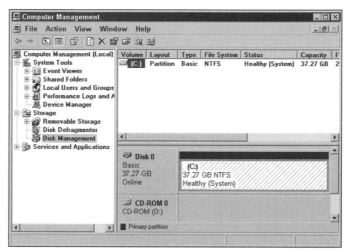

FIGURE 10-8: *The Disk Management screen of Windows XP permits adding and deleting partitions on an existing disk.*

If you are performing a clean install of Windows XP, the recommended method is to boot the system from Microsoft's distribution disc; to do so, you may have to change the boot sequence setting in the BIOS to go to the CD first. The automated installation process takes you to a Setup screen that leads to a partitioning utility. There you can create or delete partitions, choosing among NFTS, FAT32, and FAT, and assign space to them. After the partition is completed, you're prompted to format the subdivision; you can choose between full (including a scan of the disk for bad sectors) and fast.

If you install Windows on a partition formatted by using the Quick option, you can later check the health of the disk by running the chkdsk /r command. Choose Start ➪ Run and then type **chkdsk /r**.

Finally, many hard drive manufacturers include a copy of FDISK or DISKPART or their own version of partitioning software as part of their hardware kit.

The software writes a master partition boot sector to cylinder 0, head 0, sector 1. Recorded here are the starting and ending locations of each partition on the drive.

If you choose to have only a single partition on your drive, the utility will create only a primary partition, which will be the active or boot partition of the drive.

If you choose to have multiple partitions on your drive, FDISK or DISKPART will create a primary partition with a single active partition plus an extended partition that is divided into one or more logical volumes.

The minimum size for a partition is 1MB. (Older, small drives of less than that size will have all available space assigned to the primary partition.)

Under Windows 98 and later versions, the maximum size for a partition is as much as 2 terabytes (2,048GB), although hard drive manufacturers often offer workarounds that permit larger partition sizes for users that want a huge amount of real estate under a single drive letter.

Older versions of Windows and DOS will not allow partitions larger than 32MB without special software; again, you may find special versions of FDISK in the hardware kit from drive makers.

If you choose to create a second or further partition, it is called an extended partition, and it uses the space remaining after the primary partition. Extended partitions are labeled with letters from D through Z.

Many hard drive manufacturers provide a utility that automates the process of partitioning and formatting a new drive installation. Some of the utilities work in conjunction with a Windows installation or emergency startup disk that contains the Microsoft programs FDISK and FORMAT, while others use third-party programs that perform the same functions.

Nearly all current hard drive kits include installation software on diskette or CD that automates much of the process of partitioning and formatting. I recommend that you take advantage of the software's facilities.

Also very useful is a utility to help transfer data from an old disk to the new one. This sort of utility is also available as a standalone product; one example is Copy Commander from VCom, or that company's DriveWorks suite, which includes Copy Commander and other utilities. Whatever method you use — including a manual collection of files — be sure to include all essential data as well as settings, templates, favorites, address books, and e-mail.

Follow the instructions the drive maker provides. If you are installing a secondary drive in a system, most hard drive software requires you to make some changes to the BIOS and possibly the primary drive before the new hardware is put in place.

It is sometimes easier to install cables (data and power) to the new hard drive before sliding it into place in the drive cage. The standard configuration for most IDE hard drives allows you to use either the connector in the middle or at the end of the cable; however, some systems are configured to use a Cable Select specification. In such a system, the position of the hard drive on the cable indicates its assignment as a primary (end of the cable) or secondary (middle connector) hard drive.

After installing the drive, follow the maker's instructions on continuing the process for partitioning and formatting. After you complete that, you can move data from the old drive to the new.

NOTE

Some computer manufacturers make modifications to the standard BIOS setup screens to customize them to a particular configuration or product line, simplifying the options on systems marketed to entry-level computer users. In many cases, this causes no problems in ordinary use but may limit upgrading options further down the road. One example that came up during the research for this book was a Compaq computer that was based on an Award BIOS. When I wanted to add a second hard drive to the system, I found the BIOS had no provision for defining a new hard drive. The solution: I opened the case and examined the motherboard to find its model number. I then visited the manufacturer's Web site and found an available download of a flash update to the BIOS that added definable hard drives as well as a number of other modern facilities.

Operating system partition limitations

DOS 6.22 and earlier. Versions of DOS that predate the underlying code of Windows 9*x* do not support hard drives larger than 8.4GB.

Windows 95 A. Windows 95 version A (standard version) supports extended interrupt 13, allowing it to work with hard drives larger than 8.4GB up to a maximum of 32GB. However, the FAT16 file system used by the original release of Windows 95 requires that partitions be no larger than 2.048GB in size; therefore a 10GB hard drive must include at least five partitions.

Although some third-party utility makers have come up with ways to expand the capability of Windows 95A to larger drives, a better bet is to upgrade to Windows 98 or later.

Note that **Windows 95 Upgrade,** sold by Microsoft to migrate drives from Windows 3.1 or MS-DOS is not considered a standard version and does not update the PC's file system; therefore, a Windows 95 Upgrade will not support drives larger than 8.4GB.

Windows 95B (OSR2), Windows 95C, and Windows 98. Windows 95B (OSR2), Windows 95C, and Windows 98 support extended interrupt 13, allowing the use of drives larger than 8.4GB. Windows 95 systems are still officially limited to 32GB, although third-party utilities can extend their capabilities.

These operating systems also support FAT32, which permits the creation of partitions larger than 2.048GB. FAT32 can only be used on hard drives whose capacity exceeds 512MB.

Windows 2000. Windows 2000 supports FAT16, FAT32, and NTFS file systems. Under FAT16, partition sizes are limited in size to 2.048GB. The FAT32 file system supports up to 2TB (terabytes).

Windows NT 3.5. Windows NT 3.5 does not support drives greater than 8.4GB.

Windows NT 4.0. Windows NT 4.0 will support drive capacities greater than 8.4GB if the operating system has been updated to NT 4.0 Service Pack 3 or NT 4.0 Service Pack 4.

Windows XP. Under NTFS, volumes can be 2TB or larger. Under FAT32, you can format a volume up to 32GB; larger volumes are possible with third-party utilities.

High-level formatting

Logical or high-level formatting applies a file structure that the operating system uses to index the contents of the drive. Over the history of the PC, three common index structures have been used: FAT (in similar FAT12 and FAT16 versions, and the VFAT extension that recognized long filenames), FAT32, and the newest design, NTFS. The history of file systems is shown in Table 10-7.

An important element of the format is the *cluster* size, also called the *allocation unit*. The cluster is the smallest subdivision of the disk, used by the operating system for its index. Larger cluster sizes allow the operating system to work faster, because it has fewer units to keep track of; the bad news is that larger cluster sizes are generally wasteful of space. For example, if the system uses a 32KB cluster, a tiny file of a few hundred bytes would have its own 32KB space; a file of 33KB would demand two clusters, or 64KB of space.

TABLE 10-7: File Systems Used by Windows

Operating System	File System
DOS and Windows 3.*x*	FAT
Windows 95	FAT, VFAT
Windows 95 OSR2, Windows 98, Windows Me	FAT, FAT32
Windows NT v.3 and earlier	FAT, HPFS, NTFS
Windows NT v. 4	FAT, NTFS
Windows 2000, Windows XP	FAT, FAT32, NTFS

Each succeeding version of the file system brought new facilities that allow larger partitions, volumes, and filenames. A summary of some of the basics of each file system is shown in Table 10-8.

Ch 10

TABLE 10-8: File System Capabilities

File System	FAT (FAT12, FAT16)	FAT32	NTFS
Operating system compatibility	MS-DOS, all versions of Windows, Windows NT, Windows 2000, Windows XP, and OS/2	Windows 95 OSR2, Windows 98, Windows Me, Windows 2000, and Windows XP	Windows XP or Windows 2000 can access files on an NTFS partition. A computer running Windows NT 4.0 with Service Pack 4 or later might be able to access some files.
Volume size	Floppy disk size to 4GB	512MB to 2 TB (under Windows XP, volumes can be formatted to 32GB)	Recommended minimum volume size is 10MB, with maximum volumes of 2TB and larger.
File size	2GB maximum	4GB maximum	File size limited only by size of volume.
Notes	Does not support domains	Does not support domains	Cannot be used on floppy disks.

FAT16

The file system introduced with DOS 3.1 and maintained through early versions of Windows requires that partitions be no larger than 2.048GB in size.

Table 10-9 shows the FAT (file allocation table) cluster sizes under FAT16.

TABLE 10-9: FAT16 Cluster Size on Hard Drives

Drive Size (Logical volume)	Cluster Size
0–15MB	4K
16–127MB	2K
128–255MB	4K
256–511MB	8K
512–1,023MB	16K
1,024–2,047MB	32K
2,048–4,095MB	64K
4,096–8,191MB	128K (NT v4.0 only)
8,192–16,384MB	256K (NT v4.0 only)

FAT32

Microsoft's FAT32, used in Windows 98 and Windows Me, and available as an alternative file system in Windows 2000 and Windows XP, is based on a 32-bit file allocation table. FAT32 was introduced a few years into the life of Windows 95, in versions identified as Windows 95B or OEM Service Release 2. Microsoft also posted a partial patch to Windows 95 on its Web page.

Table 10-10 shows the FAT (file allocation table) cluster sizes under FAT32.

This file format can yield several hundred megabytes of additional storage over the conventional, 16-bit FAT because space isn't wasted with fixed large cluster sizes. In addition, you might see improved drive performance, perhaps as much as 50 percent improvement in some situations, according to Microsoft.

To convert a FAT16 file directory to FAT32 in Windows 98, use the built-in utility, Drive Converter: Choose Start ➪ Programs ➪ Accessories ➪ System Tools ➪ Drive Converter.

This action launches a Windows wizard that steps you through the process. Before proceeding, be sure to click the

Details button to read about what FAT32 means to your current configuration.

After you move into the 32-bit file world, you can't go back unless you're willing to reformat and repartition your drives. This, of course, means reinstalling all software — including Windows — and restoring your data files. You also cannot uninstall Windows after converting because earlier versions of Windows won't work with the new file system.

Older utilities — including drive compression, data recovery, and the like — will need to be updated.

Data on removable drives may not be accessible from other machines unless they also use the FAT32 file system.

TABLE 10-10: FAT32 Cluster Size on Hard Drives

Cluster Size	Minimum Partition Size	Maximum Partition Size
512 bytes	0	260MB
4KB	260MB	8GB
8KB	8GB	16GB
16KB	16GB	32GB
32KB	32GB	64GB

NTFS

Windows XP and Windows 2000 allow users to choose from among three file systems: FAT, FAT32, and the advanced (and recommended) NTFS.

NTFS works best with large disks, an improvement over FAT32. Other features are aimed at network administrators, including the ability to use Active Directory for control of distributed computing environment. NFTS also permits access control on files and folders.

Table 10-11 shows cluster sizes under NFTS.

If you're upgrading to Windows XP, that operating system includes utilities that make it easy to convert partitions to NTFS from FAT, FAT32, or the older version of NTFS used in Windows NT. The conversion keeps files intact.

Under Windows XP, if you do not need to maintain files created using an earlier file system, Microsoft recommends that you *format* the partition with NTFS (erasing all data within the partition) rather than *convert* it from the earlier system.

The only common reason to keep FAT or FAT32 as the file system for a PC running Windows XP is if you will also be running an earlier version of Windows that will need access to the same partitions; most earlier versions of Windows will not be able to work with files stored using the NTFS system. (Windows 2000 should be able to work with the files, while Windows NT 4.0 with Service Pack 4 will have access but with some limitations on features.)

After converting a partition or drive to NTFS, you cannot change it back to FAT or FAT32 without reformatting, which will erase all data. If you have to take this action, be sure to make copies of any files you want to keep.

TABLE 10-11: NTFS Cluster Size on Hard Drives

Cluster Size	Minimum Partition Size	Maximum Partition Size
0.5KB	0	0.5GB
1KB	0.5GB	1GB
2KB	1GB	2GB
4KB	2GB	4GB
8KB	4GB	8GB
16KB	8GB	16GB
32KB	16GB	32GB
64KB	32GB	64GB

Ch 10

Using FDISK

Under Windows 95/98 and Me, to manually partition and format a drive, boot the system from the startup disk. Then type **FDISK** and press Enter.

The first task is to set up a primary DOS partition. Choose Option 1 (Create DOS Partition or Logical DOS Drive). From the succeeding menu, choose Option 1.

You must instruct the system whether to devote the entire C: drive to the primary partition or to subdivide the drive. For simplicity, some users make the entire drive the primary partition; others prefer to organize the drive with C: devoted to the operating system and programs, and subsequent partitions used for storage of various types of files.

If you want to subdivide the drive, specify the amount of drive space you want to partition in either megabytes or a percentage of the entire drive, using a % (percent) sign.

Next, you need to make the primary partition active, holding the bootup files and instructions. From the main FDISK menu, choose Option 2 (Set Active Partition).

To create an extended partition, choose Option 1 again, and then choose Option 2 (Create Extended DOS Partition). Enter a percentage of the drive or the number of megabytes for this partition. Do not attempt to make this partition active; only one can be active.

After you create an extended partition, you can further divide it into logical drives. To do so, select the Create Logical Drives option from the extended partition menu. Follow the on-screen instructions to assign drive letters to your partitions. Bear in mind that if you choose D:, you will end up pushing the designation for any installed CD-ROM drive to higher in the alphabet; this should not cause problems but may result in some confusion when other programs, including installation utilities, assume that the D: designator refers to your CD-ROM.

You can double-check the results of your work by choosing Option 4 (Display Partition Information).

FDISK virus repair

The master boot record is a very attractive target for malicious virus makers; you should guard your machine with antivirus software and take other steps to protect the data recorded there.

Current versions of FDISK include two safety utilities that can help protect against accidental or malicious damage to your partition table.

If the master boot record is damaged, you can instruct FDISK to rewrite it based on the existing partitions on the drive, without damaging them or deleting the data records. To perform this task, boot from the startup disk and go to the A: prompt. Then type **FDISK /MBR** and press Enter.

You can also create a backup copy of the partition table on a floppy disk. From the DOS prompt, type **MIRROR /PARTN**.

The MIRROR utility copies the partition table to a file called PARTNSAV.FIL.

To restore this partition information, go to the DOS prompt and type **UNFORMAT /PARTN**.

Repartitioning a hard drive using FDISK

WARNING: Using FDISK on an existing hard drive will delete the records for everything previously stored.

Follow these steps to repartition a hard drive by using FDISK:

1. Boot the computer from your Windows startup disk, a Microsoft boot disk, or other startup disk.
2. Select the option to Start Computer with CD-ROM support.
3. The first step is to clear the Master Boot Record, which holds the partition records. At the A: prompt, type **FDISK/ mbr** and press Enter.
4. Now, you begin the process of removing the existing partitions. At the A: prompt, type **FDISK** and press Enter. On most modern machines, the operating system will ask if you want to use large disk support, which means to adapt the BIOS to work with, well, larger disks. Type **Y** and press Enter.

5. From the menu, select Option 3 (Delete the Partition) and press Enter. From the succeeding menu, select Option 1 (Delete the PRIMARY Partition).

6. Next, you're asked to confirm the partition to remove; type **1** and press Enter, and then enter the Volume Label for the partition to be removed. If it has no name, press Enter to move on.

7. At this point you have removed all partition information on the drive and made any data inaccessible. Now you need to repartition the drive. From the main menu select Option 1 (Create Partition). At the next screen, choose Option 1 (Create the PRIMARY DOS Partition).

8. The utility asks if you want to use the maximum partition space for the Primary Dos Partition. Type **Y** and then press Enter.

9. Your hard drive is now partitioned. Press the Escape key to return to the Λ: prompt.

10. The final step is to reformat the hard drive. Be sure to add the necessary system tracks. From the A: drive, type **Format C:/s** to do both.

Recovery Console (Windows 2000 and Windows XP)

Advanced users of Windows 2000 and Windows XP can perform surgery on drives — including formatting, writing data or recovery files or drivers to and from a drive, reading the data on an otherwise-inaccessible disk, and other power-tool tasks — by using the Recovery Console. You can also repair a damaged boot sector.

Two powerful uses of the Recovery Console are to repair a system by copying a file from a floppy disk or CD-ROM to the hard drive outside of Windows, and to reconfigure a service that is preventing the computer from starting properly.

You must be an administrator to use the Recovery Console.

If you are unable to start your computer, you can run the Recovery Console from the Windows XP or Windows 2000 Setup CD. Follow the text prompts to the repair or recover option.

Or, you can install the Recovery Console on your computer to make it available anytime Windows is in the process of starting. A Recovery Console option is then added to the list of available operating systems at startup.

 CROSS-REFERENCE

I discuss the Recovery Console in more detail in Chapter 22.

Alphabet Soup: Hard Drive Interfaces

Computers communicate with hard disks through an interface that is based on an industry standard that describes the adapter card, the cable, the electronics on the hard disk itself, and the electrical signals running between the hard disk and controller.

Over the years, the PC has seen a succession of steadily improving interfaces and associated hardware. In roughly chronological order, the PC has been host to ST506, ESDI, SCSI, IDE (also known as ATA), the enhanced EIDE standard (Enhanced IDE, also called ATA-2), Ultra ATA (based on Ultra DMA/33), and Wide SCSI.

Today's modern machines typically have an ATA or Ultra ATA interface. All ATA drives, including current Ultra ATA systems, employ IDE (Integrated Drive Electronics), meaning that the controller is built into the drive rather than on a separate controller card. For our purposes, IDE and ATA are the same thing.

Advanced machines may offer a SCSI interface, with some rising interest in Fibre Channel for disk arrays used in engineering, video editing, graphics, and sound applications.

Each hard drive interface handles the actual data storage in its own way.

ATA drives allow ordinary computer bus signals on the cable running from the IDE adapter card to the IDE hard drive, which has its own intelligence.

SCSI uses a separate bus (its own data and control signal path) to carry the data signals and control signals from adapter card, to hard disk, and back again. The SCSI bus is so separate, in fact, that most SCSI installations tell you to set up your computer as if no hard drives were installed. SCSI doesn't want the computer messing around with its bus, its data, or its hard disk.

Prior to the arrival of ATA drives in 1986, most early PCs used a design called ST506/412, which was introduced with the original IBM PC and still used until about 1988, and a specification called ESDI, in use from about 1983 through 1991.

The ST506 specification expected the user to instruct the computer's ROM BIOS how many heads and cylinders are on the hard disk, which read/write head should read what data, and what track on the hard disk this head should read.

These hard drive interfaces all do the same basic job (store and retrieve data, and connect to the computer motherboard) but in such different ways that none of the parts are interchangeable. SCSI drives insist on a SCSI adapter and cable; an older ESDI hard disk controller card won't work with a modern ATA drive. In addition, troubleshooting and installation techniques vary from interface to interface.

Examining Your Hard Drive and Interface

If you don't know what type of hard drive is within the case of your PC, you can consult the Hard Drive section of the Device Manager within Windows; look for a listing for an IDE or SCSI controller and driver. Most capable diagnostic programs will also produce a report that includes details of your storage system.

You can also open your computer to examine the drive, its controller/adapter, and their associated cables. Remove the cover and find the hard drive — a solid, rectangular, metal device that is usually mounted in a bay at the front of the chassis, although some designs suspend it elsewhere inside the case.

A four-wire power cable and one or two ribbon cables are attached to the back of the hard disk. Your floppy disk drive or drives also have a four-wire power cable and a ribbon cable, but it is easy to tell floppy disk drives from hard drives: Each floppy drive has a door in front to insert the floppy disks — a hard drive doesn't.

SCSI and ATA drives each use a single ribbon cable running from the hard drive adapter card or motherboard connector to the back of the hard disk. SCSI ribbon cables have 50 wires. IDE ribbon cables have 40 or 80 wires. Both of these cables are straight-through in design, with pin 1 at one end equal to pin 1 at the other. (See Figure 10-9.)

By comparison, a floppy drive cable has a twist with seven wires split off from the rest of the ribbon, flipped over, and clipped into the drive A: connector. (See Figure 10-10.)

Dinosaur tech: Because ESDI is simply a faster version of the ST506 interface (but incompatible with ST506), ESDI and ST506 drives and cables look the same. ST506 and ESDI interfaces both use two ribbon cables. One is 34 wires wide (the controller cable) and the other is 20 wires wide (the data cable). You can follow the ribbon cables back to the hard disk controller card. If you have two cables and your hard disk is less than 50MB, you probably have an ST506 interface. (The handful of exceptions includes a few small Micropolis, Rodime, and Microscience ESDI drives.)

If the hard disk is more than 200MB and has two cables, it is almost certainly an ESDI drive. Between 50 and 200MB is a gray area, because both ST506 drives (also called MFM and RLL drives) and ESDI drives have been manufactured in this size range. It makes sense to call your computer dealer or the hard drive manufacturer if you have any doubts.

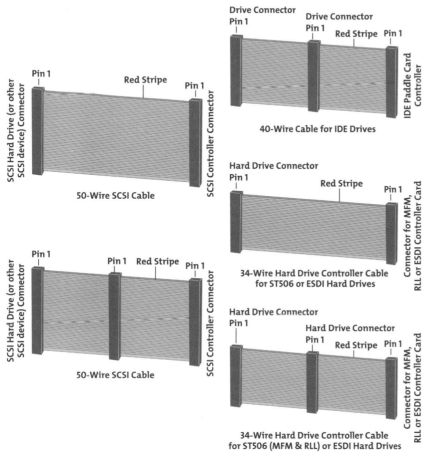

FIGURE 10-9: *Straight-through ribbon cables*

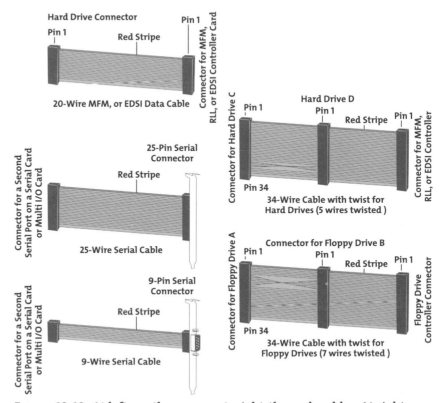

FIGURE 10-10: *At left are three more straight-through cables. At right are two ribbon cables with a twist to change drive selection.*

A dizzying alphabet soup of standards and specifications govern the recording and retrieval of data on a hard disk. For your purposes, it doesn't matter whether your drive uses MFM (modified frequency modulation) or RLL (run length limited) schemes for recording, or ST506, ESDI, IDE, EIDE, or SCSI disk controllers: The hard drive platters and heads are the same.

Modern Machine Hard Disk Drives and Interfaces

The good news is that modern machines can work with just about any drive interface previously used for PCs. The bad news is that you've got a whole bunch of choices and configurations to deal with. Table 10-12 lists the maximum possible transfer rates for modern interfaces.

TABLE 10-12: Transfer Rates for Current Hard Drive Interfaces

Interface Design	Maximum Theoretical Transfer Rate
ST506	0.625 MBps
ESDI	2.5 MBps
IDE	2–3 MBps
SCSI	10 MBps
EIDE (ATA-2)	11.1 or 16.6 MBps
FAST SCSI-2	20 MBps
Ultra SCSI	20 MBps
Ultra ATA	33.3 MBps
Ultra2 SCSI	40 MBps
Ultra ATA/66	66 MBps
SCSI-3	80 MBps
Fibre Channel	100 MBps
Ultra ATA/100	100 MBps
Ultra ATA/133	133 MBps
Ultra3 SCSI *	160 MBps
Ultra160 SCSI	160 MBps
Fibre Channel Dual Loop	200 MBps

Ultra3 SCSI is a somewhat incomplete SCSI definition from the SCSI Trade Association (STA). Although it is a 160 MBps bus, it also includes several other optional features, which has made the design and delivery of compatible devices difficult. A subset of Ultra3 SCSI, Ultra160 SCSI attempts to define compatible standards for interface manufacturers and suppliers of SCSI devices, such as hard drives.

IDE drives and adapters

Nearly all current home and small business machines use an IDE connection (including the enhanced version, EIDE). The key to understanding these controllers lies in the name: The drive electronics are integrated onto the drive itself. IDE connectors are host adapters that serve as ports into and out of the computer bus; the controller exists on the drive. This placement enables customization and upgrades by the drive manufacturer.

IDE controllers generally use one of the ATA standards, the latest of which are Ultra ATA/66, Ultra ATA/100, and Ultra ATA/133. For details of the various ATA standards, see Table 10-13.

TABLE 10-13: ATA Interface Transfer Modes and Rates

ATA Standard	Year Introduced	Transfer Speed	Notes
ATA	1986	8.33 MBps	Original BIOS limit was 528MB; updated BIOS permitted drives up to 137GB
ATA-2 (EIDE)	1995	16.67 MBps	Added ATAPI support to CD-ROMs and other devices
ATA-3	1997	16.67 MBps	Added support for SMART drives
ATA-4 (Ultra ATA, ATA/33)	1998	33.33 MBps	
ATA-5 (Ultra ATA/66)	1999	66.67 MBps	Requires use of 80-wire cable
ATA-6 (Ultra ATA/100)	2000	100 MBps	
ATA/133	2001	133 MBps	Drives as large as 144PB (petabytes), limited by current operating systems to 2TB

Current PCs come with one or two IDE connectors on the motherboard. You can plug as many as two devices into each cable that attaches to the connectors. See Figure 10-11.

If you don't want to use the motherboard IDE connector, or if it fails, the system BIOS configuration/setup program should let you turn off the onboard IDE controllers. If the IDE controller is not part of the BIOS, the motherboard should include a jumper block or a switch that disables the controller and recognizes a new controller that is plugged into the bus.

You can also purchase a separate IDE controller on an add-on card. Some manufacturers call IDE controller cards paddle cards; these replacement cards sell for as little as $20.

One reason to purchase a plug-in adapter is to upgrade your system to work with advanced standards including Ultra ATA/66, Ultra ATA/100, and Ultra ATA/133. An example of a state-of-the-art Ultra ATA/133 adapter is shown in Figure 10-12; the adapter and compatible hard drives came to market nearly a year before motherboards with the advanced circuitry were expected.

Figure 10-11: *IDE connectors on an ATX motherboard with the secondary connector nearest the rear of the board.*

 NOTE

IBM's PS/2 systems in most cases will not work with a standard IDE subsystem; IBM developed its own slightly different flavor of the specification.

IDE systems put the brains on the hard drive itself. The host adapter merely sends signals from the drive across the bus. The adapter, unlike earlier ST506 or ESDI hard disk controllers, does no data encoding or decoding. The drive's electronics also take responsibility for control signals for the read/write heads on the disk.

At the heart of the definition of IDE is the concept of the independence of the drive from its PC host. IDE drives use special registers for commands from the PC; the drives themselves have address-decoding logic used to match bus signals to the drive. In this way, a PC designer can locate an IDE subsystem at any port address with relative ease.

Because of the rapid increase in the number and types of IDE drives and to maintain compatibility with older drives and ROM BIOS chips, most modern machines do not have a drive type preconfigured in the BIOS that matches the IDE drive. Follow the drive manufacturer's instructions; depending on the system, you'll either set up the device as a user-defined drive type or allow the BIOS to automatically detect the specifications of the drive. If you want to use all the storage space available on your IDE drive, you have to tell the CMOS setup program that the IDE drive is a user-definable drive type.

Until late 2001, the fastest implementation of an IDE controller used the ATA/100 standard; Maxtor's new ATA/133 now rules the roost. Both of those high-speed protocols, as well as the ATA/66 design, are downwardly compatible with older IDE and ATAPI devices using the ATA/33 protocol.

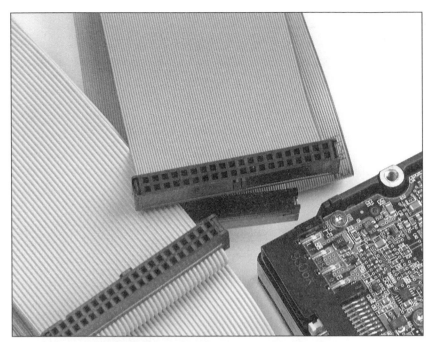

FIGURE 10-12: *An Ultra ATA cable is an unusual bridge between two specifications. It uses a 40-pin, 80-wire connection (the extra 40 wires serve as ground connections to help the parallel data stay in proper marching order). The blue connector must be plugged into the motherboard; the black end connector is used for the master drive on the cable, and the gray middle connector for a slave drive, if present. In this picture, the high-density Ultra ATA cable sits above its ATA/33 cousin.*

Ultra ATA, DMA/33, EIDE

The original IDE drive specification suffered from a few handicaps. As designed, IDE circuitry could not work with hard drives larger than 528MB, which seemed huge at the time but is way too tiny to hold even the operating system these days. Another problem was a limit of no more than two devices per IDE connector. Finally, IDE was at first only intended for use with hard drives, meaning it could not work with CD-ROM drives and tape backup devices.

Western Digital lead the effort to enhance the IDE specification, coming up with an improved variant that was named, logically, enhanced integrated drive electronics, or EIDE. Today EIDE is variously called Fast ATA, Fast IDE, ATA-2, ATA-3, and Ultra ATA. In this book, I have chosen to use the latest name, Ultra ATA.

Ultra ATA became widely available in 1998, offering data transfer rates up to 33 MBps when the proper drive was paired with an Ultra DMA/33 motherboard and controller. Ultra ATA is completely backward compatible with older Fast ATA-2 (EIDE) systems and can be used in legacy systems, albeit at the slower speed.

Most controllers can work with as many as four drives, with two on each channel. The drives can be all EIDE, all IDE, or a mix. In some systems, the entire EIDE channel will be limited to the maximum speed of the slowest device attached.

With this version of the specification, IDE included the ATA Packet Interface (ATAPI) specification that extends control to other types of devices. ATAPI drivers are available for CD-ROM drives, tape drives, and removable storage devices such as Iomega Zip drives.

The enhanced IDE standard deals with most of the limitations of IDE. It includes support for the following:

- As many as four devices from one controller, with the addition of a second connector that enables two devices on each of two channels.
- CD-ROMs and nondisk devices, as well as hard disk drives.
- High-capacity disk drives, up to 8.4GB in a single volume on a hard disk.
- High-speed host transfers, beyond that of the ISA bus. This enables a device to take full advantage of a VL or PCI local bus with data throughput of up to 11.1 MBps, which compares favorably with SCSI transfer rates of 10 MBps.

And, more importantly, Ultra ATA retains compatibility with ATA devices.

Ultra ATA/66 and Ultra ATA/100 interfaces

Modern machines on the market after 2000 now commonly support the Ultra ATA/66 or Ultra ATA/100 enhanced IDE interfaces. They are also known as Ultra DMA/66 or Ultra DMA/100.

As the names suggest, these versions double and triple the Ultra/33 burst data transfer rate to 66.6 MBps and 100 MBps, respectively.

Both of these interface standards describe how fast information can flow from your hard drive's data buffer (RAM) to your computer system; it is not a measure of how fast the hardware can actually pass data off of the disk to the system. You also need the Intel 820 chipset or a later (higher-numbered) chipset or a competitive equivalent to support the advanced standards; you can also purchase a third-party hard disk controller with its own onboard support for this high-speed IDE mode.

Although an Ultra ATA/66 and Ultra ATA/100 cable look like a conventional 40-conductor IDE interface, they are electrically different. The connectors still hold only 40 pins; there are 40 additional ground lines between each of the standard 40-pin ATA signal lines and ground lines to improve signal integrity by reducing crosstalk across data lines.

The specification calls for the connector at the drive end to be colored bright blue in order to help differentiate this interface from others in your system. You can use the new interface cables with conventional IDE drives, but, of course, you'll only get 33 MBps or less performance.

In order to run data transfer in Ultra ATA/66 or Ultra ATA/100 mode, you need the following:

■ A storage device capable of working with the Ultra ATA/66 or Ultra ATA/100 standard

■ A system board and BIOS compatible with the advanced standards

■ An 80-conductor cable designed for the Ultra ATA/66 or Ultra ATA/100 standard

■ An operating system capable of DMA transfers — support began with Windows 95 (OSR2) and continues in Windows 98, Me, 2000, and XP

In a capable system, both the motherboard and the hard drive can detect the presence of the required 80-conductor cable.

Ultra ATA/100 increases the data transfer rate and adds some enhancements to error checking. These drives also work with an expanded command set intended to work with future interfaces and enhancements.

All Ultra ATA/100 and Ultra ATA/66 drives are backward compatible with earlier ATA standards. However, some older ATA host controllers and motherboards may not work properly with Ultra ATA drives; the major disk drive manufacturers offer a utility program that sets the most advanced Ultra ATA drives to Ultra ATA/33 or Ultra ATA/66 mode to maintain compatibility. Changing the transfer mode affects only the external maximum (burst) transfer rate of the device; internal performance is not affected by the external transfer mode, so the overall sustained transfer rate is only slightly reduced.

Ultra ATA/133

In late 2001, Maxtor introduced the Ultra ATA/133 interface, which promises a 33 percent boost to 133 MBps in the top speed for data transfer to and from the interface. The interface uses the same 80-conductor, 40-pin cable used for ATA/100 and provides backward compatibility with all parallel ATA devices, including Ultra ATA/33, ATA/66 and ATA/100. The interface includes a set of tightly controlled specifications for trace lengths and timing parameters, an essential element of any high-speed parallel interface.

Maxtor filed for a patent on the technology and was first to market with devices that use the standard, but the company promised to license the interface to other drive manufacturers as it has with previous Ultra ATA technologies it developed. VIA Technologies, Silicon Integrated Systems Corp (SiS), Adaptec, Promise Technology, and Silicon Image are among early license holders for Ultra ATA/133 interface technology for systems and chipsets. An ATA/133 adapter card is shown in Figure 10-13.

FIGURE 10-13: *Maxtor's ATA/133 hard drive arrived before motherboards included the advanced circuitry it required. Pictured here is a Maxtor hard disk adaptor, based on a Promise Technology chip, to upgrade a modern machine. The large black connectors at the top of the card accept Ultra ATA cables to primary and secondary IDE drive systems.*

The next issue is the speed at which the drive can transfer data to and from the media. For example, Maxtor's DiamondMax D540X, which spins at 5400 rpm, can deal with the media at a speed of as much as 43.4 MBps; the company's DiamondMax Plus

D740X, which spins at 7200 rpm, has a media data transfer rate of as much as 54.2 MBps.

Both media transfer rates are well below the ATA/133 interface speed of 133 MBps and, for that matter, below the rates of ATA/100 and ATA/66.

However, the real interface transfer rate is actually as much as one-third slower because of overhead; one estimate is that a 32K block of data has a transfer efficiency of about 62 percent on an ATA/100 interface, meaning an effective transfer rate of 62 MBps, which is a lot closer to the maximum media data transfer rate.

According to hard drive manufacturer Maxtor, hard drive performance has been improving at about 40 percent per year, and the transfer overhead becomes more and more of an issue with larger drives and higher speeds.

Drive designers consider ATA/133 an important accomplishment because it matches the PCI bus data rate of 133 MBps exactly. In theory, even faster data transfer rates are possible, although there are obstacles, including finding a way to deliver backward compatibility to earlier interfaces. Current plans involve new designs for cables and connectors that won't work with the existing ATA interface.

For some users, the most important new element of the ATA/133 specification is breaking through the 137GB barrier for ATA hard drives. Over the history of the personal computer, there have been nearly a dozen barriers that set a maximum size for hard drives, beginning with an original limit of 528MB.

The 137GB barrier was in place because the original ATA interface provided only 28 bits of address for data, which meant that a hard disk could have no more than 268,435,456 sectors of 512 bytes of data.

ATA/133 doesn't just break through the barrier — it smashes it to bits, with a new top end of 100,000 times more data: 48-bit addressing permits a single drive with more than 144 *petabytes* (144 million gigabytes) of storage. (A petabyte is 2 to the 50th power [1,125,899,906,842,624] bytes, or 1,024 terabytes.)

And the accompanying ATA/ATAPI-6 definition also permits a boost in the maximum amount of data that can be transferred with each command for ATA devices from 256 sectors (about 131KB) to 65,536 sectors (about 33MB). This new capability will be used in multimedia applications including streaming audio and video.

However, the hardware top end of 144 petabytes is not yet matched by current operating systems. Because they are based on 32-bit addressing, Windows 95/98, Me, 2000, and XP cannot work with drives larger than 2.2 terabytes (2,200 gigabytes).

To work with the ATA/133 specification, systems need a compatible hard disk controller; Maxtor supplied a plug-in adapter with its early models of 160GB hard drives, ahead of the arrival of adapter cards from other manufacturers. Many BIOS chips also have to be updated in order to work with the advanced standard.

Serial ATA

On the horizon is a new standard, called Serial ATA, that will use the same protocol as parallel ATA but with different hardware using a smaller cable and demanding lower voltages, which is intended to allow chipset manufacturers to produced smaller and less expensive devices.

For many years, designers have been aware of the limitations of the ATA interface. The principal issue is the inherent difficulty of maintaining proper timing of the individual bits of a computer word or byte traveling alongside each other on parallel wires. ATA (which some designers have redubbed as parallel ATA) has been inching forward in potential transfer speed, most recently advancing to 133 MBps in Maxtor's ATA/133 hardware.

Serial ATA is expected to begin to arrive in late 2002 and proponents expect it to become the standard for hard drive communication in 2003. This design will begin at a data transfer rate of 150 MBps, with plans in place for a doubling and quadrupling to 300 MBps and 600 MBps in coming years.

Because of the huge installed base of machines using the existing ATA interface, motherboard manufacturers are expected to offer systems with both serial and parallel ATA ports for an extended period of transition for several years.

The new standard is intended to be 100 percent software compatible with earlier systems, requiring no changes to software and operating systems.

The parallel ATA design uses a somewhat unwieldy cable with 40 or 80 wires (ATA/66 and later standards use 80 conductors) and 40 pins in the connector. At the motherboard end, 26 signal pins go into the interface chip. The ribbon cables are 2-inches wide and can be no more than 18 inches in length.

The new Serial ATA standard uses only four signal pins to carry data in a thin cable similar in appearance to a telephone cable. The smaller cable can be as long as 3 feet, allowing for simpler design within the case and improving the system's airflow and cooling.

Parallel ATA interfaces are based on TTL circuits, which require as much as 5 volts of electrical power. Future high-speed circuitry using ultrafine traces requires much lower voltages, and Serial ATA can work with signaling voltages of as little as 250 millivolts ($\frac{1}{4}$ volt).

Devices attached to a parallel ATA interface are set up in pairs sharing a common cable in a master-slave relationship; both devices share the available bandwidth, and in some situations, both may be contending for access and data transfer at the same time.

On the other hand, Serial ATA is set up as a point-to-point interface with each device directly connected to the host with its own link and each able to use the entire bandwidth.

Finally, Serial ATA can be set up to be hot-pluggable, allowing devices to be attached to or removed from a system while it is running.

The specification was developed by an industry group lead by Intel and including Dell Computers, IBM, Maxtor Corporation, and Seagate Technologies. In late 2001, Western Digital showed off a prototype of the first hard drive designed for use with Serial ATA.

Testing IDE drives and their adapter cards

In general, IDE drives work, or they don't work.

One way that they won't work is if you fail to properly identify each device on the cable as either a primary or secondary device.

In many systems, you identify devices by setting a pin block on the rear of the drive. Consult the instructions that come with drives for proper settings.

On other systems, devices receive their primary or secondary identification depending on which of the two connectors on the cable they use; these "cable select" systems use the connector on the end of the cable for the primary device and the connector between the two ends of the cable for the secondary device.

If the drive won't read or write and the installation is new, recheck the drive jumpers and the cables. If the drive doesn't even spin, you may have a bad power connection, or you may have put the ribbon cable on upside down so that the red stripe is away from pin 1.

When installing IDE drives, users often find that their newly installed drives appear to have only a fraction of the storage capacity that they were promised. The problem almost always lies in the computer's ROM BIOS or an incorrect CMOS setup, not the IDE drive itself. The computer tries to access as many logical sectors as the CMOS indicates are in the drive. If you tell the computer there are fewer sectors in this IDE drive than actually exist, it believes you — and reports a smaller drive. (See the installation instructions in "Installing an IDE drive," later in this chapter.)

If you can read and write to your IDE drive, but it won't boot, check the standard DOS headaches. Do you have clean copies of COMMAND.COM and the DOS hidden files on your IDE drive? If you partitioned the drive, are you trying to boot from the active partition? Did you remember to make one of the partitions active? If you have two IDE drives in the system, you must boot from the master drive, not the slave.

Installing an IDE adapter card

Nearly all modern machines have two IDE ports built into the motherboard. All you have to do is connect a drive to the IDE connector on the motherboard. If there is a problem with the IDE circuitry on the motherboard or you want to upgrade to a better system, you may need to disable the adapter by using a jumper or a switch. Consult your PC's instruction manual or the manufacturer for details.

NOTE

On some early modern machines, when you disable an onboard IDE interface, each time you boot Windows you will receive a repetitive and annoying reminder that you have new hardware for which there are no drivers. When you do reboot, just click Cancel when Windows asks if you want to search for the appropriate drivers for this new hardware.

On other machines, it is necessary to install an IDE paddle card in the expansion bus. The directions follow.

Removing an existing IDE connection

If you must remove an existing IDE host adapter, begin by examining the cables attached to the card. Mark them with tape or a soft marker, and take notes before you disconnect them so that you will be able to reinstall them properly. On many machines, don't forget to mark and remove the little two-wire cable to the remote hard-drive light on the front panel of your computer case. It pulls right off the controller card and slides back onto the equivalent pins on the new card. Remove the screw holding the card to the rear of the computer chassis and pull the IDE paddle card straight up out of the bus connector.

Dinosaur note: EIDE adapters sometimes are installed in PCI local bus slots. XT-style 8-bit adapter boards with a ROM on the paddle card go in older machines to drive XT-style IDE drives.

If you are replacing a defective IDE circuit on the mother-board, consult your instruction manual to see if it must be disabled with a switch or a jumper; some systems automatically disable built-in circuitry if a new adapter is detected in the bus.

Installing an IDE cable

IDE cables are hard to install incorrectly because in most systems, the cable ends are keyed and color-coded in blue for the motherboard end, black for the master IDE drive, and gray for the slave drive that attaches to the middle connector. In addition, most controllers (and some drives) have the number 1 stenciled next to the pin-1 end of the cable connector. The cable has a red or blue stripe along one edge. Put this edge toward pin 1 on the drive and the controller. If you are attaching to an IDE circuit on the mother-board, locate the IDE connector there.

Most IDE cables have three connectors. One attaches to the IDE paddle card, and the other two are available for connection to one or two IDE drives.

You'll need to know if your system employs standard or cable select logic to identify devices. In a standard system, it doesn't matter which data connector you use for each drive; the selection of a master or slave drive is made with jumpers or switches on the drives themselves. In a cable select system, the connector you use determines whether a drive is primary or secondary.

Installing an IDE drive

Jumpers on the IDE drive tell the drive if it is one of the following:

- The only drive installed in the computer
- One of two drives installed and assigned as the first drive, or master
- One of two drives installed and assigned as the second drive, or slave
- A drive in a system that uses cable select to identify first or slave drives based on which of the two connectors they use

If you're adding a second drive to your system, do your research on Web sites and instruction manuals. You want to end up with compatible drives and be able to boot off the drive of your choice. In some rare instances, some drives may not be able to be slaves to another drive's master, or vice versa.

As you might imagine, if you have two identical drives or two similar drives from the same manufacturer, you stand a better chance of setting jumpers properly. That doesn't mean you can't mix a Seagate with a Fujitsu — just take care to read the instruction manuals of both drives.

If you're installing a new drive and controller package, check with both manufacturers to be certain they will work together.

Removing an IDE drive

Remove the system cover. Study the 40-pin ribbon cable at the back of the hard disk, mark it with tape or a soft marker, and make notes so that you'll be able to reinstall it properly. Pay special attention to the red stripe on the flat cable — this indicates the Pin 1 position on the cable to help orient it correctly in the connector. Disconnect the ribbon cable and the four-wire power cord from the hard disk.

On some space-saving desktop cases, you may need to remove the power supply and/or other components, including other drives, to gain access to the bay; this is especially true with space-saving desktop PC cases.

Most modern machines use rails screwed to the side of the hard disk that make it possible to slide the disk in and out of the chassis like a drawer. Some such installations hold the disk in place with clips on the front of the chassis that hold the hard disk. Remove the screws holding the clips in place or squeeze the spring-loaded clips and then slide the hard disk out.

Other drives are held in place by one or more screws on the sides of the drive. Regardless of which system holds your hard disk in place, save any rails, clips, or screws you remove; you will need them for the new hard disk.

On standard systems, set the jumpers or the switches on the drive to distinguish the first drive (called the master) from the second drive (the slave). Consult your instruction manual or call the manufacturer of the drive for assistance if necessary.

Sliding in the drive and connecting cables

Slide the hard disk into the chassis. Most modern machines use rails to hold the hard disk in place, but some use screws.

Connect the 40-pin ribbon cable. Be sure to connect pin 1 on the ribbon cable to pin 1 on the hard drive. If you have two IDE hard disks in your system, they will share the ribbon cable.

Plug in a four-wire power cable from the power supply. Note that the power supply cable connectors are not rectangular. Look at one carefully; two corners have been cut off on a diagonal. Examine the socket on the hard drive carefully and be sure to install the power connector correctly.

Install any screws that hold the drive into the chassis.

Using setup to tell your computer about the hard disk

Begin your configuration process by seeking information from the instruction manual for your new drive. Nearly all current hard drives come with an automatic installation program on diskette; even with this program, you may have to make settings in the BIOS. The most common BIOS setting is to instruct the system to *auto-detect* the drive; the BIOS communicates with the drive to determine the proper settings.

If your BIOS will work with auto-detect, you can skip to the next section of this chapter. Otherwise, read on.

On an older system, you will have to choose settings. Once again, consult the instruction manual for the hard drive for specific details. When you enter your computer's setup screen, you see a list of supported hard disks, complete with number of cylinders and heads. This list was stored in the ROM BIOS when it was manufactured. You may find that the exact IDE drive configuration that you have will be in this hard disk list, especially if you're dealing with a senior citizen or an older modern machine BIOS manufactured before 1990.

Many IDE drives don't fit into the standard drive list, anyway. They may, for example, break a cardinal rule of BIOS-supported hard disks by putting more sectors on the large outer tracks than on the small-diameter inner tracks. The good news is that the drive you select on the setup screen doesn't have to match the physical configuration of the IDE drive, just the logical configuration.

Multiply heads by cylinders by sectors per track to determine the number of cylinders on a hard disk (this is the logical size). An 84MB IDE drive with 6 heads, 832 cylinders, and 33 sectors per track would have 164,736 sectors. If you select a hard drive type from the BIOS list that contains the same 164,736 sectors (or fewer), the drive will work. It will work even if the drive you pick has 8 heads and 624 cylinders (a different physical configuration) because the IDE drive electronics translate your computer's instructions to read a particular logical sector (in the drive the computer believes is installed) to the actual head-and-cylinder situation in the IDE drive.

If you must choose among a limited list of drive types, pick one as close as possible to your actual IDE logical size (total number of sectors), but pick one a bit smaller rather than a hair too large. Newer ROMs now support a user-definable drive with user-defined cylinder and head counts. Thus, you can easily match the logical size of your IDE drive to the logical size of your user-defined drive by picking an ordinary number of heads (for example, 8) and an ordinary number of sectors per track (17, 39, and 53 are typical values) and calculating the nonstandard number of cylinders you need to make the total number of sectors on the drive less than or equal to the actual number of sectors on your IDE drive.

If you don't have a reasonable size match to choose from, and you don't have (or can't use) a user-definable drive type, it makes sense to get a newer BIOS rather than wasting a quarter or a third of your IDE drive's capacity by entering too small a drive in your computer's CMOS setup.

NOTE

In some situations, less-than-current network software may not run properly on user-definable drives. Check with your LAN supplier if you have any questions.

SCSI devices

Many PCs that demand very high sustained data transfer use the small computer system interface (SCSI) specification, a high-speed parallel subsystem.

The SCSI specification has been around for quite some time, appearing in minicomputers and Apple Macintosh computers before arriving on the PC. SCSI (and its faster cousins SCSI-2, SCSI-3, and their variations) offers greater speed and the capability to daisy-chain as many as 15 devices inside and outside the PC. SCSI controllers can, in theory, work with CD-ROM drives, as well as hard disks and controllers, but be forewarned: There are many different flavors of SCSI, including some proprietary versions that work only with specific devices. Make certain that any peripherals you want to attach to a SCSI chain are compatible with the version you have; check with the manufacturer of the hardware to be sure.

The difference among the various drives lies in low-level formatting, which is taken care of by special software bundled with these drives.

The SCSI (pronounced "skuzzy") interface was under development at about the same time as ESDI, and it represented (along with IDE) a new approach to the design of disk drives and controllers. The concept was intended to move much of the intelligence from the computer to the drive electronics and resulted in improved drive speed and enhanced compatibility across systems.

Because it is a higher-level interface than a mere card in the bus, you can also use SCSI to connect a wide range of other devices to the PC, including scanners and CD-ROMs. SCSI controllers add about $100 to $250 to the cost of a machine, and SCSI drives sell at a premium of about $50 to $100 more than EIDE equivalents.

The SCSI specification allows up to 15 devices on one controller, depending on the type of SCSI interface you're using, and you can put more than one controller in a system. SCSI is well suited for external drives, CD-ROMs, scanners, tape backups, and other devices that can be daisy-chained on and beneath the desk.

The original specification for SCSI had a top end of 5 MBps with an 8-bit data path and a maximum of seven devices, one of which was the SCSI controller itself. That was soon surpassed by SCSI-2 (also called Fast SCSI), which could move as much as 10 MBps in an 8-bit bus. Beyond that is Fast-Wide SCSI, which uses a 16-bit data path and moves twice as much data—20 MBps. Later SCSI standards support up to 15 devices, but one device—usually number 7—is assigned to the SCSI controller.

And SCSI-3, which includes a mode called Ultra-SCSI or Fast 20, doubles the speed of SCSI again to 20 MBps on an 8-bit bus and 40 MBps on a 16-bit bus. Dual, Ultra-Wide SCSI interfaces double that again, giving you up to 80 MBps of data transfer. However, SCSI-3 is a somewhat unclear designation these days. The industry has used the Ultra designator for fast SCSI interfaces because the official SCSI-3 designation includes a number of optional features. It is relatively easy for manufacturers to comply with the bare minimum SCSI-3 specifications and still not have what others would term a SCSI-3 device. Moreover, the availability of these options within the specifications means that controllers and SCSI devices may end up being incompatible with each other, particularly products that come from different manufacturers. Table 10-14 summarizes SCSI specifications.

For this reason, some manufacturers have developed another SCSI standard, Ultra160 SCSI, which is really a subset of SCSI-3 but a subset that carries fixed features and specifications. An Ultra160 SCSI device is capable of 160 MBps data transfers—the same as the SCSI-3 specification. Adaptec (www.adaptec.com) has introduced a range of Ultra160 SCSI controllers designed for low- to high-end servers. These cards are 32- or 64-bit PCI cards, depending on the application, and can support up to 30 devices. Like most other high-end SCSI adapters, these products also can support hard drives and other devices designed for earlier SCSI standards. Adaptec claims its SpeedFlex technology will ensure top performance from all SCSI devices on the chain, regardless of SCSI generation. However, as I have warned before, you should be careful mixing high-performance and low-performance devices on the same bus. You might degrade the performance of the fast drive to no better than the slowest drive on the bus. Just test things before you set your weight down on a permanent solution.

In 2001, manufacturers were beginning to embrace a new standard, Ultra4 SCSI (also known as Ultra320 SCSI), that doubled the speed of its predecessor to 320 MBps.

All SCSI devices are backward compatible; the fastest devices will operate at a slower speed on older controllers, and older devices will work properly when connected to a modern controller.

For more information on the latest standard, consult the Web site of the SCSI Trade Organization at `www.scsita.org`.

TABLE 10-14: SCSI Specifications

Standard	Common Name	Bus Width	Clock Speed	Maximum Transfer Rate
SCSI	SCSI	8 bit	5 MHz	5 MBps
SCSI-2	Fast SCSI	8 bit	10 MHz	10 MBps
SCSI-2	Wide SCSI	16 bit	5 MHz	10 MBps
SCSI-2	Fast-Wide SCSI	16 bit	10 MHz	20 MBps
SCSI-3	Ultra SCSI	8 bit	20 MHz	20 MBps
SCSI-3	Ultra-Wide SCSI	16 bit	20 MHz	40 MBps
SCSI-3	Ultra2 SCSI	8 bit	40 MHz	40 MBps
SCSI-3	Ultra2-Wide SCSI	16 bit	40 MHz	80 MBps
SCSI-3	Ultra3 SCSI	32/64 bit	40 MHz*	160 MBps
SCSI-3	Ultra4 SCSI	32/64 bit	40 MHz*	320 MBps

Ultra3 SCSI and Ultra4 SCSI transfer data twice on each clock cycle for an effective clock speed of 80 MHz.

SCSI disadvantages

SCSI does, though, have some limitations principally related to the complexity of configuration. SCSI requires device drivers for each operating system, operating environment, and hardware combination. And the ultimate performance of a SCSI system is greatly affected by the quality of the drive/interface combination. In certain circumstances, a SCSI system can end up being slower than an IDE package.

Hardware configuration requires that each device must be assigned a device identification number, and the last device in the SCSI chain must be set up as the termination device by changing a jumper or installing a special plug.

And finally, a SCSI device is more expensive to manufacture than an IDE equivalent because of the additional logic necessary on the controller and the SCSI device.

However, many of the original configuration problems associated with SCSI have gone away with Plug-and-Play systems under Windows 95/98. The operating system can detect and adapt itself to old and new devices.

For many users, the biggest headache associated with SCSI involves the mating of cable and connector. There are four different connectors in common use on PCs, plus a few other variants employed on Apple and other systems.

The original 8-bit SCSI specification used a standard 50-pin Centronics connector; you can easily identify it by its use of wire latches to lock into place.

With the arrival of SCSI-2, drives used a downsized attachment device that is referred to as a 50-pin high-density connector.

The next means of attachment in wide use was the high-density 68-pin SCSI connector, used to support additional pins for 16- and 32-bit data transfers. Most current drives use this scheme.

You'll also find some drives that demand an 80-pin SCSI connector that merges data signals and power lines in the same attachment; it is sometimes referred to as an SCA connector.

The good news is that you should be able to locate conversion adapters that can mate most drives with most cables.

SCSI drives and host adapter cards

The SCSI bus is completely separate from the motherboard's main bus. Unlike ATA and older ESDI and ST506 drives, which all rely on the computer's ROM BIOS to send read/write directives, SCSI drives are autonomous.

You can also use SCSI for other devices, including CD-ROMs, scanners, and removable hard drives.

When the computer boots, it checks for additional hardware ROMs (the chips that tell your computer how to interact with each piece of oddball hardware). When your computer finds that a SCSI host adapter is installed, it doesn't discover any details about the SCSI equipment attached to the SCSI host adapter.

Most modern machines are capable of interacting with multiple SCSI adapters, each with its own set of 15 devices (one of which is the SCSI adapter itself). The newest SCSI standards — Ultra160 SCSI and Ultra320 SCSI — support up to 30 devices.

The SCSI host adapter card keeps track of data flow across the SCSI bus. Each SCSI item on the bus, whether it's a host adapter card, hard disk, optical disk, or some other item, requires a unique SCSI bus address, also called a SCSI address or SCSI target address. An example of a basic SCSI card is shown in Figure 10-14.

Any two of these SCSI devices can converse on the SCSI bus, without help from your desktop computer or its microprocessor.

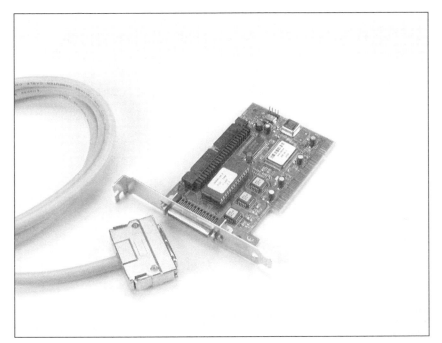

Figure 10-14: *An Adaptec AHA 2920 SCSI PCI card with a SCSI-2 cable in the foreground*

The nonstandard standard

SCSI may be a standard, but some SCSI implementations are more standard than others. First of all, there is the original SCSI; then there is SCSI-2 with both Fast and Wide variants; and SCSI-3, with Ultra, Ultra2, and Wide variants. Devices intended for the faster SCSI-2 or SCSI-3 implementation may not work reliably with the slower original if it varies in any significant way from the official description, although usually it's possible to use devices intended for SCSI-1 with SCSI-2 or SCSI-3. SCSI-3 is, in general, compatible with earlier SCSI-1 and SCSI-2 drives, as well as new devices. Figure 10-15 shows an Ultra-Wide SCSI card.

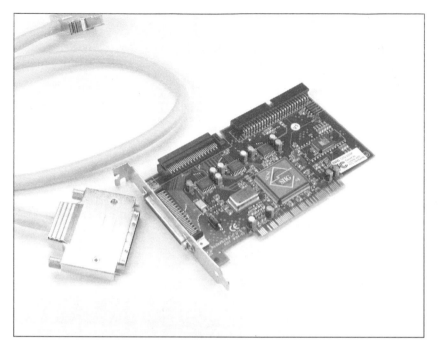

FIGURE 10-15: *A SIIG Ultra-Wide SCSI PCI card with a SCSI-3 cable in the foreground*

a proprietary SCSI drive if you want to substitute a lower-priced generic SCSI for the real thing. Two solutions that work in many cases are CorelSCSI from Corel and EasySCSI from Adaptec. You may find one or the other of these utilities bundled with adapters; they are also available for purchase separately.

There are kinks in other areas, as well. Few, if any, dinosaur PC motherboards work with SCSI adapters, and some older AT-style motherboards don't function properly with fast, 16-bit SCSI adapters.

Check the instruction manual for your SCSI adapter, or better yet, call the manufacturer — before you buy the card — to check on the pairing of the card with your system's motherboard and with any disk drives and other devices you want to attach to it.

Not all SCSI devices use the same SCSI software command set to communicate on the SCSI bus. If you have two SCSI devices that cannot seem to get along, you may have to speak to both of the hardware manufacturers to find a common language. Newer SCSI standards are helping with this level of incompatibility, as is the improved Plug and Play support built into Windows 98 and later versions of the operating system.

Testing SCSI drives and host adapter cards

You can connect as many as seven devices with older SCSI adapters, up to 15 devices with SCSI-2 controllers, and 30 devices with Ultra160 SCSI. External SCSI devices usually use a thick 50-wire cable; internal devices use flat ribbon cables.

Each SCSI device has two ports. One is used for incoming signals, and the other is used for an outgoing cable to the next device in an electronic daisy chain.

One important element of a SCSI system is that the two ends of the daisy chain must be terminated to tell the adapter where the chain ends. Most devices use a special terminator plug, which fits into the SCSI output port; some units have switches or jumpers that you can set to terminate a port.

Proprietary SCSI is often used for special devices, such as scanners, some CD-ROMs, and certain specialized hard drives, including some removable models. At the dawn of the modern age, the entire class of sound cards included a SCSI adapter on the board intended for connection to a CD-ROM; the adapter worked only with certain devices.

In addition, many computer manufacturers used proprietary extensions to the SCSI standard in the past, although this is less common now. Among companies that have gone out of their way to come up with their own versions of SCSI devices at various times in their history are Compaq and Apple. If you are saddled with a nonstandard SCSI adapter, you may be able to purchase special software that fools the computer into thinking you've installed

If your SCSI adapter is at the end of the chain—in other words, if only one outgoing cable is attached to it—the adapter itself must be terminated. If the adapter is in the middle of the chain, the devices at each end must be terminated, and the adapter must not be.

SCSI devices can do a bit of their own diagnostic work and report errors using a set of messages that have been sanctioned by the American National Standards Institute (ANSI). That's the good news; the bad news is that, like the SCSI standard itself, not all of the codes are as standardized as they could be.

Consult the instruction manual that comes with your SCSI adapter for details on the error codes used by your device.

Check to see that a modern machine's CMOS setup indicates that a hard drive is not installed.

Poorly shielded SCSI cables can cause data corruption or even prevent a computer from booting off the SCSI drive.

If the SCSI device won't read or write at all, check for proper installation, especially if you have just been working inside the computer. Perhaps you knocked a cable loose. If you have just added a new piece of equipment, make sure that it has not been given the same SCSI bus address as another device.

If you can read and write to your SCSI drive, but it won't boot, check for the usual DOS problems. Do you have clean copies of `COMMAND.COM` and the DOS hidden files on your SCSI drive? If you partitioned the drive, are you trying to boot from the active partition? You did, of course, remember to make one of the partitions active, right?

Installing a SCSI host adapter card

SCSI adapters generally reside in the computer's bus, although some motherboards offer built-in SCSI circuitry. To add a SCSI card, you need to remove an existing adapter in the bus. If you have SCSI circuitry on the motherboard, consult the instruction manual to see if it's necessary to disable the interface or make special settings for a second adapter that will go into the bus.

Removing a SCSI adapter

If you must remove a defective SCSI adapter, begin by examining the cables attached to the card. Mark them with tape or a soft marker and take notes before you disconnect them so that you will be able to reinstall them properly. Don't forget to mark and remove the little two-wire cable attached to the remote hard drive light on the front panel of many computer cases. It pulls right off the controller card and slides back onto the equivalent pins on the new card. Remove the screw holding the card to the rear of the computer chassis and then pull the card straight up, out of the bus connector.

Setting switches or jumpers

The new adapter card may be set up ready to work with your system straight out of the box, but to be on the safe side, read the manufacturer's installation instructions. One instance when you are certain to need a switch change is if you have another SCSI device that insists on being device number 7, which is the default SCSI bus address for the host adapter card.

Checking termination

The SCSI bus must be terminated at the two far ends of the SCSI cable. Each manufacturer uses its own termination technique. Read the installation booklet for your particular SCSI device or host adapter card.

Although no hard-and-fast rule exists, in general, most SCSI adapters come with a terminator installed, assuming that the board will be used with internal SCSI devices, such as hard drives and some CD-ROMs. The host adapter (one end of the bus) is terminated, and you can terminate the last drive on the internal SCSI cable.

You can also leave the terminator in place on the adapter if you install only external SCSI devices; again, the adapter is one end of the bus, and the last external device is given a terminator to end the bus there.

However, if you have one or more internal SCSI devices and decide to add an external device as well (a backup hard drive, CD-ROM, or scanner, perhaps), you must take the terminator off the SCSI host adapter card because it is now in the middle of the bus. One terminator should be on the last internal device, and the other terminator on the last external SCSI unit.

Installing the SCSI host adapter card

Press the card firmly into a slot on the motherboard. Install the screw that holds the card in place.

NOTE

You may need to attach a separate drive LED cable to SCSI drives to activate the drive activity light on the front of many computers. Consult the instruction manual with your drive and with your PC for details.

On modern machines (in general, the only type of device that can work with a SCSI bus), run the setup program and indicate for the SCSI chain that a hard drive is not installed. If you're adding a second SCSI drive or replacing both your hard disk and controller, see the section "Installing a SCSI drive," later in this chapter.

If you have an EISA computer, use the EISA configuration utility to tell your computer about the SCSI card.

Installing the SCSI cable

SCSI uses a straight-through 50-wire ribbon cable for standard SCSI devices mounted internally within a computer. Internal Wide SCSI devices use a 68-pin cable.

External SCSI drives and the external connector on the back of a SCSI host adapter card use a 25-pin connector that resembles the parallel printer port on the back of your computer, or they use a 50-pin Amphenol connector that looks like a longer version of the Centronics cable connector that is located on the back of a parallel printer.

Newer external SCSI cables for SCSI-2 or SCSI-3 may be small 50- or 68-pin D-shaped connectors. The internal pins on these connectors are quite small, but the connectors snap into place firmly. All external cables are designed so you cannot install them upside down or backward.

The internal SCSI cable is usually gray or multicolored. Gray cables ordinarily have a red or blue line along one edge to identify pin 1 of the cable connector; multicolored cables have a brown wire for pin 1. You must find pin 1 on your SCSI adapter and then install the cable with the 1 wire going to pin 1.

The manufacturer may have marked pin 1 on the adapter itself. You may be able to find a drawing with the location of pin 1 in the instruction manual for your SCSI adapter. If you have any doubts, call the card manufacturer to be sure you properly install the cable and adapter. Installing the cable backward can blow a fuse in the drive or cause other damage when you turn on the power.

SCSI drive letter assignments

If you install both an IDE drive and a SCSI drive, most PC BIOS systems will assign the IDE as drive C: and make it the boot drive. They do this because the BIOS is set up to boot from the first active primary DOS partition it encounters. Any IDE drive installed as a master device on the primary IDE channel must have a primary DOS partition and will automatically be known as C:.

On the most modern PCs, though, some BIOS chips permit you to choose between the SCSI and IDE interfaces for the boot drive. Check the documentation and online help screens of the CMOS configuration screens for details.

Installing a SCSI drive

The following sections describe the process of installing a SCSI drive.

Removing the old SCSI drive Remove the system cover. Examine the ribbon cable on the back of the hard disk, noting the red-marked edge that should face toward pin 1 on the drive. Use tape or a soft marker to mark the cables and take notes to help with reinstallation. Disconnect the ribbon cable and the four-wire power cord from the hard disk.

> **NOTE**
>
> You may need to remove the PC's power supply and/or other components, including other drives, to gain access to the bay for a new hard drive; this is especially true with space-saving desktop PC cases.

Most modern machines use rails screwed to the side of the hard disk that enable the disk to slide in and out of the chassis like a drawer. Some such installations hold the disk in place with clips on the front of the chassis that hold the hard disk. Remove the screws holding the clips in place or squeeze the spring-loaded clips and slide the hard disk out.

Other drives are held in place by one or more screws on the sides of the drive. Regardless of which system holds your hard disk in place, save any rails, clips, or screws you remove; you will need them for the new hard disk.

Setting switches or jumpers In some ways, the SCSI bus is like a small local area network (LAN), with many individual computers speaking to each other over a shared bus. As with LANs, each device on the SCSI bus must have its own device number (its own bus address).

Device 7 is traditionally reserved for the SCSI host adapter card; this convention usually is maintained even with new controllers that support 15 or 30 devices. Originally, device 7 was the last one in the chain (0 through 8). Now device 7 falls in the middle or toward the lower end of available SCSI devices. The device-7 convention helps facilitate backward compatibility with earlier systems and devices. You may pick any unused address for your hard disk. Just make certain that your host adapter card hasn't reserved special relationships with particular SCSI bus address numbers. The popular Adaptec 1542, for example, treats devices 0 and 1 differently than it treats all other devices. As a result, you might run into difficulty if you set a particular drive to device 0. Read your SCSI adapter installation manual to determine the idiosyncrasies of your particular controller. Insist on getting installation instructions with every card you buy and be sure to read them.

Checking for correct termination See the section "Checking termination," earlier in this chapter.

Sliding in the drive and connecting cables Most modern machines use rails (flat bars screwed onto the side of the hard disk) to hold the hard disk in place. If your computer requires rails, install them on the SCSI drive and slide it back into the chassis.

Connect the ribbon cable. Be sure to connect pin 1 on each ribbon cable to pin 1 on the hard drive. Plug in a four-wire power cable from the power supply. Note that the power-supply cable connectors are not rectangular. Look at one carefully: Two corners have been cut off on a diagonal. Examine the socket on the hard drive carefully and be sure to install the power connector correctly.

Install screws to hold the drive into the chassis.

Formatting a SCSI drive SCSI drives are already low-level formatted at the factory. However, you do have to partition SCSI drives with the FDISK command and then format them with the FORMAT command. (The process under Windows XP is similar, using the DISKPART command.) Your drive manufacturer should offer details.

Fibre Channel drives

Controllers for those with a real need for speed include Fibre Channel cards, which can move data at 1.06 GBps, with developing extensions to an astounding 2.12 GBps, with 4.24 GBps on the way. Fibre Channel interfaces are almost exclusively used on high-end servers, engineering machines, or computers destined for audio and video editing or high-end graphics.

The interface is built around optical cable that connects the controller and hard drive, although some devices use standard cable but substitute copper wiring.

Using a connector based on the 80-pin parallel SCSI single connector attachment (SCA), Fibre Channel disk drives attach directly to a backplane for data transfer and power. This not only eliminates cable congestion but also enables hot plugging of drives while the system is running and reduces the number of parts — and possibilities of failure — in the new class of drives.

The Fibre Channel connector determines the drive's address from the relative position of the drive on the backplane or from its unique address encoded into the drive's hardware. Each drive has its own code number that is not duplicated on any other device. The Fibre Channel interface can theoretically address as many as 126 devices, but a limit of about 60 drives is more practical with current controllers.

You may hear the term Fibre Channel (or simply Fibre) applied to a variety of different physical interfaces in the computer business today. Some of these are actually fiber-optic interfaces, and some use copper wiring. The data transport standards and hardware capabilities are similar but vary with the type of device being supported.

Fibre technology can be and is being used for computer networking and for local and long-distance backbone connections, but it also is an attractive storage interface, as well. It offers a higher speed than even the fastest SCSI interface today and has the additional advantage of long-distance connections compared to SCSI. High-performance RAID packages increasingly use Fibre Channel interfaces for reliability and speed and to eliminate distance limitations.

For the latest information on the Fibre Channel industry, consult www.fibrechannel.com.

Internal Versus External Hard Disk Drives

The original Winchester hard drives were huge washing machine-sized boxes that sat outside the even larger computers they served. (The name Winchester dates back to IBM's design for a drive subsystem with 30MB of fixed-disk storage and 30MB of removable storage; they were called 30-30s, calling to mind the famous Winchester 30-30 rifle.)

With the advent of the personal computer, nearly all hard disk drives moved inside the PCs they were associated with. Under some circumstances, though, you may want to consider adding an external hard drive to your system.

First of all, your PC may have no more available hard drive bays, or the design of the PC case may make it inconvenient to squeeze an extra device into an open bay.

Or, you may have run out of available electrical power from your PC's power supply because of a large number of internal devices and cards.

Finally, you may want to create a somewhat portable power-house of a hard drive subsystem.

You can attach an external hard drive to your system several ways, including:

- SCSI
- USB
- FireWire

I discuss USB and FireWire technology and equipment in Chapter 15, including a Plug-and-Play 40GB USB hard drive from Maxtor; the company also produces a very similar FireWire drive.

Another of the storage systems in my office is a four-bay SCSI storage box. One bay holds a 1GB Jaz cartridge drive for data backups, a second holds a CD-R, a third bay is used for a speedy Cheetah Wide SCSI drive from Seagate, and the fourth has a DVD-ROM. Each SCSI device is linked to the others by a short internal cable, with the single external cable snaking back from the box to the connector on a SCSI adapter in the PC. The entire subsystem can be transferred from one machine to another by moving just that one cable. It is also shared on the office's local area network.

The box, literally the size of a toaster, includes a small 65-watt power supply, SCSI ID switches and drive activity lights, and even a set of audio output plugs for use with a CD or DVD drive. The hard drive is used to create a mirror of the files to be installed onto the CD-R, enabling quick and uninterrupted transfer of data from one device to the other.

In Figure 10-16, you can see a two-bay SCSI enclosure about to meet a 10,000 RPM 4.5GB Seagate Cheetah SCSI ST34501 hard drive. The drive connects to power, data, SCSI ID, and drive access LEDs within the enclosure; CD-ROM drives also have a pair of audio jacks on the back with an internal connection.

This particular version of the Cheetah drive uses a relatively rare 80-pin SCA adapter that merges data, control, power, and LED connectors in a single attachment. This arrangement is intended for use in swappable hard drive cases, enabling the drive to be removed and transported, or locked away for security.

FIGURE 10-16: *An external SCSI enclosure during the assembly of the subsystem*

I consulted the back pages of computer supply catalogs to find an adapter that broke out the SCA connectors to a more standard SCSI-3 adapter with a power input and a pin block for SCSI ID and LED wiring. Figure 10-17 shows the adapter.

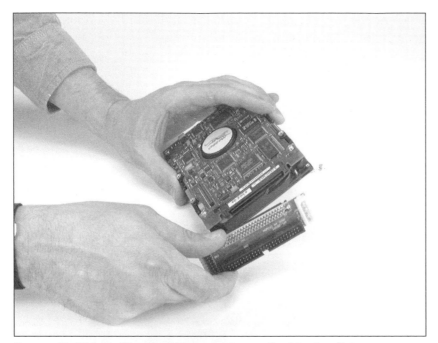

Figure 10-17: *Installing an SCA converter on the 80-pin, all-in-one connector on the Seagate Cheetah SCSI drive*

Dinosaur Hard Drive Interfaces

Early PC systems typically used ST506 controllers, which are now obsolete. If you have such a system, you may find it difficult to replace a failed controller. The solution is to substitute the ST506 controller with a new IDE controller and a paired IDE hard drive.

ST506 controllers used in the original IBM PC-XT worked only with the clunky 10MB hard drives of that machine, whereas later ST506 controllers were matched with other specific drives. Later ST506 controllers were more flexible but still severely limited in the size of drive with which they would work.

A later standard was the enhanced small device interface (ESDI), which is a much quicker system but still limited in size. In addition, an ESDI controller had to be matched carefully with a drive so that both had the same transfer rate. ESDI controllers may

also be difficult to obtain or to justify on a cost-benefit basis; you may need to substitute an IDE controller and new disk in order to fix a broken ESDI system.

Repairing or upgrading a dinosaur machine may require a visit to the dusty back shelves of your computer store or even to a used equipment dealer. You can also check for parts through the membership of a computer-users group.

ST506 and ESDI

Almost all early PCs used Seagate's ST506/ST412 interface, originally developed for Seagate's popular ST506 hard disk. ST506-compatible drives were subdivided into MFM and RLL drives because of the means by which data is encoded on the disk.

The MFM data encoding technique was used on the first IBM-XT hard drives and many systems that followed. To increase speed and data storage capacity, drive manufacturers started using RLL encoding with the ST506 interface. Because RLL encoding stores roughly 1.5 times as much information in the same space, it requires high-quality RLL-certified hard disks and a special RLL hard disk controller.

ST506 was more than adequate for the poky PC-XTs and just about good enough for the first PC-AT machines, but it ran out of a reason for being about 1984. ST506, in any form, has all but disappeared now, except for a few warehouses that hold boxes of old drives waiting to be used to repair early systems.

As the early PCs became faster and more capable, a group of hard disk manufacturers created their own improved adaptation of the ST506 design. The ESDI (enhanced standard device interface) transfers data two, three, or four times as fast as ST506 drives — as much as 20 million bits per second.

ESDI uses the same wiring system as ST506 drives, but the two types of drives cannot be interchanged under the same controller because of changes to the control signals. And ESDI drives are particularly sensitive if there is not a perfect match to a particular brand or type of ESDI controller.

In addition to significant speed pickups, ESDI improvements include reserved areas on the disk itself for the storage of setup parameters and bad track data.

ST506 MFM and RLL drives and controllers

An ST506 hard drive must match the controller card. Because ST506 is not a particularly sophisticated interface, the ST506 hard disk and controller rely on DOS for explicit read-here or write-there directions. Therefore, you must tell DOS how many heads and how many cylinders are in the hard drive you have installed. You must set up these relationships (computer-to-controller, controller-to-cable, cable-to-hard drive, hard drive-to-controller, and DOS-to-hard drive) correctly, or the drive won't work.

How ST506 hard drives and controllers work

Under the ST506 interface standard, the hard disk does none of the heavy thinking involved in data recording. The hard disk controller follows DOS instructions that tell the drive where to move the read/write heads, when to write, and when to read. The hard disk merely follows the controller's directions.

The ST506 hard disk controller mediates between DOS and one or two hard drives. DOS decides what information should be recorded and exactly where it should go on the platters, demanding a read/write action at a particular sector and track on the hard disk. The controller translates these instructions into electrical signals to the stepper motor, which moves the heads inside the hard drive.

Many modern machines use combination floppy and hard drive controller cards. Early PCs almost always use two separate cards. In either case, the floppy and hard drive controller circuitry is independent so that one system might fail while the other continues to work properly. The microprocessor sends an I/O write signal down the bus, along with the address that indicates the memory location of the hard disk controller.

Next, DOS sends the where-to-write instruction. DOS keeps track of the information on the hard disk. It knows what file has been recorded where, which sectors are empty and available to store information, and which sectors on the hard disk are locked out because they are not suitable for safe data storage. Then DOS requests a read/write operation by track and sector number. It tells the hard disk where (to what track) to move the head assembly and what sector on the track should be used to store the upcoming data. Finally, DOS sends the data it wants to record.

Various housekeeping bits — clock bits and error correction code bits, for example — must be added. The hard disk controller is responsible for packaging (encoding) the data before the hard disk records it. When the data is read back, everything recorded on the hard disk is sent to the hard disk controller. Data separation circuits, located on the controller, sort out this raw information, discard the housekeeping bits, and send a clean stream of stored data back to the microprocessor through the bus.

There are two popular ways to package information on ST506 hard disks: modified frequency modulation (MFM) and run length limited (RLL) encoding. MFM encoding uses 17 sectors per track, and the magnetic marks on the hard disk are spaced relatively far apart. The 2,7 RLL data encoding uses 26 sectors per track and packs many more magnetic marks on each track; therefore, an extremely precise hard disk is required. Faster and higher capacity drives, including ESDI, SCSI, IDE, and EIDE devices use newer versions of RLL encoding that compress the data tighter than 2,7 RLL does and allow far more sectors per track.

Testing an ST506 hard disk and controller

Occasionally, a hard disk breaks down and makes so much noise while self-destructing that there is no doubt that the hard disk, and only the hard disk, is causing the malfunction. This noise usually starts out as a scraping, squeaking sound and eventually grows much louder. If hard disk 0 is fine, but hard disk 1 is noisy and is becoming louder and beginning to exhibit read/write errors, then it makes sense to replace only hard disk 1.

Unfortunately, most troubleshooting situations are not so clear. Typically, a malfunctioning hard disk fails silently. In this case, it's hard to tell whether the hard disk itself is causing the problem.

Neither hard disks nor hard disk controllers can be tested alone. I test these devices by seeing how well they do their jobs, and both must be installed before either will do any work. Therefore, substituting a known-good hard disk or a known-good controller and then observing if the symptom has disappeared is the ideal way to determine which part is failing. However, this substitution technique does have limitations. First, hard drives are relatively expensive, and not many users have extra ones lying around on the shelf. Second, in some rare instances, a bad part can kill the good test part you've just swapped into the machine.

Despite these limitations, some troubleshooting suggestions follow:

1. Remove the system cover. Ground your body and turn the machine on, taking care not to touch any internal part of the computer unnecessarily. First, check that the hard disk platters are spinning when the power is on; put your hand on top of the hard disk to check.

2. If you have any doubts about the power connection to the disk drive, you can test the connector with a voltmeter. You're looking for + 5 and + 12 volts. If you have any doubts about how to use a voltmeter or about the internal parts of your machine, I suggest you leave this test to a technician.

3. You can usually find one or more unused power connectors in a modern machine. Substitute a different connector to rule out the possibility of a shorted or cut wire.

4. If the power connector carries voltage but the drive does not spin up when power is applied, you need to replace the drive. You may be able to bring a balky motor back to life by gently tapping on the casing. If it resumes spinning, I would consider it an unreliable business partner: Get the files off of the drive while it is working and replace it soon.

5. If the hard disk does spin when connected to power, check the ribbon cables running between the disk and the disk controller. These cables should be connected snugly to the pins on the controller card and to the flat edge connectors on the back of the hard drive.

6. If this is a new installation or if any other work has been conducted on the machine recently, double-check the cables, looking for a backward connection or a floppy drive cable mistakenly installed on the hard disk. Check also for broken or bent pins that do not provide a good connection for the data. If it's a new installation, you should also recheck the configuration of the jumpers on both the drive and the controller. Incorrect installation, rather than bad parts, is likely to be the problem, even though the error message on your screen is an intimidating Error Reading Fixed Disk, Hard Disk Failure, or HDD Controller Failure.

7. If the hard disk won't boot, try booting from a floppy disk, instead. Check to see if you can read some or all of the data on the hard disk. If you can read data, it probably means that the hard disk and its hard disk controller are okay. A likely cause is damage to the information in the boot sector of the drive — perhaps caused by a voltage spike or other transient problem. Recopy `COMMAND.COM` and the two DOS hidden files (using the DOS command SYS) and then retest.

Use FDISK to examine the drive partition setup. Did you forget to make one of the partitions active?

CROSS-REFERENCE

If the hard disk still won't boot, or it boots but is beginning to produce read or write errors, consider using a hard disk analysis and maintenance program. I describe this type of maintenance program in Chapter 22.

If none of these suggestions solves your problem, you may have to reformat the drive to restore it to working order. You maintain current backups of all of your critical data, right? Before you reformat, carefully read Chapter 21, which deals with backing up data, to make sure you haven't missed any tricks. After you low-level format the hard disk, your data is gone.

See the sections "Formatting an ST506 drive" and "Manually formatting an ST506 disk on a modern machine," later in this chapter, for directions on formatting.

If the computer won't format the hard disk, you have to replace both the hard disk and the controller. I do not recommend replacing only one unit, because a malfunctioning controller can burn out a good hard disk. It's better to replace both than to guess wrong, blow up the new disk, and end up buying two hard disks and a controller. If you absolutely need to try the cheapest solution, replace the controller first and then the hard disk.

Installing an ST506 hard disk controller

As I go deeper into ancient history, I need to pay attention to old technologies, such as 8-bit and 16-bit controllers and outmoded recording techniques. Here is a great argument for keeping every old instruction manual you ever receive from a computer or hard drive manufacturer — someday, somehow, you may need them.

Removing the old controller card Examine the cables connected to the card. Mark them with tape or a soft marker and take notes so you can properly reinstall them. Remove the screw holding the card to the rear of the computer chassis and pull the card straight up, out of the bus connector.

Choosing the right controller Before you install a hard disk controller, you should be familiar with the differences among the various types of controllers. One major difference is 8-bit versus 16-bit cards.

Eight-bit cards are for dinosaur PCs and have the short, single bus connector. These 8-bit controller cards usually regulate only hard disks. Typical 16-bit controller cards used in modern machines, by comparison, manage both the hard and the floppy drives. These dual-purpose controller cards are designed with two separate sets of circuits; they just share a single card and use only one card slot.

NOTE

As dinosaur PC/XT computers fade away, it may be difficult to find replacement 8-bit controller cards. If you cannot find a new card, you may have to purchase a used controller from a computer dealer. Be sure the dealer tests and certifies the device before you try it in your machine.

The other major difference among the various types of hard disk controllers is the data-coding scheme, something that is built right into the hardware. Both 8-bit and 16-bit cards come in MFM and RLL designs, hard-wired to follow one or the other data-coding scheme. They cannot be reconfigured or adjusted to use a different data-packaging technique.

The hard disk should be certified for the chosen controller's data-packaging method. Whatever data-coding scheme you choose, use a matched set of hard disk and hard disk controller. Don't connect an RLL controller to an MFM-type hard disk. The combination may appear to work for the first couple of weeks, but it will rapidly start losing data.

On the other hand, an RLL-certified hard disk does work with an MFM controller, but the extra quality in the hard disk will be wasted because it is underutilized when data is recorded in the MFM format.

Dinosaur PCs: Setting switches on XT controllers Early 8-bit controller cards have jumpers or dip switches that tell the controller and DOS what kind of hard disks are attached. Consult the controller manual to learn how to set these jumpers; older machines typically have about a dozen hard disk options. These include four heads and 306 cylinders, four heads and 615 cylinders, and two heads and 612 cylinders. Use the option for your particular hard disk — if it's listed.

If you have a nonstandard hard disk, choose an option slightly smaller than the actual size of the hard disk. For instance, you can approximate a hard disk with five heads and 620 cylinders by setting the controller for four heads and 615 cylinders. Some of the hard disk area (the part accessed by the fifth head and the innermost tracks) won't be used, but no read/write problems will result. Of course, buying a new controller — one that's able to manage five heads and 640 cylinders — would give you access to the full storage capacity of your hard disk.

Either solution works fine technically, so it's primarily a question of economics. If you don't know how many heads and cylinders your hard disk has, call the drive manufacturer's technical department and ask.

Modern machines: Running the setup program

Modern machine controller cards do not have jumpers to configure them to work with different hard disks; the information is instead stored on the motherboard in the CMOS memory of the clock/calendar chip. Run the setup program after you've installed the card and choose an appropriate hard disk type from the list in the motherboard ROM BIOS. Choose a drive type smaller than the actual hard drive if the choices in the setup program don't match your hard disk perfectly. Newer ROM BIOS versions have more drive types to choose from, so consider upgrading your old ROM BIOS if your drive or something close to it isn't listed. Your computer manufacturer's technical support department knows what new BIOS versions are available and whether a new BIOS can help here.

Putting the card in the slot

Press the card into a slot on the motherboard. Install the screw that holds the card in place.

Formatting the hard disk

Unless you have replaced a bad controller with the identical hard disk controller, you have to reformat the hard disk so this new controller and the hard disk can talk to each other. You must low-level format the drive, run FDISK, and then high-level format the drive. This three-step process is covered in the sections "Formatting an ST506 drive," and "Manually formatting an ST506 disk on a modern machine," later in this chapter.

If you're adding a drive or replacing your present hard disk and controller, see the section "Installing an MFM or RLL hard disk," later in this chapter, for tips about drive-select jumpers and terminating resistors.

Installing cables for ST506 and ESDI drives

A separate 20-wire ribbon data cable goes from the controller to each hard drive. The red or blue edge of the cable is for pin 1. Find the number 1 on the controller card (usually stenciled next to the data cable connector pins). Hard disks have flat-card edge connectors, with a notch cut close to the pin-1 end of the connector. Put the colored edge of the data cable toward the slot when connecting the cable to the hard disk.

All the hard disks share a single controller cable. It's a wide, 34-wire ribbon cable. Pay attention to the colored edge so that the cable will mate correctly to pin 1 at each connection. Hard disk 0 (DOS calls it drive C:) is at the end of this controller cable. The middle connector attaches to the second hard disk (if there is one). If you have only one drive and a short, straight-through ribbon cable with only two connectors, put one connector on the hard disk and the other on the controller card, making sure that you put the color-coded edge toward pin 1 at each connector.

On modern machines with 16-bit (AT-style) controller cards, you also need to attach the floppy drive controller cable. Luckily, most of these cards have the words "to floppy drive" stenciled on the card at the appropriate connector pins; if you have any doubt, consult the instruction manual or call the manufacturer. Because both floppy cable and hard disk controller cable have 34 wires, it is possible to get them mixed up. Be sure you have the floppy cable on the floppy connector and the hard disk cable on the hard disk connector.

One more cabling example, Figure 10-18, shows a pair of drives connected to a single control cable, each requiring its own data cable.

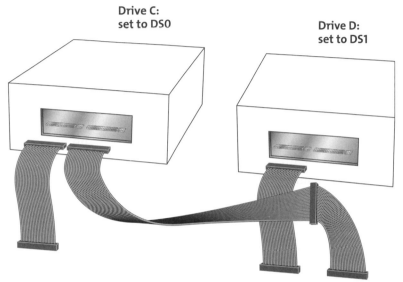

Drive C:
set to DS0

Drive D:
set to DS1

FIGURE 10-18: *A pair of ST506 or ESDI hard drives is connected with a 34-pin control cable without a twist at the C: drive. In this instance, set drive C: to DS0 and drive D: to DS1. Use separate 20-wire data control cables for each drive.*

Installing an MFM or RLL hard disk

A good habit to get into when working with old systems is to mark all cables with masking tape before you remove them from a controller or drive. Write a number on the tape and keep a notepad handy to record what went where.

Removing the old hard disk Remove the system unit cover. Examine the two ribbon cables at the back of the hard disk, marking them with tape or a soft marker and taking notes for reinstallation. Then disconnect them and the four-wire power cord from the hard disk. Remove the screws holding the hard disk to the

chassis. Early PC/XT computers usually have screws threaded into the side of the hard disk. There may also be a screw or two that is accessible through holes in the bottom of the computer chassis. Many modern machines use rails screwed to the side of the hard disk, allowing the drive to slide in and out of the chassis like a drawer. To remove a 286 or 386 hard disk, look for clips on the front of the chassis. Remove the screws holding the clips in place or squeeze the clips to release them and then slide the hard disk out. On other systems, you may have to remove screws. Save the rails, clips, and screws; you will need them for the new hard disk.

Setting jumpers or switches on the new drive Before you install a new hard disk, you must set the drive select (DS) and terminating resistor. Hard drives have jumpers (or, occasionally, dip switches) that set the drive-select number.

Some hard disk manufacturers use a 0-1-2-3 numbering system for the drive-select jumpers on their hard disks. In this case, the first hard disk is number 0. Others use 1-2-3-4 numbering so that the first unit is number 1, and the second is number 2. See the manual shipped with your hard disk for details about your drive.

Also check the settings for various jumpers. The example given here works with many systems but not all — be sure to customize it for your particular setup.

If you have a cable with a twist and two hard drives, as shown in Figure 10-19, set the DS jumper on both drives to show that each drive is the second hard drive in the computer. This doesn't make much sense, but the computer won't confuse the drives when they're set to the same DS. The twist at the end of the cable, where it plugs into the C: drive, flips the DS signals back around so that the controller thinks the C: drive is set to DS0. Arcane, isn't it? However, this is the same technique used to distinguish floppy drive A: from floppy drive B:, so it must have made sense to somebody at some point.

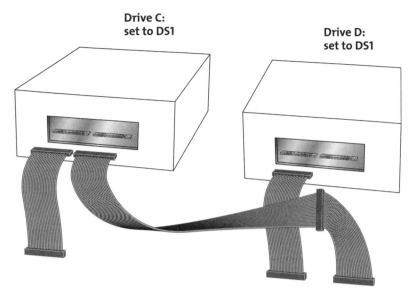

Drive C:
set to DS1

Drive D:
set to DS1

FIGURE 10-19: *Cable routing for a pair of dinosaur ST506 (MFM or RLL) or ESDI drives includes a cable twist at drive C:. Under this outmoded scheme, you need a separate 20-wire data cable for each drive, and each drive must be set to DS1.*

If you have a cable with a twist and only one hard drive, as shown in Figure 10-20, set the DS jumper on this drive to make it the second hard drive in the computer. The twist at the end of the cable, where it plugs into the C: drive, flips the DS signals back around so the controller thinks the C: drive is set to DS 0. Don't try setting the drive to 0 and using the straight-through connector in the middle of the cable. Though it sounds plausible, you'd end up with a pigtail of cable (the end with the twist) not connected to anything, which would make weird electronic echoes on the cable whenever the drive and controller tried to talk to each other.

If you have one drive and a straight-through cable, as shown in Figure 10-21, things are a bit more complicated. Clone manufacturers save money when they install a straight-through, one-hard-drive-only, controller cable on single-drive systems. If you have this cheaper controller cable (with one connector on each

end, no third connector, and no twist in the middle), set up the hard drive as if it were the first (and only) drive in the computer system. Set the drive select jumper on the first set of pins — not the second.

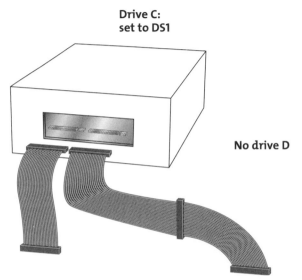

Drive C:
set to DS1

No drive D

FIGURE 10-20: *This single dinosaur ST506 or ESDI hard drive has a 20-pin data cable and a 34-pin control cable. Because the control cable has a twist, it is necessary to set the drive to DS1.*

Checking terminating resistors The first drive (the drive at the end of the hard drive controller cable) should have a terminating resistor.

Any second hard drive, if installed, should not have a resistor in place. Look for the terminating resistor in a socket on the bottom of the hard drive. Because very few hard disk components are socketed, it should be easy to identify a terminator.

If necessary, remove the terminating resistor from your second drive with your fingers or by sliding a small screwdriver between the resistor and the socket.

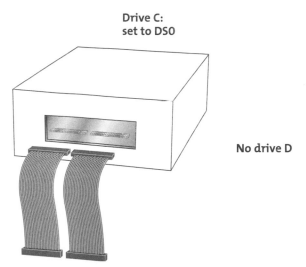

Drive C:
set to DS0

No drive D

FIGURE 10-21: *This single dinosaur ST506 or ESDI drive has a 20-pin data cable and a 34-pin control cable. If the cable does not have a twist, as shown here, set the drive to DS0.*

Be sure to use a terminating resistor on the drive at the end of the controller cable, but not on the drive in the middle of the controller cable.

Sliding in the drive and connect cables After you configure the hard disk, slide it into the chassis. Most modern machines use rails to hold the hard disk in place. If your computer requires rails, install them on the hard disk and slide it back into the chassis, following instructions in the drive's manual.

Connect the two ribbon cables to the flat-edge connectors on the back of the hard disk. Be sure to connect pin 1 on each ribbon cable to pin 1 on the hard drive. The colored edge of the cable is the number-1 end. The gold-colored hard drive edge connectors have a notch cut into the connector on one end. The end with the notch has pin 1, so put the red edge on the ribbon cable toward the notch.

If you have two hard disks in your system, they will share the 34-wire hard disk controller cable, but each disk will have its own 20-wire data cable.

After you've connected the ribbon cables, plug in any four-wire power cable from the power supply. Note that the power supply cable connectors are not rectangular. Look at one carefully; two corners have been cut off on a diagonal. Examine the socket on the hard drive carefully and be sure to install the power connector correctly. Then install screws to hold the drive into the chassis.

 NOTE

If you're working on an ESDI drive, jump ahead to the formatting instructions in the section "Formatting the ESDI drive."

Formatting an ST506 drive After you install an ST506 hard disk, you must format it. This is a three-step process: low-level formatting, FDISK, and DOS FORMAT.

Use the current version of DOS, which helps with the formatting process for disks of any size. If you have an older version of DOS, version 3.3 or earlier, you can use a program called Disk Manager to automate much of the process. If you are using Disk Manager, follow the directions that come with the program disk.

If you want to format your hard disk manually, read the directions in "Manually formatting an ST506 disk on a modern machine," later in this chapter.

Manually formatting a hard disk on an XT clone Manually formatting a hard disk involves three steps: low-level formatting, FDISK, and high-level formatting. Remember: Don't try this at home on anything but a dinosaur PC ST506 drive. The ESDI, IDE, EIDE, and SCSI drives should not ordinarily be low-level formatted by an end user.

Step 1: Low-Level Formatting. A dinosaur PC motherboard knows nothing about hard disk hardware. Modern machines, on the other hand, are engineered quite differently.

Ch
10

Within an XT, the hard disk controller ROM, not the CPU or the clone's ROM BIOS, supervises all hard disk physical control. Low-level formatting examines the hard disk for bad spots, locks out the bad spots so that they cannot be written to, and writes the sector address marks on the hard disk. In other words, it is the most hardware-specific level of hard disk preparation.

The details of low-level formatting are completely dependent on the hard disk controller. For this reason, the low-level formatting program is stored in the hard disk controller ROM. You can access the ROM format routine with the DEBUG command that is part of DOS. To do so, enter **DEBUG** and then enter **g = c800:5**.

You may have to substitute a different address for c:800:5 in the example; consult the instruction manual for the hard drive controller to see if g = c800:5 means jump to the address c800:5 and follow the instructions at that address.

Most hard disk controller ROMs have the low-level formatting utility at the address c800:5, but a few use other locations, including, but not limited to, c800:6 and c800:ccc.

A careful technician insists upon documentation whenever he or she encounters a new hard disk controller, but one of these three addresses usually works. You'll know right away if you have picked an incorrect address because the screen will be full of gibberish.

The instruction manual should also provide the drive's specifications and many of the answers to the questions posed by the low-level formatter.

Entering the correct address produces a screen of English language questions — not necessarily intelligible questions, just English. When faced with these controller questions, keep your wits about you. Those controllers that require answers in hexadecimal numbers indicate it; don't worry, most don't. Some controllers use a 0-1-2-3 numbering system for hard disks. In this case, the first hard disk (usually drive C:) is number 0. Others use 1-2-3-4 numbering, so the first unit is number 1, and the second is number 2.

When you're prompted to input an interleave factor, enter **3** for an early version PC. You'll be prompted to enter a write precompensation cylinder factor. If you have no documentation with the drive, you have to guess — one-half of the total number of cylinders is a reasonable rule of thumb. Both interleave and write precompensation are listed in the Glossary of this book, if you want more details.

Most Western Digital XT hard disk controllers display the following screen query: Are you dynamically configuring the drive? A no response means: "Don't ask me any questions, just follow the jumpers on the card." A yes response allows you to answer detailed questions about the hard disk design — in other words, to customize the installation. Unfortunately, some Western Digital XT controllers display the query, ignore your answers, and then proceed to format the hard drive according to its switch and jumper settings. To ensure that your card is set up the way you want, determine the correct jumper settings for your model of hard disk and manually configure the card correctly before you install it.

If you have to dynamically configure the drive, here are some hints. Landing zone is the track where the drive parks the head when you run a disk park program before moving the computer; this is a feature of older drives. When you're prompted for a landing zone, enter a track number equal to the number of tracks on the hard disk plus one. If absolutely no guidance is available for any of these questions, try using the defaults in the controller's low-level formatting program. They won't hurt anything and might work.

Often the low-level formatting program prompts you for a list of known-bad areas. Check the top of your hard disk for a bad track label. It is important to enter all of these bad tracks. The tests done by the hard disk manufacturer are more rigorous than those done by the low-level formatting program. Some tracks that failed at the factory after long testing might slip through the low-level formatting program's tests, be recorded on, and then eventually lose your files.

When you have answered all the questions and pressed Enter for the last time, the formatting routine starts. As the head assembly moves from cylinder to cylinder, it makes a rhythmic ticking sound. It takes a few minutes because the entire hard disk surface area must be scanned for defects. Ten to twenty minutes is not an unusually long low-level formatting time for a 40MB disk. Larger disks, of course, take longer.

Step 2: FDISK Formatting. The second step of the hard disk formatting process uses the FDISK utility of DOS to prepare one or more DOS partitions (areas on the hard disk suitable for DOS files). This is a quick process, taking about 30 seconds per partition. Up to four partitions per drive are allowed.

Unlike low-level formatting, FDISK is software-dependent. The low-level formatting program is stored inside the hard disk controller ROM so that changing controllers changes the screen messages and low-level formatting process. By comparison, FDISK is a DOS utility. Changing DOS versions changes the FDISK screen messages and, to some extent, the FDISK process. But changing the hard disk controller doesn't affect FDISK at all.

DOS versions earlier than 2.0 are unable to deal with hard disks. Versions of DOS from 2.0 to 3.2 can partition a hard drive as large as 32MB.

MS-DOS 3.3 can partition larger drives, but each partition is limited to a maximum size of 32MB. MS-DOS versions 4.01 and above can have partitions of any size. Hard disk control programs such as Disk Manager are designed to transcend the hard disk limitations imposed by older DOS versions.

Disk Manager provides a device driver that contains a software interface between DOS and the physical hard disk controller. When DOS looks at the device driver, it believes a second physical hard disk is inside the computer. It addresses the hard disk through the device driver and receives appropriate responses from drive D:.

Step 3: High-Level Formatting (FORMAT C:/S). High-level formatting (FORMAT C:/S) is covered in any DOS manual. Remember, if you've decided to partition your hard drive into two or more logical drives, you must individually format each logical drive before writing data on it.

On DOS versions through 3.2, be sure to put the DOS system files (the two hidden files plus COMMAND.COM) on the first partition. That's the only place DOS looks for boot files. MS-DOS versions 3.3 and subsequent versions allow you to specify an active partition, the one the computer will boot from. This active partition need not be the first partition. Of course, it must have DOS system files installed on it.

High-level formatting is another slow process. Allow three to five minutes for a 20MB drive; the computer must examine each track for bad sectors. A typical screen message displays cylinder number after cylinder number as each one is completed. Some DOS FORMAT programs then count back through the cylinder numbers a second time before declaring the formatting complete.

During the heyday of the dinosaurs, a number of semiautomated hard disk format programs, including Disk Manager, were available to help. Some hard drive manufacturers offered their own equivalent of this program bundled with their drives.

Manually formatting an ST506 disk on a modern machine

Formatting a hard disk manually involves three steps: low-level formatting, FDISK, and high-level formatting (FORMAT C:/S).

Step 1: Low-Level Formatting. Modern machines were designed in the age of hard disks; therefore, hard disk control functions were designed right into the motherboard ROM BIOS. To start low-level formatting a modern machine, use the AT diagnostics disk (the low-level format option) or the low-level formatting utility that's part of your computer's setup program. Choose the appropriate drive type, matching cylinders, heads, and so forth. Slower ATs should have an interleave of 2. Fast 286s, most 386s, and all 486s can use an interleave of 1.

If your drive does not match a drive type exactly, you may choose a similar, but smaller, drive and lose access to the balance of your disk.

Step 2: FDISK Formatting. The FDISK step of the hard disk formatting process prepares one or more DOS partitions (areas on the hard disk suitable for DOS files). It is a quick process, taking about 30 seconds per partition. If you're using MS-DOS version 3.3 or a subsequent version, be sure to make one of the partitions active if you want to boot from this hard disk.

Unlike low-level formatting, FDISK is software-dependent— it's a DOS utility. Changing DOS versions changes the FDISK screen messages and, to some extent, the FDISK process. However, changing the hard disk or the hard disk controller doesn't affect FDISK at all.

I've already discussed the limitations of older DOS versions when I covered formatting ST506 drives on early version PCs. I recommend that you upgrade to the current version of DOS, which is 6.22 as this book goes to press, or the 7.0 version that lies mostly hidden within Windows 95.

Step 3: High-Level Formatting (FORMAT C:/S). High-level formatting (FORMAT C:/S) is covered in any DOS manual. If you have decided to partition your hard drive into two or more logical drives, remember that you must format each logical drive individually before writing data on it.

On DOS versions through 3.2, be sure to put the DOS system files (the two hidden files plus COMMAND.COM) on the first partition. That's the only place DOS looks for boot files. MS-DOS versions 3.3 and higher allow you to specify an active partition, the one the computer will boot from. This active partition need not be the first partition. Of course, it must have DOS system files installed on it.

High-level formatting is another slow process. Allow 35 minutes for a 20MB drive; the computer must examine each track for bad sectors. A typical screen message displays cylinder after cylinder as each cylinder is completed. Some DOS versions then count back through the cylinder numbers a second time before declaring the formatting complete.

ESDI drives and controller cards

ESDI built upon the ST506 foundation to offer greater throughput. The interface had a short active life in the PC world and is now all but forgotten—that is, unless you've got one in your dinosaur.

How ESDI works

ESDI is an enhanced version of the ST506 standard. Its cables and connectors are identical to ST506 cables and connectors.

ESDI drives put the data separation circuitry (the data encoding/decoding circuits) on the hard drive; ST506 puts it on the hard disk controller. ESDI drives send clean data to the ESDI controller instead of the weird drive-writing signals that actually encode the data on the disk platters. Therefore, ESDI drives don't have to be as carefully synchronized with their controllers, and higher data transfer rates are possible. The ESDI interface transfers two, three, or four times as much data per second as the old ST506.

Some versions of DOS can't talk to more than 1,024 cylinders on a hard drive. To get around this limitation, many ESDI controllers enable translation—they lie to DOS about the physical configuration of the drive.

Theoretically, the ESDI interface can accommodate eight ESDI drives, but few controllers are designed for eight drives. If you're planning to connect more than two ESDI drives, get a special controller and then cable the drives and jumper as directed by the instructions that were shipped with the controller.

I have experienced some compatibility issues in the past between certain ESDI controllers and other devices, and with Microsoft Windows. Consult the manufacturer of your adapter about any questions you may have.

Testing an ESDI drive and ESDI controller

See "Testing an ST506 hard disk and controller," earlier in this chapter, for details. Because the interfaces are so similar, most troubleshooting techniques work for both ESDI and ST506.

Installing an ESDI controller card

ESDI drives and controllers need to be closely matched. Be sure to check instruction manuals or with a knowledgeable dealer before mixing and matching.

Removing the old controller card Begin by examining the cables attached to the controller card. Mark them with tape or a soft marker and take notes before you disconnect them so that you will be able to reinstall them properly. Don't forget the little two-wire cable attached to the remote hard drive light on the front panel of your computer case. It pulls right off the controller card and slides back onto the equivalent pins on the new card. Remove the screw holding the card to the rear of the computer chassis. Pull the ESDI card straight up and then out of the bus connector.

Choosing the right controller Not all ESDI drives and controllers work with each other. Buy them together — or check that both the drive manufacturer and the controller manufacturer certify that they work together. A slow ESDI drive works with a fast controller; but a fast drive won't work with a slow controller.

Inserting the board in the slot Line up the controller card's edge connector with an appropriate expansion slot connector on the motherboard. Press the board down and then secure it to the back of the case with a screw. Plug in the cables. If you can't just reinstall the cables in the way they were hooked up to the original ESDI controller, see the directions for installing ST506 cables in the section "Installing cables for ST506 and ESDI drives," earlier in this chapter. Because ESDI and ST506 cables are the same, this section applies.

Using setup Ordinarily, you use setup to tell the computer what kind of drive is installed so that the computer's BIOS can issue intelligent read/write commands to the hard disk controller (which, in turn, issues its own read/write signals to the hard

disk). Because ESDI hard disk controllers lie to the computer about the ESDI drive's configuration, you don't have to enter the correct number of heads and cylinders in the setup program.

The ESDI controller does, however, require you to enter a preliminary number so the computer knows that a hard disk is installed and so that the ESDI controller and the computer can start a conversation. Most ESDI controllers ask you to set the drive type to type 1 with the CMOS setup routine. To be certain your drive works properly, read and follow your ESDI drive's installation manual.

Installing the ESDI cables ESDI is a souped-up ST506 interface. ESDI uses the same cables and the same hook-up rules as ST506 (the old MFM and RLL hard drives). Read the section "Installing cables for ST506 and ESDI drives," earlier in this chapter, and then return here to proceed with installation of the drive itself.

Installing an ESDI drive

Follow the directions in the section "Installing an MFM or RLL hard disk," earlier in this chapter. Read that section and then come back to this section before you format your ESDI drive.

Formatting the ESDI drive

The hard drive controller has a low-level formatting routine built into the ROM on the ESDI card. Follow the directions in the controller's installation manual. Remember, most ESDI drives want you to set the drive type to 1 with the CMOS setup program; read the manual to make sure.

Use the DOS FDISK command to partition the drive. I recommend that you upgrade to a current version of DOS. If you have an older version of DOS, you may want to use Disk Manager to partition this disk because DOS versions lower than 4.01 limit each hard disk partition to 32MB or less, which may be an unnecessary complication for the user.

Format the disk with the DOS FORMAT command. If you intend to boot from this drive, use the /S switch or the DOS command SYS C: to copy COMMAND.COM and the DOS hidden files to the boot partition. Find directions for using FDISK, FORMAT, and SYS in your DOS manual.

Hard cards

Hard cards were an interesting side trip in the development of PCs. They are not at all exotic, except in the realm of packaging. A hard card is a small 3.5-inch hard disk bolted onto a hard drive controller and attached to a plug-in card that fits into the computer's bus.

Among its advantages was the fact that a hard card would fit into a machine that did not have an available drive bay. Also, installing a hard card was considerably easier than installing a controller card and snaking data and power cables to a new drive.

The disadvantages included that the card — although it plugged into only one slot — was sometimes fat enough to block access to two or even more slots on the motherboard. The hard card also drew its electrical power from the bus rather than directly from the computer's power supply, which sometimes caused problems in underpowered systems.

The cards were designed to be logically relocatable (their memory address could be adjusted). Therefore, they could coexist with a machine that already had a regular hard disk controller. Getting the hard card to function as this second drive, however, can require setting and resetting jumpers because you often don't know the existing hard drive controller's I/O port and ROM addresses. The hard card must use different I/O port and ROM addresses. Making sure the port and ROM addresses are unique to each controller can take some exasperating experimentation.

Hard cards served a valid purpose when the owners of the first and second generation of PCs were upgrading their machines, which often came with puny 10MB hard drives or none at all. They don't serve much purpose with modern machines that often contain large hard drives and include extra drive bays.

If you have an early version PC with two floppy disk drives, it may make sense to remove the second 5.25-inch floppy drive and install an additional hard drive in its place, if you can find one.

Troubleshooting hard drives

Problem: How do I access the CMOS system setup if I want to add information about the new drive?

Solution: The procedure to bring up the setup screen varies from one ROM BIOS to another; consult your system's instruction manual. On most systems, setup is available during system bootup. Common instructions call for pressing Esc or the F1 or F2 function keys during bootup. Some systems enable you to access setup after the system has completed bootup; common instructions to access setup for such systems include Ctrl + Alt + Esc, Alt + F2, or Ctrl + S.

Problem: The drive won't spin up, or it spins down after a few seconds.

Solution: Check to see that the drive is properly attached to a power cable from the power supply. If the power is good, this problem is probably a drive failure. Contact the manufacturer of the hard drive for assistance. (See the list of hard drive manufacturers in the previous section.)

Problem: The drive works as a slave but not as a master — or as a master but not as a slave.

Solution: Check the master/slave jumpers on the hard drive; consult your instruction manual for the proper settings.

Different drive manufacturers use different jumper assignments. In some cases, mixing two drives with different speeds or timings can cause the system not to see one of the drives. It may be necessary to swap the assignment of the two drives.

Problem: The drive has been installed and the drive parameters have been entered in the CMOS, but the drive won't boot, or the system displays a message of an HDD controller failure or indicates that a drive cannot be accessed.
Solution: The drive must be partitioned and formatted under DOS before it can be accessed.

Problem: Can hard drives be mounted at any angle?
Solution: Consult your instruction manual or hard drive manufacturer. (See Table 10-5.) Most drives can be mounted right side up or on their sides without a problem; it is generally not good practice to mount a drive upside down.

Problem: A new ATA hard disk drive is not detected by the system BIOS.
Solution: Assuming your motherboard's BIOS is capable of working with the ATA standard, here are some steps to take:

Verify the cable connections. Check that both the data cable and power supply cable are properly installed; check to see that the cables are fully seated in connectors and that no pins are bent. The stripe on one edge of the data cable should be matched up to pin #1 on the drive and pin #1 on the motherboard.

To test the data cable, use a known-good cable or try the cable from the non-functioning drive on a known-working drive.

Verify the jumper settings. If the drive is a master or a stand-alone drive (on a standard data/ribbon cable), the DS jumper needs to be installed, or the DS switch needs to be enabled.

If the drive is a slave, the DS jumper must be removed, or the DS jumper must be disabled.

If you're using an Ultra-ATA data cable that uses a Cable Select configuration, both master and slave drives must have their CS jumpers installed or the CS switch enabled. Check to see that the Ultra-ATA cables are properly installed — on most systems, the master drive is attached to the end connector, colored black; the slave is connected to the gray middle connector, and the blue connector is attached directly to the motherboard or to an ATA adapter card.

Swap the ATA adapter card or the drive. To isolate a problem not solved by working with the cables, you can try swapping a known-good adapter card into your system to see if it will recognize your drive. Or, you can temporarily install a known-good hard drive (be sure to back up any irreplaceable data).

SUMMARY

Phew! That's a lot of hard drive information, but then again, there have been quite a few steps along the evolutionary path from the day of the dinosaurs to today. I examine one more class of hard drive — removable drives used for transfer, security, and expandability — in the next chapter.

Chapter 11

Removable Hard Drives

Throughout this book, I've preached the critical importance of backing up before you go forward. The key to truly safe computing is to have copies of current data stored at a site away from the machine. I'm not just talking about the threats from hard disk failure or a complete PC meltdown. Theft can also be a serious problem. Your insurance probably covers the theft of your PC and may even repay you for the loss of your programs, but you are almost assuredly not covered for the theft of your data.

You also have the problem of how to get your data from here to there. How do you easily transport a massive graphics file, a few hundred megabytes of downloaded music, a presentation, or a complete copy of your great American novel from one system to another if you don't have a network? How do you transfer a major word processing, spreadsheet, or database file from one location to another without the time-consuming process of sending massive files over the Internet, or the oppressive process of spreading a few hundred megabytes of data across a few hundred 1.44MB floppy disks?

Of all the elements of the PC, data storage has gone through the most change during the evolution from dinosaur to modern machine. This chapter examines many of the most important backup and transport devices.

Removable Storage Devices

This hefty book consists of about 1GB of images and some 2MB of text. After I finish my work, I have to get it to the publisher 1,000 miles away. What are my choices for transporting the data?

- I could send it over the Internet. On my fast broadband cable modem connection, I'd consider doing that; if I were still using a dial-up modem, I probably wouldn't. Speaking in very rough terms, sending a file of that size at dial-up speed is going to monopolize a computer and a phone line for an unacceptable chunk of time. Assuming that I am willing to trust my files to the Internet, I also have to rely on the recipient to gather the files onto some form of media at the other end.

- I could, of course, copy the files to floppy disks. To do so, I'd have to format about 700 1.44MB floppies, at about a minute apiece (not to mention the cost of each floppy), and then copy files to them one by one. Taking off an hour for lunch, figure on spending somewhere between two days and forever.

- Or I could open up my computer, unhook the hard disk, package it up, and ship it across the country to the editor's office where it will be reinstalled into a waiting PC. I sure hope nobody drops the box.

Get the idea? The larger the data file — and they keep getting larger with the addition of more graphical information — the more difficult it is to transport it from one place to another.

So, I bet you're wondering how I decided to transport my data: I fired up my CD-R and burned a pair of 30-cent CD-Rs to hold the entire manuscript and all of the images, and I still had more than 100MB left over. As an alternative, I could have recorded the data on a single, more expensive DVD-R, or on a dozen Zip or SuperDisks, or on a single Peerless drive. Figure 11-1 shows a selection of devices.

This chapter explores several removable storage solutions:

- **Super-floppy disks.** Pioneered by Iomega's 100 and 250MB Zip drives, this category now includes the talented SuperDisk LS-120 system (which stores 120MB and can also read puny old-style 1.44MB floppies) and another Iomega offering, the PC Card 40MB Click! Drive.

- **Removable hard drive cartridges.** The latest and greatest devices in this class include Iomega's Peerless, in 10 and 20GB versions; Jaz systems, available in 1 and 2GB sizes; and Castlewood's 2.2GB and 5.7GB disks.

- **External hard drive systems.** The arrival of high-speed serial communications ports — based on SCSI, USB, and FireWire protocols — has allowed use of speedy plug-and-play hard drives that can be easily moved from machine to machine, or locked up in a safe for security purposes.

- **Flash memory.** Portable, non-volatile storage media allow quick transport of data from machine to machine.

- **Tape backup devices.** An old-fashioned backup solution that has persisted into the era of the modern machine.

- **CD-R, CD-RW, and DVD-RAM discs.** Relatively easy-to-use devices enable users to burn a disc from their desktop, storing more than 700MB of data on a CD or as much as 9.4GB on a DVD.

FIGURE 11-1: *A cornucopia of large-capacity removable storage media, including outmoded but still workable SyQuest 44MB and 270MB cartridges, a CD-R write-once read-many times disc with a capacity of more than 600MB, an older streaming tape backup cartridge with a capacity of about 60MB, an Iomega Jaz cartridge that can hold 1GB of information, and a relatively inexpensive and simple 100MB Zip disk, also from Iomega.*

CROSS-REFERENCE

I explore CD-R, CD-RW, and DVD-RAM in detail in Chapter 12.

Super-floppy disks

Iomega woke up the computer industry in 1995 with the introduction of the low-cost Zip drive, which stores an impressive 100MB of data on a special 3.5-inch floppy disk. Although not quite as fast as earlier technology, such as Bernoulli or SyQuest drives, it won converts based on its low price and simplicity of use. The Zip 100 has a data transfer rate of 1.4MB per second and an access time of 29 milliseconds (ms). At the time of this writing, you can purchase an internal Zip drive for as little as $50, an external parallel port or SCSI device for about $100, and a USB model for about $125. Zip cartridges in early 2002 cost less than $10 each, or about 10 cents per megabyte.

Zip drives suffered from an unusually high failure rate in early years, sometimes destroying disks as they failed. Current devices are more reliable. In any case, Zips are intended for transfer of data and not as the sole repository for information.

The Zip drive — widely used in graphics departments and other applications where it is necessary to transport or archive large files between clients or unrelated companies — is available in 100MB and 250MB versions. The larger-capacity drive also reads the smaller disks. Zips are sold with SCSI, USB, and parallel port connections in internal and external versions. Figure 11-2 shows an internal 100MB Zip drive. An external 250MB Zip drive is shown in Figure 11-3.

Zip 250, introduced in 1999, is a similar device that stores as much as 250MB on special disks; the units can also read and write to the original 100MB Zip disks. Zip 250 units are available in an internal version, plus FireWire, parallel port, SCSI, and USB external models. In early 2002, prices ranged from about $140 to $170 for the various models; the larger capacity disks sold for about $19 each. Details of the Zip family are shown in Table 11-1. For the latest information on Iomega products, consult www.iomega.com.

FIGURE 11-2: *An internal 100MB Zip drive. The device attaches to an EIDE connector on the motherboard or in the bus of your computer. In the setup pictured, the 3.5-inch-wide Zip drive is mounted in an available 5.25-inch bay.*

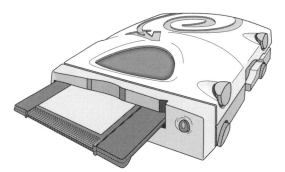

FIGURE 11-3: *An external 250MB Zip drive. Such devices are available in USB and FireWire versions. (Courtesy of Iomega Corporation)*

Ch 11

TABLE 11-1: Iomega Zip Drives		
	Zip 100	**Zip 250**
Capacity	100MB	250MB
Maximum transfer rate:		
FireWire	N/A	2.0MB/sec
IDE internal	1.4MB/sec	1.4MB/sec
Parallel port	1.4MB/sec	800KB/sec
SCSI	1.4MB/sec	2.4MB/sec
USB 1.1	1.2MB/sec	900KB/sec
Average seek time	29 ms	29 ms

A worthy competitor in recent years was SuperDisk LS-120 technology, marketed by Imation Corporation and some of its partners. Internal and external drives use 3.5-inch LS-120 floppy disks capable of holding 120MB of information; the same drives can also read from and write to old-style 1.44MB floppies. The goal of its proponents is to replace the old-style 3.5-inch drive in new and upgraded PCs and laptops. The marketing pitch is that one LS-120 disk is equivalent to the capacity of more than 83 standard 3.5-inch disks.

In recent years, some computer manufacturers offered a SuperDisk as a substitute for a standard floppy disk drive, although it is more common after an upgrade. As a standalone product, the LS-120 internal drive is priced at about $100. Imation also kept up with interface and usage trends. LS-120s are available with USB, PC Card, and parallel port interfaces and in internal and external models. Prices range up to $300 for these external models as I write this book.

In 2000, Imation introduced the 2X Speed LS-120, which — as its name suggests — offers double the transfer speed of the original device at the same price. A 240MB version of the drive was introduced in 2001 and sold in Asia; the drive is not widely available in the United States.

All along, other companies manufactured the drives; in 2001, Imation ended marketing of the drive under its own name. You should still be able to find drives from various makers for several years. Disks will continue to be available, although I recommend adding a box or two to your storage closet if you use these drives.

You can use an internal drive, like the one shown in Figure 11-4, instead of a standard 3.5-inch floppy drive. It connects to one of the EIDE connectors on a modern machine, leaving the FDD floppy connector unused.

An external SuperDisk device, such as the one shown in Figure 11-5, connects to the parallel port and includes a special device driver to instruct a modern machine to use that port to communicate with the storage device. You can daisy-chain another device, such as a printer, from the back of the SuperDisk; however, a SuperDisk can't print directly to another device on the same parallel port. A workaround is to copy a file to your hard disk and print it from there.

FIGURE 11-4: *An internal SuperDisk LS-120 drive kit from Hi-Val. The drive attaches to a standard EIDE port on the motherboard of a modern machine.*

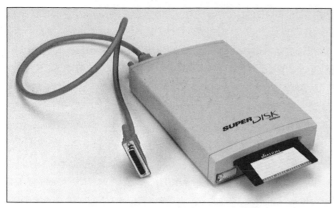

FIGURE 11-5: *An external SuperDisk LS-120 kit from Imation; the drive attaches to an EPP parallel port.*

The LS in LS-120 technology stands for *laser servo*. The disks and mechanism increase the data track density on a 3.5-inch disk from 135 tracks per inch (tpi) to 2,490 tpi. A laser-controlled servomotor accurately positions the read-write head over the correct track. Although the LS-120 disks and drives look similar to standard 1.44MB disks and drives, the technical differences are substantial. Table 11-2 shows a comparison of key specifications.

TABLE 11-2: SuperDisk versus Standard Floppy Drive

	LS-120	Standard 3.5-Inch Floppy
Capacity	120MB	1.44MB
Maximum transfer rate:		
IDE internal	484K/sec	45K/sec
Parallel port	290K/sec	
Average seek time	70 ms	84 ms
Disk rotational speed	720 rpm	300 rpm
Track density	2,490 tpi	135 tpi
Number of tracks	1,736 × two sides	80 × two sides

LS-120 technology was developed by a group of companies led by Imation, a spin-off of the 3M Company. Although Imation has ended its own production of the drive, a number of other companies continue to sell the device for PCs and portables; prices in 2002 are generally in the range of $75 to $100. The LS-120 disks sold for about $6 to $8 each in early 2002, or about 5 to 7 cents per megabyte.

CD-recordable devices

Recordable CD-ROM discs (also called CD-Rs) have become popular among software developers who can create their own masters while they're developing a product. The discs can also be used for low-volume publishing of database information; each disc can hold up to 700MB of information. One of the original names for the CD-R was WORM, an acronym for *write once, read many times*.

As with most everything else in the high-tech world, prices have tumbled even as capabilities have gone up. At the time of this writing, CD-R discs sell in quantity (on a "spindle," which means you don't get — or pay for — plastic cases or paper sleeves) for as little as 30 cents apiece, which makes them very attractive as an archival and transport media. At that price, you get roughly 23MB for a penny. So what if you can't reuse them? (When this technology first came on the market, about the time of the book's fourth edition, the discs for a CD-R sold for as much as $15 each.)

CD-RW devices add the ability to rewrite data on special CD discs. Figure 11-6 shows an example of a CD-RW. The discs dropped below $2 in 2001, still a respectable cost of about 3MB for a penny. The discs are also reusable.

Ch 11

FIGURE 11-6: *A Hi-Val CD-RW drive; the device installs in an internal bay and connects to an IDE port on the motherboard. The latest CD-RW drives are capable of recording at speeds of up to 20×, reading as fast as 40×.*

Even more capacious are DVD-RAMs and DVD-Rs, which can hold from 2.5GB to 9.4GB, depending on design. In 2001, the retail price for a 9.4GB DVD-RAM was about $50, which is about 1.8MB for a penny. As with other technologies, you can expect prices for DVD media to drop sharply over time.

CROSS-REFERENCE

I discuss CD-Rs, CD-RWs, and DVD-RAMs in detail in Chapter 12.

Removable hard drive cartridges

The leading manufacturer of removable storage is Iomega, which offers the Zip and Jaz product lines as well as CD-RW devices. In 2001, Iomega debuted the high-capacity Peerless drive.

At the time of this writing, you could purchase a Peerless drive that works with disks in 10 and 20GB sizes; the drives are Plug and Play with USB and FireWire versions. The FireWire version allows sustained transfer rates of 15MB per second.

The unique feature of this system is that each sealed Peerless disk includes a set of integrated read/write heads. As such, the removable disks are protected from contamination and the drives are considerably simpler to manufacture.

Another interesting feature of the disks is an identifying number recorded on the media, which can be used as part of a security system to protect against unauthorized attempts to read a lost or stolen disk.

In late 2001, Peerless drives sold for about $250. Disks sold for about $160 and $200 for 10GB and 20GB media, respectively. An example of a Peerless drive is shown in Figure 11-7.

FIGURE 11-7: *An Iomega Peerless drive with its 250GB disk in place. (Courtesy of Iomega Corporation)*

Iomega has had great success with its Zip and Jaz products; it is uncertain whether Peerless will become as ubiquitous as its corporate cousins.

The Jaz drive can store 1GB or 2GB of data on a removable cartridge. The original version operates at a respectable 6.6MB per second transfer rate and a 12 ms access time — just slightly slower than a typical hard drive. The newer 2GB model is 30 percent faster.

The Jaz, which requires an SCSI interface, sold for less than $300 in a 1GB internal or external model when the last edition of this book came out. Today, only the 2GB versions of the drive are available and sell for about $275 for internal or $350 for external models. Jaz cartridges are a bit pricey — at about $70 for 1GB and $125 for 2GB, 7 or 6.25 cents per megabyte, respectively. Specifications for Jaz drives are shown in Table 11-3.

TABLE 11-3: Iomega Jaz Drives

	1GB	2GB
Capacity	1.07GB	2GB
Maximum transfer rate:		
SCSI	6.62MB/sec	8.7MB/sec
Average seek time	10 ms	10 ms
Disk rotational speed	5,400 rpm	5,400 rpm

Another removable cartridge drive player is Castlewood with their line of Orb drives. The original system used a 2.2GB cartridge that sold for about $30 (less than 1.5 cents per megabyte) and the drive sold for about $150 for an EIDE interface model. The 3.5-inch hard disk cartridge is capable of a 12.2MB per second sustained data transfer rate. Orb drives also are available with EIDE, parallel port, SCSI, and USB interfaces.

In 2001, the company introduced a 5.7GB version that installs in a bay as an EIDE device. Data transfer is as much as 17.35MB per second. The drive can also read and write 2.2GB Orb cartridges. The specifications of Orb drives are shown in Table 11-4.

TABLE 11-4: Castlewood Orb Drives

	2.2GB	5.7GB
Capacity	2.2GB	5.7GB
Maximum transfer rate:		
ATA	12.2MB/sec	17.35MB/sec
Parallel	2MB/sec	N/A
SCSI	12.2MB/sec	N/A
USB 1.1	1.0MB/sec	N/A
Average seek time	11 ms	11 ms
Disk rotational speed	5,400 rpm	5,400 rpm

SyQuest was one of the pioneers of removable storage for personal computers, with a family of systems that could store 44, 88, 105, or 200MB on a 5.25-inch disk cartridge, or as much as 1.5GB on smaller, high-density Sparq systems. SyQuest hard drives captured the attention, particularly, of the Macintosh-based publishing and graphics industry as a way of exchanging data between one production house and another. As popular as they were, however, many of the SyQuest products were prone to failure — sometimes eating the data and at other times damaging the drive itself.

Much of SyQuest's core technology was sold, at fire-sale prices, to its former competitor Iomega in 1999. I can't recommend that you add a new SyQuest drive to your system under the present arrangement. If you do have a functioning SyQuest, though, you can still obtain support and repairs and you can purchase media and remaining products through a successor company, Syqt, Inc. (www.syqt.com).

External Hard Drives

Although they are not often thought of as a form of removable storage, external hard drives can also be used for that sort of purpose. Hard drives with capacities of as much as 100GB are available in versions that use USB, FireWire, or SCSI connections. These drives can be easily unplugged and moved from machine to machine or locked in a safe as a form of secure storage.

At the time of this writing, the best deals can be found on USB drives — devices that are capable of interfacing to your computer under the developing USB 2.0 standard that permits a transfer rate of 480MB per second, as much as 40 times faster than the original USB standard.

CROSS-REFERENCE

I discuss a Maxtor external USB drive in Chapter 15.

External drives are typically priced about $50 to $75 more than internal drives because of the cost of the necessary case, power supply, and cable.

Flash Memory

Flash memory is a form of nonvolatile memory, similar to the SmartMedia or CompactFlash memory modules used in digital cameras and portable digital music players. SmartMedia and CompactFlash are not in ordinary use on desktop PCs. You can, however, purchase a reader that allows you to download data from a camera or musical device to your PC; most of these readers use the USB port as an interface.

Another class of device — in some ways a solution looking for a problem, but a neat product nevertheless — is a portable plug-in block of RAM. One example is the DiskOnKey from M-Systems, shown in Figure 11-8.

FIGURE 11-8: *A block of 64MB of nonvolatile RAM resides in a Plug-and-Play container on a key ring. DiskOnKey attaches to a USB port.*

Just over two inches long and fashioned as a key fob, DiskOnKey includes its own intelligence and is capable of storing files, as well as running multiple applications directly from the product. It can be used to transport files from office to office, as a security device, and as an easy way to cross boundaries between a PC and an Apple Macintosh without making alterations to either operating system. The device is immediately recognized as a supplementary hard drive by the host computer when it is plugged into a USB port.

DiskOnKey will work with any USB-enabled PC. Windows XP, ME, and 2000 and later operating systems are prepared to work with the device; users of Windows 98 will need to install a driver, provided by M-Systems. In its initial release, DiskOnKey was compliant with USB 1.1, meaning that data transfer moves at 12 Mbps. For more information, consult www.diskonkey.com.

Tape Backup Devices

The old reliable backup scheme for a great deal of information is a tape drive, a technology first developed for the early days of mainframe computing. Tape drives lay down information on a moving strip of tape held within a cartridge.

Modern tape drives are offered in internal versions and as standalone boxes with dedicated interfaces or parallel port connections. Today's basic units have capacities of 10 to 20GB, with advanced units capable of storing as much as 500GB. With compression of stored data, those 500GB tape drives are capable of holding as much as 1.6 *terabytes* of data. Tape backups are another area in which hardware prices have dropped precipitously in recent years.

Tape devices may be appropriate for huge storage systems, but they can be painfully slow to use for anything other than middle-of-the-night automated backups. The principal reason for their slowness is the fact that tapes store information in a serial fashion — one bit after another down the length of the tape. If the information that you want is located near the beginning of the tape, you can reach it fairly quickly; if it is near the end of the tape, you may have to wait several minutes before the drive is able to fast-forward its way to that location. Think of it as trying to find a particular scene on a VCR tape.

If you purchase a tape drive, I recommend that you choose one that will work with third-party backup software, as well as those offered by the hardware manufacturer. Without such standardization of the data organization and data-encoding scheme, if the built-in tape drive failed, the backup tapes could only be read by a drive of the identical type.

Helical-scan drives

DAT and 8mm drives use rotating heads mounted on a slight angle to the width of the tape. The head records a slanted magnetic trail of data across the width of the tape, thus enabling much higher data densities than the ordinary lengthwise track used on quarter-inch tape media. But the rotating heads and sophisticated tape advance mechanism used in helical-scan tape drives are expensive. You can see the difference in recording methods in Figure 11-9.

Q/C Tape

Helical Scan Tape

FIGURE 11-9: *QIC tape versus helical-scan tape*

These devices were developed in the late 1980s for high-end audio uses, hence the name *digital audiotape*, or DAT. Most DAT drives are SCSI devices, often using the high-speed SCSI-2 version of the standard.

Both 4mm DAT drives and 8mm helical-scan tapes generally hold far more data than quarter-inch tapes. You won't be surprised to learn that the 8mm tape holds roughly twice as much data as the 4mm tape and that 8mm tape drive systems are roughly twice as expensive as 4mm tape drive systems.

Senior citizen tech: Quarter-inch cartridge (QIC)

QIC tape drives record data in ordinary linear tracks laid down parallel to the edge of the tape.

High-speed QIC systems use an IDE or SCSI interface. Some of the first QIC drives used the computer's floppy drive interface to connect to the bus, plugging into an unused B drive connector on the floppy drive cable. Other QIC tape drives use an interface board to connect the tape drive cable to the bus for an increase in speed, but again the tape drive appears to the computer to be another version (albeit a weird one) of a floppy drive. A design for an external QIC tape drive connects to the parallel port but reroutes signals inside the computer so that the floppy drive interface signals come out through the parallel port pins.

Some QIC tape systems use proprietary data-storage formats, which makes me nervous. A QIC-80 drive should theoretically be completely compatible with all other QIC-80 drives — they should be able to read and write to each other's tapes without difficulty. There is little reason to search out a QIC drive if you are setting up a new backup system; if you need to expand an existing system or replace a failed unit, be sure to buy a drive that is QIC-80-certified (one that has been tested and certified by the industry's test agents), and not merely a QIC-80-compatible drive.

Follow your tape drive vendor's installation and troubleshooting directions. When troubleshooting a QIC tape drive that uses the floppy drive interface, consider the common causes of floppy drive failure: incorrect drive select settings, incorrect termination, or the user plugging the wrong floppy drive cable connector onto the drive — for example, plugging the A: drive connector to a tape drive that is supposed to be impersonating the B: drive. These same mistakes can choke a QIC tape drive. So can a bad floppy drive, especially if the tape drive shares cables and/or a floppy drive controller with the bad floppy drive.

High-End Backup Devices

Large computer installations have broken ground with other high-speed, high-capacity backup devices, including magneto-optical recorders and transportable hard drives.

Magneto-optical recorders are similar to CD-ROM in operation. They use special, high-coercivity disks. *Coercivity* is a measure of the strength of the magnetic field needed to write data; the smaller data bits of high-capacity disks demand higher coercivity.

Transportable hard drives first came about as devices for use in high-security settings, including government agencies. At the end of the day, the entire hard drive mechanism was taken out of its holder and placed in a safe. These drives are declining in popularity, although some offices use lightweight versions with parallel interfaces as a high-capacity version of a sneaker net, picking up or delivering data to far-flung machines when carried on foot.

Dinosaur Tech: Bernoulli Drives

For many years, one of the leaders in the removable storage market was Iomega's Bernoulli drive technology — specially designed disk cartridges that connected to a PC through the parallel port or an SCSI interface. The final versions of the Bernoulli drive had capacities of 90, 150, or 230MB per cartridge. Although Bernoulli disk cartridges were expensive at the time, they promised data access time comparable to hard disk speed, allowing their use as a live storage medium as well as for backup.

Bernoulli disk cartridges used a flexible disk with a metal particle coating. Unlike most other magnetic disk media, Bernoulli drives wrote only on the top surface of the disk, using a single read/write head. At rest, the disk curved downward, hanging below the head. This space between the head and the disk made Bernoulli cartridges tough. Iomega claimed they could withstand an eight-foot drop to a hard surface without damage.

When a cartridge was installed in a Bernoulli drive, the flexible disk spun up to speed and rose close to the read/write head. If the power failed, the disk would lose lift and fall back down, away from the head.

You may still find some Bernoulli drives around in senior citizen systems, but they have been replaced, for the most part, by high-density floppies or removable hard drives. In my experience, the Bernoulli drive was never as reliable as some of the newer technology, and they never sold as well, either. When the Bernoulli first hit the market, some government agencies quickly adopted it as their standard for data exchange (before the days when local area networks were virtually universal, as they are today). Most agencies, however, quickly un-adopted the Bernoulli because of data integrity problems.

Dinosaur Tech: Floptical Disks and Drives

Floptical brand disks look much like ordinary 3.5-inch disks. Like 2.88MB floppy disks, Floptical disks are made of Mylar with a barium ferrite magnetic coating. Like ordinary 720K, 1.44MB, and 2.88MB 3.5-inch disks, Floptical disks store data magnetically. In fact, many Floptical drives are both read- and write-compatible with ordinary double-density (720K) and high-density (1.44MB) 3.5-inch floppy disks.

Unlike ordinary 3.5-inch disks, Floptical disks provide optical feedback to the drive so that the drive can accurately position the read/write head over the chosen track, even if that track has become slightly eccentric. Because data-recording tracks can be much closer together than on ordinary 3.5-inch disks, each Floptical disk stores over 20MB of data. Flopticals, once promising, have mostly been shoved aside by improvements in capacity and price for older designs that are still around and new devices, such as the Zip and SuperDisk LS-120 drives.

The Floptical disk manufacturer stamps very closely spaced concentric rings into the surface of ordinary 3.5-inch barium ferrite disks. These rings (1,250 per inch) guide the read/write heads as they position themselves over the appropriate track on the disk. Light from an LED (light-emitting diode) on the read/write head shines onto the disk, reflecting back to a photodetector that converts the light energy to electrical current. As the head moves across the disk, the light (and current) drops off over a groove and gets stronger over the flat, reflective land between the grooves. The drive can therefore distinguish one track from the next.

Using ordinary magnetic disk reading/writing technology (but using a very small read/write head suitable for the skinny tracks), the Floptical drive writes data on the flat tracks between the optical guidance grooves. Most Floptical drives are capable of multiple modes. Their read/write head contains both a small head to write tiny magnetic marks on Floptical disks and an ordinary read/write head used to read and write to ordinary 720K and 1.44MB floppy disks.

Floptical drives are SCSI devices that require an SCSI adapter in the computer. Because the SCSI standard enables up to seven devices to be chained to a single SCSI host adapter, your Floptical drive can share the adapter with a recordable CD, CD-ROM drive, or an SCSI hard disk.

Special software redirects interrupt 13h (the interrupt that the computer uses to send commands to the floppy disk) so that commands routed from the computer to the ordinary floppy drive go to the Floptical drive instead.

Troubleshooting a Removable Storage Device

The removable storage devices discussed in this chapter attach to your computer through an IDE connector; an SCSI, USB, or FireWire port, or a parallel port.

Too many types of devices and too many possible combinations of controllers, devices, and systems exist to go into step-by-step troubleshooting here. But the good news is that if you run into difficulties with a removable storage device, it is fairly easy to isolate which part of the whole package is the source of the problem.

I assume that your drive was working properly at one time, and now it doesn't. Ask yourself the following questions:

- What has changed since the last time it worked properly? (This is the first question you should ask.)
- Have you added any new hardware? Are all cables properly reinstalled and power cords attached? Are you certain that any new adapter cards are properly seated in the bus connector?

Ch 11

- Have you made changes to IRQs, I/O addresses, or DMA settings? Under Windows 95/98 and later versions, go to the Device Manager and check for conflicts. Change settings, if necessary, in order to avoid having two devices making the same demand on your PC.
- Have you installed new drivers that may have overwritten earlier ones? Try reinstalling the software and drivers for the hardware that has stopped working.
- Are you certain that the media — the disk, cartridge, or tape — has not failed? Try taking a copy to a coworker or friend with the same hardware and see if it works there; you may also be able to bring the media to a computer store and try it out on a machine there.

- Use a diagnostic program to check that the port is performing properly. Take the portable unit and install it on another machine to see if it works there.

SUMMARY

This chapter examined the growing category of high-capacity removable storage devices, which have moved from a somewhat exotic novelty to an essential add-on for the careful computer user. The next chapter covers another class of hardware that has moved from the fringes to the center of the PC market: CD and DVD devices.

Notes

Chapter 12

CD and DVD Drives

The designers of the first PC almost certainly never imagined that high-tech software programs would one day be stamped out on an assembly line alongside the latest Madonna album. And they probably never considered the possibility that users would record their own plastic disks with hundreds and thousands of megabytes of data, or hours of music and video.

The still-expanding world of CD and DVD drives present some of the most exciting opportunities for computer owners, who can now do the following:

- Load huge operating systems and office suites from a single disc.
- Make backup disks of their essential data on a CD-R, CD-RW or a DVD recorder.
- Create their own movies and animations.
- Make compilations of music downloaded from the Internet, recorded from broadcast radio, or from their personal collection of CDs, cassettes, and records.

The first CD-ROM players for PCs offered little more than large-capacity platters of text, delivered at a snail's pace of 150K per second. These early drives required complex SCSI or proprietary connections to the system and sold at eye-popping prices. Today, a modern machine can have an inexpensive CD-ROM drive that reads data up to 72 times as fast (10,800K per second) and is capable of delivering movie-like video, high-fidelity audio, and nearly instant access to full encyclopedias of data.

Or, a machine can include a CD-R, which is a device that allows you to record your own disc, or a CD-RW that can write and then rewrite data to a disc multiple times. Today, many computer manufacturers are replacing CD-ROM drives with an even more impressive DVD drive that can hold gigabytes of data. Some systems now include both a CD and a DVD drive.

The CD Story

CD-ROMs are a computer adaptation of the CDs produced for audio systems, first introduced in 1982 at about the same time that PCs were first mass-marketed. Although the potential of CD-ROMs as a storage media for computers was immediately obvious, it took a while before prices and capabilities reached acceptable levels.

When CD drives were first introduced for computer use, they were only capable of reading data or music from a CD-ROM (CD read-only memory.) Disks were manufactured by pressing a master into a soft plastic disk to imprint it with a pattern of pits and flat areas that denote the 0s and 1s of digital information.

To read the disk, a CD-ROM player focuses a narrow beam of laser light on a section of the spinning disk. Light reflects from the flat surfaces but doesn't reflect from the pits. Inside the CD-ROM drive, a photo detector converts these on/off light flashes to electric signals that are brought to your microprocessor across the bus.

Although you can still purchase a CD-ROM drive today, most users have adopted even-more-capable CD-R (CD recordable) or CD-RW (CD rewritable) devices. I discuss CD-Rs and CD-RWs shortly.

Today, a standard CD-ROM can hold 700MB of information on a platter that costs just pennies to manufacture. At the factory, CDs are very cheap to produce once the original master has been made. In other words, the first copy of a CD-ROM may cost several thousand dollars to make, but subsequent copies may cost only a few dimes. Obviously, a run of 10,000 copies brings the total price down substantially, but manufactured CDs are not cost-effective for one or two copies.

CD-ROM players sell for as little as $50 for a basic commodity device that runs at speeds of as much as 7,800K per second (52X). Players are available in internal and external varieties, with IDE, SCSI, and proprietary interfaces. Figure 12-1 shows a basic "bare" internal CD-ROM.

As I mentioned previously, CD-ROM drives are by definition read-only. The next step up in flexibility is the CD-recordable (CD-R) device, and the even-more-capable CD-rewritable (CD-RW) drives.

CD-Rs and CD-RWs use focused laser beams to melt pits or change the reflective properties of special CD blanks. They are very well suited to make a small number of copies of disks for personal use, including backups of data. CD-Rs can only be recorded once; CD-RWs can be recorded to, erased, and re-recorded much like a hard disk drive.

Most modern CD drives can read all types of discs: CDs, CD-Rs, and CD-RWs. Early CD-ROM and CD-R drives, though, do not work reliably with CD-RWs because there is less contrast between the reflective and the non-reflective areas on CD-RWs.

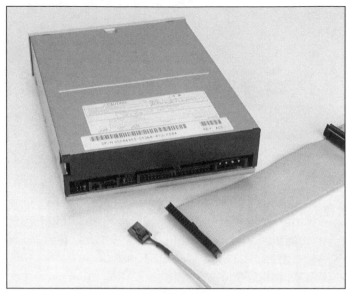

FIGURE 12-1: *Buying a "bare" kit from a computer supply house will save money, but you will have to assemble your own supporting cast of mounting hardware and cables.*

How CD-Rs and CD-RWs work

CD-Rs and CD-RWs have the same physical shape as a CD-ROM, but they are not designed to be pressed in a factory; instead, they include a special recording layer.

On a CD-R, the recording layer is made with organic dyes. Depending on the manufacturer, these dyes include compounds of green cyanine, gold phthalocyanine, or silver-blue azo. Although some disc makers claim particular advantages to their particular chemical formula, most scientists say the differences among these three dyes are miniscule.

To create a pattern of pits, a CD-R uses a focused laser beam to heat the dye to about 200 degrees Celsius (about 400 degrees Fahrenheit) to melt a permanent gap in the dye. A plastic layer alongside the dye expands into the space to make a highly reflective pit. When a CD attempts to read back information from a disc, the pit reflects back the light that is interpreted by the drive's electronics as a bit of information. The melted area on a CD-R can't be reset to its original condition, and therefore, CD-R discs can't be re-recorded or erased.

On the other hand, a CD-RW disc can be reused hundreds or even thousands of times, depending on the quality of the disc; manufacturers have made great progress in efforts to improve the lifetime of these discs.

The recording layer of a CD-RW disc is made of an alloy of silver and other metals, including indium, antimony, and tellurium. The high-powered laser in a CD-RW heats pinpoint areas to 500 to 700 degrees Celsius (about 900 to 1,300 degrees Fahrenheit). This intense heat melts the crystals at the point of focus, changing them to a non-crystalline structure that reflects back less light than the surrounding area.

To erase a CD-RW, the laser heats the recording layer to about 200 degrees Celsius, which is just enough to return the alloy to a reflective crystalline form. Erasing an entire disc requires a sustained heating period; depending on the drive and disc maker, erasing can require twenty minutes to an hour.

Instead of erasing a CD-RW disc, the medium can instead be overwritten (the rewriting in the RW label) in a process that combines erasing and recording in one step. In rewriting, the drive's laser records a new decrystalized pattern on the disc for information and new crystallized areas between the pits by alternating between high-heat, high-energy pulses for recording and low-energy pulses for erasures. Rewriting typically occurs at a slower rate than writing to a virgin disc but faster than a full-disc erase process.

A CD-RW's hardware and electronics are more complex than those of a CD-R drive, and the discs are somewhat more expensive than write-once CD-R discs.

CD disc speed ratings

In addition to a stated capacity, CD media are marketed with a speed rating. At the time of this writing, the most common ratings are 8X, 12X, or 20X. These ratings represent the manufacturer's certification of the fastest reliable recording speed for the media.

To get the best results, you should use media that matches the fastest recording speed of your CD-R or CD-RW drive. If you use a disc that is certified at a slower speed, be sure that you adjust the recording speed of your CD-burning software accordingly. Some advanced drives are able to read an identification code on the blank disc and set their recording speed accordingly. A high-speed disc won't record any faster than the top speed of the drive.

Should you use a CD-R or a CD-RW?

First of all, it is becoming increasingly difficult to find a new CD-R in the market; manufacturers have changed over to producing CD-RW devices. Again, as with other PC components, prices have continued to decline just as capabilities have improved. In early 2002, high-speed internal CD-RW drives sold for as little as $80; external FireWire and USB drives were priced at about $150 to $200.

Current CD-RW drives are very flexible — they can be used to read manufactured CDs, to read and write (once) to a CD-R disc, or to read and write multiple times to a CD-RW disc.

CD-Rs are much less expensive to manufacture than CD-RWs, although the price gap between the two types of media has narrowed considerably in recent years. In late 2001, you could purchase a spindle of 100 CD-R discs for $30 to $50, which works out to 30 to 50 cents apiece. At the same time, bulk purchase prices for CD-RWs dropped below $1 apiece, down from about $3 apiece at the time of the previous edition of this book and $20 each just a few years earlier.

CD-R discs are particularly suitable for private archiving and permanent storage. Because CD-R disks are not erasable, they provide an audit trail that is useful for some types of data, such as recording financial transactions at a bank. Each day's information can be added to a backup CD-ROM, but you can't erase previously recorded data, thus preserving the integrity of the archival backup.

Ch 12

To decide which one makes more economic sense, think about the role that CD-Rs or CD-RWs will play in your office or home system. In my office, I use CD-Rs for deep storage and to send very large files to clients outside of my office. At 30 cents for a CD-R and $1 for a CD-RW, I would have to reuse the rewritable media at least four times before I'm ahead of the game. If the disk is going out of my office, or if I intend to keep it untouched as an archive, CD-Rs are much more economical. And I have to keep in mind the fact that some of my clients don't have drives capable of reliably reading some CD-RW discs.

CD-ROM, CD-R, and CD-RW disks are sturdy, with a much longer shelf life than tapes or ordinary disks. Because the data is stored physically, magnetic fields can't erase or damage the data, and the optically readable pits are covered with clear plastic, which reduces the chance of accidental damage by abrasion. Although no one has yet been able to test this empirically because the technology is still young, engineers estimate that CD-R and CD-RW disks will remain readable for more than 15 years after being written.

CD-ROM, CD-R, CD-RW data specifications

Standard CD-ROMs, CD-Rs, and CD-RWs store information in 1.6-micron grooves. (A *micron* is one-thousandth of a millimeter. One inch contains a bit more than 25,000 microns; the average human hair is about 50 microns wide).

As is discussed previously in the chapter, a manufactured CD-ROM is pressed one disc at a time from a mold at a factory while CD-Rs and CD-RWs are created one bit at a time in a recording drive. The end result is very similar.

Unlike most other disk media, the data on a CD-ROM is written in one long spiral track, like the groove on a record. (You do remember record albums, don't you?) But unlike records, early CD-ROM drives played CD-ROMs at a constant linear velocity (CLV). To maintain constant linear velocity (a constant number of inches per second passing the read/write head), these CD-ROM drives use sophisticated drive-spinning mechanisms that spin the drive more slowly as the head gets closer to the outer edge of the disk.

Other types of WORM (write once, read many times) drives and most magneto-optical (MO) disks record data in multiple concentric rings arranged like rows of seats in a stadium rather than a single long spiral. Most other disk media (such as floppy disks, hard disks, Bernoulli cartridges, and Floptical disks) also use this concentric track system. This type of media is read and written at a constant angular velocity (CAV).

Because the outermost edge of a CD is the hardest area to manufacture accurately and the most easily damaged, a CD-ROM data track starts at the inside of the disk and spirals out toward the outer edge. Ordinary magnetic disk media, including hard disks and floppy disks, record on the outer tracks first, gradually working their way in toward the crowded central tracks.

CD-ROM speed

Just as with a hard disk, a CD-ROM drive's speed is measured in several ways, but the sorts of demands put on a CD-ROM drive are different from those of a hard drive.

The most important measure of speed for a CD-ROM drive is its *data transfer rate*, also referred to as *throughput*. Throughput tells you how quickly a CD-ROM drive can transfer data from a CD-ROM to the computer's data bus.

On a hard drive, speed of access to a bit of information is very important because users typically pick one small data record from a huge database. Because a CD-ROM is typically used to supply a long stream of information, such as audio or video for a game or other multimedia applications, data transfer rate is a more important consideration than speed of access.

When CD-ROMs first arrived on the PC scene, the original data transfer rate standard was 150K per second, which is considerably

Ch 12

slower than most other data storage devices. That speed was extremely limiting in multimedia applications, thus preventing PCs from displaying streaming video effectively and requiring more than an hour to record a full disc.

Several years later, a new generation of CD-ROM drives was introduced. They were capable of data transfer at 300K per second and became known as double-speed, or 2X, devices. Within a few years, triple-speed (450K per second) and quad-speed (600K per second) drives appeared, and then in short order, 6X-speed (900K per second), 8X-speed (1,200K per second), and 10X-speed (1,500K per second) drives arrived.

In early 2002, the top end of consumer CD drives runs at speeds of up to 72X (10,800K per second). The most advanced CD-R and CD-RW drives typically read at speeds of up to 40X, and are capable of writing at speeds of 24X and rewriting at 10X.

NOTE

Some exceptionally honest drive makers list their reading speeds as a range, such as 40X-52X. This is due to the fact that on a spinning disc, the grooves at or near the center move slower than the grooves toward the outer edge; more data is available at the outer tracks than on the inner ones. Unfortunately, because the data spiral begins on the inside and most CD-ROMs are not full, these new, fast CD-ROM drives are rarely called upon to deliver data at their highest through-put. But, in general, faster is better.

Early designs for CD-ROMs varied the speed of rotation so that all data passed under the head at the same speed. This required some extra electronics and put some strain on the motor. Modern CD-ROMs, though, have added sophisticated electronics and memory buffers that allow the drive to run at a constant speed while dealing with differing rates of data acquisition in various parts of the disc.

Another reason for multiple spin or retrieval rates for CD-ROM drives is that computer data and audio data must be read at different rates on double-speed and faster drives. The standard speed for audio information was set at 153.6K per second (usually rounded to 150K per second) when the first CDs were created. Computer data was originally intended to be read at the same rate, but as CD-ROM technology advanced, the reading speed of data doubled, doubled again, and then doubled again. However, the standard for audio data transfer has remained unchanged. If you were to read a song at 600K per second, it would sound like Alvin the Chipmunk on helium. So when a CD-ROM needs to transfer audio information, the drive must slow down to 150K per second. When it goes back to data, it speeds up.

In Table 12-1 you'll find a guide to the meaning of "X" in CD drive speeds.

TABLE 12-1: The Meaning of X

Drive Speed	Data Transfer Rate	Access Time
1X	150KB/second	400 ms
2X	300KB/second	300 ms
3X	450KB/second	200 ms
4X	600KB/second	150 ms
6X	900KB/second	150 ms
8X to 12X	1.2MB/second to 1.8MB/second	100 ms
16X to 24X	2.4MB/second to 3.6MB/second	90 ms
32X to 52X	4.8MB/second to 7.8MB/second	85 ms

CD-R and CD-RW drives list their speeds for their various functions. The specifications for a CD-R tell you how fast they record and how fast they read a disc with data already in place. A CD-RW lists three speeds: recording on a write-once CD-R disc, recording on a multiple-write CD-RW, and reading a disc with data.

What does the writing speed of a CD-R mean in actual time? Data recorded to disk at 1X moves at about 150KB/second, or about 9MB/minute. A fast CD-R drive will save you more than an hour per disk, as Table 12-2 shows.

TABLE 12-2: The Value of X	
Recording Speed	**Time Required**
CD 1X recording 650MB of data	74 minutes
CD 2X recording 650MB of data	37 minutes
CD 4X recording 650MB of data	18.5 minutes
CD 8X recording 650MB of data	9.2 minutes
CD 12X recording 650MB of data	6 minutes
CD 16X recording 650MB of data	4.6 minutes
CD 24X recording 650MB of data	3 minutes

Access speed is the other critical indication of the meaningful speed of a CD-ROM drive. This specification tells you, on average, how long it takes the drive mechanism to locate a particular block of information and move its read head into position to begin data transfer.

Access speed is most important for applications, such as a database, in which you need to pick up a number of small blocks of data in rapid succession. It is generally less important in playing audio, video, and multimedia games because once the drive locates a particular section, all the CD-ROM has to do is unload a large section of contiguous video and audio.

The lower the access speed, the faster the CD-ROM drive responds to requests for information. Therefore, look for the best combination of high throughput and low access speed.

Data buffer

In general, a bigger data buffer is better, assuming that the buffer is properly designed. Think of a buffer as a first-in, first-out staging area. When the system is momentarily busy and can't accept data, data read from the CD-ROM is held in the buffer. When the system is ready for the data, the information held in the memory chips that make up the buffer can be delivered many times faster than data that must be fetched from the CD-ROM. With a buffer, a CD-ROM drive does not have to stop and then resume delivering data as often as it does without a buffer. (The system does have other chores to attend to and can't always just serve the CD-ROM drive.)

Early CD-ROM drives had no buffer, but then moved to 64K and then 256K memory chips. New models include 1MB buffers.

CD-ROM capacity

The capacity of a CD-ROM disk depends on two factors: the data encoding specification used by the publisher of the disk, and how much of the available space the publisher actually uses. The range of maximum capacities for consumer products runs from about 540MB to 700MB.

The nature of the material recorded on the disk can also affect its capacity. Data that is intended to be read in a continuous stream — such as audio and video — may take up slightly less space than data that is intended to be taken in many small chunks, such as database entries.

Because CDs are written in a spiral, the amount of data that you can get on a disc is affected by how tightly spaced the "groove" is. A standard Red Book audio CD or Yellow Book CD-ROM permits recording as much as 74 minutes of data. An 80-minute disc has roughly 360,000 sectors instead of the usual 333,000, a theoretical increase in data capacity from 650MB to 703MB.

Of course, this doesn't guarantee that all CD devices will be able to read or write to an 80-minute disc reliably. In fact, you should expect some modern drives and most older devices to have difficulty with them. And consumer CD players in your stereo system or your car are all but certain to balk at playing back an expanded 80-minute disc.

One other issue: a 650MB CD disc actually has a capacity of about 747MB of audio; that's because audio sectors hold 2,352 bytes per sector, while data sectors hold only 2,048 bytes, using the remainder for error correction.

At the time of this writing, manufacturers are experimenting with 90-minute and 99-minute CD-R discs, with capacities of about 791MB and 870MB, respectively. This form of media is all but certain to be unreadable on most CD devices now in use.

Multisession Photo CDs

Kodak's Photo CD specification enables users to store and view photographs and slides. Professional photographers and publishers, as well as amateurs, have adopted the system that lets them manipulate and alter the photos on the CD by using advanced software.

One Photo CD can hold as many as 100 photos in standard size and resolution. Very large and very high-resolution versions for professional applications take up more space.

All CD-ROM drives can retrieve images from a Photo CD that was recorded in one session. But if you choose to have two or more rolls of film recorded onto a Photo CD at different times, the Kodak system creates multiple directories to those files; such a disk is called a *multisession Photo CD*. Only later-generation CD-ROM drives that are identified as multisession-capable can retrieve the images added at a later session to an original Photo CD.

In addition to multisession capability in the firmware of the CD-ROM drive, your interface board and software device driver must also support multisession Photo CDs.

Multisession capability is useful as you write CDROM data because it lets you accumulate data over a period of time, adding new information to the previously recorded disk. You can use multisession features for any data, not just photographs. The negative side of multisession recording is that about 13MB of storage is used to store beginning and ending information about each session. So if your CD-ROM disk holds two sessions, you waste some 26MB of space. Four sessions recorded on a multisession drive use up about 52MB of space to store this data, and so on. The good news is that a newer writing technique, called *packet writing*, reduces this multisession overhead by supporting the writing of shorter data increments. Still, while multisession recording is useful — and quite common in today's hardware — if you want to

get the most data on a single CD-ROM disk, write the disk in a single session.

Audio disks must also be written in a single session if you intend to play them on standard CD players in your rec room or your car.

> **NOTE**
>
> Extended architecture (XA) is a specification without much use. XA disks were supposed to enable the interleaving of audio and data information on the same track of a CD-ROM disk, thus enabling greater capacity and transfer speed. Such a capability would be valuable for multimedia applications in which the computer has to work hard to merge audio and video from a standard CD-ROM. Very few XA disks were ever produced, though, and are not likely to be produced in the future. Kodak's Photo CD is a subset of the XA format, although it does not require additional hardware. In any case, nearly all current CD-ROM drives claim they are XA-compatible or XA-ready.

Unusual drive mechanisms

Many early CD-ROM drives used caddies to hold the disks. The caddies, which slipped into an opening on the front of the drive, helped stabilize the disks in the drive. Caddies also protected disks stored in them when not in use. Extra caddies were cheap enough that you could have several extras on hand. When these drives were popular, sellers said that caddies helped to protect the media and provided more reliable read/write operations from the drive.

Today, however, modern CD-ROM drives are much more mechanically and electrically stable, even as they have dropped in price by a factor of ten. CD caddies have been mostly relegated to the used computer racks. As cheap as CD-ROM drives are today, it makes sense to dump the caddy drive if you're upgrading other parts of your system anyway.

Ch 12

If you have an older and slower CD-ROM drive that you insist on using, you may be able to find caddies for sale in some catalogs. (I can give you a great price on a couple dozen that are sitting in the back of a closet here in my office.)

Most current CD-ROM drives use a slide-out drawer similar to those in most audio drives. This design is slightly less expensive to produce, and some users may find it easier to use. The sliding drawer, though, is a point of potential failure for the drive. And seriously, dear reader, the slide-out drawer is not a coffee-cup holder.

Several CD-ROM drive makers have introduced multiple-disk caddies that enable users to load three or more disks in a single carrier for easier access. Only one disk is available at one time, but a software command can instruct the drive to swap among the available disks. Changing disks requires a few seconds. You've probably used the same kind of design in an audio CD changer.

Finally, heavy users of CD-ROMs may want to consider a multiple-CD drive system. With an SCSI adapter, you can install as many as 14 drives in an external cabinet with a single connecting cable to the PC itself. A single IDE channel can support two CD-ROM drives with a master and slave on the same cable.

Playing music CDs on a computer CD-ROM drive

Because computer CD drives are direct descendants of audio CDs, all of the mechanical and electronic elements to play music CDs exist. You need to add a proper device driver and software program that enables the selection of specific tracks.

Most modern CD units have an external jack for directly attaching a headphone; there is usually a volume control but no other facilities to adjust the quality of the sound.

Microsoft Windows users can play CD music tracks with the Windows Media Player that is part of the operating system. For more fancy options, including the capability to shuffle tracks, make random selections, or create a directory of songs by name, you can use a specialized music CD program starting with applications shipped as part of a package with sound cards from most makers.

An internal analog output connects the CD to your sound card, allowing you to use the sound card to drive speakers attached to your PC. You can also use the sound card to record tracks or samples from a CD onto your hard drive. Keep in mind that in doing so, you are sending the data on the original CD through two conversions: from digital information on the disc through a digital-to-analog converter on the CD and then through an analog-to-digital converter on the sound card. You are also giving up a lot of the precision that is part of a digitally recorded and stored music file.

Most modern CD drives also allow you to directly output the digital audio files from a disc, in what is called *digital audio extraction*. You can use this facility to directly record digital files on your hard drive, or output a signal to an advanced home stereo system with digital inputs.

New CD-R technologies

Even with the advent of DVDs, manufacturers continue to push the boundaries of CDs. In 2001, a pair of advanced technologies were introduced, one boosting the potential speed of recording and the other creating yet another incompatible standard for storage of data.

Yamaha brought to market the CRW2200EZ, which is the first consumer-level CD-R able to record discs at 20X. The device uses a technology called Partial CAV that adapts the drive's recording speed so that the motor spins faster as the write head moves to the outer portions of the disc. The drive includes a capacious 8MB buffer to help avoid buffer underruns. The drive can read discs made on other machines, and the discs that it creates can be used on other modern CD drives.

In mid-2001, Sony introduced the first double-density CD-RW device, the CRX200E. This drive uses a specialized double-density CD-R or CD-RW disc that can store as much as 1.3GB of data. The discs sold for as much as $3 at the time of this writing, and the resulting discs can be read only on a Sony Double Density drive. (The drive can also read and write standard CD-R and CD-RW discs.)

High-Capacity DVD

A DVD is just like a CD, only more so; *much* more so, actually. CDs record only on one side and have only a single layer of information, but DVDs can have two layers on either side of the disc. And the spiral tracks of the disc are less than half the width used on a CD. The net result is discs that can hold 9.4GB, with even larger capacities including a 17GB disc under plan.

Just as the CD-ROM was an outgrowth of a consumer audio disc system, DVD traces its roots back to a scheme for a consumer video delivery technology called *digital video disk*. Today, DVD officially stands for *digital versatile disk*. The video part was dropped as the industry realized that this technology was, indeed, more versatile than just video. DVD is a fast-rising technology destined to change the way you store data on your computer and the way you entertain yourself in front of the tube.

This technology crosses the boundary between entertainment and data storage, promising the possibility of a single device that can work with your computer and your television for music, movies, and data. The original DVD standard was developed to link a special entertainment player to a television set. DVD-ROM is the computer industry's adaptation of that standard for use in PCs. DVD drives for televisions can't play DVD-ROMs, but DVD-ROM drives attached to a computer are capable of playing DVD video disks.

Today's DVD represents an extraordinarily capable hodge-podge of sometimes conflicting aims and standards.

The computer, consumer electronics, movie, and record industries embraced DVDs for various purposes. Many of the incompatible standards have been resolved, although at the time of this writing, two standards groups continue to compete, the predominant DVD Forum and the smaller but aggressive DVD+RW Alliance. The good news is that the latest DVD devices incorporate support for many—if not all—of the various standards.

Pre-recorded discs, which are the same physical size and shape as a CD, can hold about 4.7GB, about seven times as much as a CD.

Recordable DVDs were introduced in 1998; the first DVD-RAM units could record 2.6GB per side. The high cost of these devices, though, prevented wide acceptance. A year later, the DVD Forum introduced the DVD-RAM 2.0 specification, which boosted capacity of the recordable drives to the same 4.7GB capacity as prerecorded discs. A subsequent DVD RAM 2.1 standard embraced 1.45GB per side mini discs for use in digital cameras and appliances.

As with CD-ROMs, recording and playback speeds are measured as they relate to the speed of the original device in the class. The first generation of DVD-ROMs was able to read data from discs at about 1.3MB per second. Current technology allows DVD-ROMs to read at two and four times that rate; they are referred to as 2X and 4X devices. Faster DVD-ROMs are also capable of reading CD-ROM discs at greater speeds, equivalent to about a 32X CD-ROM device.

As with CDs, several types of drives are in circulation. And as in the early days of the CD, several competing and not-fully compatible versions of DVD recorders are available. Here are the three basic types of drives:

- **DVDs (also called DVD-Video)** are used for the storage of video, and are capable of holding an entire movie with added interactive features, including interviews with actors, directors, and critics. At the time of this writing, though, consumer DVD players can't read DVD-ROMs.

Ch 12

- **DVD-ROMs** in a computer can read prerecorded DVDs holding video, audio, and data. They can also read DVDs created by some types of DVD recorders.
- **DVD recorders** in a computer can create data, audio, and video discs.

The basic technology of DVDs is similar to that of CDs. Data is stored in the form of tiny bumps (called *lands*) and holes (called *pits*) recorded along a single spiral track that runs from the interior of the disc to the outside. A laser beam focuses on the spiral as it spins; the lands reflect light while the pits do not. A converter in the drive converts the pulses into the 0s and 1s that make up the binary code used for data in a computer.

DVDs are able to store much more information than a CD because they use tracks that are much closer together: 0.74 microns wide, compared to 1.6 microns for a CD.

To record the data in such a narrow track, DVDs use a different type of laser than employed by a CD. This same laser is unable to read the various types of CDs, and so modern DVD-ROM manufacturers put a second CD-only laser in the drive. The DVD's recording laser heats spots on special recordable discs to change a land into a pit.

Recording-capable DVD drives let you store data on special discs called *blanks*. When the recording laser in these drives hits the light-sensitive material on the disc surface, tiny reflective blocks become nonreflective, like the pits on commercially pressed DVDs. The following types of recording-capable DVD drives are available:

- **DVD-R** devices could initially read and write (just once) DVD-R discs at 3.95GB, later increased to 4.7GB. This class of machines can also read and write CD-R and CD-RW discs at 650MB. Single-sided DVD-R media take about half an hour to record at double speed. The first DVD-R machines were priced at as much as $15,000. At the time of this writing,

prices of DVD-Rs from Pioneer dropped below $1,000 for the first time; as with most other technologies, you can expect prices to decline over time as speeds and capabilities increase. The DVD Forum has subdivided the standard into DVD-R(A) for commercial authoring, and DVD-R(G) for general or consumer use. DVD-R(A) is intended for creation of master for mass duplication. Discs for the consumer DVD-R(G) sold for as little as $15 in 2002. Developed primarily by Pioneer, this standard is similar to CD-R in its design. It uses an organic dye for write-once recording.

- The **DVD-RAM** allows multiple writing and rewriting sessions on special discs loaded in cartridges; the original discs could hold as much as 2.6GB per side. At the time of this writing, DVD-RAM devices had advanced to 4.7GB in single-sided cartridges and 9.4GB in double-sided holders. Single-sided discs sold for about $30. A combination 4.7/9.4 DVD-RAM sold for about $500; the most current units were capable of reading from and writing to DVD-RAM, CD-R, and CD-RW discs and reading from DVD-ROM and CD format discs. Developed by Panasonic, Toshiba, and Hitachi. The discs use a phase-change chemical allowing for multiple writing and rewriting. The resulting discs are not compatible with standard DVD-ROM drives.
- **DVD-RW (DVD-Rewritable)** was first developed for use in consumer electronics devices, including DVD video recorders; it, too, has a capacity of 4.7GB. This format uses the simplest standard, and does not support full random access or defect management. Although some computer DVD recorders may incorporate support for reading and writing to this standard, this standard is not well suited for storage of data. Developed by Pioneer, similar to CD-RW in design, it uses a phase-change chemical for multiple recording. Sold in Japan as a home video recorder.

■ **DVD + RW (DVD Plus Rewritable)** is backed by the rival DVD + RW Alliance, which is primarily backed by Hewlett-Packard, Philips, Ricoh, and Thomson Multimedia. It can be used for data as well as video and consumer electronics applications, and as first released, it supports storage of as much as 4.7GB on single-sided discs and 9.4GB on double-sided media. DVD + RW units are capable of reading and multiple writes to DVD + RW media, as well as the ability to record CD-R and CD-RW discs and read DVD-R and DVD-RW discs.

One potential advantage of DVD + RW is the ability to transparently switch between data and video modes, allowing use for interactive training and entertainment. A future enhancement of the standard will include support for DVD + R (write-once) media. Developed by Sony, HP, Yamaha, and Philips. Uses a phase-change chemical for multiple recording; high-frequency wobbled grooves allow discs to be used in DVD-ROM drives.

How DVD drives work

DVD drives and recorders work similarly to their CD equivalents. Data is written by using phase-change recording; the heat of a laser changes a spot from crystalline to a less-reflective form. When the disc is read, the laser detects differences between reflective and non-reflective areas and converts them to 0s and 1s. To erase or rewrite a block of data, a lower-powered laser reheats portions of the disc to change them back to crystalline form.

The main difference between the two types of systems is the density of data. A conventional CD-ROM platter has a single substrate on a 1.2mm-thick disk, while DVDs layer two 0.6mm substrates on the same 1.2mm platter. The DVD drives use a shorter wavelength of light as well. CD-ROM drive lasers operate at about 780 nanometers, in the infrared range, and DVD drives use a light source between 650 and 635 nanometers (red light).

DVD *track pitch* (the space between tracks), at 0.74 micrometers, is about half that of a CD, and DVD recorders can write pits and lands as small as 0.4 micrometers, compared to a CD-ROM's 0.83 micrometer lands and pits. Also, DVDs can use two data layers on one side of a disc, for a top capacity of up to 8.5GB. That's up to four hours of high-quality video and a whole lot of computer information. The DVD standard actually specifies formats that range from 2.6 to 17GB:

Single-sided, single layer	2.6GB
Double-sided, single layer	5.2GB
Single-sided, single layer Version 2	4.7GB
Single-sided, double layer Version 2	8.5GB
Double-sided, single layer Version 2	9.4GB
Double-sided, double layer Version 2	17GB

Nearly all designs for high-capacity double-sided DVDs require the discs to reside in cartridges or caddies, although (like early CD-ROM designs) this may change over time.

You can see Hollywood's influence on these specifications in the fact that early DVD drives were designed to accommodate a feature film's typical running length of about two hours. But the DVD-ROM specification goes beyond mere picture and sound.

With compression, a full-motion image requires about 3,500 kilobits per second to display. Stereo surround-sound demands an additional 384 kilobits per second. But the international entertainment industry lobbied for three additional sound tracks for foreign language dubbing, plus four tracks of information to enable the inclusion of a quartet of subtitles. Another use of the image storage space would be to offer different versions of the same film — perhaps a PG-13 and an R version, with a password protection device on the player so that parents can provide guidance. The total space envisioned for video and audio entertainment would then require about 4,692 kilobits per second; multiply that by two hours, and you have space for a full motion picture with bells and whistles on one side of a DVD disk.

Ch 12

DVD is also set up to display movies in three different ways, depending on personal preference and the artistic judgment of the director. The wide screen version yields an anamorphic video signal that can be used with a special wide-screen television set to fill the entire screen as if it were a movie screen. The pan and scan version uses current methodology to fill the screen of a traditional television with a specially edited version of the film that does not cut off the parts of the image that would otherwise appear off the edges of the screen. The letterbox mode displays the full image across the width of a traditional TV screen and fills the top and bottom with black bands.

The DVD-ROM specification includes MPEG-2 compression to pack as much image information as possible on the disk. MPEG is a form of differencing compression. A basic frame is stored, and then subsequent bits of information describe the difference between the reference frame and subsequent frames.

System requirements for a DVD

If you're buying a new PC, chances are you have a DVD drive or at least were offered the option of putting one on when you ordered it. If you're working with an older machine and you are enticed into upgrading from a CD-ROM to DVD drive, just make sure you have the CPU horsepower required to make it work adequately.

Consumer-grade DVD-ROMs use the computer's CPU to do the processing of MPEG-2 video for movies and multimedia applications; this is not a strain for computers with microprocessors running at about 300 MHz and faster. On slower computers, movies may drop frames or not run at all.

If you have an older machine, you can take the load off your CPU by installing an inexpensive MPEG-2 card, which has its own dedicated processor for video purposes.

When it comes to playing back a video DVD, your computer monitor offers better resolution than a television set. To get the best sound quality, connect the output of the DVD to an audio system that accepts digital audio input and can process Dolby Digital surround sound (sometimes referred to as 5.1-channel sound).

CD and DVD Interfaces

Today, five common interface designs are used to connect CD and DVD drives to your PC: IDE, USB, FireWire, SCSI, and parallel port.

The simplest way to add a CD or DVD drive is to attach an external device to a USB and FireWire, both Plug-and-Play connections. If you already have an SCSI interface in your machine, it can easily be extended to additional devices.

Making a connection to an IDE port is relatively easy using standardized connectors. The process does require opening the computer's case and connecting cables and power supplies. Some manufacturers strongly recommend that your CD drive not be installed on the same IDE interface with a hard drive, so that the hard drive is not slowed down because of the lower access and transfer speed of the CD drive.

A group of CD-ROM drives also connects to a PC through an EPP (enhanced parallel port). I worked with one such device, a Backpack portable CD-ROM drive, shown in Figure 12-2. Other models include serial, USB (as previously mentioned), and PC Card connections; one model combines all three means of access.

The first wave of external CD drives were notably slower than internal devices, but current units come close to matching their speed. Modern external CD-R, CD-RW, and DVD drives are now available using high-speed connections, including SCSI, USB, and FireWire connections. The advantage of USB and FireWire connections is Plug-and-Play installation. Early USB drives were hampered by the slow throughput of USB 1.1, but the new USB 2.0 interface delivers blazing speed; you'll need USB 2.0 circuitry on the motherboard or in an adapter card. And you will need USB 2.0 drivers for Windows; the first release of the driver was intended for Windows XP. External units typically cost $50 to $100 more than internal equivalents; the extra money pays for a case, cable, and power supply. Figure 12-3 shows a CD-R unit that connects to an SCSI port.

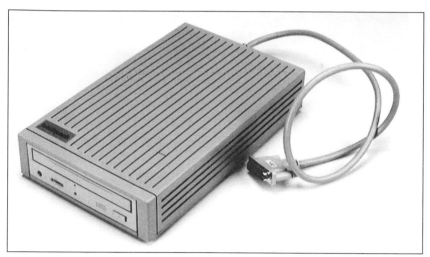

FIGURE 12-2: *This Backpack external CD-ROM drive connects to a modern machine's parallel port, without the need to install internal adapters or cables. Other external portables connect to USB or PC Card ports.*

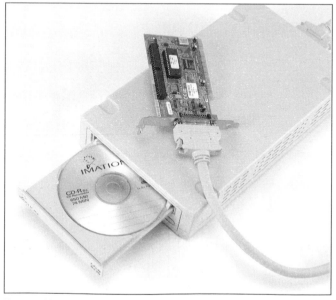

FIGURE 12-3: *An external CD-R from Imation that uses an SCSI connection to record at speeds up to 8X and play back at a respectable 20X rate.*

Installing a CD or DVD drive

All CD and DVD drives install in the same way. Internal devices connect to a data stream from an IDE/ATAPI controller or an SCSI adapter, and in most cases, to the audio input and output of a sound card or sound circuitry integrated on the motherboard.

The typical drive requires three connecting cables: a power line that branches off the power supply, a large data cable that connects to an IDE or SCSI adapter, and a small cable that delivers audio to or from the sound card. A typical set of connectors for a CD-R is shown in Figure 12-4.

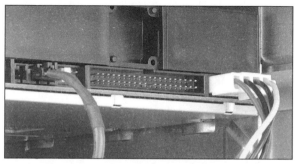

FIGURE 12-4: *The connectors on the back of this internal CD-RW are, from left to right, an empty connector for Digital Audio output (SPDIF) for some advanced sound card functions; a CD Audio analog output for playing standard audio through a sound card; a set of jumpers for configuration adjustments; an open connector for an IDE data cable, and a power cable.*

Internal drives, such as hard drives, should be mounted in the computer with screws or rails. A drive kit should include rails plus data and audio cables. If you purchase a bare drive from a computer supply house, you will need to assemble your own cables and rails; they are available for separate purchase.

Many senior citizen CD-ROMs used a proprietary SCSI channel provided as a component of some sound cards. The proprietary interfaces are rarely faster than standard SCSI or even IDE and are by design limited in expandability; they are, however, less costly to manufacture. Start with an analysis of any interface cards you may already have in your system. You don't want to unnecessarily give up one of the relatively few available slots on the motherboard.

If you have a sound card with a proprietary interface, check with the manufacturer to determine which CD-ROM drives it works with. Also be sure to find out about any necessary cables or adapters. If you intend to use an SCSI port that is part of a sound card, make sure that the SCSI adapter is at least a 16-bit model. Don't be confused by the description of the sound capabilities of the board, which may refer to the width of the board's audio channel. Check the specs or call the manufacturer to determine the nature of the SCSI portion of the card. Be aware, too, that the SCSI adapter included with many sound cards is designed to work only with a CD-ROM drive, and sometimes only a specific CD-ROM drive. It may not be a fully functioning, standard SCSI interface that you can use with other SCSI devices, such as hard drives.

In summary, this class of proprietary drives is too slow and limited in its facilities for modern machines; if you have such a setup, you should consider installing a new CD or DVD drive. CD-ROMs that connect to IDE ports are available for as little as $40, and CD-RWs for as little as $99 at the time of this writing.

NOTE

If you install a drive to an IDE controller, try installing it as a master on the secondary IDE connector (assuming it uses an IDE interface). Many of these drives may not work well as the slave drive on an IDE bus. They also may not work well if they share the same IDE connector as a hard disk drive. Here's a place to pay close attention to the instruction manual for the installation of the CD drive.

Installing and testing drives and adapter cards

The hard part of installing a CD-ROM or DVD drive usually comes from the software, not the hardware side. While an IDE adapter is already set up for use with a CD drive, if you are working with an SCSI adapter card, in most cases, you must properly configure the adapter as well as properly set up Windows or other operating systems to work with the drive.

SCSI adapter cards

To install or test the adapter card, use standard SCSI device troubleshooting and installation techniques. If your CD-ROM drive and sound card were sold as a packaged set, they are sure to be set up to enable the disk to communicate both data and sound.

If you have mixed and matched an SCSI or other controller and the CD-ROM drive, you have to make another internal connection between the audio output of your CD-ROM drive to the sound card. Unfortunately, no single standard exists for the construction of the cable that runs between the two devices; consult the instruction manuals for your CD-ROM or DVD drive and sound card or call the manufacturers for information.

Software considerations

When CDs first arrived on the scene, they were a completely alien species to the operating system. As such, users had to install Microsoft's MSCDEX extension drivers to expand DOS and Windows. If you're still working with Windows 3.1, you'll need to make sure that the driver is added to the operating system; the latest version is available through www.microsoft.com (search for MSCDEX) and should also be a part of installation diskettes or CDs provided by the CD-ROM maker.

Today, MSCDEX is an integrated part of Windows 95/98 and later versions, including Windows XP. The driver should automatically recognize nearly all CD and DVD drives. Any unusual drives should come with their own installation software that will adapt the operating system.

An essential component of any CD-R or CD-RW installation is a capable software program to manage burning data and audio discs. Many drives come equipped with a basic program, such as Roxio's Easy CD Creator, and Windows XP includes its own basic version of such software. For more advanced facilities, including the ability to create MP3 audio discs and video and digital still slideshow discs, a program such as Roxio's Easy CD Creator Platinum is required.

Troubleshooting a CD or DVD Installation

If your CD or DVD drive doesn't work after installation, consider taking the following troubleshooting steps:

- Use the Device Properties reports of Windows 95/98 and later Windows versions to check for conflicts among IRQs, DMAs, and I/O ports that may have slipped through, despite the best efforts of the Plug-and-Play wizard. See Chapter 23 for details on troubleshooting Windows.
- Does the unit show up in the Device Manager display of Windows? If not, it may not be receiving electrical power or be properly connected to the data bus.
- To check if the drive is receiving power, press its eject button to see if the door will open or one of its front panel lights will flash.
- The next step is to disconnect the power from the PC and remove the covers. Confirm that the power connector is properly attached to the pins on the CD or DVD; most power connectors click into a holder and are unlikely to work themselves out of the socket, but they can be dislodged if they were not fully seated when installed.
- Next check the gray or beige IDE ribbon cable that carries data to and from the computer bus. On nearly all internal storage devices, the red stripe on the cable should be facing the power connector. Check to see that the cable is properly seated and that pins on the socket are not bent out of position.

- Follow the data cable from the CD or DVD to the connector on the motherboard (or in some cases, a connector on a plug-in IDE controller in the bus). Make sure that it is properly installed and that the pins on the socket are not bent out of position.
- If your CD or DVD is receiving power but the drive door won't open, the device may possibly have a mechanical problem. In some instances, a CD or DVD that is not centered properly in the drawer can jam the mechanism. Most devices have a small pinhole on the front to manually eject the drawer; insert a straightened paper clip or small screwdriver into the hole and push gently to open the drawer.
- On a newly installed drive, it is possible that mounting screws tightened too firmly on the mounting rails can block the movement of the drawer. Try loosening the screws slightly.

Problems recording a disc

When everything goes well, burning a CD-R, CD-RW, or DVD-R is more-or-less a point and click operation. However, a recording process can be disrupted or ruined in many, many ways. The main source of the problem is that the making of CDs or DVDs, especially audio or video discs, requires nearly all of the computer's attention. Any other process can interrupt the stream of data to the recorder, resulting in a corrupted disc or an aborted session.

CD and DVD recorders have a small block of memory that serves as a buffer to keep a constant supply of data. Think of the buffer as a bucket; new data comes into the top, while the recorder draws out stored data from the bottom. If the flow of data to the buffer is interrupted long enough to result in a gap, the recording session will stop because of a *buffer underrun*.

Ch 12

Here are some tips on safe recording:

- Disconnect from the Internet.
- Turn off screen savers.
- Disable antivirus software for the duration of the session.
- Turn off any other software that may come to life during the recording session.
- If your hard disk is more than 5 percent fragmented, run a defragmenter before burning a CD or DVD.
- Make sure that you have enough free space on your hard drive. Most CD-recording software needs temporary space equivalent to the size of the CD that it will create, at least 700 MB; DVD-recording software works in a similar manner, although files are typically divided into segments smaller than the total size of the drive, and recorded segment by segment.
- Use the facilities of your recording software to test the facilities of your recorder and the capabilities of your PC before you write your first disc and after any significant change to your setup.
- Keep all discs clean, especially unrecorded ones. Smudges, fingerprints, or dust on a virgin disc can affect the recording process.
- Use a soft-tip marker to label a disc on the top or printed side of a CD or DVD. Don't write on the bottom where the data tracks of a CD are recorded. Never apply an ordinary paper label to a disc; sooner or later they will come off and jam inside your player or recorder.

Note that if a recording session is interrupted, the CD-R is most likely unusable and should be thrown away. A CD-RW or DVD-R can most likely be reformatted and used again.

If you are concerned about the security of the data on a CD that you are throwing away, the best way to disable a disc is to cut it in half. But please be very careful in doing so: the disc can shatter into very sharp pieces. Use a heavy-duty paper cutter or shears, holding the disc at arms length and away from your eyes and face.

Changing the drive letter for a CD-ROM or DVD

When you install additional drives in a system, other drives may have their identifying drive letters changed. IDE hard drives will automatically occupy the lowest letters, beginning with C.

If you want to adjust the designation for other drives, you can change the Reserved Drive Letter for each. From the desktop, right-click on My Computer. From the menu, choose Properties, and select the Device Manager tab. Expand the listing for the drive that you want to adjust.

Under Windows XP, click on Start, then right-click on My Computer. From the menu, choose Properties. Select the Hardware tab and then choose Device Manager.

For example, to specify a setting for your CD-ROM, expand the listing for that class of device by clicking on the + symbol. Select your particular device and click on the Properties button and then on the Settings tab.

At the bottom of the panel is the Reserved Drive Letters section. Here you can set a start and end for a range of letters, or you can specify a particular available letter by using the same character for both start and end.

Reboot the system after any change.

SUMMARY

This chapter completes my spin through the world of CDs and DVDS. In the next two chapters, I look at video adapters and computer monitors.

Notes

Ch
12

Chapter 13

Tools Needed:

- Phillips screwdriver

Video Display Adapters and Standards

The video monitor is your view into the computer. No matter how impressive the PC, no matter how dazzling the software, if your monitor is too fuzzy for you to view what's on the screen or too slow to keep up with your work pace, you're looking straight into frustration and aggravation.

Computer video uses different standards and specifications than the Panasonic in your family room. To begin with, your computer monitor receives only one channel — the signal coming from the video card of the PC. The adapter is responsible for converting the information within your computer into a stream of information that can be displayed on your monitor.

This chapter examines the commonly available display standards for modern machines, including the current, ubiquitous standard, SVGA, and the previous champion, VGA. It also helps with troubleshooting and upgrading from dinosaur standards, including MDA, CGA, and EGA. (A modern display adapter includes both graphics and text-mode abilities, whereas a dinosaur text-mode adapter has only the one function of displaying predefined characters.) I review such arcane standards as 8514/A, XGA, and TIGA, and I also introduce the state-of-the-art accelerated graphics port (AGP), a nonstop throughway from your video display adapter to the CPU and system memory.

What Makes Good Video?

A good place to begin is with a quick description of how monitors work. When you look at a computer screen, as well as at a television, you are looking through the front glass at an image that is drawn on its backside. The image is made up of hundreds of thousands or even millions of little phosphor dots that glow when they are struck by a moving electron beam produced by the monitor's electronics, controlled by the video display adapter, and based on data produced by the computer.

Why am I beginning a discussion of video display adapters by describing how a monitor works? Because a good display is a function of the highest capabilities of both the display adapter and the monitor. Today's PCs have all but abandoned text-mode displays, so I'm concentrating on graphics. The next sections describe the elements of monitors.

CROSS-REFERENCE

Chapter 14 goes into more detail on how monitors work.

Pixels

A *pixel* (the term comes from *picture element*) is an individually controllable set of dot triads on a traditional monitor screen. Each triad consists of one red dot, one green dot, and one blue dot. The number of dot triads in one pixel depends on the size of the pixel and on how close together the dots are located. The video display adapter tells the monitor what color each pixel should be, and the monitor's electronics energize each pixel's red, green, and blue dots to produce the desired color. A pixel on a monitor using Sony's Trinitron technology, which covers the screen with thousands of thin vertical stripes of red, green, and blue phosphor, consists of a short vertical portion of three adjacent stripes.

Another monitor, NEC's ChromaClear, blends dot triads and Trinitron features by using vertical oval phosphors. When combined with a slot mask, the phosphors appear elliptical in shape, compared to round phosphors of dot triads and stripes of a Trinitron.

Resolution

Resolution is a measure of the number of individually controllable pixels on a monitor screen. The higher the stated resolution, the more information can theoretically be displayed, but this is just one part of the sharpness equation. Maximum resolution is determined by the highest capability of the video display adapter and the monitor. A monitor can't display more pixels than a video adapter is capable of describing, and a video display adapter can't command a monitor to use more pixels than the monitor was designed to use.

Resolution is generally described in terms of the number of horizontal dots and the number of vertical dots that a screen can hold. The basic PC resolution is expressed as 640 x 480 pixels, meaning 640 pixels horizontally and 480 pixels vertically. Modern display adapter and monitor combinations routinely display 1,024 x 768 pixels or 1,280 x 1,024 pixels. On current larger monitor screens, resolution generally reaches as much as 1,920 x 1,440 pixels.

Dot pitch

Dot pitch is a monitor specification that tells you how closely together the dots are located. The finer the dot pitch (the lower the number), theoretically, the finer the image. Today's better monitors have a dot pitch of 0.28 mm or less, and as fine as 0.24 mm on some consumer-grade devices. Sometimes monitors are measured in *mask pitch*, which gives a slightly smaller measurement than the monitor's dot pitch, but is otherwise comparable. One exception to dot or mask pitch measurement comes from monitors that use Sony's Trinitron technology; these screens use a grille of fine vertical wires that keep electrons from unintentionally striking neighboring stripes. Specifications for Trinitron devices are measured in *aperture grille pitch*, and 0.24 mm is considered quite good. Another exception is NEC's ChromaClear technology and other dot-mask/Trinitron hybrids, which express the fineness of their screens in mask or *slot pitch*, and like the Trinitron, 0.24 mm is quite good.

Refresh rate

Also called vertical scanning rate, *refresh rate* is a measure of how often the monitor rewrites the screen. The higher the refresh rate, the more stable the image appears and the less chance of apparent flicker.

Image quality

Some monitors are simply higher quality than others, using better and brighter phosphors or better electronics that can produce whiter whites and more brilliant colors. On monochrome monitors, the best displays are capable of producing a wide range of grayscale hues that improve the quality of graphics and text. Image quality is mostly in the eye of the beholder, although reviews of monitors can measure brightness and color intensity.

In my opinion, one of the most important and telling measures of image quality is the whiteness of whites and the blackness of blacks, even on a color monitor. Open a word processor application, for example, and set the background color to paper white if it isn't already the default. If black text on this white background doesn't have a crisp black-on-white, printed appearance, the rest of the monitor may not be up to par. Some low-end monitors tend to produce a gray-cast white and black that isn't sharp and distinct.

Number of colors

The more colors a monitor produces, the more apparent depth and realism an onscreen image has. Think of colors as information. The capability of a display to show 30 variations of forest green, for example, makes it possible to have much more detail in a wildlife scene. The number of colors that a monitor can produce is dependent upon the video display adapter. To use more colors, a display adapter needs a great deal of video memory.

Like resolution, the number of colors that an adapter displays affects overall image quality, as well as user acceptability — particularly with today's graphical operating systems and software applications.

The most basic display adapters display 16 colors. This range is enough to determine that color is present on the screen, but you won't be happy with that limited selection after you've had a look at your neighbor's machine, or at a television screen, for that matter. The next step up is 256 colors, which is, by most opinions, the absolute minimum setting for Windows. After you've seen screens capable of displaying thousands or millions of colors, however, you'll set your goals higher.

Most display adapters delivered with today's modern machines contain at least 8MB of RAM — many have 16MB or 32MB, and some advanced adapters offer 64MB — so you can get much better color rendition than was possible with earlier display adapters that contained only 1 or 2MB of RAM.

To see what your computer is using, in Windows 95/98 and later versions including Windows XP, right-click anywhere on the desktop and choose Properties. Click the Settings tab and note the

Colors group in the lower-left corner of the dialog box. You can pull down a list of settings by clicking the down arrow to the right of this field to see what your display adapter is capable of displaying. If you see 16 or 256 in this field, try a higher setting, true color (16 bit for 65K colors) at the minimum, and true color (32 bit for over 4 billion colors) if you have it. These settings provide the best color rendition with most operating systems and application combinations.

Speed

The speed at which a video display adapter can construct graphic images and send them to the monitor for display becomes an important measure for graphics programs and graphical user interfaces, such as Windows. The more colors and the greater the resolution, the harder the video display adapter has to work to produce images. Modern adapters, especially those connected to the local bus of the CPU and/or equipped with a graphics accelerator, work much faster than earlier adapters. For any adapter working at its top speed, however, the more information (resolution and/or colors) it displays onscreen, the slower those scenes are constructed and displayed (refresh rate).

Designers boost the speed of video adapters in several ways:

- By tightly integrating the circuitry into a chipset
- By using specialized high-speed memory
- By widening the video bus width on the card

The video bus width is the highway between the chipset and the memory. The top end of video adapters offer a 64-bit or 128-bit bus; the video bus width still has to meet up with and work with the 32-bit or 64-bit PCI or AGP bus on the computer's motherboard.

The Video Display Adapter

The video display adapter has most of the brains of the team; the monitor mostly follows orders. The adapter controls the resolution, the scan rate, and the colors or shades of gray available on a particular monitor. Of course, the adapter can't order color on a monochrome monitor, nor can it ask for a screen resolution greater than the physical capability of the display. On the same token, a monitor with extraordinary facilities is underutilized by working with a low-end display adapter or one with insufficient memory to display a full range of colors.

In the early days of the PC, video standards were based on a *digital signal*—a redirection of the internal bit map within the computer. This delivered a high-quality signal, but one that had to precisely describe every color; until recent years, the cost of memory limited the ability of adapters to work with thousands and millions of colors. With the arrival of the VGA specification, adapters changed over to an analog design that converted the bitmap from digital to analog and opened the door to more colors and gradations. Today, improved electronics and the sharp drop in the cost of memory are fueling a return to digital adapters; they are already used for many LCDs, and future designs for monitors show a changeover to digital sources.

In the original design of the PC and on many modern machines, the display adapter is a card that fits into a slot on the expansion bus or—in a local bus or accelerated-graphics-port design—into a slot that connects more or less directly to the CPU. Some modern machines place the display adapter circuitry on the motherboard itself; this move typically saves a bit on cost, but may reduce flexibility when it comes to upgrades or repairs.

Until 1997, nearly all modern machines used a PCI slot for the video display adapter, helping to boost speed in a graphics-intensive world. An older but still capable PCI card is shown in Figure 13-1. Beginning with the advent of ATX-design motherboards, most modern machines offer a high-speed, accelerated graphics port (AGP) connector for video display adapters that meet its specifications.

FIGURE 13-1: *Diamond Stealth 3-D PCI bus video display adapter card*

However, you don't have to use an AGP card on a system with an AGP port; you can still plug a video adapter into the PCI bus. (And if you plan on using two monitors, you'll need a second video adapter in the PCI bus.) On the other hand, if you have an older industry standard architecture (ISA) bus machine, you may find it difficult to obtain state-of-the art video display adapters; you may have to search sources for used computer parts, or specialty computer suppliers.

NOTE

Nearly all modern display cards have their own ROM BIOS chips that extend the basic video graphics facilities of your PC. The ROM chips are much slower than the RAM that makes up your system memory. Most modern machine BIOS configuration programs have facilities to automatically duplicate the display adapter's ROM code in RAM at startup so that the code can be run from the faster RAM. If you have an older machine, you may be able to obtain a utility from the maker of your display card that relocates the contents of the display BIOS into system memory. Check your instruction manual for details.

Video display adapters also often require device drivers that are added to your operating system to let your operating system know about the capabilities of the card. The instruction manual for the card should give details on installation of the drivers.

Keep in touch with the maker of your display adapter, especially if you have purchased a state-of-the-art device or if your operating system goes through any significant changes. Most display adapter makers regularly post updated or improved versions of their device drivers on the Internet, or will send them to registered users. Newer drivers can improve speed, add features, or fix bugs in previous releases.

In any case, it pays to have a fully capable display adapter and as good a monitor as you can justify buying. If you're upgrading in stages, buy the display adapter first. As noted previously, if the monitor's capabilities are greater than those of the adapter, you won't be able to take advantage of the monitor's capabilities.

You should also realize that many dinosaur PCs can't be upgraded to VGA and SVGA because of limitations in their ROM BIOS. Check with the PC manufacturer or the maker of the video display adapter to be sure. In some cases, you may be able to upgrade the BIOS of an old machine.

AGP: Getting Graphics off the Bus

PCI bus video adapters were — and are — able to perform quite well with standard business software, but the increased demands of graphics programs and especially 3-D gaming and design applications have moved well beyond their capabilities. Intel introduced the accelerated graphics port (AGP) design on motherboards in 1997.

AGP is not a replacement for the PCI bus as a general I/O interface. AGP is physically, logically, and electrically independent of the PCI bus; it is designed solely for the use of a graphics controller. Table 13-1 shows a comparison of AGP to the PCI bus.

TABLE 13-1: Video Bus Comparison	
Bus	**Maximum Theoretical Throughput**
PCI	132MB/second on 66MHz system bus
	200MB/second on 100MHz system bus
AGP	266MB/second
AGP2X	533MB/second
AGP4X	1.06GB/second
AGP8X	2.12GB/second

The original AGP bus extension ran at 66MHz, which was twice the speed of the PCI bus at the time of its introduction. The next step was AGP2X, which ran at 133MHz. Today, modern systems offer AGP4X ports; AGP8X technology is on its way. Like AGP4X, AGP8X implements a 32-bit wide bus, but the new specification allows a doubling of speed to 533 MHz and supports a data rate of two gigabytes per second (2GB/second).

Among the ways AGP speeds video processing is to use main PC memory to hold large 3-D images and their associated complex texture data — in effect, giving the AGP video card an unlimited amount of video memory (or at least up to the limits of available main PC memory). Accordingly, the AGP was intended to be accompanied by a large amount of system memory; happily for PC users, the price of most forms of RAM has dropped precipitously just as the need for more memory has increased.

To speed up data transfer, Intel designed the port as a direct path to the PC's main memory by using a design called Direct Memory Execute, or DIME. AGP uses a 32-bit connector, like a PCI device, but the video bus connector has 64 contacts and a 64-bit-wide data path between the graphics chipset on the card and the specialized graphics memory nearby. Figure 13-2 shows a current AGP card based on the nVidia2 chipset.

On an ATX-format motherboard, the AGP slot is positioned between the CPU's support chipsets and the graphics controller. This enables rapid transfer of information between the PC's graphics controller and system memory. Conventional technology uses the PCI bus (or whatever expansion bus is part of the design) to prefetch graphics data from system memory and deliver it to the graphics controller's RAM; AGP uses a separate high-speed bus for this memory-to-controller data interchange.

FIGURE 13-2: *This modern 4X AGP card includes 32MB of memory and offers an analog port for a computer monitor, as well as an S-VHS connector to display an image on a television set.*

With AGP, the graphics controller can execute texture maps directly from system memory rather than caching them in the controller's local RAM. AGP also facilitates transfer and display of motion video, an increasing part of the online and desktop computing experience.

The AGP design enables main system memory to be allocated to support 3-D facilities, enabling high-speed image creation and transport. This sort of design has been previously used in graphics workstations, but not in PCs.

AGP enables 3-D textures to be stored in the computer's memory and transferred to the graphics accelerator at high speed. Because memory in the PC itself can be used to supplement onboard graphics memory, there is less need for more costly specialized graphics memory on the card.

Remember that you need both a motherboard with an AGP slot and an operating system that supports its facilities. Windows 95

does not fully support AGP, and in many cases, Device Manager will report device conflict errors if you attempt to use such a card. If the card works despite the error message, you can continue to use the older operating system; if not, you'll need to update to Windows 98 or a later version.

Step by Step: How a Video Display Adapter Works

When an application or the operating system calls for the display of an image on your monitor, it sends a request to an element of the operating system, the *graphics driver interface* (GDI). The GDI hooks into the graphics driver designed specifically for your particular video display adapter. The graphics driver translates the request from the operating system into instructions that can be executed by the video display adapter.

NOTE

An outdated or corrupted driver is a common cause for problems with video display adapters, sometimes spilling over to cause problems with other devices, including a mouse or other pointing device. Take the time to check for updates to drivers on the Web site of the manufacturer of your card and on the Windows Update page offered by Microsoft.

Next, the PC moves data from memory across the bus to the video display adapter. On most modern PCs, the data travels from a special slot on the motherboard called the Accelerated Graphics Port. On older PCs, video display adapters plug into PCI or ISA slots.

The board's specialized processor, the *graphics processing unit*, converts the digital data into pixels. At a screen resolution of 1,024 x 768, the processing unit calculates the colors and then creates 786,432 pixels, updating the data 30 to 90 times each second. The pixels are then sent back to the system memory for storage.

Before the image can be displayed on most monitors, the data has to be converted from digital to analog form—changed from precise numerical values to a set of red, green, and blue rising and falling wave signals. The conversion is performed by the video display adapter's random access memory digital-to-analog converter, or *RAMDAC*. The faster the RAMDAC, the higher the potential resolution of the video display adapter and the faster it can refresh the image.

TIP

Most LCD screens and a handful of high-end monitors work directly with digital signals; you'll need a specialized video display adapter to avoid a situation in which pixels are converted from digital to analog and back to digital before display.

The speed at which the board paints pixels is called the *fill rate;* a typical current card can spit out information at about one gigapixel (more than one billion pixels) per second. The screen is painted one line at a time; a fast fill rate permits a fast *frame rate,* also called a *screen refresh rate,* which is a measurement of how many times per second the entire screen is redrawn. Computer video uses a frame rate of at least 30 frames per second, which creates the illusion of movement.

The higher the resolution, the more pixels the video display adapter must produce per frame. The greater the color depth (the number of potential colors) the more information that the card must process. A combination of both can push the video display adapter's GPU and RAMDAC to full capacity, resulting in a slow-down in frame rate.

Video display memory

Display adapters define how many colors your monitor can use to display an image. The more colors the card uses, the more bits of information are necessary to describe each color.

Cards are sometimes categorized by the following color depths: 8 bit (capable of describing as many as 256 colors because $2^8 = 256$), 16 bit (65,536 or 65K), or 24 bit (16,777,216 or 16.8 million).

You will also find some cards described as being 32-bit devices; in theory, this could allow as many as 4,294, 967,296 or 4.3 billion colors. In actuality, however, this is a special graphics mode used by certain games and digital video applications for special effects. In this scheme, 24 bits are used for 16.8 million possible colors, and the other 8 bits are used as a separate layer to represent levels of translucency in an object or image.

Just to make things complex, some cards can also simulate 12 bit and other unusual sizes for computing power. Table 13-2 summarizes common color depths.

TABLE 13-2: Color Depths	
Bit-Depth	**Number of Colors**
1	2 (monochrome)
2	4 (CGA)
4	16 (EGA)
8	256 (VGA)
16	65,536 (High color, XGA)
24	16,777,216 (True color, SVGA)
32	16,777,216 (True color plus alpha channel)

How much memory do you need?

Not sure how much memory you need? In general, more memory is better than less memory; I recommend a minimum of 16MB for a modern machine; 32MB is a more reasonable level for any user working with graphics or games. You'll find current video cards on the market with as little as 4MB and as much as 64MB.

As Table 13-3 demonstrates, all you need to display 16.8 million colors at 1,280 x 1,024 pixel resolution is 4MB of video RAM.

But if you do so, your card has no room left over for advanced graphics manipulation. You really don't want to run most of today's applications with a 2 to 4MB display memory that was common just a few years ago.

TABLE 13-3: Minimum Video Memory Requirements for a Display Adapter				
Resolution	Color Depth	Colors	Memory Needs	RAM Required
640 x 480	4 bit	16	153,600 bytes	256K
640 x 480	8 bit	256	307,200 bytes	512K
640 x 480	16 bit	65,536	614,400 bytes	1MB
640 x 480	24 bit	16,777,216	921,600 bytes	1MB
800 x 600	4 bit	16	240,000 bytes	256K
800 x 600	8 bit	256	480,000 bytes	512K
800 x 600	16 bit	65,536	960,000 bytes	1MB
800 x 600	24 bit	16,777,216	1,440,000 bytes	2MB
1,024 x 768	4 bit	16	393,216 bytes	512K
1,024 x 768	8 bit	256	786,432 bytes	1MB
1,024 x 768	16 bit	65,536	1,572,864 bytes	2MB
1,024 x 768	24 bit	16,777,216	2,359,296 bytes	4MB
1,280 x 1,024	4 bit	16	655,360 bytes	1MB
1,280 x 1,024	8 bit	256	1,310,720 bytes	2MB
1,280 x 1,024	16 bit	65,536	2,621,440 bytes	4MB
1,280 x 1,024	24 bit	16,777,216	3,932,160 bytes	4MB

Here's how to calculate your memory wants and needs: Multiply horizontal resolution by vertical resolution to get the total number of pixels and then multiply this figure by the number of bytes of color. (Remember, 256 possible colors is 8-bit color, which equals 1 byte; 65,536 colors is 16-bit color or 2 bytes; 16.8 million colors is 24-bit color, or true color, and uses 24 bits or 3 bytes.)

For example, the basic 640 x 480 pixel resolution requires about 600K of RAM at 16 bits, just under 1MB of RAM at 24-bit color, and about 1.23MB of RAM for 32-bit color. If you're working with a larger monitor and want to use the higher 800 x 600 pixel resolution, you need about 1MB for 16-bit color, almost 1.4MB for 24 bits, and around 2MB for 32 bits of color depth. Of course, PC RAM, including that on a display adapter, comes only in sizes that are a power of 2. Therefore, the display adapter has 2MB of RAM to support display needs of 1.4MB.

Table 13-4 presents the same information, but this time rearranged to show how the amount of available RAM dictates the number of colors an adapter can show.

TABLE 13-4: How Video Memory Affects Available Colors				
RAM	Resolution	Color Depth	Colors	Memory Needs
256K	640 x 480	4 bit	16	153,600 bytes
256K	800 x 600	4 bit	16	240,000 bytes
512K	640 x 480	8 bit	256	307,200 bytes
512K	800 x 600	8 bit	256	480,000 bytes
512K	1,024 x 768	4 bit	16	393,216 bytes
1MB	640 x 480	16 bit	65,536	614,400 bytes
1MB	640 x 480	24 bit	16,777,216	921,600 bytes
1MB	800 x 600	16 bit	65,536	960,000 bytes
1MB	1,024 x 768	8 bit	256	786,432 bytes
1MB	1,280 x 1,024	4 bit	16	655,360 bytes
2MB	800 x 600	24 bit	16,777,216	1,440,000 bytes
2MB	1,024 x 768	16 bit	65,536	1,572,864 bytes
2MB	1,280 x 1,024	8 bit	256	1,310,720 bytes
4MB	1,024 x 768	24 bit	16,777,216	2,359,296 bytes
4MB	1,280 x 1,024	16 bit	65,536	2,621,440 bytes
4MB	1,280 x 1,024	24 bit	16,777,216	3,932,160 bytes

The values in this table are minimum values. As previously stated, I recommend a minimum of 8MB of video memory if you work at high resolutions and high numbers of colors. And for the latest and greatest in games and high-end graphics applications, my baseline is a 32MB AGP video display card. As you work with display-intensive applications, such as page layout, graphics generation, or games, you'll need memory beyond the basics to realize reasonable speed from the application.

The good news is that the plummeting price of RAM has made video memory inexpensive; and the popularity of AGP has made this addition virtually free. For example, at the time of this writing, you could buy an 8MB AGP card for about $40, the same price as a 4MB card of two years before. In early 2002, you could purchase a basic AGP card with 64MB for about $100 to $130; more advanced high-end video display adapters sold for as much as $400.

Types of memory

Memory on a video card is the electronic scratch pad used by the computer to construct images. The higher the resolution, and the more colors in the palette, the more information that must be stored and then transmitted to the display. Add to this the element of *refresh rate* — the number of times per second the image on the display is redrawn. The combination of all these factors puts a tremendous demand on memory.

Basic video memory from dinosaur days is called DRAM (dynamic RAM) and is the same as the DRAM popularly used for system memory. Either the digital-to-analog converter (called a RAMDAC) or the graphics controller can access DRAM on a display adapter, but they can't access it at the same time. DRAM is too slow to deliver high-resolution, high-color, and a high refresh rate for a modern machine.

In the evolution of PC display adapters, the next form of memory was VRAM (video RAM, an unfortunate name because any kind of display adapter RAM is also called video RAM). VRAM is *dual ported*, meaning that two devices can access it simultaneously,

thus allowing the processor to write to memory at the same time that it is refreshing the image on the display. Dual-ported RAM enables the display adapter to perform faster because the graphics controller and the RAMDAC don't have to take turns. The faster performance enables higher refresh rates for a given resolution.

Next up the line were forms of EDO memory. EDO stands for *extended data out*, an indication of an expanded bandwidth for its data. DRAM and VRAM versions of EDO chips were about 10 to 25 percent faster than equivalent standard chips. EDO memory improves speed by enabling the next cycle of memory to begin before the previous cycle finishes its job. On the downside, EDO RAM can cause slowdowns any time you use color depths of more than 8 bits per pixel.

A slight improvement over VRAM was WRAM (Window RAM), which is specifically intended for systems running graphical user interfaces, such as Windows. WRAM is dual ported (like VRAM) and includes logic that speeds bit-block transfers and pattern fills.

SGRAM (synchronous graphics RAM) is clock-synchronized, single-ported RAM designed for video memory, aimed for use in low-cost adapters. The technology uses *masked write*, which enables selected data to be modified in a single operation rather than as a sequence of read, update, and write operations.

At the time of this writing, some high-end adapters were based on SDRAM (synchronous DRAM), able to work at bus speeds of as much as 200 MHz, and slightly faster DDR SDRAM (double data rate SDRAM). A new class of adapters uses RDRAM (rambus dynamic RAM), a system that uses a proprietary bus that speeds up the data flow between video RAM and the frame buffer. RDRAM is especially well suited to video streaming applications.

Video display resolution

The more individually controllable pixels are on a monitor screen, the crisper the image. Resolution is indicated as horizontal pixels

Ch
13

times vertical pixels on the screen. Whatever the capability of the monitor, though, it is still up to the video display adapter to produce the signal that drives it. All of the video modes are the result of a partnership between the display adapter and the monitor.

Table 13-5 shows many of the video modes available throughout the history of the PC. Early adapters had both a text and a graphics mode. The text mode was based around predefined character sets; characters were drawn within a specified character box of a particular number of pixels in width and height. Today, nearly every modern PC uses the SVGA standard in one or another of its advanced modes.

TABLE 13-5: Video Standards

Resolution	Colors	Mode	Character Box	Vertical Frequency	Horizontal Frequency	Hardware Compatible
MDA Monochrome Display Adapter (1981)						
720 x 350	1	Text	9 x 14	50	18.43	None
CGA Color Graphics Adapter (1981)						
640 x 200	16	Text	8 x 8	60	15.75	None
320 x 200	16	Text	8 x 8	60	15.75	None
160 x 200	16	Graphics	N/A	60	15.75	None
320 x 200	4	Graphics	N/A	60	15.75	None
640 x 200	2	Graphics	N/A	60	15.75	None
HGC Hercules Graphics Card (1982)						
720 x 350	1	Text	9 x 14	50	18.1	MDA
720 x 348	2	Graphics	N/A	50	18.1	MDA
EGA Enhanced Graphics Adapter (1984)						
640 x 350	16	Text	8 x 14	60	21.85	CGA, MDA
720 x 350	4	Text	9 x 14	60	21.85	CGA, MDA
640 x 350	16	Graphics	N/A	60	21.85	CGA, MDA
320 x 200	16	Graphics	N/A	60	21.85	CGA, MDA
640 x 200	16	Graphics	N/A	60	21.85	CGA, MDA
640 x 350	16	Graphics	N/A	60	21.85	CGA, MDA
PGA Professional Graphics Adapter (1984)						
640 x 480	256	Graphics	N/A	60	30.5	CGA

Resolution	Colors	Mode	Character Box	Vertical Frequency	Horizontal Frequency	Hardware Compatible
VGA Video Graphics Array (1987)						
720 x 400	16	Text	9 x 16	70	31.5	CGA, EGA
360 x 400	16	Text	9 x 16	70	31.5	CGA, EGA
640 x 480	2, 16	Graphics	N/A	60	31.5	CGA, EGA
320 x 200	256	Graphics	N/A	70	31.5	CGA, EGA
MCGA Memory Controller Gate Array (1987)						
320 x 400	4	Text	8 x 16	70	31.5	CGA, EGA
640 x 400	2	Text	8 x 16	70	31.5	CGA, EGA
640 x 480	2	Graphics	N/A	60	31.5	CGA, EGA
320 x 200	256	Graphics	N/A	70	31.5	CGA, EGA
8514/A (1987)						
1,024 x 768	16, 256	Graphics	N/A	43–48	35–52	VGA passthrough
640 x 480	256	Graphics	N/A	43–48	35–52	VGA passthrough
XGA Extended Graphics Array (1990)						
640 x 480	256	Graphics	N/A	43–48	35–52	VGA
1,024 x 768	256	Graphics	N/A	43–48	35–52	VGA
640 x 480	65,536	Graphics	N/A	43–48	35–52	VGA
1,056 x 400	16	Text	8 x 16	43–48	35–52	VGA
SVGA Super VGA or VESA Specification (1989 and subsequent expansions)						
640 x 480	256–16.8 million	Graphics	N/A	50–120	24–86	VGA, CGA, EGA
800 x 600	16–16.8 million	Graphics	N/A	50–120	25–86	None
1,024 x 768	16–16.8 million	Graphics	N/A	76–100	24–86	None
1,280 x 1,024	16–16.8 million	Graphics	N/A	76–100	24–86	None
1,600 x 1,280	16–16.8 million	Graphics	N/A	76–150	24–86	None

Ch
13

Each step along the way from CGA to today's amazing SVGA adapters brought dramatic change. It is almost comical how crude and unimpressive a CGA screen looks in comparison to a multimedia screen from SVGA today. Everything has changed: resolution, number of colors, and speed. In addition, prices have plummeted.

Resolving resolution issues

Using a monitor at a 1,280 x 1,024 pixel resolution gives you more than four times as much viewable information as can be presented on a standard 640 x 480 pixel setting — four times as many cells in a spreadsheet, four windows with four word processing documents, or any other wide-screen or ultra-sharp use you can conjure. That's the good news. The bad news is that individual elements on the screen are less than one-fourth as large.

Although high resolution may be essential in certain applications, such as desktop publishing and graphic arts work, for many users, text may be simply too small for comfortable writing and editing. However, you should be able to adjust the "view" of a screen from within many applications, including word processors, to adjust what you see on the screen to a comfortable size. Another solution is to use a zoom feature that may be an element of the driver for your particular graphics adapter or available as a separate graphics utility software package. Using a zoom or a view is a compromise, adding some extra keystrokes or mouse clicks to views of the screen and giving up some of the advantage of high resolution in the first place.

When you enable higher resolutions, you can improve readability of text by turning on large fonts. To do this, right-click on the desktop and choose Properties. From the Properties dialog box, choose Settings and click on Advanced. In the Display group, choose Large Fonts. Click OK twice to close the Advanced and Properties dialogs. Older versions of Windows may ask you to re-boot your computer before the new display settings become effective.

Of course, the higher resolutions of modern graphics adapters have been accompanied by an increase in the size of the monitors on the desk. At one time, a 13-inch monitor was considered large. Today, a 14-inch screen is considered hopelessly small. Serious computers seem to begin with 15-inch screens and move quickly to 17-inch and 19-inch models. At the time of this writing, the largest consumer-grade monitors are 21-inch and 22-inch models; these sizes are more expensive and generally a bit less sharp than smaller models. (Monitors are measured along the diagonal from one upper corner of the CRT to the lower opposite corner.)

Super Video Graphics Arrays

At the consumer level, the current state-of-the-art in video display adapters is the Super Video Graphics Array (SVGA). SVGA is an extension of the VGA standard developed by third-party manufacturers and is in common use on nearly every modern machine. IBM's XGA was intended as its own improvement on the standard, but it has not migrated to AT-bus machines.

SVGA was originally defined as a small improvement over standard VGA, with resolutions of as high as 800 x 600 pixels. As it turned out, that particular resolution level was considered insufficient by many Windows users, and the SVGA definition was expanded and improved to include specifications of 1,024 x 768 pixels, 1,280 x 1,024 pixels, and higher. SVGA also extends down, including a superset of all of the modes and specifications of VGA, which included most of the earlier EGA and CGA modes.

Another term, Ultra VGA (UVGA), is sometimes used for displays with resolution of 1,024 x 768 pixels or greater.

To view information at SVGA settings, you need both an SVGA-capable monitor and an SVGA graphics adapter.

The SVGA standard was developed by an industry group, VESA (Video Electronics Standards Association). The standard is not a law, though, and some display adapters may support only selected elements of the SVGA definition or may offer some features that go beyond its official limits. Be sure to ask the manufacturer or seller for display specifications to understand exactly what you are buying.

3-D SVGA graphics adapters

Are you ready to enter the PC third dimension? Hot and flashy 3-D graphics accelerators are now available as part of new systems and as upgrades to existing computers. They are yet another extension to the flexible SVGA standard.

All of the new cards offer impressive gains in speed and visual quality on 3-D software. You can also reasonably expect speed improvements of 25 percent or more over 2-D graphics accelerators that run equivalent applications.

However, you must understand one thing right up front: What you see onscreen is not really 3-D, at least not in the special-glasses, reach-out-and-touch-the-butterfly-hovering-in-front-of-your-nose kind of way. Instead, think of 3-D graphics as the difference between an old Road Runner cartoon and the modern state of cartoon art in computer animation movies, such as *Toy Story*.

When designers and marketers speak of 3-D today, they are talking about the capability of a video display adapter to produce and manipulate 3-D objects — mathematical representations of width, height, and depth of a shape. The addition of depth opens the door to the next great advance in graphics.

Add this new term to your PC lexicon: *texels*. Texels are pixels with a third layer of information defining the pixel's texture.

One current graphics adapter is the All-in-Wonder 128 Pro, which combines computer graphics, video, and TV signals. Based on the Rage 128 Pro chipset, it includes 32MB of memory and connects to the system through an AGP 4X/2X slot. Features include a 125-channel TV-tuner with digital VCR, still image, and MPEG-2 motion video capture. TV-on-Demand enables you to watch TV on your PC when you want it and the Guide Plus+ interactive program guide searches for programs at the click of a mouse.

The ATI Radeon 8500 is a high-end board aimed at power gamers and graphics users. Based on the Radeon 8500 graphics processing unit, it includes 64MB of double data rate (DDR) memory and connects through an AGP 4X/2X slot. It includes dual monitor, video output, and digital flat panel (DVI) support. The Radeon supports 3-D resolutions (32-bit color) up to a resolution of 2,048 x 1,536.

Figure 13-3 shows an example of a 2D/3-D video display adapter that also includes TV input and output.

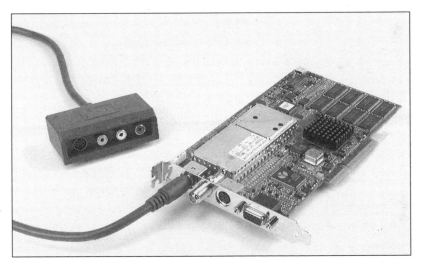

FIGURE 13-3: *ATI's All-in-Wonder 128 is a 2-D/3-D AGP graphics adapter and video accelerator that also brings together the worlds of television and computers. The card can display television, VCR, and DVD images on a computer, and it can output computer graphics to a TV or VCR.*

What are 3-D graphics?

Three-dimensional cards bring together a combination of specialized graphics processing, high-speed dedicated memory, and advanced software schemes. It all comes down to the addition of depth to graphics images. In mathematical terms, width and height are called X and Y dimensions, while depth is the sought-after Z dimension.

To achieve this addition of depth on the software side, you can use half a dozen impressive extensions to the graphics capabilities of the PC. At the heart of the improvements are texture mapping, Gouraud shading, and z-buffering. The first two improvements are ways to use a computer to apply realistic textures, color shadings, and light shadings to the basic shapes that constitute images; the effect is to enable the complex simulation of perspective and shadow.

Texture mapping gives the most eye-popping effects. Textures, with variations for perspective and changing atmospheric conditions, are applied to a shape and modified as action demands. Texture mapping is much slower to produce and manage than flat or Gouraud shading because it adds one full, additional level of information to be generated, manipulated, and stored in a new block of memory called the z-buffer.

Gouraud shading is a step up from flat shading, which assigns a single shade and intensity to fill the interior of a computer-generated shape. Although flat shading is fast, it robs an image of the variations that give the appearance of depth and reality. Gouraud interpolates color or grayshades across an object to make it seem to have depth.

Z-buffering is a scheme that assigns the computer the task of keeping track of the depth of each shape, including hidden surfaces that can't be seen in the current view, and managing the shape's appearance as the view changes. Most graphics chips use information in the z-buffer to determine whether pixels in an object are in front of (and thus displayed) or behind (and thus hidden) another object.

In a 3-D world, the entire database representing the modeled world is processed for every frame displayed, with the relative position and orientation of every object recalculated in every frame. Just as in the real world, you may be looking at just the portion of an object that is in direct view, but the rest of the object—its depth and mass—exists nevertheless.

How 3-D video display adapters work

Three-dimensional images are created in what designers call the *3-D graphics pipeline*, a connection that starts at the computer's CPU and passes through the graphics adapter en route to your monitor. Despite the impressive raw power of a current CPU, most users would not be satisfied with the slowdown in image creation that would result if the CPU rendered advanced 3-D graphics all alone.

To accomplish their magic without bringing your PC to a halt, most 3-D video display adapters offload some of the intensive number-crunching assignments from the computer's CPU to a specialized chip on the video display adapter itself. Not only does this reduce the load on the CPU, it also makes it possible for tasks to take place simultaneously. While the rendering engine produces the current frame using the dedicated processor on the 3-D card, the Pentium's CPU is calculating the geometries of the next frame.

Figure 13-4 shows an example of a 3-D PCI video adapter.

FIGURE 13-4: *ATI 3-D Xpression adapter being installed in a PCI slot. This video card includes a graphics accelerator and 3-D functions.*

The operating system is the highest-level control for your PC, controlling the disk and system memory operations of your computer. An API (application program interface) stands between your operating system and your 3-D graphics accelerator to translate specific demands of the software to the capabilities of your graphics hardware.

The next element in the production of 3-D images is the *geometry engine*, which translates descriptions of an image into smaller polygons — triangles and other vector graphics (geometric forms that are drawn from point to point, much like the way you draw a triangle on a piece of paper). Generating the polygons and rotating them in a scene to support the 30-frames-per-second imagery of an advanced game is a calculation-intensive assignment, a task that is well suited to floating-point unit CPUs like all current microprocessors.

The third element in the production of 3-D images is the *rendering engine*, which has the assignment of pixel processing. These tasks include rendering polygons with shading; attaching textures; overlaying atmospheric effects, such as fog or lighting; correcting perspective; and removing hidden surfaces. The end result is a pixel-by-pixel description for an image, ready to be transmitted to the monitor.

Each board works with a driver that stands between the operating system and the card, directing appropriate calls from the operating system directly to the hardware. The controller converts information into a pixel-by-pixel description of the image.

From the controller, the graphics information is sent to the memory on the card itself, a so-called *frame buffer* that prepares the image as a grid. Finally, a chip or chipset called the RAMDAC (random access memory digital-analog converter) changes the digital pixels to the analog signal required by nearly all monitors.

CROSS-REFERENCE

For a graphical presentation on 3-D video display adapters, point your Web browser to http://developer.intel.com/technology/3-D/docs/index.htm.

Video Daughtercards and Video Feature Connectors

At one point in the evolution of the PC, some video card manufacturers chose to design their products to accept specialized *daughtercards* as a means to expand their basic functions. In a way, this is similar to the use of adapter cards in a computer's system bus. Some uses of daughterboards were to add TV tuners that display television images on a computer monitor and video capture devices that convert the output of video cameras or other video devices into images that can be used by the computer. Figure 13-5 shows an example of a TV tuner daughtercard.

FIGURE 13-5: *This TV tuner and video input card from ATI is an example of a video daughtercard. It attaches to a connector on many current ATI video display adapters, enabling users to watch TV or videos on a computer monitor and to capture still frames and movie clips from the video feed. The card can also perform advanced functions, including creating transcripts based on closed-captioned broadcasts.*

Modern video display adapters may offer an industry standard Video Feature Connector (VFC), or a more recent version called the VESA Video Interface Port (VESA VIP) that is intended to work with a wide range of external video devices.

Today, many advanced video cards squeeze extended capabilities — video output to a TV set or VCR or other systems, such as MPEG-2 decoders, video digitizers, HDTV converters, and more — onto the card itself. Others require you to connect the output of a standard video card to the input of a second video display adapter with special features.

Television in the United States, Canada, Japan, and some other countries uses the NTSC standard that delivers 525 lines of resolution at 60 fields per second. In the United Kingdom, West Germany, and many other countries, the standard is called PAL, and delivers a finer resolution of 625 lines at 50 fields per second. France, as it does in many other matters, goes its own way with another standard, called SECAM, that also works at 625 lines.

The varying television standards are not a concern to most PC users, although you do need to keep them in mind if you travel with a laptop with a television output and use your portable computer to produce large-screen PowerPoint presentations, for example, or if you work with videotapes that may have been recorded in a different standard.

Video adapters with television output work with only one TV standard; if you need to display computer output on more than one type of television, you'll need to install an additional video adapter or use an external conversion box that changes one type of TV output to another.

Installing Multiple Video Display Adapters

Among the advanced features of Windows 98 and later versions of Windows is the ability to run multiple display adapters and monitors on the same system. You can use the monitors to display a different program on each, or you can use the facilities of some applications to display some elements of the program on one monitor and other elements on another.

For example, if you perform intensive graphics editing using a program such as Photoshop, you can display the image on one monitor and all of the menus and control panels on the other. Look for some advanced games to display one view on one screen and another view on a second screen.

Using two monitors under Windows 98

Windows 98 permits use of two display adapters and two monitors. You can set the two display adapters to the same or different resolutions and color depths. Begin by installing and configuring one video adapter and monitor, and make sure that both are functioning properly. Then simply install the second card in an available slot. Windows then automatically designates one of the cards as the primary graphics controller and the other card as secondary. Certain 3-D and multimedia features may be available only on the primary card.

If you install both a PCI and an AGP display card in the same system, in most cases, the PCI card will be designated as the primary and the AGP as the secondary controller. Some motherboards may have a BIOS that allows you to override this automatic selection and choose the much faster AGP as the primary.

If you install two PCI cards, the primary video display adapter is usually the one installed in the PCI slot with the lowest number. On most motherboards, this is the PCI slot farthest from the ISA slots.

Multiple monitors under Windows XP

Windows XP is even more accommodating to set up with more than one monitor — in fact, it can work with as many as ten monitors displaying the same or different programs or windows. You can open a different file on each monitor, or you can stretch one item across several monitors, such as a massive Excel spreadsheet.

Under Windows XP, you can choose which of the monitors to use as the primary device for log in and to start programs.

If you want to work with multiple monitors under Windows XP, take the following steps:

1. Install a new video adapter, one that supports multiple monitors, on a system running Windows XP. The system will detect the new video adapter and monitor and install appropriate drivers.
2. After drivers are installed, open Display in Control Panel and go to the Settings tab. There, click on the icon for the monitor that you want to use as a secondary monitor.
3. Select the check box "Extend my Windows desktop onto this monitor" to permit dragging items across your screen onto alternate monitors.
4. To adjust the relative position of one monitor to another, click on the monitor icons and place them alongside each other, or one above the other as you prefer.

The Windows XP operating system also includes a feature called Dualview that is primarily aimed at use on laptops that include connection to a second monitor; under Dualview, the primary display is always the laptop's LCD screen.

Troubleshooting VGA or SVGA Cards

To troubleshoot a video card and monitor, follow these steps:

1. Before you do anything rash, such as taking apart your computer, make sure that the display adapter is properly connected by cable to the monitor. Is the cable firmly attached at both ends and not partially connected?
2. Check that the monitor is plugged into a source of wall current. It may be plugged into a special outlet on the back panel of some dinosaur machines, or it may connect directly to the wall outlet.

3. Make sure that the monitor is turned on. Do you see an indicator light on the monitor? If not, check to see if a fuse is present on the monitor and that the wall outlet is live. Notice also that many modern monitors include multicolor indicator lights that show yellow when they are receiving power but not receiving a signal from the CPU. They show a green light when power is present and they are receiving a signal from the computer.
4. Finally, check that the contrast and brightness settings on the monitor are not turned all the way off.

Here are some common software issues to check before you suspect the hardware:

- **Windows won't permit a setting better than basic video VGA resolution of 640 x 480 with 16 colors.** If your card is capable of more (as most are), check the level of hardware acceleration that Windows has set. Go to Control Panel, and Display, and then click the Settings tab. Click Advanced, and then click the Performance tab. Drag the Hardware acceleration slider to None. Click OK.
- **Certain display setting options are missing in the Display Properties dialog box.** Make sure that Windows has properly detected your specific monitor manufacturer and model. An incorrect or generic setting may limit your available choices. Windows includes listings for most major manufacturers; newer monitors come with disks or CDs with hardware information for Windows.

Testing SVGA or VGA cards

The display adapter, the monitor, or a multitude of difficulties in the computer system unit can produce a display problem. The troubleshooting charts in Appendix G provide a plan to help you identify the culprit.

Before you go too far in diagnosing a display problem, try out an extra monitor (if you have one) on the troublesome system.

Ch
13

You can plug a monitor that you know is good into a questionable PC system or try the suspect monitor on a PC that you know is good. If the suspect monitor comes to life on another machine, the problem is likely with the display adapter or internal chips of the original PC. If the good monitor fails on the suspect machine, you have the same clues.

If you are running Windows 98, the first thing to check for is conflicts with the system resource settings for your card. Of course, this raises a question: How can you see the settings if your display adapter is not working?

If you have absolutely no video signal on the display, then you must open the system and explore for hardware problems. In many cases, Windows 95/98 and later versions are capable of booting up in Safe Mode, which makes minimal demands on the system, usually as a generic VGA mode using ordinary Windows drivers.

If you can get into the operating system this way, the problem probably lies with an improper display card driver or a conflict of resources. Go to the Device Manager and use its facilities to look for the source of the problem. Try resetting the video display adapter to a basic configuration, such as 640 x 480 and 256 colors, and then rebooting to Windows; if you are able to proceed from there, you can make other adjustments within Windows.

One other software option is to attempt to reinstall the drivers for your card from the floppy disk or CD-ROM provided by the manufacturer.

If you need to check out the hardware, first unplug the cables from the back of the PC, including the power cord, and then remove the cover.

NOTE

A class of all-in-one senior citizens and low-level modern machines had video circuitry on the motherboard. In these systems, the video adapter can't be repaired, but in most systems, a replacement card can be installed in the expansion bus. Check your instruction manual for details.

Because the monitor is attached to the display adapter card, look on the back of the system unit to find the 15-pin female connector that your monitor's data cable plugs into. The 15-pin connector, called a DB-15, is the video port located on the display card or located on the motherboard. The first thing to check is that the card is firmly seated in the bus.

Many SVGA or VGA cards come packaged with diagnostic software. This software is helpful if the display card is working but misbehaving. CheckIt or another diagnostics package also can test a card for subtle malfunctions.

If you can, try installing the suspect display card into a computer that you know to be good and that is configured for the same type of card. If you have one or two incorrect characters on an otherwise good screen, the video memory located on the display card is likely at fault.

Note also that an older monitor may not be capable of the higher refresh rates delivered by modern cards, including AGP adapters. You should be able to continue to use an older monitor if you instruct Windows to install and work with generic SVGA drivers, but you will lose the advanced functions of the AGP card.

Removing and installing video cards

Before you remove a video card, you must turn off the computer and the monitor. Disconnect the data cable (it runs from the video card to the monitor) at the video card end. You will probably have to remove two small screws that are used to hold the cable connector tight to the card. Remove the system unit cover. The card itself is secured to the back wall of the system unit chassis with a single screw. Remove and save the screw. Remove the card. Lift the card straight up; it should require only moderate force.

Installation is the reverse of removal. As already noted, nearly all SVGA cards are designed to plug into a PCI slot, moving toward AGP slots over time. You may have difficulty finding a state-of-the-art card for an ISA slot, although older models may be offered at a full-line dealer or mail-order house.

Line up the slot connector on the card with the slot on the motherboard and then press down firmly. When the card is in place, the screw hole on the card lines up with the screw hole in the back of the chassis. Reinstall the screw and test the machine.

If you are installing a different type of display card—for example, if you're replacing the original VGA card with a new SVGA card—be sure to consult your PC's instruction manual to see if you need to set any switches or jumpers on the motherboard to reflect the new display adapter.

If you have a modern machine, you may need to run the setup program to store the new hardware information in CMOS on the motherboard. Windows 95/98 and later versions should recognize a Plug-and-Play card. Owners of senior citizens may need to check with the manufacturer of their motherboard or system to determine if they need to upgrade the system BIOS.

Nearly all newly installed modern display cards will initially power up in basic VGA mode of 640 x 480 resolution and 16 colors. Plug-and-Play under Windows 98 and later versions should identify most new adapters and install drivers that are part of Windows or prompt you to install drivers from a disk or CD provided by the manufacturer. Be sure to consult the instruction manual for the new card.

If you are installing a new card in an older system, or one running Windows 95 or earlier, change the display adapter setting to the generic "Standard Display Adapter (VGA)" before removing the old card and installing the new one. After the machine is up and running, use the new driver to change resolution and color settings.

Dinosaur Video Standards

Older computer video standards, including CGA and MDA, were technological marvels at the time, but they seem hopelessly outdated today. In fact, many current programs don't support these older display adapters. At the same time, many older PCs can't be upgraded to more modern video standards. This section explores the additional elements that make up the dinosaurs.

I begin with VGA, the immediate predecessor to the current standard SVGA. Although VGA is still supported by today's monitors and will function under Windows, it is too limited for most current applications. You will still see some VGA and even CGA monitors in text-only environments including control systems in laboratories.

Video Graphics Array

Video Graphics Array (VGA) is another IBM-developed standard, originally included as part of the early Micro Channel Architecture PS/2s and introduced in 1987. In many ways, the arrival of the VGA defined the birth of the video portion of the modern machine; today's SVGA is built upon its foundation.

VGA gains its name from the VLSI (very large-scale integration) chip that is its engine; the processor was called the *video graphics array*. A VGA card is capable of producing a graphics image of as much as 640 x 480, or a text-only mode of 720 x 400. As many as 256 different colors can be simultaneously displayed on the screen.

The VGA card converts the computer's internal digital information into an analog (variable voltage) signal; VGA-compatible monitors must also be analog. Although it may seem a step backwards to go from precise digital to purposely imprecise analog, this scheme actually permits more combinations of colors and gradations of gray scale.

The VGA standard supports 16 colors at 640 x 480 resolution, or 256 colors at 320 x 200 resolution. Colors are chosen from a palette of 262,144 colors (not 16.7 million) because VGA uses 6 bits to specify each color, instead of the 8 bits used by SVGA.

VGA cards and monitors use a 15-pin DB-15 monitor cable connector instead of the standard 9-pin DB-9 used on dinosaur monochrome, CGA, or EGA adapters.

It is very important to have the proper software driver; most dinosaur VGA cards will work with a generic driver from within Windows. You can usually obtain specific drivers through Web sites maintained by manufacturers, assuming that the company is

Ch
13

still in business. A well-written graphics adapter driver can increase the response speed of your monitor. Screens scroll quicker, graphics redraw faster, and you won't go gray watching the Windows hourglass.

Original VGA cards had very limited memory resources, meaning that at its highest resolution, it could only display 256 or 16 colors. One solution to the slow processor and limited memory of VGA was the use of a graphics accelerator card or coprocessor. These cards have the brains to recalculate which pixels should be lit as text or graphics, to scroll up the screen, to draw a shape on the screen by themselves, or to fill a shape with color. They are also much faster than the CPU. Some accelerators were built onto the VGA cards, others were added as daughtercards, and still others occupied their own slot in the bus and were connected to the VGA card by cable.

Enhanced graphics adapter cards

The enhanced graphics adapter card (EGA) is a footnote to history; it was an advanced graphics and text card that stood between the popular CGA and the pervasive VGA standards. It failed to deliver the huge palette of colors that the coming multimedia revolution demanded, and today it is almost forgotten.

The EGA card provides medium- and high-resolution color or monochrome video display. It operates in either text mode (for word processing) or graphics mode (where charts and pictures can be drawn onscreen dot by dot). It is capable of producing 256 different colors when teamed with an EGA monitor, but the EGA card can display only 16 of those colors onscreen at one time. A data cable connects an EGA monitor to the EGA card, using a 9-pin (DB-9) socket on the card.

How EGA cards work

An EGA video display adapter is capable of multiple display modes. One mode, EGA monochrome, treats the screen as a 720 x 350-pixel grid. The grid has 720 pixels per horizontal line and 350 lines per screen. In this monochrome mode, the EGA card drives a simple monochrome monitor in order to replicate the features of a Hercules graphics card. Many color modes are possible, ranging from 320 x 200-pixel (emulating a CGA graphics adapter) to 640 x 350-pixel screens with 16 different colors onscreen simultaneously. Extended EGA cards have added two display modes, both with 16-color, VGA-quality resolution. Most color modes work with either an EGA color monitor or a multiscanning monitor, but extended EGA requires a multiscanning monitor.

The monitor is a servant of the display adapter; it turns a pixel on or passes over it, and it leaves the pixel blank at the explicit pixel-by-pixel direction of the EGA card. EGA cards provide two on/off signals to each of the three electron guns. One signal is high intensity (bright) and one is low intensity. The result is a potential of 16 colors from a palette of 64 hues, including black and shades of gray.

At a 640 x 350-pixel resolution, the screen contains more than 200,000 pixels. All this video information must be stored somewhere, so EGA cards have as much as 256K of video memory on the card. (Original IBM EGA cards had only 64K, but performance was limited, so 256K soon became the standard.)

The computer sends data to the display card. When the card is in text mode, the computer sends alphanumeric character codes, which are stored in video memory. The display card's character generator changes each character code into a pattern of pixels and then sends that data to the monitor, pixel by pixel.

In graphics mode, the computer sends pixel-by-pixel instructions directly to the video card memory. The card then transmits that information to the monitor, which displays and redisplays the contents of video memory. The monitor refreshes the screen (re-energizes the pixels) 60 times per second, providing a fairly stable image.

Testing EGA cards

To locate the EGA card, first remove the cover from the computer system unit. Because the monitor is attached to the graphics adapter card, look on the back of the system unit to find the 9-pin, female connector that your monitor data cable plugs into.

EGA adapters and EGA monitors use DB-9 connectors. Monochrome (MDA, MGA, and MGP) display cards and color (CGA) graphics cards use a DB-9 connector. Therefore, it isn't easy to distinguish these display cards by looking at the outside of the computer. If you have doubts about your display card's identity, take off the system unit cover and look at the card. Most EGA boards have DIP switches that set the various possible EGA video modes. In addition, most EGA board manufacturers provide a prominent decal or other label on the EGA card.

Whenever you install a new EGA card or have doubts about an old one, you should test all the separate EGA modes — both monochrome and color. Luckily, EGA cards are usually sold with diagnostic software that make this testing easy.

Suppose, however, that you have no display at all, or the screen displays snow or other gibberish. See Chapter 14 for information about testing a monitor. By using the information in that chapter, you usually can find the solution to the problem.

If the information from Chapter 14 doesn't help, here are some other ideas. EGA cards have many modes, with the initial boot mode usually controlled by DIP switches or jumpers. Make sure that the motherboard setting of these switches or jumpers matches the EGA card setting. Remember that many 286 and 386 PCs and some older 486 computers have a jumper on the motherboard for color versus monochrome video. You also have to make changes to the setup information in the CMOS chip. Finally, make sure that the EGA card is set to work with the monitor that you're using. Check your EGA card and computer motherboard manuals for the correct switch settings.

With more advanced display cards, it becomes more valuable to have a good diagnostics program for testing its various modes. As with any other display card, the most likely culprit for many display problems is a failure in video memory on the card. Run diagnostics before considering replacing the memory — held in sockets on many EGA cards — or the more expensive card itself.

Removing and installing EGA cards

Before you remove the EGA card, turn off the computer and the monitor. Disconnect the data cable that connects the display card to the monitor at the display card end. You will probably have to remove two small screws used to hold the cable connector tight to the card. Remove the system unit cover. The card itself is secured to the back wall of the system unit chassis with a single screw. Remove and save that screw. Lift the card straight up; it shouldn't require great force.

Before you install an EGA card, read the manual and set the DIP switches as necessary. You may also need to reset the motherboard DIP switches if you are changing from monochrome or from RGB color to EGA.

Remember that installation is the reverse of removal. Because EGA graphics cards are 8-bit cards, any bus connector from any clone is appropriate. When the card is in place, the screw hole on the card lines up with the screw hole in the back of the chassis. Reinstall the screw and test the machine.

If you are installing a different type of display card — if, for example, you're replacing the original CGA card with an EGA or a VGA card — be sure to set any switches or jumpers on the motherboard to reflect the new graphics adapter. See your motherboard manual for further instructions.

It may be difficult to find a replacement EGA card because card manufacturers have abandoned that standard. You may have luck locating a used card at a computer repair shop. And some ROM BIOS chips on early PCs and older modern machines may be able to accommodate a VGA adapter, so you could move up from the older EGA standard if you are willing to purchase a new monitor as well. Check with the manufacturer of your PC or a BIOS manufacturer.

Color graphics adapter cards

The color graphics adapter (CGA) was the first bitmapped display adapter for the PC and dates back to the introduction of the IBM

Ch 13

PC. A CGA adapter drives an RGB monitor, which draws its name from the fact that it receives separate red, green, and blue signals for the corresponding color phosphors that are painted on the inside surface of a picture tube.

WARNING

A CGA adapter is not compatible with a current SVGA or VGA monitor, and most current monitors don't work with an outdated CGA adapter.

The CGA card was the first IBM PC video card. It worked with an 8- or 16-color display and had the pixel-by-pixel screen control necessary to display graphics. CGA adapters treat the screen as a grid that is 200 pixels (picture elements) tall and 320 pixels wide. When working in the 320 x 200-pixel mode, the CGA card is able to display 4 of the 16 available colors on the screen at any one time. Because it can manage relatively few pixels, which therefore are quite large, a CGA card has much poorer resolution than a monochrome card. Nevertheless, color display and the potential to draw pictures or graphs dot-by-dot onscreen made the CGA popular.

CGA cards also offer a special high-resolution mode that provides two colors (for example, black and white) onscreen at a time. The two-color mode uses a 640 x 200-pixel grid, enabling reasonably sharp display, although it is still coarser than the 720 x 348-pixel resolution available with a Hercules graphics card, and it functions far below the capabilities of a modern adapter.

How CGA cards work

A CGA board contains enough memory (16K) to store information for each pixel on the color monitor screen. For the sake of comparison, consider that modern machines typically sport SVGA cards that start at 8MB and often begin at 64MB or even more video RAM.

All display data, whether text or graphics, is stored pixel-by-pixel in the video memory. The display adapter reads the video memory 60 times per second and sends its contents to the monitor. To display a simple letter, a capital *T* for instance, the electron beam in the monitor excites one horizontal row of pixels and one vertical column of pixels.

A program can display text either by creating the text font out of individual pixels or by asking the ROM BIOS to display text using its standard font. In the first case, the text is stored in the video memory as a collection of dots, and not as a complete character.

To display a *graphic* (a picture composed of many little dots of color), individual pixels are excited. As previously noted, only four colors can be used on the screen at any one time, but two palettes of four colors are always available and ready to be switched into place. Three of the four colors in a given palette are predetermined by the video adapter circuitry. Any of the 13 other colors in the basic set of 16 can be chosen as the fourth color in either palette.

Testing CGA cards

See the introduction to the "Troubleshooting VGA or SVGA Cards" for test instructions for the electrical and signal connectors of the card and the monitor.

On a dinosaur, the CGA card is often—but not always—located on the far left, as far away from the disk drives and the power supply as possible. Because the monitor is attached to the CGA card, look on the back of the system unit to find the 9-pin female connector that your monitor's data cable plugs into.

If the problem is that you have no display at all, check for an incorrect match between the monitor and the display card. Don't use CGA cards with monochrome text monitors. That mismatch causes snow on the monitor because the display data transmitted for a line of color text is gibberish to a monochrome text monitor.

If you have a dinosaur XT clone, check for proper dual-in-line-package (DIP) switch settings on the motherboard. Modern machines must have the display adapter type set correctly in their CMOS setup memory chip, but these machines are able to display an initial error message, such as "Incorrect setup. Wrong video adapter."

If you have one or two incorrect characters on an otherwise good screen, the video memory located on the display adapter is likely at fault. You can use CheckIt or other diagnostic software to test the video memory before you consider acquiring a new card.

You may have a hard time finding a replacement CGA card, although you may have luck obtaining a used relic from a computer repair shop. Check with the manufacturer of your computer or the maker of the ROM BIOS to see if the machine is capable of working with a more advanced video display adapter, such as a VGA.

Removing and installing CGA cards

Before you remove the CGA card, you must turn off the computer and the monitor. Disconnect the data cable that connects the CGA card to the monitor at the CGA card end. You will probably have to remove two small screws that hold the cable connector tight to the card.

The card itself is secured to the back wall of the system unit chassis with a single screw. Remove and save that screw. Lift the card straight up; it shouldn't require great force.

Again, installation is the reverse of removal. Because CGA cards are 8-bit cards, any bus connector in any of the clones is appropriate, although some systems suggest keeping the display adapter as far away from the power supply as possible. Carefully line up the card edge connector with the slot on the motherboard and then press down firmly. When the card is in place, the screw hole on the card lines up with the screw hole in the back of the chassis. Reinstall the screw, reattach the monitor cable, and test the machine.

If you are installing a different type of display adapter, be sure to set any switches or jumpers on the motherboard to reflect the new display adapter. See your motherboard manual and the section of this chapter that covers your new card for more details.

Monochrome display adapters

Even older than the CGA card by a few months, this text-only monochrome card is officially known as the *monochrome display/parallel printer adapter* (MDA). The MDA was the original display adapter offered with IBM's first computer, the IBM PC. It was intended to work with IBM's own text-only monochrome monitor. Only a handful of early clone makers bothered to adopt the MDA, and only a few monitor makers emulated IBM's design for the monitor.

Soon after the introduction of the IBM PC, the color graphics adapter (with lower resolution but the capability to draw graphics and to use color) arrived. The first major third-party adapter was the Hercules graphics adapter, which had the functions of both IBM cards: It was a high-resolution monochrome text card that could also display monochrome graphics.

MDA is all but abandoned by most modern software. Microsoft Windows does not work with MDA at all because the adapter can't display bit-mapped graphics. You can probably continue to perform text-oriented applications, such as word processing and some database work, but not much else.

NOTE

If you have an MDA adapter, check with the manufacturer of your PC, if it is still in business, or with a ROM BIOS manufacturer to see if the ROM BIOS can be upgraded to work with a VGA adapter. If not, the only solution to improving your computing capabilities is to retire your Old Faithful PC to the closet. It's not likely that you will be able to use the adapter cards or the monochrome monitor with a modern machine.

If your MDA adapter has failed, you may find it difficult to find a replacement that works with your ROM BIOS and your system, but it may be possible to obtain a used part from a computer shop. You may also be able to obtain a Hercules graphics card or a card that emulates the Hercules card.

The monochrome text-only video adapter card is technically considered a character-mapped system, capable of displaying only 256 preformed characters—called the *IBM PC character set*—in standard positions on the screen. The card can't draw free-form graphics images on the screen because it is not capable of pixel-by-pixel (dot-by-dot) control of the monitor screen. It is capable of driving only a monochrome monitor. Hooking it to an RGB color monitor produces only snow on the screen and may damage the monitor, the card, or both.

The card treats the monitor screen as if it were a grid of 80 columns of characters by 25 rows. Each of these positions may contain one of the preformed characters and nothing else. This text-only card is also capable of a 40-character wide by 25-row format. Programmers rarely used this alternative format, but you occasionally see it in old programs and games that somehow managed to coax a bit of a picture out of some of the symbols in the IBM PC character set.

How monochrome text-only video adapter cards work

The video card contains enough memory (4K) to store information for each character position on the screen. The monitor is continuously placing data from the video memory onscreen. A monochrome display adapter reads the video memory and sends its contents onto the monitor approximately 50 times per second. When a program needs to write characters to the display screen, it may put data directly into video memory, or it may ask the ROM to write the characters on the screen and rely on the ROM to put the necessary data in video memory. In either case, the video memory holds a record of the character (including the null character for blanks) to be displayed at each position on the screen.

Testing monochrome text-only video adapter cards

Many diagnostic disks provide video troubleshooting help. CheckIt and QA Plus, for example, include video test programs. Of course, you have to be able to see some video onscreen in order to use them.

If you have no display at all and have made any changes under the covers of the computer since the last time the monitor worked, check for an incorrect match between the monitor and the display card. Check for proper switch settings on the motherboard of a dinosaur PC. On modern machines, the BIOS checks that the display adapter type is set correctly in the CMOS setup memory chip. Modern machines are able to display an initial error message, such as "Incorrect setup. Wrong video adapter."

One indication of the failure of an MDA is that characters change on the monitor all by themselves. A Greek character, a face, or a punctuation mark suddenly appears on the monitor in the midst of text, replacing the original letter of the alphabet. If you reload the text from the PC, the screen may be fine, or the problem characters may appear somewhere else.

If you suspect that your monitor is malfunctioning, try connecting it to another MDA that you know to be good, if you can find one, or connect a good monitor to your MDA.

Removing and installing monochrome text-only video adapter cards

To locate the card, you must first remove the cover from the computer system unit. The display adapter card is often, but not always, on the far left—as far away from the disk drives and the power supply as possible. The monitor is attached to the display adapter card, so look on the back of the system unit to find the 9-pin female connector that your monitor plugs into. That 9-pin connector, called a DB-9, is on the display card.

To remove the monochrome text card, first turn off the computer and monitor. Disconnect the data cable, which runs from the display adapter to the monitor, at the display card end. You will probably have to remove the two small screws that hold the cable connector tight. The card itself is secured to the back wall of the system unit chassis with a single screw. Remove and save this screw. Lift the card straight up; it shouldn't require much force.

Installation is the reverse of removal. Because MDA cards are 8-bit cards, any bus connector in any clone is appropriate, although I suggest you use a slot as far as possible from the power supply. Line up the slot connector (card edge connector) on the card with the slot on the motherboard carefully and press down firmly. When the card is in place, the screw hole on the card lines up with the screw hole in the back of the chassis. Reinstall the screw, reattach the monitor cable, and test the machine.

If you are installing a different type of display adapter, be sure to set any switches or jumpers on the motherboard to reflect the new adapter. See your motherboard manual and the section of this chapter dedicated to your new display card (VGA, SVGA, and so on) for more details.

Hercules graphics cards or monochrome graphics adapter cards

Hercules introduced its graphics and text hybrid about a year after the birth of the dinosaur IBM PC. The Hercules graphic card (HGC); monochrome graphics adapter cards (MGAs), which are non-Hercules clones of the HGC; and the MGP (a version of an MGA that includes a parallel port) combine the best aspects of both monochrome text and color video adapters: well-defined, crisp characters, as well as pixel-by-pixel control of monitor display.

How HGC, MGA, and MGP cards work

HGC and compatible cards produce two video modes: text and graphics. In text mode, the cards display clear, crisp, predrawn

characters. This mode uses an 80 x 25-line character grid on the display screen. An MGA board has sufficient video memory to store a character for each of the 80 positions per line and for all 25 lines on the screen. The adapter reads data from the video memory and sends it to the monitor 50 times per second.

When a program needs to write characters to the screen in text mode, it can put data directly into video memory, or it can ask the ROM to write the characters onscreen and rely on the ROM to put the necessary data in video memory. In either case, the video memory holds a record of the character — including the null character for blanks — to be displayed at each position on the screen.

The card includes 64K of video memory, which is enough memory to store up to 16 text screens or pages; or in graphics mode, enough memory for two full-screen pages of monochrome graphics. The additional stored pages in text mode can be used to predraw succeeding screens of data. This technique provides extremely quick page-down capability because the information for succeeding pages is already in memory and is ready to be displayed instantly. Some monochrome software uses this feature, but quick screen changes are not generally a high priority for monochrome applications.

In graphics mode, HGCs and MGAs control each pixel on the display screen individually. The screen is divided into 720 pixels horizontally and 348 pixels vertically.

Compare this to the CGA. CGA boards can show only half that resolution, having 320 x 200 pixels. But CGA cards store color information for each individual pixel in the video display adapters memory, and color uses up more space than monochrome information.

Characters can be displayed when the MGA or MGP card is in graphics mode, but they are individually drawn onto the screen pixel by pixel. Pictures are also drawn pixel by pixel.

Testing HGC, MGA, or MGP cards

To locate the HGC, MGA, or MGP card, first remove the cover from the computer system unit. The display adapter card is often, but not always, on the far left, as far away from the disk drives and the power supply as possible. Because the monitor is attached to the display adapter card, look on the back of the system unit to find the 9-pin female connector that your monitor plugs into.

If you have no display at all, check for an incorrect match between the monitor and the display adapter. Don't attach MGA and MGP cards to color monitors. Mismatches between the display adapter and the monitor usually result in snow on the monitor screen.

If you have an early PC, check the DIP-switch settings on the motherboard. DIP-switches control the memory address range where the PC expects to find display information. Incorrect DIP-switch settings usually produce a flashing cursor, with no additional video display. Modern machines need to have the display adapter type set correctly in their CMOS setup memory chip, but these machines are able to display an initial error message, such as "Incorrect setup. Wrong video adapter."

If you have one or two incorrect characters on an otherwise good screen, the video memory located on the display adapter is most likely at fault. You can use a diagnostic program to test the video RAM before you buy a new card. Many diagnostic disks provide video troubleshooting help. CheckIt, for example, contains video test programs.

Removing and installing HGC, MGA, or MGP cards

Before you remove the HGC, MGA, or MGP card, turn off the computer and monitor. Disconnect the data cable that connects the display adapter to the monitor at the display card end. You will probably have to remove two small screws that hold the cable connector tight to the card. Remove the system unit cover.

The card itself is secured to the back wall of the system unit chassis with a single screw. Remove and save the screw. Lift the card straight up; it shouldn't require extreme force.

Installation is the reverse of removal. Because HGC and MGA graphics cards are 8-bit cards, any bus connector in any clone is

appropriate. If you are replacing the card with another type of card, you may have to use a 16-bit slot on a modern machine. Carefully line up the card edge connector with the slot on the motherboard and then press down firmly. When the card is in place, the screw hole on the card lines up with the screw hole in the back of the chassis. Reinstall the screw, attach the monitor cable, and test the machine.

If you are installing a different type of display adapter — if you're replacing your old card with a VGA or a color card, for example — be sure to set any switches or jumpers on the motherboard to reflect the new display adapter. See your motherboard manual for more details.

Exotic Video Cards

In the years leading up to the arrival of the SVGA standard, several interim standards were introduced. Few of them are still in use today, and many current software programs may not work well with them. Your best bet for replacement cards may be used computer stores.

Extended Graphics Array cards

IBM introduced Extended Graphics Array (XGA) cards with its advanced 486 PS/2 computers in 1990. IBM designed the XGA card as an extension to its 8514/A standard. The XGA standard requires a Micro Channel Architecture (MCA) computer, which was used only on high-level PS/2s and a tiny handful of clones.

XGA cards provide high resolution (1,024 x 768 pixels per monitor screen) and the potential to display 65,536 colors onscreen simultaneously if you choose 640 x 480-pixel (standard VGA) resolution. In addition, XGA cards can be switched to emulate an ordinary VGA card with 16 colors and 640 x 480-pixel resolution. XGA cards use a microprocessor on the card to do most of the routine work associated with screen redraws. The 8514/A,

TIGA (Texas Instruments Graphics Architecture) cards, and VGA cards with accelerators also use video card microprocessors for fast video response.

How XGA cards work

XGA cards use the 32-bit MCA bus and MCA bus mastering (the card can take over the bus to speed up data transfer into the card). Therefore, they are surprisingly fast but limited to the PS/2 family.

Each pixel of an XGA-compatible color monitor is really a number of phosphor dot triads. Each triad is composed of one red, one green, and one blue phosphor dot. When excited by an electron beam, the dots glow. Inside the monitor, three separate electron beams scan across the CRT screen. Each beam is responsible for exciting a single color of phosphor in each pixel.

The XGA card provides an analog signal to each of the three electron guns for each of the 307,200 (640 x 480) pixels or 786,432 (1,024 x 768) pixels on the screen.

High-resolution monitors use much video memory. Remember that the specifications for each pixel are stored in the XGA card's memory, and these high resolutions have many pixels. Color uses up video memory, too. Sixteen-color modes require half as much memory as 256-color modes. Keep in mind that I'm talking about dedicated video memory (memory chips on the video card or in the sockets on the motherboard dedicated to video memory, if the XGA card is built into the motherboard) — not system memory (ordinary memory chips on the motherboard or on a memory expansion card).

Testing XGA cards

Some PS/2s feature XGA integrated on the motherboard, whereas others use a separate XGA card. However, many mid-level or low-priced PS/2s feature VGA graphics, so don't jump to the conclusion that your PS/2 has XGA merely because it is a PS/2. PS/2 computers come with diagnostic software. Use this software to check your XGA card and monitor.

Remove the cover from the computer system unit. Because the monitor is attached to the graphics adapter card or to the graphics connector on the motherboard, look on the back of the system unit to find the 15-pin female connector that your monitor data cable plugs into.

Replacement XGA adapters can be obtained from IBM; you should also be able to install a VGA or SVGA card in its place. Check with IBM if you have any questions. If the XGA adapter is part of the motherboard of your PC, you should be able to disable it with a jumper setting and have the computer recognize a card installed in the bus instead.

The 8514/A video cards

IBM introduced 8514/A in 1987 on PS/2 computers with Micro Channel Architecture. The original IBM standard provided 1,024 x 768-pixel resolution but used an interlaced monitor. *Interlacing* (painting the monitor screen in two passes of the electron gun rather than all at once) enables high-resolution graphics on moderately priced monitors, but interlaced displays tend to flicker.

The Video Electronics Standards Association (VESA) 8514/A adaptation of the 8514/A standard calls for noninterlaced monitors and a vertical scan rate of at least 70 screen refreshes per second. Many 8514/A graphics cards provide 72 or 76 Hz scan rates for crisp, flicker-free pictures on large monitors.

How 8514/A video cards work

The 8514/A uses the same monitor-to-graphics-card interface as Super VGA and extended VGA. In other words, a multiscanning VGA monitor that works fine with a high-resolution VGA card will work fine with an 8514/A card. However, your computer communicates with an 8514/A card quite differently than with a VGA card.

Your computer tells the 8514/A card to please draw a box or rotate this box; this is vector graphics. The CPU issues a high-level command, and the 8514/A graphics card figures out how to execute it. By comparison, monochrome graphics, CGA, EGA, and frame-buffer VGA cards use raster graphics and rely on the computer's main CPU for most video processing. In raster graphics, the computer's CPU figures out pixel by pixel what should be on the monitor screen.

The 8514/A cards are much faster than raster graphics cards, especially when running Windows and CAD software. TIGA cards also use vector graphics, but TIGA cards are built around a microprocessor from the Texas Instruments 34010 and 34020 families of graphics chips. TIGA is particularly fast for CAD applications. IBM's XGA video standard was designed particularly for the Microsoft Windows market. Any of these coprocessor graphics cards (8514/A, TIGA, and XGA) are dramatically faster in graphics-intensive applications than is the ordinary raster-graphics VGA card.

Testing 8514/A cards

Remove the cover from the computer system unit. Because the monitor is attached to the graphics adapter card or to the graphics connector on the motherboard, look on the back of the system unit to find the 15-pin female connector that your monitor data cable plugs into.

If the computer has no display at all, first check the switches and cables. Make sure that the computer and monitor are both plugged in and turned on. Check the monitor data cable from the 8514/A card to the monitor. It must be plugged in tight and screwed down at the video card end. You should also check the brightness and contrast controls on the monitor, but don't adjust these controls and then accidentally leave them in the dim position. The monitor is usually brightest when the knob is as far clockwise as possible.

Some 8514/A cards have VGA support built in. Other 8514/A cards are designed for a computer with a separate VGA card or with VGA on the motherboard. In either case, the computer runs in VGA mode while booting and then switches over to 8514/A mode.

In order to properly configure an 8514/A card and to troubleshoot problems, you need to know if you have a secondary VGA card installed, and if the 8514/A card requires a separate VGA card.

Memory Controller Gate Arrays

The Memory Controller Gate Array (MCGA) adapter is a hybrid of a hybrid, and it is all but forgotten in the history of PC video, except by those owners of a small group of low-end IBM PS/2 models that used it. The adapter offered a mix of VGA, MDA, and CGA. Two text modes are available — one mode close to the CGA standard and another somewhat like VGA. For graphics, several CGA-like modes are available, as well as a pair of severely limited VGA modes that are hamstrung by the 64K total RAM associated with the adapter.

An MCGA-based system uses VGA-style connectors and can be used with standard VGA displays. The system is capable of detecting color or monochrome monitors, and the system can reset its mode automatically.

Use IBM's supplied diagnostics to test the MCGA circuitry. Be sure that the monitor is attached, turned on, and properly adjusted before concluding that the problem lies with the adapter.

The MCGA is integrated into the motherboard of the PS/2, and therefore can't be repaired or upgraded. Instead, you can bypass it completely by plugging a PS/2 VGA adapter into the display adapter slot of the MCA expansion bus; the MCGA will be automatically disabled.

Texas Instruments Graphics Architecture cards

Texas Instruments launched its own graphics interface, called TIGA (Texas Instruments graphics architecture). These TIGA graphics cards use a Texas Instruments 34010 or 34020 graphics microprocessor chip and vector graphics.

Many of the early users of TIGA cards were design professionals who needed 24-bit, photo-quality color. Super VGA cards have adopted most of the TIGA standard's advantages. TIGA cards provide high resolution (1,024 x 768 pixels per monitor screen or higher) and improved speed.

How TIGA cards work

TIGA cards use a high-speed, VGA-style analog monitor. The monitor turns a pixel on or passes over it and then leaves it blank at the explicit pixel-by-pixel direction of the graphics adapter card. The TIGA card provides an analog signal to each of the three electron guns for each of the 786,432 (1,024 x 768) onscreen pixels. The resolution of 1,280 x 1,024 pixels has 1.3 million pixels, almost twice as many pixels as the 1,024 x 768-pixel resolution.

Though TIGA uses the same monitor-to-graphics-card interface as Super VGA and Extended VGA, your computer communicates with a TIGA card quite differently than with a VGA card. Your computer tells the TIGA card to please draw a box or rotate this box, which, as explained previously, is termed *vector graphics*. Most other video cards use raster graphics, a pixel-by-pixel technique in which, as explained earlier in the chapter, the computer's CPU figures out pixel by pixel what should be on the monitor screen. Frame buffer VGA cards (ordinary VGA cards without an accelerator), EGA cards, MGP cards, and CGA cards use raster graphics.

Because most TIGA cards come with Windows drivers, any program that you run from within Microsoft Windows should be able to use the TIGA card's fast graphics microprocessor. Other DOS-based software, however, may not have a TIGA driver.

Testing TIGA cards

Remove the cover from the computer system unit. Because the monitor is attached to the graphics adapter card or to the graphics connector on the motherboard, look on the back of the system unit to find the 15-pin, female connector that your monitor data cable plugs into.

If the computer has no display at all, first check the switches and cables. Make sure that the computer and monitor are both plugged in and turned on. Check the monitor data cable that connects the TIGA card to the monitor. It must be plugged in tightly and screwed down at the video display adapter end. You should also check the brightness and contrast controls on the monitor, but don't adjust these controls and then accidentally leave them in the dim position. In general, the monitor is brightest with the knob turned clockwise.

Some TIGA cards have VGA support built in; others are designed for a computer with a separate VGA card or with VGA on the motherboard. In either case, the computer runs in VGA mode while booting and then switches to TIGA mode. For troubleshooting purposes, ask yourself the following questions: Do you have a VGA card installed? Do you need one? Does it work?

SUMMARY

This chapter explored the transmitter to your PC's monitor. I also spent a good deal of time discussing various older display adapter technologies. You can see from the specifications on these older devices that using them for anything but the most basic computer tasks would be difficult or impossible. Nevertheless, I know a fair number of people who continue to use older computer hardware. They purchased PCs several years ago, on which they installed basic word processing or accounting or spreadsheet software that continues to do what they want done. After you decide to move beyond early versions of Windows, or move up from DOS to Windows, you'll want to install newer display technology.

The next chapter moves on to the monitor itself.

Ch
13

Chapter 14

Monitors and LCDs

You may not know much about the electronics of video monitors, but you almost certainly know what you like. Modern displays are Rembrandts compared to the cave scrawls of dinosaur systems. The current state-of-the-art for modern machines is a high-resolution SVGA monitor or a flat liquid crystal display (better known by the acronym, *LCD*).

Most PC buyers today consider a 15-inch monitor the minimum acceptable size, and many low-end to medium-priced systems from major vendors now come with 17-inch or 19-inch displays. For graphics-intensive computing, such as photo and video editing, a 19-, 20-, or 21-inch device is considered essential. In many offices, high-quality LCDs have taken their place on the crowded desktop; they are popular because they require less space and generate less heat. Like most other parts of the modern PC system, the prices of monitors have also dropped sharply in recent years, even as they have become larger and of better quality.

Any modern machine should readily work with high-resolution SVGA monitors or LCDs. Some senior citizens may require new video display adapters and, possibly, upgrades to ROM BIOS chips to work with high-resolution monitors or LCDs. The oldest of the dinosaurs may not have BIOS fixes or motherboard circuitry to enable them to work with advanced video systems.

If you intend to use high-resolution settings on your monitor, make sure that the display device and your graphics adapter are a good match for each other. You can't view more pixels than your monitor can display, and you can't ask a graphics adapter to address more pixels than it is capable of rendering in memory.

Another issue for some users in choosing a monitor is the physical size of the monitor itself. The depth of a monitor in its case is roughly equal to the diagonal measurement of the tube; a 21-inch monitor will take up a lot of space on a typical 30-inch-deep desktop. Monitor weight also increases with size, with some monsters weighing in at 75 pounds or more. The good news is that monitor technology, like the technology in other parts of the computer, is improving. So-called short or short-depth monitors are available today that considerably reduce the demands of older monitors on your desktop real estate. Some 19-inch monitors today are no deeper than previous 14- and 15-inch screens.

And as I've noted, many users have shifted their sights from video display tube monitors to flat-panel LCD displays. These devices are smaller, considerably more lightweight, and in some uses, sharper and brighter than monitors. When the previous edition of this book was published, I celebrated the fact that 14-inch LCDs had dropped below the $1,000 price line; as this seventh edition goes to press, 15-inch LCDs sell for as little as $400.

After you've chosen your monitor, maintaining it becomes the focus. For the most part, monitors are not repairable — at least not by anyone other than a highly skilled technician. That's the bad news; the good news is that monitors are generally very reliable.

> **TIP**
>
> I've found that getting a monitor repaired at a computer store — even one that may have quite capable technicians — isn't a cost-effective solution. On the other hand, I've had really good luck finding old-fashioned television repair shops that are well equipped to solve many monitor problems. Look for a shop that seems to have a history in its location. If old parts and dozens of TV sets awaiting pickup or repair are scattered around the shop, give them a try. The shops I've found will charge no fee or a very low fee to at least look at your monitor and give you an estimate on repair. If the estimate is too high, just leave it with them; these shops sometimes can sell the parts or the whole monitor at salvage. George, my favorite repairman, is a master at mixing and matching on-off switches and other controls from devices never intended to work together.

Here are four things that you can do to help your monitor have a long and healthy life:

- Make sure to plug it into a good-quality surge protector. (This is the best thing you can do to protect the life of your monitor.)
- Make sure that the cable between the monitor and the video card is firmly attached at each end and not crimped or pinched.
- Be sure that the monitor is safely installed on a sturdy desk with its cable properly out of tripping range of passersby.
- Keep your workplace tidy: Don't place any papers on top of the ventilating holes on the back and side of the monitor. Periodically use a new paintbrush to remove accumulated dust on the monitor's ventilation holes. And I don't have to warn you about placing cups of coffee or soda anywhere in the vicinity, right?

Choosing the right monitor or LCD and understanding it are the topics at issue in this chapter.

How a Monitor Works

Amateurs — including this author — should not attempt to repair a monitor. High voltage, delicate glass, and toxic chemicals are inside. Confine your troubleshooting to the outside of the box, please, and bring your monitor to a capable repair shop if necessary. The troubleshooting process will go much easier for you if you have a basic understanding of the way a monitor works.

A monitor is, at heart, a very high-quality television set that is tuned to just one channel: the signal coming out of the PC's video adapter. The inside of the glass front of the monitor is coated with phosphor compounds that glow whenever an electron beam strikes them. The monitor's electronics view the screen as a grid of dots to be painted with light. Each group of red, green, and blue dots is called a *pixel*, which stands for picture element.

A color monitor creates color display by combining the three primary colors of light: red, green, and blue. Black is the absence of any color. Combining green light and blue light creates yellow. Combining all three light sources creates white.

Inside a monitor, an electron beam is aimed toward a phosphor-coated screen. The phosphor glows whenever the electrons hit it, producing lighted images on the screen. When the monitor is plugged into a video adapter card, it receives a signal called the *scan frequency*. The monitor must lock in on the scan signal; in other words, the electron beam must cross the screen in synchronization with the scan signal.

The electron beam starts at the top left of the screen. It scans across the screen from left to right, exciting some dots of phosphor and bypassing others. When the beam reaches the right side of the screen, it quickly returns to the left and scans another line directly beneath the first one. An ordinary monochrome monitor has 350 of these scan lines per screen.

When the electron beam reaches the bottom right of the screen, it leaps up to the top-left corner and traces the 350 scan lines from the top again. This set of 350 scan lines—often visible when the brightness control is turned up too high—is called the *raster pattern* (or *raster*).

A basic SVGA monitor refreshes the screen (rescans the complete raster) 60 to 75 times a second. The refresh or vertical scan rate is, therefore, 60 to 75 Hz. By comparison, the horizontal scan rate is 31,500 to 60,000 times per second (31.5 to 60 KHz).

The video adapter card, located in the computer system unit, provides explicit directions to the electron gun in the monitor. As the electron beam scans across the screen, the video card calls for a burst of electrons here to excite this pixel or a burst of electrons there to excite that pixel. A match must exist between the capabilities of the video card and the monitor or else the monitor may not be able to work at its optimum resolution or other settings.

The higher the resolution you select, the faster the horizontal scan rate that the video card must produce. Table 14-1 contains the requirements for the most common video standards; in Chapter 13, you can find a more detailed listing of standards and their requirements.

Video Standard	Resolution	Horizontal Scan Rate (KHz)	Vertical Scan (Refresh) Rate (Hz)
SVGA	1,024 x 768	48.3 KHz	60 Hz
VESA	1,024 x 768	60 KHz	75 Hz
VESA	1,280 x 1,024	80 KHz	75 Hz

Nearly all modern monitors deliver SVGA specifications, an extension of the VGA standard that is one of the demarcation lines between dinosaurs and senior citizens. Dinosaur RGB monitors are no longer supported by modern machines, and EGA screens have very limited utility today.

Each monitor must be paired with an appropriate video display adapter card located in the computer system unit. *Multiscanning* circuitry—nearly ubiquitous today—allows monitors to lock onto multiple vertical and horizontal scanning frequencies, so a single multiscanning monitor is compatible with many different video cards.

Monitor components

The main internal components of a monitor are as follows:

- **CRT.** The cathode ray tube (CRT) is a sealed glass vacuum tube. Within it is an electron gun that emits a beam of electrons. A deflection yoke moves the beam horizontally and vertically as it strikes the phosphor-coated screen on the inside of the tube's front. Each of the points struck by the electron beam emits a red, blue, or green light for a fraction of a second.
- **Flyback transformer.** This component generates the high voltage needed to produce the electron beam within the CRT.
- **Power supply.** Circuitry within the CRT changes the incoming alternating voltage into necessary direct current.

TABLE 14-1: Horizontal and Vertical Scan Rates

Video Standard	Resolution	Horizontal Scan Rate (KHz)	Vertical Scan (Refresh) Rate (Hz)
CGA	640 x 200	15.75 KHz	60 Hz
EGA	640 x 350	21.5 KHz	60 Hz
VGA	640 x 480	31.5 KHz	60 Hz
VESA	640 x 480	37.5 KHz	75 Hz
SVGA	800 x 600	37.5 KHz	60 Hz
VESA	800 x 600	48 KHz	72 Hz
XGA	1,024 x 768	56.6 KHz	44 Hz (interlaced)

Ch 14

- **Video amplifier.** The incoming video signal from the computer, usually about 0.7 volts, must be amplified to a level needed by the CRT to generate an image, usually above 40 volts.
- **Degaussing coil.** Circuitry here removes from the CRT any stray magnetic field, which can cause signal impurities.
- **CPU (central processing unit).** Modern monitors have their own brain to manage special features, including screen adjustments.

How a monitor draws an image

Monitors use one of three ways to draw an image or a character on the screen:

- One way uses simple instructions from the CPU that tell the video card and the monitor to display the letter J at position 12,180. The card needs to have a definition for each letter and a particular style for that letter; the description is then communicated to the monitor in the form of instructions about which individual dots to illuminate. The original monochrome display adapter for the first IBM PC used such a scheme. Although very few modern users work in "text mode," all subsequent improvements to graphics modes maintain this facility as part of their repertoire.
- Another means of drawing images uses a video display adapter that maintains a library of shapes and colors that are then communicated to the monitor.
- Modern graphical user interfaces (GUIs) like Windows produce the entire screen as a bitmap in memory, drawing all characters and graphics. The video card transfers this bitmap to the monitor for display as a series of illuminated dots. Bitmaps are not nearly as fast as direct display of characters, but offer other significant advantages, such as the ability to draw any type of imaginable image and to use an unlimited number of type styles and sizes.

One additional, essential element of monitor quality is *resolution*, which is a measurement of the size of the pixels. On two monitors of the same size, the one that displays more pixels is the one with higher resolution because the pixels must be smaller to fit in the same space. A set of tiny pixels on a small screen yields a high-resolution display; those same pixels on a huge room-sized screen won't yield as sharp an image.

Types of Monitors

Inexpensive monochrome monitors, the kind that were standard on PCs through the 1980s, are capable of displaying only one color — usually white, green, or amber against a black background.

Some very capable monochrome displays exist for modern machines. Higher-priced monochrome monitors — for example, VGA monochrome monitors — are available with very high resolution and multiple shades of gray. Ultra-high-resolution monochrome monitors with proprietary video systems, intended for desktop publishing and computer-aided design, usually have extra-large screens designed to show two facing pages or a vertical page in true proportions.

But high-resolution color video really took off in the 1990s. SVGA color monitors are now standard equipment on PCs, with resolutions of up to $1,600 \times 1,280$ pixels on home machines. In fact, the designation of monitor specifications by labels such as SVGA, VGA, and other tags is declining; manufacturers instead market primarily on the basis of resolution.

Microsoft Windows, large spreadsheet, and desktop publishing users appreciate a full-page view of their work. In addition, high-level graphics users are choosing to manipulate photos, video, and animation with 32-bit color video cards capable of displaying millions of subtle color shades.

LCD Displays

LCDs produce images on a flat surface by shining or reflecting light through changeable liquid crystals and colored filters. LCDs offer a number of advantages over a traditional cathode ray tube, including:

- They take up less space.
- They consume much less power, perhaps 30 to 50 watts compared to a video display tube's need for 100 to 125 watts.
- They produce much less heat.
- They don't flicker or strobe, thus reducing eyestrain.
- Screen surfaces produce little or no glare.
- LCD screens require a much smaller frame around their edges, yielding more usable display space than a cathode ray tube of the same nominal size. The viewable area of a typical 15-inch LCD is about the same as that of a typical 17-inch CRT.

The disadvantages of LCDs are relatively few:

- An LCD costs more than a CRT of equivalent size. Until recently, that statement would have read "much more," but like almost every other part of the modern PC, LCDs have begun to drop in price. In 2002, 15-inch LCDs are expected to drop below $400, down from over $1,000 a year earlier.
- Some LCD devices may not have as wide a viewing angle as a conventional CRT monitor. Early LCD displays had to be viewed at close to a head-on angle. Moving more than about 10 degrees to the left or right, or sitting at a chair too high or low could result in a dimmed or distorted image. Today, however, the situation is much better, with viewing angles from 60 degrees or so to as high as 160 degrees in more expensive high-end devices.
- Good-quality LCDs are very sharp and easy to read, but even the best models can't display colors as brightly or as well-defined as a good CRT can. Because each pixel can be addressed individually, LCDs are capable of creating sharper text than CRTs, which depend on a moving beam of electrons that must be kept in focus and controlled properly. Those same sharp edges, however, make graphics a bit less lifelike than those shown on a CRT, where various tricks can be used to create subtle gradations of color and brightness.
- LCDs are capable of working with only one physical resolution, limited by the number of pixels that are built into the display. If you need to work at a particular non-standard resolution, the LCD must work with emulation software; some display-software combinations work better than others.

The technology behind LCDs goes back to experiments with liquid crystals as early as 1888. Scientists found that certain liquid chemicals can be made to align precisely when they are subjected to electrical current; think of the way metal shavings will align at the poles of a magnet.

An LCD works by energizing or de-energizing liquid crystals to act like shutters to block or permit the passage of light. Early LCDs, still used in inexpensive calculators, some cell phone screens, and some of the first laptops, depended on light penetrating through the screen to reach a reflective surface and then to be bounced back at the viewer. Modern LCDs typically use a powered fluorescent backlight to shine through the crystals. Light from the backlight passes through one or more polarizing filters and then through a layer that contains many thousands of tiny spots of liquid crystal arrayed in tiny cells.

The frame of the LCD screen contains thousands of tiny electrical connectors that connect to tracings that extend across the rows of cells. When the display's controller sends an electric current to a particular row and column, the liquid crystals at that cell twist into a position that permits the polarized light to pass through. Modern LCDs, like the one shown in Figure 14-1, use a *thin-film transistor* to deliver current to individual cells; these active-matrix systems are much improved over earlier passive-matrix systems.

Ch
14

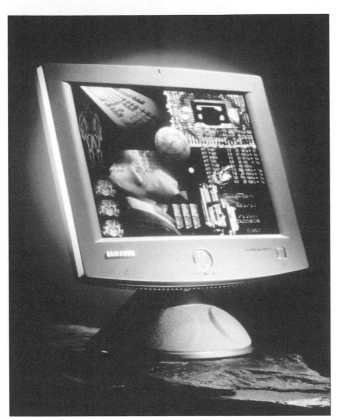

FIGURE 14-1: *A monitor without a video display tube, the Samsung SyncMaster is a flat-panel LCD display.*

On a monochrome screen, the crystals block the passage of light to display black. Color LCDs use similar technology. Each pixel is made up of three cells of liquid crystal; each of these cells has a red, green, or blue filter allowing creation of almost every hue by the additive color process.

Within an LCD, the addressing of the pixels is done digitally. Although the PC itself manipulates a graphics bitmap digitally, a standard video adapter then converts the information to an analog signal. Nearly all early LCDs converted this analog signal back to digital form, adding circuitry that minimizes ghosting and

fluttering that can be caused by the conversion from digital to analog and back to digital.

The best quality, though, comes with designs that stay digital all the way, working with specialized digital video adapters. Today, many LCD designs use the Digital Visual Interface (DVI) standard, ending several years of incompatible digital standards between the Digital Flat Panel standard, put forth by the Video Electronics Association, and the DVI standard promulgated by the Digital Display Working Group. The standard regularizes connectors and electrical signals for digital video controllers. Older LCDs do exist; they must be mated with the appropriate display adapter and cable to work properly.

> **NOTE**
>
> Because LCDs don't require a wide supporting frame around the display, a 15-inch LCD presents nearly the same viewable surface as a 17-inch cathode ray tube monitor.

Monitor Size

What exactly is a 15-inch monitor? In theory, *screen size* is measured as the diagonal distance from top-left to bottom-right corners, or top-right to bottom-left corners. However, not all screens are shaped the same, and in any case, the plastic frame around the screen (called a *bezel*) can crop as much as an inch on all sides of the tube.

Partly as the result of some consumer lawsuits, monitor makers now are a bit more careful in their claims. Look for the manufacturer's specification of maximum viewable image size. Often, a 15-inch screen has viewable sizes in the range of 13.5 to 13.9 inches; 17-inch screens are usually in the range of 15.5 to 16 inches.

Probably more important is the difference in square inches of screen real estate offered by monitors of various sizes. Going from a 14-inch monitor to a 15-inch box yields about a 12 percent boost in size, from 84 square inches to 94 square inches. Going from a

15-inch monitor to a 21-inch behemoth doubles the view, from about 94 square inches to about 185 square inches. All of these numbers are rough because no two monitor makers frame their tubes with the same width of plastic bezel.

Also consider the fact that very few monitors actually send electrons all the way to the edges of the tube. Additionally, those that are capable of doing so may deliver a distorted picture at the edges. You need to adjust the picture to deliver the best view, usually resulting in a frame of about a quarter-inch on all sides. Note also that on some monitors, each time you adjust the resolution, the side-to-side and diagonal measurements of the image may change.

On my desktop, I use a 19-inch monitor that delivers a diagonal viewable image size of about 18 inches; it is capable of displaying a clean and crisp image at 1,024 × 768 resolution. Table 14-2 compares real estate for monitors from 14 to 21 inches diagonal measure.

The fact that a monitor is technically capable of operating at a high resolution does not mean that it will present a usable image. For example, a 14-inch monitor looks best at a 640 × 480 resolution and will give you an electronic headache at 1,280 × 1,024 or higher. By the same token, some very large monitors are optimized for use at higher resolutions and may look too blocky at lower resolutions. It all comes down to personal preference; some users like to use large characters on a large screen, while others prefer to see more information.

LCD monitors have a very narrow frame around their screens; for all intents and purposes, the entire screen is viewable. Table 14-3 contains a comparison of available real estate on LCDs. More displayable real estate is available at every size.

TABLE 14-2: Monitor Real Estate Comparison

Monitor Size*	Typical Viewable Image Size*	Typical Square Inches	Real Estate Index**	Typical Maximum Resolution
14-inch	13.2 inches	84 inches	100	1,024 × 768
15-inch	13.7 inches	94 inches	112	1,024 × 768
17-inch	15.7 inches	130 inches	155	1,280 × 1,024
19-inch	18 inches	156 inches	186	1,280 × 1,024 to 1,600 × 1,280
20-inch	19 inches	168 inches	200	1,280 × 1,024 to 1,600 × 1,280
21-inch	19.8 inches	185 inches	220	1,280 × 1,024 to 1,600 × 1,280

Measured diagonally.
**Fix Your Own PC Real Estate Index: Square-inch measurements of viewable image size are compared to a 14-inch monitor. For example, the 21-inch monitor listed here is approximately 2.2 times larger than a 14-inch monitor.*

TABLE 14-3: LCD Real Estate Comparison

LCD Size*	Typical Viewable Image Size*	Typical Square Inches	Real Estate Index**	Typical Maximum Resolution
14-inch	14 inches	88 inches	100	1,024 × 768
15-inch	15 inches	119 inches	135	1,024 × 768
17-inch	17 inches	140 inches	159	1,280 × 1,024
18-inch	18 inches	156 inches	177	1,280 × 1,024
20-inch	20 inches	192 inches	219	1,280 × 1,024

Measured diagonally.
**Fix Your Own PC Real Estate Index: Square-inch measurements of viewable image size are compared to a 14-inch LCD. For example, the 20-inch LCD listed here is approximately 2.19 times larger than a 14-inch LCD.*

Table 14-4 is a chart of typical best settings. However, what is best in any given situation depends to some degree on the application that you are running. Highly graphical applications certainly will do better at higher resolutions, but you won't see much difference if you are using text-only applications all the time.

Ch 14

TABLE 14-4: Best Resolution by Display Size

Display Size (Nominal size)	640 × 480	800 × 600	1,024 × 768	1,280 × 1,024	1,600 × 1,200
14-inch	**Best**	Good	Fair	Poor	Poor
15-inch	Good	Good	**Best**	Poor	Poor
17-inch	Fair–Good	Good	**Best**	Fair	Poor
19-inch	Fair	Fair	Good	**Best**	Fair
21-inch	Poor	Fair	Good	**Best**	Good

The Elements of a High-Quality Display

Four important specifications make up the elements of a high-quality display:

- Dot pitch
- Refresh or scan rate
- Interlace or noninterlace scan
- Screen shape

The following sections describe each element in detail.

Dot pitch

The first element that most monitor buyers consider is the *dot pitch*, a measurement of how close together the dots of phosphor are placed to make up a video monitor's image. The finer the dot pitch (the lower the number), the finer the image — theoretically. Today's better monitors have a dot pitch of 0.28mm or less.

On traditional monitors using dot masks, dot pitch is measured as the diagonal or vertical distance between two dots of the same color. The smaller the dot pitch, the finer the image. I wouldn't choose to strain my eyes with anything coarser than 0.28mm for a video monitor or LCD panel. (Dot pitch is sometimes called *pixel pitch* in LCD specs.)

As with everything else in personal computing, specs are getting better. In late 2001, some 21-inch monitors were on the market with 0.24mm dot pitch or better, so check the specifications before you buy.

Trinitron and similar tubes are measured by stripe pitch; NEC ChromaClear and Panasonic Pure Flat tubes present measurements of mask or slot pitch. Both represent the horizontal distance between two stripes of the same color. Look for pitches of 0.25mm or less for desktop monitors, and 0.24mm or less for 20- and 21-inch models.

One specialized class of monitors is large presentation devices used in instructional settings and as part of a family room PC/entertainment center system. These monitors are big, even by television standards — up to 42 or 48 inches in size — and are intended to be viewed at some distance from the screen. Typical dot pitches for these room-size monitors can be in the 0.75mm to 0.90mm range and larger. One design uses a smaller dot pitch at the center and a larger dot pitch at the corners, where information is presumably less important.

Someday, the prices of another type of monitor — the plasma display — may drop to a reasonable range. Plasma displays use charged gas to create separate light sources for each pixel, like a tiny neon light. Displays are as perfectly flat as an LCD, and as bright or brighter than a video display tube. These devices — just a few inches thick — can be produced in giant sizes. In 2001, a 50-inch plasma display from Pioneer sold for just under $10,000.

Refresh or scan rate

Refresh rate, also called *vertical frequency* or *vertical scan rate*, tells you how many times per second the monitor redraws the image on screen. Most current users find that refresh rates below 75 Hz (75 refreshes per second) cause visible and annoying flicker. Slow scan rates produce flicker because of the decay of phosphor illumination between passes of the beam. High scan rates produce a rock-solid image, but monitors capable of high scan rates are more expensive. A scan rate that is adequate on a 14-inch monitor will seem to flicker on a big 17- or 20-inch monitor because the high-resolution video modes often used on these large monitors need a higher scan rate.

For most monitors, the refresh rate declines as the resolution increases. In other words, a monitor may be capable of 100 to 150 Hz at 640 × 480 resolution, but only 75 to 85 Hz at the 1,280 × 1,024 setting. Put another way, when you see a high refresh rate advertised for a monitor, it almost always refers to the display's capability at its lowest resolution. Pay attention to its specifications at the resolution you intend to use most often.

The original IBM PC's monochrome card rewrote the monitor screen 50 times per second. A vertical scan rate of 50 Hz is too slow for most people's eyes, so IBM specified long-persistence phosphor compounds on the monitor screen. Once excited, these phosphors continue to glow for a while even after the electron beam has moved on to another part of the screen. This cures the flickering, but the monitor displays annoying ghosts when the user scrolls text.

Modern monitors adjust refresh rate according to the display resolution. You may see specs for a 21-inch monitor, such as the ViewSonic PT813, for example, that show a 130 Hz refresh rate at 640 × 480 resolution, and an 85 Hz refresh rate at 1,600 × 1,200 resolution.

An RGB color monitor, the color monitor paired with the CGA video card on the early IBM PC, refreshes the screen 60 times per second. High-resolution VGA and multiscanning monitors refresh at rates of as much as 80 times per second.

Do you see a pattern in these numbers? A high vertical scan rate is better. Monitors that can handle Super VGA (800 × 600) screen resolutions at 70 or 72 refreshes per second look good. The same Super VGA resolution on a lower-quality Super VGA monitor that refreshes the screen 56 times per second will look jumpy and appear to flicker.

Interlaced versus noninterlaced monitors

In the high-tech equivalent of the search for a free lunch, monitor designers came up with interlaced monitors, displays that refresh only the odd-numbered rows of pixels in one pass, and then refresh the even-numbered rows of pixels in a second pass. Interlaced monitors can display high-resolution video (many rows of pixels on the screen), yet at the time they were introduced, they cost much less than noninterlaced monitors.

It's a subjective decision—some viewers don't mind the flicker inherent in the design; others can't abide interlaced monitors, especially if they spend many hours in front of the screen. Because the overall price of monitors has gone down at the same time that quality has gone up, interlaced monitors are now relatively rare and really not worth buying.

Screen shape

The sheet of paper in the book that you are reading is more or less flat. Monitors, on the other hand, are more or less curved. Designers add curvature to television and computer monitor screens to deal with the fact that the edges of the screen are farther away from the electron gun than the center of the screen. Think of it this way: at the center of the screen, the angle between the electron gun and the front face of the tube is flat. However, to illuminate a pixel in the upper-right corner, for example, the electron gun has to point up and to the right. A pixel located at the exact center of the tube, therefore, may be perfectly round, while a pixel in one of the corners receives a relatively oblique pulse that results in an oblong or *astigmatic* illumination. Therefore, the larger the screen, the wider the angle between the electron gun and the corners.

Some of that physics problem has been solved by modern electronics, but nearly all tubes still have a bit of curve today. Tube designs include spherical, cylindrical, and flat.

- **Spherical tubes** present a face like a slice of a ball, with curves at the top, bottom, and sides. They are generally the least expensive, but often the least pleasing to critical eyes. They are usually seen on 14-inch models; some 20-inch monitors use spherical tubes to present a lower-cost alternative to 21-inch behemoths.
- **Cylindrical screens** are like a slice taken from the side of a large barrel, resulting in a nearly flat vertical and a slightly curved horizontal shape. Cylindrical tubes are well suited to Trinitron designs. (Sony's original design has since been licensed and adapted by Mitsubishi and other manufacturers.)
- **Flat screens,** for the most part, are close enough to claim the name but still deserving of quotation marks. These designs are a slice of a very large sphere, so large that the curves are barely perceptible. Some of these designs sacrifice a bit of sharpness at the edges. Panasonic has introduced what it calls a Pure Flat CRT design, which is, as the name suggests, truly level in all dimensions. This design uses a "pre-stretched" slot mask held flat by tension, and an ultra-fine 0.24mm stripe pitch.

Color and shades of gray

The number of colors offered on a monitor is determined by the capabilities of the video adapter. More color does not make the monitor display any sharper, but it does make it easier to read or easier to pick out details in an image, which may make additional colors the functional equivalent of sharpness.

A total of 16 colors was once the standard for text work and simple graphics, and was considered adequate for those tasks. Today, I don't think anybody with a modern machine would be satisfied with a 16-color display. A 256-color display was once considered the minimum for multimedia work, but today's users want more than that even for text displays. Even the most basic graphics display card is capable of 65K colors (16-bit color) and most can go to 16.7 million colors (24-bit color) or more (32-bit color). If you perform any graphics editing, including retouching and manipulation of photographs, you need a high-resolution video card and monitor.

WARNING

Higher color counts come at a price, though, and I'm not merely referring to purchase cost. The more colors the system has to draw with and transfer, the slower the screen redraws and the slower the general video response.

A high number of colors places a great demand on video display adapters. Many modern machine graphics cards now begin with 4MB of DRAM (dynamic RAM), but upgrades offer as much as 64MB to add more colors and speed at higher resolutions.

CROSS-REFERENCE

See Chapter 13 for more on DRAM, VRAM, WRAM, and video display adapters.

If you have a monochrome monitor—almost impossible to replace—the equivalent of a monitor's number of colors is the range of shades of gray. Gray shades can make the display seem much sharper, even though you are still working with the original number of pixels per screen. Clever font designers use gray shades strategically on the edges of characters to fool the eye, a technique called *antialiasing*. The user perceives noticeably crisper fonts with cleaner, smoother curves.

Antiglare

One not-so-minor issue for monitor owners is dealing with glare from office lighting and open windows. The cheapest monitors can be so shiny that you can comb your hair in the reflected glare.

You can do a number of things to reduce interference from outside light sources. The first issue is often to deal with the lighting situation at your workplace. Some users find a good solution in turning off overhead lights and replacing them with smaller, focused task lights on or alongside your desk. You can also install light-filtering shades or curtains to reduce glare from outside sources. Monitor makers can mount their devices on a tilt-and-pivot stand that allows for adjustment.

The lowest level of glare protection is a coating that is sprayed onto the outside or inside of the glass that faces the user. Newer techniques called *spin coating* can apply a very thin, optically clear protection.

One recent advance is *microfilter CRTs*. In this scheme, a tiny, colored filter over each phosphor dot absorbs light bouncing off the filter. An added plus for this design is that the tubes can be made of clear instead of tinted glass, allowing the monitors to be slightly brighter than standard devices.

The importance of maintaining control

Buying a monitor that has only an on-off switch is not a wise decision. No two offices or rec rooms have the same lighting conditions, your eyes may be different from mine, and two models of the same monitor may have different brightness, contrast, or color levels. And finally, everything is subject to change over time.

Therefore, I recommend that you buy a monitor with a full set of controls. The best location for these controls is on the front side of the monitor; you want to be looking at the screen at a standard reading distance as you make adjustments.

The original design for computer monitors used knobs or wheels to make analog adjustments; lower-priced (and mostly outdated) models still offer these controls. The problem with knobs is that the settings you make affect only the current resolution. Any time you change resolution—which includes bouncing out of Windows to DOS—the image size, centering, brightness, contrast, and other settings may bounce around.

Modern monitors use digital controls with digital memories that store the precise settings you make for each resolution or graphics mode. The monitor senses changes and uses stored settings automatically. Other advanced features include onscreen menus that display instructions for making settings on the monitor, and in some cases, produce test patterns for adjustment purposes.

The monitor should at least include controls for brightness, contrast, vertical size, horizontal size, and position. Some less-expensive monitors may offer a switch to turn overscan on or off, which expands the image vertically and horizontally, but gives you less flexibility than separate controls. You may have a situation where text is placed off the displayable face of the monitor.

Better monitors include a degaussing circuit that clears up color and convergence problems caused by magnetic fields. The process can take place automatically each time you turn the

Ch
14

monitor on, or you can initiate it by pressing a button among the controls.

An advanced color adjustment, offered in addition to color level, lets you set a monitor's white balance. Photographers sometimes refer to this sort of adjustment as *color temperature*. A white balance setting can add a slight pink (warm) tint or a slight blue (cool) tint to what may otherwise be pure white. This sort of feature is valuable if the particular monitor has a warm or cool tint as delivered.

Other advanced image controls are intended to compensate for distortions such as pincushioning in which vertical lines bow outward or barrel distortion in which the lines bow inward. A trapezoid control can improve trapezoidal distortion that gives an image varying widths at top and bottom.

Why bad things happen to good monitors

Why does the monitor that got such good reviews in a computer magazine, or the one that shone with uncommon excellence on the shelf at the dealer, look like a 1956 Philco when you plug it in at home or at your office?

The fact is that monitors are subject to variations in assembly and are also vulnerable to mishandling in shipping or setup. Because a bit of hand work is involved in finishing display tubes and in placing and adjusting the electromagnets that aim electrons at the screen, a minor misplacement or a shift in location after a monitor leaves the factory can throw a monitor out of focus, shift its image off-center, or otherwise affect image quality.

WARNING

Over time, power supplies age and change characteristics, and the stress and strain a monitor undergoes as it is turned on and off can have an effect. One indicator of a failing power supply is a shrunken display that no longer can extend to the corners of the screen; another indicator is a reduction in the intensity of the whitest whites or other bright colors.

Be sure to test your monitor meticulously when you first plug it in. And don't be afraid to reject a monitor that doesn't live up to your expectations. For that reason, be sure to buy the screen from a reputable dealer willing to give you a money-back guarantee that will be in effect for a reasonable period of time after purchase. Compare the potential savings you may obtain from a mail-order house to the cost of returning a bad display if necessary.

Also, go back and make adjustments to the controls for your monitor every six months or so to tune it up in that way.

Green monitors

Green monitors can display hundreds of colors—not just the color of the forests or money. The term *green* refers to a standard intended to reduce electrical usage by devices. These monitors have their own internal hardware that reduces power draw or even shuts down the device entirely if the user ceases activity for a particular period of time. Green monitors often also work with software and BIOS-based controls.

Look for compliance with the Energy Star standards for consumption in sleep modes and the Display Power Management Signaling (DPMS) standard that allows a DPMS-compliant graphics card to initiate sleep modes. Some monitors support the Swedish Nutek standards, which are even more stringent in power consumption controls.

If you are concerned about electromagnetic emissions from monitors, look for compliance with the current MPR-II specifications or the even more stringent TCO standard. Your best defense against electromagnetic emissions is to sit at a proper distance from your monitor, generally about an arm's length, and never to operate a monitor with its cover off or with a crack or other opening in the shielding.

Plug-and-Play monitors

With the arrival of the Plug-and-Play standard came monitors that can communicate with the PC when they are plugged in.

Nearly all monitors now offered for sale support this standard. These monitors use an adaptation of the common DB-15 VGA cable and connector to send information about the monitor's capabilities to the graphics adapter in the PC and vice versa. The biggest problem addressed by this new intelligent connection is avoiding refresh rate mismatches between monitor and adapter.

The cables use four rarely used data lines in the cable for this purpose, but the monitor and adapter must subscribe to the VESA Display Data Channel (DDC) protocol. Some monitors indicate compliance with DDC by coloring their cable connectors bright blue.

The original standard here was DDC1, which has Plug-and-Play monitors continuously sending information back up the wire to the graphics adapter. The more advanced DDC2B specification has the monitor send information to the PC only when it is requested to do so by the graphics adapter. Monitors must support both DDC versions 1 and 2B, while the adapter can support either specification.

NOTE

A DDC monitor will work without problem on a PC that doesn't have Plug-and-Play capabilities and with an adapter that does not support DDC. The system will simply be as dumb as it always was before the new specification.

Even further advanced is the DDC2AB specification that allows software control of monitor features, including color settings and size and distortion adjustments.

The Universal Serial Bus can offer the same facilities, and can also permit daisy-chaining of peripherals including mice, keyboards, and printers. Today, though, monitors that connect to the PC through the USB port are rare, although some models that use a standard SVGA connector also attach to a computer's USB port so that the monitor can offer a convenient desktop USB hub for various devices.

Monitor Prices

Here's another area where your computer dollar goes farther than ever before. In recent years, the prices of monitors began to drop sharply at the same time that buyers became more demanding of quality, resolution, and size.

Table 14-5 contains the price range from discount sources for a selected group of noninterlaced monitors in standard and Trinitron mask versions, updated in 2002 and including average price changes since 2000. As with other types of products, the biggest declines in prices come among high-end large monitors.

TABLE 14-5: Monitor Prices

Consumer-Quality Monitor	Price Range in Early 2002	Average Price Change Since 2000
15-inch SVGA 0.28mm dot pitch, 1,280 × 1,024	$140–$150	Down 5 percent
17-inch SVGA 0.28mm dot pitch, 1,280 × 1,024	$170–$220	Down 24 percent
17-inch SVGA 0.24mm Trinitron, 1,600 × 1,200	$330	Down 25 percent
19-inch SVGA 0.26mm dot pitch, 1,600 × 1,200	$220–$260	Down 40 to 50 percent
19-inch SVGA 0.25mm Trinitron, 1,800 × 1,440	$480	Down 18 percent
21-inch SVGA 0.28mm dot pitch, 1,600 × 1,280	$560	Down 40 to 50 percent
21-inch SVGA 0.22mm Trinitron, 2,048 × 1,536	$850	Down 40 to 50 percent

Based on today's prices, I would recommend a 17-inch monitor to get the most for your money, and a 19-inch monitor if you can spare a few dollars more. If you spend your entire day in front of a monitor, consider an investment in a 21-inch screen.

Ch 14

Table 14-6 presents similar information for LCDs.

TABLE 14-6: LCD Prices	
Consumer-Quality LCD	**Price Range in Early 2002**
15-inch, 1,024 × 768	$339–$639
17-inch, 1,280 × 1,024	$599–$1,299
18-inch, 1,280 × 1,024	$1,429
19-inch, 1,280 × 1,024	$1,999–$2,499

Testing a Monitor

If your monitor has no video, it's best to start with a quick switch and cable check. Are both the computer and the monitor plugged in and turned on? Look for an indicator light to tell you that the monitor is receiving power. For a cruder but more interesting way to test whether your monitor is powering up, you can try the following manual test. Monitors develop a big electrostatic field in the first couple of seconds after they are turned on, so turn off the power to the monitor, and then hold the back of your hand to the monitor screen and power it back on. The hair on the back of your hand will stand up as the electrostatic field develops.

Check the video data cable from the video card to the monitor. It must be plugged in tight and screwed down at the video card end.

If your monitor suddenly seems to have lost the ability to think in more than one color, the problem could be serious — the failure of the electron gun or the tube itself — or it could be no more than a loose connection.

Just hope that the problem is simple: Make sure that the cable that runs between the PC and the monitor is properly seated at both ends; look for pins that may be misaligned; see whether the cable has been crimped or cut somehow by a piece of furniture. If you have another working graphics cable, try substituting it to see if the problem goes away. You can also try another working monitor to see if the problem lies in the original cable.

The next things to check are the brightness and contrast controls on the monitor. Many, but not all, monochrome monitors show a raster pattern when they are powered on and the brightness knob or a digital control is turned all the way up — whether the monitor is connected to a computer or not. Don't adjust these controls and then accidentally leave them in the dim position; we've all done this. It can be very frustrating to finally fix a video problem without realizing you have fixed it because the monitor brightness is adjusted so low that no characters are visible. In general, full-stop clockwise is the brightest position.

 CROSS-REFERENCE

The video card, the monitor, or a multitude of problems in the computer system unit can cause an absence of video. The troubleshooting charts in Appendix G provide a plan to help you identify the culprit.

Before jumping into the troubleshooting charts, try a couple of quick swaps if you have duplicate monitors or comparably equipped computers available. Try attaching the suspect monitor to a computer that you know works. If the monitor works on the comparable computer (one that has the same video adapter card), then test the suspect computer and the video card. For testing ideas, check the troubleshooting charts in Appendix G of this book.

If you have snow (a fuzzy, random-dot effect) on your monitor, the most likely problem is an incompatible video card. The card is sending signals, but signals from a CGA card with a 15.75 KHz scan rate are gibberish to an MDA monitor with a scan rate of 18.43 KHz. Make sure that you've hooked up your monitor to a compatible card.

If you have a dinosaur using an 8088 or 8086 CPU chip and you have a flashing cursor and no other video, check the DIP switch settings on the motherboard. DIP switches control the video address that the motherboard is trying to use. The monitor is usually smart enough to put a cursor on the screen — even without any direction from the computer — but incorrect DIP switch settings send the data to the wrong place in video memory (for example, to the nonexistent color video adapter). As a result, the actual video card gets absolutely no information from the computer and puts nothing besides the cursor on the video display screen. The 286, 386, and 486 computers also need to have the video type set correctly in their CMOS setup memory chip, but these machines are smart enough to switch to the monitor's display mode long enough to display an initial error message, such as "Incorrect setup. Wrong video adapter."

If your problem is one or two incorrect characters in an otherwise good screen, the video memory located on the video card is at fault. Replace the card. If you feel like double-checking before buying a new video card, use diagnostic software to test the video RAM (video memory).

Sometimes the screen will roll upward or downward. An incorrect vertical sync adjustment causes this problem. Most monochrome monitors have an external vertical sync knob. When you adjust it, first change the misadjustment to a slow upward roll, and then try to stop the roll completely. If you go too far and the screen starts to roll downward, try to slow and then stop the downward roll. On modern monitors, it's hard to get into a situation where the screen rolls; if you do end up with one, it may be necessary to reset all settings and redo them.

Horizontal misalignment is usually slight, but occasionally it is so severe that the screen message appears to have rolled entirely around so that it is displayed as a mirror image of itself. If your computer has an external horizontal sync knob, use this knob to correct the problem.

Monitors are very similar to television sets. If you have a horizontal or vertical sync problem that seems too intimidating, or if the bottom line of letters is much larger than the top line (a sign of poor linearity adjustment), a good computer repair shop — or possibly a TV repair shop — should be able to correct the problem. Monochrome monitors tend to be inexpensive, so more than an hour of repair work is not likely to be cost-effective.

Color monitors are also susceptible to convergence problems. Each pixel is really a trio of phosphor dots. It is important to have these dots bunched closely together or the display will be fuzzy, with one or more colors bleeding off the edges of white text. On older monitors, a television technician could adjust the convergence by slightly altering the angle of the three electron beams to target the trio of dots in each pixel more precisely. Modern monitors include electronics that can automatically adjust the convergence; consult the monitor's instruction manual for more details.

Monitor diagnostics

Most diagnostic programs include a set of test screens that allow you to explore the capabilities of your monitor and video card; some card or monitor makers include a few specialized demo programs with their products.

For more precise adjustment and testing of your monitor and card, you can check out the DisplayMate products from DisplayMate Technologies (`www.displaymate.com`). DisplayMate for Windows is an end-user video utility for setting up and tuning up a monitor for optimum image and picture quality. The program walks you through more than a dozen detailed exercises using the monitor's adjustments to display as much detail in as sharp a presentation as possible.

The program supports modes from 16 colors to 24-bit, 16.7-million colors; all resolutions up to 4,096 × 4,096; and all screen shapes and aspect ratios including landscape, portrait, and HDTV. It runs under any video board and monitor supported by Windows. You can use the program's all-purpose diagnostic screen as your Windows opening screen for a daily checkup.

The next steps up are DisplayMate and DisplayMate Professional, which are comprehensive video system hardware diagnostics that test every aspect of a computer's video system including monitor, video board hardware and registers, video

Ch 14

BIOS, and video data area. They include more than 200 test patterns and 200 diagnostic tests. The program can check accurate timing and frequency measurements for all monitor-scanning parameters.

Removing and installing a monitor

Turn off the monitor and the computer. It is not good practice to attach a cable to a computer that is powered up — a slight misalignment of the plug can result in a short that can damage the video adapter, the monitor, the motherboard, or all three.

Unscrew the two tiny screws holding the monitor data cable to the video card. Disconnect the video cable and power cables, and then replace the malfunctioning monitor with an equivalent good one.

If you are replacing both the monitor and the video card, refer to the section in Chapter 13 that covers your particular video card for card installation hints. Remember that you may need to reset both the motherboard and the video card DIP switches and/or jumpers if you are changing the video display type from monochrome to color or from MDA monochrome to EGA or VGA monochrome. Check your video card manual and your motherboard/computer owner's manual for details.

The History of PC Monitors

When IBM introduced the PC in 1981, the standard video setup was a monochrome text-only video card (the monochrome display adapter (MDA) board) and a monochrome (green phosphor) monitor. The MDA video system could produce 25 lines of text with 80 characters per line. The display was quite readable — but only if all you needed to see were lines of text; it was well suited for database retrieval and simple spreadsheets and word processing.

IBM simultaneously introduced the CGA video card, a much coarser, grainy display that bleared a lot of eyes. It was intended for hobbyists who liked the color and crude graphics and could put up with the lower resolution.

Improvements in monochrome video cards began almost immediately. The Hercules card, also called a monochrome graphics adapter (MGA) or monochrome graphics adapter with printer port (MGP) card, provided monochrome graphics on a simple monochrome MDA-style monitor because it allowed pixel-by-pixel (dot-by-dot), as well as character-by-character, control of the display. The Hercules design permitted the board to display Lotus 1-2-3 graphics while still allowing a high-resolution text display.

The next improvement was IBM's EGA in 1985, which proved to be a short-lived halfway measure. EGA featured both color and monochrome modes with pixel-by-pixel video control. EGA color was very popular, but hardly any software was written for EGA monochrome.

These three video adapter cards — MDA, MGA, and EGA (in monochrome mode) — use a horizontal scan rate of 18.43 MHz and a vertical scan rate of 50 Hz (50 refreshes per second).

MDA, MGA, and EGA monochrome resolution is 720 × 348 pixels (MGA) or 720 × 350 pixels (MDA and EGA). For an 80-character, 25-line screen of data, that means each character is allocated an area with dimensions of 9 × 14 pixels. Spacing between lines and between characters eats up some of these pixels, so the actual character is formed out of a 7 × 9 pixel rectangle with two more rows of pixels available for letters with *descenders* (tails below the line, such as p and q).

Beyond MDA, MGA, and EGA, the next higher monochrome resolution is VGA monochrome, which requires both a VGA card and a higher-priced VGA monochrome monitor. VGA provides 720 × 400 pixel resolution in text mode. That adds two horizontal rows of dots per character. In graphics mode, VGA works with a 640 × 480 pixel grid, which provides significantly more pixels per screen than the 720 × 348 pixels available with an MGA (Hercules) card. The distinguishing feature of VGA monochrome monitors, though, is their gray scales. An analog monitor displays these multiple shades of gray with a 15-pin video data cable connecting the monitor to the computer system unit. VGA monitors use a horizontal scan rate of 31.5 KHz — well outside the operating range of simple MDA monochrome monitors.

Computers dedicated to desktop publishing can be equipped with ultra-high-resolution monochrome monitors that allow you to view two complete pages of text side-by-side. Many of these sophisticated monitors require a proprietary video card and special video drivers.

The imprecise big-pixel color monitors, first found on IBM PCs in 1981, had 200 scan lines across the screen. These RGB color monitors, driven by CGA video cards, had a resolution of 320×200 pixels, which is very crude by modern standards. Higher-priced color video systems (such as EGA, VGA, XGA, and 8514) have many tiny pixels on the screen, so subtle curves seem smooth, and individual pixels are unnoticeable. CGA video cards and the RGB monitor did introduce graphics to the PC world. CGA cards allow pixel-by-pixel control of the monitor screen. The PC's original monochrome display, by contrast, could display only pre-formatted characters in an 80-column-x-25-row grid.

In 1985, IBM introduced EGA color with more pixels per scan line and more scan lines per screen than RGB monitors used. The highest resolution color EGA mode treats the screen as a 640×350-pixel grid.

IBM's 1987 VGA video standard had a maximum resolution of 640×480 pixels. The VGA standard has four video modes, all with a horizontal scan rate of 31.5 KHz. Two different vertical scan rates are required, though, so VGA monitors must be capable of either 60 or 70 Hz (60 or 70 complete refreshes per second).

The general pattern is to offer more pixels per screen and more screen refreshes per second. In the early CGA/EGA/VGA days, people were content to buy a new monitor when they upgraded to a new video standard. Each new video standard used dramatically different technology — for example, different wires in the monitor-to-video-card cable and different signals carried on those wires.

The improvement from VGA to super VGA was different. Super VGA is hard to define precisely because it has a virtually unlimited upside. It originally was an industry specification for 800×600-pixel displays, but has zoomed well past that.

Super VGA monitors are simply capable of processing the video card's instructions faster, refreshing the screen more often and displaying more individual pixels on each screen. Therefore, multiscanning monitors compatible with multiple video standards became attractive to buyers who didn't want to lock themselves into a particular video standard when they bought a monitor.

IBM's 8514/A (1987) and XGA (1990) video standards are optimized for CAD and Windows, respectively. But 8514/A and XGA don't demand a qualitatively different monitor. They both run on high-end VGA-compatible multiscanning monitors.

Dinosaur technology: RGB monitors

The original color monitor, called an RGB monitor, was a wonder at the time, way back in the early 1980s. By today's standards, it has ridiculously low resolution and a pathetic palette of 16 less-than-crisp colors. Add to that the fact that early video controllers were painfully slow.

RGB color monitors have relatively few pixels. These pixels are also relatively large, and each contains a trio of phosphor dots: one red, one green, and one blue. There are three separate electron beams, each dedicated to stimulating a single color of phosphor. As mentioned previously, mixing red, green, and blue light in the appropriate proportions makes other colors. Red is displayed by exciting only the red phosphor portion of the pixel. Purple (or magenta) is produced when both blue and red dots are glowing. When all three phosphor dots in a pixel are excited, the three colors of light combine to show white on the screen.

To display a simple letter, for example, a capital T, the electron beam excites one horizontal row and one vertical column of pixels. Resolution (crispness of image) is not very good on an RGB color monitor. If you look closely, you can see the individual pixels, and with a magnifying glass, you can see the individual dots inside a single pixel.

The three primary colors of light are controlled by simple TTL (on/off) signals; therefore, subtle color shadings are not available. RGB monitors can produce 16 colors. The monitor has a 9-pin connector on the cable running from the monitor to the video card, and it is compatible with the CGA video card.

Dinosaur technology: EGA monitors

EGA monitors also have a 9-pin cable carrying data from the video card to the monitor, but they must be paired with an EGA video card in order to work. EGA monitors are capable of substantially better resolution than RGB monitors, and they have two intensity (brightness) signal levels available for each primary-color light source. These intensity variables allow more color selections; EGA monitors can produce 64 colors.

Dinosaur technology: VGA monitors

You can readily distinguish VGA monitors from CGA and EGA monitors because VGA monitors have a 15-pin video data cable. These monitors use an analog signal, which can be adjusted anywhere in a voltage range. If CGA and EGA monitors use simple binary (on/off) signals, analog monitors use a continuously variable signal (like a dimmer switch). This analog signal allows precise brightness control at each of the three primary-color light sources, yielding many delicate color shadings. A VGA monitor can display millions of colors, but few video cards can push the monitor that far.

VGA, CGA, and EGA monitors are not interchangeable. A VGA monitor won't even plug into a CGA or EGA card, much less work properly with it. In most cases, an SVGA monitor will not work, or will not work at its optimum settings, when connected to a VGA adapter. Consult the instruction manual for the monitor and the display adapter for any makeshift arrangements that may allow mating an SVGA monitor to a VGA adapter.

SUMMARY

Now that you understand how your computer visually displays its operations and results, it's time to move on to the mechanics behind communications with devices outside of the box. In the next chapter, I explore serial communication, including asynchronous serial, USB, and FireWire specifications for use with modems, certain printers, external storage devices, and high-bandwidth digital video cameras and other accessories.

Notes

Chapter 15

Tools Needed:

- Phillips or flat-blade screwdriver

Serial, USB, and FireWire Connections

It's the morning commute, and thousands of cars, trucks, and buses speed along in a thick river on an eight-lane limited-access superhighway. Then the entire column comes to a single tollbooth with a gate at the entrance to a two-lane tunnel. This scenario is pretty close to the situation inside your computer when data is forced to switch over from the 8-, 16-, or 32-bit-wide parallel superhighway that connects the CPU, memory, and most internal devices to the local road that exits to most modems and some other external peripherals.

The two-lane roads are called *serial lines* because the data is forced to march one bit behind the other. One road runs from the computer to a device, and the other from the device back to the computer. The PC adds marker signals to indicate the beginning and end of each word of data and, in many cases, also adds error-detecting codes so that it has a reasonable chance to correct errors in transmission.

In theory, a parallel interface is much faster than a serial interface, just as an eight-lane superhighway can carry more vehicles than a two-lane back road. Within a computer, a short parallel pathway — like the computer bus — is indeed the fastest way to communicate information. When you take the parallel path out of the PC, a parallel cable is also very fast when it is in direct connection to a device that is very close.

Parallel pathways face limitations of physics: Although 8 or 16 bits of information may be sent from the interface at the exact same moment, various problems — including interference, crosstalk, and flaws in the wire or the metal itself — can result in tiny delays at the receiving end. Technicians call this *skew* and the more the delay, or the more information being forced down the wire, the more problems skew can engender. Problems with parallel communications increase with the clock speed, the drumbeat that paces the transmission of packets of information across the wires.

Designers attempt to deal with the problems of parallel communication by using more robust construction of the cables and added shielding between wires and in the connectors. SCSI interfaces, which are a form of very high-speed parallel communication, require especially heavy-duty components.

Serial cables are much simpler, essentially using just two wires for carrying information. Although data must be converted from its parallel form as it exists on the computer bus, high-speed circuits and specialized memory caches are able to keep up with that task. Also, because only two data wires are present, the chance of interference is much less. It is therefore easier to boost the clock speed of communication on a serial cable than on a parallel cable.

Serial connections were a holdover from the early days of computerdom, when the massive room-sized machines were so relatively slow that forcing data into a single line didn't have that much effect on overall speed. With the debut of the PC, most machines switched to parallel ports in order to communicate with printers; serial ports were used with devices such as modems that move data in serial fashion.

Today, though, the pendulum has very much swung back in the direction of serial communications. The state of the art in communication interfaces for consumer products from printers to modems to just about anything else is the Universal Serial Bus 2.0 (USB 2.0). Very close in capability, but not in as wide use, is IEEE 1394, better known by its Apple marketing name of FireWire.

In this chapter, I describe the original serial connection, then the speedy and easy-to-use Universal Serial Bus, and finally the IEEE 1394 (FireWire) standard.

The PC Serial Port

An 8-bit byte of information is carried in parallel form on the computer bus; in other words, all 8 bits are transmitted from place to place simultaneously across eight side-by-side wires. With a 16-bit bus, all 16 bits of data (two bytes) run side by side to their destination. On a 32-bit bus system, you get a 32-bit run (four bytes), and so on.

A serial port must repackage this information in order to send it down its one-lane road. Each byte is broken into eight separate data bits that are stacked up so that they follow one behind the other; the byte is preceded and followed by one or two stop/start bits that bracket the package of information and is usually followed by a parity-checking bit that helps with error detection. The communication is *asynchronous*, meaning that the transmission of information does not depend upon timing but instead upon a start and stop bit that is attached to each character; as such, it is a bit easier to work with, but the size of transmitted files are increased by 20 percent because of the extra bits employed.

The official specification for serial communication states that serial cables should not extend more than 50 feet. Modern improvements to cables and interfaces, however, allow distances of 200 or more feet between devices (compared with the 15- to 25-foot maximum for unamplified parallel cables). The length of a serial connection can be extended to great distances with the use of amplifiers and repeaters (in computer terminology, called *line drivers*).

Serial cables are often used to communicate with remote printers. Another area in which serial connections are still an essential part of PCs is modem-to-modem communication. A computer modem uses the telephone wire to send and receive information. A telephone connection is comprised of a single pair of thin wires, with information sent down only one of the wires. Serial ports are also commonly used to communicate with devices such as mice, which don't need to send a tremendous amount of information at one time. Serial ports are used with devices that have particularly unusual communication requirements. As I've noted previously, serial communication is sometimes difficult to set up, but it is much more flexible in configuration than parallel links.

I return to the topic of configuring and troubleshooting a serial port later in this chapter, but at this point, you should know that many of the devices that have traditionally used serial ports have been redesigned in recent years to work with the Universal Serial Bus, a high-speed and easy-to-configure successor.

Universal Serial Bus

For the first decade and a half of the PC age, the typical computer had one parallel port, a serial port, a keyboard connector, and a mouse port. If you attached a printer, a mouse, a keyboard, and an external modem, you would have used up all your standard external connections. To add more devices — such as video cameras, touchpads, secondary printers, external CD-ROMs or hard drives — you would have had to install a new I/O card. And then you'd have to tangle with reallocating IRQs, DMA channels, and memory resources; all of this was made even more complex if your system also included a needful sound card or network interface card. This process became much simpler with the arrival of the Universal Serial Bus, or USB. This all-in-one connector allows as many as 127 devices to share a single port.

USB is a bus, meaning that devices can share a common interface for interconnection and data transfer. In theory, you can hook almost anything to a USB — a keyboard, mouse, modem, plotter, printer, camera, joystick, and so on. Like a FireWire or SCSI port, several devices can share a USB port in a daisy-chain connection. Modern PCs typically come with two or four USB ports.

USB is what technical types call *PC-centric* or *managed*. The PC is the host, and all peripherals are slaves to it; in this scheme, the PC manages transfers and peripherals can only respond. Inside the four-wire cable, two wires handle data transmission, another provides as much as five volts of power to peripherals, and the fourth wire is an electrical ground.

Although parallel and serial ports send data in the form of individual pulses of data, USB operates in a manner more like a network or the Internet. Data is gathered into *packets* — packages with a beginning, an end, and a destination and return address. The technology employs *non-return to zero invert* encoding; simply put, this means that a USB interface sends out an efficient signal that does not require a return to a particular voltage level between bits. High voltage means 1, and low voltage means 0, and a continued high voltage level can be interpreted by the system to mean a string of 1s.

Beyond its speed, though, one of the principal advantages of USB is its simplicity of use. As many as 127 devices can be daisy-chained together through a single connection. The USB adapter in

the PC creates what is called the root hub. Outside of the PC, the USB chain can be further split off into smaller branches through the use of hubs. The hubs split off pieces of bandwidth as well as subdivide available electrical current to operate devices. All attached devices are designed to be automatically recognized by the Plug-and-Play components of the hardware and the operating system. In addition, all of the devices on the chain communicate through a single USB port that demands only one of the computer's limited supply of IRQs. Also, one of the advantages of USB is the ability to hot swap devices, which means you don't have to turn off your computer to add new devices.

On most modern machines, two USB ports exit from the rear panel of current motherboards, including motherboards that follow ATX specification, as shown in Figure 15-1. Some designers run cables from the motherboard to a USB port on the front of the machine, making it easier to attach devices. If you add a USB hub, you can place that connector on your desktop or in another convenient location to allow for quick connection.

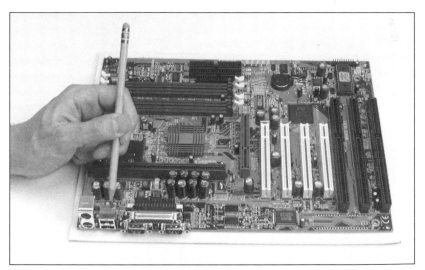

FIGURE 15-1: *An addition to modern motherboards is a dual Universal Serial Bus (USB) port.*

The USB cables use only four wires. Two wires are used for voltage and ground, and two are used for sending and receiving data. The small connectors to the USB, as shown in Figure 15-2, are flat rectangles. USB cables have an up and a downside: Connectors don't allow cables to be inserted incorrectly.

FIGURE 15-2: *The rectangular USB connectors are stacked like a pizza oven at the rear of an ATX motherboard.*

USB development

An industry group finalized the first specification for USB in 1996; two years later, the specification was refined. USB 1.0 and 1.1 run at a top speed of 12 megabits per second. In other words, if the chain contains one device, it could theoretically take all that available bandwidth for itself. If two devices were attached, they would have to split the capacity. A system packed with 127 devices would have to divide the bandwidth into tiny fractions. However, even though several or dozens of devices may be plugged into a USB chain, they will very rarely make demands at the same time.

In its original release, Windows 95 did not recognize USB devices; Windows 95 OSR 2.1 adapted the operating system to add support, but not all peripherals will work under that adaptation. Full support for USB 1.1 did not arrive until Windows 98, and continues in Windows 2000 and Windows XP.

The original version, USB 1.0, and the slightly improved USB 1.1 were designed to handle data transfer at a maximum rate of 12 Mbps or 1.5 MBps, about the speed of a T1 high-speed data communication line.

USB 2.0, marketed as High-Speed USB, arrived in 2001, offering a possible top speed of 480 megabits per second — 40 times faster than the original USB standard. This specification allows use of the USB for external hard drives, CD and DVD drives, digital cameras, and other devices that demand a great deal of bandwidth. However, the advanced standard maintains backward compatibility with USB 1.0, meaning older devices will operate (at their original slower speed) when connected to either a 2.0 or 1.0 USB system.

Additionally, the PC actively manages the assignment of bandwidth, querying attached devices to identify them and dividing them into those with the need for high-speed and those (like keyboards and mice) that can work well with a smaller pipe. Each time a device is attached to the bus, the PC reconfigures the bandwidth and assigns each device its own identification number that is used to label the packets of data.

Modern motherboards now ship with chipsets that support USB 2.0; older motherboards can generally be upgraded by the installation of an adapter that brings the new functionality. An example of a USB 2.0 card is shown in Figure 15-3. Adapter cards can also be used to add USB to a system that doesn't include circuitry on the motherboard; you can also use the card to add additional USB ports.

On the software side, you need to have an operating system that will work with USB 2.0 and appropriate drivers for this class of device. Microsoft added drivers for USB 2.0 to Windows XP in 2002; without support for USB 2.0, devices automatically revert to the earlier USB 1.1 specification. After the operating system recognizes the presence of a USB 2.0 port, you need to update drivers for the operating system.

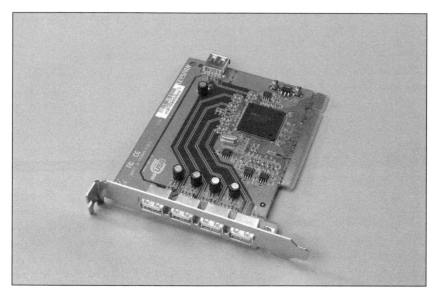

FIGURE 15-3: *Keyspan's USB 2.0 PCI card is a Plug-and-Play update that delivers four high-speed USB ports.*

Cables designed to be fully compliant with USB 1.1 should work properly at USB 2.0 speeds. If you are uncertain about the quality or design of a hub or cable, however, you may want to consider replacing them with current connectors specifically labeled as appropriate for USB 2.0.

Although USB storage and recording devices have been available since the arrival of the first version of the standard, the introduction of 40-times-faster USB 2.0 guarantees a new crop of valuable products.

Among the first was Maxtor's Personal Storage 3000LE, a 40GB external drive intended for use with a USB 2.0 interface and shown in Figure 15-4. Within the box is a solid performer, a 5,400 RPM, 3.5-inch IDE drive with a 2MB cache buffer. Unlike many other USB devices, the drive requires its own power supply because of the needs of the drive motor. At its introduction, the drive was priced at about $199, about $100 more than the price of a bare internal IDE drive; I would expect the price gap to narrow with time.

Devices designed for the USB 2.0 standard are downwardly compatible with USB 1.1; if you plug the drive into a slower port, it will operate at that speed. Similarly, if you use a USB 1.1 hub on a USB 2.0 link, all devices attached to the hub will operate at the slower speed.

Maxtor also has announced plans to offer a line of similar drives using the FireWire interface.

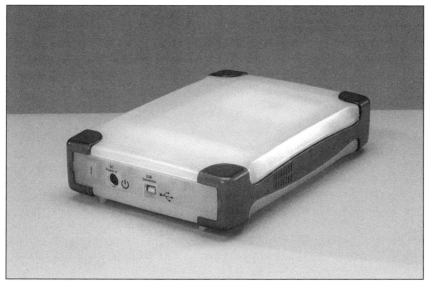

FIGURE 15-4: *This Maxtor 40GB USB drive can be hot-plugged into a running system, an unusual feature for a storage device.*

USB hubs and peripherals

Devices plugged into a USB port draw both data signals and electrical power from the computer's bus. That works perfectly well for low-power devices like mice and keyboards. Other devices, such as amplified speakers, video cameras, and printers, may need to connect to an external power supply.

To connect more than one device to a USB port, you'll need to split the signal from the port. To do that, you'll use a device called a *hub*, which connects on one side to the USB port on the computer and commonly offers two, four, or seven connectors for devices. Typical hubs sell for about $30 to $50. Figure 15-5 shows a basic USB hub. Figure 15-6 shows an unusual mini-hub that can be used with a portable PC or a desktop.

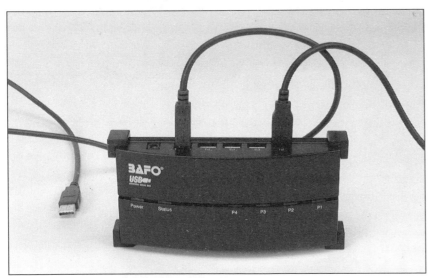

FIGURE 15-5: *A USB hub that splits one port on the computer into four ports on the desktop or floor*

Hubs designed to be compliant with the USB 1.1 specification will operate at speeds of up to 12 Mbps. USB 2.0 devices work with an older hub at the original, slower speed; however, to run at 480 Mbps, you need a USB 2.0 hub. Some USB devices, including

keyboards and monitors, include hubs that allow easy desktop connection of more peripherals.

 TIP

If devices plugged into your USB port sometimes operate but sometimes fail, the most common problem is insufficient power.

Hubs are available in two types: an unpowered hub that merely splits the signals and power, and a powered hub that connects to an electrical outlet and boosts the current available to devices. Hubs without their own power source, or those with insufficient power, can restrict the number of peripherals you can use on a USB channel or can cause intermittent failures. I suggest that you use self-powered USB hubs with at least 500 milliamps per channel. Another important feature to look for when considering hubs is per-port switching, which prevents the failure of one device from shutting down all devices attached to a hub.

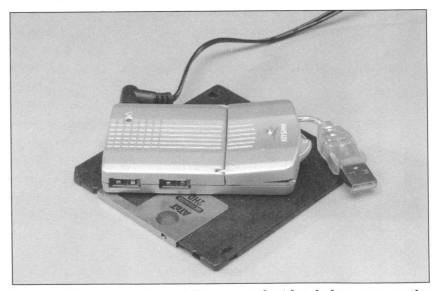

FIGURE 15-6: *A tiny hub from Belkin can work with a desktop or go on the road with a portable.*

TIP

Don't use cables longer than necessary because signals and electrical power can be degraded. In most cases, the cable length should be no more than 15 feet or 5 meters.

Some older motherboards offered USB circuitry, but not a USB port. If you have one of these older motherboards, you need to connect an adapter cable and bracket like the one shown in Figure 15-7.

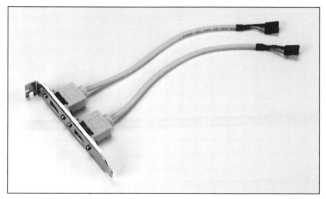

FIGURE 15-7: *An external Universal Serial Board adapter for motherboards that don't include attached USB ports*

Manufacturers now offer nearly every peripheral in a USB version. You'll find printers, mice, keyboards, scanners, CD-ROMs, DVDs, and even monitors designed to use the port. Some PC makers, with the encouragement of Intel and Microsoft, have begun to offer "legacy-free" computers that dispense with built-in serial and parallel ports, replacing them with USB circuitry. (Apple has already done this with many models of its popular iMac machine.)

If you have older peripherals that you want to connect to a USB port, you may be able to work with adapters such as the USB-to-parallel converter cable, shown in Figure 15-8. This simple device requires no settings; it simply takes in USB at the computer

or hub and outputs bidirectional parallel signals at the other end. On the PC, Windows printer drivers believe that they are communicating with a USB device; at the printer end, the device believes that it is working with a standard parallel port.

FIGURE 15-8: *USB to IEEE-1284 parallel printer converter*

Another interesting product is Keyspan's USB Serial Adapter, a short cable that plugs into a USB port at one end and terminates in a DB9 serial connector at the other. The Plug-and-Play installation gives you a serial port that is capable of communication at rates of as much as 230 Kbps, twice the speed of a standard serial port. The adapter is shown in Figure 15-9.

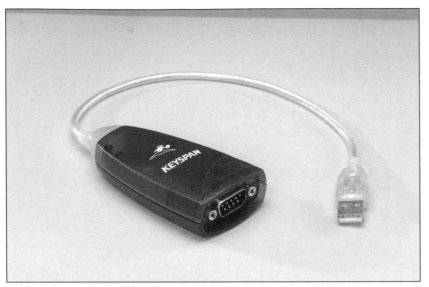

FIGURE 15-9: *Keyspan's USB Serial Adapter is compatible with serial modems, tablets, cameras, and other devices.*

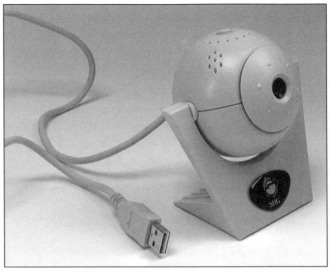

FIGURE 15-10: *This USB PC camera from SIIG includes a 350-pixel CCD (charge couple device) sensor that can be used to create snapshots for e-mail or for live video conferencing.*

The following devices are among those I've worked with in the Word Association laboratory:

- USB color PC camera from SIIG, shown in Figure 15-10
- USB wheel mouse from Logitech, shown in Figure 15-11
- USB 56K data/fax/voice modem, shown in Figure 15-12

As USB devices become more and more common, I've become happier and happier with the new devices that have arrived in my laboratory. These accessories are exactly what Plug-and-Play promises: Attach them to the system and Windows recognizes them and loads necessary drivers.

IEEE 1394 FireWire

The IEEE 1394 high-speed serial bus is based on a specification that enables connection of as many as 63 nodes to the computer through a single port. Initial implementations provided I/O speeds of 100 and 200 Mbps; that was later expanded to 400 Mbps. An expanded specification able to move data at 800 Mbps was due in stores by early 2002, and future plans call for 1,600 and 3,200 Mbps versions using optical fiber instead of copper wire.

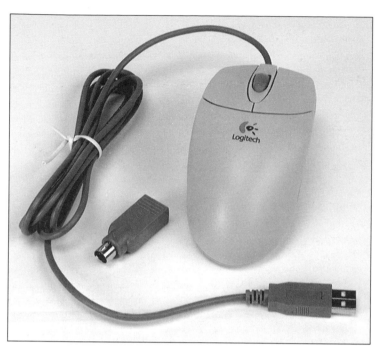

FIGURE 15-11: *The Logitech USB Wheel Mouse connects to a USB port or to a PS/2 port with the included adapter. The scroll wheel enables you to move screen displays without having to click the scroll bar in an application or a Web page.*

FIGURE 15-12: *The 56K data/fax/voice USB modem is a capable, generic device. The modem includes support for both V.90 and K56flex standards for 56K data communication.*

The official name for the specification is IEEE 1394 (100, 200, and 400 Mbps) and IEEE 1394b (800, 1,600, and 3,200 Mbps), but most users have adopted Apple Computer's zippy marketing name, FireWire. Sony has released video products that use the same interface — but a different cable — under the i.Link name.

The bus uses a six-wire cable for most computer devices; two lines deliver power, and two pairs of lines are used for clock and data signals. In addition, a four-wire version of the cable is used with self-powered devices such as camcorders.

As the time of this writing, very few motherboards included a FireWire port. However, you can easily add a set of them with a plug-in adapter, such as the one shown in Figure 15-13.

FIGURE 15-13: *This PCI adapter from Belkin is a Plug-and-Play upgrade that adds three FireWire ports to a modern machine. It includes an optional connection to the PC's power supply to provide additional power to FireWire devices.*

The IEEE 1394 standard theoretically can be expanded to thousands of devices. I'm having a hard time picturing exactly what sort of a network would have tens of thousands of nodes — perhaps some future manufacturing line — but the basic point is that FireWire is very flexible in its organizational structure. Devices created for the new 1394b standard can be designed either to support only that standard or to also work with the original version of FireWire by using "bilingual" chips.

By the end of 2001, FireWire had not caught on in wide use in modern PCs, and the standard's position was further threatened by the arrival of USB 2.0, which is capable of exchanging data as fast as 480 Mbps, a bit faster than the original FireWire system.

Data is broken into packets encased within a block that includes identification of the sender and receiver. The design of the cable includes shielding for the wires that reduces noise and

interference. FireWire cables are not supposed to be more than 4.5 meters (just under 15 feet) long.

As with USB, one FireWire device can be daisy-chained to the next. However, unlike USB, the result is a peer-to-peer network between and among the devices on the node without active control by the PC at its heart; devices can even communicate with each other without management by the computer. The design also permits two computers to share a single peripheral. An example of a FireWire hub is shown in Figure 15-14.

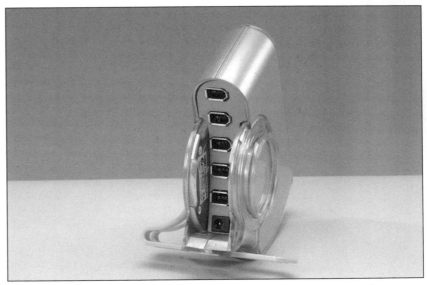

FIGURE 15-14: *Belkin's elegant FireWire 6-port hub operates as a bus-powered or self-powered repeater; the rear panel contains five ports and another one is hidden behind a panel on the front. A docking ring on the side allows you to attach multiple hubs, routers, and other devices from Belkin.*

Like USB, FireWire can divide the available bandwidth *isochronously*, dedicating a particular slice of the spectrum to particular devices — useful in such applications as streaming video. FireWire can also operate *asynchronously*, a more flexible means of communication for devices that can accept information broken into packets and able to deal with sometimes-changing conditions along the shared cable as other devices request access to the stream of data.

Finally, like USB devices, FireWire devices are hot-pluggable, allowing them to be attached or disconnected to a PC without rebooting. Devices broadcast their unique identification number to other devices on the network and obtain a place on the network.

To obtain all of the facilities of FireWire, you need Windows 98 SE or later versions of Windows, including Windows 2000, Windows Me, and Windows XP. Windows 95 and the original version of Windows 98 deliver only limited functionality.

 CROSS-REFERENCE

For more information on FireWire, you can consult the trade association's page at www.1394ta.org.

Troubleshooting a Serial Port

In Chapter 4, I explore the concept of interrupts in the computer; to review, the PC uses IRQs (interrupt requests) to signal the CPU and request that it deal with incoming information from a particular device.

Modern machine PCs have 16 interrupts, numbered from 0 to 15. Each serial port generally needs its own IRQ. Note, however, that the standard settings for serial ports — shown in Table 15-1 — have multiple uses of IRQs 3 and 4. Although that is permissible, it may cause problems; some technicians routinely set COM 3 to IRQ 10 and COM 4 to IRQ 11 if those interrupts are available. If you must have more than two serial ports, consider installing a multi-port serial card that permits sharing of interrupts. Most current users have changed over to the Universal Serial Bus (USB) instead; as explained previously in this chapter, this high-speed system allows as many as 127 devices to share a single port and interrupt.

TABLE 15-1: Standard Serial Port Resources

COM Name	IRQ	I/O Starting Address
COM 1	IRQ 4	3F8
COM 2	IRQ 3	2F8
COM 3	IRQ 4	3E8
COM 4	IRQ 3	2E8
COM 5	IRQ 4	3E0
COM 6	IRQ 3	2E0
COM 7	IRQ 4	338
COM 8	IRQ3	238

Serial ports also require a unique input/output (I/O) address. The port address is a sort of inbox for the device, a place where information is held before it is processed. In theory, current versions of Windows are supposed to be able to automatically assign IRQs and I/O addresses, but the occasional inconsistency is more than enough to drive you nuts.

You should avoid reassigning the IRQ and I/O addresses of COM 1 and COM 2 unless it is absolutely necessary to do so. These first two ports use standard settings that are referenced in many other pieces of hardware and software. COM ports 3 and above, though, are fair game. Table 15-1 lists standard serial port resource assignments.

The role of the serial port is complicated by the many different package designs for computer data. These package designs are called *parameters* or *protocols*. Modern PC serial communication can use either 7 or 8 data bits, with either 1 or 2 stop bits appended. The serial device may use either even or odd parity, or use no parity checking at all. In addition, many different transmission speeds — ranging from 110 bps to a hardware maximum of 115,200 bps — are allowed.

Before any two serial devices can communicate, the parameters must be set and agreed upon by the devices at both ends of the connection. Many serial port problems can be traced to incorrect parameter setup. At the computer end, parameters are set with software, using communications software for a modem or occasionally through the facilities of the DOS MODE command.

A modem device is usually pretty flexible in working with whatever parameters the modem sends its way, but serial printers and some other devices may be more hidebound. Check the instruction manual carefully for any serial device to see whether any DIP switches or other settings must be adjusted.

Reassigning COM port settings in current versions of Windows

If one of your devices is not compliant with Plug and Play, or if the system's smarts are not quite smart enough to avoid conflicts, you may need to take matters into your own hands. To reassign COM port settings in Windows 95/98 and later versions, start by checking the port settings from the Device Manager. Here's how to get there:

1. Select Start ⇨ Settings ⇨ Control Panel.
2. Click the System icon and then select the Device Manager tab. (In Windows XP, you'll need to click the Hardware tab and then choose Device Manager.)
3. Click the + mark next to Ports (COM & LPT) to expand the display of ports.

You're looking for yellow circles with an exclamation mark (!), an indication of a possible conflict among devices. If you find an exclamation mark, double-click it, click the Properties button, and then click the Resources tab. Look in the Conflicting device list for a report on what Windows thinks it knows about the source of the conflict.

To resolve the problem, you have to manually reassign the IRQ, I/O port address, or both for one of the devices. You can find

a list of unused IRQs and I/O addresses by going back to the Device Manager and double-clicking Computer.

CROSS-REFERENCE

You can find more details about making changes to the resource setting in Chapter 23.

Serial port UARTs

The hard work of chopping up parallel data bytes and sending them out in a serial stream and putting the received stream back together is performed by an electronic circuit called a *universal asynchronous receiver/transmitter* (UART).

Today, most modern machines have the circuitry included within the Super I/O Controller or equivalent, part of the motherboard's chipset. The Super I/O chip typically emulates a pair of 16550A UARTs (I discuss this more later in the chapter) and also provides support circuitry for a bidirectional parallel port, the floppy disk controller, the keyboard and mouse controller, and infrared communications interface. As part of the chipset, the Super I/O Controller is not something that the user can repair or directly replace, although a plug-in adapter can augment a PC's communications facilities.

Throughout most of the history of the PC, though, the UART was a separate chip that plugged directly into the bus on the motherboard. In many cases, the chip could be updated or repaired by removing it from its socket and installing an updated version.

NOTE

You can find the identity of your UART chip by running a system diagnostics program. Under Windows, you can also go through the Control Panel to the Device Manager. Once there, select the Ports listing and right-click and select Properties to learn about the Communications Port (COM1).

The current rulers of the serial world are the 16550 and its improved cousin, the 16550A; each is capable of a maximum throughput of 115,200 bits per second (115 Kbps). These chips improve on the earlier UARTs with the addition of a 16-byte first-in, first-out buffer, which is just enough to keep the serial port busy in a multitasking environment. In other words, if your modern machine's CPU is working on several tasks under Microsoft Windows and dividing its attention between one device and another, the buffers on the 16550 and 16550A are big enough in most instances to enable your CPU to continue working without interruption.

Specialized systems may use a version of the 16550 with larger buffers: They may use the 16650 with a 32-byte buffer, the 16750 with a 64-byte buffer, or the 16850 with a 128-byte buffer.

If your machine is very modern, you won't find a separate UART chip at all. Instead, the functions of the UART are integrated into the I/O section of the motherboard's chipset. One such current chip is the Intel 82801BA LPC Interface Controller, a component of the Intel 850 chipset. The LPC Interface includes both serial and parallel circuitry; it emulates the 16550A UART.

The original PC used a chip labeled the 8250; this device is not reliable for modem speeds beyond 9,600 bps and is, therefore, a hopeless dinosaur. A slightly improved chip was the 16450, which should accommodate 14,400 bps modems — also well behind today's 56K dial-up modems.

CROSS-REFERENCE

A good diagnostic program can help you easily find some of your system information all in one place. See Chapter 22 for details about some popular diagnostic programs.

The 8250, 16450, 16550, and 16550A chips are pin-for-pin compatible with each other, and it is easy to upgrade from an earlier UART to a state-of-the-art chip if the UART is mounted in a socket. If the UART is soldered into place, you can't directly upgrade it.

The solution for systems that don't enable you to simply remove and replace the UART chip is to install a high-speed serial communications card. These devices can add one, two, or even four serial ports; combination cards can also add a bidirectional parallel port.

If you add one of these special serial I/O cards, you will probably have to disable one or more of the serial ports on your PC to avoid interrupt and I/O conflicts with the original ports. Such I/O cards are priced from about $25 to $100. Be sure that you get a 16550 or 16550A for your money — there is no good reason to put in a new 8250 or 16450.

One backdoor way to give an instant modem communications boost to an older PC with an 8250- or 16450-based UART system is to install a modern internal modem. These devices go around your system's existing serial ports and include their own high-speed UART.

Internal modems have two parts: a dedicated serial port of their own, and a telecommunications section. Nearly every high-speed modem is based on a 16550 or 16550A UART. Another advantage of an internal modem is that it can usually be set to be COM 3 or COM 4, and therefore may not be in conflict with existing serial ports.

The disadvantages of internal modems include that they use a bus slot, draw internal power, lack visible status indicators like those on an external unit, and don't offer an on/off or reset switch. On most internal modems, the only way to clear an unusual condition is to turn off the power to the PC itself. For these reasons, I generally prefer external modems, except for situations like the one outlined previously, in which your system needs to go around or replace an 8250 UART.

Serial port address

Up to this point in the chapter, I have covered parameters, which along with cables, are among the trickier elements of setting up a serial port. The last consideration is serial port addresses. Early DOS versions allowed two serial ports, called COM 1 and COM 2 — each at a different address.

Under current operating systems, users can have two additional ports, called COM 3 and COM 4. Each of these serial ports has an associated physical port address — a place where the OS sends data that it's trying to shove out the serial port. With some low-end or older devices, you use switches or jumpers on the serial card or modem to set up the card to use a particular port address. Most current cards use Plug-and-Play technology to set these parameters for you automatically. However, even modern multiport cards will use jumper or switch settings because of the complexity of their possible configuration settings. After you set the port address (the physical address), you use the MODE command to tell the OS where to send serial output. It makes sense to set the first serial port in a computer to COM 1 because it is the default setting.

Each serial port must have a different port address. If you don't set up different addresses, your modem software tries to send dialing instructions to your mouse. Each physical port also has a corresponding interrupt number.

CROSS-REFERENCE

Appendix D helps you to choose the interrupt that matches the port address that you selected. Serial cards, modems, and other serial devices are shipped with installation manuals. Read them.

Add-On Serial Port Expansion Cards

Several simple, but capable, serial port expansions are available for modern machines.

The High-IRQ I/O-I/O Professional Plus from SIIG, Inc., shown in Figure 15-15, is an all-in-one communications upgrade and expansion that includes two high-speed UART serial ports and a high-speed EPP/ECP parallel port. Each of the serial ports can be jumpered to work as COM 1 through COM 4 or disabled. The parallel port can be set up with a standard I/O port address or relocated.

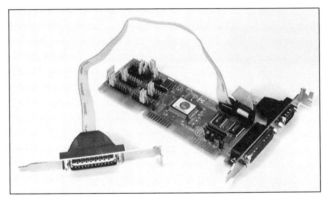

FIGURE 15-15: *A High-IRQ I/O card from SIIG*

The CyberPro Quad I/O, shown in Figure 15-16, is a serial port turbocharger that includes four 16550 UART serial ports that can be independently configured from COM 1 through COM 8 with a full range of IRQ and I/O choices. The CyberPro is also available from SIIG.

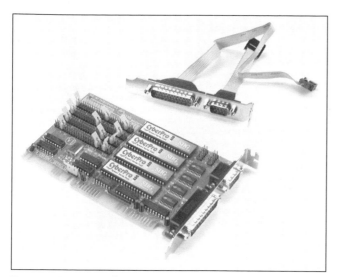

FIGURE 15-16: *A CyberPro Quad I/O card from SIIG. Note the thicket of jumpers, used to customize the card to extend your system without running into IRQ and resource conflicts.*

SIIG is also among suppliers of serial cards based on the 16850 UART, which includes a 128-byte buffer and offers advantages in use with external ISDN modems and may also improve performance of external 56K dial-up modems. The PCI Expander 4S 850 features two of the high-speed, high-capacity UARTs and can be upgraded to offer four.

Serial Cables

Although 25 pins on the DB-25 connector were originally used for serial communications, in almost every use of a serial connection on a PC, only 9 pins are ever used, and most implementations use less than that.

Most modern serial devices use standard cables that you can purchase off the shelf or from mail-order houses. You should also be able to rely on the recommendation of the dealer who sold you the printer, modem, or other device that you are connecting to. Figure 15-17 shows the serial connectors on the back of an ATX motherboard.

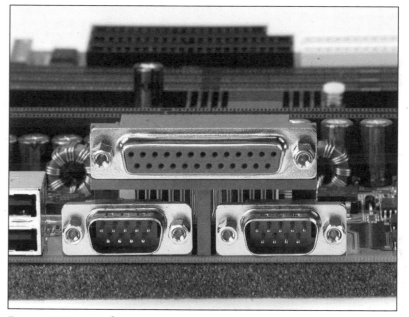

FIGURE 15-17: *Serial connectors on a modern machine based on an ATX form factor motherboard*

Your computer may have a 25-pin male, 9-pin male, or 25-pin female serial port. When you have to, you can patch the mismatches with gender menders and 9- to 25-pin pigtails, leaving interesting tangles hanging out the back of the machine. Figure 15-18 shows the standard serial connectors on most senior citizen PCs.

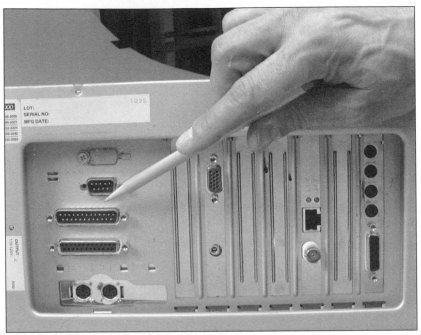

FIGURE 15-18: *Serial connectors COM 1 and COM 2 on the back panel of a senior citizen PC. One connector is a 9-pin male, and the other is a 25-pin female, a standard combination. Some PCs offer a pair of 9-pin connectors.*

You can find a mind-boggling array of cables and connectors from specialty stores such as Dalco Electronics or Micro Warehouse and offerings from specialty hardware vendors in publications, such as *Computer Shopper* magazine. If necessary, most computer shops will make a custom serial cable for you, although the price can be prohibitive. A better solution is to use a configurable cable, such as the Smart Cable from Smart Cable Company (www.smart-cable.com), which I discuss further in the next section. Still, the simplest solution to using a serial port is to purchase a device that comes packaged with its own serial cable. In this case, all you have to do is plug it in.

Serial cable black magic

In the early PC days, a serial cable was a concept and not a standard. All serial cables were based on the idea of bits of data moving one behind the other down the length of a wire, but choosing which wire was to be used for which purpose was often inconsistent from device to device.

It was very common in the early days to have to buy a Hayes cable for a particular class of modems, an HP cable for a group of plotters, an Epson cable for certain printers, and so on. The closet of my lab is filled with these orphaned cables.

Most of these problems are gone for modern machine peripherals. Today, nearly all printers use the standardized parallel interface, and most modems and specialized serial devices use straight-through cables, with pin 1 at one end directly connected to pin 1 at the other end, and so on. An exception to this scheme is null modem cables that are used to directly connect one PC to another and are used by software programs, such as LapLink or the Windows Direct Connect program. These cables connect the receive wires of one PC to the send wires of the other so that the two machines can communicate. A straight-through connection for send and receive works on other devices because the devices themselves change which pin is a receive pin and which is a transmit pin. When you connect two devices of the same kind — such as two PCs — you need the crossover cable.

Nevertheless, in some situations, you may need an unusual serial cable connection. Two examples that are of special interest to readers of this book are the problem of matching a dinosaur-era device to a modern machine or replacing a failed dinosaur-era cable.

One extremely interesting solution to serial cable connections is the Smart Cable, a bit of electronic magic that is able to look to its left and look to its right and help you to figure out which wires need to be connected to each other with the flick of two switches, following the simple logic of the LED lights on the Smart Cable. You can use a Smart Cable, which costs only slightly more than standard cables, to temporarily link two devices until a custom cable is constructed, or you can leave it in place. I keep a 9-pin and 25-pin Smart Cable on the shelf in the lab at all times. For more information, consult www.smart-cable.com. Figure 15-19 shows one model of Smart Cable.

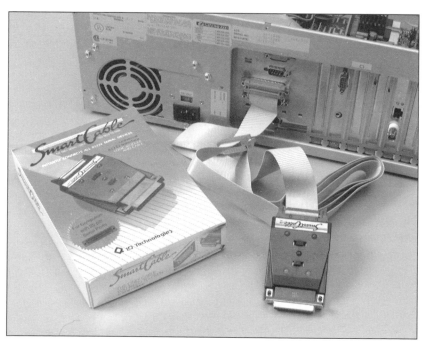

FIGURE 15-19: *A Smart Cable from Smart Cable Company performs an electronic balancing act, matching the wires on one side of a serial cable with the needs of the wires on the other side.*

Another form of black magic involves the use of a box that converts one type of signal to another. Going from serial to parallel, it bunches up data bits to send them in parallel. From parallel to serial, it buffers bits that arrive together and sends them out one behind the other.

In a pinch, you can convert most serial devices to parallel, or the other way around, with the use of an interface converter. These devices generally perform well but may result in the loss of some speed and may also block full bidirectional communication for the most modern of devices.

Serial port connectors

Most PCs include two serial ports. On dinosaur machines, the ports were typically a part of an I/O or multifunction card. On modern machines, the ports are usually part of the motherboard itself.

The official description for serial ports, called the RS-232C specification, described specifications for a DB-25 connector, which was commonly used on the original PC. (The DB-25 is a D-shaped device with 25 pins on the port and 25 pinholes on the cable.) The parallel connection on the PC also used a DB-25, with a female connector on the port and a male connector on the cable.

As previously discussed, a serial connection comes down to just a single wire for the transmission of data, but a computer serial port uses a total of nine wires for most communication with devices such as printers and modems. The extra wires are used to control the port or machine.

As the PC began to grow in popularity and capability, designers began to run into a problem with fitting two or three DB-25 connectors on an expansion card. Therefore, IBM made a change with the introduction of its PC-AT machine, substituting a 9-pin connector (the DB-9) for the use of the serial port.

Many older machines used a DB-9 for the first serial port and a DB-25 for the second port; other machines offered both DB-9 and DB-25 connectors for both ports. Cable manufacturers also offered converters that enabled a 25-pin cable to connect with a 9-pin port, or the other way around.

Finding the serial port

Serial port connectors come in three styles: the original DB-25 male connector with 25 pins as shipped with dinosaur PCs, the modern machine's 9-pin serial connector fitted with a DB-9 connector, and — just for confusion's sake — a 25-pin female serial port connector shipped with several (but not all) IBM PS/2 models. The DB-9 socket on a modern machine has a male DB-9 connector with nine holes; it is intended to mate with a cable with a female DB-9 connector. If you don't find a 9-pin male serial port, look for a 25-pin male connector with protruding pins in the rear of the computer.

NOTE

Once again, a reminder: If you find a female DB-25 connector on the back of your computer, it's most likely the socket for a parallel port. If you have any doubts about ports, consult the instruction manual for your PC and any add-in cards in the system. It's a good idea to label your ports with a marker or tape after you've confirmed their identity.

One of the most useful types of devices to keep around your PC is a cable converter, also known as a *gender changer*, and more colorfully, as a *gender bender*. Cable converters are small adapters or short lengths of cable with the same sex connector at each end. A male-male gender bender would mate with a female cable or connector at each end; a female-female gender bender expects to connect with male devices at both ends. Figure 15-20 shows examples of these devices.

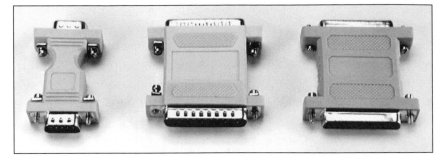

FIGURE 15-20: *Gender benders: from left to right, DB-9 male to male, DB-25 male to male, and DB-25 female to female*

Testing a serial connection

The first step in testing a serial connection is to check how many serial ports the computer believes it has. If you have two physical serial ports, but a diagnostic program shows only one, then clearly the device-addressing switches on one or the other are not set correctly.

When a diagnostic program checks the serial ports, it reads the equipment list — a file that the BIOS assembles as it boots the computer. The BIOS checks serial port addresses, but doesn't compare each physical card with its address, so it is possible to set up two serial ports so that they have the same address (both set to COM 1, for instance). The BIOS never catches this problem.

It is also possible to accidentally set parameters on the CMOS setup (or on a senior citizen or dinosaur, on the switches on a serial port) so that its I/O address is one that the system can't recognize. Because the BIOS doesn't see this serial port, it doesn't include it in the equipment list.

Next, rethink the links among physical address, interrupt, software setup, and other parameters. Make sure that you're not trying something illogical like sending data to COM 1 when the printer cable is connected to COM 2. It's also a common mistake to send modem commands to the port used by the mouse.

The BIOS can talk to only two serial ports: COM 1 and COM 2. However, some software can bypass the BIOS and address two more communications ports directly; some internal modems are routinely set to COM 3 or COM 4. If you are mixing and matching hardware and software, be sure that your software enables you to set the serial card to one of these nonstandard addresses.

Plug-and-Play serial cards should be able to negotiate with other devices in your system in search of a compatible set of resources, although you may run into problems with a machine that has a full set of demanding adapters, including sound cards, network cards, and multifunction video cards.

Older add-on serial cards are packaged with instruction manuals that give suggested address switch (or jumper) settings. You will be responsible for giving a serial port a unique I/O address. The OS simplifies things for you at this point by dealing with the logical address: COM 1, COM 2, COM 3, and so on.

Some serial port manuals refer to hexadecimal addresses instead of the COM *x* names. COM 1, for example, is the physical I/O address 03F8 and is paired with interrupt 4. COM 2 is the I/O address 02F8 and is paired with interrupt 3.

Be sure that you receive and hold on to all the instruction manuals for the parts of a computer when you take delivery. If you've got a system with an add-on serial port or a multifunction card, they're probably accompanied by minimal documentation because these devices are commodities imported from the lowest bidder. I have encountered situations in which the addresses printed on the card and in the manual were both different and were both wrong. Check the jumpers on the serial card or the modem against the manual.

If these steps don't reveal an obvious problem, use a serial test program with wrap (loopback) plug capability. CheckIt is one program that can send data out the transmit data (TX) line and check to see that it has been properly received on the receive data (RX) line.

These tests require a wrap plug, which is sometimes provided with the diagnostics software. You can also purchase one from an electronics supply house. If you want to make your own, you can construct one out of a female RS232 plug or a female DB-9 plug. You have to make three soldered connections. Table 15-2 tells you which signal pins you must solder to other signal pins. Use short jumper wires or clean solder bridges to connect the pins electrically.

TABLE 15-2: Making a Serial Port Wrap (Loopback) Plug

Solder This Signal *...	...to This Signal	...and This Signal
TXD	RXD	
RTS	CTS	CD
DTR	DSR	RI

Please see Tables 15-3 and 15-4 for explanations of each abbreviation.

If a serial port passes the wrap plug test, it is fair to assume that the port is good and that the problem lies in a configuration error or in another problem with the system. Look again for mismatched COM port and interrupt or for an incorrect MODE command in a legacy program.

 CROSS-REFERENCE

The troubleshooting charts in Appendix G lead you step-by-step through serial port diagnostic/repair procedures.

Table 15-3 is a pinout diagram for DB-25 serial ports showing which pin carries which signal. Table 15-4 is the pinout diagram for the most common (modern) DB-9 male serial ports. A few nonstandard 9-pin designs were made in the early 1980s, but they are not currently manufactured.

Ch 15

TABLE 15-3: 25-Pin Serial Port Pinouts, Male or Female

Pin	Name	Protocol Code
1	Chassis ground	
2	Transmit data	TXD
3	Receive data	RXD
4	Request to send	RTS
5	Clear to send	CTS
6	Data set ready	DSR
7	Signal ground	SG
8	Carrier detect	CD
9	+ Transmit current loop return (obsolete IBM asynch adapter)	
11	− Transmit current loop data (obsolete IBM asynch adapter)	
18	+ Receive current loop data (obsolete IBM asynch adapter)	
20	Data terminal ready	DTR
22	Ring indicator	RI
25	− Receive current loop return (obsolete IBM asynch adapter)	

TABLE 15-4: 9-Pin Serial Port Pinouts, Male

Pin	Name	Protocol Code
1	Carrier detect	CD
2	Receive data	RXD
3	Transmit data	TXD
4	Data terminal ready	DTR
5	Signal ground	GND
6	Data set ready	DSR
7	Request to send	RTS
8	Clear to send	CTS
9	Ring indicator	RI

One way to make temporary cable setups for testing or short-term work is to use a solderless jumpbox like the one shown in Figure 15-21.

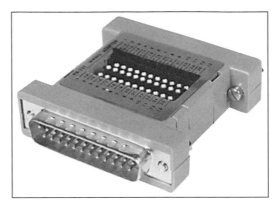

FIGURE 15-21: *You can use a solderless jumpbox to make custom serial cables. Insert a prestripped wire into sockets to connect pins.*

Null modems

A *null modem* is not a modem but actually a special cable that you can use to directly connect two serial ports as if they had a pair of modems between them. The special cable is necessary because a serial port is designed so that the transmitted data coming out of one machine is switched over to the received data input on the other. Actually, because serial communication is two-way, both transmit and receive lines are crossed within the cable.

Null modems are used in many simple network and data transfer programs, including applications such as LapLink, used for temporary connections between a portable or laptop computer and a desktop device. You also need a null modem cable to use the Direct Cable Connection utility, a very low-end network substitute that is included as part of Windows.

LapLink and many other such programs are shipped with a null modem, but in some cases, you may need to order one from an electronics supply house.

You can also build your own. Table 15-5 shows the details of the pin-to-pin connections of a null modem. You may find it easier to sacrifice an existing serial cable and cross some of its wires rather than starting from scratch.

TABLE 15-5: Null Modem

25-Pin Number on Connector A	25-Pin Number on Connector B
1	1
2	3
3	2
4	5
5	4
6 and 8	20
20	6 and 8
7	7

Removing and installing a serial port

If you have a serial port on the motherboard, you may have to disable it by setting a jumper or switch before you attach a new I/O card in the bus. On a modern machine, you should be able to disable a serial port on the motherboard by turning it off at the CMOS Setup screen.

The following instructions apply to removal and installation of add-in cards with I/O functions.

1. Remove the cables and computer cover. Disconnect the serial cable (if installed) and remove the system unit cover.

2. Remove the old card. Remove the single screw holding the card to the back of the system unit chassis and save it. Pull the old serial card straight up out of its slot.

3. Set switches and jumpers. Before you install a serial card, read the instruction manual that comes with the card.

4. Install the new card. Modern serial cards will use a PCI slot; dinosaur cards generally used an 8-bit ISA slot. Line the card up with the expansion slot connector, and then press it down firmly. When the card has settled into the bus connector on the motherboard and the screw hole lines up with the hole on the top or back of the chassis, reinstall the screw.

5. Test the new serial card. Test the machine with the cover off first, taking care not to touch anything inside the machine while the computer is on. If the computer tests well, reinstall the cover and screws. On an older card that requires you to set switches or jumpers, it's not unusual to have to make several attempts to find the proper setting. If you have problems getting the new card to work properly, the troubleshooting charts in Appendix G should help.

SUMMARY

In this chapter, I explored serial communications, including standard serial, USB, and FireWire technologies. In the next chapter, I examine in some detail the most common peripheral to use serial signals: the modem.

Chapter 16

Modems

A modem is your entrance ramp to the global information superhighway. The purpose of a modem is to *MO*dulate the digital signals of your PC so they can be sent in analog fashion over a telephone wire; incoming analog signals are then *DEM*odulated to become digital.

Your computer stores information in the form of 0s and 1s. This stream of digits is assembled into a stream of information by the PC's UART (universal asynchronous receiver/transmitter) and sent as a serial signal to a modem. There the modem's electronics change the bits into a warbling soundwave that indicates 1s with its peaks and 0s with its valleys; this signal is an analog of changes in values between the bits. At the other end of the connection, another modem receives the wave and converts the peaks and valleys back into 1s and 0s for the recipient.

Consumer modems, like those I write about in this book, are considered *asynchronous* devices in that the data stream is not tied to timing; rather, it is defined by the start and stop bits of each byte. Specialized modems used in direct connection or leased-line communication are sometimes *synchronous*, moving to the beat of a clock.

Modems are available in several forms:

- Dial-up devices that use standard telephone lines
- High-speed broadband cable modems that use coaxial and fiber optic links through cable television providers
- High-speed broadband DSL modems that use special telephone circuits
- High-speed broadband satellite links for download, in combination with dial-up links for upload

Modems attach to your computer in three ways:

- As internal cards that attach to the bus as a serial device
- As external devices that connect to a serial port, a USB port, or a parallel port
- As external devices that connect to an Ethernet

Each style has some significant benefits. In this chapter, I discuss considerations for buying a modem, as well as different modem standards.

Dial-up Modems

The majority of PC users still connect to the Internet and other communications services through "old" technology. Dial-up modems attempt to eke every possible bit of capability from technology that is more than a century old: a pair of copper wires that stretch from your home or office to a central telephone switch. (Sometime in the next few years, though, broadband cable and DSL modems — discussed later in this chapter — are expected to predominate.)

Ch 16

Throughout the history of the PC, dozens of modem manufacturers have been on the scene, some claiming higher speed, better quality, or improved features while others have marketed on the basis of price alone. Today, though, dial-up modems have reached a technological wall at 56K and a marketing chasm: Modems are now mostly a commodity — nearly all modems perform comparably. All modems have to go through the same computer gateway — a serial, parallel, or USB port at one end and the antique two-wire copper telephone line at the other — and none of them can perform better than the facilities on either side of them.

CROSS-REFERENCE

I discuss UARTs in detail in Chapter 15. Be sure you know the capabilities of your system before you purchase an external modem so that you don't buy one that's beyond the capabilities of your PC.

Even the most capable modem still has to deal with the quality of the phone line between your home or office and the telephone company's central office. From there, it still has to travel to the central office nearest the call's destination, and then over the local lines to the destination. The very best modem will be slow and problematic if it uses phone lines of poor quality. (From my very rural office, the best we can expect to get from a 56 Kbps modem is about 40K, and then only when the weather does not interfere with the signal to and from the phone company's microwave tower.)

Only a limited number of primary manufacturers produce the chipsets used in most modern modems. The brain of nearly every modem comes from Rockwell International, Texas Instruments, Motorola, Lucent, or IBM. Literally dozens of modems are on the market, with tremendous change from month to month in price and capabilities. Over time, the trend has been falling prices and increasing functionality.

The state of the art for dial-up modems in terms of speed and capability today are 56 Kbps devices built to adhere to the V.92 standard. I discuss real and potential speed later in this chapter.

Modem quality

I divide dial-up modems into the following three classes:

- **Consumer-quality modems:** In general, I have had better luck with these devices. They are usually more flexible in configuration, use more current technologies, and are supported with up-to-date device drivers. Also, the makers of these modems are more likely to be in business a year or so down the road when the next revolution in technologies comes along. With luck, you'll be able to upgrade your modem to keep current; a good feature in a modem is the presence of flash memory that you can update from a disk or even over the phone lines.

  In early 2002, brand-name consumer-quality modems were priced from about $50 to $60 for an internal modem to about $80 to $100 for external devices. A few trusted names for modems include Best Data, Boca Research, CNet, Creative Labs, Diamond Multimedia, MultiTech, 3Com, U.S. Robotics, and Zoom Telephonics. In 1999, Zoom acquired most of the assets of modem pioneer Hayes Corporation, including the Hayes, Practical Peripherals, Accura, Optima, Century 2, and Cardinal brands. 3Com owns U.S. Robotics.

- **Commodity modems:** These are the least expensive models. They often use older technologies or cut corners by using off-the-shelf components instead of custom-designed devices. This is not to say that they won't work. In fact, over the years, one of the most reliable modems in the Word Association laboratories was a no-name metal box that was able to hold onto the sometimes-weak phone lines in our remote location better than a few of the more expensive brand-name devices. As this book goes to press, no-name internal modems are available for as little as $19 and external units for about $60. Figure 16-1 shows a basic internal modem card.

Take the time to test a few modems if you can. Paying $25 more for a better modem can turn out to be a very good deal if the more robust device ends up saving you hours of time.

- **High-end devices:** These are mostly intended for use with network servers or with mission-critical systems. Some such units offer special features, including Caller ID recognition, password, and callback security.

Nearly all senior citizen modems and most modern ones are internal serial devices, or connect to an external serial port. Older modem cards installed in ISA slots, requiring careful management of interrupts and memory allocation; a basic ISA modem is shown in Figure 16-1.

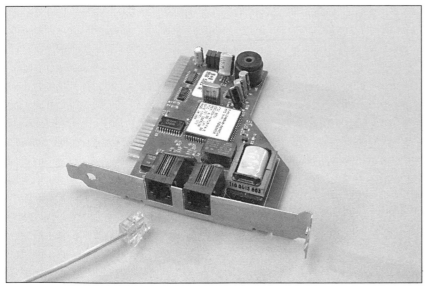

FIGURE 16-1: *A basic no-frills internal modem card for an ISA slot*

Most modern modems now use a PCI slot, which allows Plug-and-Play ease of configuration. These modems may also include connections to link to a sound card for answering machine facilities. A relative handful of machines have a specialized internal slot called an AMR (Audio Modem Riser) and can accept modem cards in that format without giving up a bus slot.

Today, though, many buyers are opting for Universal Serial Bus (USB) modems. The self-configuring nature of USB makes setting up these modems a breeze.

CROSS-REFERENCE

I show an example of a USB modem in Chapter 15 (Figure 15-12).

Before the arrival of the USB, some manufacturers introduced devices that connected to the parallel port of the PC, avoiding problems with outmoded UART chips and also leaving existing serial ports untouched. One example was the Deskporte line, originally offered by Microcom (now part of Compaq) and still available from the back bins of some dealers. These devices use a special device driver that redirects communications to the parallel port.

Modem speed

It would be perfectly logical to think that a 56K modem is capable of receiving and transmitting data at twice the speed of a 28.8 Kbps, but the truth is a little bit short of that.

Technical and regulatory speed limits set the maximum download speed for a V.90 and V.92 modem at about 53,000 bits per second (bps). The upload speed — from your computer to the Internet — is notably slower: V.90 sends data up the line at as much as 33,600 bps, while the newer V.92 standard theoretically is capable of transmitting at as much as 48,000 bps.

To begin with, 56K technology only works if a completely digital line is present between the two ends of the connection or if no more than one analog/digital conversion is present along the way. If you work or live in a big city with a good telephone company, you may have part of the equation in place — a good connection from your PC to the central office and a digital line from there.

Today, nearly every major ISP offers 56 Kbps dial-up nodes for their customers and should offer a digital link to the phone company at their end. This doesn't mean that some tiny, financially weak ISP doesn't have a few or many slower modems or lower-quality phone lines.

If you are unable to connect at 56 Kbps, a current modem will still be able to downshift to slower speeds covered under earlier standards.

You may still find a few 33.6 Kbps and slower modems for a few dollars less, but in today's marketplace, I wouldn't bother. The small amount of money you save would quickly be eaten up in lost productivity. The latest widely accepted modem standards, V.90 and V.92, not only offer the possibility of supporting 53 Kbps, but have other desirable connectivity features that will provide a better online experience at any connection speed. A no-name internal modem is shown in Figure 16-2.

You should expect 19.2 Kbps fax facilities to be included with any modem. Don't accept a slower and outmoded 9600 bps fax component on the modem.

If you have only a single telephone line in your home or small office, you may want to look for a modem that includes support for distinctive-ring services offered by most telephone companies. With such a setup, you can obtain a second telephone number for the same single line and devote that number to incoming faxes or telecommunications. The second number, which costs less to install and use than a separate phone line, has a different sound or pattern to its ring, and you can instruct a sophisticated modem to automatically answer calls to the second number only.

In addition, many modems today include sophisticated voice facilities for a few dollars more. You can use your modem to answer your telephone, for example, and the software provided with the hardware lets you set up multiple voicemail boxes. Some modems even support simultaneous voice and data connections on the same phone line — a real plus when you have only a single line and you need help troubleshooting your Internet connection.

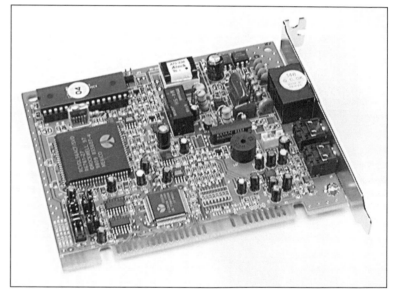

FIGURE 16-2: *A generic 56 Kbps internal modem awaits installation in a PCI slot.*

External versus internal modems

External modems have LEDs or other indicators that make it easier to diagnose problems, and you can turn off external modems to reset them without having to shut down the computer. They also don't draw power from the PC bus, produce heat under the covers, or use one of the computer's limited bus slots. Figure 16-3 shows an external modem.

Internal modems are usually a bit less expensive because they don't require a case, power supply, and cable. And though they use one of the internal slots, they don't necessarily use up one of the PC's two standard COM ports. With the proper software, you can set them to COM 3 or COM 4.

Table 16-1 compares external with internal devices.

Although modems are increasingly standardized, it is sometimes necessary to communicate with another modem of the same connection. If the modem uses an optional data-compression standard, such as MNP (discussed later in this chapter), you need another MNP modem to get the benefits of the data compression. Some very fast proprietary modems will only speak to another identical model.

FIGURE 16-3: *An external modem connects to a serial or USB port, without demanding an internal slot. External modems also provide visible indicators of telecommunication status.*

TABLE 16-1: A Comparison of External and Internal Modems

	External Serial Modem	External USB Modem	Internal Modem
Slots	+ Does not occupy an internal slot	+ Does not occupy an internal slot	– Requires an internal slot
Ports	– Uses a serial port	+ Shares a USB port with other devices	+ Usually supplies own serial port
Power, Heat	+ Does not draw on PC's power supply; does not add to internal heat; can be turned off	–/+ Draws small amount of power from USB bus or hub but does not add heat within case; can be turned off	– Draws power from internal power supply and adds some heat within case; generally cannot be turned off
Indicators	+ Usually offers range of indicator lights to show progress of session	+ Usually offers range of indicator lights to show progress of session	– Some models offer an onscreen display of the progression of the session
High speed with old UART?	– No. UART must be upgraded, or a separate serial adapter must be installed, requiring a slot in bus	+ Yes; provides its own high-speed UART	+ Yes; provides its own high-speed UART

Continued

Ch 16

TABLE 16-1: *Continued*

	External Serial Modem	External USB Modem	Internal Modem
Reset	+ Can be reset by turning off power switch or unplugging	+ Can be reset by turning off power switch or unplugging	− In some situations, lock-up of modem can only be cured by resetting entire computer
Cost	− More expensive because of case, power supply, cable	−/+ Slightly higher price than internal, but may not require power supply	+ Least expensive form

WinModems

A modem consists of certain basic components to enable the necessary send-and-receive data conversion and to conduct transmission and reception of information over the telephone line. Recall that the UART is one necessary component for the serial communications part of the modem. The other devices are part of a fairly standardized chipset supplied by one of several manufacturers. Each of these chipsets has its own features, but they all work pretty much the same and are all quite good.

Some modem manufacturers save money during construction by cutting redundancy, by using lower-cost support components, and so on, but all hardware modem manufacturers must start with one of these core chipsets. The fact is that hardware costs money. In a competitive computer marketplace, where consumers pretty much expect a modem as part of the computer hardware package, manufacturers are always looking for ways to reduce the cost of the package to the consumer.

Manufacturers have found one way in the software or soft modem. Most are meant to operate under Windows 95/98 and later, and usually are referred to as WinModems.

Soft modems work by offloading some of the work normally done by modem chips to the computer's main CPU; you'll need a modern machine with a Pentium II or later CPU. This means that the microprocessor is taking on other duties normally handled

elsewhere, and that information must travel along the PCI bus to and from the modem to get the work done.

3COM's WinModem design eliminates one hardware component — the controller — but still has a hardware data pump, the modem piece that takes care of the basic modulation/demodulation tasks. The controller handles protocols for error correction, data transfer, and so on. I suppose that this model could be called a "half-soft modem."

Other designs, however, replace both the controller and the data pump with software running on the host computer (HSP modems, for host signal processor). These are more difficult to configure and, in my experience, the least likely to provide reliable service.

 NOTE

A number of manufacturers supply software modems. The 3COM WinModem is one example, and the 3COM chips are supplied to a number of other vendors as an OEM product. The designation *WinModem* is a certain sign that the modem is at least partly based on software. If a modem is advertised for Windows only, it probably is a soft modem. If the manufacturer calls it a *controllerless modem*, it certainly isn't playing with all the hardware it really needs. Rockwell's RPI modem series are software-based modems, as are Lucent's LT WinModems.

I'm not saying you can't get satisfactory performance out of a software-driven modem. Many designs are available, and some units work better than others. Some use more hardware and less software, and some locations accept a software modem better than others. However, if you're having trouble getting online or having problems getting the kind of speed your modem was designed to deliver, consider upgrading to a better, hardware-based modem. It can save a lot of troubleshooting headaches and, in the end, save you money.

Windows-only modems (sometimes called WinModems) are internal Plug-and-Play devices that usually share system memory and are dependent on drivers in the Windows operating system to function properly. As an internal device, WinModems use system resources including an I/O address and IRQ. In addition, many WinModems also use a DMA channel. If the modem attempts to use the same resources as another device, there will be a resource conflict and either or both devices may not work.

You can check on resource conflicts from the Device Manager. Click Start ➪ Settings ➪ Control Panel. Double-click System, and then click the Device Manager tab. In most cases, a resource conflict or other problem with a device is indicated by an exclamation point in a yellow circle.

Fax Modems

Nearly all modern internal modems and external modems include fax capabilities, allowing you to send anything you see on the screen over a telephone line to a fax machine or another fax modem.

Perhaps the most important component here is a capable piece of software that converts the screen display to a faxable image and manages the transmission and receipt facilities of the modem. I nominate Symantec's Winfax as the best consumer product. In recent years, a basic version of Winfax has been bundled as a component of suites, such as Norton Systemworks.

If you want to send a copy of a piece of paper, you need to add a scanner to the mix. You scan whatever you want to send, save it as a graphics file, and then use your fax software to send it over the phone lines to another fax. Alternatively, you can send the graphics file as a stream of data to a standard modem, where the recipient can print out the image using a graphics program and a printer. You can use your printer to make hard copies of any faxes that you receive.

To use your fax modem to receive incoming faxes, you have to leave the modem and PC on all the time, with the modem set to auto answer.

If you're like me, you've switched to a broadband cable or DSL modem for direct connection to the Internet; your ability to send and receive faxes with your PC takes a different route. You'll either need to keep a dial-up modem available just for faxing, or subscribe to one of several Internet-based fax services that will link your Internet address to a phone line at their end.

Modern Dial-up Modem Standards

Over the years, modem designers had succeeded in pushing communication in exciting but relatively small increments: from 300 bps when the IBM PC first arrived to 1,200, and then 2,400, 4,800, 9,600, and finally 14,400. When modem manufacturers figured out a way to double communications speed to 28,800 bps (28.8 Kbps) in 1993, they did so with a warning that technology was nearing the maximum speed limit. That seemed to be proving true in 1996 when modem makers came out with a very small, incremental increase to 33.6 Kbps.

In fact, 33.6 Kbps may well prove to be as fast as many people can push data over the pair of copper wires that run from their homes or offices.

Modems supporting the 56 Kbps standard began arriving on the scene in 1998. Although the modem is capable of working at

Ch 16

56,000 bits per second, technical restrictions limit download to no more than 53,000 bps. Uploading from your machine to another 56K modem, the potential top speed is 33.6 Kbps. This design element works well in an Internet environment where the bulk of the traffic is from a Web site to your PC.

For top speed, it is also essential that only one analog segment be present in the communication path from your PC to its destination or the other direction. Remember that the purpose of a dial-up modem is to convert the digital information within your PC to an analog wave signal that can travel the simple two-wire telephone circuit from your home or office to the phone company's nearest central switching office. After the signal arrives at the phone company facility, in most cases, it is converted to digital form. If the signal has to be reconverted from digital to analog at the central office nearest the destination of your Internet communication (and then back from analog to digital at the receiving computer) the throughput will be reduced markedly.

When 56K modems were first introduced, competing manufacturers divided the market into two incompatible camps: those using the X2 standard and those using the K56Flex standard. If you have a modem that uses one of these standards, you will only be able to connect at 56 Kbps if your modem finds a like-minded device at the other end of the phone line.

In 1998, the industry came together behind a single standard called V.90. Some, but not all, of the original 56K modems can be upgraded to work under V.90. Contact your modem manufacturer or check the company's Web site for details.

Along the way, some modems supported at least two and sometimes three of these standards, automatically switching to the correct one depending on the kind of hardware they encounter on the other end. A V.90 modem that includes X2 in its name, for example, adheres to the V.90 standard, but can also communicate with devices that are capable of using only X2 on the other end. Likewise, a V.90/K56 modem supports those two standards.

V.92 and V.44 modems

Two new standards offer the possibility of squeezing out a bit more data from the effective dial-up speed limit of 56 Kbps modems.

V.92 ekes out a bit more speed, allowing uploads at as much as 48 Kbps, up from V.90's theoretical maximum of 33 Kbps. Modems using this standard can work with call-waiting services on your telephone to put the Internet on hold, in order to allow you to answer an incoming voice call. And V.92 promises to perform its "handshaking" connection to an Internet provider faster than previous standards.

The second new standard, V.44, provides an improved means of data compression. Systems using V.44 can compress Web pages at the ISP and decompress them at the receiving modem. In some situations, use of V.44 can double or even triple the speed of download of Web pages. The compression, though, won't speed up streaming video or audio data.

Although both are improvements over previous modem standards, there is one important gotcha: To make use of its advanced features, a compatible modem must be present at both ends of the connection. If you have a V.92 modem but your ISP has not upgraded beyond V.90, you will end up using the older V.90 standard in your communications. The same goes for V.44 compression.

New modems using the standards are now available, and as this book goes to press, they cost only slightly more than older models; over time, the price differential will likely disappear as the new standards supplant the older standards entirely.

Some current modems can use software upgrades to migrate from the V.90 to the V.92 standard. However, many older modems don't have sufficient speed to handle the needs of the V.44 decompression.

NOTE

If one pipe full of information is good, two pipes are twice as good. This is the thinking behind multimodem technology or "Shotgun" devices, which combine two modems over two phone lines for a theoretical throughput of up to 112 Kbps. This sophisticated technology requires that both ends of the communication have a set of Shotgun-compatible modems. The information is split in two and sent down both pipelines to be recombined at the receiving end. This interesting technology has not been widely adopted, however. Instead, users have gone to broadband solutions, such as DSL or cable modems.

CCITT standards

The International Telephone and Telegraph Consultative Committee (known by the French acronym CCITT) is an international association that establishes and oversees worldwide communications standards. CCITT standards begin with the letter V and are followed by a numeric code.

Bell Labs developed the original American standards in the 1960s and 1970s. The newer CCITT standards generally cover the same protocols. The newest modem standard is V.90, which describes the 56 Kbps protocol.

Table 16-2 gives a listing of modem standards.

TABLE 16-2: Modem Standards

Standard	Description
V.22	1,200 bps. Synchronous or asynchronous data transmission with full-duplex operations over two-wire leased or dial-up lines. Comparable to Bell 212A.
V.22bis	2,400 bps.
V.32	9,600 bps, fallback to 4,800 bps. The first universal standard for 9,600 bps modems on dial-up or leased lines.

Standard	Description
V.32bis	14,400 bps. Includes the ability to retrain connected modems to reduce transmission speed to deal with line noise, if necessary.
V.34	28,800 to 33,600 bps. This standard began at 28.8 Kbps, but firmware improvements allowed modems to eke out a bit of extra speed, moving from 28.8 Kbps to 33.6 Kbps in good conditions.
V.90	56,000 bps. Download at as much as 53 Kbps; upload at as much as 33.6 Kbps in good conditions. Most designs are backward compatible to allow communications with earlier devices, and many support the other 56K protocols, 56Kflex, and X2.
V.92	56,000 bps. Download at as much as 53 Kbps; upload at as much as 48 Kbps in good conditions. As this book goes to press, this is the current published standard.

Error correction and data compression

After the transmission speed for the bits of information has been set, you can add protocols that help ensure error-free transmission of data, or that compress data so that the effective rate of transmission is even greater. Data compression is one way to increase the speed of the modem without having to deal with the physical limitations of the wiring used. A compression ratio of 6:1 (the ultimate potential rate of V.44) effectively converts a 56 Kbps modem to nearly 200,000 bps in throughput. Two caveats: you must have the same protocols installed at both ends of the modem connection for the information to be properly encoded and decoded, and not all data can be compressed. Some data is already shrunk by application software and some types of information don't lend themselves to high ratios of compression.

Ch 16

Table 16-3 shows a listing of current telecommunication protocols.

TABLE 16-3: Current Telecommunication Protocols

Protocol	Description
MNP Levels 1-4	The Microcom Networking Protocols permit error-free asynchronous transmission of data.
MNP Level 5	This protocol adds a data compression algorithm to the error-correction code. Data is compressed by a factor of about 2:1.
MNP-10	Includes previous levels and adds features to support cellular data connections.
V.42, V.42bis	The CCITT definition for a protocol that is comparable to MNP Level 5. The V.42 protocol offers error correction with MNP levels 2-4 and LAPM (link access procedure for modems), while V.42bis adds compression.
V.44	Improved data compression; systems using V.44 can compress Web pages at the ISP and decompress them at the receiving modem.

Troubleshooting an External Modem

When it comes to troubleshooting an external modem, you should test the following separate components:

- **Port:** Test the port by using a diagnostic program, such as AMI Diags. By examining Device Manager from within Windows, you can check whether the port is disabled because of a resource conflict.

- **Modem:** Is the modem plugged in and turned on? Do the modem lights turn on when power is applied? Some modems have a self-test that should generate an OK or other message after you turn on the device.

- **Software settings in your telecommunications program:** Check the settings in your software program. Is it set to use the proper COM port?

- **The cable to the PC:** Check the cable running from the serial port to the modem by substituting a new or replacement cable that you know to be good.

- **The cable to the telephone socket:** Test the connection from the computer to the modem by going into the Hyper Terminal program that is available from within Windows. By default, this little-used program is part of the Communications subgroup in the Accessories group of Windows. Load the terminal emulation program. Type **AT** and press the Enter key. If your modem is working and is properly attached to a working serial port through a working cable, the software program should report an OK message onscreen.

- **The phone line:** Is the modem properly plugged into the phone jack? Swap a phone cable that you know to be good for the one in use. Try plugging a telephone into the jack to confirm that a dial tone is on the line. If the jack itself is dead, you may have to troubleshoot the phone line within your home or office. If the problem lies at the network interface between your building and the phone company's incoming line, it's time to call the phone repairman. You can also purchase an inexpensive telephone line tester that will tell you whether the line is active, and if the + or − wires are reversed; a telephone will generally work with the lines reversed, but some high-tech devices, including answering machines and modems, may not. An example of a line tester is shown in Figure 16-4.

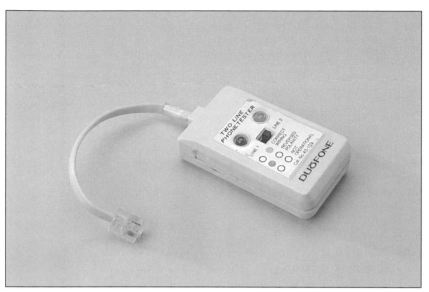

FIGURE 16-4: *A simple telephone line tester will tell you whether the line is live and whether the internal wiring is properly installed.*

Modem cables

You can have the speediest PC in town, equipped with a state-of-the-art dial-up, cable, or DSL modem and a subscription to the best Internet provider in town — and still end up with bad connections, disconnects, and corrupted files.

The problem may lie in the easy-to-overlook, inexpensive cables that hook it all together.

If you're like me, you have a couple dozen of the cheap, two- or four-wire telephone cables that connect a dial-up modem to a wall jack sitting in a drawer — the leftover pieces from various telephones and modems I have purchased over the years.

It's very easy to think that these cables will last forever and always perform as if new. This is simply not true. Here are a few ways that a simple phone cable can go bad:

- It can be pinched beneath a desk or chair, causing a short circuit or break in the wires.

- It can be made fragile by proximity to a radiator or heater. Repeated heating and cooling can cause the wire to shrink, or damage the insulation around the wire.
- Wires can be stretched or connectors damaged if they are pulled when a computer or desk is moved.

Any time you experience problems with a modem, I suggest that you carefully examine phone wires for damage. Try replacing the cables to see if a fresh wire will fix the problem.

It is also possible that a problem with a cable, telephone, or wall jack elsewhere in your home or office can short out the phone line throughout your operation. To attempt to solve a mystery phone or modem problem, start by confirming that your phone line is operating properly. Do so by plugging a working telephone into the Network Interface installed by the phone company at the point where it enters your home or office. A phone that does not work properly indicates that the problem lies in telephone company wiring and equipment. A phone that's working properly indicates that problems exist between the incoming phone line and the various devices plugged into the system in your home and office.

To find problems on your side of the network interface, start by unplugging every phone device. Then plug them in one at a time, checking for problems one at a time. If your modem operates well until a particular phone, answering machine, or other device is plugged into the phone line, you can assume that the problem is with the last device you attached.

Although modern devices are pretty well shielded against interference, you may be able to fix problems with modems by eliminating radio frequency interference from monitors, modems, and other peripherals. Some of these devices come with small iron rings, called *ferrite chokes*, that reduce interference when attached to cables; if you can't find a set in your kit of leftover bits and pieces of equipment, you can purchase ferrite chokes from most electronics stores.

Troubleshooting an Internal Modem

In theory, the Plug-and-Play facility of Windows 95/98 and later will set up an internal PCI bus modem to avoid conflicts with IRQ and I/O port addresses. Follow the instructions that come with the modem.

Older cards, including all ISA bus devices, require you to physically make these settings by using jumpers or switches. Here's the procedure for most of them: Examine the Device Manager to look for available IRQs and I/O port addresses and then change the jumpers on the board if necessary. Then install the modem and go to the Modems setup screen of Windows to assign IRQs and I/O port addresses.

Test the machine before reinstalling the cover — it's easy to make a mistake here. The I/O port address must be unique — it must not interfere with another device already installed in the machine. If your telecommunications software supports COM 3 and/or COM 4, set the modem to COM 3. You are unlikely to have another serial device set to COM 3. Be sure to set the IRQ for the I/O port address that you are using (each I/O port address is paired, by tradition, with a particular interrupt).

CROSS-REFERENCE

See Appendix D for a list of common I/O port addresses and their associated interrupts.

NOTE

If your modem suddenly stops working, remember this basic rule of troubleshooting: Figure out what changes have been made since the last time it worked. If you've installed a sound card (a regular offender), check to see if it has glommed onto the modem's IRQ or port addresses.

Then check the phone line. Is the modem properly plugged into the phone jack? Swap a phone cable that you know to be good for the one in use. Try plugging a telephone into the jack to confirm that a dial tone is on the line. If the jack itself is dead, you may have to troubleshoot the phone line within your home or office; if the problem lies at the network interface between your building and the phone company's incoming line, it's time to call the phone repairman.

Telecom Problems

Whether you use an external or internal modem, your telecommunications software must be set up correctly. A minor baud rate error or the incorrect I/O port address will make your perfectly good modem appear to be stone-cold dead. Modems are just that way; they either work fine or they don't work at all. Some pieces of communications software are very picky about the brand of telecommunications hardware in your system.

The call-waiting headache

The call-waiting tone unfortunately can disrupt modem communications. The result can be a simple loss of characters, a corruption of a file that you're transmitting, or a complete loss of the connection.

On most phone networks, you can disable call waiting by manually entering *70 from the dialing pad of a telephone before you place the call. As soon as you hang up, though, call waiting goes back into effect.

Some telecommunications programs have a setting for automatically including the disable signal before any call is dialed. For other applications, type **70,** (include the comma) at the end of the dialing prefix.

Modem troubleshooting

Here are some suggestions to determine the source of your modem's ills:

Modem is recognized but cuts off before connecting.

- If your modem seems to be working properly but cuts off before a connection is successfully negotiated, try instructing Windows to be a bit more patient.
    1. Click Start ➪ Settings ➪ Control Panel, and then double-click Modems. On the General tab, click the name of the modem you are using. Then click Properties ➪ Connection tab.
    2. Add 15 seconds to the value for "Cancel the call if not connected within *xx* secs value." Click OK, and then click Close.
    3. Try the call again. If the problem recurs, repeat the steps until you are at the Properties tab, and turn off the waiting period entirely. Clear the Cancel the call if not connected within *xx* secs check box. Click OK, and then click Close. Try the call again.
- Another important modem checkup: Make sure you are using the most current device driver.
    1. To update a modem driver, click Start ➪ Settings ➪ Control Panel, and then double-click System. Click the Device Manager tab. If a Modem branch is displayed, double-click to expand it. Double-click your modem, click the Driver tab, and then click Update Driver.
    2. If you have an updated driver on a disk, you can specify a location. If you're using Windows 98, you can launch the Update Device Driver Wizard to search for a driver on a Web page maintained by Microsoft.

Modem does not connect at its full speed.

- Consider the quality of your phone line. If your voice telephone is regularly scratchy or disconnects by itself, your data modem is going to do no better.
- In most homes and offices, telephone companies have installed a box called the *network interface*; it may be located on the outside of the house, in the basement, or in a utility closet. The incoming telephone line comes into the box and from there it is split off to serve your home or office.
- The first task in checking a telephone line is to determine whether the problem lies in the phone company's connection to your home or office, or in the wiring that you own. Go to the network interface and plug a telephone directly into the interface and make a call. If the connection is clear and clean, your problem is probably on your side of the interface; if the line is bad, contact your telephone company and have them test the line.
- You can also call your telephone company and request a report on the possible top data connection speed for your line.
- In most cases, a problem on the telephone company's side of the interface is the responsibility of the utility. You will have to repair a problem within your home or office, or you can pay the phone company or a communications specialist to do the repair. Check the telephone directory supplied by your phone company — not one of the independent directories — for details about network interfaces and repair policies.
- If the phone line seems okay on both sides of the network interface and Windows finds the modem and does not report a resource conflict, the problem may lie in the settings that you have made for the Internet connection or the dial-up line you are using. Here you should enlist the assistance of your Internet Service Provider if possible; call customer service and go through all the settings you have made. Make certain your modem is compatible with the ISP's modem.

Testing your line for 56K capability

The only sure way to test whether your phone line is capable of connecting at 56K is to install a 56K modem and try it out. See if you can borrow a high-speed modem from a friend or colleague or a demo model from a store.

Dial into an ISP or a modem link that promises 56K compatibility, but make certain that your model matches the protocol used by that service. Today, that's probably V.90, but some earlier 56K devices may still be out there.

If the connection is successful at anything above 40K, you're all set — that is, unless line conditions change. Remember that most phone companies don't guarantee high-speed or digital connections unless you pay extra for a specific type of service. If you want to find out how fast your connection actually is, contact your modem manufacturer or visit the manufacturer's Web page. Many companies offer a dial-in testing service that can verify whether your modem is operating correctly. Software utilities available on the Internet can show you how fast you are exchanging data with other hosts.

Check out Table 16-4 for a comparison of modem speeds.

TABLE 16-4: A Comparison of Modem Communication Speed (Download)	
Type of Connection	**Description**
Dial-up modem	V.92 56 Kbps modem can download at 48 Kbps
ISDN	64 Kbps (1 B-channel) or 128 Kbps (2 B-channels)
Satellite	700 Kbps
DSL	256 Kbps to 1.5 Mbps (1500 Kbps)
Cable modem	1.5 to 3 Mbps
T1	1.544 Mbps (point-to-point dedicated line)
T2	6.312 Mbps (point-to-point dedicated line)
T3	44.736 Mbps (point-to-point dedicated digital line)

Cable Modems

For many users, cable modems represent the simplest route to high-speed Internet connection. Other options include advanced phone line solutions, including ISDN and DSL, and dedicated line systems including T1, T2, and T3. An out-of-this-world method involves satellite downlinks combined with dial-up uplinks. For a comparison of modem speeds, see Table 16-4.

In theory, the "fat" cable television wire that comes into many homes and offices offers a superhighway for Internet information. Almost all of the systems are unbalanced, devoting more space (and therefore greater speed) to the download stream from the Web to your PC than to the upload from your PC to the Internet. Still, you should be able to receive the Internet at speeds of 8 to 20 times the speed of a standard 56K dial-up modem.

Cable modems offer other advantages as well. To begin with, there is no dial-up; the Internet is available all the time. (In practice, it takes a few seconds for your computer to connect to the cable modem the first time you boot up; after then, the link is active and very quick to respond.) Figure 16-5 shows a Toshiba PCX1100 cable modem.

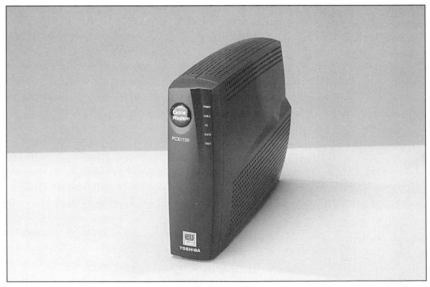

FIGURE 16-5: *A Toshiba PCX1100 cable modem, a DOCSIS broadband device in wide use*

The Internet signals don't interfere with your cable television reception. You'll need a good quality splitter to divide the incoming cable between the needs of your televisions and your PCs.

That's the good news. Here are a few areas of possible bad news:

- **The connection between your home or office and the central switch for the cable television company is a shared wire.** Unlike a telephone connection, which essentially creates a dedicated circuit between your PC and your ISP, cable systems use a "branching network" that splits the Internet signal into successively smaller feeder lines. All users along a feeder line share the available Internet bandwidth. You may find that you have a consistently fast connection, or you may find that a neighbor or group of neighbors may be grabbing large chunks of bandwidth for other purposes, such as streaming audio or video. On my system, I find the cable link to be fast and responsive all the day until late afternoon when, it seems, youngsters further along the line turn on their machines after school. Speed drops noticeably for a few hours, but is still six or eight times faster than a 56K modem at that time. Check with your cable company to see what kind of guaranteed minimum speed they will offer.
- **You'll have to make a judgment about the reliability and responsiveness of your cable television provider.** Some systems are very stable with few outages, while others seem to have constant breakdowns.
- **The constantly connected nature of the cable modem makes an attractive target for malicious and mischievous hackers who troll the Internet for ways to break into computers.** I absolutely recommend that you install a firewall to protect your system from intruders — either a hardware firewall that is part of a router for a small network, or a software firewall. And you will also want to install and keep current an antivirus program to scan e-mail and incoming files.

- **Cable modem Internet service is not available everywhere.** Older cable providers that have not upgraded their systems to fiber optics and high-speed switches are generally not able to offer high-speed service; they may offer a slower hybrid system that uses a dial-up telephone link to send information *from* your PC to the Internet and the cable television system for downloading information.
- **In general, you will have to use your cable company's ISP once you're online.** This doesn't mean that you can't connect to any Web page or check your mail from other sources. However, you may end up with redundant mail accounts and Web hosting accounts if you want to hold on to existing addresses you had before the cable company wired your PC. Lawsuits filed by some ISPs and concerns about antitrust rulings have begun to convince cable television companies to open their wires to other service providers.

Installing a cable modem

In theory, a cable television wire can bring in the Internet at speeds of as much as 38 megabits per second. A more realistic expectation is in the range from 300 kilobits to 3 megabits per second. (My office connection runs in the range from 1 to 1.7 megabits per second.) Compare this to a typical throughput of about 44 kilobits per second using a dial-up 56K modem.

The cable modem converts incoming signals into data that your computer can understand. Most cable modems connect to the PC through an Ethernet network interface card; a smaller number of cable modems connect to a USB port on the PC.

Cable modems sell for about $150 to $300. You can purchase one through some specialty PC suppliers and at some computer retail outlets. At this early stage of the cable modem technology, though, I suggest that you look into renting the modem from your provider. You'll pay about $10 to $15 per month for the rental, but you will also have the security of knowing that if the modem fails or if the provider upgrades to a new protocol or hardware, you can arrange for a quick swap at no additional cost.

Several protocols are available for cable modems, but in 2000, the industry came to an agreement to use a standard called the Data Over Cable Service Interface Specification (DOCSIS). Any DOCSIS modem is supposed to be interchangeable with another. I will only consider purchasing a cable modem when prices drop well below $100.

Cable companies may offer a free do-it-yourself installation kit or free connection by a technician, or they may demand a service charge of as much as $100 for running a cable to your PC and providing a splitter and other hardware.

Before you sign up, though, be sure you are satisfied with the quality of the cable television signal you see on your television sets. If you have a weak, snowy picture on the Sony in your bedroom, chances are the signal to your PC will be slow or unreliable.

When the technician came to my office to wire my system, I asked him to measure the signal strength on the incoming cable. He found that the signal was unacceptably weak; I asked for, and received, a new incoming cable from the road. The technician ran the new cable directly to my PC, splitting it off to the televisions just short of the computer.

DSL Modems

Digital subscriber line (DSL) technology delivers high-speed data and Internet connections over regular phone lines. Here are the facts about DSL modems:

- DSL works by taking advantage of previously little-used frequencies on telephone wires. Standard voice telephone calls are sent at frequencies from 0 KHz to 4 KHz, a relatively narrow band that works well over long distances; it's that narrow band that makes phone calls less than high-fidelity in sound. Traditional dial-up modems modulate their information into analog sounds that travel in the same frequency range as voice.

- DSL moves its data at a higher frequency in a much broader bandwidth between 25 KHz and 1 MHz. This allows transmission of much more information without interfering with voice calls.

- In addition to speed — as much as 52 megabits per second in optimal settings — DSL offers an always-on connection that is not shared with other users. This avoids one of the downsides of cable modems, which share their connection with other users between a central office and subscriber. DSL users can also continue to use existing wires for voice calls.

- The most common DSL connection for home and small business users is capable of 384 Kbps, about eight times faster than a 56K modem; higher speeds are available in some locations at higher prices.

The potential bad news, though, is that DSL is a somewhat tricky technology to install and maintain, and may not be available at all in some areas:

- The farther your home or office is from the central office, the slower and potentially more problematic your connection is. If you are right next door to a phone company switching office, you may be able to purchase 1.5 Mbps service; most users will be offered 384 Kbps service. If you are more than two miles away from the central office, DSL may not be available at all.

- Not all telephone companies offer DSL service, or may be in competition with other companies that are permitted to use their wires. You may even find a three-party setup where one company sells you the DSL service, the phone company provides the physical link, and a third business serves as the Internet Service Provider. If this sounds like an invitation to trouble, that's because it usually is; many early users of DSL found themselves in the midst of a buck-passing battle when they sought technical support.

- As with a cable modem system, you'll need to appraise the quality of the phone service you receive. If your phone lines regularly fail or if the quality of signal is poor, you can expect slow or poor DSL service. (In my rural neighborhood, our fiber optic cable television system is many decades younger than the copper telephone wires, and DSL does not seem like a good choice.)

How DSL works

A DSL modem operates similarly to a dial-up or cable modem, converting the digital information of your computer to an analog signal that moves across the phone lines. At the telephone company's central office, a Digital Subscriber Line Access Multiplexer (DSLAM) separates the data signal from voice, connecting the computer's signal to an ISP.

The most common form of DSL for homes and small businesses is Asymmetric Digital Subscriber Line (ADSL), a technology that uses an unbalanced set of channels devoting more space and yielding more speed for downstream information coming in from the Internet and a smaller proportional share to the upstream channel, used for sending data from the user to the Internet. For many users, this asymmetric design works well because most upstream traffic consists of small files and requests to the Internet for the download of information. Typical real world speeds are about 375 Kbps downstream and 284 Kbps upstream.

Symmetric Digital Subscriber Line (SDSL) devotes the same amount of bandwidth in both directions. If your home or office is within two miles of a central office, this could allow as much as 750 Kbps in each direction, or 1.5 Mbps in total. IDSL (ISDN Digital Subscriber Line) is another symmetrical technology that may work better (but at a slower speed) when the home or office is distant from the central office. IDSL, also known as ISDN over DSL, transmits at 144 Kbps in both directions.

HDSL (High-Data-Rate Digital Subscriber Line) is an expensive high-speed solution for some businesses, requiring installation of a direct T-1 phone line. Another high-speed solution is VDSL (Very-High-Rate Digital Subscriber Line), but this technology has a very limited range. VDSL is capable of speeds of as much as 52 Mbps downstream and 1.5 Mbps upstream.

Another type of DSL service is RADSL (Rate Adaptive Digital Subscriber Line), a system that continuously samples the quality of the phone line and then automatically adjusts the access speed based upon its condition.

For consumers, one of the advantages of ADSL is that it permits you to use a single phone line for both voice and data. To do so, you may need to have a splitter installed on the incoming line to send voice frequencies to the telephones and data frequencies to the DSL modem; an alternative is to install a microfilter at each phone jack. Some providers require a technician to install splitters; do-it-yourself kits with microfilters may save the cost of a service visit.

As with cable modems, you may find it better to rent a DSL modem from a service provider instead of purchasing one; by renting you leave compatibility, upgrade, and repair or replacement headaches to the provider. After you are certain that DSL works well for you, and that your provider seems to be well established, you can consider purchasing your own modem.

SUMMARY

I've explored the current state of modems for telecommunications into and out of a PC. In the next chapter, I move on to a different form of mass transport within the PC: the parallel interface, used primarily for printers but also for devices including scanners, external storage devices, and a specialized category of modems.

Chapter 17

Tools Needed:

- Phillips or flat-blade screwdriver

The Parallel Interface

A *parallel port* is a continuation of the computer data bus that can carry 8 bits of information (one byte) along an eight-lane wired highway, one alongside each other. In theory, a parallel port can deliver information eight times as fast as a basic serial port, which sends those same 8 bits one after another down a single wire. However, as is discussed in Chapter 15, parallel ports tend to run into trouble when the speed of those bits is increased or the length of the cable passes a certain point.

The original PC used a parallel port as a quick and simple way to attach a nearby printer, and that is still the case for many modern machines. Meanwhile, designers have found more and more ways to use the parallel port for devices from scanners to modems to external CD-ROM drives and hard drives. However, an increasing number of peripheral manufacturers are changing some or all of their products to use the speedy and convenient USB port, a serial specification that in its 1.1 version, is nearly as fast and in its 2.0 version, is potentially nearly 40 times faster than parallel ports.

This chapter explores how parallel ports work and offers advice on troubleshooting and replacing parallel port hardware.

Going Parallel

The original PC parallel port had one basic function: to send data in one direction, from computer to printer. An adapter called a parallel card collected data from the computer bus and sent it 8 bits at a time to the printer.

For years, the PC's parallel port was called the *printer port*, which was an appropriate name because very few parallel devices existed other than printers. In fact, in the early days, this port was frequently called the *Centronics port* because the Centronics company provided one of the first printers with a parallel interface and designed a 36-pin connection scheme for parallel ports that was called the Centronics connector. Devices that, at the time, were considered very sophisticated were capable of sending a small amount of data back up the wire to communicate from the printer to the PC. For example, the computer could receive an out-of-paper or printer-busy signal from the printer, but that signal held up data transmission.

Modern machines have true two-way parallel ports (also called *enhanced parallel port*, or *enhanced capabilities port*) so that data can flow freely into and out of the computer. The two-way parallel port has spawned a whole raft of parallel-interface peripherals. You can now buy modems, network adapters, CD-ROM drives, backup drives, and even external hard disks and tape backup units that communicate with the host computer through a parallel port. Figure 17-1 shows a D-shaped, 25-pin, female parallel connector on a PC.

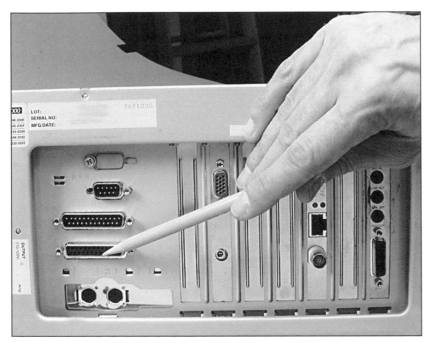

FIGURE 17-1: *A parallel connector on the back panel of a PC*

Despite the new class of flashy parallel peripherals, printers are still the most common peripheral on a parallel port. However, consumer printers are increasingly offered in high-speed USB versions. Also, some specialty printers use serial ports.

Parallel Port Designs

Four basic types of parallel ports are available for the modern machine, each with differing speeds and capabilities. The good

news is that current systems offer ports that include all four modes. Here are the elements:

- **Unidirectional.** The original definition for the port, enabling one-way flow of data from a PC to a printer and occasionally to other devices. The top speed under this mode is about 50 Kbps.
- **Bidirectional.** In addition to the potential for two-way communication, this protocol boosts the possible transfer rate to as much as 300 Kbps. The bidirectional signal is mostly used to communicate status back from the device to the PC. Such information can include an out-of-paper signal from a printer.
- **EPP (enhanced parallel port).** An expansion of the protocol to speeds from 500 Kbps to more than 2 Mbps. The EPP is widely used by a new class of external devices that include hard drives, removable storage devices, and network adapters.
- **ECP (extended capabilities port).** A further extension of the EPP to improve two-way communications between peripherals and the PC.

Your best bet to avoid confusion is to follow carefully the advice in instruction manuals for your PC and devices attached to it. If your PC and peripherals support ECP, you have no reason not to use this most current and fastest implementation of the parallel port. Device drivers and setup programs should automatically prepare your machine for use with new hardware. You can also make changes using the Device Manager under Windows. You may also need to enter your computer's ROM BIOS to configure some types of new hardware. If Plug-and-Play doesn't catch your hardware, try configuring it from inside the BIOS.

How a Parallel Port Works

Because computers store information in 8-bit bytes, the simplest way to send a byte of information to a printer is to use eight separate wires from computer to printer. Each of the 8 bits is sent on its own wire, parallel to other wires within the cable.

Nearly every modern motherboard offers only a single parallel port, although a standard motherboard is capable of having as many as three parallel ports, numbered as LPT 1 through LPT 3. Under Windows 98 and later versions, the Plug-and-Play function should assign IRQs, I/O port addresses, and DMA channels automatically, although the occasional conflict still slips by. If you have more than one LPT port in your system, they should have resource settings that are unique to each other, as well as different from those of other devices in the PC.

Table 17-1 shows the standard resource settings for parallel ports. Note that the standard settings for LPT 1 and LPT 2 both use IRQ 7. One or the other (preferably LPT 2) should be given a different IRQ to avoid conflicts.

TABLE 17-1: Standard Resource Settings for Parallel Ports

Port Name	IRQ	I/O Port Address
LPT 1	IRQ 7	3BC-3BFh
LPT 2	IRQ 7	378-37Ah
LPT 3	IRQ 5	278-27Ah

Many modern parallel port devices include a pass-through cabling system that enables you to daisy-chain at least one more peripheral. For example, you can use a parallel port to communicate with an external CD-ROM drive and plug a printer cable into the back of the CD-ROM case to serve a printer. In theory, this is another Plug-and-Play solution, but in practice you may find occasional conflicts if both devices seek the attention of the PC at the same time. In the case cited here, for example, you may have problems printing information from the CD-ROM to the printer that is daisy-chained through it. One solution is to print to a file on your hard disk, and then resend the file to the printer.

Three signal lines on early parallel ports were assigned to the printer to send out-of-paper, printer-busy, and data-acknowledgment signals back to the computer. The parallel port could transmit signals on the eight data lines, but not receive them. New parallel ports can send and receive on all lines.

A standard parallel printer cable—sometimes called a Centronics cable for the 36-pin Centronics connector at the printer end—connects the parallel card to the printer. (Some of the most modern devices have begun to use a smaller, high-density 36-pin connector at the printer end; the specification is called IEEE 1284-C.)

 NOTE

Unlike serial ports, all parallel ports send the same signals on each particular pin, so no custom parallel cables are needed.

If you are going to use an ECP or EPP parallel device, though, your hardware may demand a high-quality bidirectional cable. Some devices use high-density connectors that are smaller than the traditional DB-25 connector used on earlier PCs.

Extended Capabilities Port/Enhanced Parallel Port

ECP and EPP ports offer improved throughput for some peripherals and add to the number of ports that you can have on your PC. This high-speed parallel specification (also referred to as IEEE 1284) can transfer data in parallel fashion up to 50 to 100 times faster than traditional parallel (Centronics) interfaces.

The 1284 specification provides for five basic port modes:

■ **Compatibility.** A one-way mode that sends data only from the host to a peripheral. Sometimes called Centronics or standard mode, this is the way parallel ports worked in the beginning.

■ **Nybble.** A 4-bit bidirectional mode, but somewhat limited, and most often used to get information back from a printer, such as out-of-paper, offline, or other status information. A peripheral can send a full byte of information to the host, but it takes two 4-bit transmissions to do it.

- **Byte.** The bidirectional port mode. Eight bits at a time are transferred bidirectionally.
- **EPP.** A bidirectional, 8-bit mode. This is a fast data-transfer mode that can achieve transfer rates from 500K to 2MB per second. Transfer requires only a single ISA bus cycle. With this data rate, the parallel port peripheral can operate at about the same speed as an ISA bus card.
- **ECP.** Also a high-speed data interchange mode, designed for host-peripheral data transfer with printers, scanners, and other peripherals.

Although ECP/EPP ports offer much faster transfer and bidirectionality, they also maintain compatibility with older peripherals, so you can upgrade your PC with a new parallel port board and still hook up your older printer or other parallel device.

On the other hand, don't expect to see dramatic changes in printer speed (or the speed of other peripherals) just because you have installed an IEEE 1284-compliant interface. You must have the proper drivers to support the port and the applications that you want to use with it, and, of course, your peripheral must be designed to handle the faster host communications.

Table 17-2 describes the signals that take ownership of each of the lines in a 25-wire parallel connector.

TABLE 17-2: Signals on a 25-Pin Parallel Port Connector

Pin	Name	Direction
1	– Strobe	Out
2	+ Data bit 0	Out
3	+ Data bit 1	Out
4	+ Data bit 2	Out
5	+ Data bit 3	Out
6	+ Data bit 4	Out
7	+ Data bit 5	Out
8	+ Data bit 6	Out
9	+ Data bit 7	Out
10	– Acknowledge	In
11	+ Busy	In
12	+ Paper out	In
13	+ Select	In
14	– Auto line feed	Out
15	– Error	In
16	– Initialize printer	Out
17	– Select input	Out
18	– Data bit 0 Return (Ground)	In
19	– Data bit 1 Return (Ground)	In
20	– Data bit 2 Return (Ground)	In
21	– Data bit 3 Return (Ground)	In
22	– Data bit 4 Return (Ground)	In
23	– Data bit 5 Return (Ground)	In
24	– Data bit 6 Return (Ground)	In
25	– Data bit 7 Return (Ground)	In

Unfortunately, parallel cables are only guaranteed to be accurate for short runs of 12 to 15 feet, though users sometimes successfully use cables as long as 25 feet. Each case is different. If it works, it works.

If a longer run does not function reliably, several solutions may help. One involves the use of a *parallel line booster*, which is a specialized amplifier that can extend the useful transmission distance of a parallel signal as much as 2,000 feet. These relatively inexpensive devices (costing less than $100 from mail-order sources) essentially convert the parallel signal into a specialized high-speed serial signal and send it over a standard telephone cable to a receiver where the signal is changed back to a parallel signal.

Finding a Parallel Port

If you have a printer, follow the printer cable to the back of your computer and examine that connector first. Nearly all parallel ports use 25-pin connectors (called *DB-25 connectors*). The parallel port on the computer system is a female DB-25 socket. The cable to the printer has a male DB-25 connector for the computer end of the link. (Male DB-25 connectors have protruding pins; female DB-25 connectors have openings to accept the pins.)

Just to make things interesting, serial ports can also use a DB-25 connector, although modern machines have mostly changed over to smaller DB-9 connectors. For users of the oldest PCs, serious confusion often occurred because some serial ports used female DB-25 sockets identical to the parallel port socket. All modern machines and most PCs manufactured after that period of initial confusion use male connectors for serial ports.

The DB-9 connector on a modern machine is male. You may still find a second DB-25 socket on the back of your PC for a second serial port, but it will have a male socket — with protruding pins — to differentiate it from the parallel printer port. IBM, which has almost always marched to its own drummer, reintroduced the confusion with some of its PS/2 computers in the early 1990s. If you're lucky, your machine has labels identifying the nature of all connectors on the back panel. Consult the PC's instruction manual if you have any doubts. Among dinosaurs, you will also find parallel ports on some video cards, multifunction cards, and on separate I/O (input/output) cards.

Figure 17-2 shows an add-on parallel port card that can be used to upgrade an older machine or to replace failed circuitry on a more current machine.

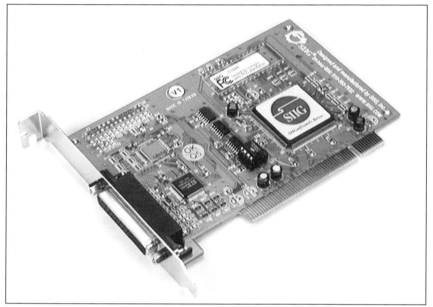

FIGURE 17-2: *You can add an enhanced parallel port card, such as this CyberParallel PCI card from SIIG, Inc., to an older machine to get the benefits of bidirectional parallel communication.*

Testing a Parallel Port

Parallel ports seldom fail. If you have a problem, it is more likely that the cable has worked loose, been crimped, or shorted out, or that a change to a software setting or a driver has caused it to stop responding. In my experience, however, the most likely cause is a failed cable. I recommend that you keep replacement parallel and serial cables in your supply cabinet. Here are some logical steps for troubleshooting parallel port problems:

1. Check the power cable to the printer. Most printers have a self-test capability; check the instruction manual to run the self-test. If the printer is plugged in and the self-test does not work, your printer has a problem.

2. Next, check the data cable connections between the parallel port and the printer. Is the cable firmly attached at both ends? Try using your new cable or a spare cable that you know to be good. If changing the cable fixes the problem, throw away the old cable.

3. Take the printer and the cable to another machine that has a working parallel port. If the printer and the cable work, then you can assume that the parallel port on the original PC has either failed or has an improper setting.

4. Try printing from another application. I have experienced printer failure from within application software many times. The software simply doesn't recognize the printer for some reason, even if it has worked properly before. (Okay, it shouldn't be that way, but these are computers, after all. Stuff happens!)

5. Try re-installing the printer driver software. For reasons probably nobody understands, printer drivers that worked fine yesterday can stop working today. Under Windows versions through Windows 98, use Start ⇨ Settings ⇨ Printers to display the printer dialog box, then right-click the icon that represents the printer that is not functioning properly and select remove or delete from the pop-up menu. Then choose Add a printer from this dialog box and follow instructions for re-installing the printer driver. This may, indeed, correct your printer errors. Under Windows 2000 and Windows XP, go to Start ⇨ Printers and Faxes.

CROSS-REFERENCE

Reference the troubleshooting charts in Appendix G for more hints on how to test a parallel port. See Chapter 18 for additional information on printers and printer configuration.

If the printer and the cable are good, and changing applications and printer drivers doesn't fix the problem, use a diagnostic disk to see what parallel ports the computer thinks are installed. If you have two physical parallel ports, but your Windows System Information utility or a troubleshooting utility such as Norton's System Information shows only one, the switches and interrupts on one of the ports are probably not set correctly.

The earliest versions of video with parallel port cards have a port enable/disable jumper. Check the manual for such a jumper. In addition, the physical port address and the interrupt assigned to the card are set with jumpers on some parallel cards. Again, check the manual.

As with serial ports, you must be careful to give each parallel port a unique hardware address. The operating system refers to these different addresses as LPT 1, LPT 2, and LPT 3, as I mentioned previously. Be sure that your software is set up correctly to send information to the appropriate parallel port. The printer cabled to LPT 1 won't print your document if the word processor is sending the text to LPT 2.

If you find no obvious problems, investigate the parallel port further. Try the CheckIt printer port tests. They require a wrap plug (also called a *loopback plug*). Wrap plugs sometimes come with the software, you can purchase one from an electronics supplier, or you can construct one out of a spare male RS232 plug (also available at an electronics supplier).

If you want to make your own wrap plug, you can short out the pins of a DB-25 connector with solder or connect the wires in a short parallel cable. Use short jumper wires or clean solder bridges to connect the pins electrically. You must make five solder connections. Details are shown in Table 17-3.

TABLE 17-3: Parallel Loopback Plug Combinations

Solder Pin	To Pin
2	15
3	13
4	12
5	10
6	11

If the parallel port passes the wrap plug test, the port is probably good. Check again for a mismatched LPT port and interrupt and for mismatched word processor output parameters. If you still can't find the problem, try the troubleshooting charts in Appendix G, which have complete, step-by-step, parallel port diagnostic/repair procedures.

Removing and Installing a Parallel Port

Many modern machines have serial and parallel circuitry built into the motherboard, with the ports extending out the back of the chassis. If a problem occurs with the parallel adapter on the motherboard, or if you want to upgrade to a better system, you may need to disable the adapter with a jumper or switch; modern machines usually allow you to turn off a parallel port on the motherboard through a setting on the CMOS Setup screen. Consult your PC's instruction manual or the manufacturer for details.

The following instructions apply to parallel ports on an add-in card plugged into the bus:

1. Before you remove a parallel port, turn off the computer and unplug it from the wall. Remove the cables and computer cover. Disconnect the printer cable (the cable from computer to printer) at the parallel port end. The cable may have two long, threaded knobs on the card end or a pair of narrow, thin screws to hold the cable connector tight to the card. Unscrew the knobs or screws by turning them counterclockwise. If the parallel port is part of the video card (a dinosaur-era design), remove the video cable, too. After you disconnect the cables, remove the system cover.

2. Remove the old card. The card is secured to the back wall of the system unit chassis with a single screw. Remove this screw and save it. Lift the card straight up; it shouldn't require too much force.

3. Install the new card. Installation is the reverse of removal. Old-style parallel, video-with-parallel, and multifunction cards are 8-bit cards that used the ISA bus. Modern add-in cards use PCI slots. Carefully line up the edge connector on the card with the slot on the motherboard and press down firmly. When the card is in place, the screw hole on the card lines up with the screw hole in the back of the chassis. Re-install the screw and test the machine.

Adding a New Parallel Port

You can upgrade your modern machine with a new ECC/EPP parallel port or add a second port to a PC with add-on cards, such as the CyberParallel PCI card from SIIG. This Plug-and-Play PCI card gives you an IEEE 1284-1994 parallel port that supports all current types of devices, including printers, removable cartridge drives, CD-ROM drives, scanners, and more. The board includes an intelligent IRQ-sharing feature to eliminate conflicts, and it works with Windows 95/98 and later to automatically assign the next available I/O port address.

Ch 17

Another unusual route to adding a parallel port to a modern machine is to use a USB-to-parallel conversion cable. The special electronics in the cable store up the incoming serial data from the computer and put them out the other end through a parallel plug. One example of this sort of converter is shown in Figure 17-3.

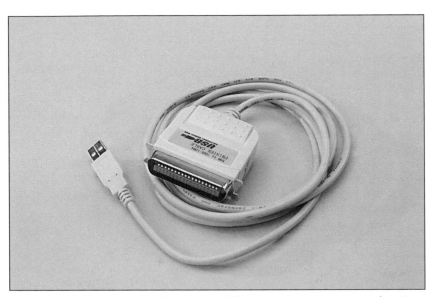

FIGURE 17-3: *This specialized printer cable connects to a computer's USB port and converts serial data to output through a standard Centronics connector.*

You can also purchase a converter that changes the output of a bidirectional parallel port to work with a SCSI chain. Note, however, that the result is a SCSI subsystem that will operate at the significantly slower speed of the parallel port, about 2 MB per second.

SUMMARY

In this chapter, I completed the exploration of the parallel port. In the next chapter, I move on to the process of using a printer to produce hard-copy printouts.

Notes

Chapter 18

Hard Copy

In the early days of computers, printers were expensive, large, slow, and loud mechanical devices, falling somewhere between a lawnmower and a Smith Corona typewriter. The most common design used a mechanism with a spinning "daisywheel" that had typewriter-like molds for each character. (IBM's hugely successful variant was the Selectric ball.) A hammer struck the character through a ribbon and onto the paper. These devices were called *character* printers.

Computer mainframes used huge printers that had a set of wheels or a metal band a full page in width, allowing them to print a line at a time. These devices were called *line printers*, and that name lives on in the official name for the parallel port on personal computers, LPT 1.

All of these devices were *character-oriented*. The computer sent a signal that told the printer to hit the letter *J* mold against the ribbon. If you wanted to type an italic J, you had to change the type wheel or ball to one that had an italic J.

Both line printers and character printers also carry another designation: impact printers. The reason for this moniker should be obvious: A mechanical mechanism causes whatever device that holds the characters to move quickly against a ribbon and strike the paper, causing ink in the shape of the selected character or characters to be deposited on the paper.

Soon after personal computers arrived on the scene, printer manufacturers introduced a whole new type of design. These devices are called *dot-matrix* printers. Nearly every printer now sold for use with PCs uses this technology, which is cheaper, smaller, faster, and quieter than character printers. Not all of these dot-matrix printers are impact printers, however, which I discuss later in this chapter. Newer technology laser and ink jet printers also are dot-matrix printers because the characters are formed by a series of dots; they certainly do not use impact technology to form the characters.

Early dot-matrix printers used the impact of tiny pins or wires inside a movable print head. Instead of slamming fully formed characters against a ribbon and then into the paper, dot-matrix printers created each character by forming a character from a set of dots. As technology improved, the grid of dots was made denser and the quality of character output and simple graphics improved.

This chapter examines all the major technologies for printers and offers advice on tracking down the source of problems with hard-copy output devices.

Types of Printers

Modern machines use three major types of printers: impact, ink jet, and laser. All three are dot-matrix printers.

Keep in mind that the recipient of a letter you send, a report you prepare, or a graphic that you produce knows little about all that went into its preparation; they do, however, make a judgment about the quality of your work based on the quality of the page in front of them.

As with every other component of a personal computer, printer prices have fallen as quality, speed, and capability have increased. At the time of this writing, you can purchase a capable inkjet printer for $75, a color photo printer for $150, a personal laser printer for as little as $179, and a high-end office laser for about $700. If those prices don't impress you, perhaps you would be interested in buying one of half a dozen old machines in my closet, each of which cost more than $1,000 when new.

The principal difference between machines at the high and low end of the price spectrum today is speed and what manufacturers call a *duty cycle*. An inexpensive machine is generally not intended to be in constant, heavy use; parts may wear down, and the cost of consumables — ink, toner, ribbons, or drums — may be unacceptable.

For most modern users, the machines of choice are laser printers and their cousins, LED and inkjet printers. I discuss all of these in this chapter.

Inkjet printers

Inkjet printers squirt tiny droplets of ink in programmable patterns. They are similar in concept to dot-matrix impact printers, except that they replace hammers and pins with ink nozzles. Characters, however, are still made up of dots.

Current models can work with a wide range of types of paper, including ordinary office copy paper, and have dropped in price to a few hundred dollars for good quality printers with a number of options, to less than $100 for the most basic designs.

Inkjet printers are every bit as impressive as a low-end laser printer — with the same 600-dot-per-inch resolution — at least when you first take them out of the box. Quality can fall off slightly if you don't keep the nozzles clean, if you use poor quality paper, or if you operate the printer in extremely humid conditions.

As with conventional impact dot-matrix printers, most common machines today emulate a few common designs. Look for Hewlett-Packard Ink Jet or Canon emulation to be sure of compatibility with a wide range of software packages.

Before you buy an inkjet printer, check the price and availability of ink cartridges for the printer. You should also compare the per-page cost for inkjet devices. The printers' specifications should give you the information that you need. In other words, some printer manufacturers have embraced an old theory of American marketing: Give away the razor to sell the blades. Some low-cost printers require expensive cartridges or other supplies, making their total cost of operation comparable to printers that may have a higher initial price tag.

Color inkjet printers use three or four reservoirs of ink, creating pictures by overlaying color in an additive process. Simple color inkjets for business presentations will work with most smooth papers; sophisticated devices intended to print out photo-quality images usually require specialized expensive coated paper.

Color printers have one additional cost issue: the sometimes-inefficient use of ink reservoirs. The worst design, from the standpoint of economics, is an all-in-one cartridge that includes black and several color inks. If you use up one color, you have to replace the entire cartridge. A better design uses separate ink cartridges for each color. A good compromise is a design that uses a separate black cartridge and a multicolor cartridge.

Laser and LED printers

Laser printers have become as commonplace in the office as copy machines. The differences between the two are not as great as you may think. You can think of a laser printer as a computerized copy machine, requiring the same kind of care.

The creation of this class of printers begins with a dot matrix of characters or graphics in a bank of memory. When the full page is ready to be printed, electronics in the device control the output of a tiny laser beam that pulses out flashes of light. In most such devices, the laser beam is moved around on a metallic drum by a system of tiny moving mirrors and lenses.

A light-sensitive drum within the laser printer is given a positive electrical charge by a *corona wire* or *corona roller*. As the drum rolls, the tiny focused dot of light from the laser beam strikes it at certain points; each place touched by the light loses its positive electrical charge. The result is an electrostatic image of the entire page to be printed.

Next, the drum is coated with positively charged toner. If you can remember back to high school physics, you will recall that opposite charges attract each other while same charges repel each other. The toner sticks only in the places where the laser has created a negative charge.

The drum then meets up with a sheet of paper that is moved into position by the printer mechanism. The paper is given a stronger negative charge than the drum, which forces the toner to move across to it.

Finally, the paper is passed through a set of heated rollers, called a *fuser,* which melts the toner. Meanwhile, the drum is exposed to a bright discharge lamp that erases the electrostatic image and readies it for another use.

An LED printer uses the same drum and toner concept, but uses a light emitting diode printhead as a light source within the imaging device. The printhead is solid-state and has no moving parts; it pulse-flashes across the entire page width and creates the image on the print drum as it moves down. As far as the user is concerned, the operation is identical to that of a laser printer. In general, LED printers are a bit slower but less expensive than an equivalent laser device. Some manufacturers claim that they have a longer service life because they have fewer moving parts.

The important specifications for a printer are resolution (with 600 dots per inch the current minimum, and 1,200 dpi increasingly common), pages per minute (based on the output of simple text pages, and usually starting at about 4 or 6 ppm), and printer memory (1MB is a minimum, but 8 to 12MB is more realistic if you are going to print graphics of any complexity). You will also find differences related to the particular page description language in use: For example, PostScript generally requires more memory to construct a page than does PCL.

 NOTE

Bear in mind that the page-per-minute rating is based on plain text pages. It can take quite a while — sometimes several minutes — for the computer to compose a complex bitmap and send it to your printer for output. In such a case, a 4 ppm printer is just as fast as a 20 ppm device — they both put out only a single page at a time. Also, some printer manufacturers quote page-per-minute rates based on printing the same page over and over again. Copier manufacturers use this same scheme. It takes longer to send a succession of different pages to the printer because the printer electronics have to accept and digest the new data before putting it onto paper. Assume page-per-minute specifications are the maximum that your printer can do. Actual throughput will fall off under a variety of conditions.

Insufficient memory can slow down printing, or cause the device to refuse to work at all with complex pages that contain graphics or multiple fonts. Some printers accept standard memory in SIMM format, making it easy and inexpensive to upgrade the device; other printers demand proprietary memory modules, raising the cost for consumers. You should check the memory design and default memory size before making a purchase.

Another critical difference between laser printers involves the quality of construction and the cost of consumables. You can often gauge the quality of construction by looking at the length of warranty offered by the manufacturer and checking the reviews in computer magazines.

Many laser printer makers put many of the mechanical elements, including the light-sensitive drum, in a removable cartridge that also contains a supply of toner; typical prices for one of these all-inclusive cartridges is about $100. You replace the cartridge after printing a certain number of pages. Another design uses inexpensive toner cartridges and more expensive separate drum packages; you replace an image drum after every dozen or so toner cartridges. Both schemes work, and in many cases work out to about the same cost per page.

One note about toner: You can save some money by purchasing refilled cartridges from companies other than the original manufacturer. Exercise caution when doing so, however, for the following reasons:

- The cartridges for many printers include the image drum and other moving parts, and you have no idea of the condition of those parts in a used package.
- The replacement toner is usually a generic formula that may not be a perfect match for the material sold by the original equipment manufacturer.

For these reasons, I stay away from "garage" refillers, but I have had success with refills from national brand name office supply houses. If you want to experiment here, buy one replacement cartridge and test it in your machine before filling your supply closet with third-party units.

Page description languages

Laser, LED, and most inkjet printers are *page printers* that assemble a full page in memory — either within the printer or in the computer — before producing an image on paper. Early printers used a scheme called *escape codes* to communicate commands; these specialized characters instruct the printer to produce a limited set of features.

The two most prevalent modern page description languages are PCL, developed by Hewlett-Packard, and PostScript from Adobe. For most users, all that matters is that your printer comes with a driver that interprets commands from your application — a word processor, a spreadsheet, an Internet browser, and the like — and applies a proper set of instructions for your printer.

At one time, PostScript was the leading printer language for high-quality desktop publishing and graphics. PostScript is an *object-oriented language*, meaning that pages are created using the assembly of geometric shapes rather than as bitmaps or individual characters. Fonts are described as an outline, and the printer generates images based on this mathematical description. As such, fonts are scalable in size and alterable to versions such as italic and bold forms. Because the printer is generating the shapes, quality of output is dependent on the resolution of the printer; for example, a 600 dpi laser printer will be a noticeable improvement over a 300 dpi model, while a 2,400 dpi device used in a print shop will be good enough for publication. PostScript exists in several versions; at the time of this writing, the current version is PostScript 3.

Adobe has licensed PostScript to many printer manufacturers. You will also find several "PostScript emulators" offered with hardware; in general, this sort of clone software will work well with most applications, but if you are preparing work to be sent to a service bureau for professional purposes, I suggest you stay with Adobe's brand.

Hewlett-Packard's Printer Control Language (PCL) was developed for use with the company's well-respected DeskJet, LaserJet, and other printers; a number of other makers have since licensed the code for their own drivers. Current versions of PCL deliver most of the functionality of PostScript, even surpassing it in some ways. Be sure to keep your printer drivers up to date under Windows. For more information, consult www.hp.com.

Senior-citizen technology: Dot-matrix printers

Dot-matrix printers draw characters by making tiny dots that are close enough to seem to merge into a continuous line. The same principle is used to draw an image on a television screen or monitor and to produce a printed photograph in a book or newspaper. A dot-matrix printer can create a character of any design, limited only by the fineness of the dots and the number of dots that can fit in a particular area. The dots can also make pictures and other graphics. The first dot-matrix printers used small hammers that tapped on inked ribbons to construct letters and images.

Dot-matrix impact printers today are relatively rare — not because they don't still work, but they do suffer severely in comparison to inkjet printers. Impact dot-matrix printers are noisy and the quality of their output is, by comparison, crude. However, nothing else can print multicopy carbon and carbonless forms. You still see workhorse impact dot-matrix printers at airports, insurance companies, and other places where multipart hard copy forms are produced.

The major distinction among impact dot-matrix printers is the number of pins that are used to draw the dots for each letter. A 24-pin printer is capable of drawing much finer characters and graphics than a 9-pin device.

The other distinction involves which printer specification the printer most closely emulates. The most common printer designs are Epson devices and IBM Proprinter machines. Very few dot-matrix printers are offered that are not capable of acting like one or the other of these devices. Stay away from an oddball printer unless its manufacturer can convince you of a good reason to use it and provides drivers to work with the software that you use.

Dinosaur technology: Daisywheel printers

This book no longer provides detailed troubleshooting for daisywheel printers. They are generally not worth repairing if they break down. If you do have a problem with a daisywheel, spend a few minutes to check the following: Is the printer plugged into a powered outlet? Has the printer blown a fuse on its back panel? Is the printer properly connected to the computer with a data cable? (Try substituting a cable that you know to be good.) And do your applications and programs have a proper printer driver or description to work with the daisywheel device? One quick way to test a daisywheel is to go to the DOS prompt. (In Windows, click Start ➪ Run, type **command**, and press Enter.) Type the command **DIR** and press Enter to ask for the display of a directory of the current disk, and then press the Print Screen key (or Shift + Print Screen) on your keyboard. If the printer is functioning and properly cabled to the computer, it should print a copy of the directory.

Sharing printers on a single parallel port

Many home and office users need more than one printer — you may need a laser printer for office correspondence and a color inkjet printer for presentations and artwork, for example. The problem is that nearly all PCs have only one parallel port.

Two solutions can work here. One solution is to install a second parallel port, as described in Chapter 17. In some cases, though, you may run into problems with redirecting the output of specialized printer drivers to a secondary port.

Another solution is to use a data switch that enables the output of a single parallel port to be directed to one of two (or more) parallel devices. Once again, there may be a small gotcha here: Many data switches don't work with bidirectional signals. You can send data to a printer, but you may not be able to receive messages back from the device. It is also a good idea to turn off the power to your printer before making the switch to avoid the slight possibility of sending an electrical spike that could damage the unit. Figure 18-1 shows an example of a data switch.

FIGURE 18-1: *Data switches, such as this A/B device from Dalco Electronics, enable one computer to work with several devices vying for the attention of a single serial or parallel port, or enable several computers to share a single device.*

Networked printers

If you use printers in a business setting — or if you have two or more computers networked at home — then you are a candidate for a networked printer. Attaching a printer to a network connection instead of directly to a PC gives you the following advantages:

- You free up the parallel port on your PC for something else.
- Physical placement can be much more flexible because you can run network cable virtually anywhere without the length limitations of a parallel cable.
- A PC isn't used as a printer server, which requires memory and CPU resources.

The simplest arrangement, then, is to attach a printer to one of the computers on your network, and set up that printer under Windows to be shared by other devices. The major downside here is that both the sending and receiving computers must be turned on and functioning as part of the network to permit printing.

You can purchase printers with built-in network interfaces, or you can buy separate network boxes that include a network port and one or more parallel printer ports. You can also purchase a network box that supports one or more parallel printers. The cost is about $100 to $250 in early 2002. The main difference in price is the speed of the network. Low cost network printer interfaces are generally designed for 10 Mbps networks, while devices at the high end of the price scale can work on 100 Mbps networks. At the time of this writing, you can even purchase a Bluetooth printer interface for around $140. Bluetooth is the relatively new, low-power RF networking scheme designed to provide flexible connectivity to a wide range of electronic devices, including personal digital assistants (PDAs), mobile phones, and even household and business appliances, such as refrigerators, television sets, and soft drink machines.

If you are already working with networked computers, then attaching a networked printer is an easy task. The printer simply becomes one more device on your network, like another computer. Software spoofs applications into believing that they are printing to a local printer attached to LPT 1 when, in fact, they print to this remote device. It works the same as printing to a printer connected directly to another PC on your network.

Determining the Source of a Printer Problem

A parallel or serial printer port rarely breaks. The most common sources of problems for hard-copy output are cables, switches, and the printers themselves; a functioning parallel or serial port can be knocked out of commission by resource conflicts.

To identify the source of a problem, first run the printer's self-test. Consult your instruction manual or call the manufacturer to learn how to test the machine. If the self-test fails, your printer needs servicing. If the self-test works, move on to test your printer interface and cable.

To send a test page to the printer from within Windows, start by turning on the printer and continue by following these steps:

1. Click Start ⇨ Settings ⇨ Printers. (Under Windows XP, click Start ⇨ Printers and Faxes.)
2. Highlight the printer that you want to test, and then right-click it.
3. Choose Properties.
4. Select the General tab, and then click Print Test Page.

If the printer delivers the test page, your problem is most likely a setting within an application, such as your word processor or office suite. Try resetting printer options from within that application.

If the printer does not work, test to see whether the problem may lie in the Windows operating system. Go to DOS. One way to do this is to choose Start ⇨ Programs, and then click the MS-DOS prompt. Another route to the DOS prompt is to restart the system; click Start ⇨ Shutdown and then select Restart in MS-DOS mode.

Under Windows XP, you can reach a version of the operating system prompt by clicking Start ⇨ All Programs ⇨ Accessories ⇨ Command Prompt.

Turn on the printer. From the prompt, type **DIR > LPT1** to send a copy of the folder directory to be printed. The printer should produce the directory. Some devices may require you to turn the printer from On Line to Off Line and then press Form Feed to manually eject a page from the printer. If the printer works in this test, your problem is probably related to a setting in your operating system or in the printer driver.

If the printer fails both tests, try substituting a data cable that you know to be good and running the same test. If the printer now works, the original cable has failed and should be replaced.

If the cable is not the problem, try hooking up the printer to another computer. Try the printer from an application and from DOS, as described previously. If the printer doesn't work, take it in for service. If it works properly, your problem lies with the original computer.

Test the serial or parallel port of your computer as appropriate, using a diagnostic software program.

If you have a very old printer, you may have a nonstandard serial cable. Consult the instruction manual for details. Chapter 15 discusses one almost-foolproof solution to serial cable problems — a magical device called the Smart Cable. The Smart Cable can adjust to match the needs of either end of the connection.

 CROSS-REFERENCE

See Chapter 15 for more serial connection troubleshooting tips.

Hardware checks for parallel port printers

The first hardware question you should ask yourself: "Is the printer turned on and connected by cable to the parallel port of my PC?"

If the answer to that question is "Yes," then start by making sure that the printer itself is functioning by performing a self-test. Each printer has its own way to produce a test page; consult your instruction manual for details.

Next, check the connection from your PC to the printer by sending a simple file from DOS. You can open a prompt window — choose Start ⇨ Programs ⇨ MS-DOS Prompt from within Windows 95/98, or exit Windows to the DOS prompt. From Windows XP, choose Start ⇨ All Programs ⇨ Accessories ⇨ Command Prompt.

Type the following two commands and then press Enter. The first creates a small file consisting of a copy of the directory of the subfolder; the second sends a copy to the printer.

```
Dir > dir
COPY C:\dir LPT1
```

If C: is not your boot drive, or if your printer is not connected to LPT 1 — the standard parallel port designation — then make the appropriate changes to the command. You can send any file to the printer.

You may need to manually eject a page from your printer to see the results. On most devices, press the On Line button (to set the printer offline) and then the Form Feed button. If the printer produces a copy of your file, you have established that the printer, its cable, and the PC's parallel port are all functioning properly.

NOTE

If you have more than one printer and therefore more than one logical printer port configured under Windows, this test may not work because DOS may not be able to identify your printer hardware correctly. If you suspect a problem with your computer hardware, use the Printers utility in the Control Panel to remove all printers except the one you are testing. Reboot your computer and try this DOS-level test again.

Next, eliminate problems with any advanced text-processing application. If you are running Windows 95/98 or XP, click Start ➪ Programs ➪ Accessories ➪ Notepad (or WordPad). Type some text on the screen, and then attempt to print.

If you can't print from either of the accessories, check the settings for the printer port by using Device Manager. (Choose Start ➪ Settings ➪ Control Panel ➪ System.) Scroll down to Ports (COM & LPT), click its plus sign, and then double-click the port for your printer — usually Printer Port (LPT 1).

Click the Resources tab and check that the conflicting devices list does not indicate a conflict. Examine the settings for the port.

The usual input/output range for a standard LPT 1 port is 0378-037A. If a second parallel port is installed, LPT 2 is ordinarily assigned to 0278.

If there appears to be a conflict or if the port settings are incorrect, use the Device Manager program to remove the printer port from the system and then restart the computer. When Windows is running again, click Start ➪ Settings ➪ Control Panel. Then double-click Add New Hardware to enable Windows to detect the hardware again.

Windows also includes a printer test facility that you can access from the Properties dialog box of most printers. Click Start ➪ Settings ➪ Printers to display the Printers dialog box. Right-click the printer that you're having problems with and choose Properties. At the bottom of the General tab, you should see a button labeled Send Test Page to Printer. Click this button. Windows then asks if everything printed normally. If it did not print normally, choose "No," and then follow the onscreen instructions for testing your printer.

Printer software issues

If you can print from a DOS command prompt but not from within Windows-based programs, and you have already examined port settings, you may have a problem with spool settings or bidirectional communication. A print spool holds information prepared by the PC for printing. Copying information to the spooler enables the computer to get back to other tasks and leave output as a background function.

Experiment to see if the problem lies in the spool settings. Click Start ➪ Settings ➪ Printers; then point to the printer that you're attempting to use and right-click it to bring up a submenu. Click Properties, and then click Details and the Spool Settings button. Finally, click the Print Directly to the Printer option button to turn off spooling.

If the Details tab indicates that the printer is set up to support bidirectional communication, try turning off that advanced facility. Click the Disable Bidirectional Support for this Printer button. Click OK, and then try to print from Notepad or WordPad. If the printer now functions properly, experiment with other settings for the spooler in combination with the bidirectional printing option.

Bidirectional printing requires an improved parallel printer cable, one that conforms to the IEEE 1284 specification. You may need to replace your printer cable to use its facilities. Bidirectional printing may also fail if the cable is too long. And you may lose bidirectionality if the parallel cable goes through a switch box or line extender.

Printer drivers

Printers vary in the way they handle hard returns and line feeds and the way they interpret escape codes for fonts and print size. To accommodate these differences, you must install a software program called a *printer driver*.

The most common reason for printer problems is an incorrect printer driver installation. This doesn't mean that you've installed the printer incorrectly, but that you've installed the wrong printer driver while setting up the software. The result can be some truly odd characters that appear when you print bold or underlined words. When you first use the software, you must select the correct printer driver to copy into the program. If you don't see the exact model number and guess wrong, or if you inadvertently type the wrong choice, you will install the wrong printer driver.

Application settings

Too many applications exist and too many combinations of problems are possible to address here. However, you can explore a few basic questions before you call the software maker.

First, determine the nature of the printing problem. Are you able to produce text, but not graphics? Will text print, but not in proper fonts? Does the problem only occur in one document?

NOTE

One interesting test is to attempt to print a blank page to the printer. If the empty page goes through the printer, this may indicate a problem with memory or fonts.

You may need to reinstall the applications, or you may have a problem with the System Registry (used for 32-bit applications) or an .INI file (an initialization file used for a 16-bit program).

If you're trying to use an application written for an older operating system, consult the maker to see whether any updates or patches are available.

Finally, you may have a problem with the printer driver for your hardware. Windows supports more than a thousand printers directly. When you install Windows on a system with a connected printer, Windows will use the printer driver it has for that printer. Contact the maker of the printer to see whether an updated driver is available.

Printer speed

Printers, like hard disk drives and CPUs, sometimes exist in an Alice-in-Wonderland world when it comes to measures of speed. A dot-matrix printer may, in fact, be capable of zipping along at 192 characters per second (cps) on a small-sized font, but may slow to 160 cps on a larger font. And dot-matrix printers usually make a distinction between draft and letter-quality printing. The difference in characters per second can be significant; the same printer in the preceding example may be able to produce its best type at a relatively slow 45 cps. A truer measure is the number of hammer strikes per second, but by itself this won't tell you how long your resumé will take to exit from the printer. And neither specification will easily inform you how long it will take to print out a graphic.

Here's a real-world appraisal: A typical single-spaced page of manuscript for this book contains 381 words or 1,762 characters. (In the English language, the average word length is about 5 characters.) At 192 cps, a dot-matrix printer would require about 9.2 seconds to spit out a draft-quality copy of the page. At the (near) letter-quality speed of 45 cps, the page would require a fairly slow 39 seconds.

Similarly, a laser printer may be advertised as an 8 ppm device. However, laser printers are page printers in that they form the entire page in their internal memory (or in some designs, in the memory of the PC) and then produce the page in a single pass. The 8 ppm specification refers to the speed of continuous pieces of paper through the printer after the pages have been formed in memory. Each page requires 7.5 seconds, which works out to something like 235 cps. However, creating the first page of a text document typically requires 20 to 30 seconds. A more reasonable ppm rating for an eight-page document is about 6.6. Remember, though, that a laser printer is *always* producing letter-quality pages.

TIP

Modern laser printers may have settings that let you adjust the dpi settings and darkness levels of printed pages. These settings work similar to the way the draft and letter-quality settings on older impact printers work, except that for text output on a laser printer, you can rarely see the difference. By choosing an economy or draft setting in your printer's control panel, you may improve throughput and almost certainly will save toner, allowing you to get more pages out of a single toner cartridge. Save the high-quality output for graphics or photographs.

Creating a complex graphic image can slow a laser printer to a crawl, sometimes requiring a minute or more to create the page. After that page is completed, it will be spit out at the ppm rate — 7.5 seconds in the supposed 8 ppm example.

What can you do to improve printer speed? A laser printer will benefit from the addition of RAM. The memory will either speed the creation of the page being printed or enable creation of the next page in the background as the current one is being produced.

One device that improves your computing environment is a hardware printer cache or a software printer buffer. Either one will enable you to move on to new tasks while pages are created and stored in the background. Neither solution speeds up the production of the pages themselves, but they do improve your personal productivity.

Printing speed in Windows

In some cases, you can improve the performance of your printers under Windows 95/98 and later editions by adjusting the spool file setting. When you print a document from an application, Windows creates a temporary spool file on your hard disk and copies the document to that file using a special format. After the spool file has been created, Windows returns control to your application and then manages the printing of the document in the background.

You can use one of several routes to the Printers folder, where you can make changes to the settings for the spool file. Here's the most direct:

1. Click Start ⇨ Settings ⇨ Printers.
2. Right-click the icon for the active printer, and click Properties.
3. On the Details tab, click the Spool Settings button to display the Spool Settings dialog box. An example is shown in Figure 18-2. By default, the settings are intended to allow you to get back to work as quickly as possible.

The first option — Spool Print Jobs so Program Finishes Printing Faster — turns on spooling, returning control to your application while printing goes on in the background.

The next two options present an either/or choice. The default choice is Start printing after first page is spooled, which gets the printer to work as soon as the first page has been copied to the spool; additional pages are put in the temporary storage while printing continues. The other option makes the printer wait until the last page has been spooled. This speeds up the spooling process but slows down the return of control to Windows; it also requires more hard disk space for the spooled pages.

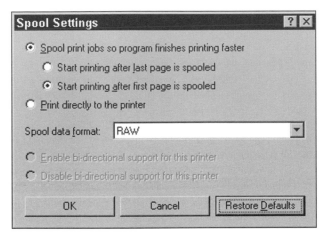

FIGURE 18-2: *The Spool Settings screen of Windows*

Depending on the model of printer you have installed, you may also be able to select Print Directly to the Printer. With this option, Windows devotes all of its attention to sending pages to the printer; the printer responds as fast as it is able to do so, but you won't be able to perform other tasks until the last page has been sent.

Another option available only with certain printers is a choice of Spool Data Format. If available on the printer, Windows will try to work with a file format called *enhanced metafile format* (EMF), which is smaller than a RAW format, which takes a bit longer to load but is customized for each printer.

Windows 2000 and XP work in a similar fashion:

1. Choose Start ⇨ Printers and Faxes, and then right-click the printer you want to adjust.
2. On the Advanced tab, make changes to the spool settings. Note that the screen you see is specific to the type of printer you have installed on your system. And if you are working with a machine located on a network, the network administrator may have disabled some options or preselected settings.

Troubleshooting a troubled printer

Ask yourself the following questions when troubleshooting your printer:

Are you using an appropriate printer driver? A printer can freeze, or produce garbled output, if you use an incorrect, outdated, or corrupted printer driver.

To check printer properties: Click Start ⇨ Settings ⇨ Printers. Right-click the icon that represents the printer that you want to use, click Properties, and then click the Details tab. Check that the driver settings are correct and that an appropriate driver is being used. Under Windows 98, the Driver tab offers the option to check the Windows Update Web site for an updated driver. Under Windows 2000 and XP, the driver update is accomplished through the Advanced tab.

Are your printer driver graphics settings correct? Consult your printer documentation to determine the correct settings for your printer. Click Start ⇨ Settings ⇨ Printers. Right-click your printer icon, and then click Properties.

Depending on the particular driver for your printer, you may see a Graphics tab, a Device Options tab, or an Advanced button. Start by changing any settings back to the recommended defaults for your printer; consult the device's instruction manual for suggestions on changes.

Do you have enough paper, toner, or ink? Some printers are smart enough to stop the job when you run out of supplies, but may not be communicative enough to tell you why. Study the printer's instruction manual to learn the meaning of error codes on the printer or messages that may be displayed on your PC.

Has the quality of output degraded? Uneven darkness across a page is often an indication of low toner on a laser printer. You can usually eke out a few dozen more pages from a cartridge by removing it and gently shaking it from side to side and back and forth to redistribute the toner. Another possible cause for uneven printing is damage to the photoreceptor, or a light leak into the receptor from a nearby lamp or window.

Dark lines down the length of a laser-printed page may be caused by a scratch or other damage on the drum; the drum is usually part of the laser cartridge that is replaced when toner is depleted. White gaps or lines down the length of the page may be caused by damage to the toner cartridge or debris in the path between the cartridge and the drum. It may be possible to remove obstacles; otherwise, the cartridge will need to be replaced.

Blotches of black or white on the paper may indicate contamination of the drum or the fusing roller. The drum is not easily cleaned; if your cartridge includes a drum, the problem will be fixed when you replace it. Most printers include a small brush and sometimes a cleaning solution for the fusing roller. Consult the printer's instruction manual for advice.

An inkjet printer is prone to clogs in the print head that can result in loss of resolution, or dropouts in text or graphics. Many modern printers include a utility to clean the inkjet head; consult the instruction manual for details. On most machines, the manufacturer recommends removal of the ink cartridge if a printer is left unused for a lengthy period of time.

Are you using an inappropriate grade of paper? Different printing technologies and resolutions require various paper qualities. To get the most out of a laser printer, you want to use a good quality copy paper certified for a laser printer or copying machine.

Inkjet printers generally require an even smoother paper surface because the ink is applied wet and the text or image can become fuzzy if the ink is absorbed into the paper; photorealistic inkjet printers work best with glossy or coated stock.

Does paper jam in the printer regularly? Paper jams are usually caused by one of three conditions: debris (including pieces of paper) stuck in the paper path; high humidity causing paper to stick together or to rollers; or inappropriate paper. Consult the instruction manual for advice on cleaning the paper path; use a vacuum with a soft brush to remove debris. One way to deal with high humidity is to store your paper in a sealed box, installing only as much as you need to print a job. Finally, check the specifications for your printer for acceptable weights and grades of paper; stock that is too thin, too thick, or too glossy can jam a printer.

Does your printer have enough memory? Try printing a small, simple document from the same program. If it works properly, the problem may lie in the printer's memory. You can also run any self-test routine that is part of the printer to check for error messages.

You can adjust printer settings to minimize the amount of memory that the document requires. If that doesn't work, or results in unacceptable print quality, your choice may come down to reducing the complexity of the document or adding more memory to your printer. Consult the instruction manual for your printer for specifics on how to adjust settings.

Are your printer time-out settings long enough? A very complex printing job — or a slow printer — may take longer to be ready to print than the time allotted under Windows.

To lengthen the time-out settings for the printer, click Start ➪ Settings ➪ Printers. Right-click your printer icon, click Properties, and then click the Details tab. Increase all of the values under Timeout settings. Under Windows XP, go to Start ➪ Printers and Faxes ➪ Device Settings.

NOTE

You can adjust time-out settings only for printers that are local to your PC; devices on a network are under the control of network settings.

Do you have enough free space on your hard disk? If you have enabled a printer spooler under Windows, the operating system will need space to prepare pages for printing; your system will likely grind to a halt if you have less than 10MB of available space.

You may be able to free up some space by emptying the Recycle Bin, deleting unneeded temporary files, removing programs that are not needed, and defragmenting the drive. And, of course, you can install an additional hard drive or upgrade to a new larger storage device.

SUMMARY

Now you've completed the exploration of hard-copy output devices — better known as printers. In the next chapter, you explore how mice and scanners bring hands and eyes to your PC.

Ch 18

Chapter 19

Tools Needed:
- Phillips or flat-blade screwdriver

Your Computer's Hands, Eyes, and Ears

Your fabulously capable, high-speed personal computer would be no better than a high-tech boat anchor if not for its capability to communicate with the outside world. We use PCs by printing out their products, by sending data over a telephone wire, or by using a network connection.

Additionally, your PC would not be all that impressive if it couldn't respond to input that it receives from the outside world through devices such as keyboards, mice, scanners, laboratory control devices, and more.

For the first decade of the history of the PC, input devices generally connected to the computer through the serial port. Then came devices that spoke with the computer through a specialized SCSI adapter. In recent years, a new class of scanners and other devices began to connect to the PC through the parallel port. Most modern machines and current operating systems support the USB standard, allowing easy connection of a wide range of devices to that port system.

In this chapter, I discuss important input and output devices — a hand, an eye, and a set of ears for the computer. I explore various species of keyboards — the computer mouse, game controllers, scanners, digital and PC cameras, and sound cards.

The Keyboard

It's easy to overlook the keyboard, but don't do that. The device that sits beneath your fingers is critical to the operation of your computer, and it's also essential that it fit your style of work like a glove.

Keyboards have two basic types of feel — soft and click. The original IBM PC came with Big Blue's computer equivalent of its famed Selectric typewriter keyboard; each press of the keys was a smooth passage to a firm bottom, accompanied by a solid click. Soon thereafter, though, many PC clone makers began adopting a soft-touch keyboard, on which the key presses did not reach a bottom and the click was gone. Both types of keyboards work, and some users barely notice the difference between the two types of feel. Some people are strong partisans of one style or another.

Two commonly used keyboard connectors are an older-style large DIN plug and a smaller PS/2-style connector, shown in Figure 19-1. Adapters are available to convert cables to the proper connector.

On some modern machines, keyboards attach to the USB port; some include built-in hubs or connectors for mice and other desktop devices, a nicety that reduces the number of cables snaking across or under your desk.

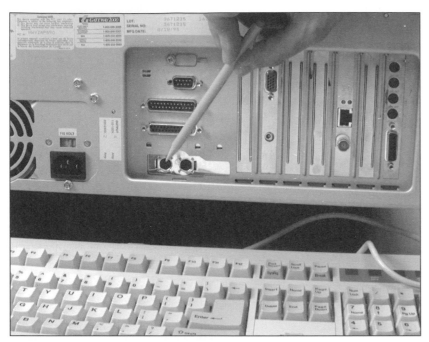

FIGURE 19-1: *A small PS/2-style keyboard connector on the back panel of a PC. Older machines use a larger AT-style connector. Adapter plugs convert cables to work with either type of connector.*

NOTE

Some systems may not recognize the presence of a new USB peripheral until Windows has loaded the associated drivers for the bus. If this is the case, a USB keyboard or mouse may not be active during bootup, which may prevent access to the CMOS Setup and could also block keystrokes for the Windows logon. You may need to keep a standard keyboard or mouse, or both, attached during the first bootup. After Windows has loaded, its Plug-and-Play facilities should locate the new USB device.

You'll also find some wireless keyboards that use a small infrared or radio transmitter to communicate with a receiver mounted in a convenient location on your desktop or on the PC itself. These devices, along with wireless mice and trackballs, may be of value in classroom or boardroom settings, allowing a speaker to control the computer at a reasonable distance.

One example is the Intel Wireless Series, which uses a digital spread spectrum radio with frequency-hopping technology (similar to the system used by portable phones) to communicate at distances of as much as three meters (about ten feet). RF-based systems don't require a direct line of sight to the PC or the base station.

Infrared wireless keyboards use the same sort of technology employed by the remote controller for your television set, with a range of as much as 25 feet. These keyboards must have a clear line of sight between the transmitter and receiver, or have the lucky coincidence of walls or ceilings that bounce the signal in the right direction.

After you have decided the keyboard feel you want and the type of connection you want to use, you need to choose a keyboard maker. Dozens of keyboard makers — most of them in Asia — proliferate the market. Two schools of thought exist on buying strategies. One is to search high and low for the highest quality keyboard you can find. The other idea is to go for low price and consider the keyboard an expendable part of the system — like tires on a car. I generally place myself in the latter group; I look for a comfortable, inexpensive keyboard and plan on replacing it once a year or so.

Some folks, however, prefer the solid, heavy-duty feel of the original IBM PC keyboard, a sturdy click-style device that was derived from the famed IBM Selectric keyboard. IBM moved on to light, mushier keyboards for most of its systems. The company spun off its keyboard and printer division to a separate company called Lexmark, and in 1996, that company sold off its technology to Unicomp. Today you can purchase several derivatives of the IBM/Lexmark click keyboards directly from Unicomp and through distributors.

In technical terms, the IBM click design is called "buckling spring key" technology. I worked with the EnduraPro, which is a power tool of a keyboard. The keyboard is shown in Figure 19-2. The 104-key device, which weighs in at nearly six pounds, includes an integrated pressure-sensitive pointing stick that can substitute for a mouse, as well as a port for an external PS/2 mouse on the board.

FIGURE 19-2: *The Unicomp EnduraPro keeps alive the heavy-duty design and click feel of the original IBM keyboard along with a versatile pointing stick that substitutes for a mouse.*

Table 19-1 contains a listing of major keyboard manufacturers. Several no-name makers in Asia will sell directly to computer makers and retailers.

TABLE 19-1: Major Replacement Keyboard Manufacturers		
Manufacturer	**How Sold**	**Web Site**
Cherry	Distributors	www.cherry corp.com
Chicony	Distributors	www.chicony.com
IBM	Distributors and direct	www.pc.ibm.com/ us/accessories/ access.html
Key Tronics	Distributors and direct	www.keytronic. com/home/ keyboards/ keyboards.html
SIIG	Distributors	www.siig.com
Unicomp	Direct	www.pckeyboard.com

NOTE

There is absolutely no reason why you can't select the keyboard of your choice to work with your old or new PC. With only a few exceptions, all keyboards are interchangeable. You may have to purchase conversion plugs to adapt a keyboard with one sort of connector to the appropriate port on your PC.

The next issue in choosing your keyboard involves the layout of the board. Some keyboards are available full-sized with 101 to 105 keys including numeric keypads, separate cursor-movement keys, and 12 function keys; others are 80- to 84-key small footprint models that give you just the basics. Again, they all work; I prefer full-size models, like the one shown in Figures 19-3 and 19-4, because I spend hours at the keyboard, but the choice is yours.

In addition to the basic keyboard, you may also see some variations that are aimed at making use a bit easier on human shoulders, wrists, and elbows.

Ch 19

FIGURE 19-3: *A modern replacement keyboard with a few special keys for Windows. This model is standard issue for current Dell computers; similar boards are available for other brands and generic PCs.*

FIGURE 19-4: *The extra keys on a Windows keyboard bring up the Start menu and can also be programmed to bring up a specific menu within an application. On this Dell keyboard, four extra buttons are recessed into the board: above F8, a button to open the default mail program; above F10, a button to summon the home page of the default Internet browser; above F12, a button to call for the default search engine for the browser, and above the backspace key, a button to put the PC into sleep mode.*

One design uses a tiny round button set into the middle of the keys that is used as the controller for the mouse cursor. Slight pressure on the button in any direction moves the cursor just as sliding a mouse on a desktop does. The built-in controller began as a space-saving solution for laptop computers, but is beginning to show up in some desktop models. It's an acquired taste, but for some users it is faster and less fatiguing than removing a hand to operate the mouse.

Ergonomic keyboards reject the rectangular, straight-line layout of the keyboard in favor of one that is said to be more like the shape of the human hands. One design, the Microsoft Natural Keyboard, splits the left and right sides of the keyboard along a curved shape and adds an extended wrist support in front, intended to help avoid strains in the hands.

In my experience, though, long-time users of traditional keyboards have a long and sometimes difficult adjustment period to ergonomic keyboards. In my case, I never became comfortable with the split design.

Finally, keyboards that offer Windows-specific keys include a button that summons a popup Start menu and another that duplicates the context-sensitive effect of pressing the right mouse button. The advantage of the Windows keyboard is that it allows users to keep their hands on the board in order to initiate many common commands.

Most such keyboards include two Windows logo keys, one to the left of the left Alt key and the other to the right of the right Alt key. A special Application key is located between the right Windows logo key and the right Ctrl key. Pressing the Application key generally brings up the same context-sensitive menu that you see by clicking the right mouse button within a program; press the Esc key to remove the menu. However, software programmers can assign special functions to that key; check instruction manuals for your applications.

Pressing and releasing either one of the Windows logo keys opens the Start menu. If you press the Windows key and hold it and then press additional keys, you can initiate operating systems commands, as shown in Table 19-2.

TABLE 19-2: Windows Keyboard Special Commands

Key or Combination	Function
Application key	Display context-sensitive menu
Windows key	Open Start menu
Windows key+F1	Display Help menu
Windows key+Tab	Activate next taskbar button
Windows key+D	Show Desktop, or Undo minimize all
Windows key+E	Explore My Computer
Windows key+F	Find files or folder
Windows key+Ctrl+F	Find computer
Windows key+L	Lock computer on network domain
Windows key+M	Minimize all
Windows key+Shift+M	Undo minimize all
Windows key+Pause/Break	Display System Properties
Windows key+R	Display Run dialog box
Windows key+U	Open Utility Manager (Windows XP)

How the keyboard works

A keyboard is essentially a box full of switches. When you press or release a keyboard key, the keyboard sends a signal to the computer over a cable (or through a wireless link in a few models) to a keyboard port on the motherboard. Various designs keep the two halves of the switch apart with springs, rubber domes, and spongy foam.

Beneath the keys on the keyboard is a grid of circuits. When you press a key, two wires on the grid are connected. These wires send a signal to the keyboard microprocessor, which converts the grid signals to standard scan codes (signals identifying which key you pressed or released). The scan codes are sent through the keyboard cable to the motherboard.

Inside dinosaur PCs, the ROM converts the keyboard scan code into an ASCII character code representing letters, numbers, and function keys. Modern machines have a dedicated keyboard controller on the motherboard to make this translation.

Because dinosaur XT and AT machines use the five pins of the keyboard cable for different signals, many keyboards are manufactured with an XT/AT switch on the back. A keyboard set to work with an XT and plugged into a modern machine sends only gibberish. If the monitor displays a keyboard error message on bootup, this XT/AT switch is the first place to check.

The original PC keyboard used a large round DIN 5-pin plug to connect to the keyboard port; modern models use a smaller Mini-DIN 6-pin plug or a USB connector. Over the years, a small number of keyboard makers have used some non-standard connectors, including telephone cable connectors and flat 6-pin SDL (Shielded Data Link) connectors. You must match the cable and port to your setup. Conversion devices are available that plug into the end of the keyboard cable to make it fit in an unfriendly port.

Ch 19

Preventive maintenance for keyboards

Every few months, run the keyboard test that is part of most diagnostic programs to test the electronic logic of the keyboard and the motherboard's keyboard controller. The test also forces you to run through all the keys on the board, including a few you may not ordinarily use.

NOTE

Keeping your keyboard clean and dry is essential to its health. You shouldn't have a cup of coffee, a can of soda, or anything else liquid or sticky anywhere near your keyboard — or your PC, for that matter. Although it may be possible to clean a keyboard that has been doused with a soda, this is a problem you don't need. If your keyboard is bound to be in a wet or sloppy environment — in a kitchen or a restaurant, for example — you should look into purchasing a keyboard skin that covers all the keys with an impervious plastic that you can peck through.

To clean a keyboard, turn off the power to the PC, unplug the keyboard, and turn it over to shake out dust and dirt. For an even better cleaning, use a can of compressed air to blow between individual keys or a vacuum to suck it clean.

You can use a cloth dampened with a weak plastic cleaner to polish the keys; the most fastidious among us may want to use a cotton-tipped stick to clean between them. If it is absolutely necessary, you can also remove individual keys using a special tool that is supplied with many keyboards. Do so very carefully to avoid breaking the plastic keycaps or the somewhat delicate switches beneath.

TIP

An excellent tool for cleaning the keyboard, the screen, and other parts of the computer is a soft, unused paintbrush. I keep a couple of different sizes on or near my desk at all times. The soft bristles won't scratch hardware or screen surfaces, and they can reach down between keys and into other cracks and crevices to remove dust and other undesirable debris.

In some keyboard designs, it is reasonable to remove all keys for extended cleaning except the spacebar. In newer keyboards, construction may be too delicate to permit the safe removal of key caps. Besides, for $10 to $20, you can just buy a new keyboard.

Finally, I recommend that you always have a replacement keyboard on hand. Like hard drives and other mechanical elements of the PC, keyboards are bound to fail sooner or later. A keyboard in the closet can save you time and aggravation.

To remove the keyboard, turn off the PC, and simply unplug it from the system unit. To install a keyboard, do this in reverse. Rotate the new keyboard's plug until the pins fit into the connector on the motherboard and then push it in firmly. USB keyboards can be unplugged or attached while the system is running. The flat USB connector has a top and bottom; be sure not to force the connector in place in the wrong orientation.

WARNING

It is not a good practice to attach or remove a keyboard while the PC power is on. It is possible to generate a short or static surge that could damage the PC or the keyboard.

Testing the keyboard

Before you try to correct a keyboard problem, analyze the situation. Does the problem involve just one or two keys? If so, try cleaning the bad keys with compressed air or with a good quality, noncorrosive electronic circuit cleaner to clean out the contamination.

If you have any working keys and a whole row or column of nonworking keys, the grid has failed because of a broken wire or short. This is not worth repairing; you have to replace the whole keyboard.

Sometimes no portion of the keyboard works properly. It's possible that a bad microprocessor chip is in the keyboard, but before you discard the keyboard, check that the keyboard is tightly plugged in at the system motherboard. On an older system, see that the XT/AT switch is properly set. On a system that uses

PS/2-style connectors, check that the keyboard is plugged into the keyboard port and not into the nearby mouse port, which is the same size.

Also don't forget to check for a stuck key. If you can't fix the problem at the plug or through the keys, it's time for a new keyboard.

Mice and Trackballs

A mouse gives your computer a hand. This electronic rodent changes small hand motions into pointer motions onscreen. Although the general concept has been around for many years, it was with the arrival and acceptance of graphical user interfaces, such as Microsoft Windows, that mice went from an option to a necessity on most modern machines. A close relative of the mouse is the trackball, which places a large ball on top of a stationary pointing device.

Five types of connections enable a mouse to communicate with the computer:

- A *serial mouse* uses a standard serial port.
- A *bus mouse* uses a dedicated controller card that plugs into the bus and has a unique port address of its own.
- A *PS/2-compatible mouse port* is a special connection that does not use one of the system's standard serial ports.
- A *USB mouse* attaches to the system's USB port or a hub.
- An *infrared mouse* uses the computer's infrared port, or a special port that is part of the mouse system.

All five are still serial devices, but PS/2, bus, infrared, and USB mice don't use the system's standard serial ports, their port addresses, or their interrupts — leaving these system resources free for other purposes.

PS/2 ports ordinarily use IRQ 12 and I/O (input/output) port addresses 60h and 64h, usually free on standard PCs. Figure 19-5 shows a PS/2 connector.

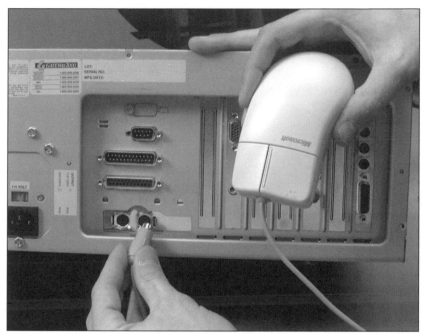

FIGURE 19-5: *A PS/2-style mouse connector on the back panel of an older PC. Modern ATX motherboards cluster the mouse and keyboard connector with the serial and parallel ports.*

Nearly every modern PC comes with a mouse; in most cases, these are basic, inexpensive models. If you're a power user, you'll want to consider an upgrade to a sturdier or more comfortable device. Like keyboards, mice have a finite life and will eventually need replacement. I always keep a replacement model in my supply closet in anticipation of the day when my mouse won't skitter anymore.

The two most significant manufacturers of mice are Microsoft and Logitech; each offers mechanical and optical models of mice and trackballs. You'll also find many other manufacturers offering either very inexpensive simple replacement models or advanced special-purpose devices. Kensington is a leading maker of trackballs.

How a mouse works

When you slide a mouse across the desktop or a mouse pad, the mouse detects this motion in horizontal and in vertical directions. The mouse sends this information to the computer along a cable attached to one of the serial port alternatives mentioned previously. Wireless models use infrared or radio signals to communicate between the mouse and a receiver that attaches to the computer. Inside the computer, a device driver (a software program designed to interface the mouse to the computer) translates the mouse signal into instructions the computer can read.

Mice can detect hand motion in many ways. Most mice use a ball that rolls as your hand slides the mouse across a flat surface. In all, four types of mice are available, and three related devices are worth considering:

- Mechanical mice
- Optical mice
- Optomechanical mice
- Wheel mice
- Pointing sticks
- Trackballs
- Joysticks

Common to all mouse designs are one or more microswitches that lie beneath the buttons on the mice. Pressing the button closes the switch and sends a signal (a click). The mouse software interprets the signals to determine whether the user has double-clicked the button.

Mechanical mice have a hard rubber ball inside that rests loosely in a chamber surrounded by sensing rollers. As you move the mouse along a desktop or a mouse pad, the ball rolls, and the rolling ball moves the rollers (Microsoft calls its internal parts *shafts*), causing copper contacts or brushes to sweep across a segmented conductor. In function, the arrangement is somewhat like the brushes of an electric motor, except that the rotating contacts within the mouse are circuit board lands. As an electric

circuit makes and breaks contact, electronics in the mouse can count the number of clicks electrically. By knowing the distance between each electrical contact, the diameter of the shafts, and so on, it is fairly easy to calculate where the mouse is moving — how far and how fast.

The conducting strips are attached to a circular board in a spoke-like arrangement. The conducting wheel is called an *encoder*. As the moving conductor goes across the segmented contacts, electrical impulses are generated and the signals are counted in the attached electronic circuitry.

The impulses can be either negative or positive, depending on the direction of rotation. The polarity of the pulses tells the electronics the direction the mouse is moving, and the speed of the pulses shows how fast the mouse is moving.

In most designs, the two rollers inside the mouse ball cavity are opposed at 90 degrees to each other, enabling them to differentiate between horizontal and vertical movement. If both rollers turn, the movement is interpreted as oblique, and the electronics of the mouse interpret the relative speed and polarity of the pulses to compute a precise direction of movement.

Optical mice have no moving parts and offer very high resolution. They are used in applications requiring very fine motions, such as certain art and graphics programs. Optical mice may use a special grid pad with a reflective surface, or they may use a high-intensity, light-emitting diode (LED) that bounces off of a desk or other surface and is picked up by an optical receiver inside the body of the mouse. Sensitive electronics inside these newer designs can find enough texture on virtually any surface to judge mouse movement through the reflected light. When the user moves the mouse on this surface, an LED shines light onto the pad, and photosensors in the mouse detect motion from the streaks of light reflected back. After the pulses are received and counted, the optical mouse functions similarly to mechanical and optomechanical designs. However, because the optical mouse has no mechanical components, to the user it feels very different from a mechanical device, and little — if any — mechanical maintenance is required.

Optomechanical mice use a hybrid design that lies between mechanical and optical devices. With this device, the movement of the ball is translated into an electrical signal by an optical device. The mechanical ball turns rollers, just as with a mechanical mouse, but instead of using mechanical electrical contacts, the optomechanical design rotates slotted or perforated wheels. An LED shines through the openings on the wheel, and optical sensors on the other side count the resulting pulses.

Wheel mice (Microsoft's name for this type of device is IntelliMouse) are becoming the standard on modern machines. This two-button mouse, like the one shown in Figure 19-6, has a small wheel mounted between the buttons. You can easily spin this wheel forward and backward with your index finger while you manipulate the mouse. Beneath the wheel is a microswitch that serves as a third button. The default setting is for the wheel to control document or page scrolling. Rotate the wheel forward (away from you) and the current page of information moves down to reveal data farther up in the document; pull the wheel towards you and the page of information scrolls up to display data farther down in the document. The wheel performs the same function as the up and down arrows on the vertical scroll bar displayed in many applications and dialog boxes.

Although the microswitch beneath the wheel is programmed by default to enable a fixed scrolling function, you can use included utility software to program the function of the wheel and switch. When these mice first started to appear, some applications wouldn't work with them. Today I find that virtually every display that supports scroll bars recognizes the wheel. You do have to install supplemental driver software to support the wheel function in Windows 95 and in early versions of Windows 98. A wheel mouse can be either mechanical, optical, or optomechanical for its basic functions; the wheel just adds additional convenience and functionality.

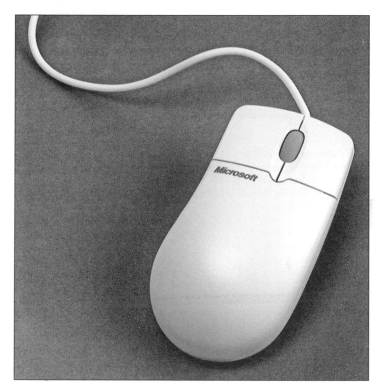

FIGURE 19-6: *A Microsoft IntelliMouse. You can use the wheel between the buttons to scroll onscreen displays.*

A *pointing stick* is a specialized version of a mouse, a pencil-eraser-like nub that sits on the keyboard, usually centered in the lower third of the keys above the letter *B*. (IBM, which patented one design for this sort of pointer, calls its product the TrackPoint.) The little stick interprets finger pressure as it is pushed in one direction or another; the harder the stick is pressed, the faster the onscreen cursor moves. Keyboards that employ this system have one connector that runs to the PS/2 port on the PC and a second connector that attaches to a PS/2 mouse port. For some users, a pointing stick is a great way to avoid having to remove their hands from the keyboard to make mouse movements. An example of a modern keyboard with a pointing stick is seen earlier in this chapter in Figure 19-2. Some users love this sort of design, while others can never quite master moving the cursor with their index finger; I would suggest you take one of these keyboards for a test drive before making a commitment. Pointing sticks require no special maintenance, although the little rubber nub usually wears down with use; most keyboard makers provide a package of replacement nubs.

Trackballs are upside-down mechanical mice. The ball rests loosely in a cavity and sensors track horizontal and vertical movement. Instead of moving the hardware across the desk, you use your hand to spin the ball in place.

Trackballs have three advantages. The first is that you can place them on a desktop and they take up just a small amount of valuable real estate. The second advantage is that a trackball can be incorporated into a keyboard. And finally, an ergonomic advantage for some users (including me) is the fact it puts less strain on the shoulder and wrist because a trackball is stationary on the desk. Two rather different interpretations of a trackball are shown in Figure 19-7.

Joysticks work in a manner similar to the pointer devices. Instead of rollers, joysticks use pressure-sensitive electronics or mechanical potentiometers that vary voltage by changing resistance in an electronic circuit.

Mouse tracking resolution

Mice and other pointing devices can differ in their capability to read very small movements. Older mice were usually able to discern differences in location as small as $1/200$ of an inch; this capability is called resolution. High-resolution models send more motion signals to the computer per inch of hand motion, with resolution as great as $1/1200$ inch. Some specialty pointing devices for artists and designers have even finer resolution.

FIGURE 19-7: *At left, the Kensington Orbit trackball. A right-hander would use the thumb for the left-click, the index or middle finger to move the trackball, and the ring finger for the right-click; the trackball can easily be used with the left hand. At right, Microsoft's Trackball Optical, which uses the thumb for the trackball with the rest of the right hand draped around its curved body. Be sure to test-drive a trackball before making a commitment.*

With an optical mouse, resolution is determined by the ability of the mouse electronics to read motion from the reflected light. With a mechanical or optomechanical mouse, higher resolution requires more holes in the light wheel or more physical segments for the mechanical brush to pass over.

Some designers improve effective resolution by sophisticated software routines. By counting the actual pulses and then interpolating what would fall between the physical pulses, higher-resolution performance can be simulated.

NOTE

For most desktop applications, including moving the onscreen pointer under Microsoft Windows, the difference between 200 points per inch (ppi) and 400 or 1,200 ppi may not matter enough to be worth the extra expense. If you are using the mouse for drawing or other fine graphics manipulation, though, higher resolution may be worthwhile.

One other difference between high- and low-resolution pointing devices is the speed of onscreen movement. Most high-resolution devices seem much faster.

Many input devices enable you to vary the *sensitivity* — the relationship between the distance moved on the desktop and the distance moved on the screen. Similarly, you often can control acceleration with a software setting. Acceleration is the relationship between the speed and distance of mouse movement and the speed and distance of cursor movement. As you move the physical mouse faster, the onscreen pointer or cursor picks up speed and moves farther than when you move the mouse at slower speeds.

Connecting the mouse

Serial mice don't require system resources of their own; instead, they use the I/O port address and assigned IRQ interrupt of an existing serial port. A serial mouse, shown in Figure 19-8, requires a unique port address because it gets control signals from the bus. The microprocessor speaks to a device by sending a port address down the bus. All the devices are looking at the bus, waiting for their distinctive port address. When a device recognizes its own port address on the bus, it pays attention to the subsequent data signals.

FIGURE 19-8: *This older three-button serial mouse connects to a standard serial port on a PC.*

Most of the time, the mouse is trying to send, not receive, information. When a mouse is ready to transmit data, it sends an interrupt to the microprocessor. The microprocessor looks up the interrupt number in the interrupt vector table, which tells the microprocessor to start using mouse-specific routines to accept the incoming data.

NOTE

A mouse sends an interrupt when you move it or press a button; for that reason, a system with a conflict between interrupts may seem to be working properly some of the time. It may freeze in situations where the mouse issues an interrupt at the same time as another device that conflicts with it.

PS/2 mice attach directly to a port on the motherboard; this is the most common design in use on modern machines. (The pointer received its name because IBM first introduced it as a component of its PS/2 systems; the connection became a generic element of most subsequent motherboards.) The PS/2 connector is wired to the motherboard's keyboard controller, which converts the mouse signals to a form that the computer can interpret; as such, it does not require the assignment of a separate port and IRQ for the mouse. Most such mouse port devices use IRQ 12. Note that the mouse connector is identical in size and shape to the keyboard connector; you should avoid mistakes here, although reversed plugs will probably not damage the computer — the mouse or keyboard will not work, however, if attached incorrectly.

USB mice use the facilities of the USB port that is common on modern machines. As with all USB devices, they offer the benefit of not requiring their own system resources, and they can be part of a long daisy chain of devices attached to the port. Finally, USB devices are hot-swappable, meaning they can be attached or removed while the system is running.

Bus mice need a unique port address and a unique interrupt, attaching to special-purpose serial adapters that plug into the expansion bus. This design was used for a period of time during the late senior citizen era, but has since been replaced by PS/2 and USB models. The mouse card required its own interrupt, and mouse cards can conflict with the other hardware installed in the computer if they demand the same IRQ.

Your computer supplier can help you with a common problem — a mouse with a connector that doesn't match available connectors on the PC. For example, you can purchase an adapter to convert a DB-9 serial plug to a PS/2 connector, like the one shown in Figure 19-9. Adapters also are available to convert a USB mouse to a PS/2 or serial mouse connection. They're usually supplied with the USB mouse hardware package.

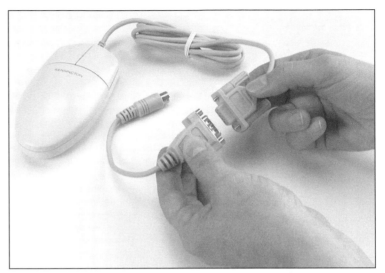

FIGURE 19-9: *This adapter converts a DB-9 serial connector to a PS/2 connector.*

Basic mice will work with the built-in drivers that are supplied with current editions of Windows. However, any special features — including Microsoft's IntelliMouse facilities — require the installation of drivers that are supplied with the pointer, or available over the Internet. If you hope to use a mouse within a DOS window, you may need to install a generic driver such as Mouse.com and reference it in an `Autoexec.bat` file; the instruction manual for the mouse should include instructions on this procedure. Some advanced mice intended for the Windows environment — including Microsoft's IntelliMouse — include support for use of the mouse in DOS as part of their Windows driver.

Spend the time to keep your drivers up to date, especially if you update or change your operating system. Check the Web site for the mouse manufacturer or the Windows Update facility of `www.microsoft.com`. In some cases, conflicts can occur between the drivers for video adapters and mice; check the instruction manuals for both devices or the manufacturer's Web site for assistance in resolving problems.

Testing a mouse

If you have trouble with a mouse attached to a serial port, first try testing the serial port alone. If you find no problem with the serial port (if it works with a modem, for example), check the mouse setup (port address, interrupts, driver, and so on) to make sure that another serial device in the machine doesn't conflict with the mouse. If you suspect a conflict, test the mouse with the other device temporarily pulled out of the computer.

If you're trying to fix a dinosaur bus mouse, double-check the setup. Most bus mice required the installation of a special driver and possibly settings in the `config.sys` or `autoexec.bat` files of DOS or older Windows versions. Consult the instruction manual for details, or upgrade to a more current design.

An early optical mouse can't work properly without the special optical pad. The pad must be correctly oriented as well.

MOUSE SKITTERS

If your mouse pointer no longer seems to follow your commands — especially if you've recently made a change in screen resolution or color depth — the problem may be related to a conflict between the device drivers for the mouse and the display driver.

To check for a conflict, go to the desktop and right-click My Computer. Click Properties, and then select the Performance tab. Click the Graphics button and slide the Hardware acceleration pointer one notch to the left. If your mouse now works properly, this is an indication of a driver conflict. Contact the manufacturer of your mouse and display adapter for more current drivers and bug fixes.

Installing a mouse

Mice come packaged with mouse device drivers and test software. Be sure that you are using the correct mouse driver. A Microsoft mouse must have a Microsoft mouse driver and probably won't work with Logitech mouse drivers. However, a Logitech mouse and mice from other makers usually work with Microsoft drivers.

If you are running Windows, the operating system comes with a driver that works with most pointing devices. If you have an unusual device, you should expect to receive a custom driver from the manufacturer, along with instructions for installing it in Windows.

Under older operating systems, including DOS and Windows 3.1, you need to install the mouse driver in the `config.sys` or `autoexec.bat` file. Most mice are shipped with two drivers, one suitable for the `config.sys` file and one for the `autoexec.bat` file. You can use either. Read the installation manual for your mouse.

Good mousekeeping

Your mouse travels miles and miles, sliding back and forth on your desktop. Along the way, it's likely to pick up dust, cookie crumbs, oils, and whatever else is floating around in your office. Sooner or later, the going is going to get a bit sticky.

The solution is to practice good mousekeeping — keep your desk as clean as possible and every few months take apart the mouse, as shown in Figure 19-10, and clean the roller or ball. To do so, unplug the mouse from the computer. You can get to the roller ball in most mouse designs by rotating a ring to release it. Clean the ball (and rollers, if there are any) with alcohol and a lint-free cloth. Check the instruction manual for your mouse for details.

Ch
19

If an optomechanical or a mechanical mouse works but seems jerky and less fluid than it should be, check the roller ball and associated shafts for contamination.

Cleaning an optical mouse is simpler because it contains no moving parts. Use an alcohol cleaner or a small spray of window cleaner to remove any buildup from the sensor on its bottom.

To be truly fastidious about your mouse's personal hygiene, you can purchase a mouse cleaning kit from specialty computer stores. The fully equipped office also includes a vacuum cleaner to remove dirt from crevices, an air cleaner to remove dust from the air, and even antistatic mats and sprays to reduce dust-collection charges from the carpeting and other surfaces.

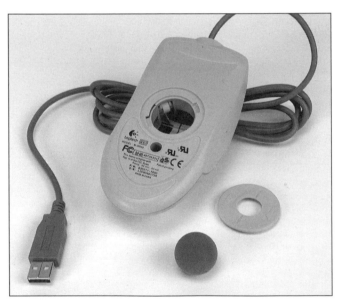

FIGURE 19-10: *If your mouse finds the going a bit sticky, it may be worthwhile to remove the mouse roller and clean it with soap and water or alcohol. In most designs, a simple twist-release mechanism on the bottom of the mouse frees the ball.*

Game Controllers

Advanced gamers will want to give their computer a hand with a joystick or other game controllers including roller balls, video-game-like pads, and even specialized simulations of airplane yokes for flight simulators and steering wheels for driving games. All of these devices work by transmitting to the computer a set of X and Y coordinates representing a position on the screen, which itself is a display of a bitmap in memory.

The most modern of game controllers use the USB port, allowing for easily changeable, advanced devices that are specific to particular types of games. USB also operates much faster than an original serial port, allowing more responsive controllers.

Older game controllers require you to add a game port to your system. Most modern sound cards include a DB15 game port among their features; in some cases the game port performs double duty as a MIDI breakout port. The game port, a large DB15 connector that will work with a MIDI device, is at the left end of the Sound Blaster Live! card (shown later in this chapter in Figure 19-16).

You may also find a game port as part of a multi-I/O card that adds enhanced serial, parallel, and IDE ports to an older machine.

Owners of dinosaurs and senior citizens can also add an inexpensive game port card to their systems. Figure 19-11 shows an example of a simple ISA bus game port card.

Figure 19-11: *Serious gamers will want to install a game port card to enable use of one or two joysticks or other controllers. You can also find multifunction cards that include serial, parallel, IDE, floppy, and game ports to upgrade older machines to near state-of-the-art I/O functions.*

Scanners

A scanner gives your computer eyes. You can use a scanner to capture drawings and photographs for use in your printed or onscreen work. A scanner can also work in conjunction with an optical character recognition (OCR) program to convert typed or printed text into computer files that you can edit and change.

How a scanner works

Scanners bounce light off a target — which may be either a picture or text — and measure the amount of reflected light. Most of this light is reflected from white paper, less from halftones in a photograph, and almost none from black text characters. The scanner sends this information to a scanner interface card in the computer, where either OCR or graphics software takes over. The software processes the light level measurements. You can save the resulting file as a standard bitmap file for further manipulation by the computer.

Color scanners shine three separate lights (red, green, and blue) on the image or use a single light with a set of red, green, and blue filters.

These are the two essential elements of a high-quality scanner:

- **Resolution.** The scanner converts an analog image to a digital representation, presented as a series of tiny dots. The finer the dots, the sharper the image. Modern scanners for graphics work start at 300 dots per inch (dpi) and progress upward from there. Devices at that resolution are more than sufficient for Web-page images, but may be less than optimal for a high-resolution printer.
- **Bit depth.** This is a measure of how many samples of colors or grays the scanner records. The higher the bit depth, the more lifelike the representation of colors. For desktop users, a 24-bit depth is a minimal level with 30 bits an up-and-coming standard.

NOTE

Scanners and OCRs work with any computer, although both make very heavy demands upon the microprocessor, video, and hard disk systems. This is not the sort of work you would want to perform using an early PC.

OCR software converts light gray shades to white and dark gray to black. Then, using this two-color image, the OCR software tries to identify the letter written on the paper. Character recognition software uses one of two techniques: font matching and feature recognition. Font matching compares the character against all memorized fonts, similar to using tracing paper to match an unknown shape against stored standard patterns. Feature recognition uses logic and piece-by-piece analysis of a character to deduce what letter it really is. Feature recognition relies on questions such as, "Does an extender protrude below the line of type?" (The letters *p*, *q*, *g*, *y*, and *j* all share this characteristic feature.) By asking itself successive questions, the software is able to systematically eliminate characters. Pattern recognition software is more flexible because proportional spacing and new fonts are less likely to throw it off stride. It is also more expensive.

Graphics software retains the middle range of signal values — the ones that represent gray tones in an image. Some scanners convert the intermediate gray tones to dithered patterns (prepared patterns of black and white dots that match the approximate light/dark ratio of the gray tone). Other scanners retain up to 64 levels of gray in the stored image (called *grayscaling*).

Scanner interfaces

Consumer-level scanning devices commonly use one of four high-speed, high-bandwidth interface connections:

- A modern machine's USB port
- A SCSI card, with the scanner capable of being one of seven devices in a chain
- A proprietary interface card specific to the scanner that in many cases is an adaptation of SCSI, but does not enable other devices to be used with the specialized card
- The PC's parallel port

Scanners connected to a parallel port or USB port

Parallel port devices are very easy to install and use, but their throughput is generally a bit slower than using a dedicated SCSI card or a USB port. Both require installation of a driver to allow Windows to work with the device.

 CROSS-REFERENCE

For the details on parallel port connections, see Chapter 17. For the details on the USB, see Chapter 15.

To troubleshoot a parallel port or USB device, begin by checking that the cable is properly attached to the scanner at one end and the PC at the other. Check the System display of Windows to be sure the port is not experiencing a resource conflict. You can also run a diagnostic program to test the function of the I/O ports.

Installing a scanner interface card

A scanner interface card — either a standard SCSI card or an adapted preconfigured SCSI adapter — installs in the system bus like other expansion cards. Here's how to do it:

1. Remove the old card. If you need to remove an old scanner card, remove the screw and pull the card straight up out of the bus connector on the motherboard.
2. Set switches and jumpers on the scanner interface card. If you are attaching to a standard SCSI host adapter card, you have to assign the scanning device a SCSI ID number and may have to make other adjustments to the adapter card. See the sections about SCSI adapters in Chapter 10. If you are using a proprietary interface card, before you install it, consider possible interference from the equipment already in

the computer. The interface board must have a unique interrupt number and a unique port address. Unfortunately, many scanners use the interrupts assigned to parallel or serial ports. Most of these interface boards enable you to choose among a number of possible interrupts and a number of port addresses. Nevertheless, careful planning, with scanner manual in hand, is required. Diagnostic software (I discuss a number of brands in Chapter 22) can scan the peripheral equipment in your computer and report what port address and interrupt each peripheral is using. This information can really help.

3. Install the card. Select a suitable expansion slot. Line up the card with the expansion slot connector and press down firmly. The card should slip into the connector. Reinstall the screw so that the card is snug in the computer case.
4. Plug in the scanner and test it. The installation manual tells you how to set the scanner switches and how to hook up the cables. The scanner manufacturer gives you test software or troubleshooting information customized for your particular scanner.

Digital Cameras

One of the most exciting extensions of the personal computer into daily life is the broadening intersection with photography. If you have any doubt about how traditional camera makers view the future, consider the names of the manufacturers of the most popular digital cameras and film scanners now on the market: start with Kodak, and then there's Canon, Fuji, Minolta, Nikon, Olympus, and others. Going the other way, many of the major consumer electronics and computer makers realize the appeal of digital photography: Hewlett Packard and Sony among them.

Digital photography converts images into the dots or pixels of a computer memory where you can manipulate them with an editing program such as Adobe Photoshop, Microsoft Photo Editor, or other similar application. You can print the result on a high-resolution photo printer, present it on the computer in a slideshow using programs like Microsoft PowerPoint, or output it to a television set or VCR.

At the time of this writing, I classify digital cameras in four groups: point-and-shoot, advanced hobbyist, semi-professional, and professional. As with other computer components, though, yesterday's advanced capability quickly becomes today's entry-level specification.

The principal differences among the four classes are resolution, lens design, and controls.

- **Point-and-shoot:** A basic version has a simple lens with a fixed focal length and autofocus logic. The first group of cameras in this group could capture images of 640 × 480, good enough for e-mailing small images and making small snapshot-sized prints. Today, cameras in this class typically can capture four times as much detail, at 1,280 × 960 or 1.3 megapixels in total. Oh, and the prices have declined by 50 percent or more: the typical range here is from about $199 to $399.
- **Advanced hobbyist:** Delivers cameras that can capture from 2.1 megapixels to 4.1 megapixels or so, more than sufficient to produce high-quality 8 × 10 prints. This class of camera typically includes an optical zoom that doubles or triples the focal length of the lens, giving a range from a moderate wide angle to a moderate telephoto view. These cameras also offer advanced controls, including manual focus, aperture or shutter speed settings, and variable file sizes for captured images. Expect to pay about $399 to $999 for cameras in this class. In the last edition of this book, I worked with an Olympus C-2020 digital camera, shown in Figure 19-12.
- **Semi-professional cameras:** Bridge the narrowing gap between the most advanced hobbyist device and expensive cameras used by professional photographers. This is another area where the gap has narrowed markedly in recent years.

Cameras in this class include SLR designs that allow you to look through the lens as you compose the picture (most lesser cameras use an optical viewfinder that is separate from the image capture system, something that causes difficulties in certain situations including close-ups). You can also expect resolution of 4.1 to 6 megapixels, improved lenses with wide ranges of zoom, and a host of controls that allow an experienced photographer to make adjustments to exposure, focus, color balance, and more. Prices for cameras in this group start at about $1,000 and reach to about $2,500.

- **Professional cameras:** Intended for photojournalists, portrait photographers, and studio workers. Most of these cameras are adapted versions of high-end film cameras, capable of working with a wide range of changeable lenses. Image resolution runs from about 2 to 6 megapixels. Prices range from about $3000 to $10,000.

FIGURE 19-12: *The Olympus C-2020 digital camera is an example of an advanced hobbyist device.*

Most digital cameras store images on a matchbook-size SmartMedia or CompactFlash card. At the time of this writing, prices are similar for the two types of storage. SmartMedia cards were available in sizes up to 128MB, while CompactFlash units were as large as 320MB. A third memory device is Sony's Memory Stick, used in devices manufactured by that company.

Most digital cameras are capable of downloading their images to a PC through a USB port; early cameras used a serial port. You can also purchase a reader to attach to your PC that can directly read the card's contents. Also available are adapters that accept a SmartMedia or CompactFlash card or Memory Stick and then plug into the USB port or other connector on your computer for transferring information.

Sony also offers a line of digital cameras that stores information on standard floppy disk drives. Although the simplicity and convenience of that system is appealing, the 1.44MB capacity of the floppy disk limits the resolution of the images that can be captured. Sony also offers a more capable version that stores images on a mini CD-R or CD-RW disc.

When you go shopping for a digital camera, these are the criteria you should consider:

- First and most important, how many pixels can the camera capture? If you're only taking pictures to post on Web pages, you can get away with a lower resolution camera of 1 megapixel or less. If you're planning to make prints, you want as many pixels as possible.
- What is the quality of the lens? Inexpensive cameras often scrimp on the lens, using no-name plastic optics with limited zoom capabilities. Again, for Web pages, the lens quality is less important. But for prints, I would look for a name-brand lens. For high-end applications, you may also want to look for a camera that can use standard lenses from 35mm cameras. Only a few digital products can accommodate these lenses, and they are generally at the upper end of the price range, but if you need such functionality, you can find it.

- How does the camera store images and transfer them to a computer? Is the standard memory device (SmartMedia, CompactFlash, Memory Stick, or other system) sufficient, or do you need to immediately purchase additional memory or a larger replacement memory unit? How easy is it to download the images to your computer?
- It's great to have a fully automated camera for most occasions, but serious hobbyists and professionals also want the ability to make their own decisions about exposure, shutter speed, focus, depth of field, color balance, and other elements.
- After you find a camera that has all the bells and whistles you want, try it out for a while to see how easy it is to use. Special features have no value if you can't get them to work when you need them.

PC Cameras

A PC camera turns your desktop into a broadcast studio — not quite up to network standards, but quite acceptable for such tasks as making Internet video phone calls and producing e-mail postcards.

A simple PC camera perches atop your computer, linked to digital capture software and your Internet mail program. Figure 19-13 shows two examples of inexpensive, capable cameras from Intel and Logitech.

Intel's line of PC cameras is among the best, offering CCD sensors capable of VGA (640 × 480) resolution, 24-bit (16.8 million) color, and automatic exposure over a wide range of lighting conditions. The cameras can be used to capture individual images or as much as 30 frames per second of video.

The camera attaches to a USB port. You'll need an Internet connection to make video phone calls. For information, consult `www.intel.com/pccamera/index.htm`.

Another leading maker is Logitech, which offers products of similar capability; the company's inexpensive QuickCam Express uses a CMOS sensor, which generally yields slightly lower-quality results compared to a CCD sensor. For information, consult `www.logitech.com`.

Most cameras come packaged with software for basic capture and editing. You will also find packages that include hardware and more sophisticated functions; one such deal is offered by 01 Communique. The Communicate! Package includes a Logitech camera and the Video i2000 software that includes advanced features, such as live video phone conferencing, home monitoring with motion detection, telephone answering software, and a set of data communications applications including an unattended bulletin board system. For information, consult `www.01com.com`.

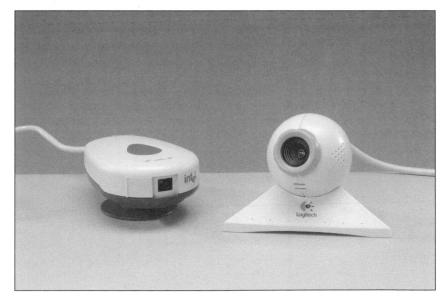

FIGURE 19-13: *The Intel PC Camera Pro, at left, is based on a CCD sensor. The simple and less expensive Logitech QuickCam Express uses a CMOS sensor.*

Ch 19

Film Scanners

Another way to bring photographs into your PC is with a film scanner. These devices use a high-resolution scanner to produce a bitmap of negatives or slides that you can store and manipulate on the computer.

A film scanner represents a good compromise for many photographers. You can continue to use your existing traditional film cameras and lenses (many of which are capable of producing higher-quality images than consumer-grade digital cameras), and you can also have access to a lifetime's worth of old negatives or slides stored under your bed.

One example is the Olympus ES-10, shown in Figure 19-14. This device can scan 35mm and Advanced Photo System (APS) negatives and slides at a maximum resolution of 1,770 dpi. The resulting image files at top resolution are about 11MB in size, more than sufficient for printing an 8-x-10-inch print or larger. Compare this to a 2.1 megapixel camera that yields an image file of about 6MB at its highest resolution setting.

This scanner is available with a SCSI interface or with a simple parallel port connection. Either way, the supplied driver attaches to the TWAIN or TWAIN32 scanner controls of a Windows machine. The scanner includes Adobe's low-end Photo Deluxe software, but any other major image manipulation program, including Adobe Photoshop, can also directly import images from the scanner.

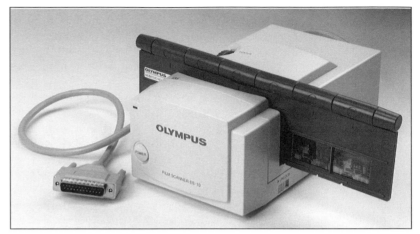

FIGURE 19-14: *The Olympus ES-10 film scanner bridges the worlds of traditional film photography and digital computer image editing.*

Sound Cards

A sound card gives your computer a voice and a set of ears.

The first PC had a silver dollar-sized speaker capable of producing little more than annoying beeps and pathetic squawks. Today, a modern machine can have a symphony orchestra within its covers, with rich sound booming forth from tabletop speakers with powered subwoofers.

With a sound card, the PC can speak to you by playing back recorded digital speech or through a text-to-speech program. The PC can listen to you with voice recording and voice recognition features. A sound card can also play audio from a music CD or produce a wide range of sounds for business, education, and gaming applications.

Music, sound effects, and speech are essential parts of the multimedia revolution. However, don't think for a minute that the tiny little beeper of a speaker within a standard PC is capable of making beautiful music. To produce multimedia audio, you need a capable sound card. Windows also enables sound recording and playback from within documents.

Some of these sound boards pipe music and voice to your stereo. Others enable recording as well through a microphone input or a line input that can accept a signal from a tape recorder or CD player. Top-of-the-line sound boards provide multiple interfaces, such as CD-ROM drive, CD player, microphone, joystick, portable speakers, AUX jack on your stereo, and MIDI.

To some users, the quality of a sound card is a critical element of their entire computer system. These folks are the high-tech cousins of audiophiles who claim to be able to distinguish between pairs of $5,000 speakers for their home stereo systems. I guess if you really can hear the difference, it's worth the effort.

For the rest of us, though, follow these hard-and-fast specifications that tell a great deal about the quality of a sound card.

- Modern machines should use a 16-bit card for recording and playing back music; an 8-bit card will disappoint. I'm not talking about the bus design here — cards can plug into ISA or PCI slots — but instead the bit depth of the audio sample. Think of this as equivalent to the number of colors used by a video adapter to draw a picture; a picture or a sound will be recognizable in 8-bit form but richer and more subtly shaded using 16 bits of information. An 8-bit card describes sounds in 256 steps, while a 16-bit card is capable of 65,536 gradations. Be sure that the card offers a reasonable range of frequencies. Most humans can hear sounds from as low as a deep rumble at about 20 Hz to a high-pitch squeal around 20 KHz. Just for

perspective, consider that a standard piano has a range from 27 Hz to 4.2 KHz; the voice frequency band on a telephone runs from 300 Hz to 3400 Hz.

Sound purists will tell you that even subaudible frequencies or those slightly above the ordinary hearing range have an effect on the quality of the sound we perceive from a speaker. I suggest that you look for a sound card capable of producing signals from 20 Hz to 20 KHz or better.

- Consider the signal-to-noise ratio, a measurement of the strength of the signal in comparison to background or underlying noise. The greater the S/N ratio, the cleaner the sound. Look for a ratio of at least 95DB for good quality.
- Another indicator of quality is total harmonic distortion, a measurement of undesirable harmonics present in an audio signal. Expressed as a percentage, the lower the THD, the better.

Most modern cards give users a range of options for the quality of sound file. Just as you can choose the resolution of a digital camera file or the screen resolution of a picture displayed on your monitor, the higher the quality of sound file you select the larger its size. The quality of a sound file is related to the *frequency* (the number of samples taken per second) and the *bandwidth* (the amount of information collected). And, of course, the quality of the computer file is related to the quality of sound you are recording; garbage in, garbage out . . . at least until you use some of the facilities of advanced sound editing programs to repair problems.

Sound files are stored as digital representations of the waveforms of an analog sound. The most common file format is WAV, used by Microsoft for many sounds within Windows as well as for extended recordings of music; most users call them "wave" files.

At CD-quality recording, a five-minute song recorded as a stereo WAV file occupies about 50MB on your hard disk. In Table 19-3, I present some of the most common sound file settings.

Nearly all modern sound cards also include *data compression* facilities that can be used to reduce the size of a recorded file by a factor of as much as 4:1. Specialized adapters can use even more powerful compression schemes such as the MPEG standard that can compress a file as much as 30:1.

Compression does not come without a price. In general, the higher the compression rate, the more information is lost. Most begin by chopping off sounds at frequencies most humans cannot hear; audio purists, though, will tell you they believe that even inaudible sounds have an effect on the overall quality of a piece of music or recorded voice. Then a scheme may play with the phrasing of music, trimming off parts of notes that are longer than a standard beat. The bottom line: if you have the space on your hard drive and a desire for the highest quality sound reproduction, avoid data compression and use a CD-quality sampling rate.

TABLE 19-3: Sound File Resolution

Type	Frequency	Bandwidth	File Requirements
Basic	7,418 Hz	8-bit mono	7KB/second
Basic	7,418 Hz	8-bit stereo	14KB/second
Telephone quality	11,025 Hz	8-bit mono	11KB/second
Telephone quality	11,025 Hz	8-bit stereo	22KB/second
Radio quality	22,050 Hz	8-bit mono	22KB/second
Radio quality	22,050 Hz	8-bit stereo	44KB/second
CD quality	44,100 Hz	16-bit stereo	172KB/second
DVD audio/ Dolby Digital 5.1	48,000 Hz	16-bit stereo	188KB/second

Here are two other noteworthy forms of files for music:

■ MIDI (musical instrument digital interface) files contain digital notations of instructions for special types of hardware; the notations may call for the playing of a sampled sound, or for a particular frequency and volume. As such you are not playing back a recording, but rather a set of instructions for a device to create sound using its own facilities. MIDI devices include synthesizers; many capable sound cards include small synthesizers for creation of music for games and multimedia purposes. Note that MIDI files are not intended to reproduce voices, or at least not ones that are very close to real ones. MIDI files are much smaller than waveforms. A five-minute selection of music in MIDI form might occupy 42K of storage.

■ Another form of digital-only file format is MP3, most commonly used in portable music players. A high-quality MP3 file records at 128 kilobits per second, near the resolution of a CD-quality waveform. The recording is "ripped" (converted to digital form) and then compressed; a typical five-minute song occupies about 4MB of space. Microsoft pushes WMA, which is capable of producing CD-quality sound with a recording rate of 64 kilobits per second, half that of MP3.

The sound card de facto standard are cards in the Sound Blaster family from Creative Labs. That doesn't necessarily mean that the Sound Blaster provides the best quality or the most features — although Creative Labs' cards have led the industry almost from the start. However, if you buy a card from another maker, be certain that it promises full Sound Blaster compatibility. Without it, you cannot be sure that all multimedia software will work properly with your card. Though third-party cards may perform quite well, and even surpass Sound Blaster in some capabilities, they may occupy different memory addresses or interrupts and may confuse some games and multimedia programs. Be sure to insist on a full explanation of the meaning of compatibility from any card maker. One example of a compatible card from another maker is the SIIG card, shown in Figure 19-15.

Some motherboards come with "integrated" sound facilities that are an element of the chipset or otherwise installed on the board. Among chipsets offering these facilities are the Intel 810,

815, and 820. This sort of setup should deliver acceptable basic performance, but rarely equal the quality or breadth of features offered by a plug-in card. You should be able to upgrade to a plug-in sound card; depending on the BIOS, the motherboard will either automatically disable the onboard sound facilities or you will have to set a jumper to turn it off.

FIGURE 19-15: *SIIG's SoundWave Pro PCI card is compatible with Sound Blaster and other standards and includes 64-voice stereo channels, true hardware wave table synthesis, and a digital signal processor that delivers 3-D positional sound effects.*

In recent years, Microsoft has simplified life for multimedia developers and users by interposing the DirectX suite of Application Program Interfaces between hardware and applications. Before the arrival of DirectX, software writers had to choose which design of hardware to support, or attempt (usually with only limited success) to work with many different standards. Today developers of hardware and software both write to the requirements of DirectX. As a user, your responsibility is to make sure you have the latest most appropriate version of DirectX installed on your machine under Windows; the easiest way to do this is to use the facilities of Window3s Update (a component of Windows 98 and later versions) or to visit **www.microsoft.com** every month or so and allow Microsoft to probe your system to make certain components are current.

You should also devote the effort to keep your drivers up to date, especially if you have upgraded the PC's operating system. Check the Web site for the manufacturer of the sound card as well as the Windows Update page.

About MP3

MP3, which draws its name from the standard it is based on, MPEG-1, Layer 3, is a compression standard that creates relatively small high-quality digital audio files for playback on a computer or a specialty portable music player.

A typical uncompressed .wav file under Windows can require about 10MB of hard disk space for each minute of CD-quality sound. An MP3 file of the same minute of sound compressed at 128 kilobits per second needs only about one-tenth that space.

MP3 encoders perform their magic by getting rid of unnecessary audio information. Part of the conversion is the filtering out of audio signals that are above or below the average human's range of hearing; in theory, this shouldn't be noticeable, except perhaps by your pet sheepdog, but audio purists maintain that even inaudible frequencies have an effect on the sound we do hear.

In any case, because some of the data is thrown away, MP3 is considered *lossy compression.*

MP3 files can be compressed at several settings. Most files are encoded at 128 kilobits per second. At a setting of 96 kilobits per second the files are smaller still but often include discernible distortion and unwanted noise; a higher-quality setting of 160 kilobits per second is usually regarded as nearly equivalent to a CD.

You can download files encoded as MP3s; some advanced audio programs include encoders to create your own files. You'll also need an MP3 decoder to play back the files. A number of decoders are available as free files on the Internet.

Future refinements of MP3 may include an adaptation of MPEG-2 Advanced Audio Coding, which can compress files at 96 kilobits per second at a higher quality.

Setting up a sound card

When recording sound, the board feeds audio from the in jack (microphone, CD player, whatever) through an analog-to-digital converter (ADC). To play sound, the sound board converts digitized audio or digital descriptions of sounds to an analog signal that enables a speaker to reproduce sound.

A modern sound card is a jack-of-all-trades when it comes to multimedia. The state-of-the-art Sound Blaster Live! card included in the demonstration system in Chapter 6 makes its primary connection to the system through a PCI slot, but beyond that, it has 13 additional connectors for various functions.

Many problems in using a sound card are related to inserting the wrong plug into connectors on the card. Card manufacturers, prodded by Intel and Microsoft with the PC99 Design Specifications, have begun color-coding the connectors on the hardware; the connectors are also marked with (tiny) symbols or descriptions of their intended use. I list a modern sound card's connectors in Table 19-4. You can find a full listing of the color assignments of PC99 in Chapter 1 of this book. Figure 19-16 shows the external panel of a current card.

Some advanced sound cards have so many available facilities that they end up being forced to share connectors for more than one purpose. They may use a breakout box that expands available connectors to an external box. In Figure 19-17 is a fully featured current card.

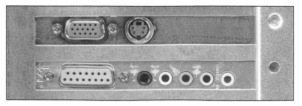

FIGURE 19-16: *On the external panel of this Creative Labs Sound Blaster Live! card you find, from left to right, the DB15 game controller/MIDI connector, rear out, line out, microphone in, line in, and digital out. Above the sound card is an AGP video adapter with a DB9 for a monitor and an S-VHS connector for use with a television.*

FIGURE 19-17: *Sound cards have become among the most highly integrated devices of a modern PC. In addition to the six connectors on the rear panel of this current Creative Labs Sound Blaster Live! card, it also includes seven more connectors for internal devices.*

Ch 19

TABLE 19-4: Jacks and Connectors on a Modern Sound Card

Type	Location	Purpose
Line In (blue)	Rear bracket	Connects to the output of an amplified external device such as a cassette recorder, CD player, DAT, or MiniDisc player.
Microphone In (red)	Rear bracket	Connects to the output of an external microphone for recording voice or other audio. Most cards record from microphone in monaural only.
Line Out (green)	Rear bracket	Connects to powered speakers, headphones, or an external amplifier for playback.
Digital Out (white)	Rear bracket	Connects to an external digital device, such as a Digital Audio Tape (DAT) recorder that uses the SPDIF digital device specification.
Rear Out (black)	Rear bracket	Provides an amplified signal to basic speakers, or for rear speakers in a four-speaker setup. Avoid using this connector with powered speakers unless the sound card's amplifier is turned off.
Joystick/ MIDI (yellow)	Rear bracket	DB15 connector for a joystick or a MIDI music device; can be adapted to work with both at the same time.
PCI	Internal base of card	Provides electrical power for the card, plus data interchange with hard drive, and carries instructions from the microprocessor.

Type	Location	Purpose
AUX (white)	Internal	Links the card to internal audio sources including a TV tuner, MPEG converter, and other devices.
CD Audio (black)	Internal	Connects to the analog audio output of an internal CD-ROM or DVD-ROM, using a CD audio cable.
Telephone Answering Device (green)	Internal	Monaural connection of audio to and from an internal voice modem.
Modem	Internal	A pin header that connects to certain classes of modem cards.
PC Speaker	Internal	Connects to the internal speaker on the motherboard.
CD SPDIF	Internal	Connects to a SPDIF (digital audio) output of an internal CD-ROM or DVD-ROM.
Audio Extension (Digital I/O)	Internal	A pin header that connects to a specialized digital I/O card.

Sound cards have gone through a great deal of change in the course of a few years on the scene, always in the direction of improved capabilities. The biggest points of difference are between 16- and 32-bit cards and FM synthesis versus wave table synthesis. Older, 8-bit cards are still around, too, and an even wider gap separates these and the newer offerings.

In general, 16-bit cards are capable of using more memory to describe and prepare notes than an 8-bit card; a 32-bit card offers still more definition and produces better sound.

Ch
19

FM synthesis creates sounds by using algorithms to produce mixed sine waves that are analogs of real instruments. Depending on the capabilities of the card, the quality of output can range from Game Boy–like beeps and squawks to decent, but artificial, sound. Wave table synthesis is based on actual recorded instrument samples that can be called upon and manipulated by MIDI commands.

When you record music or sound from an outside source, such as a tape deck, video recorder, or the analog output of a CD player, the information travels to the sound card as an analog audio signal that plugs into an input jack on the back of the sound card.

However, if you want to play the digital audio output of a CD-ROM player installed internally, you'll need to connect an audio cable inside the PC between the sound card and the digital output of the CD-ROM.

Other features to look for include the power of the internal amplifier. Many sound cards produce as little as 1 watt per channel, which is barely enough power for use with external speakers that have their own amplifiers. More modern cards generate as much as 4 watts per channel, but this is still insufficient for clean sound — they are likely to produce noise along with the signal. If you are a sound purist, look for a card that adds a low-level (unamplified) line-out connector that you can attach to a more generous external amplifier.

WARNING

On many sound cards, it is very important to disable the onboard audio amplifier if you will be using the card with an active or powered external speaker system. Consult the instruction manual for more information.

Many multimedia kits come with a pair of speakers. In my experience, the quality of these devices ranges between symphonic and spectacularly awful. Try to audition your speakers at a retail store or at a friend's setup; at the very least, buy the best pair you can afford and be prepared to send them back if they don't meet the needs of your ears.

It is generally not a good idea to use ordinary home stereo speakers directly connected to your PC for two reasons: Their magnetic coils are not shielded and can cause disturbances to your monitor or damage to floppy disks, and they may require greater wattage than is produced by the tiny amplifiers of sound cards. A good compromise, and a very appropriate choice for users who don't want to disturb others, is a quality set of headphones instead of speakers.

Prices for sound cards, like most everything else related to computers, have come down sharply. You can get pretty good sound — good enough for games, audio response to your application programs, and even music CD playback — for $20 or so. Figure 19-18 shows a very basic Sound Blaster 16 card from Creative Labs.

FIGURE 19-18: *A basic Sound Blaster 16 card*

A more advanced version of the Sound Blaster is shown in Figure 19-19, offering a way to add an EIDE controller along with audio features. In this book's test system, which I disassemble in Chapter 6, I work with a Sound Blaster Live! card.

You also face the problem brought about by all of the possible functions of a fully featured card: too many choices to easily control. One interesting solution is a remote control, similar to the multifunction remote for your VCR and cable box. Keyspan offers a Digital Media Remote that offers wireless access to PowerPoint, QuickTime, DVD, CD, and MP3 software. The device is shown in Figure 19-20.

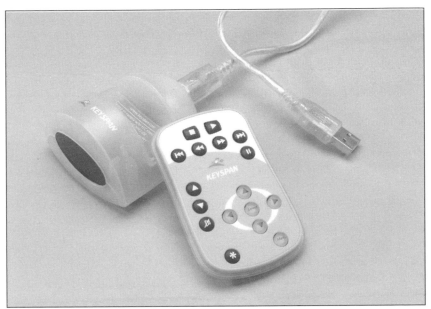

FIGURE 19-20: *Keyspan's Digital Media Remote includes a receiver that plugs into a USB port and a matchbook-sized wireless infrared remote. Included software allows users to customize commands for multimedia software.*

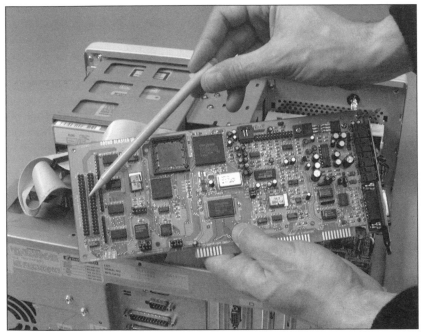

FIGURE 19-19: *Another model of the Sound Blaster 16, this older card includes an EIDE controller that can be used with certain brands of CD-ROM drives. Modern PCs offer an EIDE controller on the motherboard for CD-ROM drives.*

Installing and testing a sound board

Although CD-ROM drives, DVD-ROM drives, and sound cards are individually very different types of peripherals — the first two are storage devices and the last is an electronic orchestra and sound effects generator — they are very much linked in modern machines in that they are essential elements of the burgeoning multimedia explosion.

Many sound cards are electronically linked to CD-ROM drives as interfaces to the bus and as amplifiers for CD- and DVD-based audio.

Most current cards require a PCI slot; if you have a choice between a PCI or an ISA slot, use a faster and more capable PCI adapter. ISA cards make it more difficult to configure interrupts and system resources, and lack other advanced features.

On a modern machine, Plug and Play should do most or all of the heavy thinking when it comes to configuring a PCI card. Most PCI sound cards use IRQ5 and DMA 5 for all native and emulated modes.

Older ISA cards often employed jumpers or switches on the card for the assignment of IRQs and memory segments; you'll have to experiment with offerings in search of conflict-free settings. ISA cards generally require separate IRQs for emulated modes, making them difficult to fit into a well-equipped machine.

EISA sound boards (which are relatively rare, by the way) use level-sensitive interrupts, so that an EISA sound board in an EISA computer could theoretically share an interrupt with another EISA device, but most sound boards are ISA and require a unique interrupt.

In most cases, you'll need to attach an analog audio cable from your internal CD-ROM to the sound card's CD Audio In connector. A number of different designs are available for this cable; this is one reason to use an industry card like those offered by Creative Labs or a card that adheres closely to the Sound Blaster standard.

Advanced CD-ROMs and DVD-ROMs also offer a digital audio connector that attaches to the sound card's S/PDIF or digital audio input, allowing you to play digital audio CDs.

 WARNING

Be sure that your CD-ROM drive and sound board work together. If you purchase a package that includes both, you have a reasonable expectation that they will be able to talk to each other and will include necessary audio cables to connect them. If you're buying à la carte or upgrading one or the other, check with the maker of the CD-ROM drive and your sound board before you make the purchase. Connecting the two may be as simple as plugging in a provided cable, or you may have to acquire (or build) a custom cable to match the connectors on the two devices. This is not difficult, because the output of your sound card is probably compatible with the input of your CD-ROM drive, even if the connectors don't match. However, it is a lot easier if you start with matching connectors and a cable that works out of the box.

You also have to install device drivers to Windows and DOS to inform your operating system of the presence of the sound card. Consult the instruction manual for the card for details. Most sound cards include their own diagnostic programs to test their settings and performance.

Troubleshooting a sound card

Before you curse the silence, check the most obvious sources of problems.

Speak to me. First of all, are your speakers plugged into the output of the sound card? If the speakers have a power amplifier, check to see that they are turned on and that they are connected to a power source — usually a DC transformer. Some speakers use batteries, and these must be in place and holding sufficient power.

Next, check to see that the sound card is enabled, and configured as the active preferred device.

Verify that your sound card is enabled. Click Start ⇨ Settings ⇨ Control Panel. Double-click System, and then click the Device Manager tab. Double-click Sound, video and game controllers, and then click on your sound card.

Click Properties. If the Disable in this hardware profile check box is selected, click on the check box to clear that choice and enable the card. Click OK, and then click OK again. Restart your computer if the system requests you to do so.

Verify that your sound card is the preferred device. Click Start, point to Settings, click Control Panel, and then double-click Multimedia.

In the Preferred device boxes under Playback and Recording, click on your sound card. Click OK.

Verify that Windows is configured to use the audio features of your sound card. Click Start, point to Settings, click Control Panel, and then double-click Multimedia. Click the Devices tab, and then double-click Audio Devices. Click on your sound card, and then click Properties. Click Use audio features on this device.

Click OK to return to the Control Panel window. Restart your computer.

Check for corrupt sound files. If you are having a problem playing a particular .wav or .mid sound file, try playing another similar file to see if it is the file itself that is causing the problem.

You'll find wave (*.wav) files in the Windows System folder. You can locate other wave or MIDI files on your computer by clicking on Start and then pointing to Find. Click on Files or Folders and type in *.wav or *.mid.

Verify you are using current sound drivers. Update the driver from within Windows if possible, go to the manufacturer's Web site, or call the manufacturer to obtain a current driver.

Check for hardware conflicts. Click Start, point to Settings, and then click Control Panel. Double-click System, and then click the Device Manager tab.

Double-click Sound, video and game controllers, and check to see that your sound card is listed; if it is not there it has not been recognized by Windows. It may not be physically installed properly or may have failed.

If you see your sound card listed, check for an exclamation point in a yellow circle; if you see this symbol, Windows is reporting a problem with the device. The source of the problem can include a resource conflict, a corrupted or absent driver, or a hardware problem with the device itself.

To attempt to resolve the problem, double-click on the sound card, and then click the Resources tab. Check the panel that displays the Conflicting device list. If Windows reports a conflict here, you'll have to reconfigure the sound card or one or more other conflicting devices to use different IRQ or memory resources. Check instruction manuals or contact the manufacturer for information on suggestions to end the conflict.

TIP

In all Windows versions — at least since late Windows 98 — you may have success letting Windows reconfigure things for you. Open the Device manager as described earlier and right-click your sound card listing and choose Remove. Now reboot Windows. The operating system should locate this new hardware and attempt to reinstall it for you. The previous driver software you used should be on the hard drive, where Windows will find it and set up your sound card again. If Plug and Play works properly, the previous resource conflict should be cleared automatically.

More sound card fix-its

After you have dealt with issues of resource conflict, you may run into some other problems to be fixed. Here are some common issues for sound cards, with typical solutions.

No sound or low volume. Are the speakers plugged into the proper output of the sound card; double-check that they use the line-out or speaker jack. If the speakers have an amplifier, is it plugged into the wall current and turned on? Is the volume control of the speakers set to a middle or high position for testing?

Check the settings of the Windows sound mixer. See that the mixer doesn't mute the output of the sound card, and that volume settings are at a middle or high position for testing.

Try using a different application to generate sound. For example, try the Windows sounds, configurable and testable from the Control Panel. If you hear sounds from another source, the problem is likely with whatever software you first tried.

Scratchy or weak sound. Poor quality sound may be the result of the device's DMA setting not matching the DMA setting under Windows; Plug-and-Play should prevent this situation, but problems still occur. Follow these steps to determine if the DMA settings are correct:

1. Right-click My Computer and then click Properties.
2. On the Device Manager tab, click Sound, video and game controllers. Then click Remove.
3. Restart the computer. Once Windows is up and running again, click Start ⇨ Settings ⇨ Control Panel. Then double-click the Add New Hardware icon and reinstall the sound card.

Be sure to let Windows search for new hardware first. If it finds it, you'll stand a better chance of getting the right driver installed. If this doesn't work, choose manual and try to point to the right driver on the manufacturer's disk or CD-ROM included with the product.

Another possible cause for poor sound performance is an attempt to mix wave file formats. For example, you cannot play a 16-bit wave file on an 8-bit sound card.

Monaural sound or one channel. If you hear sound through only one side of the speaker pair, or if you can determine that the sound you hear is monaural and not stereo, check to see that you are using a stereo jack in the sound card's speaker output. A mono jack combines the left and right signals into a single stream; as you look at a jack, you will see three segments for a stereo unit and two segments on a mono unit. Check the sound card's drivers and support software for any configuration errors, including a manual assignment of monaural sound. Check, too, that the Windows sound mixer is not set up to mute one of the two channels of a stereo signal. If you are replaying the output of an external device, check to see that its balance setting is not turning off one channel and that switches are not set to produce a mono signal.

Hum or distortion in the signal. Tracking down the source of a hum can be very tricky. One common source of the problem is placement of the speakers too close to the monitor, or to a poorly shielded television or FM receiver. The problem can also be caused by a pinch in the cable or damage to one of the connectors. Check to be sure the plug is fully inserted into the connector. In some instances, the sound card itself may be receiving interference from another component within the PC; if possible, move the card to another slot away from other adapters.

Are you overpowering your speakers? If you overpower the speakers with too much power, sound will be distorted. It is best to adjust the volume from within Windows or on the sound card before the signal travels to the sound card.

Adjust the volume control on the speakers to a middle position. If your sound card has a volume control, adjust it to a middle position. Then adjust the volume within any audio control panel put in your system by the sound card; look for a volume control icon on the desktop.

Or, check for a volume control within Windows. Click Start, point to Programs, then Accessories, and then Entertainment. Click Volume Control, and then adjust the volume.

Speakers

Consider the quality of the speakers you use to reproduce sound. A great sound card coupled with a tinny pair of speakers will sound tinny, just as a superior set of speakers used with an inadequate sound card won't satisfy most ears.

Computer speakers are generally lightweight and small. A proper design shields the magnetic coil on the speaker to prevent distortion of the image on a computer monitor and distortion of the audio because of leaking magnetic waves and radio frequency radiation.

The best quality speakers have their own small amplifiers; even better than a simple two-speaker setup is a system that uses a third speaker called a *subwoofer*. Subwoofers deliver clean, resonant bass; because low frequency sounds are relatively nondirectional, this sort of speaker can be placed on the floor or corner in the general area of the left and right speakers. Amplified

Ch 19

speakers obviously require a source of power; tiny and tinny speakers may use batteries, while more impressive models require power from an AC to DC adapter. We can also expect to see some speakers that draw power from the USB system in modern PCs.

To judge the quality of speakers, you should pay attention to the frequency range and the total harmonic distortion, just as you do for the sound card. The third most important element is the wattage of the built-in amplifier. Within reason, the more wattage the better; most consumer-grade speaker systems offer amplifiers yielding from 10 to 100 watts.

You'll also want to use connecting cables of decent quality. Cheap wire or connectors can result in distortion.

The current ultimate in computer audio is 5.1 Surround Sound, also known as Dolby Digital. This scheme, similar to that used in a high-end home theater, uses six speakers. Two speakers are located in "front" of the user, usually on either side of the monitor. A third front speaker delivers a computer-derived "middle" channel that fills in the sound between left and right. Two more speakers are placed behind the user. A subwoofer is placed on the floor.

After your speaker system is in place, use the facilities of the sound card's software to define the sound setup. Most applications can make adjustments to the sound to adjust it to the size of room, type of music, and number of speakers.

Microphones

To record voice or to use a voice-recognition or dictation system with a PC, you'll need a microphone. The price and quality of mikes varies tremendously, but if you're planning on basic tasks, an inexpensive model should suffice. If you're planning on recording music, you'll need a more professional model and you may want to invest in a specialized sound card and an external mixer.

To judge the quality of a microphone, look at the same specifications you consulted for a speaker: frequency range and signal-to-noise ratio.

Be sure to plug the microphone into the correct connector on the sound card, and check to make sure the cable does not become crimped or damaged. Some microphones include a small battery-powered amplifier; be sure the batteries are fresh and that an on-off switch is in the proper position.

TV Output

So, you'd like to be the next David Letterman with your own television studio? Modern PCs can work with a variety of hardware and software products that enable you to edit videotapes on the screen of your computer and output them back to a VCR.

The time may also come when you want to get your fancy PC-based presentation from the computer to a large-screen television or projection TV for a business meeting. Or perhaps you want to make your own training tape for a sales meeting or scan in a collection of photos to produce a nifty electronic photo album that can be distributed by videotape at the next family reunion.

You have two relatively simple solutions. One is to work with a video adapter card that includes a TV-out port; for example, the 32MB NVIDIA GeForce2 MX 4X AGP Graphics Card with TV-Out is part of my demonstration system in Chapter 6; this device has an S-VHS output alongside the standard computer video connector. Another major manufacturer of cards with TV-out ports is ATI.

Another way to accomplish the same task is to use a converter that takes the output of a standard computer video card and splits off a television signal. I worked with one such solution from AITech, the MultiPro Plus PC-to-TV Digital Converter. For information, consult www.aitech.com.

The MultiPro is a true electronic magic box, capable of giving and taking in most any direction. It works with PCs and most current Macs and outputs to NTSC or PAL television standards. NTSC is used in the United States, Canada, and parts of Asia and Latin America, while the slightly higher-resolution PAL system is used in Europe and parts of Asia.

Ch 19

The MultiPro Plus supports as many as 16 million colors at computer screen resolutions of 640×480 pixels and 800×600 pixels, as well as a virtual resolution of $1,024 \times 768$ pixels at a refresh rate of up to 75 Hz.

Due to the differences in VGA and TV signals, converted images are sometimes unstable and flickering. AITech's Flic-Free filter provides eight selectable settings to produce a clear and stable image.

One advantage of an external converter is that it requires no software on your PC. It accepts the VGA output of the computer at one plug and outputs a television signal and a pass-through to your computer monitor. The touch panel on the converter lets you adjust underscan or overscan on the television, perform image centering, and zoom in on a portion of an image.

The box includes a unique 1:1 perspective (square pixel) conversion that eliminates distortion when going from the PC's screen to the TV, which has a different aspect ratio. An intelligent circuit automatically powers-down when the computer is switched off or the VGA signal is not present; all user settings are preserved in this mode.

For the highest quality results, connect the output of the MultiPro to an S-VHS cable, which connects to the most current televisions and video recorders. S-VHS (also called S-Video) signals separate luminance and chrominance video signals to provide the highest image quality.

SUMMARY

This chapter concludes the hardware tour of PCs, from dinosaurs to modern machines. In the next few chapters, I look at some good software and operating system practices that help you keep your hardware working properly and protect you against losing your data when hardware fails.

Ch 19

Notes

Ch
19

Chapter 20

Networks, Gateways, and Routers

Sooner or later, nearly every home or office ends up with more than one computer: one in the den and one in the home office, or one in the front office and another on the desk of the sales manager. In many situations, you can find more than just a handful; very few offices are without a computer on each desk, and many families end up with PCs for each child in school and one or more for mom and dad.

It has always been possible for a PC to stand on its own without a network to other machines. Files and programs can be stored on local disks, and you can equip the computer with its own modem, printer, and other peripherals. However, equipping each computer with its own peripherals is not very economical. Printers are rarely in constant use and can be shared easily. Similarly, a single Internet connection can usually be shared among many machines without significant degradation in speed, saving the cost of phone lines and subscriptions.

Additionally, consider the exchange of information among multiple machines. In an office, the sales force needs to know the status of inventory in the warehouse; the warehouse should be up-to-date on the status of the assembly line at the manufacturing plant, and so on. In a home, parents may want to check on the kids' homework or share the information in the computerized checking account.

The low-tech solution is to make copies of files on floppy disks or other portable media and move them from machine to machine by hand. Wags dub this solution a *sneaker net*.

A much better solution is the creation of a local area network (LAN), a system that links multiple machines to allow users to exchange files and programs and share devices. In the early days of the PC, establishing a LAN was a black-magic task left to the technicians. Today, a basic office or home network is close to a Plug-and-Play application.

In this chapter, I'll explore the hardware side of networking including network interfaces, hubs, switches, routers, and gateways.

I also touch on some of the basics of software protocols. Microsoft Windows includes extensive information on configuring a network after the hardware is in place. You can also obtain assistance from makers of network cards and other devices.

Additionally, I discuss a related critical security issue for networks connected to the Internet with an introduction to hardware and software firewalls.

The Components of a Network

To become part of a local area network each computer needs three principal components:

- A network interface. Hardware on a plug-in adapter card, a chipset on the motherboard, or an external device that attaches through a USB connection that bundles data into packets to be sent out onto the network and collects packets addressed to it from other devices.
- A system of wires (or a wireless equivalent) to link one computer to another.
- A software protocol to manage the operation of the network.

For most of today's personal computers, networks are based around the Ethernet specification, which defines the hardware and the communications protocol that encases chunks of data between a sender's address and a receiver's address and other information.

The current state-of-the-art in Ethernet is called 100Base-T, or Fast Ethernet, which is capable of passing as much as 100 megabits of data per second. Fast Ethernet superceded 10Base-T, which could move at 10 megabits per second. Higher speed 1 gigabit Ethernet also is available, primarily for commercial application. Eventually 10-gigabit-per-second versions will be fairly commonplace.

NOTE

Other less commonly used transport mechanisms include token ring and ArcNet. Indeed, these technologies are virtually a thing of the past, with the exception of existing installations.

The Ethernet interface uses a protocol called Carrier Sense Multiple Access With Collision Detection, which means that the network interface card monitors the stream of traffic moving past on the network and looks for an opening. Think of merging your car onto a crowded expressway. You can't just plow ahead blindly.

You must wait for an opening at least as large as your car and within the capabilities of your engine's ability to catch up with it.

In an Ethernet system, each computer listens in on the network in search of a gap in the stream of data and then transmits its short packet; if two devices happen to send a packet at the same moment, there will be a collision and both computers will be instructed to resend the packet after a randomly assigned wait.

Ethernet was originally envisioned for use for PCs located near each other in a LAN. However, the system has been expanded into use across wider groups and as the mechanism behind connections between a PC and such devices as a cable modem network and shared printers.

Within a network, packets flow along cables arranged in a particular *topology*. The most common design is a *hub and spoke* or *star* topology that connects each of the computers in the network to a central hub. The hub reroutes the packets out to the other computers in the network.

A *passive hub* sends every incoming packet out on the network where it passes all of the computers until it comes to the proper address. A *switched hub* sends packets only to the particular hub to which it has been addressed; as such it operates considerably faster than a passive hub.

Another design for a network is a *bus* topology in which all computers branch off of a single main line.

Wireless networks mimic hardware cable designs. Data is transmitted by each computer to a receiver that functions as the hub of the network. The receiver retransmits data to the addressed computer.

The specification also sets the details of the type of cable for the network, and the speed of transmission. Until recent years, the standard Ethernet specification was called 10Base-T, which was capable of moving data at 10 megabits of data per second. Today, the most common standard has been 100Base-T, also known as Fast Ethernet; as its name suggests, it can move data at 100 megabits per second.

On the horizon are home and small office versions of Ethernet able to communicate at 1 gigabit and 10 gigabits per second. Network savvy businesses today are installing or converting to gigabit Ethernet. By the time home users find gigabit Ethernet fairly common, 10 gigabit will be common in the workplace.

Note that an Ethernet is only capable of working at the speed of its slowest component. For example, if you have 100Base-T network interface cards but a 10Base-T hub, the network will move no faster than 10 megabits per second. If you have a 100Base-T hub that connects to a 10Base-T NIC in a computer on the network, you'll also be limited to that slower speed.

For that reason, purchasing a 10/100Base-T hub or switch capable of working at both speeds makes sense.

Network Topologies

The physical design of the connections between network components is called its *topology*. Several designs are commonly used, including bus, star, and ring. Most simple networks use the star design.

Star topology

A *star topology* — also called a hub and spoke — is centered around a server, a hub, or a switch. Each computer is connected by a cable to the hub or server; the path from one computer to another passes through the central device.

The principal advantage of this design is that the failure of any spoke — a computer or a networked device such as a printer or broadband modem — does not bring down the entire network. A star topology typically requires much more cabling than a bus, because machines that may sit next to each other do not connect directly to each other but instead must be linked to the central device.

If the server — an active PC — or the hub or switch fails, the network will not operate but individual machines can work independently.

Bus topology

A *bus topology* uses a single cable with workstations and peripheral devices connected anywhere along the way. In a typical setup where Windows is the only networking software you are using, the system is a *peer-to-peer* network in which each PC on the network is essentially equal to every other one.

The bus must remain unbroken from one end to the other with hardware termination at each end. The network won't work if the cable is damaged, a connector comes undone, or a network interface fails.

Again, because each member of the network is a computer capable of functioning on its own, the individual network components can still work in the event of a failure, but they won't be able to communicate with each other. Data can be shared via floppy disk or other removable media, but there will be no direct connection.

Ring topology

A *ring topology* is a closed system, a form of bus without any termination. Each PC or other network component attaches to the continuous network wiring, with the ends of the loop connected to each other to form a ring.

All of the components — cables, connectors, and interfaces — must be working properly for the network to operate. (Think of a Christmas tree light set with the lamps wired in serial form; the failure of one lamp brings down the entire string.) Unlike the Christmas tree light example, however, individual components — because they are intelligent entities in their own right — can still function, but without network communications.

Ch 20

Network Interface Cards

The network interface card, sometimes called a *NIC*, is the hardware that provides the physical connection between your computer and the network. A NIC works with the networking software to establish and manage the protocol that chops up data into packets and adds a destination address to each piece.

Although the device is commonly referred to as a bus adapter card, network interface card, or a NIC, it can also exist as a set of chips on the motherboard or as a plug-in module that attaches using the USB port of a modern machine. Portable computers can use a USB device or a network interface on a PC Card.

NICs work well with Plug-and-Play, in most cases allocating hardware resources automatically.

Cards are very inexpensive — as little as $15 for a no-name brand, and you should have no reason to purchase or reuse an older card that may require you to move some jumpers on the card to set resources.

USB interfaces are even simpler to use, requiring no hardware settings; USB devices cost less than $100.

As noted, a 100Base-T NIC connected to a 10Base-T hub, or a 100Base-T hub linked to a 10Base-T NIC will operate at the slower speed. For a new system, it makes sense to purchase the devices capable of working at the highest speed; if you have a mixed system, buy *autonegotiating* hardware that can adjust to the speed of the network. Such devices are sometimes advertised as 10/100 devices.

Figures 20-1 through 20-3 show a selection of modern network interfaces, in a PCI bus version, an external USB adapter, and a PC card for use in portables.

Ch
20

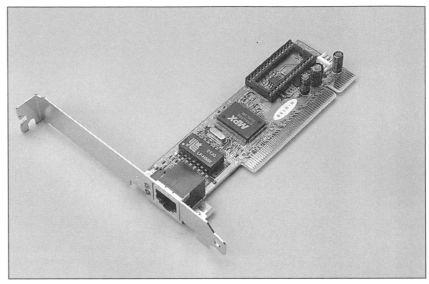

FIGURE 20-1: *The Belkin Network PCI Card is an example of a basic plug-and-play NIC for modern machines. It includes support for 10Mbps and 100Mbps networking.*

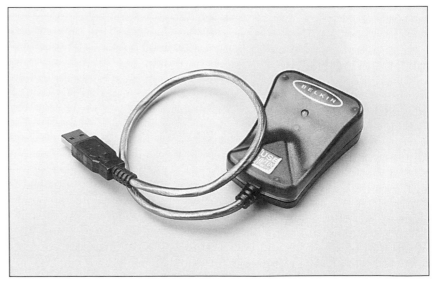

FIGURE 20-2: *USB NICs, such as this Belkin 10/100 Ethernet Adapter, do not require any system resources other than those already claimed by the USB chain.*

FIGURE 20-3: *A 32-bit CardBus or PC Card network adapter like this model from Belkin allow attachment of a portable computer to a home or office network, and to broadband modems.*

Hubs, Switches, and Gateway/Routers

A *hub* (known to some techies as a *concentrator*) is an external hardware device that serves as a central connection point for cables from PCs and other devices; to connect from one to another, the cable goes to the hub and then back out.

A hub can also be used to convert from one type cable to another, such as linking a section of a network using 10Base-2 coaxial to a device or network segment that requires a 10Base-T connection. And it can merge together segments that are based on differing speeds, such as 10Base-T and 100Base-T; a slower device will continue to operate at its base speed, and a slow hub will reduce all segments to its speed limit.

Hubs are a bit like an unguarded highway intersection, with as many as 24 lanes of traffic on some models. Packets of information are brought together from sending devices to join the stream of data that visits every machine on the network.

A much better solution is the use of an intelligent switch; until recently, though, these devices were too expensive and too complex for small office and home networks. Now, though, network switches are widely available at reasonable prices — less than $100 for an eight-port switch, not much more than an equivalent hub.

A switch works by reading the distinct address of an incoming packet and then selecting a path to send it directly to the intended recipient instead of sending it out on the network to every attached device. As such, each sender and receiver has access to the full bandwidth of the network rather than having to share it with all of the other traffic. The direct path also reduces the chances for collisions between the packets, resulting in a greater efficiency rate.

For this book, I worked with three capable switches, each flawless in operation and Plug-and-Play in setup.

One switch, Belkin's network switch, is available in both five-port and eight-port versions, with auto-sensing RJ45 ports capable of working with either 10Base-T or 100Base-T segments; LEDs on the front indicate the speed of each port. An uplink port allows connection to additional switches or to a router to extend the system; one of the hallmarks of the Belkin products is a swoopy Art Deco-like design. Various components in the Belkin line can dock together to form a desktop panel.

A more capable device is a combination gateway and router, sometimes called a residential gateway. These devices combine a switch to link together the devices on a network with a gateway router that permits an entire network to share a single cable or DSL modem Internet account. All modern versions of a gateway router also include a hardware firewall to protect against unwanted intrusion by hackers.

Ch 20

Belkin's Cable/DSL Gateway Router includes four ports for network devices; one of those ports can be used to connect to a network switch to expand the size of the network and the number of devices that can share the Internet connection.

A Belkin gateway router and network switch can be seen in Figure 20-4. For more information on Belkin, consult `www.belkin.com`.

FIGURE 20-4: *The Belkin Cable/DSL Gateway Router, at left, can function alone to link four PCs to a single broadband Internet connection or can attach to a network switch to expand to a larger group of machines.*

I built the test network for this edition of *Fix Your Own PC* around the Linksys EtherFast Cable/DSL Router. This eight-port switch and gateway includes a broad range of firewall and security facilities including packet filtering. The Linksys device, shown in Figure 20-5, is set up and managed from a Web page accessed through the browser of an attached computer on the network.

Both gateways use Network Address Translation to convert multiple IP addresses on a private local area network to a single public address that is sent out on the Internet. This adds security to your operations because the addresses of PCs on the network are not transmitted on the Internet.

Linksys offers a wide range of products aimed at small office and home networks. In addition to hubs, switches, and gateways of various sizes, the company also is among the leading makers of wireless networking devices as well as phone line and power line systems. For information on Linksys, consult `www.linksys.com`.

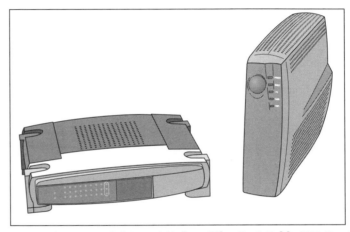

FIGURE 20-5: *An eight-port Linksys EtherFast Cable/DSL Router, alongside a Toshiba PCX1100 cable modem*

Cabling

The simplest type of cable for use in home and small office PC networks is twisted pair wiring, a more robust version of the familiar two- or four-wire telephone cable. Networking cable uses eight wires, configured in pairs of wires, twisted together to reduce interference. Twisted-pair cables use a slightly larger version of the familiar plastic snap-in connector of a telephone, too, and in an office installation can be wired to connection boxes in the wall. Cables are rated by quality and capacity; Category 5 is the most common high-quality design.

In larger offices, coaxial cable is commonly used. The cable is made up of a center connector surrounded by a plastic dielectric (insulator). A copper braid is woven around the dielectric sheath and is covered by a thin plastic outer layer. This cable is similar to the wiring used by cable television providers; on computer networks, the wire attaches to network interfaces and hubs with a twist-on BNC connector. Coaxial cables are sturdier than twisted-pair and may be required by some fire codes for in-wall installation. But in most cases, the coaxial backbone will be converted to twisted pair before connecting the network to individual PCs.

Coaxial networks using Ethernet can extend for about 2,000 feet in total; a twisted pair network is limited to about 300 feet. Some hub designs can improve on — or reduce — total distances.

Many offices and large installations now use fiber optic cable, which offers greater security and speed; it is, however, difficult to install and more expensive than other technologies. And because few PCs have the ability to connect directly to a fiber backbone, you need adapters to convert fiber to copper before attaching it to your computer.

In this book, I'll concentrate on twisted-pair protocols, 10Base-T and 100Base-T.

Network Software and Protocols

On the software side, you'll need a driver to connect your NIC to the operating system and a network-capable operating system.

For most users, current versions of Windows from Windows 95 onward will provide both software components. Windows includes drivers for most current network interfaces; some manufacturers supply customized drivers along with their hardware.

Windows can support multiple protocols on the same system. The operating system includes these built-in network protocols:

- **Microsoft TCP/IP.** The Transmission Control Protocol/Internet Protocol is well suited to link computers with a mix of hardware architectures and operating systems, including the Internet and Unix-based hosts. Under Windows XP, this protocol is recommended for a local area network.
- **Microsoft NetBEUI.** The native networking protocol for Windows through Windows 98, NetBEUI is a NETBIOS-compatible (**NET**work **B**asic **I**nput/**O**utput **S**ystem) protocol — pronounced by techies as "net-buoy" — that facilitates communication with other NETBIOS machines, including Windows for Workgroups and Windows NT server.
- **Microsoft IPX/SPX.** A Novell NetWare-compatible protocol that you can use with an existing Novell network; Novell also offers its own version of the protocol that may offer some advantages to users.

Telephone Line Networks

A specialized form of interconnection is a telephone line network that uses existing telephone wiring in a home or small office to share files, printers, or Internet access.

Although they are a bit slower and sometimes subject to more problems than a traditional 10Base-T network, phone line networks are inexpensive and easier to set up in places where you can't or don't want to run cables through the walls.

Current specifications for phone line networks let you network as many as 25 computers and permit transfer of data at the same time as the wires are used for phone calls.

The principal difference between a phone line network and a local area network is that the phone line adapter (like a modem) converts digital data into analog waves to travel along the two-wire phone lines.

Phone line adapters use the same small plastic plugs, called an RJ-11, employed by telephones.

The adapters employ a technology called *frequency division multiplexing* that splits the available bandwidth on the telephone line into slices. This technology takes advantage of the fact that a basic telephone call uses only a small portion of the available

Ch
20

range of frequencies on the wires in your home or office. The system maintains the slice for voice communication, allowing data and voice to use the same set of wires. (You can even use the same phone line for a DSL Internet connection, because that technology uses yet another section of the bandwidth.)

Most telephone line networks use a peer-to-peer topology in which every computer on the network is connected to every other device; packets pass from PC to PC and other devices until they reach the address specified in the packet.

The original specification for home phone networks, HomePNA 1.0, had a speed limit of 1 megabit per second; HomePNA 2.0 boosted the top speed to 10 megabits per second, the same as 10Base-T. Under development are devices able to communicate at 100 megabits per second.

As I have noted, telephone networks can be problematic if the quality of the wires or connectors in your home or office is less than optimal. If you have more than one telephone line, you'll have to ensure that all devices in the network are attached to the same pair of wires. And the total length of wire within the phone network cannot exceed about 500 feet, which is probably not a problem in a home but may exceed the distance in a medium-sized office.

Power Line Networks

Yet another alternative to laying cable to connect devices within the home is to use the electrical grid; after years of attempts, this technology has been perfected for most installations.

In theory, this technology is similar to phone line networking, applying its own modulated signal to the electrical current already moving through the wires. In practice, though, electrical power line networking faces some difficult challenges due to challenges from appliances and other electronic equipment on the same circuit. Among the noisiest devices in the house—in electrical terms—are halogen lamps, large-draw motors, such as refrigerators and air conditioners, and electric heaters and hair dryers. And

unlike the controlled, closed loop of an Ethernet system, devices turn on and off and the electricity itself can vary in voltage and other characteristics.

One of the leading product lines is the Linksys family of Instant PowerLine products. They are capable of transporting up to 14 megabits per second of voice, video, and Internet data over residential wiring. Linksys employs a technology called Orthogonal Frequency Division Multiplexing, which combines a number of frequencies to form a single signal for transmission on the medium; the scheme allows the network to adjust to changing conditions on the wire, turning on or off appropriate frequencies.

Data carried on the electrical wiring of a house travels as far as the nearest transformer, which could mean that information might be accessible in neighboring homes. The Linksys system minimizes transmission out of the local system and adds encryption to protect the security of the data.

Wireless Networks

A wireless LAN is similar to a wired Ethernet, except without the wires. Data is transmitted over radio waves, with information broken up into packets that identify the address of the sender and recipient.

Each network adapter has its own ID number that serves as an address. Transmitters monitor the stream of traffic on the network, waiting for a break in which to send out a packet of information.

In a peer-to-peer network, each PC has its own transmitter and receiver capable of communication with other devices within the same network and within its operating range.

In a hub-and-spoke network, each PC has its own adapter that communicates with a fixed access point transceiver with its own antenna. In this design, the transmitter can send packets to other devices or link to a wired Ethernet network.

Bluetooth and Wi-Fi Wireless

To hear from its supporters, Bluetooth will be the greatest thing since sliced microprocessor wafers. This technology is a way to cut the cord between PCs, printers, telephones, and the Internet.

Bluetooth is a low-power communication medium that uses the 2.4 GHz radio band at a data transmission speed of 1 Mbps; actual throughput is about 720 Kbps. The maximum distance between a Bluetooth device and an access point is 30 feet.

The 2.4 GHz band is considered an industrial, scientific, and medical band, open to unlicensed devices for short-range communication. Other devices in that band include garage door openers, recent cordless phones, and baby monitors. Bluetooth employs several high-tech solutions to attempt to avoid interference, including frequency hopping.

In a Bluetooth world, computers would meet and greet cell phones and PDAs as their owners entered a room, laptops and handhelds could surf the Web in airports, hotel lobbies, and meeting rooms, and eventually nearly every consumer appliance — microwaves, refrigerators, and televisions, to name a few — could communicate with other devices about needs and wants.

The market, though, responded with a very cautious wait-and-see attitude.

Two reasons were given for the slower-than-expected embrace. In its first version, the technology proved prone to interference and incompatibility, and the price for production of the Bluetooth chipset was higher than hoped for through the end of 2001.

Bluetooth was developed in 1994 at Ericsson labs where researchers were working on new cell phone technologies. Several years later, an Intel technician and amateur historian gave the standard its unusual name in remembrance of Harald Bluetooth, a Scandinavian king who brought together the two warring communities of Denmark and Norway in the tenth century.

But competition from another wireless technology, originally envisioned as complementary to Bluetooth, may become a serious impediment to its success.

IEEE 802.11b, or *Wi-Fi*, is a wireless local area network that directly connects devices to an Internet network at speeds approaching broadband cable or DSL connections.

Wi-Fi can link devices as far as 300 feet away from the access point and can communicate at speeds of up to 11 Mbps; on the downside, Wi-Fi requires much more power than Bluetooth. Wi-Fi uses the same 2.4 GHz band.

If transmitters are close together, Bluetooth radio waves sometimes disrupt Wi-Fi connections. Future versions of Wi-Fi are expected to move up to the less-used 5 GHz band.

Both technologies could coexist if, for example, Bluetooth connects small, battery-powered devices, such as cell phones and PDAs, to an access point and Wi-Fi links laptops to the Internet.

Microsoft chose to have it both ways, at least at first, backing both Bluetooth and Wi-Fi, but then supporting only Wi-Fi in Windows XP.

Infrared Systems

Infrared, most familiar to users of television remote controls, is used to connect individual pairs of devices, such as laptops and PCs and PCs and printers.

HomeRF is intended for use in homes to connect computers and multimedia devices. An adaptation of the 802.11 standard, it can communicate at speeds of about 1.6 Mbps.

An *infrared (IR) port* is a serial connection that dispenses with cables between the PC and devices.

Infrared connections have a lot of appeal as offices become more and more complex, and electronic clutter on the desktop and the floor becomes more of an issue.

IR ports are essentially serial ports. They use similar connectivity protocols, and their speed is similar to a serial port. The difference is that you don't have to physically connect two devices for them to exchange information.

Ch 20

Even if you don't have an IR port on your computer (or if you have one and haven't used it), you probably use IR interfaces every day. Most television remote controls use infrared signaling, for example.

Infrared controllers and data I/O ports use IR radiation as the carrier of information. IR radiation is at a frequency lower than visible light (below red light) but higher than microwaves. The low end of the visible spectrum starts with radiation that has a wavelength over about 700 nanometers (a nanometer is one-billionth of a meter). Microwaves top out with a wavelength of 1 millimeter and range down to about 30 centimeters. IR communications devices range in wavelength from 0.85 micrometer to 0.90 micrometer. A micrometer is one-millionth of a meter.

You may have heard about IR radiation in connection with low-light or no-light photography or remote sensing imaging. All objects give off IR radiation directly proportional to their temperature.

The bottom line is that IR radiation is at a pretty high frequency. It has limited range as a communication tool, but it can be modulated in much the same way as RF waves or laser light. This invisible light communication enables you to place a peripheral device, such as a printer, personal information manager, calculator, or a laptop computer, close to your desktop or laptop machine and send and receive information.

IR ports are similar to USB ports in that a lot of laptops and other devices include the port, but any two devices may or may not be compatible with each other. Windows 98 and later versions include built-in support for IR ports, resulting in improved functionality and better compatibility.

Many manufacturers and equipment designers work with the specifications of the IrDA, the Infrared Data Association, which is an organization of some 160 companies. The organization's stated purpose is "to create an interoperable, low cost, low power, half-duplex serial data interconnection standard that supports a walk-up, point-to-point user model that is adaptable to a wide range of appliances and devices."

IrDA specifications detail IR frequencies, communications distances, and other physical characteristics of the interface as well as the software specifications used to conduct the actual data transfer. For example, IrDA specifications say that the IR interface is designed for communications over a one-meter range with a +/− 15-degree cone from the center of the transmitting device. This standard is important, because you want to be able to connect two devices without having to carefully place them, just so, beside each other, but at the same time you don't want to connect simultaneously to all the IR devices in the office around you. A 15-degree spread was determined to be just about right.

Additional hardware specifications ensure that IR ports use as little power as possible to make them go easy on the batteries in your laptop or other devices, and they should be virtually immune to external noise and interference while achieving data transfer rates of 115.2 Kbps. The standard also allows for a medium speed of 1.152 Mbps (standard serial port speed, expressed a little differently) and a high-speed, 4 Mbps mode that uses PPM (pulse position modulation) connections. The higher speeds are used for such applications as printer interfaces. The lower rates may be used for computer-to-computer connections. But with technology evolution, the higher rates are likely to become more common. With older devices you may connect at speeds of 9,600 bps or even slower.

The IR interface is basically a serial port that uses an 8N1 (8 data bit, no parity, and one stop bit) much like your modem or serial printer. Special hardware may also use a parallel port connection at the higher data rates as well.

A couple of differences exist between your IR port and your conventional serial port. The transmit cycles (the amount of time the interface is up or on to represent a 1 data bit) are much shorter with IR, and IR interfaces are capable of only half-duplex operation. In other words, information can flow in only one direction at a time.

The software protocol used to transfer data is similar to a network with different layers designed to handle different parts of the communications task. Lower layers are dedicated to establishing a connection, error control, and other tasks. At the top is something called tiny TP, a subset of TCP/IP (transfer control protocol/Internet protocol), which is the standard of communications on Unix networks and the Internet, and some FTP (file transfer protocol) functionality. Tiny TP is basically a flow control protocol layer that performs the actual file transfer between devices.

Increasingly, laptop computers and other mobile devices include IR interfaces. You also can add an IR interface to your desktop machine if it doesn't already have one.

Support for infrared communication is included from Windows 98 through current versions; the W95IR.EXE infrared port driver can be added to Windows 95. (The driver file is available through Microsoft's Knowledge Base at `www.microsoft.com/support`).

At the Web site, click the Search button on the toolbar, type infrared driver, and press Enter. Choose the driver download from the resulting articles and follow the on-screen instructions from there. Of course you need this driver and an IR port installation on both devices that you want to communicate with each other. Use Add/Remove Programs from the Control Panel to install this file after it is downloaded.

After you have this driver installed, installing IR port connectivity is relatively simple:

1. **Open the Control Panel.**
2. **Double-click the Infrared icon.** The Infrared Device Wizard launches.
3. **Click Next to move to the next Wizard screen where you can choose the manufacturer of your infrared device.** Doing this is akin to installing a modem. Yes, there are modem standards and, yes, all modems use a serial connection but no, all modems are not created equal. You have to configure your IR port in much the same way as you would a new modem. If your IR hardware isn't listed, choose Have Disk on the Wizard dialog. Hopefully you have an install disk that came with your computer or IR port.

4. **Continue the Wizard install.** Follow instructions as they are presented.

If you have problems with your IR port, the most likely gremlins are the driver software (you've chosen the wrong manufacturer, for example), a loose power connection, or physical interference with the IR beam. Check the software installation from the System folder in the Control Panel. Click the Device Manager tab and select Infrared Communication Device. If a yellow exclamation point appears beside the driver information, something is wrong with the driver. Click the device entry and choose Properties for more information. If you see an error message in the General tab of the Properties dialog box, you have either a driver or hardware problem.

Check the Driver tab of the Properties dialog box to make sure that the correct driver is installed. If so, look to the hardware. Maybe a connection from the external IR LED to the motherboard or other internal device is loose. Is there an obstruction in front of the IR LED? Carrying a laptop or other device around in a case and using it in different locations can result in lint or other foreign material inside the tiny LED port. The IR interface is designed to be tolerant of such interference, but it can't stand an outright obstruction.

Be sure to run these same checks on both devices. Both devices must be functioning properly for communication to take place.

Internet Security

As I have noted, cable modem and DSL connections are especially vulnerable to attacks because they are connected to the Internet anytime they are turned on; they receive an IP (Internet Protocol) address from the service provider and hold on to that address for as long as they are powered on and connected to the cable or telephone line. In addition, in most cases, that IP address is assigned from a particular range that belongs to major ISPs, making it that much easier for a malevolent hacker to troll through a group of

Ch 20

addresses in search of an open door. And the high bandwidth of a cable or DSL mode — the capacity behind the term broadband — makes it easier for some hackers to pump a huge amount of code through an open machine in a very short period of time.

By contrast, a dial-up telephone connection to the Internet is usually transitory, existing only for the length of a session and using a new IP address each time.

Many broadband connections attach to a computer through an Ethernet connection. Further, many broadband links are shared over a network. For that reason, I'll deal with Internet security here as a network issue.

About TCP/IP ports

To understand a bit about the security vulnerability of a PC connected to the Internet, it's worthwhile to learn about the "ports" that a computer opens to the world under the TCP/IP scheme.

For example, to connect as a client to an e-mail application running on a remote server your computer connects to the port associated with the Simple Mail Transfer Protocol (SMTP), typically assigned to port 25.

Similarly, the Hypertext Transfer Protocol (HTTP), the key to the World Wide Web, uses TCP port 80. A list of some of the most common assigned TCP ports is in Table 20-TCPTCP.

TABLE 20-1: Common TCP/IP Services With Assigned Port Numbers	
PING	7
FTP	20 and 21
Telnet	23
HTTP (World Wide Web)	80
SMTP (E-mail)	25
Windows file and print sharing	137-139
Registered ports	1024-49151
Dynamic or private ports	49152-65535

When a computer opens a port, it monitors that location for appropriately addressed packets; a packet arriving at port 25, for example, is sent to the computer's e-mail application.

A hacker looks for open ports. In addition to doorways for the Web and e-mail, one of the most commonly attacked ports on client computers is 137, used by Windows for file and print sharing over a local area network (LAN). Microsoft — the creator of this vulnerability — and many security experts recommend that sharing be disabled on the Internet connection of any computer directly connected to the Internet. Of course, that could disrupt the facilities of a LAN; in practice, a hardware firewall should provide sufficient protection from intrusion, especially in combination with a software equivalent.

Other areas of particular danger include open FTP ports, personal Web sites, and remote-access programs, such as pcAnywhere.

Some virus programs, including so-called Trojan horse programs, sneak into machines as attachments to e-mail or downloaded programs; some of these programs open a port to the Internet without the user's knowledge.

I recommend that you check the status of your computer's ports — and their ability to hide behind a hardware or software firewall — by visiting a port-checking site. One such site is Shields Up at www.grc.com, operated by longtime utility programmer Steve Gibson and Gibson Research Corporation.

Internet firewalls

A firewall is intended to stop the spread of damage. Cars have a firewall between the engine and the interior of the passenger cabin. Big buildings and cruise ships have them in strategic locations.

In personal computer terms, a firewall is a barrier against intrusion and leakage by outsiders trying to gain access to your data or cause mischief on your system.

Every Internet user, especially those using broadband connections, such as cable modems and DSL links, needs to pay attention to security. Broadband links are usually on all the time, making them especially attractive targets for malevolent snoops trolling the Internet.

The Internet is a fast-moving stream of billions of small snippets of information, called packets. When your PC is connected, it is sticking an electronic toe into the stream looking for packets that are addressed to you. Going the other way, when you click an Internet link or send a page of information, your machine is creating a packet with your return address and a recipient.

Hackers and snoops let loose on the Internet packets that are like skeleton keys, jiggling the doors of millions of PCs until they find one they can open. The odds of one of these packets breaking into a specific machine in this way are very low; however, the fact that so many millions of machines are connected to the Internet makes it likely that sooner or later some machine somewhere is going to be attacked.

A firewall works by standing between your computer and the Internet, examining every data packet sent to or from your PC. Based on a set of criteria established by the manufacturer and updated and adjusted by the user, the firewall decides whether to block a packet or let it pass.

The most common type of device is called an application gateway firewall, also known as a *proxy*. The rules for the firewall can be set to check packets against a particular list of addresses or to set specific limits on the actions of particular applications. For example, the proxy could block downloads or prevent a packet from initiating a deletion or change of a file.

Other firewall designs include *packet filters*, which only allow entrance to packets from specified addresses, and *circuit-level* firewalls that only permit communication with specific computers and Internet service providers.

The newest and most advanced design is stateful inspection firewalls; these devices actually read the contents of packets and block those that are determined to be harmful or an unauthorized threat to privacy.

Software firewalls

A slightly less expensive alternative is a software-based personal firewall.

These programs run within your PC, so they are much closer to your data than is an external hardware firewall. But a properly designed and maintained software firewall is able to monitor against intrusion attempts and block most assaults. It can also provide security settings that protect your private information.

You can purchase a standalone personal firewall or obtain one as part of a suite of utilities.

I worked with Norton Internet Security from Symantec (www.symantec.com), which includes a firewall, antivirus software, and other utilities including the ability to block or control pop-up ads and cookies.

Other well-regarded utilities are BlackIce Defender from Network Ice (www.networkice.com), ZoneAlarm from Zone Labs (www.zonelabs.com), and McAfee.com Personal Firewall (www.mcafee.com).

How a firewall works

The two most common designs for software firewalls are *packet-filtering routers* and *proxy servers*.

Packet filters exist at the network level of the seven-layer Open System Interconnection (OSI) model or the equivalent IP level of the TCP/IP model. They work by examining the source and destination addresses and ports in individual IP packets and comparing them against known threats and suspected sources. They work quickly and do not affect network performance greatly.

Proxy servers offer a higher level of security, monitoring Internet traffic at the highest, application level of the OSI or

Ch 20

TCP/IP model. Users can specify which applications can access the Internet, and which types of incoming packets can get past the firewall. The price for the extra safety is a more significant effect on network performance.

Firewalls also set up machines to block intrusions at specific ports unless you allow them; for example, port 7 would otherwise respond to "pinging" by port scanners in search of open ports. A ping utility sends a packet to a particular address and measures the time it takes for a reply from that site to arrive; the name comes from a utility called Packet Internet Groper.

Hardware firewalls often use a technique called Network Address Translation (NAT), acting as a physical gateway between the Internet and a local area network. The entire LAN appears as a single IP address on the Internet; on the network side, each client PC receives its own private IP address, and that information is not available to the Internet. Intruders cannot find open ports on attached computers because the Internet appears to end at the gateway.

An expansion of NAT is called *stateful* port inspection; in this design the firewall also examines all inbound packets to make sure that they match the source of an earlier outbound request. Inbound traffic from the Internet is only allowed to the computers on the network when the firewall finds a matching entry in its internal records that shows that the communication exchange began on your side of the firewall.

Yet another firewall design is a piece of software that makes the PC emulate a hardware gateway, acting as a "proxy" for a computer. Examples of this include WinProxy. Microsoft Windows 98SE, Windows 2000, Windows Me, and Windows XP allow Internet Connection Sharing, a form of proxy software. Experts recommend the addition of a software firewall to proxy software to fully protect the system.

Windows XP includes a basic personal firewall called Internet Connection Firewall (ICF). The built-in firewall is intended to work in conjunction with Internet Connection Sharing (ICS), a software component of current versions of Windows that allows multiple PCs to work with a single Internet connection. Microsoft recommends enabling ICF on the Internet connection of any computer directly connected to the Internet. ICF should not be enabled on other computers on the network because it will interfere with some network functions; the other computers will be protected by the firewall on the PC with the direct connection.

ICF can also be enabled on a single computer connected to the Internet through a dial-up, DSL, or cable modem; however, it should not be used on a virtual private network because it will interfere with file sharing. As a stateful firewall, it will block any incoming traffic that was not initiated by one of the computers on your network; you can allow specific inbound traffic by making an entry in the Services tab.

And ICF is not needed and can cause some problems if your network already has a hardware or software firewall or a proxy server in place.

 WARNING

If you have a network in which computers share an Internet connection but also have the ability to make a direct dial-up connection using a modem, you should enable ICF for the dial-up connection. If you don't, your entire network will be vulnerable through that unprotected connection.

A belt and suspenders solution

On my office network, eight PCs are connected to the Internet through a cable modem.

When I first installed the cable modem, I experimented by having just a single PC connected to the broadband link. On that machine, I installed Norton Internet Security as a software firewall.

The good news is that my machine was never successfully violated, and my personal data did not leak out on the Internet without my permission.

The bad news was the discovery that my system was under regular attack. The firewall reported an average of three attempts at breaking into my machine each day.

The next step was the installation of a Linksys EtherFast 8-port Cable/DSL Router. This device combines an eight-port Ethernet switch to bring together the PCs in my office with a hardware firewall.

I kept the Norton Internet Security in place on the machine at the hub of the network. With both hardware and software firewalls in place, the software firewall has not reported a single attempted intrusion.

Does this mean that you can get by with either a software or a hardware firewall? Probably. If I had to choose between the two, I would take the hardware device because it sits physically outside of my computer rather than on the hard drive within. But being a cautious user, I'm very happy with my inside-and-out, belt-and-suspenders solution. The Linksys hardware device stands guard between the cable modem and my PC, while the Norton Internet Security software sits between Windows and the Internet, receiving regular updates from the Symantec Web site.

SUMMARY

In this chapter, you learned about networks, gateways, and routers. In the next chapter, I explore the rules of backing up regularly.

Ch 20

Chapter 21

Living the Good Life: Backing Up Regularly

When it comes to the safety of the data on my machine, I choose to adopt a belt-and-suspenders philosophy. They may not make for the most stylish wardrobe, but your pants won't ever fall down — and your computer data will never completely disappear.

My goal in computer life is to strive toward a fail-safe world where a hardware failure, a software error, or a slip of the fingers at the keyboard is a mere annoyance and not a job-threatening disaster.

Remember that if you're lucky, your hard drive will have a full, healthy, and productive life. And then it will die. It may be tomorrow, or it may be in 10 years, but it will fail. It's up to you to be prepared for the hereafter.

In this chapter, I explore the best methods for protecting your data before a problem occurs, and some utilities to recover data from a system that has failed.

CROSS-REFERENCE

In Chapter 11, I discuss some of the hardware devices that can be employed for backup.

A Basic Data Protection Strategy

To protect your data, follow these steps:

1. Make backups of essential data onto removable media, such as CDs, Zip disks, tapes, or other devices.
2. Install and keep current a disk diagnostic and maintenance utility.
3. Run defragmenting and surface analyzer utilities regularly.
4. Enable the Windows Recycle Bin to allow you to undelete files that were mistakenly trashed.
5. Perform Step 1 regularly, and test your backup data on the original machine and on another machine.

You can prevent most data loss with good backup habits. If you keep copies of your data that are only a few hours old, the worst thing that can happen if the computer or one of its disk drives fails is the loss of a few hours' worth of work. I describe the three levels of backup in the following sections.

Current document backup

The first level is current document backup, a feature common to many advanced application programs.

This book was written using Microsoft Word 2002. In that program — and most other major word processors — you can instruct the application to make backups of your files as you work on them. In the latest version of Word, the facility is called Auto Recover. Other programs refer to the same sort of function as Automatic Save or Timed Document Backup.

In my office, I ask Word to update its temporary backup file every three minutes. So if Word, Windows, the operating system, or a piece of hardware causes the PC to lock up, I have a copy of the file that is no more than roughly 2 minutes and 59 seconds old and usually younger.

A current document backup, however, does not protect against the failure of the storage media. If the hard drive fails, you may lose any work since the last time a copy was stored on different media.

Version backup

The second type of backup is version backup.

Microsoft Word has an option called Always Create Backup Copy, and other programs have similar facilities. With this option enabled, any time you save a file, the program makes a copy of the previous version of the file. (The standard filename for the backup under Word is `Backup of {filename}.wbk`.) If you decide that the changes or additions you have made to the current version are not what you want to keep, you can revert to the previous version.

Again, version backup does not protect against the failure of the storage media. If the hard drive fails, you may lose any work since the last time a copy was stored on different media.

Deep storage backups

The third type of backup is what I call "deep storage." These are copies of all your important data files that you maintain on some sort of removable media and keep on a shelf, in a fireproof safe, or in a safe deposit box inside a bank's fireproof safe.

Deep storage guards against the failure of the hard drive in the original machine or the theft of the machine.

Removable media include floppy disks for individual files, high-capacity Zip or Jaz drives, portable hard disks, tape backups, and recordable CD-ROMs.

What files should be backed up?

Concentrate on the data. Everything else can be reconstructed, and a good renovation may be healthy for your system every once in a while.

Here's what I include in my data backups:

- Every data file from my applications, including those from the word processor, spreadsheet, personal finance, and the calendar and address book from my personal data assistant
- Personalized dictionaries and customized Windows desktop and sound themes
- All of the downloaded image files from my digital camera
- Copies of e-mails sent and received
- The address book from my e-mail program

Beyond the data, your operating system also contains hundreds of settings for appearance and actions. Your Internet browser and e-mail program are also customized for appearance, security and privacy, subscriptions, and accounts.

Although you can choose to make a full-mirrored backup of your entire hard drive, including the operating system and applications, you should know some good reasons not to do so. To begin with, you may have difficulty reinstalling an image back to a new or reformatted hard drive. Also, if your operating system or one of its applications was the cause of your system crash — because of a corrupted file or a virus, for example — reinstalling a mirror of the hard drive will simply give you a new copy of the original problem.

A much better plan of action is this: Set up a safe and secure storage place for original installation CDs or diskettes for your Windows operating system and all applications and device drivers.

Keep a notebook nearby in which you list every program, update, and upgrade that you make to your system. If you download a program or a driver over the Internet, make a copy of the pre-installation file and store it with your other originals.

Making deep-storage backups of valuable data presents a logical and procedural dilemma for most users. The whole goal is to make copies that are as current as possible and yet are physically separated from your main computer so that a failure (or theft) does not take away irreplaceable information.

How should you back up?

How often is enough? Answer this question immediately after your hard drive dies.

Every user can come up with his or her best answer. Some users make a backup an unvarying assignment at the end of every day: In my office, I perform backups each night before I straggle out of the office, and I have been known to do an extra backup in the middle of the day any time I've been working on an especially important project.

Over the course of two decades of personal computing, I've used half a dozen different backup devices — beginning with a stack of floppy disks, moving on to a few designs of removable platter hard drives, a tape drive, and most recently, a combination of a recordable CD drive and a large external hard drive.

Floppy disk backups

Once upon a time, floppy disks were a viable option for backups, back when an IBM PC-AT came equipped with a 20MB hard drive. The entire disk could be backed up to a stack of about 15 floppies.

Today, though, it is ridiculous to consider storing the contents of a 20GB hard drive on a set of 15,000 or so disks.

However, some users use floppy disks to make copies of individual files they worked on over the course of a day to serve as a short-term repository between full backups. The downside: Files can't be larger than 1.44MB (or about 2.8MB if you use a disk-doubling utility). Also, floppy disks are fragile and easily misplaced, which can be a threat to the security of your files.

Removable storage backups

Removable storage media, including devices like recordable CDs or DVDs, Peerless disks, and tape cartridges, are excellent ways to create backups of your files.

 CROSS-REFERENCE

I discuss many of the available storage devices in Chapter 11.

As previously discussed, most users don't need to store the entire contents of a drive in backup. Also, very few users will ever create more than a few hundred megabytes of data per day. In fact, unless you're working with graphics, video, or audio files, the chances are your daily output of new and changed files is only a few tens of megabytes or less.

With today's large hard drives — new machines ship with a basic disk of 40GB — I consider a CD-R as the smallest reasonable size for a backup device. Recordable CDs can store as much as 800MB of data per disk, and they offer a reasonable recording speed. DVD-Rs can store as much as 4.7GB and will become very attractive for backup purposes in coming years as prices of the drives and media decline toward the level of today's CD-Rs.

CD-Rs are not reusable, but they are inexpensive, thus allowing users to maintain an archive of the day-by-day or week-by-week status of their files.

Iomega's Peerless disks store 10GB or 20GB on a removable cartridge, making them very attractive for large files.

Another easy-to-use backup device is an external hard drive. Modern machines can connect to these standalone drives through a USB, FireWire, or SCSI port. The drives can remain in place atop the PC, or they can be disconnected and stored in a fireproof safe, in a briefcase that you take with you, or anywhere else away from the machine that they back up.

For huge hard drives and commercial operations where it is important to maintain a continuous stream of transaction-by-transaction changes to a database, the solution often involves tape drives, capable of storing hundreds of gigabytes of data. Tape drives, however, are slow and data is not stored in a random-access form; the tape must be fast-forwarded or rewound to particular locations to yield a particular block.

A Real-Life Backup Policy

Analyze the patterns of work in your own office to see what scheme makes the most sense for you. In my office, my backup procedure in 2002 works like this:

- **Daily.** As I write them, all files are backed up elsewhere on the hard drive every three minutes by Microsoft Word. At the end of each day, I use a CD-R to burn a disc that contains the folders for the projects I worked on that day.
- **Every other day.** I make a copy of the complete contents of the My Documents folder of my machine on a Maxtor 40GB external USB 2.0 hard drive.
- **Every Friday.** I send a complete image of the My Documents folder across my office Ethernet to a SCSI drive on a file server machine.

If you are really concerned about the security of your data — whether you worry about loss caused by the failure of a hard drive, the theft of a computer, or from fire — I suggest that you store your removable media backups in a fireproof safe.

 WARNING

Remember that backup media will eventually fail, just like any floppy disk or hard drive. Plan on retiring backup tapes or removable disks at least once a year. Most CD-Rs are expected to have a shelf life of five to ten years.

I routinely practice one special backup task: If I am going to be out of the office on a long trip, I create a CD-R with a complete image of my document subdirectory on a CD-ROM and throw it in my briefcase. This is a protection against a catastrophe while I am away and a most valuable emergency disk in case I absolutely must get into one of my files while I am on the road. Sometimes I also copy active files to my laptop computer for the same reason.

Backup Utilities

If you are careful and consistent in organizing your hard drive and understand the types of files in your system, it is possible to manually identify files to be backed up by using the facilities of Windows Explorer.

However, the Windows operating system offers some niceties that allow you to make automated, selective backups. The operating system can distinguish between new files and those that have already been archived (backed up). This allows you to make incremental backups that make copies of just those files that are not already in storage.

You can also purchase third-party backup programs that include many customizable settings and advanced features.

Windows Backup Utility

The ever-engulfing Microsoft maw added a file backup program to Windows 95/98, adding new features in later versions, including the current Windows XP.

The Windows Backup Utility can copy the entire contents of your hard disk or specific files; as part of a program of regular backups, it can also manage the archiving of just those files that have been changed since the last backup operation was performed.

As is the case with most of the utilities that have been added to Windows over the years, Backup performs well and reliably but lacks some of the features and polish of third-party equivalents.

To start Backup, go to the Start menu and point to Programs, then Accessories, and then System Tools. Then click on Backup.

Note that Backup is not automatically a part of Windows 98 or Windows XP Home Edition; if the utility is not listed in System Tools, you'll have to add it from the Windows installation disk. Under Windows XP Professional, you must sign in as an administrator or backup operator to perform backup tasks.

The Windows XP version includes an option to back up all data plus the System State, which includes essential configuration information in the registry and the Active Directory database, if used. (System State can be backed only on a local computer, and not on a remote device.)

Windows XP and 2000 users also need to note that although it is possible to back up and restore data on FAT16, FAT32, or NTFS volumes, if your original data is held on an NTFS volume, it is possible to lose data and some file and folder features if the backup file is later restored to FAT16 or FAT32.

By default, Backup files are given the filename extension of .bkf, although you can choose any extension.

Third-party backup utilities

You may find some specialized backup products more convenient than Microsoft's offerings. Many of these programs use compression and speed-up routines.

Many hardware vendors offer a backup utility along with removable drive devices. For example, Iomega includes a set of Windows utilities with the company's Zip drives.

Among leading backup utility products is Retrospect Backup, from Dantz Development Corporation; for more information, consult www.dantz.com or www.betterbackup.com. Retrospect Backup schedules progressive backups to hard drives, tape drives, and CD drives, and includes network facilities for systems and portables.

Norton Ghost 2002, from Symantec, provides high-performance utilities for system upgrading, backup, and recovery. It writes disk images directly to many popular CD-R/CD-RW drives. Facilities include fast PC-to-PC cloning by using high-speed parallel, USB, or network connections.

You can add files to previously created images, thus eliminating the need to reclone the entire disk to back up new contents. The program can automatically size destination partitions to help streamline the cloning process. Norton Ghost is sold as a standalone product and is also included as a component of the Norton Systemworks suite. For more information, consult www.symantec.com.

Veritas Backup MyPC provides automated protection with point-and-click scheduling. The program restores data and applications during disaster recovery without the need to reinstall the operating system or backup software. For information, consult www.veritas.com.

Backing Up Outlook Express E-mail Files

For many users, your e-mail correspondence makes up an important part of your business or personal life. Ask yourself this question: Would it be a problem if one day you turned on your machine and all of the mail you have received and sent for the past year or so had disappeared?

It's good practice to make backup copies of your e-mail files on a regular basis, so in case of disaster you can reconstruct them. And when you upgrade to a new computer or a new hard drive, you can also bring your old e-mail files with you.

Windows XP includes a Files and Settings Transfer Wizard that will bring over e-mail as well as preferences and settings for your Internet connection and other applications. You can also purchase utility programs from third parties that will do the same for earlier versions of Windows.

Your e-mail files are stored in special file formats, stored away in a less-than-obvious location on your hard drive.

Here are the steps to back up your e-mail in Outlook Express; other mail programs are organized similarly.

1. Minimize or close all applications.
2. Right-click on an empty section of the desktop, and select New and then click Folder.
3. Right-click the new folder and select Rename; type a name for the folder, such as **OE_BACKUP**.
4. Open Outlook Express and click the Inbox that you want to back up.
5. Click Edit and then Select All; all mail in the box should be highlighted;
6. Right-click the selected e-mail and drag it into the new folder on your desktop; release the mouse button and click Copy Here.

To back up your Address Book from Outlook Express:

1. Minimize or close all applications.
2. Right-click on an empty section of the desktop, and select New and then click Folder.
3. Right-click the new folder and select Rename; type a name for the folder, such as **OE_ADDRESS**.
4. Open Outlook Express and click Address on the toolbar.
5. Click one of the Addresses in the Address Book to highlight it, and then click Edit and Select All to highlight all of the contacts.
6. Right-click the highlighted items and select Copy.
7. Double-click the new folder to open it; right-click anywhere inside the folder and select Paste.

Testing Your Backups

I know from personal experience that a good backup policy carried out according to plan is only part of what you need to help ensure against data loss. I know of at least two fairly large companies who learned this lesson the hard way. One particular company was storing many gigabytes of company and customer data in a RAID assembly across multiple computers and hard drives. The RAID configuration by itself should have been enough to ensure against losing any data. After all, the information was automatically mirrored across multiple computers on the network, using multiple disk drives. Even so, this company conducted daily, automatic backup to high-capacity streaming tape. The backup tapes were removed from the office each morning and a full weekly set was stored onsite, as well as at a remote location.

Foolproof, right?

Wrong!

Something went wrong with the RAID system one day and the data couldn't be recovered. No one was particularly worried. A new, high-speed computer was positioned on the network, a very large capacity hard drive was installed, and the current backup tape (only hours old) was put in the tape drive. After a full day's work and despite receiving help from the manufacturers of the tape drive, the backup software, and the computer, this company's backup files could not be restored. Though employees had religiously made backups, they had never tried to restore files from them. The tapes were useless.

The lesson: You should regularly take one of your backup disks or tapes and restore the data to a hard drive that you aren't using for live data, an extra drive on the network, or a spare drive or directory on your primary computer. If you can restore and read the data satisfactorily, then your backup plan really is complete. Otherwise, you need to find out what is causing problems and fix it before you really need this backup information.

Summary

This chapter discussed ways to protect and recover your data. After making copies to protect against disaster, the careful computer user does everything possible to guard against them ever being needed. In the next chapter, I explore some capable electronic physician's assistants that give your system a checkup and help repair small problems before they become major headaches.

Chapter 22

Antivirus, Utility, and Diagnostic Programs

When the ship's doctor of a Federation starship needs to find out what's going on inside an injured or ill Star Trek crewmember, he or she waves a tricorder over the patient's body. When you're on your own trek to figure out what ails your PC, the best thing you've got is a good diagnostic program.

When it comes time to fix whatever the diagnostic has found, the best tool may be a specialized utility program.

And when it comes to guarding against disease — of the computer sort — no computer user should turn on the power switch without an antivirus program in place.

This chapter examines the various types of diagnostic programs available, plus configuration utilities used to prevent hardware conflicts when you are installing new boards. In the next chapter of this book, I explore some of the very useful utilities that are part of current editions of Windows.

The Modern Plague: Viruses and Worms

A *virus* is a self-replicating piece of computer code that can attach itself to files or applications with the intent of making your computer do something that you don't want it to do.

And then there are just-slightly less annoying worms and Trojan horse files.

A *worm* is a self-replicating program that insinuates itself into computers and out through network connections to infect any machine on the network, taking storage space and slowing down the computer but not altering or deleting other files.

A *Trojan horse* doesn't replicate itself but instead sneaks into your machine and searches out information, such as passwords, e-mail addresses, and account names and numbers, with the goal of transmitting that data back to the author.

Whatever they are called, these malicious codes are sometimes annoyances and sometimes major disruptions to the way we run our businesses and our personal lives. Several times in the past few years a new virus has swept around the world, spread over the burgeoning links of the Internet. Thousands of other times, minor outbreaks have infected clusters of computers in offices or on networks.

You must understand two things in order to protect your machine and fix your PC when it becomes infected: how viruses spread, and how you can inoculate and doctor your machine.

Malicious code can enter a PC through almost any connection that it has to the outside: The most common ways are through an infected floppy disk, e-mail, or a downloaded file. A hacker coming in through an Internet connection can also plant an infection.

Viruses are generally classified into five major types:

- **Boot Sector Virus.** A piece of code that hides in the boot sector — the place on a hard drive or floppy disk that the operating system goes to first to boot up the machine. This sort of virus can make it impossible to boot the disk, or can damage the essential file attribute table that keeps track of the location of files on the drive.
- **File Virus.** This code attaches itself to executable applications.
- **Macro Virus.** A simple but effective code that hides within a data file, including word processor and spreadsheet files, and modifies a common embedded command to do something else, usually malicious.
- **Multipartite Virus.** A hybrid code that infects both executable files and the boot sector, allowing it to spread quickly and reinfect your system repeatedly.
- **Polymorphic Virus.** A code that changes some of its elements each time it replicates in an attempt to defeat antivirus scanners.

Adding an antivirus program

The good news is that capable antivirus software can detect nearly all types of known viruses and sniff out new ones, but it is absolutely essential that the software is updated regularly to keep it current with the latest known and anticipated threats.

Even with antivirus software in place, you also need to practice safe computing. Scan any shareware manually, and make sure you never leave a floppy disk in your computer when you turn off the machine where it may attempt to boot — and infect — your machine the next time you start up the PC.

Be very wary of any e-mail with attachments, especially if they are from people you don't know. Delete any suspect e-mails without opening them; send messages to people you know to confirm that they sent you a file and that they believe it to be virus-free. (And make sure your antivirus software scans your e-mail anyway.)

Choosing your antivirus software

Antivirus software generally works in two ways: by scanning for known viruses in search of *signatures* (identified blocks of code), and by employing heuristic intelligence that looks for virus-like activity by any program.

Either way, you'll want to set up your software to automatically stop the progress of a virus or virus-like program and confirm with you whether you want to zap the bug or let the innocent program proceed.

Any antivirus program is better than none at all. Here are some of the best programs:

- **Norton Antivirus.** Available as a standalone product, or as part of a utilities suite such as Norton SystemWorks or Norton Internet Security. The package includes automatic updating of virus definitions as well as protection for incoming and outgoing e-mail and a guard against malicious Internet scripts. For more information, consult `www.symantec.com`.
- **McAfee VirusScan.** This capable antivirus program also includes an integrated personal firewall. For more information, consult `www.mcafeeathome.com/products/virusscan`.
- **PC-cillin 2000.** Another worthy competitor with claims of greater speed and smaller memory demands. For more information, consult `www.antivirus.com/pc-cillin/products`.

You can purchase antivirus software over the Web, from mail order houses, and from many local computer and office supply stores. In addition, you can purchase Web-based subscriptions to some antivirus software that update your virus database automatically via the Internet. Check all of the Web sites noted in the previous list for this feature. In many cases, the annual fee for this continuous update feature costs about the same as purchasing the software once, but you can get daily database updates. If you spend a lot of time on the Internet or if you install a lot of software — especially shareware or software swapped among friends — I recommend a subscription service as the best way to avoid virus infections.

Diagnostic Utilities

Diagnostic programs can give your machine a checkup and help you with treatment, but they're not much good at autopsies. Here's what I mean: Your PC has to be able to start up and boot from a floppy or hard disk in order to run a software-based diagnostic program. If all you hear when you flick the switch is stony silence, you're going to have to figure out what is wrong by yourself (with the help of this book, of course).

Some diagnostic programs are also dependent on the presence of a working copy of DOS or Windows; others are capable of running off their own limited equivalent to DOS or with the assistance of an emergency boot disk that you were asked to create when you first installed the diagnostic.

Here's another unfortunate fact: Even the very best diagnostic program still requires a capable supercomputer to interpret its findings. That supercomputer is your brain.

No matter how good the diagnostic program, none is able to test every last modular element of your PC. Here are a few examples of real-world problems that are generally beneath a diagnostic program's radar:

- **The health of your power supply.** I've heard the story of one inexperienced technician who replaced four or five hard drives in a row because his diagnostic disk kept reporting sector read/write errors on the drive. A new drive would function well when first installed and then report increasing errors during the all-night read/write testing that the

technician conducted to confirm that the repair was done correctly. Each morning, he examined the error log, saw the new read/write errors, and assumed that the hard disk replacement that he had installed the previous day was defective. Many hard drives later, the true cause was discovered: a bad power supply. The most up-to-date motherboards, though, include a set of diagnostics that can check heat buildup and certain voltage readings.

- **Intermittent hardware problems.** This problem can take the form of a transitory short in a card that happens only when the system is hot, for example. You may be able to deal with the situation by putting a diagnostic program into a repetitive loop and running the machine all night.

- **An interrupt or memory conflict for a device that appears to be turned off or is electrically malfunctioning.** This category includes problems in external cables. For example, a parallel port may be functioning perfectly, but the cable that runs from it to a printer may have a short or may be only partially attached. Once again, the path to diagnostic joy here involves using your own logic — swapping with cables you know to be good or changing printers, for example.

Whole machine, disk/data diagnostics, and system snoopers

I'm going to divide the world of diagnostic programs into the following three categories:

- **Whole machine diagnostics.** These products attempt to test the entire machine. They test memory, the microprocessor, the DMA chips, the numeric coprocessor, the floppy and hard drives, the serial and parallel ports, the video, the mouse, and the keyboard. They also provide full system configuration information, including the interrupt, input/output (I/O) port settings, and memory addresses used by each piece of hardware.

- **Disk/data diagnostics.** These products concentrate on the disk drives and the data structures of the hard disk and/or the floppy disk, painstakingly reading each sector in search of corrupted data. These programs usually include sophisticated data recovery utilities. A typical disk/data diagnostic program provides intensive testing routines, bad sector lockout, file-moving utilities, and a sector-by-sector hard disk editor.

- **System snoopers.** These products report on the hardware and software installed in the computer plus the interrupts, I/O port settings, and addresses used by that hardware; however, they don't attempt to test them. You must know which interrupts, I/O port settings, and memory addresses are in use when you install new cards — especially network, MIDI, fax, and other exotic hardware items. Each expansion card needs its own exclusive interrupt and I/O port setting; a card with a ROM may need a unique memory address range as well. Products in this class are sometimes called *configuration utilities* or *system information utilities.*

Diagnostic programs can't tell you everything, but they are very useful. Because each of these diagnostic programs uncovers slightly different types of problems, you are probably best off investing in one of the disk/data diagnostic programs as well as a whole-machine diagnostic. These diagnostic programs are good, but always remember that your brain, especially if you are an experienced technician, is better. And nothing beats the eyeball when troubleshooting installation problems such as cables, switches, and jumpers. Use the diagnostics and consider their repair recommendations, but don't follow them blindly.

Imagine that your computer is a patient in the hospital. Diagnostic programs are excellent at testing one limb at a time — the serial port, extended memory, or keyboard, for example. The patient must be conscious, though, to report to the doctor, or the tests are useless.

Limitations inherent in the testing process

Suppose that your diagnostic disk tells you that something in a particular system — the floppy drive, for example — is malfunctioning. Is this true? Maybe.

One thing you can be sure of is that something is wrong. It may not be exactly what the diagnostic program is reporting, though. Diagnostics often don't identify which part is bad, only that a particular subsystem is bad. Because any one of several components may cause a given symptom, it is often impossible to know from the diagnostic report exactly which component is to blame. Instead, use the report as your starting point in exploring the system by using the techniques described in this book and in the troubleshooting flowcharts in Appendix G.

System reporting utilities

In many instances, the key to resolving problems in a Windows-based system is the ability to let the operating system count its fingers and toes and tell you what it finds — and what it can't find.

 CROSS-REFERENCE

In Chapter 23, I discuss Device Manager and other essential utilities in current versions of Windows.

Diagnostic and Data Recovery Utilities

Hard disk diagnosis and data recovery are closely allied. You may choose to buy separate programs to perform each function, or you can look for products that combine all features. This section includes descriptions of some of the best products; be sure to check the utilities shelf of your computer retailer or a mail-order catalog for the latest and greatest.

Diagnostic program error messages, your computer's BIOS ROM error messages, and DOS error messages are all based on educated guesses. Use the information that these error messages give you, but remember that they are not infallible. I've listed common error messages in Appendix B, along with suggestions for approaches to try if one of these messages appears on your screen.

American Megatrends, maker of the AMI BIOS as well as a range of utilities and special-purpose hardware, offers AMIDiag, one of the more complete sets of generic hardware diagnostics for consumers. The program detects and checks CPUs from Intel, AMD, Cyrix, SGS Thompson, and Texas Instruments. Component tests examine the processor, memory, floppy and hard drives, CD and DVD drives, video, USB, serial and parallel ports, sound cards, network interfaces, and more. For more information, consult www.ami.com.

Another well-regarded set of generic diagnostic programs is CheckIt, offered by Smith Micro Software (the latest in a series of publishers). The program also includes the Clean & Zip File Management Utility and InoculateIT Antivirus from Computer Associates. For more information, consult www.smithmicro.com/checkit.

Because almost all diagnostic tests require a living, breathing patient (a functioning computer) to run the test and to communicate with the diagnostic software, this sort of software is ideal for torture-testing a running computer. If you must certify that a particular computer is good, you can't beat a good diagnostic program that can be set to test all day or all night without any supervision.

Even this sort of extensive automated checkup has a flaw. The diagnostics programs can test the machine longer, in greater depth, and more creatively than any user ever could — except by using the machine — and therein lies the potential problem. Many technicians run 72 hours of sophisticated diagnostics on a particular machine and then hand the machine to the user, swearing that everything is perfect. Within five minutes of normal use, the machine breaks, and the technician looks like a fool. Nothing is wrong with the diagnostic program, nothing is wrong with the technician, and nothing is wrong with the user. It's just that the user may be asking the computer to do something that the diagnostic program didn't check.

Peter Norton began his empire selling a rather simple unerase utility to computer enthusiasts and clubs when the IBM PC was first introduced. Other products may have some individual elements that are better or offer some specific bells and whistles that may hold special appeal, but overall, Symantec's Norton Utilities offers a pretty complete and well-polished package. The utilities are sold as a standalone package and as part of a suite within Norton SystemWorks.

At the heart of the utility are Norton Disk Doctor and Norton System Doctor, which operate in the background to search out disk and system problems and can launch utilities to repair many problems. System Watch monitors system resources under Windows and alerts you to potential and real problems. Other programs in the Norton series include Norton Uninstall Deluxe, which helps you to remove all of the disparate pieces of programs that were scattered in the far corners of your PC's hard disk during installation under Windows. Norton CrashGuard Deluxe helps protect against many types of PC crashes and screen freezes and includes a system checkup module that looks for problems with files and settings on your system. For more information, consult www.symantec.com.

Another set of utilities is McAfee Utilities, the successor to CyberMedia's First Aid 98. For more information, consult www.mcafee.com.

Disk Analyzers

Surface analysis programs analyze your hard drive by performing a read/write test to see whether the entire surface can reliably hold data. Using ingenious data-repair algorithms, they reconstruct the data in the suspect areas that DOS can't read.

If the boot cluster is damaged, the operating system won't be able to recognize the disk and will display a message such as Non-System Disk, if it can give any message at all. Usually, the machine just locks up. If the FAT is slightly damaged, the DOS command CHKDSK, the improved DOS program SCANDISK, or a data-recovery program may be able to reconstruct the *pointers* (the directions to the next cluster in the chain). If the FAT is unreadable, the pointer information and whatever data the disk contains are lost. Even though the information is actually still on the disk, there is no way to access it in any meaningful form.

CHKDSK, which dates back to the very early versions of DOS, has been in place in the underlying system for Windows from the very start. Under Windows 95/98, Microsoft recommended use of the enhanced SCANDISK program. With the arrival of Windows XP, Microsoft updated CHKDSK, including facilities that make repairs and display information about partitions that use the NTFS system.

Third-party surface analyzers include more complex and thorough tests. Such products include Norton Utilities and SpinRite. You can count on any of these programs to find bad spots, move the data to a safe part of the disk, and mark the bad spots so that they won't be reused. These programs are easy to use and take less than an hour to run on an average-size drive. Their value is in catching bad spots before you lose data.

The best thing about third-party programs like Norton SystemWorks and Norton Utilities is their ability to reconstruct data from a drive that suffers from a corrupted file attribute table or other problems. If the problem seems to be one-of-a-kind, you can thank your foresight in installing the program; if the hard drive is failing, you should make a backup to another drive and replace the failing drive.

If the disk has been damaged by fire or water or if the disk surface has been damaged by the actual crash of the read/write head into the surface, I recommend that you use a commercial data recovery service. You can find listings of such companies in the back pages of many of the major computer magazines and on the Web.

Aside from physical damage to a disk, probably the trickiest data recovery problem is a bad sector in the middle of a long file. If the sector is totally unreadable, the rest of the file may be lost. For example, a tiny error equivalent to an inkblot covering two bad characters on page 13 can make the hard disk lose the rest of this book. DOS and Windows can correct small errors—the equivalent of one bad character—on their own. But no consumer-level program can correct more than 11 bad bits (that's about one-and-a-half 8-bit characters). You did remember to make backups to your data files, right?

Defragmenting Utilities

When you store a file on disk, the operating system puts the file in an available space on the disk. On a freshly formatted disk, the file is stored in a contiguous fashion—one sector after another from the beginning to the end. When you store your next file, it may well begin right at the end of the previous file and continue from there.

Fragmentation occurs when you reopen an existing file and expand it. The operating system may not be able to place the additional sectors of the file immediately after the end of the original file. In fact, for files that you open and change regularly—and most data files are altered many times between creation and completion—the data may be scattered across several places on the disk.

The file attribute table keeps track of where the pieces of each file are and tells the hard drive how to attach the pieces when you ask it to read the file.

However, fragmented files take a bit longer for the hard drive to read and present a danger if the file attribute table is ever damaged. The solution is to defragment files from time to time as part of your regular maintenance duties.

Under Windows, you can initiate a defragmenting process by going to My Computer and highlighting a drive. Right-click and choose Properties and then go to the Tools Tab and choose Defragmentation.

The Windows defrag program will do the job just fine, although on a large drive it can take hours to complete — this is a job I usually leave running overnight.

Several third-party programs do the same work faster and with some additional bells and whistles. Norton Utilities and Norton SystemWorks include Norton Disk Doctor that monitors the status and health of your drives and can manage a faster version of a defragmentation utility. For more information, consult `www.symantec.com`.

A specialized tool is Diskeeper, which claims to be as much as 300 to 500 percent faster than Windows equivalents. It also includes the ability to run invisibly in the background and can prioritize defragmentation to concentrate on essential system files. For more information, consult `www.execsoft.com`.

Sometimes the most useful tools in your kit are things you never thought you'd ever need. DiskMapper from MicroLogic is a road map for your hard disk. It churns away for a while and then returns with a graphical representation of the contents of your drive. You can zoom in on any directory or subdirectory, remove or archive a file, and even launch files from the display. For more information, consult `www.miclog.com`.

SUMMARY

The next chapter examines the extensive troubleshooting and configuration utilities that are built into current versions of Windows.

Chapter 23

In This Chapter:

Windows Troubleshooting and Repairs

Someday, operating systems will meet up with science fiction dreams. "Good morning, Corey," my machine will declare. "I've been feeling a bit slow lately, and I really feel bad about the work you lost yesterday when I had a system crash. I've figured it out, though: That new sound card you installed the other day was arguing with my network interface card. I've rearranged the interrupts, and all is well. While I was at it, I figured out why the Microsoft Office taskbar was hanging up; the driver was corrupted, so I downloaded an updated version. The hard drive was also very badly fragmented so I ran a utility during the night so I'd be ready to fly this morning. Would you like me to compose a symphony in your honor?"

Actually, we are almost there: Modern operating systems, beginning with Windows 95/98 and accelerating with the arrival of Windows XP, include a broad range of tools that allow them to self-configure, make repairs, and help the most complex and capable brain in your office or home — that would be you — troubleshoot more complex problems and make repairs.

At the heart of the magic is Plug-and-Play, which interlinks the system BIOS, hardware devices, and the operating system in a way that allows the computer to configure new hardware components automatically by assigning interrupts, DMA channels, and memory resources without conflicts, and to manage the installation, monitoring, and update of device drivers.

Plug-and-Play began with features incorporated into nearly every PCI adapter; these cards needed to be able to announce their presence to the PC and to be flexible in their demands for system resources. The computer's BIOS was then able to work its way through the various devices installed in the bus and choose the best combination of settings. Most ISA cards are not capable of negotiating with a Plug-and-Play system.

Included in the specification is a wide range of external devices that can identify themselves to the system and work out the kinks of configuration. Plug-and-Play equipment includes intelligent monitors, PC Cards, USB devices, FireWire devices, bidirectional parallel ports, and the latest SCSI hardware.

In some cases, an older ISA card can gain some of the flexibility and functionality of modern devices by using an updated Plug-and-Play driver; check manufacturer's Web sites for updates.

USB devices and most pieces of FireWire equipment are *hot-pluggable*, which means that they can be attached to a computer that is running and will be automatically configured. SCSI devices that are certified for Plug-and-Play use permit automatic configuration of device ID and termination settings as well as dynamic changes to the adapter.

The Device Manager

Current versions of Windows do a pretty good job of spotting many problems with drivers, system resources, some hardware devices, and the operating system itself. The Device Manager, a key component of the System utility on the Control Panel, does much of the snooping and reporting.

As I noted previously in this chapter, the most complex and capable brain in your home or office is not the computer — it's you — at least for the foreseeable future. The Device Manager facility allows users to deal with problems beyond the abilities of the computer to fix, and to make the occasional manual assignment of resources or to force the use of a different device driver.

To display the Device Manager, go to the Control Panel and choose System.

Device Manager is a report card on nearly every piece of hardware in your system, as well as hardware settings, device drivers, and resource allocations.

The facilities of Device Manager allow you to do the following:

- See at a glance an indication of whether Windows believes the hardware on your computer is working properly.
- Disable, enable, and uninstall devices.
- Determine major hardware configuration settings and properties, and make changes to them.
- Learn the identity of device drivers for each device, and see information including the maker of the driver and its version.
- Install updated device drivers, and (in the most current versions of Windows) roll back to the previous version of the driver to undo problems caused by updates.
- Print a summary report of the devices that are installed on your computer; with your permission, (usually) the same information can be supplied over the Internet to support desks or registration systems.

Note that under Windows XP and Windows 2000, you must have administrator status to manage device drivers and make certain changes to configurations and settings.

You can take several routes to open the Device Manager; the most commonly used is to click Start ➪ Control Panel, then double-click System, then on the Hardware tab, click Device Manager.

The goal of the software engineers at Microsoft, in conjunction with Intel and other hardware makers, is an unalloyed world of Plug-and-Play devices, with Windows automatically configuring every device so that it will work without conflicts with other devices when assigning IRQ lines, DMA channels, I/O port addresses, and memory address ranges.

A modern motherboard, in conjunction with current adapters and a current Windows operating system, should allow automatic configuration of almost every device. I say *almost* every device because you can make almost an infinite number of different combinations of devices, chipsets, resources, and configurations; sooner or later, most users run into some sort of conflict. In theory, the chances of conflicts should be less and less over time — we can hope.

If two devices require the same resources, the result is a *device conflict*. Sometimes this causes one or both devices to stop functioning or to act unpredictably. In the worst case, the operating system or the system itself may come to a halt — often displaying the "blue screen of death."

If you use an older adapter card that does not support Plug-and-Play, the system won't be able to automatically set resources. You may have to live with the default setting that the card's designers have assigned or (if permitted) make changes to those settings by moving jumpers or setting switches on the card. Consult the instruction manual and Web sites for card makers in search of assistance.

The other alternative is to use the facilities of Device Manager to manually assign resources.

By setting the resources on a non-Plug-and-Play adapter or assigning them under Device Manager, you may solve one problem but cause another, because Windows will end up with less flexibility when it comes to dynamically allocating resources to other devices.

Figure 23-1 shows the General tab of the display under Windows 98; tabs behind it open the way to the Device Manager as well as other controls. The XP version of System Properties is shown in Figure 23-2; under that operating system, the Device Manager is accessible through the Hardware tab of System Properties.

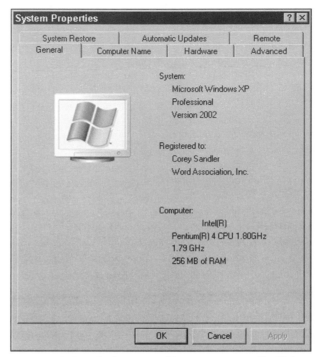

FIGURE 23-2: *Windows XP offers even more facilities, including System Restore and Automatic Updates. Performance settings were moved under the Advanced tab.*

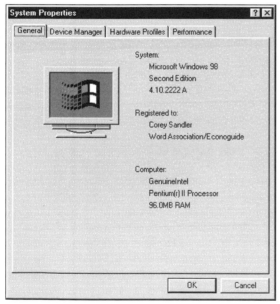

FIGURE 23-1: *The General tab of the System Properties dialog box in Windows 98*

Click Device Manager to show a list of devices by type or by connections, as shown in Figure 23-3.

You can expand the tree layout of Device Manager by clicking the plus sign (+) to the left of the device names, as shown in Figure 23-4, in the Windows 98 version. Click the minus sign (–) to collapse the tree back to its original appearance.

Check the hardware tree list under Computer for devices with a problem. An exclamation point (!) in a yellow circle indicates a potential conflict; an *X* in a red circle tells you that an ill-behaved device has been disabled.

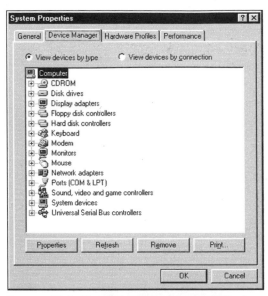

FIGURE 23-3: *The Device Manager of Windows 98 with devices sorted by type. Windows XP has a similar page with some additional functions available through pulldown menus.*

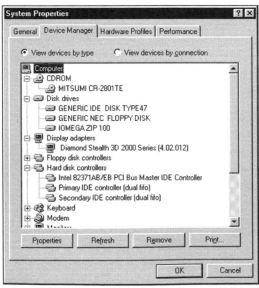

FIGURE 23-4: *Click the plus sign (+) to expand the tree of Device Manager and examine a specific piece of hardware.*

Double-click a device to check its properties; Device Manager tells you a bit about the hardware itself and whether it appears to be working properly. Actually, the report only tells you whether the device is communicating clearly with the system. Figure 23-5 shows a typical General tab of system properties; the Windows XP version shown here includes a link to troubleshooting scripts for many important devices.

FIGURE 23-5: *Double-clicking a device brings up its Properties dialog box. Here, in the General tab of the Windows XP version, you learn whether the hardware appears to be working properly and have access to a troubleshooter.*

Click the "View devices by connection" radio button to sort the device list differently. Sometimes during Plug-and-Play installation, the system gives unfamiliar names to some devices that you have installed. Changing the way you look at this information can help you to understand what's installed and what each device does.

Located under the Resources tab is a window indicating which resources are available for the selected device. The scroll box at the bottom of the page shows a Conflicting Device list. With the information in the two windows, you should be able to figure out the source of the conflict and a solution.

If you're having problems with a sound card, CD-ROM drive, or another device that could be classified as a multimedia device, simply open Multimedia from the Control Panel to display the Multimedia Properties dialog box. Click the Devices tab of this dialog box to see a list similar to the System list.

In order for Windows to successfully assign resources to a detected device, the Use Automatic Settings check box on the Resources tab of the Device Manager has to be checked. Depending on the device and the associated driver, you may be able to uncheck the automatic configuration to manually adjust elements of the resource settings. Figure 23-6 shows the Resources tab.

You can scroll through available interrupts or memory addresses using the arrow keys. Pay attention to the report of possible conflicts with other hardware. A dialog box can help you choose an interrupt that does not conflict with other devices.

If you believe a problem lies with an incorrect or corrupted device driver, restart Windows in Safe Mode and remove the conflicting drivers under Device Manager. Then restart Windows normally and start the Add New Hardware Wizard from the Control Panel. To completely disable a device in Device Manager but leave it in place in the system — one step in an advanced troubleshooting process — click the Original Configuration (Current) check box on the General tab to clear it. You can later enable the check box after you've cleared up the conflict.

To check the status of a device

Open Device Manager and double-click on the type of device that you want to view. Right-click on the specific device and then click Properties. Go to the General tab; under Device status is a report on the functioning of the device.

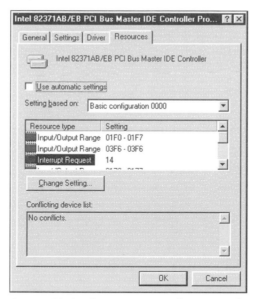

FIGURE 23-6: *The Resources tab reports the I/O range, interrupt, DMA (if used), and other information for a particular piece of hardware. Look in the lower section to see whether Windows reports that the device is conflicting with the resources used by another device.*

If the device is not working properly or has a potential conflict, the status box will display the problem. Depending on the device and manufacturer, additional information may include a problem code or number and a suggested fix.

Under Windows XP, many devices are also linked to a hardware troubleshooter.

Uninstalling or disabling devices

Another advantage offered by the Plug-and-Play design is that it allows you to uninstall most devices by merely removing them from the system when it is turned off; when the system is next powered on, the operating system should be able to note the absence of the device and adjust the allocation of resources if necessary. Be sure to consult the instruction manual for your device for details.

If it is a hot-swappable USB or FireWire device, you can merely detach it from the port. For devices installed in the bus, turn off the computer, unplug it, and remove the cover. Remove the adapter from the bus.

For a non-Plug-and-Play device, you may need to go to Device Manager and uninstall the device. Then turn off the machine and physically remove the adapter or device from the system or from an attached port. Again, check the instruction manual for the device for any specific additional recommendations.

In some situations — such as an attempt to identify the source of a conflict — you can use Device Manager to temporarily disable a Plug-and-Play device. The device remains in place in the bus or attached to a port, but the Windows Registry is changed so that device drivers are not loaded when the computer is started. If the device is later re-enabled, the Registry is changed again and the device drivers load at startup.

To disable a device driver (and thus turn off the device itself) without removing the driver, go to its Drivers tab under Device Manager and choose the disable box. (The option to disable differs slightly in wording across the various versions of Windows, but the effect is the same.)

To enable a device, open Device Manager and double-click on the type of device that you want to enable. Right-click on a specific device and then click Enable.

Hardware profiles

Device Manager also allows creation of multiple hardware profiles, allowing you to choose from two or more user profiles that might have different sets of devices enabled or disabled.

Windows sets up Profile 1 to include all devices installed in the computer when the operating system is first set up, or when you first set up a second profile. You can instruct Windows to ask which profile to use when you start the computer, or you can

swap profiles from a running system and reboot to enable the differing devices.

NOTE

Windows 2000 and its descendant, Windows XP, extends the concept of Plug-and-Play with Universal Plug-and-Play, which allows a PC to look beyond its own bus and ports to locate and control networked devices and services, including network-attached printers, Internet gateways, and consumer electronics equipment. This scheme allows the PC to join an up-and-running network, obtain an IP address, announce itself to the other devices on the network, and find out about — and connect to — everything else on the network.

For example, with Universal Plug-and-Play, a user can add a new printer or a storage device to a system and it will immediately be made available to any other PCs on the network at that time or in the future. A word of warning, though: Soon after Windows XP was released, security experts warned that Universal Plug-and-Play opened new portals for evildoers to hack into a system. Be sure to keep your system current with Windows Update from the Microsoft Web site and protect your system behind a firewall and antivirus software.

Windows System Information Utility

Windows 98 and later versions, including Windows XP, offer another utility that may prove useful if you try to diagnose system problems caused by non-Plug-and-Play hardware or by unknown sources. Use the System Information utility — also accessible from the System Tools menu under Accessories — to display a variety of data about your system configuration, as shown in Figure 23-7.

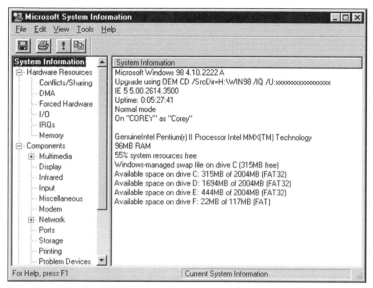

FIGURE 23-7: *The Windows 98 System Information window*

The System Information display is similar to a Windows directory tree, with plus signs (+) beside any entry that includes additional information. Click the plus signs to expand the display and show information about the selected topic. You can browse system settings through this facility to determine IRQ settings for various devices, to see which devices are using what memory segments, and to learn about other hardware settings.

Under Windows 98, you can open a software window that shows which drivers are loaded and whether they are 16-bit or 32-bit, as shown in Figure 23-8.

Windows XP offers other details about drivers, including details of *digital signing*—a security measure that assures that drivers have passed Microsoft compatibility tests and to help alert users to corruption or tampering. Figure 23-9 shows a Windows XP report on signed drivers. An associated tool within System Information is File Signature Verification, which checks to see which system files and device driver files are digitally signed; if you enable logging, the search results are also written to a log file.

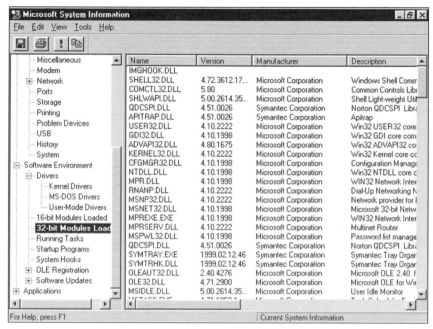

FIGURE 23-8: *A more detailed look at Windows 98's System Information window reveals details about device drivers.*

The Registry Checker — available in Windows 98 only — scans your current Registry for errors and then gives you an opportunity to back up the registry if you want.

The Version Conflict Manager, another Windows 98 facility, may be useful if you're having software problems. It displays a list of file versions that are different from the versions Windows would have installed. You can back up these files and restore the Windows originals, a move that sometimes can fix flaky Windows operation. If it doesn't solve your current problem, then copy the newer files back to where they belong.

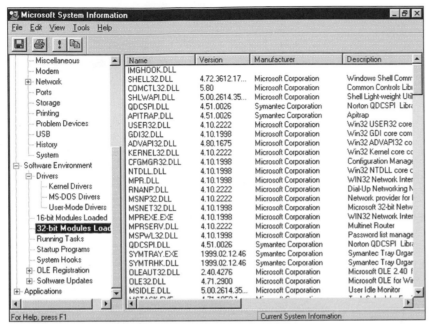

FIGURE 23-9: *Windows XP includes a detailed report on the provenance of device drivers.*

System Restore (XP)

Most computer users have come to dread the installation of a new application or even an update to a device driver, knowing that many times the latest "improvement" to your system may end up causing all sorts of new problems or even bringing everything to a complete halt. It seems that too many combinations of hardware, software, and settings are available for developers to anticipate every possible conflict that may arise.

One of the most useful new facilities of Windows XP is System Restore, a utility that takes an electronic snapshot of your system settings and many application files. If you run into a problem, you can instruct System Restore to reset the computer to a previous, properly operating state. Personal data files, such as word

processor files, e-mail, and other application files, are not affected by the rollback.

System Restore automatically creates *restore points* — identified by a time and date — anytime you install a new application or install a new or updated driver. You can also instruct the utility to automatically take snapshots at specific intervals, and you can manually create a restore point at any time before you make a change to your system.

The utility requires a minimum of 200MB of space within the system partition; the program automatically manages the space, purging the oldest restore points to make room for new ones, thus creating what Microsoft calls a "rolling safety net" under the user.

Device Driver Roll Back (XP)

Another safety net within Windows XP is the Device Driver Roll Back, which does exactly what its name promises. If you install a device driver and later find that the system has become unusable or a piece of hardware becomes unreliable, you can reinstall the driver previously in use and restore any driver settings that were changed when the new driver was installed. No other files or settings are altered.

This specialized form of a system restore utility does not work with printer drivers.

You'll find Device Driver Roll Back on the same Drivers tab of Device Manager in Windows XP.

Last Known Good Configuration (XP)

What happens if your computer won't come to life at all? Assuming that the machine's hardware — the hard drive, CPU, memory, video adapter, and BIOS chips as a minimum — is performing properly, the problem may be due to a change to the configuration.

Windows XP includes a feature called Last Known Good that restores Registry settings and drivers that were in effect the last time the computer successfully started. This is not quite the same as System Restore, which can be invoked days or weeks later to reset a system to a previous configuration; however, System Restore can only be used on a PC that is up and running.

To use the Last Known Good Configuration, start the machine (or restart it from a cold shutdown) and press F8 as the operating system begins to load to display a screen with startup options. (If the system identifies a problem as it is starting, you may see a message that says, "For troubleshooting and advanced startup options for Windows XP, press F8." This will take you to the same screen.

Your options include:

- Safe Mode
- Safe Mode with Networking
- Safe Mode with Command Prompt
- Enable Boot Logging
- Enable VGA Mode
- Last Known Good Configuration (Your most recent settings that worked)
- Directory Services Restore Mode (Windows domain controllers only)
- Debugging Mode
- Start Windows Normally
- Reboot
- Return to OS Choices Menu

The Last Known Good Configuration will allow you to recover from improper newly added drivers; it won't, however, solve problems caused by corrupted or missing drivers or files.

Restarting Windows in Safe Mode

In a current Windows system, Safe Mode is an excellent way to attempt to determine the source of problems or to undo changes made to configurations that may be causing problems.

To go to safe mode, restart the system or start it from a cold boot and press and hold F8 until the first Windows message leaves the screen. On some Windows 98 systems, the same process will work with the Ctrl key. Select the option for Safe Mode, and then press Enter.

Safe Mode helps you to diagnose problems. You will have access to basic files and drives, including those for the mouse, monitor, keyboard, hard drives, and basic VGA video. If your system is performing properly after you start the system in safe mode, this is an indication that default settings and minimum device drivers are not the cause; instead, this should point you toward settings or configurations that you have recently made or to new drivers or devices recently added to the system.

While the PC is operating in safe mode, you can remove drivers or make changes to configurations to fix problems.

You can also select the "Safe Mode with Command Prompt" option, which loads basic drivers but goes to a DOS or DOS-like command prompt instead of the graphical user interface or Windows.

Under Windows 95/98, your machine won't be able to access a connected network. With the debut of Windows XP, though, a new startup option is available — "Safe Mode with Networking," which adds essential services and drivers to join an existing network. Another XP option available is to restart to the "Last Known Good Configuration," which starts the computer by using Registry information saved at the last orderly shutdown.

If Windows does not come to life, then the files are likely damaged beyond repair; your best bet here would be to attempt to restart using the Windows boot disk that you should have created when the operating system was installed. You may also be able to bring the system back to life by booting from the Windows installation disc or from a specialized recovery CD provided by some computer manufacturers.

Under Windows XP, you can also use the Recovery Console to restore many corrupted or damaged Windows facilities.

Recovery Console (2000 and XP)

If you are unable to use Last Known Good Configuration, or if you can't start the computer in Safe Mode, you can use the advanced facilities of the Recovery Console. The Recovery Console, available in Windows 2000 and Windows XP, is essentially an enhanced version of a DOS system prompt.

From the Recovery Console, you can access FAT, FAT32, and NTFS volumes on the drives of your computer without starting Windows. You can also enable or disable device drivers, copy files from the Windows installation disc for the operating system or from a hardware installation disc, or create a new boot sector and master boot record to repair damage to the file organization of a hard drive.

You can start Windows Recovery in two ways:

- Load the console from the Windows installation disc. At the Welcome to Setup screen, press F10 or type **R** to repair, and then type **C** to initiate the console.
- Add the Windows Recovery Console to the Windows Startup folder. Consult the Windows help screens for assistance on installation. If you go this route, the console will be readily available any time you boot up without need for the Windows installation disc.

Automated System Recovery (XP Professional)

If you are unable to restart your computer by other means, or if you have had to replace a damaged system hard drive, you can use a previously created Windows Backup file that includes an Automated System Recovery set.

This facility is available only in Windows XP Professional; it replaces the Emergency Repair Disk option of Windows 2000 and Windows NT 4.0.

Automated System Recovery restores all disk signatures, volumes, and partitions on the disks required to start the computer, plus a basic version of Windows capable of restoring the backup file that you created.

Performing a Clean Boot

One of the most valuable diagnostic and repair tools in current Windows systems is the ability to restart the system with a Clean Boot. In other words, you will load the operating system with only the drivers and startup programs you choose to have running. This amounts to a selective version of a Safe Mode restart.

The key to this power tool is the System Configuration Utility, available in Windows 98 and Windows XP. Under Windows 98, you can launch the utility in two ways:

- From within Windows 98 or Windows 2000, choose Start ⇨ Programs ⇨ Accessories ⇨ System Tools ⇨ System Information. On the Tools menu, click System Configuration Utility.
- To run the same program from a command prompt under Windows 98, choose Start ⇨ Run. Type **msconfig.exe** in the Open box, and then click OK.

After the program is displayed, go to the General tab and then click Selective Startup. From here you can click to clear or restore the following check boxes: Process Config.sys File, Process Autoexec.bat File, Process Winstart.bat File (if available), Process System.ini File, Process Win.ini File, and Load Startup Group Items. Click OK, then restart your computer when you are prompted to do so.

To perform a clean boot in Windows XP, you must be logged on as an administrator. Choose Start ➪ Run, type **msconfig** in the Open box, and then click OK. On the General tab, click Selective Startup, and then clear the check boxes that are available to you. Click OK, and then click Restart to restart your computer.

After Windows 98 or XP has restarted, you can check whether you are still having problems. If all is well, you can then selectively turn on drivers and configuration files — one at a time. Go back to the System Configuration Utility and enable an item by checking its box.

Your goal is to keep adding more back to the ordinary startup group until the problem recurs; when it does, you can hone in on your detective work on the contents of that file or driver.

If all of this sounds time-consuming and tedious, that's because it is. However, it may be the only way to determine the source of a problem caused by an unusual combination of programs, drivers, or settings on your machine. Many technical support desks — including Microsoft — will point you in this direction when your problem does not match one of the usual suspects in their knowledge base.

Note, though, that Microsoft strongly recommends against using System Configuration Utility to modify the Boot.ini file on your computer unless you are doing so with the assistance of one of their support staffers.

To return from a clean boot state, load the System Configuration Utility one more time and go to the General tab. There click on "Normal Startup (load all device drivers and services)." Click OK and then Restart.

Creating a Boot Disk

If your primary hard drive sustains damage to the outermost tracks where the system keeps its all-important bootup information — or if your operating system files are somehow damaged — your computer is going to be unable to start.

Depending on your system's configuration, you should be able to bring the computer to life by using a *bootable floppy disk* or another medium, such as a CD-ROM or Zip disk.

With current versions of the operating system (Windows 98, Windows NT 4, and later), you can boot from the installation copy of Windows. Doing so will automatically begin the process of reinstalling your operating system.

If you just want to reboot your system to examine the contents of the hard drive or to make repairs, the best way is to use a bootable floppy disk created under Windows or with the assistance of a Windows utility available in Windows 95/98, ME, and NT. Under Windows XP, the installation CD includes the Recovery Console that can be used for this purpose.

To make a floppy to be bootable, the computer's system files need to be copied to the floppy disk from a properly functioning system. You'll be offered the opportunity to create a bootable floppy as part of the Windows installation process; you can also create one later from within Windows.

To create a boot disk from within Windows 95/98:

1. Choose Start ➪ Settings, and then choose the Control Panel.
2. Click on Add/Remove Programs and then choose the Startup Disk tab.
3. Insert a disk into your computer's floppy disk drive and then click on Create Disk. The process will automatically create a bootable disk with necessary system files.

You can also choose to manually create a startup disk from within Windows:

1. Insert a disk in the floppy disk drive. Go to the desktop and double-click on the My Computer icon.
2. Click once on the A: drive to select it, and then right-click to bring up a pop-up menu. Under Format Type, choose Full.
3. Under Other Options, choose Copy System Files. Click the Start button.
4. When Windows is finished formatting the disk, close the format window. Now you will need to manually copy some additional system files to the floppy. Use Windows Explorer to identify and copy the following files to the floppy drive: from within the Command folder, copy `Fdisk.exe` and `Format.exe`.

Several Windows utility programs, including Norton Utilities, Norton SystemWorks, and other applications, can also create a bootable floppy. These disks will usually also include antivirus cleanup files and access to a CD-ROM if one is installed in your system.

Whichever way you create your bootup floppy, be sure to conduct a test to make sure that the system will boot from it. Install the floppy in the floppy disk drive and restart Windows; the disk should bring the system to life and allow you access to your hard drive.

Booting from a CD

To boot from a CD, restart the computer with the Windows CD in the CD-ROM drive.

If you are unable to boot, your PC may not be set up to look for a bootable disk in the CD-ROM. You may need to instruct the BIOS to check the CD-ROM as well as the floppy disk drive and the hard drive.

Restart the computer and go to the system BIOS before the PC begins to load Windows. When the BIOS menu is displayed, locate the section that lists available boot devices; this is often an element of Advanced Features in the BIOS.

On this screen, you can instruct the computer where to look for bootable disks, and the order in which to search. If you want to force the system to go to the CD-ROM first, change the setting for Boot Device 1 to CD-ROM.

If you want to have the system attempt to boot from the hard drive first, and if it is unsuccessful there to look at the CD-ROM next, set Boot Device 1 to IDE1 and Boot Device 2 to CD-ROM.

You can also include the floppy disk drive as one of the boot devices; most modern machine BIOS systems allow selection of three or four boot devices.

On dinosaur machines, you may have to set switches on the motherboard or run a configuration disk to instruct the system to check a drive other than C: first.

To make a CD-ROM drive accessible in Safe Mode under Windows 95/98, restart the computer to safe mode and choose "Command Prompt Only." At the command prompt, type **win /d:m** and press Enter.

Emergency boot disk

You can bring any version of Windows back to some semblance of life by using an *emergency boot disk*. This is a disk that you can install in a bootable drive on your machine to bring the PC to life if your hard drive refuses to do the job. (Users of Windows 2000 and XP can use the Recovery Console for the same purpose.)

Depending on the components of your PC system, the bootable drive may be a floppy drive, a CD-ROM, a Zip drive, or an external SCSI hard drive. The concept is the same: This is another drive that your system can be instructed to check for boot files and then the operating system and hardware drivers.

Windows 95/98, Windows ME, and Windows 2000 give you the option to create a startup disk as part of their installation or upgrade process. To create the disk, go to Control Panel, then Add/Remove Programs. Select the Startup Disk panel and follow the instructions.

A number of PC utility programs, including Symantec's Norton Utilities and McAfee Antivirus, automate the process of making an emergency or rescue disk for the same purpose.

You want your emergency disk to include the low-level boot tracks and as much of the operating system as necessary to bring the system to life. It should also include any necessary device drivers to enable the BIOS to recognize the presence of a hard drive and CD-ROM drive. On most systems, you also need `config.sys` and `autoexec.bat` files that refer to those drivers on the emergency disk.

Recovering from an Accidental Deletion or Format

Deleting a file or reformatting a disk full of data sounds like capital punishment, but in the world of personal computing, reprieves are available. However, the reprieves only work if you act quickly after performing the offending act. This section explores some critical lifesaving utilities.

Undeleting

When you erase or delete a file, the operating system doesn't actually remove the file from the disk. Instead, it first changes the name of the file in the directory by writing hex code E5 (written E5H in computer-speak) over the name's first character. The old file and the details of its size and date and time of creation are still on the disk, but the DOS or Windows directory doesn't display this information because it has been programmed to ignore any filename that begins with E5H.

After completing this first step, DOS zeroes out the FAT entries of the clusters that still contain the deleted file to indicate to the system that those clusters are now available for a new file. When DOS examines the FAT, it now sees the zeroed-out entries as permission to use the associated clusters for new data.

As long as you have a reasonable amount of space available on your hard drive, it's likely to take a while before the system overwrites the space held by the "deleted" file.

Soon after the birth of the PC and its first DOS, several utilities were offered that could "undelete" these files — they located filenames that began with E5H and allowed users to change that first letter back to an allowable character, and made necessary changes to the FAT. The entire Norton Utilities empire — now part of Symantec — was born from such a program.

Microsoft Undelete became part of DOS and was offered through early versions of Windows.

Today, Windows 95/98 and all subsequent versions of Windows include a Recycle Bin that holds the contents of recently deleted files. You can open the bin and restore a deleted file with a few clicks of the mouse. You can adjust the size of the bin — the larger it is, the longer it will take for the oldest file in the bin to be overwritten by new materials.

Some utility programs, including Norton SystemWorks, expand the facilities of the Recycle Bin with new features including added, configurable data protection.

Unformatting

In certain circumstances, it is possible to unformat a disk that has been reformatted. Windows versions from Windows 95/98 through Windows ME extend a DOS command to UNFORMAT a disk, although you can only recover an accidentally erased drive if new files have not written over the older ones. The utility was not continued into Windows XP.

Some third-party utilities, including Norton Utilities and Norton SystemWorks, include enhanced versions of the Unformat command. Most are based around a data-loss prevention program that makes copies of the FAT and root directory. If your FAT or root directory gets corrupted, the second part of the program uses these copies to recover data from the disk.

When Your Computer Loses Its Setup

On many modern machines and senior citizens, an unwelcome visitor is a bootup error message of "Invalid Configuration Information" followed by "Hard Disk Failure."

Among the possibilities in this case is an accidental trashing of the PC's setup information, something that can happen as the result of a power spike or that can occasionally be caused by a poorly behaved piece of software. On the other hand, the problem may be as simple as dead batteries.

Begin by rebooting the machine and go to the setup or configuration screen. Check the entries against the copy of settings you maintain in a notebook alongside your computer. If that advice catches you by surprise, run out, get a notebook, and write down the settings now. On many setup screens for modern machines, you can ask the computer to autodetect your hard drives and make its own settings. Save your changes (the method varies based on the BIOS maker and version of setup provided, but you should find instructions on the screen) and then reboot the system to see whether it now comes to life.

If this fails, or if setup holds the configuration only for a while until it loses it again, you may have a dead battery connected to the clock-calendar chip that holds the setup information. Check the instruction manual for your motherboard or call the manufacturer for advice.

Open the case, replace the batteries with fresh ones, and run the setup program.

Missing Device Drivers

The symptoms of a missing device driver are usually something like this: Your computer boots, but drive D: has disappeared, the scanner has stopped scanning, or you can't get back on the network.

If you are working under Windows 95/98, go to the Device Manager (discussed previously in this chapter) and check for the presence of proper drivers for your devices. You can update a driver from the properties page for a hardware device.

Under Windows XP, Microsoft has made several valuable improvements. First of all, Windows device drivers and operating system files are now digitally signed by Microsoft to ensure their quality to indicate they have passed compatibility testing and that the file has not been altered or overwritten by another program's installation process.

The new operating system also includes a facility to roll back a driver when a driver upgrade doesn't work properly or causes interference with other components of the PC. When you update a driver, Windows XP stores information about the previous driver, and choosing "Roll Back Driver" from the properties page for a piece of hardware will revert to the earlier version.

If you are working under DOS or Windows 3.1, you should first direct your attention to the `config.sys` and `autoexec.bat` files to check for a problem with the driver references located there. Have drivers been removed, renamed, or moved? When you check your `config.sys` file, see that it includes all the DEVICE= statements required to load all your device drivers. Add-on peripherals and boards are often shipped with installation disks that make alterations to the `autoexec.bat` and `config.sys` files. Before you install an add-on, first copy your files to `autoexec.old` and `config.old`. Then rewrite the originals or run the installation program to add the necessary DEVICE= statements. The lines required by the device driver are now in your `config.sys` file, but you have the backup files in case something goes wrong and you want to look at the old instructions.

A corresponding problem crops up in the `win.ini` file of Windows 3.1, which contains specific instructions about the Windows setup. New software writes additional lines into `win.ini`. Well-mannered software makes a copy of the old file in case you uninstall or need to make other changes. If you get strange symptoms, something may have zapped your `win.ini` file.

System Crashes: Rounding Up the Usual Suspects

At the heart of the Windows operating system is its ability to work with many programs open at the same time; the microprocessor is able to shift its attention from one to the other as needed, dividing up jobs as needed to give the appearance of everything happening at once.

That's the good news; the bad news is that the number of programs running in the background can begin to grow to unmanageable size, and even worse, may cause minor to major problems without you even being aware that they were loaded.

To see how many programs are running on your PC at startup, load Windows. After it is running, hit the Ctrl + Alt + Del key combination once to bring up the Close Program box. (Under Windows XP, the more capable equivalent is the Windows Task Manager, which includes information about Processes running in the background and also gives access to CPU and network usage reports.)

Be careful not to hit the keys a second time to avoid resetting the computer.

Each of the programs that you see listed is currently active and demanding a bit of your CPU's attention. Among the programs that you are likely to see are utilities to support your mouse, keyboard, advanced graphics card, and other hardware. If you're running an antivirus program (and you should) you'll see one or more components of that application monitoring the activities of your computer.

All of these programs are part of your startup group. After you load an application, such as Microsoft Word, Internet Explorer, or Quicken, they will be added to the list of open programs.

If you suspect problems caused by one of the startup programs, you'll need to put on your sleuth's hat and try disabling the programs one at a time to try to isolate the one at fault.

If you are running Windows 95, you'll have to do all of the work by yourself; identify each program and look for a menu command to disable it. Keep track of all changes you make so that you can track your progress and undo the process later.

Under Windows 98, you can use the included System Configuration Utility to disable and enable programs one at a time. To launch the utility, click Start ⇨ Run. Type **MSCONFIG** and press Enter.

Before you test each program individually, a process that can take a while, find out if the problem is in one of your startup programs. From the System Configuration Utility, go to the General tab and remove the check mark in front of "Load startup group items."

Now reboot the system. Your computer will come to life without any of the startup programs running. If the problem persists, it is very likely that it is not caused by one of the programs in the startup list. If the problem goes away, go back to the General tab and put the check mark back.

At this point, your assignment is to disable all of the startup programs and then enable them one at a time until the problem comes back. You'll have to reboot the computer each time you re-enable a startup item.

With the System Configuration Utility panel displayed, click on the Startup tab to see the list of programs that automatically start each time the system is booted. Check or uncheck the boxes alongside the program names to include or disable programs from the startup process.

Remember that deselecting a program here does not remove it from your system. You can later return it to the startup list by checking its box.

With luck, you'll find the offending program. When you do, decide if you really need to have it running. Check with the manufacturer for an updated version or for a bug fix.

And while you're in the neighborhood, disable any startup items that you don't need. Each slows down the loading of Windows and uses system resources.

Resetting a Windows XP Password

If you plan ahead, you can recover from a forgotten password using the aptly named Forgotten Password Wizard of Windows XP.

The utility lets you create a password reset disk that you can use to recover your user account and personalized computer settings.

Open User Accounts from the Control Panel and click on your account name. Under Related Tasks, click "Prevent a forgotten password." Follow the instructions to create a floppy disk with a back door into your system; store the disk with your Windows CD.

If your Windows XP machine is on a domain, press Ctrl + Alt + Delete to open the Windows Security dialog box. Click Change Password and then click Backup to open the Forgotten Password Wizard. Follow the instructions on the screen.

Operating System Housecleaning

This book concentrates on the hardware side of the computer equation, but it is a basic fact of PC life that the hardware and the operating system are inextricable. Each can cause the other trouble, and determining the source of the problem is sometimes as easy as herding cats.

In this section, you'll find a few operating system tips and tricks that will help you keep the software side of your system healthy.

Clean up the System Tray

Too many programs on the System Tray (known as the Notification Area in Windows XP) of the taskbar can slow down startup and steal clock cycles from your CPU, slowing down the system.

You can remove or disable some of the programs you find there by right-clicking on each icon; look for an option to disable or remove the program.

Under Windows 95, you can remove any program from the Startup folder in this way: Open Windows Explorer and click on Windows ⇨ Start Menu ⇨ Programs ⇨ Startup folder.

Under Windows 98, run the Microsoft System Configuration utility. Click Start/Run and open MSCONFIG. Open the Startup tab and unclick the box next to any program that you don't want to start with Windows. (Note that this does not remove the program from your system; your action merely disables it as part of the startup process.)

Under Windows XP, right-click on the Notification Area and then choose the Customize button. You can then choose to hide, or hide when inactive, components of the tray.

Empty the Temp folder

Windows stores working files and placemarkers in a file folder at `C:\Windows\Temp` and other locations.

Depending on the sort of programs you run and your working practices, this folder can rapidly fill with hundreds or even thousands of files. Some programs will clean out entries they place in the folder, and others create tiny or even empty files there. In some cases, the swelling folder can waste space on your hard drive and even slow down the start-up process.

You can check the contents of the folder by clicking on Start ⇨ Find ⇨ Files or Folders. Under Named, enter ***.tmp** and Look in the C: drive.

You can individually delete files here, or select all files for deletion. Either way, the best practice is to reboot your system after deletions.

Under Windows 98 and later versions, including Windows XP, you can also clear out temporary files by going to a Windows utility. Choose Start ➪ All Programs ➪ Accessories ➪ System Tools and Disk Cleanup. Open the Select Drive box and choose a drive to clean up, and then click OK to open the Disk Cleanup box.

Windows 95/98 users can also add a command to the `Autoexec.bat` file that is executed by the operating system each time you boot up.

Under Windows 95 and earlier operating systems, find the `Autoexec.bat` file in the root directory of the C: drive and open it for editing in Windows Notepad.

Under Windows 98 and XP, run the Microsoft System Configuration utility. Click Start ➪ Run and open MSCONFIG. Click on the Autoexec tab and add a new line. Enter the following new command: `del C:\Windows\Temp\*.tmp > nul`.

With this command in place, your operating system will sweep out the contents of the Temp folder each time you start your machine.

Learn how to safely shut down Windows

You should always follow official procedure when you shut down Windows; click on Start and then Shut Down under Windows 95, 98, and 2000. Under Windows XP, click on Start and then Turn Off Computer.

While Windows operates, it stores information about configuration and settings in temporary files. If you merely turn off the power, these files may be left in place or corrupted.

Of course, if your machine freezes and you can't perform an orderly shutdown, you'll have to turn off the power or press the reset button on the case and hope that Windows can (as it usually does) repair problems caused by the shutdown.

One common annoying problem with Windows 98 is a hangup during shutdown. The good news is that this is a fairly common problem, and well known to Microsoft. The bad news is that it can have many causes and is not easily fixed.

In many cases, you can solve the problem by disabling a Windows feature called "fast shutdown." This facility reduces the time Windows requires to close down files it has opened for its own needs. However, there may be some incompatibilities between fast shutdown and some hardware devices.

To disable fast shutdown, click on Start ➪ Run, and type **MSCONFIG**. Press Enter to run the utility program. After it is displayed, click on the Advanced button (on the General tab) and click on the check box to disable fast shutdown. Restart your computer and test again for proper shutdown.

NOTE

Some older BIOS systems may not offer fast shutdown.

If the problem persists, visit Microsoft's Knowledge Base on the Internet and follow the steps in article Q202633 for Windows 98 or Q238096 for Windows 98 SE. Among the files that Microsoft suggests you check is the Windows shutdown sound.

Other usual suspects include devices that require a great deal of system resources, such as sound cards and network interface cards: You can experiment by disabling devices one by one to see if the problem goes away. When you identify the problematic device, you should contact its manufacturer for assistance.

To temporarily disable a device, right-click on My Computer, and then click Properties. Click the Device Manager tab, and then double-click on a class of devices.

For sound cards, choose Sound ➪ Video and game controllers. For network cards, double-click Network adapters. Click the first device in the list, and then click Properties. Select the Disable in this hardware profile check box, and then click OK. Restart the computer and check for the effect of your changes.

If the problem does not go away, repeat these steps and choose another device.

You should also investigate whether Advanced Power Management (APM) is causing the problem. This feature is intended to help reduce the use of electrical power by the computer, shutting down hard drives, monitors, and other devices, but it may not be fully compatible with all devices installed in your system.

To determine whether APM is causing a problem at shutdown, try disabling it. To do so, click Start ⇨ Settings ⇨ Control Panel, and then double-click System. Click the Device Manager tab, and then double-click System Devices. (In Windows 2000, click the Hardware tab of the System dialog box, and then click on the Device Manger button on this dialog box.) Double-click Advanced Power Management in the device list, then click the Settings tab. Clear the check box in front of Enable Power Management.

NOTE

Some BIOS systems don't offer this feature, and Advanced Power Management won't be listed.

Restart your computer and test shutdown. If disabling APM seems to fix your problem, keep it shut off.

Store a copy of Windows 98

When you add some devices or make changes to certain elements of system configuration, you will be asked to direct the operating system to the location of the original installation files for Windows. If you have the CD-ROM disc at hand, you can make the files available from there.

If you can't find the disc, however, or if your CD-ROM is not functioning, you may find yourself in trouble.

Windows 98 users: Before you have a problem, take the time to make copies of the essential Windows installation files in a folder on your hard disk. Create a folder, name it CABS, and copy the .cab files from the WIN98 and DRIVERS folders on the Windows installation disk (.cab files use a special Microsoft compression scheme; the necessary files occupy about 275 MB).

Uninstall programs properly

When you install a program under Windows, elements of the application are typically spread across a number of different folders on your hard drive, and changes are made to the System Registry and other configuration files. For that reason, it is not a proper — or safe — procedure to attempt to remove a program by merely deleting its main executable file.

If you want to remove a program, check whether it has its own uninstall option by looking in the application's Start Menu group or within Add/Remove Programs in the Control Panel. This will usually get rid of the program.

Internet Troubleshooting

If your Internet connection slows down markedly, begin with this basic question: Have you changed any settings or added any programs or software since the last time it functioned properly? If so, you should double-check your work, and consider reinstalling software.

If you have made no changes to your system, check with your Internet Service Provider. If you can get online to the ISP's home page, look for reports of technical problems or scheduled maintenance; some companies, including cable and DSL services, offer utility programs that monitor the condition of your connection and deliver messages.

Another way to gauge the performance of your system is to use Ping, a DOS utility that is included in most versions of Windows. Ping sends a small packet of data from your PC to a Web site of your choice and then reports how long it takes for a response.

To run Ping, you need to be running Windows and have an Internet connection open.

Click on Start ⇨ Programs ⇨ MS-DOS Prompt, and then open a DOS window. You will be greeted with a command prompt from DOS, the operating system that underlines much of Windows. Type **Ping** followed by the name of a Web site you want to test, and press Return.

If the Ping is successful in reaching the Web site, you will receive a report. For example:

```
C:\WINDOWS>ping Econoguide.com
Pinging Econoguide.com [64.82.99.19] with 32 bytes of data
Reply from 64.82.99.19: bytes = 32, time = 44ms, TTL = 42
Reply from 64.82.99.19: bytes = 32, time = 42ms, TTL = 42
Reply from 64.82.99.19: bytes = 32, time = 46ms, TTL = 42
Reply from 64.82.99.19: bytes = 32, time = 46ms, TTL = 42
Ping statistics for 64.82.99.19:
    Packets: Sent = 4, Received = 4, Lost = 0 (0% loss)
Approximate round trip times in milli-seconds:
    Minimum = 42ms, Maximum = 46ms, Average = 44 ms
```

From this report, I learned that my Web site, www.econoguide.com, was reachable and that the average roundtrip time for the transmission of 32 bytes of data and a response was about 44 ms, a typical time period at a busy time of day on the Internet.

One other test: Ping 127.0.0.1 to check your system's TCP/IP settings. You should receive an almost instant response; if not, your TCP/IP settings are probably incorrect. Check with your Internet Service Provider for assistance.

Tracking the Registry

When you install new hardware and software, Windows keeps track of it in a special database file called the Registry. The Registry is a crucial component of any Windows installation because it stores configuration information about everything you have on your machine. Unfortunately, not all third-party programs (or even Windows itself, if the truth be known) always do a good job of keeping the Registry current with the real world. If your computer starts acting flaky and you've eliminated a virus as the problem, chances are you have a corrupted Registry.

The Registry can become corrupted by a number of causes, but the most common are hardware problems that physically damage data in the Registry database, or software that you install or remove that doesn't properly update the Registry. Remember that uninstalling is different from simply deleting software. Uninstalling cleans up all the parts of a software program that may exist on your system. If you simply delete a file or program, you may not be aware of related files that should also be deleted. You'll certainly encounter Registry problems if you just delete a program directory without uninstalling the software. Deleting leaves instructions and configuration information in the Registry about software that no longer exists.

You can use a built-in Windows utility called RegEdit to view Registry information and change it. However, I recommend that you stay away from this editor unless you are working under the direct supervision of a technician at a support desk. It is simply too easy to cause more problems than you fix unless you have experience in this area.

You can use a number of commercial utilities to help track or repair the Registry. Microsoft offered its own utility, RegClean, for systems from Windows 95 through Windows 2000; that product was withdrawn in 2001.

For users of Windows XP, the best solution is to become a regular user of System Restore. Set up that utility to record regular snapshots of your Registry and other system settings. Then before you make any major change to your system, including installation of new software or hardware, manually instruct System Restore to create a restore point. If your system does not perform properly after a change, go back to System Restore and revert to one of the saved points in time.

Users of earlier versions of Windows may need to consider occasionally reinstalling Windows. If you notice software problems, you can try reinstalling Windows in the same directory where it currently resides. This preserves all of your installed software and data files that reside in the Windows directory. If this doesn't correct the problem, then consider a fresh installation.

Run the Windows setup program and specify a different directory for your Windows software. Doing this ensures that you start with a clean Registry and that all extraneous DLL files are removed. Of course, it also means that you have to reinstall all of the software that you want to use.

If you decide to reinstall Windows in this way, make sure to back up any data files that you need before you erase the files in the original directory.

Finally, once in a while, you should take the ultimate step in system tuning. Make a startup disk, back up any data files you need to save, and then run FORMAT to completely remove everything on your hard drive before reinstalling Windows. Sound drastic? It is, but you'd be amazed at how clean and fast your system will become after you do this. An additional benefit is that this tactic forces you to organize and store what you need and to throw away what you don't. I usually end up with several hundred megabytes of free space after a format because I don't put back everything I took off. Think of it as cleaning out the garage: You don't like to do it, you don't do it often enough, but after it's done, you feel really good about having a clean, clear space to park your car.

SUMMARY

The advanced utilities of Windows offer valuable tools to help you figure out the source of many problems with your system. In the next chapter, I explore some hard-won hints and tips from long-time users.

Notes

Chapter 24

Common-Sense Solutions to Common Problems

Throughout this book, you've explored some very technical solutions to computer problems. At the same time, many users also know that one way to get a balky hard drive to start spinning is to whack the side of the case in just the right spot, that the solution to a noisy cooling fan may be to put an old floppy disk under the front of the case to change its position slightly, or that an aging monitor may work best at a refresh rate other than its original recommended setting. These are the sorts of lessons that come with experience; they are common-sense solutions to common problems.

In this chapter, I disclose some of the best tips and techniques that you can use to solve many problems that cause big headaches.

Top Ten Crimes against Your Computer

Don't go looking for trouble; trouble will find you. But you can do some things to make yourself less of a target. Here are the top ten crimes a user can commit against his or her computer. (Let's be careful out there, people.)

1. **Failing to back up your files.** You can do dozens of things to try to keep your PC's hardware and software in good working order, and you should do as many of them as you possibly can. However, the most foolproof preventative measure is having a good set of backup files of all of your essential data in case of disaster.

   Analyze your work habits and consider the amount of data that you create each day. Depending on the size of your files, you should back up copies to some form of removable storage: a Zip or Jaz disk, a CD-R, a tape cartridge, or a superfloppy among them.

2. **Not inoculating against infection.** Computer viruses are out there; it's a crime to operate a computer that is any way connected to the outside world without having a proper antivirus program in place. This includes nearly every PC: if your machine is connected to the Internet, to AOL, or to a home or office network, it is at risk. And, if you load software or data files from a floppy disk, you risk infection in that way.

   At the very least, install a capable antivirus program. Even better, add a software or hardware firewall.

3. **Playing with unfinished software.** Many software companies — including Microsoft — offer individuals and

companies the "opportunity" to work with pre-release or "beta" software. In a way, users who agree to do so become unpaid testers for the software companies. Unless you have a very good reason to do so, I advise against trying these products. They are considered beta versions because they may cause problems with your system.

Having stated that, I regularly try out beta versions of operating systems and applications for my books. However, I do so on a machine separate from my mission-critical systems, and I fully expect the need to reformat and reinstall operating systems on that machine regularly. I never mix beta software with my irreplaceable data files.

4. **Fixing things that aren't broken.** Stop and think before you apply the latest upgrade or update to your software applications; sometimes the cure is worse than any illness it may be applied to. Sometimes the best policy is to wait a few weeks or months before upgrading to allow other users to be the guinea pigs for the software maker.

On the other hand, be sure to keep your antivirus software up-to-date, and install any critical security updates available from Microsoft for Windows.

5. **Performing improper housecleaning.** Life as a PC user would be so much easier if the process of adding or removing a piece of software was as simple as copying the application onto your hard drive. Alas, although the original DOS more or less worked like that, the arrival of the multitasking Windows environment and the concept of the interlinked office suite put an end to that.

Under Windows, components of an application are typically spread across many places in the computer, and additions or alterations are made to numerous components of the operating system, including the System Registry.

However, you can cause damage to your operating environment by installing or uninstalling software without regard to the proper procedure. Follow all instructions at installation,

including shutting down any other unnecessary Windows applications while new programs are put in place.

If you choose to uninstall a program, use the facilities of the Add/Remove Programs option that is part of the Control Panel. Or, use the program's own uninstaller, or a third-party program "sweeper."

6. **Not playing doctor with your drives.** Even the largest hard drive will eventually become cluttered with fragmented files, wasted clusters, and errors, such as crosslinked files. The prudent user regularly employs ScanDisk (built into Microsoft Windows), or a third-party disk utility, such as Norton Systemworks from Symantec or Diskeeper from Executive Software.

There is nothing magical about the work that these programs perform — the creation of fragmented files and wasted clusters is an ordinary consequence of the way the file attribute table works. In an ordinary home or office, it is good practice to defragment your hard drive anytime more than 10 percent of the files are inefficiently scattered.

7. **Failing to keep your system high and dry.** Put most simply: Don't drink and compute. And eating around the keyboard is not such a great idea, either.

Speaking just for myself, I figure I drop a glass or spill a can of soda once every few months. It's no big deal if that happens on the beach or in my kitchen. But if I spill a can into my PC or monitor, the consequences can be catastrophic. Later in this chapter, I present some common-sense solutions that *might* undo the damage. But the only way to be sure food and drink don't damage any of your components is to simply keep them away from your system.

8. **Not keeping your cool.** Heat is one of the principal enemies of your computer and your monitor.

Never block the inflow and outflow openings on your PC's case. A well-designed case is part of the cooling system for your computer, and most systems don't cool properly without the case in place.

Never operate a PC without its cooling fan properly operating. Monitors produce a great deal of heat that is normally vented through its top. Never place papers or other objects on top of the case. One of the dumbest office products I have ever seen is a set of plastic shelves intended to encase your monitor and allow you to place a telephone and books above it. This sort of device is almost guaranteed to cause the monitor to overheat and shorten its life; in the worst case, it could cause a fire.

9. **Mispowering your system.** Electricity is a flowing river, but like a waterway, it sometimes surges and wanes.
   A power surge or spike can fry your PC. A brownout can shut down your system or cause damage. Don't connect your PC directly to the wall outlet. Every system should have a surge protector in place on the power line. Even better is an uninterruptible power supply that isolates the system from the power line; a UPS powers the PC from a large battery, all the while recharging the storage device.

10. **Not keeping your system clean.** Cigarettes, hair spray, pet hair, dirt, and dust are unfriendly neighbors for a PC. They can cause a hard drive to crash, make it difficult to read an optical CD-ROM, and block the air vents for cooling. Vacuum your office or workspace regularly, and consider using an air cleaner in especially dirty environments.

Getting Good Technical Support

As part of any purchase decision, include an assessment of the quality and availability of technical support. If you're considering making a major purchase of an application, make a call to the support desk with a question about configuration or system requirements; if you're not satisfied with the quality of the response you get before you buy the product, you have no reason to expect good service after your check has been cashed.

Here are some more tips:

1. Make a record of error messages. Keep a notepad by your computer, and write down any error messages that you receive.

2. Make notes on what you were doing before the error occurred. Which programs were open? What key combinations or mouse clicks had you just entered? How long had the machine been powered on?

3. Keep copies of every instruction manual, program installation disk, and driver file. I keep all of these materials in large envelopes on one level of the bookshelf in my office, organized by type of device. If you have multiple machines, be sure to attach a note indicating in which machine the device is installed, and the date of installation.

4. Prepare for your technical support call. Know the system specifications for your machine, including the operating system and version, the type of processor, and internal devices. Have your machine running, and call from a telephone near the keyboard so that you can perform any actions asked of you by a technician. Keep a notebook to keep track of actions that you are asked to make.

5. If possible, call when support desks are least busy. In general, it's not a good idea to call on Monday morning after a weekend's pent-up problems, or late in the afternoon when a day's issues are before them. When does that leave? I've had the best luck calling early in the day during the week.

6. Write down the name of the technician you speak with, and see whether you can obtain a direct telephone number or an e-mail address for follow-up questions. Find out whether the support desk assigns a case number that documents your interaction with the support desk, and be sure to record that information. If you call back another time, a technician can read the entire history of your case.

7. Be polite, but firm. There's no point to losing your cool. But if you feel you are not getting good advice, politely ask whether you can speak to another technician or a supervisor who may be able to help.

Ch 24

Secrets of the Hardware Gurus

There is hardware and then there is hardware: The lack of a simple machine screw — about a penny's worth of metal — can cause an adapter card not to seat properly in the system bus and cause your $2,000 PC to resemble an electric paperweight. Or a sudden spike in electricity — caused by a lightning storm or your kid opening the refrigerator — can fry your PC in an instant.

The following sections give some hard-won solutions to knotty problems that computer manufacturers — and the writers of instruction manuals — somehow seem to ignore year after year.

Resetting a system password

Many modern BIOS systems offer the chance to set a system password that must be entered before the PC begins to load an operating system. This is a good way to protect a machine from mischief, but can be a danger if you happen to forget the password or if the CMOS memory for the BIOS becomes corrupted.

If you are unable to get past a system password, your options are limited; the password is not stored in a file, but rather in a small segment of specialized memory on the CMOS.

Consult the instruction manual for the BIOS or contact the manufacturer of your system to determine whether there is a default password that supercedes your private entry. Ask also whether there is a reset button on the motherboard or a jumper that can be changed to reset all of the entries in the CMOS. One last step is to find out whether the battery that keeps the CMOS memory alive can be disconnected or removed to cancel all settings for the BIOS.

If you end up clearing the BIOS, you will need to enter new settings, including those that allow your system to recognize the hard drive and other peripherals. It's a good idea when you first purchase a machine to walk through the BIOS settings and write down critical entries, including hard drive type and all of the specifications that accompany it, memory and display settings, and anything else that the system may not be able to determine automatically if this data is lost during a hardware problem.

Check the cables first

Before you think I'm trying to embarrass you with a problem I haven't had myself, let me assure you that sooner or later every computer owner — including authors of PC repair books — has a moment of sheer panic caused by something as simple as an unplugged PC or monitor or a blown fuse caused by a disagreement between the vacuum cleaner and the color TV.

Always check the electrical connection first if your computer appears to be dead. Is the PC plugged into the wall and is the other end of the power cable properly attached to the PC? Check the power outlet by plugging a lamp or radio into the socket. If your computer is plugged into a spike protector, line conditioner, or uninterruptible power supply (something I highly recommend), check that one of these protective devices hasn't blown a fuse.

The next thing to check is the jumble of cables worming out of the back of the computer. It's easy for one of them to get unplugged by a vacuum cleaner, your cat, or a tug from the other end of the cable.

Check all the connections to make sure that they are firmly seated on their sockets. Screw cables into connectors where possible, making certain that the plugs go into place evenly without one side off-center.

A loosely connected video cable, for example, can sometimes cause blurred characters or a color shift. A wobbly printer cable can make "Now is the time for all good men to come to the aid of the party" come out as "Mpe od yjr yo,r gpt s;; hppf ,rm yp vp,r yp yje sof pg yjr [sryu."

Power supply

Your computer, depending on the design of its power supply, has the right to expect a steady and reliable source of electricity in the range of 110 to 120 volts at 50 to 60 cycles per second. (Your power supply may also be able to work with foreign current sources of 240 volts.)

Modern machine power supplies are pretty good at dealing with current that dips slightly below that range momentarily or that surges a bit above the top end for a few milliseconds. Power supplies are not designed to work with long-term overvoltage or undervoltage situations, however. Severe spikes can pass through some power supplies and travel through the low-voltage DC lines to the chips. Long-term overvoltage conditions stress every motor and every chip in the computer.

Chronic undervoltage produces its own set of symptoms. A hard disk that is getting less than 12 volts, for example, may not come up to speed the first three times you turn on the computer in the morning. The fourth time, though, it may work fine and seem okay all day. Low voltage can also cause mysterious intermittent computer lockups.

If you are constantly replacing parts, I suggest that you buy or borrow a voltmeter or other line voltage-testing device and plug it into your wall socket. If the meter reads outside the expected range (about 100 to 120 volts) for no good reason, call the electric company or an electrician.

What can cause power fluctuations? The reasons run from the ordinary — a brownout on the hottest day of the summer or power line interference by major appliances — to just plain bad electrical service. When an air conditioner or a refrigerator turns on, the draw caused by its motor may produce a momentary dip in the line voltage, followed by a spike as the power comes back up. Thunderstorms are also notorious for the voltage spikes that they cause.

A momentary dip in current can cause the voltage to drop so low that the memory chips start to forget things. When this happens, the computer locks up. Perhaps you didn't see the lights brown out for an instant during the voltage drop. It doesn't matter, because a voltage drop lasting only a thousandth of a second can lock up an older computer.

Similarly, a momentary voltage spike to the hard disk head may write gibberish in the middle of a file, or, much worse, to the boot sector or the FAT (file allocation table). You won't notice this problem until you go back and try to read the file or boot from the hard disk. This is where routine use of disk maintenance programs can pay off. Run a disk utility such as Norton Utilities on a regular basis so it can catch and repair these problems. If the boot sector is trashed, these utilities may be able to repair the boot sector or help you recover the FAT and files.

Every system in any home or office should, at the very least, be plugged into a *spike protector*. These units, which sell for $10 to $50, are electronic sacrificial lambs. They are intended to blow a fuse or even blow up themselves to shut down the line to your computer if a dangerous spike is headed its way. A *line conditioner* is a device (priced less than $100) that boosts the power during momentary drops and acts as a surge protector as well.

Uninterruptible power supply (UPS) systems are electronic guarantors of a reliable source of power in brownouts, overvoltage situations, and even power failures. They generally include line-conditioning circuitry, as well as a large internal battery and a regulator. UPSs come in two designs: a standby style that includes a very fast switch that can jump into the fray to substitute battery power for line current in an emergency, and a true uninterruptible style that constantly feeds your computer from its battery at the same time that it uses line current to keep the battery charged. UPS systems sell for about $100 to $300 for units intended to work with single PCs.

In my very rural office, the electrical system is rather unreliable. Undervoltage is common, storms bring the occasional spike, and brief — and sometimes extended — outages pop up regularly. All of the computers in my office are plugged into uninterruptible power supply (UPS) boxes, and electric spike protectors or line conditioners protect every other major device. The UPSs protect from under- and overvoltage incidents and provide about 15 minutes of battery power in the case of a complete outage — enough time to conduct an orderly shutdown. I also have all of my major applications programs, including my word processor, configured to automatically save files in progress every five minutes. This means that the most I could lose in the event of an unexpected shutdown (or system crash) is whatever work I have done in the last 4 minutes and 59 seconds.

After the power gets past the surge protector, line conditioner, or UPS, the computer's power supply is in charge of converting AC to DC and stepping down the voltage. In general, power supplies are usually good for many years of use; the entire PC will typically be out of date before the supply will fail.

But power supplies can fail, especially if they are not well-protected from over- or undervoltage. They can also break down if the cooling fan does not work or if vents are blocked. Here are some signs of the failure of a power supply:

- A completely dead system with no cooling fans running on the power supply or elsewhere in the case
- Repeated failure of the system to bootup
- Unexpected rebooting or shutdown of an operating machine
- Repeated parity check or other memory errors

You can test the output of a power supply with a voltmeter. As with floppy drives, it does not make economic sense to repair a faulty power supply within your PC. Replacement units sell for about $30 to $100 and installation is simple. Be sure to match the same physical size and design; you can, though, increase the wattage of the replacement unit.

Hard disk or hard disk controller problem?

Before you consider replacing a dead hard drive, ask yourself the basic troubleshooting question: What has changed since the last time the system worked properly?

If you have been recently working under the covers of the PC, go back in (unplug the PC and turn off the power first) and see whether you accidentally dislodged or failed to reconnect a power or data cable at the hard drive or at the controller end on the motherboard or in the bus.

A diagnostic program can tell you whether the hard disk controller is functioning properly; it can also give information about any problems it finds on the drive itself. The utility can't, however, give information about a dead controller or a dead hard drive.

Check the BIOS setup screen to make sure it has not become corrupted and that it properly identifies hard drives and controllers in your system.

The next step is to try substituting a replacement hard drive that you know to be good in your system or testing your suspect hard drive in a properly functioning PC.

 CROSS-REFERENCE

Other sources of hard disk problems are a damaged boot track, damaged system files, or a failure of the disk mechanism itself. Explore those possibilities in Chapter 10.

Floppy drives

Floppy disk drives are cheaper, smaller, and more reliable than they ever used to be. They're also used a lot less now than in the early pre-hard-disk days of PCs.

Therefore, floppy disk alignment problems and outright failures are uncommon now. When one occurs, it generally makes much more sense to replace the drive—about a 15-minute and a $25 investment—than to attempt to make a repair.

 CROSS-REFERENCE

See Chapter 9 for more details on floppy drives.

The most common problems with floppy drives are failures of mechanical parts, such as latches and springs. I've also lost a few drives to human failure: An insistent shove of an upside-down or backwards floppy disk into a slot will chew up a drive.

Before you replace the drive, however, you can check a few things. If you've recently been working inside the computer, go back inside to see whether you dislodged or disconnected the data or power cable to the floppy drive.

You can purchase diagnostic programs that include drive alignment tests and a factory-formatted floppy test disk that is certified as correct. However, the cost of the software and the cost of a repair — if you can find someone who will take the job — is much more than the cost of a replacement unit.

You don't need specialized tools, though, to figure out whether your floppy disk drive has lost its will to store and retrieve data reliably. Create a disk using a floppy drive that you believe to be working properly — if you don't have another PC, ask a friend or business acquaintance or a computer retailer for 30 seconds of their machine's time. Format the disk and copy a few files of varying sizes to the floppy.

Try the good floppy on the suspect drive, and try a disk created with the suspect drive on a PC that you know to be functioning properly. If the suspected drive can't work reliably with the good diskette, or a good drive can't reliably read the suspect disk, it is reasonable to assume that the drive is out of alignment or working improperly. Although it may pain you to do so, the best solution is to throw away the drive and replace it with a new one.

Although I don't recommend repairing broken floppy disk drives, you can take a couple steps to help your floppy drives live long and prosper:

- Keep the disk drives clean. Use a vacuum cleaner to suck out the dust that may have worked its way into the drives. Don't use floppy disks with broken covers, sticky labels, or other damage.

- If you make heavy use of the floppy disk drive — not all that common anymore — you can purchase a disk-cleaning kit to treat dirty drive heads. Follow the manufacturer's directions carefully and be sure not to overdo the amount of solution or frequency of cleanings.

 NOTE

A noisy floppy disk drive is not always an indication of trouble. The poor thing may have been born that way. The only real test is whether it reads and writes to its own diskettes and those produced by other machines.

Solving printer problems

The good news about printer problems is that you can usually isolate the hardware from the software. Most printers have self-tests that can tell you whether they are working properly, and you can also try plugging them into another PC to see whether they work with a different machine. Don't forget to rule out the cable as the source of the problem. After you are satisfied that the printer is working, you can turn your attention to the operating system and software.

The causes of a printer malfunction can range from a broken or disconnected cable (most likely) to a bad printer port (the least likely). The printer itself can fail to operate properly because of paper jams — from huge wads of crumpled paper to tiny shards stuck at critical sections of the paper path. Ink or toner cartridges can also gum up the process.

Test the possible causes, in this order:

- Cables and power
- Switch box or parallel pass-through device (if you have one)
- Printer
- System configuration

Ch
24

Cables and power

See whether the data cables are properly attached at each end; a cable that is not squarely seated on its connector may result in garbled or unreliable operation. Be sure that the printer is receiving electrical power; check any suspect wall outlet by plugging in a radio or lamp.

Test the cable by substituting one you know to be good. That's one good reason to stock your closet with a few extra pieces of hardware—mine includes cables, connectors, and keyboards.

Switch box

If you use a switch box to share a printer between two computers or to share the use of a single parallel or serial port, test the setup by removing the box from the circuit and attaching the cable directly to the computer and printer. If the printer works now, you either have a failed switch or a problem with one of the extension cables used with the box.

Many switch boxes don't fully support bidirectional cables; they may be able to transmit data to the printer but not report back on paper supply, ink or toner, or other information.

If you have a parallel pass-through device, like a scanner, cabled between the PC and the printer, make sure that it's on and the cables connected to it are seated properly. If your printer still has a problem, remove the device from the circuit and attach the cable directly to the computer and printer. If the printer works now, you either have a failed pass-through device or a problem with one of the extension cables used with it.

Printer

Run your printer's self-test. If the printer appears to be working properly, test it by hooking it up to another computer in your office or take it to a friend's setup. If you purchased the printer from a retail store, you may be able to take it to the shop to test it there. That option may or may not be possible if you bought the printer or your computer from an electronics superstore.

System configuration

Before you break out your screwdriver, take a moment to check whether your computer has done anything to disable or redirect the parallel, serial, or USB port used by the printer. Have you installed a new operating system, utility, or application since the last time the program worked?

Go to the Windows Device Manager and check to see whether the port is operating properly without any system resource conflicts. If there are any conflicts with IRQs, DMAs, or memory resources, they need to be fixed.

To test the port, use a diagnostics software package. The best utilities require use of a loopback plug that attaches to the parallel and serial ports and simulates an attached device for the purposes of the test.

CROSS-REFERENCE

For more information about troubleshooting printers, consult Chapter 18.

Monitors

Make sure that your monitor is properly connected to the video adapter of the PC and plugged into a working wall circuit. Check the brightness and contrast settings on the monitor; an accidental turn of a knob may make the screen dark and unreadable.

CROSS-REFERENCE

You can find more information about monitors in Chapter 14.

Some monitors have an external fuse. Unplug the unit and remove the fuse. Examine it carefully and replace it if it has blown. If it appears to be good, the fuse may have come unseated because of heat or vibration. Reinstall the fuse and try the monitor again.

Windows should be able to identify current monitors as Plug-and-Play devices and install proper device drivers — either from the ones provided by Microsoft as part of Windows or from an installation disk that comes from the monitor manufacturer. If Windows has not recognized your monitor, or if somehow the driver has become corrupted, the system may be attempting to communicate with your monitor at a resolution or refresh rate that it does not support.

Reboot the system into Safe Mode, which will load generic VGA monitor drivers. Go to the Display item of Control Panel and make appropriate adjustments there.

WARNING

If your monitor has failed, do not attempt to make internal repairs yourself. The video circuitry can retain deadly high voltage, even when off and unplugged, and any adjustments require specialized training and equipment. It probably does not make sense to repair a basic monitor; new models will likely cost less than the repair bill. On the other hand, I have had good luck in getting monitors repaired at old-fashioned TV repair shops. If you use a lot of computers and monitors — as I do — it might make sense to establish a relationship with the proprietor of such a shop if you can find one. An older, 15-inch monitor can be thrown away, but a new 19-inch device that quits working may be worth fixing if you can find someone who really knows their way around the inside of the thing. Chances are you won't find anybody at a computer store or computer repair facility with these qualifications.

Liquid on the computer

As mentioned previously, your computer and liquids are a dangerous combination, so your best bet is to keep the two of them apart. However, accidents do happen, so consider the following information if a spill does occur on your system.

If a can of soda or a cup of coffee has spilled on your keyboard, you may be out of luck. After all, water and electricity don't get along well, and soda and coffee are corrosive. However, replacement keyboards sell for as little as $10 for a cheap model to about $125 for a deluxe replacement.

Water or soda on a keyboard may be something that can be cleaned up. First of all, unplug the board. Next, you have a couple of choices:

1. Try to clean off the liquid
2. Throw it away and buy an inexpensive ($10 to $25) new one

If you've spilled water, your best bet is to let the keyboard dry off. For other liquids, consider popping the keys off the board, taking care to keep track of springs and plastic parts that underlay each key. After the caps are removed, you can attempt to clean up the spill with a damp cloth; some fixer-uppers wash the board under running water. As far as I am concerned, I would rather buy a new board.

If you do spill something onto your computer, shut it down immediately and let it dry off completely. To be very safe, remove or at least disconnect your hard drive; in case your computer is fried, you should be able to install the hard drive in a new PC and recover the data that it held.

A spill into an electrified monitor is almost always a fatal event; if it were my display, I wouldn't even try to find out if it worked anymore. If the monitor is worth the fee that a service department will charge, bring it to a technician for testing.

Page fault errors

Most computer users are unhappily familiar with the dreaded Page Fault Error, one of the blue screens of death that from time to time crashes Windows 98 and earlier operating systems. (Windows 2000 and Windows XP promise to be less likely to crash, and to be able to isolate the death of a particular application so that it does not bring down the entire computer. In my experience, however, even these newest of operating systems will sometimes quit for no apparent reason.)

A page fault is generated when a virtual address established by an application points to a page that is not in physical memory. When that happens, the Virtual Memory Manager attempts to load the page from the hard disk or other storage medium into memory. If there is not enough free memory to hold the page, or if it can't be found, an error occurs.

You have several solutions to prevent future page fault errors:

- Add more RAM to the system
- Work with fewer programs open at the same time
- Make any available setting within the offending program so that it uses less memory

Slow display

Windows applications make heavy demands on the computer, especially the video card. Waiting for the screen to catch up can drive you nuts, especially in graphics-intensive programs such as drawing or image-editing software.

Graphics and publishing packages can use as fast a video card as you can afford. The plummeting price of memory has made it reasonable to consider 16MB of RAM a minimal level of memory for a new graphics card. The additional memory enables greater resolution levels and a larger number of colors.

Be sure to take advantage of any special-purpose bus extensions your PC may offer, including AGP on a current motherboard, or VESA local (VL) bus on a senior citizen. Graphics cards can pick up significant speed boosts by direct connection to the CPU through these slots.

Nearly all modern graphics cards lay claim to an accelerated graphics label. Computer magazine reviews of the latest crop of cards show their rankings on standardized benchmark tests.

I recommend that you stay away from no-name video cards at the bottom of the price lists. Some storefront PC makers who concentrate entirely on price use these cards in their systems. The price difference between brand X and an established name is usually not all that much, and for the extra money, you can expect more current and advanced technology, better technical support and warranty, and availability of software driver and hardware upgrades.

As soon as you install a new graphics card, contact the card's manufacturer to determine whether you have received and installed the latest device driver. Companies often produce new drivers after boxes of hardware are in the sales channel and often update drivers to improve speed and fix bugs. You can find the new drivers on the Web sites of many display adapter manufacturers.

Memory

With today's prices on RAM, you have no good reason to scrimp on memory for Windows; you'll pay a lot more in lost time and system crashes. I recommend at least 64MB for Windows; the machines in my office begin at 128MB and go up from there to 256MB and beyond.

Consult the instruction manual for your motherboard or contact the maker of your PC to determine the type of RAM, its module design (RIMM, DIMM, SIMM, SIP), its speed, and the upgrade path.

 CROSS-REFERENCE

For more information about considering types of memory and troubleshooting the memory in your system, check out Chapter 8.

Some motherboards require you to upgrade in blocks of a particular amount. Other PCs cheat their owners by inefficient use of the motherboard; these designs may require you to throw away perfectly good SIMMs or DIMMs of small capacity and replace them with larger blocks of memory. But do you really have to throw away perfectly good memory? No. Check the ads in the back pages of computer magazines for memory specialists who may buy used memory or accept it in trade for new, larger blocks of memory.

Memory prices are sometimes very volatile; the best price for RAM can shift from one source to another based on supply. In general, you can find good prices at mail-order companies that specialize in memory during times when RAM is plentiful. These companies usually buy on the spot market and can take advantage of downturns quickly. When RAM is scarce, you may find better prices through major manufacturers who have long-term contracts with memory makers that may predate current price increases.

Bigger hard drives

Don't bother to upgrade from a 1GB drive to a 2GB device; the prices of hard drives have dropped so steeply in recent years and the storage demands of modern applications have grown so sharply that it makes no sense to skimp here. In fact, you'll have a hard time finding new hard drives smaller than 10GB anymore.

 CROSS-REFERENCE

Chapter 10 shows you how to replace a hard drive and controller.

Take the opportunity to upgrade to a serious 40GB hard drive; as this book goes to press, they are available for about $100.

In previous editions, I have recommended consideration of compression software programs such as Microsoft's DoubleSpace or DriveSpace or third-party products including Stacker. These products can compress the size of many programs and data files by as much as half, effectively doubling the capacity of a drive (including floppy disks and some backup storage devices).

The products perform their magic by using codes to represent blocks of repeated data and interposing a device driver between the output of the disk controller and memory that expands information back to its real size. They also create a compressed drive that occupies a partition on your physical drive; it is not directly readable without the use of the disk compression program.

Some users swear by disk-doubling software, while others swear at them. In the early days of these products, users did encounter some problems with corrupted data, but current versions seem stable. With a fast processor, the small amount of extra CPU time required to deal with doubled disks is hardly noticeable. In my opinion, the sharp drop in cost of hard disk drives makes disk-doubling software less important and not worth the extra human brainpower required to deal with it.

SUMMARY

This chapter covered some basic troubleshooting solutions. See the troubleshooting flowcharts in Appendix G for even more help in determining the proper steps to walk through a series of common problems.

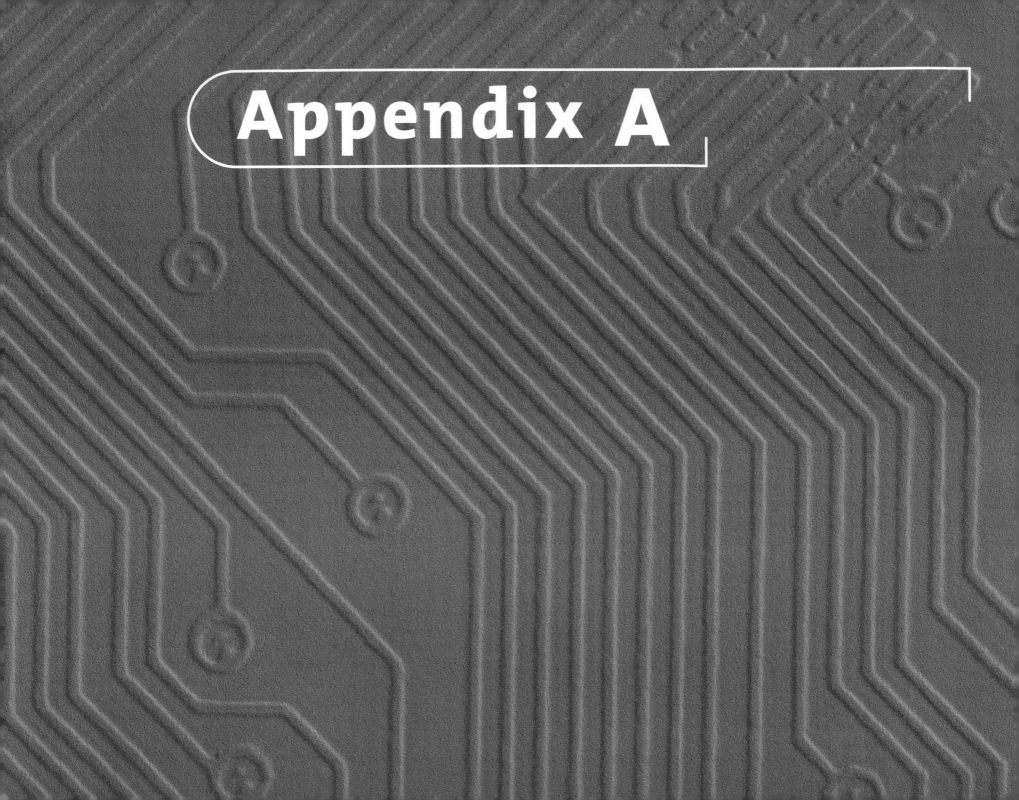

Appendix A

Numeric Codes and Text Messages

IBM produced the first PC. Within a year came the dawn of the clones from companies such as Compaq; Dell, Gateway, and many others arrived on the scene later. (Some early clonemakers that have fallen by the wayside include Columbia, Corona, and CompuAdd.) To report problems with the motherboard and adapters, IBM included a set of codes called *power-on self-test* (POST) codes in its BIOS. Similar systems were adopted by most other makers and continue to this day.

This appendix lists common numeric code or text messages that you may see during the bootup of your machine. The text may differ slightly over the years and from one BIOS maker to another. In the section of Basic POST Codes, I have mixed together early PC, PS/2, and common clone codes.

Check the instruction manuals that came with your computer to see whether the maker was kind enough to provide a current list of codes for your particular machine. You can also ask the manufacturers' technical support departments for information and check the Web sites maintained by most major BIOS makers.

Basic POST Codes

Here are the basic building blocks for power-on self-test codes as used in the original dinosaur computers and as adopted and adapted by some subsequent BIOS makers.

101 System Interrupt Failed

On dinosaur PCs based on 8008 or 8086 CPU chips, this error code indicates a motherboard failure. If you're lucky, this could simply be a transitory problem related to an unusual condition, such as cold or warm temperatures that can make electrical contacts shrink away from each other or expand to short out a trace, or loose wires in one of the many connections to the board. The problem may go away the next time you boot the system, or you may be able to fix the problem by removing the cover, grounding yourself, reseating connecting cables, and pressing down on CPU, memory, BIOS, and other socketed chips.

If you can't get past a 101 code, though, you will have to replace the motherboard. On true dinosaurs, it may be time to retire the entire system because it is not cost-effective to buy a new motherboard.

If you have a computer based on a later CPU, this error code reports an unusual condition where a failed motherboard or an add-in board is interfering with the interrupt controller chip. Once again, you will have to replace the motherboard if the error seems permanent.

102 System Timer Failed

The motherboard has a bad timer chip; you may have to replace the motherboard if the error seems permanent.

103 System Timer Interrupt Failed

The timer chip can't get the interrupt controller chip to send interrupt zero (the timer interrupt). Once again, if the error persists, the motherboard is bad and must be replaced.

104 Protected Mode Operation Failed

This error code applies to the AT only. The computer must switch into protected mode to count and check the extended memory in an AT, even if it has no extended memory (it must check that it has zero kilobytes of extended memory). A bad motherboard can cause a failure to switch into protected mode.

Another possible source of this problem is a failing keyboard that can direct its internal 8042 controller chip to keep sending signals on address line 20 to the processor. The processor needs to use address line 20 as a regular address line when it is in protected mode, but the 8042 chip won't get off the line. Eventually, the BIOS ROM sends the error message. A Phoenix BIOS sends a similar error, Gate A20 failure, to complain about a continuously busy address line 20.

Check the keyboard switches to see if they are set incorrectly, and be sure that the keyboard cable is properly connected. Next, try a new keyboard. If you can't make the error go away, you will have to install a new motherboard.

105 8042 Command Not Accepted. Keyboard Communication Failure

You have a bad 8042 keyboard controller chip or a bad keyboard. Try another keyboard that you know to be good. If the new keyboard does not work, this indicates a probable failure of the 8042 chip on the motherboard. If the chip is socketed, you can replace it; if it is soldered in place, the motherboard will have to be replaced.

106 Post Logic Test Problem, or Logic Test Failure

Some problems have catch-all error codes, covering situations found during the power-on self-test (POST) that don't fit into any of the other categories, but are believed to be caused by a bad system motherboard. Other factors, such as faulty cards, can also cause this error.

Turn off the computer, pull all the cards except the video card out of the machine, and then turn the computer back on. If the error has gone away, try replacing one card at a time and retesting until you isolate the bad card. Don't worry about additional error messages that appear when your cards are removed. If the 106 error message doesn't go away when only the video card is installed, then you probably have to replace the motherboard. A slight chance exists, though, that the video card is the culprit. To check this, try installing a good video card. If the error is still present, you must replace the motherboard.

107 NMI Test Failed

This error means that a nonmaskable interrupt (NMI) test of the microprocessor failed. An NMI is an interrupt that can't be disabled by another interrupt. If this error persists, you must replace the microprocessor. Motherboards with sockets for the CPUs enable users to swap the CPU; those that have the microprocessor soldered into place require a service call or replacement of the motherboard. Be sure to compare the cost of a new motherboard to the price of a single CPU chip.

CROSS-REFERENCE

I provide more details on NMI detection and recovery in Chapters 5 and 7.

108 Failed System Timer Test

The timer chip on the motherboard is not working. You can replace the chip on some motherboards; otherwise, you must replace the motherboard.

109 Problem with First 64K RAM

This code indicates a problem within the first 64K of RAM, which was the entire capacity of the motherboard in the original PC. You will have to track down and replace the faulty chip or chips, or replace the motherboard.

Some older PCs have the first block of memory soldered to the motherboard so the user can't replace the chips. More contemporary computers have all memory in sockets and the chips can be easily replaced.

On old 8088-based motherboards, a 109 code indicates that one or more chips in the first row of 9 — marked Bank 0 — are bad. Locate and replace these 9 chips.

If you have an 80286- or 8086-based motherboard, the code indicates that one or more of the chips in the first two rows of 9 chips are bad; locate and replace these 18 chips.

If you have a 386- or an older 486-based motherboard, the 109 code indicates that any of the first 36 memory chips could be bad. You may be able to consult your PC's instruction manual to locate and replace the proper chips. However, not all manuals are complete enough to show you a meaningful diagram of hardware, such as the memory chips, to help you isolate a problem with a specific memory chip. You could replace all memory chips, or find a chip that you know to be good from another machine and move it one step at a time through memory locations until things return to normal. This is a tedious task — not unlike trying to find the one light in the set of cheap Christmas tree lights that doesn't work when a whole line is out — but it can be done.

Modern machines with 486 and Pentium processors use SIMMs or DIMMs to hold large blocks of memory, and you can easily replace these strips. One way to isolate the problem is to swap SIMMs from higher blocks (Block 1, 2, or 3) for the lowest range of memory held in Block 0. If the problem goes away, you can assume that the SIMM originally in Block 0 is the source of the problem.

PS/2 and Some Clones

System board errors

110 PS/2 System Board Error. Parity check.
111 PS/2 Memory Adapter error.
112 PS/2 MicroChannel arbitration error, system board.
113 PS/2 MicroChannel arbitration error, system board.
115 System board, CPU error.
118 System board memory error.
119 2.88MB diskette drive installed but not supported.
120 System board processor, cache error.
121 Unexpected hardware interrupts occurred.
130 POST — no operating system, check diskettes, configuration.
131 Cassette interface test failed, PS/2 system board.
132 DMA extended registers error. Run diagnostics.
133 DMA error. Run diagnostics.
134 DMA error. Run diagnostics.

CMOS memory

161 System Option Not Set, or Possible Bad Battery.
162 System Option Not Set, or Invalid Checksum, or Configuration Incorrect.
163 Time and Date Not Set.

The CMOS memory has forgotten the PC's setup configuration. This problem can be caused by the failure of backup memory for the CMOS, a short in the motherboard (rare), or an unusual software condition.

Try first to reset the CMOS to its proper settings. Consult your instruction manual and your printed backup listing of correct settings (you do have one ready at all times, right?).

The next step is to replace the battery and rerun the setup program. If replacing the battery does not fix the problem, you may have a faulty power supply. Another possibility is a failed RTC-CMOS chip, which you can replace if it is in a socket on the motherboard. If it is soldered into place, you have to replace the motherboard.

164 Memory Size Error

This error is another indicator of a problem with your battery-backed CMOS memory, which stores your system configuration.

Run your setup program and retest. If the error is still there, remove the covers of the PC, replace the battery, and run your setup program again.

If you still have the error, turn off the computer, ground yourself, open the case, and press down on all of the memory chips or the SIMM, SIPP, or DIMM chip carriers to make sure they are all firmly seated into their sockets. Then turn on the computer and retest. If the error continues, you may want to remove all of the memory chips or carriers and bring them to a repair shop equipped with a memory-testing device. Replace any chips/modules that fail the test and install them in the machine.

If no RAM chips/modules fail in the memory tester, the problem may lie in a faulty power supply. Replace it with a unit that you know to be good, or test the memory chips in another computer that uses the same type of RAM. If these steps don't solve the problem, you may have an unusual and rare problem with your motherboard.

Configuration errors

165 PS/2 System options not set.
166 PS/2 MicroChannel adapter timeout error.
199 Configuration not correct. Check Setup.

Advanced memory errors

201 Memory Error

For an XT (8008 or 8086 CPU chips), this error code means that something is wrong with the RAM on the motherboard. No further details are available from the computer's self-tests; you have to manually test the RAM chips, replacing memory as necessary. A worst-case scenario is a failure of the memory addressing chips on the motherboard, which means that you must replace the motherboard.

If you have an AT-class machine (80286 and above), this error code means that you have one or more bad memory chips. Turn off the computer, ground yourself, open the case, and press down on all the memory chips. Make sure they are firmly seated in their sockets, and then close the case and turn on the computer to retest the memory. If the error persists, remove all the memory chips and take them to a repair shop equipped with a memory-testing device. Replace any chips that fail the test and install them in the machine.

Some machines, including original IBMs and some earlier Compaqs, have at least the first 64K or 256K soldered in place on the motherboard. With such machines, test any socketed RAM first in the hope that you will find the problem there; otherwise, you may have to replace the motherboard or (if it makes economic sense) have it professionally repaired.

202 Memory Address Error Lines 0–15, or 203 Memory Address Error Lines 16–23

These errors indicate one or more bad memory chips. Turn off the computer, open the case, ground yourself, and press down on all the memory chips to make sure that they are firmly seated in their sockets. Close the case, turn on the computer, and retest it. If the error is still present, remove all the memory chips and take them to a repair shop equipped with a memory-testing device. Replace any chips that fail the test and install them in the machine.

Some machines, including original IBMs and some earlier Compaqs, have at least the first 64K or 256K soldered in place on the motherboard. With such machines, test any socketed RAM first in the hope that you will find the problem there; otherwise, you may have to replace the motherboard or (if it makes economic sense) have it professionally repaired.

Keyboard problems

301 Keyboard Error

Make sure that the keyboard is connected properly; check that the cable is plugged in at both ends and that the wire has no cuts or crimps. Check to see whether any keys are stuck, or whether books or other objects are resting on the keyboard. Turn off the computer and turn it back on again. If the error is still there, test the PC with a keyboard that you know to be good, and test the suspect keyboard with a PC that you know to be good before you replace a possibly failing unit.

302 System Unit Keylock Is Locked

The keylock on the front of modern PCs may be locked in the off position, grounding out the keyboard-to-motherboard circuit. Turn the key to the on position. (If you don't use the keylock, store the system keys with your system documentation so your PC does not become accidentally disabled.)

You may have accidentally disconnected the jumper wires from the keyboard lock to the motherboard while installing a new hard disk or internal card.

Another possibility is a faulty keylock switch or a keyboard key stuck down.

303 Keyboard or System Unit Error, or 304 Keyboard or System Unit Error, Keyboard Clockline Error

The keyboard controller chip tests the keyboard during the power-on self-test. Error codes 303 and 304 indicate that the keyboard is not sending the right replies to the POST queries. Check for stuck keys. The keyboard cord or the keyboard itself may be bad. Check also that the XT/AT switch on the bottom of many keyboards is in the proper position.

Dinosaur video adapter problems

401 CRT Error #1, or 501 CRT Error #2

This XT code indicates that a monochrome display adapter (Code 401) or the color graphic adapter (Code 501) is malfunctioning. Check that the card is properly seated in its bus slot. If the error continues, replace the card.

Floppy and hard disk problems

601 Disk Error

A broad description of disk problems, this error can be caused by the computer looking for a nonexistent floppy drive — a situation that can occur if setup contains information about a drive that has been removed from the machine or unplugged. A bad floppy disk can also cause the problem.

More serious causes are failed disk drives or controllers. Check first that cards are properly seated in their bus slots and that power and data cables are attached correctly. You can also test the devices by swapping units known to be good.

602 Disk Boot Record Error

Error 602 is another vague but threatening message that can be caused by a number of problems, from a bad floppy disk to a bad floppy disk controller.

Try using a new floppy boot disk that you know to be good. (Test the boot disk in another PC.)

If you have recently been working inside the computer case, chances are good that you have knocked a cable loose or installed a drive cable improperly.

If the problem continues, the most likely cause is a bad floppy drive; try swapping with a good floppy drive. If the machine still doesn't boot, replace the controller.

1701 Hard Disk Failure

Somewhere between a headache and a nightmare, this error indicates that a dinosaur-era hard disk controller has not received the response from the hard disk that it expected.

Possible causes include the following: (1) the power cable may not be properly connected to the hard disk; (2) the data cables connecting the hard disk to the controller may be installed incorrectly; (3) the drive-select jumper on the hard disk may be set wrong; (4) the hard disk may be dead; or (5) the hard disk controller may be dead. The first three possibilities are more likely if you have recently been working under the covers of the PC.

After you have checked all cables and jumpers, try swapping with a good controller to see whether it solves the problem. If nothing else solves the problem, suspect a failed hard drive. In most cases, it doesn't pay to repair a hard disk, but you may be able to recover the data by using companies that specialize in retrieving data stored on failed drives. These companies advertise in PC magazines.

Note that 1701 is an error message programmed into the BIOS of the hard disk controller card, and therefore can vary from system to system. Some messages are more specific about the source of the problem; consult your hard disk and controller instruction manuals or call the manufacturers for more information.

1780 Disk 0 Failure
1790 Disk 0 Error
1781 Disk 1 Failure
1791 Disk 1 Error

The hard disk controller has not received the response from hard disk 0 or 1 that it expected. Possible causes include the following: (1) the power cord may not be connected to the hard disk; (2) the cables connecting the hard disk and its controller may be installed incorrectly; (3) the drive-select jumper on the hard disk may be set wrong; (4) the hard disk may be dead; or (5) the hard disk controller may be dead. The first three possibilities are more likely if you have recently been working under the covers of the PC.

Check that the controller and power and data cables are properly attached and examine the settings on the controller. Swap with a controller that you know to be good and see whether the problem is solved. If all else fails, suspect a bad hard drive.

Hard disk 0, the first physical hard disk, is always named logical drive C:; hard disk 1, the second physical hard disk, is usually named logical drive D:.

Sometimes the hard disk is split into more than one logical drive. In other words, the computer treats it as if two or more separate drives were present, each with its own directory tree and its own physical space.

Error codes 1780 and 1790 don't refer to any particular logical drive, just to the first physical hard disk assembly, whether mounted inside the computer case or attached externally via a cable to a hard disk controller card inside the computer. Similarly, error codes 1781 and 1791 don't refer to any particular logical drive, but merely to the second physical hard disk assembly.

1782 Disk Controller Failure

If you see this error, the hard disk controller may be bad, although some controllers report this error if hard disk cables are improperly installed. Another possibility is that you have installed a new card in your PC that has its ROM BIOS at the same memory address area as the hard disk controller card's ROM. Remove the new card to see whether the controller works. If that solves the problem, consult the maker of the new card to see whether you can set that card's BIOS to a new location.

AMI Advanced Numeric Codes

01x Non-defined error
02x Error in Power Supply
1xx Mainboard error

101 Interrupt error
102 Timer error
103 Timer interrupt error
104 Defective Protected Mode (AT)
105 Last 8042 command not accepted
106 Expansion Bus defective
107 Stuck NMI

108 Defective bus timer
109 DMA error
110 Parity error (PS/2)
111 Defective expanded memory (PS/2)
121 Unexpected hardware interrupt
161 CMOS checksum error
162 Defective CMOS configuration
163 Wrong Date/Time CMOS
164 Defective memory size CMOS
199 Specified configuration defective

2xx Memory errors
201 Memory error, address specified
202 Address error, A0 - A15
203 Address error A16 - A23
215 Memory error (PS/2)
216 Memory error (PS/2)

3xx Keyboard errors
301 Keyboard reset defective or key stuck
302 Keyboard locked
303 Keyboard defective
304 Defective keyboard control

4xx MDA errors
401 Defective adapter self test, memory error
408 Defective character attributes
416 Defective character set
424 Cannot set text mode 80×25
432 Defective parallel port (PS/2)

5xx CGA errors
501 Defective adapter self test, memory error
508 Defective character attributes
516 Defective character set

524 Cannot set text mode 80×25

532 Cannot set text mode 40×25

540 Cannot set graphics mode 320×200

548 Cannot set graphics mode 640×200

6xx Disk drive errors

601 Defective disk drive self test

602 Invalid boot sector

606 Diskette change not displayed

607 Write protect

608 Defective diskette status

610 Formatting not possible

611 Disk drive not reacting, timeout

612 Defective controller chip

613 DMA error

616 Defective number of rotations

621 Defective positioning

622 CRC error

623 Sector not found

624 Defective address

625 Defective positioning, controller error

626 Defective data compare

7xx Coprocessor errors

9xx Error in parallel port (LPT:1)

901 Defective port self test

10xx Error in parallel port (LPT:2)

1001 Defective port self test

11xx Error in serial port (COM:1)

1101 Defective port self test

12xx Error in serial port (COM:2)

1201 Defective port self test

13xx Error in game port

1301 Defective port self test

1302 Defective joystick

14xx Printer error

1401 Defective printer self test

1404 Defective Dot Matrix printer

15xx SDLC adaptor error

16xx Terminal emulation error

17xx Hard drive error

1701 Defective hard drive self test

1702 Defective controller

1703 Defective hard drive

1704 Non localizable error

1780 Defective hard drive 0

1781 Defective hard drive 1

1782 Defective controller

1790 Defective hard drive 0

1791 Defective hard drive 1

18xx Expansion board errors

1801 Defective card self test

1810 Defective enable/disable

1811 Defective extender card

1812 Defective addressing

1813 Error in wait state

1814 Defective enable/disable

1815 Error in wait state

1818 Defective disable

1819 Defective wait request

1821 Defective addressing

19xx 3270 PC attachment card errors

20xx Errors in first BSC adaptor

21xx Errors in second BSC adaptor

22xx Cluster adaptor errors (LANs)

24xx EGA error (on PS/2 VGA error)
2401 Defective adaptor self test, memory error
2408 Defective character attributes

26xx XT/370 emulation error

27xx AT/370 emulation error

28xx 3278/79 emulation adaptor error

29xx Color printer errors

30xx First PC network adaptor error

31xx Second PC network adaptor error

33xx Compact printer errors

36xx Errors on General Purpose Interface Bus

38xx Data Acquisition Adaptor errors

39xx PGA error
3901 Defective adaptor self test, memory error

71xx Voice Communication adaptor errors

73xx External 3.5 inch disc drive errors

7301 Defective disc drive self test
7306 Diskette change not displayed
7307 Write protect
7308 Defective diskette status
7310 Formatting not possible
7311 Disc drive doesn't react, timeout
7312 Defective controller chip
7313 DMA error
7316 Defective number of revolutions
7321 Defective positioning
7322 CRC error
7323 Sector not found
7324 Defective address
7325 Defective positioning, controller error
7326 Defective data compare

74xx VGA error
7401 Defective adaptor self test, memory error

85xx Expanded memory errors

86xx Digitizer errors on PS/2

89xx Music Feature card errors

104xx ESDI controller errors PS/2
10401 Defective self test
10402 Defective controller
10403 Defective hard drive
10404 Non-localizable errors
10480 Defective hard drive 0
10481 Defective hard drive 1
10482 Defective controller
10490 Defective hard drive 0
10491 Defective hard drive 1

Appendix B

Text Error Messages

On modern machines, text error messages from the BIOS are more common than the original IBM-style numeric error codes. This appendix lists some sample Phoenix BIOS ROM error messages and American Megatrends, Inc., AMIBIOS messages. Some other manufacturers of BIOS chips use similar error messages.

This appendix is primarily about error messages from the BIOS. However, DOS and later versions of Windows also display some messages that report on problems with hardware; in most cases, these messages are self-explanatory. You can also use the Help systems of Windows to research more detail on hardware messages.

DOS error messages (and remember that DOS underlies Windows through Windows 98) may vary slightly from version to version and not match the MS-DOS, AMIBIOS, or Phoenix BIOS examples word-for-word. Later versions of Windows — Windows 2000, Me, and XP — may have completely different messages. Use the information here as it applies to your system.

Each entry includes the error message displayed on the screen, followed by a description of the possible causes of the error and my recommendations for how to correct it. I list error messages that start with a variable number — for example, "xx = scancode, check keyboard" — under the first word in the message (in this case *scancode*). Messages that start with a fixed number — for example, "128 not OK, Parity Disabled" — appear at the beginning of the list in numeric order.

CROSS-REFERENCE

If you have a numeric error message (numbers only, or numbers plus a short phrase), refer to Appendix A, where I list the IBM-style numeric ROM error messages. Appendix C has a catalog of computer beep error codes.

Sometimes, you may have difficulty determining from an error code the actual cause of the condition and the best course for correction. If you're running Windows 98 or a more current version of Windows, you can access some built-in features that will help you troubleshoot hardware and software problems. Try using these tools as you work through resolution of error codes and other error or malfunction conditions.

In Windows 95/98 the Automatic Skip Driver, for example, tells Windows to quit reporting errors on devices that cause the operating system boot to halt. You may have a fault in one or more devices that won't necessarily affect operations for what you need to do. The Automatic Skip Driver won't fix malfunctioning devices; instead, it allows Windows to bypass some problems in loading caused by the devices. You can access this utility and other troubleshooting features from the Windows Help system:

1. Click Start ➪ Help.
2. Click the Index tab if it is not already above the Help display.
3. Type the word **errors** in the "Type in the keyword to find" field of this dialog box to see a listing of several conditions, including errors on startup. You can also type in **automatic skip driver** (in Windows 95/98) to go directly to that help screen.
4. Click the Display button. Follow instructions for accessing the feature you have specified in the Keyword field.

Windows also includes a number of troubleshooting wizards, step-by-step utilities that help you to identify the cause of an error, whether it is hardware or software. Some of these troubleshooters pop up automatically when errors happen; you can access others through the help system. Simply conduct the first three steps in the preceding list, and choose another error type, such as "during startup," in Windows 95/98. Windows will offer to load a troubleshooter that helps you to solve startup issues. Later versions of Windows have changed the terminology for some of these features. Windows 2000, for example, contains a section in the Help system labeled "Startup Failures."

Windows 2000 and Windows XP have an even more powerful tool, the Driver Verifier. This utility examines an individual driver, or the full set of drivers you have installed in your system, to make sure that they follow all the rules of the operating system and, most importantly, that they play well together. The verifier, an adaptation of Microsoft's internal tools for certifying drivers for use with Windows, examines the way drivers access and use memory and system resources.

The Driver Verifier is buried within the Windows code and not described in help screens. To load the program, choose Start ➪ Run, and then enter **Verifier** in the Open field of the Run dialog box.

Available options on the opening screen of the utility include:

- **Create standard settings**. Appropriate for most users, this selects a standard set of tests for the drivers you will select for examination.
- **Create custom settings.** Technicians may choose to manually select the tests for drivers.
- **Display information about the currently-verified drivers.** This option displays statistics about the currently selected drivers and assigned tests.
  The settings you make within Verifier will take effect the next time you boot your system; the utility will run in the background until and unless it comes across a problem with one or more of your drivers.

The Windows System File Checker, also available through the Windows Help system, will back up your existing system files and create new copies from your Windows CD. This facility is available under Windows 98, 2000, and XP. If you are experiencing occasional errors on startup, unexplained system lockups, or other problems that you can't resolve through other means, one or more of your system files could be the problem. Use this utility to solve the problem or at least to eliminate one more possible cause of your difficulties.

One more Windows tool that may be helpful: Dr. Watson. This utility was designed to help developers and beta testers report problems they encountered during the early stages of the development of Windows 95 and Windows 98. It remains with your Windows system as a potentially useful tool. Dr. Watson takes a snapshot of key system settings at the time an error condition occurs. You can study the Dr. Watson log file for guidance in solving the problem or preventing its recurrence.

Launch Dr. Watson by choosing Start ➪ Run and then typing **DrWatson.exe** in the Open field of the Run dialog box. Click OK to start the program. Dr. Watson runs in the background. You won't see anything happening unless you have a system-level error, but the Dr. Watson program icon will appear in the tray at the right of your task bar (or on the task bar itself in Windows 2000). You can click the icon to view the log file or to create a system snapshot at any time. To create a snapshot, click the Dr. Watson icon and choose Dr. Watson from the popup list. Dr. Watson creates and displays a snapshot onscreen. For more detailed information, click the View menu on the snapshot screen, choose Advanced view, and then browse the tabbed dialog box for current system settings and status. Use the File Save command to save the snapshot to a file.

Windows XP offers an enhanced version of Dr. Watson that can help technical support experts to diagnose problems. To open Dr. Watson, choose Start ⇨ Run. In the Open field of the Run dialog box, type **drwtsn32** and then click Enter. The utility will automatically start when there is a system or program failure, recording the system state and events in a log file.

128K NOT OK, PARITY DISABLED

The first 128K of RAM has failed the power-on self-test. Turn off the computer, turn it back on, and then reboot. If the error message repeats, a problem exists with the RAM.

For some reason, the first 128K of RAM is not responding to the CPU. The memory chips may be bad. Remove the first 128K and take the chips to a computer repair shop for testing. Or you can try switching the high and low memory on your motherboard. In 8086 and 8088 machines, the first bank of memory contains the first 64K (or the first 256K, if the computer is using 256K chips), so that switching the first and second banks (or the third and fourth banks) may solve the problem. Read your PC's instruction manual in order to find out which bank on your motherboard is considered the first bank.

A bad motherboard can also cause this problem. If testing indicates that the memory chips are all good, you will have to replace the motherboard itself.

8087 NMI AT *XXXX:XXXX*. TYPE (S)HUT OFF NMI, (R)EBOOT, OTHER KEYS TO CONTINUE

The 8087 math coprocessor chip (an add-on chip in some systems) has generated a nonmaskable interrupt (NMI) error. The 8087 chip must be tested thoroughly and replaced if it has failed. Before you turn off the system, you should attempt to save the data you were working on when you received this error message. Press S to shut off the NMI message, and you will be able to proceed with your work temporarily. Perform an orderly shutdown of your task and then test the 8087 by using a specialized math coprocessor test program.

ACCESS DENIED

You tried to replace a write-protected, read-only, or locked file.

If this error occurs because a particular file is write-protected or read-only, you can use the DOS ATTRIB command or a utility to change the file's attributes, if you need to.

You may also receive this error if you try to access a directory name as if it were a file.

Check to see whether the disk is write-protected. Sometimes the part of the floppy drive responsible for detecting the write-enable notch (on a 5.25-inch disk) or the covered write-enable slide (on a 3.5-inch disk) is broken. If so, the drive will assume that all disks are write-protected. Floppy disk drives are not easily or efficiently repaired; replacement units sell for $25 or less.

ADDRESS LINE SHORT!

This could be a problem with memory chips; reseat the chips and test again. If the problem continues, you can try to replace the memory with new chips or known-good chips, but you're probably dealing with a faulty motherboard that must be replaced.

ALLOCATION ERROR, SIZE ADJUSTED

CHKDSK compared the apparent physical file size on this disk to the allocated size in the disk directory, and the two didn't match. If the physical file seemed too long, CHKDSK truncated the file (cut off the tail end of the cluster chain) to match the size allocated in the directory. If the physical file seemed too short, CHKDSK changed the directory entry to reflect the real file size.

This error can happen to any user on rare occasions. If you get this error more than once in a six-month period, you should be concerned that your hard disk drive is starting to act up. Read the information about the "Hard Disk Read Failure" message in this appendix and take steps to safeguard your data. Back up everything, run a hard disk diagnostic/repair utility, and keep alert to possible new symptoms.

Next time, use SCANDISK (available in DOS 6.2 and more current versions of DOS) or Norton Disk Doctor rather than CHKDSK because they are capable of saving more of your data instead of arbitrarily truncating files.

ATTEMPTED WRITE-PROTECT VIOLATION

You tried to format a write-protected floppy disk. See "Access Denied" for a discussion of possible hardware problems with the floppy disk drive that may have caused this error.

BAD DMA PORT = *xx*

The direct memory access (DMA) controller chip has failed the POST. The motherboard will probably have to be replaced because the DMA chip is soldered into place.

BAD OR MISSING COMMAND INTERPRETER

Your computer can't find the essential COMMAND.COM file of DOS.

This message appears if you attempt to boot from a floppy disk that does not have system tracks, a common occurrence if you leave a data disk in the drive when you turn on your machine.

The error can also be generated if you somehow have altered the correct path to the location of COMMAND.COM in the root directory of your hard disk. Another possibility can arise if you are using a shell program and have the wrong path listed in CONFIG.SYS.

BAD PARTITION TABLE, or
ERROR READING (or WRITING) THE PARTITION TABLE

You should see this error message only as part of the process to format the hard disk; it means you ran the FDISK program improperly. Rerun FDISK and then try to format the disk again. If you receive the message again, you may have low-level formatted the drive improperly. Go back to the beginning of the format instructions for your machine, which are listed in Chapter 10. Read the instructions carefully, and retry the entire format sequence. You can also use an automated formatting utility, such as Disk Manager.

Another possibility is that your PC has picked up a computer virus. Run a virus checker and if it finds a virus, follow the program's instructions to isolate and remove the virus.

If you are certain you have low-level formatted correctly, run FDISK and FORMAT correctly, and tried the other fixes listed in this section, the remote possibility exists of a hard disk controller error. Try substituting a controller that you know to be good to see if it fixes the problem.

Otherwise, you most likely have a bad hard disk that will have to be replaced because it is incapable of recording a readable partition table.

BASE MEMORY SIZE = *nn*K, or
*nnn*K Base Memory

These are not error messages. They are informational messages from your computer at boot, reporting that it has successfully tested *nnn* kilobytes of base (system) memory.

BUS TIMEOUT NMI AT SLOT *X*

This is an EISA bus error. Run the EISA configuration utility, making certain you have correctly configured the EISA boards in your computer. If that doesn't fix the problem, consult the manufacturer of the card installed in slot *X*. A faulty card is more likely than a failed motherboard, although both are possible.

C: DRIVE ERROR, or
D: DRIVE ERROR

The hard disk C:, the first hard disk in your machine, is not set up properly in CMOS, or the second hard disk, drive D:, is not set up properly in CMOS.

Run the CMOS setup program. See also, "Disk Configuration Error."

C: DRIVE FAILURE, or
D: DRIVE FAILURE

See "Hard Disk Failure."

CACHE MEMORY BAD, DO NOT ENABLE CACHE!

The cache memory on the motherboard is malfunctioning; consult your instruction manual to find the location of the cache chips. Reseat the cache memory chips and try again.

This is an AMIBIOS error message. Run AMIDiag if it's available. If not, try replacing the cache memory. Though the cache controller chip on the motherboard could also cause this problem, it's not likely; replace the motherboard only as a last resort.

CANNOT CHDIR TO (pathname). TREE PAST THIS POINT NOT PROCESSED

One of your directory files has been trashed.

CANNOT CHDIR TO ROOT

Your root directory file has been trashed.

CANNOT RECOVER (.) ENTRY PROCESSING CONTINUED

The entry (working directory) has been trashed.

CANNOT RECOVER (..) ENTRY PROCESSING CONTINUED, or
CANNOT RECOVER (..) ENTRY, ENTRY HAS A BAD ATTRIBUTE (OR LINK SIZE), or
CHDIR (..) FAILED, TRYING ALTERNATE METHOD

The entry (parent directory) has been trashed.

A third-party utility, such as the Norton Utilities, should be able to correct this sort of problem. Also read the information about the "Hard Disk Read Failure" message. Directory files should not fail; this is an early warning of possible hard disk troubles. Back up your data, run hard disk diagnostic/repair utilities, and watch for possible new symptoms.

CH-2 TIMER ERROR

The timer chip 2 or interrupt controller logic on the motherboard is malfunctioning. Replace the motherboard.

CMOS BATTERY STATE LOW

Replace the clock/CMOS battery.

CMOS CHECKSUM FAILURE

The checksum error correction method used to check the CMOS setup chip's data integrity shows that the CMOS data is corrupted. Replace your clock/CMOS battery and run setup. If you still receive the error, the CMOS chip must be bad and the motherboard will have to be replaced.

CMOS DISPLAY TYPE MISMATCH

The CMOS chip thinks you have a monochrome video card installed, but you actually have CGA or VGA, or vice versa. Run setup so that the CMOS information matches the actual video card installed.

CMOS MEMORY SIZE MISMATCH

The CMOS chip thinks you have more or less memory installed than you actually have. Run setup.

Poorly seated memory chips or SIMM memory modules may not show up when the computer examines its physical memory during the boot process. If you know for sure how much memory is in the computer, and you know for sure that you gave the proper information to the CMOS chip during setup, better turn off the computer and carefully examine each memory chip and SIMM strip, because one is probably loose. See also the error message "Errors Found; Incorrect Configuration Information Memory Size Miscompare." However, note that you are likely to see this message if you have just replaced memory or added memory to your machine.

CMOS SYSTEM OPTIONS NOT SET, or CMOS TIME & DATE NOT SET

The CMOS setup chip's data is corrupted. Run setup. You must use the correct setup program for your computer, not any old setup diskette lying around. Most new computers have setup in ROM BIOS (you'll see a message, such as "Hit Delete if you want to run Setup," or "Press Delete if you want to run Setup or Diags," whenever your boot the computer.) Some dinosaurs use disks with setup programs that often malfunction if they are used in a different brand of computer.

If you get this error, you need to determine why. Errors such as this could indicate a low or bad CMOS backup battery, for example. If the battery is good, then you may have a more serious

problem with your motherboard or the CMOS system. As always, it is a good idea to write down the variable settings in your CMOS system and to keep current data backups.

COM PORT DOES NOT EXIST

You are attempting to use an invalid COM port. Check all the COM ports in your machine by using diagnostic utilities, such as CheckIt, QA+, or Norton Utilities, to make sure your computer recognizes the COM port you are trying to use. For example, you get this error on a machine with two physical serial ports that are both set to COM 1 if you try to send printer output through COM 2. For more information about serial port setup, see Chapter 15.

CONFIGURATION ERROR FOR SLOT *n*

You have just added an EISA card and haven't configured it, you unplugged your CMOS backup battery, or the battery power is low. In all cases, you must run the ECU (EISA configuration utility). If the battery is bad, replace it first and then run the ECU.

CONVERT DIRECTORY TO FILE?

Stop! Tell CHKDSK "No" or you will lose the entire directory with all of its files. Instead, use the Norton Disk Doctor or another disk repair utility to save the directory and its files.

CONVERT LOST CHAINS TO FILES (Y/N)?, or ERRORS FOUND, F PARAMETER NOT SPECIFIED. CORRECTIONS WILL NOT BE WRITTEN TO DISK, or *X* LOST CLUSTER(S) FOUND IN *Y* CHAINS. CONVERT LOST CHAINS TO FILES (Y/N)?

You receive these error messages if CHKDSK finds lost chains while inspecting a disk; a similar message comes from the more capable SCANDISK program that is a part of DOS 6.2 and later versions of DOS. A *lost chain* is a group of clusters that is marked as in use by the file allocation table (FAT) but not connected to any known file.

In most instances, lost chains are not significant. When you delete a number of files, the delete process may miss a link in the file chain. (A power dip or surge during an operation may also cause the computer to write a tiny blip of trash information to the FAT.)

Run CHKDSK/F or answer "Yes" to SCANDISK's query in order to fix the problem.

You should not receive this sort of error message often; regular FAT problems are early indicators of hard disk controller problems or hard disk drive problems.

DATA ERROR READING DRIVE *X:*, or
DISK ERROR READING (or WRITING) DRIVE *X:*

Most disk drives eventually begin to go out of alignment and cause the generation of one of these errors. Disk utilities, such as SpinRite, Norton Disk Doctor, QA/WIN, and QA+, can read the data and enable the rewriting of the data using the current alignment of the read/write heads. It is also possible that a spot in a sector has gone bad and can no longer hold data. Those same utilities can also help with this problem.

DECREASING AVAILABLE MEMORY

This informational message usually appears together with a memory or CMOS memory configuration error. Read the error message to determine the problem.

DISK BAD

Some part of the hard disk system is bad. As usual, you should check the cheapest possibilities first. Check the hard drive cables inside the computer. If you have recently been working inside the computer, you may have knocked one of the hard drive cables loose.

Next, check that the hard disk is spinning. You can feel a slight vibration or hear a low whine when the hard disk is on. Try unplugging the four-wire power connector at the hard disk and then plugging it back in — this makes it easy to distinguish the hard disk noise from other computer sounds.

If the hard disk is not spinning, try plugging in a different power cable from the power supply (all of the four-wire cables are identical). Next, try removing the drive, holding it with your fingers around all its sides, and giving your wrist a few quick twists. Plug it back in. If there's still no spin, you have a bad hard disk.

For older machines, I recommend that you replace both the hard disk and the hard disk controller together. See Chapter 10.

If the hard disk is spinning, you may be able to get away with replacing only the hard disk controller, but I still suggest replacing both elements.

DISK BOOT ERROR, REPLACE AND STRIKE KEY TO RETRY

The computer is attempting to boot but can't find a system disk. Check to make sure drive A: contains a system disk that you know is good. Or, if you want to boot from the hard drive, check that there's no disk in drive A:.

If drive A: contains no disk, your hard disk's system files are probably missing or damaged. System tracks can be reinstalled to a hard drive without reformatting the disk. See Chapter 10 for direction on installing hard disks and Chapter 21 to learn how to recover hard disk data.

DISK BOOT FAILURE

The boot disk, or its controller, is probably bad; the system CMOS is not configured properly. Try another boot disk. If that doesn't solve the problem, see "Disk Read Failure — Strike F1 to Retry Boot."

DISK CONFIGURATION ERROR, or HARD DISK CONFIGURATION ERROR

The CMOS chip, which holds the hardware configuration information for 286 through Pentium computers, is reporting an improper code stored within. The BIOS ROM on the system motherboard must read the information inside the CMOS chip each time the computer boots.

One example of how this sort of error could be generated is if you have installed a 1.44MB, 3.5-inch floppy drive in an old 286 machine, a computer built before such high-density drives existed. When the old ROM consults the information stored in the CMOS chip, it runs into a code that it doesn't recognize.

Older PCs were developed before today's wide range of hard disk choices were available, and the ROM may refuse to work with one of today's high-capacity or high-speed designs.

You may be able to update the ROM on your motherboard in order to fix such a problem.

DISK DRIVE 0 SEEK FAILURE, or DISK DRIVE 1 SEEK FAILURE

Check the A: drive cables (Drive 0) or the B: drive cables (Drive 1) first. Most manuals say a bad disk drive or controller causes this error, but I have most often seen it when the computer looks for a nonexistent floppy drive.

If you have an XT machine, check for a bad or unformatted floppy disk. If you have an AT-class or EISA computer, note that the CMOS chip contains setup information about a drive. If you have removed the drive from the machine or unplugged a data or power cable from the drive, the computer reports this error during boot.

DISK DRIVE FAILURE, or DISKETTE DRIVE X FAILURE

See "Disk Drive 0 Seek Failure or Disk Drive 1 Seek Failure."

DISK DRIVE RESET FAILED

The floppy disk controller is unable to reset. Try turning off the power to the machine, waiting a few seconds, and then turning it back on. If the problem is still present, you will have to replace the controller card.

DISK ERROR READING (or WRITING) FAT

A bad sector exists in the FAT. Luckily, DOS creates and stores two copies of the FAT and simply starts using the second copy.

This is a warning, though, that the fail-safe mechanism is already in use. You don't have any additional copies of the FAT if this second one goes bad.

If the problem is on a hard drive, use a disk repair utility, such as Norton Utilities or SpinRite, on the drive. If the failing disk is a floppy, just save the data that you want to a new floppy and trash the failing floppy.

DISK READ FAILURE — STRIKE F1 TO RETRY BOOT, or DISKETTE READ FAILURE

Many things can cause this problem, beginning with a simple bad disk. Try several new boot disks that you know to be good; test them on another computer equipped with an equivalent drive.

Have you just been working inside the computer? In most cases, this error is caused by knocking loose a cable or by a mistake in installing the data or power cable. See "Floppy Drives" in Chapter 9 for full cable installation directions.

If the problem persists, a bad floppy drive is the most likely cause. Try swapping in a replacement floppy drive that you know to be good. If the machine still does not boot, replace the disk controller.

DISPLAY ADAPTER FAILED; USING ALTERNATE, or DISPLAY SWITCH NOT SET PROPERLY

The mono/color jumper switch on many AT/286/386/486 motherboards has been set incorrectly. Check your manual for the location and proper setting for this jumper.

DIVIDE OVERFLOW

A numerical error has occurred in the processing of a software program. Reboot the computer; if you receive the error message again, contact the manufacturer of the software. This sort of message is often the result of a software programmer playing a bit fast-and-loose with the rules. The programmer likely tried to pick up a bit of speed by going directly to the hardware instead of through the operating system.

DMA BUS TIMEOUT

This is a message from an AMI ROM BIOS indicating that the reply to a signal on a bus did not happen in the allotted time. This may be a random or rare occurrence; reboot the PC and continue.

If you receive the message again, it may be a problem with an add-on card or with the DMA chip of your computer. If you have just added a new card, consider it a prime suspect. Turn off the computer and ground yourself. Remove the covers, take out one card at a time (starting with the most sophisticated devices), and try running the machine until you have isolated the problem. You may need to install a video card that you know to be good in order to continue your testing. If all the cards appear to be working properly, the problem may lie with the motherboard. Some diagnostic programs can check the status of the DMA controller.

DMA ERROR, or DMA 1 ERROR, or DMA 2 ERROR

The DMA chip has failed. In most cases, you will have to replace the motherboard because the DMA chip is usually soldered in place.

(.)(..) DOES NOT EXIST, or (.)(..) ENTRY HAS A BAD ATTRIBUTE (or LINK or SIZE)

The (.) entry (current directory) of the (..) entry (parent directory) has been trashed. Run a disk-repair utility, such as SpinRite or Norton Utilities.

Directory files should not fail in this manner. Read the information about the "Hard Disk Read Failure" error message; this may be an early indication of hard disk troubles. Back up your data, run hard disk diagnostic/repair utilities, and keep alert for possible new problems.

DRIVE NOT READY. ABORT, RETRY, IGNORE, FAIL?, or DRIVE X: NOT READY. MAKE SURE A DISK IS INSERTED INTO THE DRIVE AND THE DOOR IS CLOSED

If drive X: is a floppy drive, make sure that the disk is properly installed. Try the disk in another drive to be sure it is working properly and try a disk known to be good in the suspect drive. If the error continues, the floppy drive cable may be damaged, or the drive's disk sensor may be broken. Try reinstalling the cable and retesting. If this fails, try installing a new cable before you install a new disk drive.

If it turns out that the floppy disk itself was damaged, use a disk repair utility, such as Norton Disk Doctor, to repair the disk.

This same error will occasionally be reported by a hard drive. In this case, a SCSI or an ESDI controller may be having trouble talking to your motherboard — usually due to a timing incompatibility. You will often be able to get past the problem by pressing R for Retry; the problem will often go away with the second read attempt. If the hard disk does not respond after the first or second retry, you should run a disk repair utility.

EISA CMOS CHECKSUM FAILURE, or EISA CMOS INOPERATIONAL

The data in an EISA bus CMOS setup chip is corrupted and has failed a checksum test, or a read/write error has occurred. The CMOS chip holds its information with the aid of a battery, and the first suspect is a low battery. Read the discussions under "Invalid Configuration Information. Please Run Setup Program" and "Invalid EISA Configuration Storage. Please Run the Configuration Utility."

ERRORS FOUND; DISK *X*: FAILED INITIALIZATION

The hard disk has not reported back properly on initialization. The possible causes range from a simple CMOS configuration error to a major hardware catastrophe. As always, try to cure the problem with the simplest and cheapest fix. Run your setup program and enter correct hard disk configuration information. If this doesn't work, start checking the hardware.

Possible causes include the following:

- The power cable may be improperly connected to the hard disk.
- The cables connecting the hard disk to its controller may be improperly installed or may have come loose.
- The drive select jumper on the hard disk may be incorrectly set.

- The hard disk may be dead.
- The hard disk controller may be dead.

ERRORS FOUND; INCORRECT CONFIGURATION INFORMATION MEMORY SIZE MISCOMPARE

The CMOS memory has probably forgotten the setup information. Run the setup program and retest. If the error is still there, turn off the system, remove the case, and replace the CMOS battery. Run the setup program one more time.

If the error continues, turn off the power, remove the case, and press down on all of the memory chips to ensure they are firmly seated in their sockets. Then turn on the computer and retest; if the error is still present, remove all of the socketed memory chips and take them to a repair shop that has a memory tester.

If none of the RAM chips fail the memory test, or if all of the RAM chips are soldered into place, you may have to replace the motherboard. But first try swapping with a power supply that you know to be good. If this doesn't work, you have to replace the motherboard.

ERRORS ON LIST DEVICE INDICATE THAT IT MAY BE OFF-LINE. PLEASE CHECK IT

This obscure message refers to the printer; make sure it is not turned off or offline. Next check the printer cable — it should be tightly plugged into the back of the printer and tightly connected to the printer port on the back of the computer. If you have a parallel printer, refer to Chapters 17 and 18. If you have a serial printer, look at Chapters 15 and 18.

ERROR WRITING FAT

See "Disk Error Reading (or Writing) FAT."

***nnn*K EXPANDED MEMORY, or**
***nnn*K EXTENDED MEMORY, or**
***nnn*K EXTRA MEMORY, or**
EXTENDED MEMORY SIZE = *nnnnnn*K

These are informational messages. Your computer has successfully tested *nnn* kilobytes of expanded or extended memory.

EXPANSION BOARD DISABLED AT SLOT *X*

This is an informational message. The board in slot *X* has been disabled. Use the EISA configuration utility to disable or enable a board.

EXPANSION BOARD NMI AT SLOT *X*

The board in slot *X* generated a nonmaskable interrupt error, which is a significant problem. Remove the card and examine it for obvious problems. Consult your instruction manual for the card to determine if the configuration settings are wrong, and contact the manufacturer, if necessary.

EXPANSION BOARD NOT READY AT SLOT *X*

The computer does not a see a board in slot *X*, but it is expecting to find one because of information in the EISA configuration utility.

FAIL-SAFE TIMER NMI

This EISA message indicates that a device has gone wild and is hogging the bus. It may be a random event; try rebooting and retesting.

If you receive the message again, try isolating the offending card. If you have just added a new card, consider it a prime suspect. Turn off the computer, ground yourself, remove the cover, and take out one card at a time (starting with the new card and then the most sophisticated device). Try running the machine, and

repeat until you have isolated the problem. You may need to install a video card that you know to be good in order to continue with your testing. If all of the cards appear to be working properly, the problem may lie in the motherboard. The problem could be, for example, a bad DMA controller chip.

FAIL-SAFE TIMER NMI INOPERATIONAL

The fail-safe timer on your EISA board has failed. You'll probably have to replace the motherboard.

FDD A IS NOT INSTALLED, or
FDD B IS NOT INSTALLED, or
FDD CONTROLLER FAILURE

These errors generally point to a bad floppy disk drive or a bad floppy disk drive controller subsystem. For an old PC or XT, the problem could be incorrectly set configuration switches on the motherboard (see Chapter 5). Make sure that the controller card is seated firmly in the bus slot. Check for missing or incorrectly installed cables before replacing the controller.

FILE ALLOCATION TABLE BAD, or
FILE ALLOCATION TABLE BAD DRIVE *X*:

A problem exists with the FAT. Try repairing the disk with a program, such as Norton Disk Doctor. See Chapter 22 for information on data protection and recovery.

FIRST CLUSTER NUMBER IS INVALID, ENTRY TRUNCATED

CHKDSK has effectively deleted the file. It has zero clusters and now exists only as a name in the disk directory. The file is probably lost; you can try running a hard disk diagnostic or repair utility to see whether it can be repaired. Next time, use a more sophisticated disk diagnostic, such as Norton Disk Doctor or SCANDISK from DOS.

Truncating should not happen often and may be an indication of controller problems.

FIXED DISK CONFIGURATION ERROR, or
FIXED DISK CONTROLLER FAILURE

See "Disk Configuration Error."

FIXED DISK FAILURE

See "Hard Disk Failure."

FIXED DISK READ FAILURE

See "Hard Disk Read Failure — Strike F1 to Retry Boot."

GATE A20 FAILURE, or
SHUTDOWN FAILURE

An AT clone machine can generate this error message. The computer must switch into protected mode to count and check for extended memory in an AT clone (whether or not such memory is actually present). A bad motherboard or keyboard can cause a failure to switch into protected mode.

The error code may also include "8042" as a pointer to the keyboard controller chip, which may be the source of the problem.

A faulty keyboard can cause the 8042 keyboard controller chip to keep sending signals to the processor on address line 20. Check the keyboard's switches (on the bottom of the keyboard) to make certain they are properly set and then try a working keyboard. If that does not solve the problem, you will have to replace the motherboard.

GENERAL FAILURE READING (or WRITING) DRIVE *X*:
(A)BORT, (R)ETRY, (I)GNORE?

Press I (Ignore) first. If the drive reads properly afterwards, run diagnostic tests on it. Some such errors are transient or random and don't cause a problem with corrupted data; in other cases, you may have a failing controller or disk drive.

If I (Ignore) doesn't work, press A (Abort) to exit from the error message and start looking for a hardware problem. Turn off the computer, ground yourself, and remove the cover. Check the power cable and the ribbon cables to the drive. Make sure that the disk controller is firmly seated in the bus.

The error can also be caused by a bad floppy disk. Try several good floppy disks in the same drive and run a diagnostics program. See Chapter 9 for more testing suggestions.

If the problem drive is a hard disk, see Chapter 10 for testing and repair suggestions, and Chapter 21 for data protection and resurrection ideas.

HARD DISK FAILURE

The hard disk controller has not received the response from the hard disk that it expected. The controller attempts a seek on the last head on the last cylinder of the hard disk. If the head can successfully move to that last cylinder, the system BIOS assumes the hard disk type has been correctly set, the hard disk is working, and all is well.

Sometimes, however, the system BIOS sends out the command but doesn't get a response in the maximum time allotted. The BIOS then responds with a time-out error and displays the dreaded Hard Disk Failure message.

Possible causes include the following:

- The power cable may not be properly connected to the hard disk.
- The data cables connecting the hard disk and its controller may be improperly installed.
- The drive-select jumper on the hard disk may be incorrectly set.
- The hard disk may be dead.
- The hard disk controller may be dead.

In most cases, this message refers to the first hard disk (logical drive C:), but it could be either hard drive.

HARD DISK READ FAILURE — STRIKE F1 TO RETRY BOOT

Many possible causes exist for this message. If you've recently been working inside the computer, you may have knocked a cable loose or improperly installed a hard drive cable. See the installation information in your instruction manual and in Chapter 10.

If you haven't been under the covers recently, try pressing F1 to see whether the computer boots on the second try; if it does, the problem may be transitory. Run hard disk software, such as Norton Disk Doctor or SpinRite, that will read and rewrite the boot segment on the hard disk drive. If the drive is moving slightly out of alignment, using diagnostic/correction software often heads off more serious and expensive data losses.

If the hard drive won't boot after you press F1 a second time, you'll have to boot from a floppy disk with the system on it. Press C to look at the hard disk. If you get an Invalid Drive message, the computer can't read the C: drive. Run the setup program to make sure that the configuration information for the hard disk is correctly stored in the CMOS; you may have a failing CMOS battery or power supply. Try to boot again. If it still won't boot, check that the drive's data and power cables are fully connected, properly oriented, and working. (Is the drive getting power? Has the data cable been pinched?) Try the hard drive in a system with a working controller and try a working hard drive in your system.

If you are fully backed up, reformat the hard disk with system tracks and reload your programs and data. Try booting again. If the system doesn't work now, the hard disk and controller should be replaced.

If you are not backed up, you may still be able to rescue your data by sending it to a data-recovery service. And next time, back up your data.

HAS INVALID CLUSTER, FILE TRUNCATED

CHKDSK has found an invalid cluster — a reference to a nonexistent cluster, for example. It has deleted the tail end of the file, from the bad cluster to the end. The end of the file is probably gone, but a disk repair program can sometimes recover it.

Use Norton Disk Doctor, SpinRite, or the DOS SCANDISK program regularly, instead of CHKDSK, to look for developing disk problems.

ID INFORMATION MISMATCH FOR SLOT *n*

This EISA message indicates that the computer believes that cards have been moved to a slot different from the one listed in setup. Run the EISA configuration utility (ECU) to tell the computer where cards are located. If you haven't moved any cards, replace the backup battery for the CMOS memory and retest.

INFINITE RETRY ON PARALLEL PRINTER TIMEOUT, or PRINTER DEVICE FAILURE

Your printer is not turned on or is not online.

INSUFFICIENT MEMORY, or NOT ENOUGH MEMORY

These are software errors generated if you try to use more memory than is physically installed in the machine.

INTERNAL CACHE TEST FAILED — CACHE IS DISABLED

Reboot your computer. If the message recurs, run a diagnostic program to test your motherboard. Your 486 or Pentium CPU chip may have partially worked its way out of its socket, or it may be damaged beyond repair.

INTERNAL ERROR, or INTERNAL STACK OVERFLOW

These are generally software errors. Check your DOS manual for assistance. If the memory persists, check the memory on your motherboard — it could be any kind of memory problem in the lower 64K of memory.

INTR1 ERROR, or INTR2 ERROR

The interrupt controller logic has failed; the motherboard must be replaced.

INVALID BOOT DISKETTE

See "Not a Boot Disk — Strike F1 to Retry Boot."

INVALID CONFIGURATION INFORMATION. PLEASE RUN SETUP PROGRAM

If you have additional error messages displayed along with this one, try to eliminate them. You can then deal with the message listed previously.

Begin by running your setup program. Are you certain that you are entering the correct answers to the setup questions? (Check the video adapter information, disk description, keyboard specification, and other options.)

If the problem disappears when you run the setup program and then returns when you turn the computer off and on again, replace the battery and run the setup program again.

Another possible cause of this problem is a bad power supply. After you have replaced the battery for the setup memory and run the tests, try swapping the power supply on your system with a good power supply and running setup one more time.

If you install a new expansion board, you may see this error. Remove the board to see whether the error goes away. If it does,

check the board configuration and, if required by the board, set the CMOS configuration for it.

The final possibility — a rare event — would be the failure of the CMOS chip or chips themselves. In most cases, the CMOS chips are soldered into place and you will have to replace the motherboard to solve a problem with them.

INVALID CONFIGURATION INFORMATION FOR SLOT *X*, or INVALID EISA CONFIGURATION STORAGE. PLEASE RUN THE CONFIGURATION UTILITY

Rerun the ECU, making certain you have entered the correct information for the board and the correct slot number. Double-check your CMOS battery backup. If the battery power level is low, your computer can lose setup information.

I/O CARD NMI AT *XXXX:XXXX*. TYPE (S)HUT OFF NMI, (R)EBOOT, OTHER KEYS TO CONTINUE, or I/O CARD PARITY ERROR AT *XXXX* (R), or I/O CARD PARITY INTERRUPT AT *XXXX:XXXX*. TYPE (S)HUT OFF NMI, (R)EBOOT, OTHER KEYS TO CONTINUE

Your system has a bad peripheral card. First, you must figure out which card is bad. If you absolutely must continue to work, press S to shut off the nonmaskable interrupt (NMI) and save the file. The message will go away, but you haven't fixed the source of the problem.

When you are ready, turn off the computer, ground yourself, pull out all of the cards except the video adapter card, and reboot. If the error message does not reappear, reinstall the cards one at a time — turning the computer off after you install each card — and test until you find the bad card. If the error remains with only the video card installed, replace the video card and then retest. The last possibility to check for is a bad motherboard. Before you do this, though, try installing a good, basic video card so that you can eliminate that device as the source of the problem.

KEYBOARD BAD

The keyboard has failed the POST. Make certain that the keyboard is properly connected to the PC. Turn off the computer, turn it back on, and reboot. Check the AT/XT switch on the bottom of the keyboard and make sure it is in the proper position for your machine. If the message persists, you have a bad keyboard that must be replaced.

KEYBOARD CLOCK LINE FAILURE, or
KEYBOARD CONTROLLER FAILURE, or
KEYBOARD DATA LINE FAILURE, or
KEYBOARD STUCK KEY FAILURE

The keyboard controller chip tests the keyboard during POST. These messages indicate that the keyboard is sending incorrect replies to the controller's POST signals. Either the keyboard cable or the keyboard itself is bad. Check for stuck keys. Check the AT/XT switch on the bottom of the keyboard and make sure it is in the proper position for your machine. Consult your instruction manual for information.

KEYBOARD ERROR

If your computer has an older American Megatrends, Inc. AMIBIOS, the keyboard may be incompatible with the BIOS ROM. American Megatrends suggests that the keyboard may have a timing problem. One way to get around this problem is to set the keyboard in standard CMOS setup to Not Installed so that it skips the keyboard POST test.

LAST BOOT INCOMPLETE

This message is generated by a malfunctioning chip in the Intel 82335 chipset, which is used in some older AT clone motherboards.

These chips have extended features that need to be set in the extended CMOS. Run your Intel 82335 setup program, paying particular attention to the memory interweaving and EMS configuration parameters. Consult your PC's instruction manual for more details.

MEMORY ADDRESS LINE FAILURE AT *XXXX:XXXX*, READ HEX VALUE *XXXX*, EXPECTING *XXXX*

The good news is this error message is telling you a great deal of information about where it found a problem with your PC's bus; the bad news is that it is nearly impossible to repair such a problem. If the message recurs, the motherboard will have to be replaced.

MEMORY ALLOCATION ERROR. CANNOT LOAD DOS, SYSTEM HALTED

This is a software error. You may have a trashed DOS boot disk or damaged boot files on your hard drive. Try booting from a new floppy drive. Run SYS to copy COMMAND.COM and boot tracks to the hard drive.

MEMORY DATA LINE FAILURE AT *XXXX:XXXX*, READ *XXXX*, EXPECTING *XXXX*, or
MEMORY DOUBLE WORD LOGIC FAILURE AT (*hex value*), READ (*hex value*), EXPECTING (*hex value*), or MEMORY FAILURE AT *XXXX:XXXX*, READ *XXXX*, EXPECTING *XXXX*

A bad or slow memory chip causes this problem. The hexadecimal number in the first line of this error message tells you what row of memory chips contains the defective chip or chips. The message provides enough information to locate the malfunctioning chip.

You — or a computer repair technician — can figure out which chip is the problem by converting the hexadecimal number or by pulling out whole banks of memory and checking them in a memory tester.

Some diagnostic software programs, including CheckIt, can identify the problem chip. Trust me, it's much easier than manually trying to figure out the chip's address.

Here's how to convert the hexadecimal address to a particular memory address in K (kilobytes) by hand. This example uses the hexadecimal address 1EAF:45FF.

1. Shift the segment—the first half of the number (before the colon)—one place to the left. For example: 1EAF becomes 1EAF0 hexadecimal.

2. Add the offset—the second part of the number (after the colon)—to the shifted number. Now remember, you are adding hexadecimal numbers, which are base 16 and use 0 through 9, plus A through F. You can use a calculator that handles scientific math; Windows also has a capable computer calculator that can do the math for you. For example:

```
  1EAF0 hexadecimal
+ 45FF hexadecimal
= 230EF hexadecimal
```

The sum reveals the address of the bad chip. The first numeral (number 2 in the example) tells you which memory bank is the problem.

Here is a list of hex addresses and the associated memory chips:

- **0xxxx** = error in the first 64K of memory
- **1xxxx** = error in the second 64K of memory
- **2xxxx** = error in the third 64K of memory
- **3xxxx** = error in the fourth 64K of memory
- **4xxxx** = error in the fifth 64K of memory
- **5xxxx** = error in the sixth 64K of memory
- **6xxxx** = error in the seventh 64K of memory
- **7xxxx** = error in the eighth 64K of memory
- **8xxxx** = error in the ninth 64K of memory
- **9xxxx** = error in the tenth 64K of memory

Thus, for this example with a sum of 230EF hexadecimal, you know that the problem is in the third 64K of memory because the first numeral (number 2 in the example) indicates an error in the third 64K of memory.

3. Locate the correct row of chips. When computers were built with only 64K chips, this step was easy. Each bank of nine 64K chips corresponded to one segment. Now that 256K, 1MB, and 4MB chips are popular, you'll have to do some calculating. Each 256K chip contains four 64K segments (64 × 4 = 256K). A simple XT clone equipped with 640K of system memory may have two rows of 256K chips, each with four segments of 64K, and two banks of 64K for the final two segments. A more modern 386 or a better computer loaded with memory may have eight or more banks of 1MB or 4MB chips on the motherboard. The entire 640K (ten 64K segments) is located in a single bank of 1MB chips. Each motherboard manufacturer handles memory mounting slightly differently; read your computer's instruction manual to determine which bank has the problem.

4. After you have located the correct row of chips, locate the specific bad chip by using the hex data values in the second line of the error message. You do this by comparing the data that the computer attempted to store with the hexadecimal number it read back from memory. The difference between the two numbers points to the bad chip.

For example: If you have the error message "Memory Data Line Failure at Hex Value 1EAF:45FF, Read C3B6, Expecting B3B6," subtract the smaller number from the larger number:

```
  C3B6
- B3B6
= 1000. (a hexadecimal number that must be converted to
binary)
```

1000H (1000 hexadecimal) = *xxxx xxxx xxxx xxxx* with each hexadecimal digit equal to a group of four binary digits. So, 1000H is 0001 0000 0000 0000 in binary—the number that points to the bad chip.

Each digit of the 16-digit binary number corresponds to a particular chip. Counting from the right to left, you learn that the problem lies in the 13th (out of 16) chip in the row of RAM that you have already identified.

That was simple, right?

After you have determined the bad chip, you must now physically locate it on the motherboard or on the memory expansion card, if a memory expansion card is used.

Sometimes you're lucky—some motherboard manufacturers screen the bit numbers on the board. If so, you see 0, 1, 2, 3, 4, 5, 6, 7, and P. The next bank is numbered 8, 9, 10, 11, 12, 13, 14, 15, and P. Other manufacturers use hex numbers. (*P* stands for parity, which is used on most older PCs as part of an error-checking algorithm; many modern PCs have dispensed with parity checking.)

However, many board manufacturers don't bother to print this information on the board; consult your instruction manual for assistance.

MEMORY HIGH ADDRESS LINE FAILURE AT *XXXX:XXXX*. READ *XXXX*, EXPECTING *XXXX*, or MEMORY ODD/EVEN LOGIC FAILURE AT (*hex value*), READ (*hex value*), EXPECTING (*hex value*)

If either of these is a recurring error, your motherboard has failed and must be replaced.

MEMORY PARITY ERROR AT (*hex value*)

You have a bad memory chip. It could be either a data-storing memory chip or a memory chip dedicated to parity checking on most motherboards. Read the directions for the error "Memory Data Line Failure at *xxxx:xxxx*, Read *xxxx*, Expecting *xxxx*,"

remembering that the problem could be either the data-storing chip or the parity chip in the suspect bank of memory chips.

MEMORY PARITY INTERRUPT AT *XXXX:XXXX*. TYPE (S)HUT OFF NMI, (R)EBOOT, OTHER KEYS TO CONTINUE, or MEMORY PARITY NMI AT *XXXX:XXXX*. TYPE (S)HUT OFF NMI, (R)EBOOT, OTHER KEYS TO CONTINUE

This error is most often the result of a bad memory chip, and this is the first potential cause you should explore.

First, press **S** to shut off the NMI. Then save the file you have been working on. The error message will go away, but the error has not been fixed.

The bad memory chip will almost certainly not be at the address mentioned in the error message. You may choose to take all memory chips (from the motherboard and any memory expansion cards) to the repair shop for checking in a memory tester. You can also bring the entire machine to the shop for testing. I suggest that memory chips be tested at 20 nanoseconds faster than the minimum speed recommended for your motherboard.

If none of the memory chips test as bad, another unusual event may be causing the display of this message. I know of one computer that routinely displayed this message when it was formatting a disk; my guess is that the floppy disk controller card was drawing more power than expected, bringing down the power for the memory chips.

MEMORY TESTS TERMINATED BY KEYSTROKE

You are allowed to halt the initial POST memory tests on most computers by pressing the spacebar during boot. After you press the spacebar, the computer displays this message and proceeds with the rest of the POST routine.

MEMORY WRITE/READ FAILURE AT (*hex value*), READ (*hex value*), EXPECTING (*hex value*)

You have a bad memory chip. Read the directions for the error, "Memory Data Line Failure at *xxxx:xxxx*, Read *xxxx*, Expecting *xxxx*."

NO BOOT DEVICE AVAILABLE — STRIKE F1 TO RETRY BOOT

The computer is unable to boot, a problem that may have many causes.

Many machines are set up to examine the contents of drive A: first, looking for a bootable system disk. If a disk is found but the machine can't find system tracks on that disk, this error message displays. If no disk is found in the A: drive, the PC will try to boot from the C: drive (the hard disk). If the system has no hard disk or the hard disk won't boot, then the ROM BIOS displays this message.

If you recently worked inside the computer, you may have knocked a cable loose or improperly installed a hard or floppy drive cable. See Chapter 9 (floppy drives) and Chapter 10 hard drives) for cable installation directions.

Make sure you don't have an unbootable disk in drive A:. If you're sure the disk in the floppy drive is bootable, try some other disks. If your computer still does not boot, test the disks in another computer with a floppy drive of the same size and capacity.

What happens if you don't have a disk in the floppy drive, and you still receive this error? When the computer sees no disk in drive A:, it tries to boot from the hard disk. You can watch the machine turn on the red light in the floppy drive, look for a floppy, turn off that light and then turn on the indicator light associated with the hard drive.

Try pressing F1 to see whether the computer will boot on a second try. If it does — great. But you still haven't solved the mystery of why it failed the first time. Run hard disk diagnostic/ correction software, such as SpinRite or Norton Disk Doctor. Any of these programs will read and rewrite the boot segment on the hard disk drive. If the drive is moving slightly out of alignment, using this software will often head off more expensive data losses.

If the hard drive won't boot even after you've pressed F1 several times, you will need to boot from a floppy disk with the DOS system files on it to get the computer to retry the hard disk. If this works, you might be able to run a hard disk diagnostic/repair software program.

If you receive an Invalid Drive message, this is an indication that the computer can't read drive C:. Run the setup program to make certain that the configuration information for the hard disk is correctly stored in the CMOS. Try to boot again; if your PC still won't boot, your next step depends on whether you have a recent backup of your data.

If you are fully backed up, reformat the hard disk with system tracks and reload your programs and data. Retry booting. If the system does not work now, the hard disk and controller should be replaced.

If you are not backed up, you may still be able to rescue your data by sending it to a data-recovery service. And next time, back up your data.

NO FAIL-SAFE TIMER NMI

The fail-safe timer on your EISA board has failed. Run a diagnostics program, such as QA+ or QA+Win, to check your system board. If the error is real, you will have to replace your motherboard.

NO SCAN CODE FROM THE KEYBOARD

This message is generated only by certain XT class machines and indicates that the keyboard is locked out or not connected to the computer.

NO SOFTWARE PORT NMI

Run a diagnostics program, such as QA+ or QA+Win, to check your system board. If the error is real, you will have to replace your motherboard.

NON-DOS DISK ERROR READING (or WRITING) DRIVE *X*:

The boot track on this disk is dead, so DOS is unable to recognize the disk. Disk repair software may be able to fix the problem. If not, you may have to boot from a floppy disk and either use SYS to add tracks to the hard drive or remove all data to a backup medium and then reformat the hard disk with system tracks.

NON-SYSTEM DISK OR DISK ERROR. REPLACE AND STRIKE ANY KEY WHEN READY, or
NON-SYSTEM DISK OR DISK ERROR. PRESS A KEY TO CONTINUE

Normally, these errors are caused by trying to boot from a nonsystem (nonbootable) floppy disk. If you receive one of these messages when trying to access your hard disk, use SYS to reinstall COMMAND.COM and system tracks to your hard disk.

NO TIMER TICK INTERRUPT

The timer chip can't get the interrupt controller chip to send interrupt 0 (the timer interrupt). This means you have a bad motherboard; it will have to be replaced.

NOT A BOOT DISK — STRIKE F1 TO RETRY BOOT

The computer is unable to boot from the floppy drive. Make sure that your drive contains a bootable disk. If you're sure the disk is bootable, try a couple of other disks. Test all of these boot disks in another computer that is equipped with a floppy disk drive of the same size and capacity.

If the disks test as good, the error may be caused by the floppy disk controller or by a bad floppy drive. Have you had similar problems in the past? For example, have you occasionally received data-error messages inside DOS—messages that pointed to read/write problems with this drive? If so, try replacing the drive first. The second step would be to replace the controller.

NOT READY ERROR READING (OR WRITING) DRIVE *X*:, or
NOT READY READING DRIVE *X*:

The drive door is probably not closed. If the error message persists after you close the door, try a couple of different disks that you know to be good. If that doesn't work, you may have a bad door-closed sensor on the drive; the drive itself can also fail.

If the disk is the problem, not the drive, or if drive *X*: is a hard drive, try a disk-repair software program.

According to the DOS manual, you can also receive the writing to version of this error if the printer is offline or turned off, and the computer is attempting to send data.

(*hex value*) OPTIONAL ROM BAD CHECKSUM = (*hex value*)

The ROM on an optional expansion card is corrupted or destroyed. Likely candidates are ROM on the hard disk controller or a video card.

Check the instruction manual for the ROM location of your expansion card. Not all ROM locations for particular types of cards are standardized, and technicians or users can also reassign memory addresses to avoid conflict. The best defense is to keep a record of all assignments for all cards as they are installed; a good diagnostic program can also examine your machine and give you a listing of which memory locations contain what assignments.

Typical assignments for equipment include the following:

- C800, CA00, and D800 are used for hard disk controllers.
- C000 is often used for video cards.
- CE00 is used for high-density floppy controllers.
- DC00 is often taken by network cards.

If the ROMs on your computer have other addresses and you can't determine their location by using a diagnostic program, you may have to experiment. Turn off the computer, remove the cover, and take out all cards except the video card. If you still have the error when the power is turned back on, the problem must be with the video card. If the error is not displayed, turn off the computer and then reinstall and test the other cards one by one until you find the culprit.

OUT OF ENVIRONMENT SPACE

This is a software error related to a setting in your CONFIG.SYS file. See your DOS manual.

PARITY CHECK 1, or PARITY CHECK 2

Check 1 is an indication of a parity error on an expansion card. Hard disk controller cards, memory expansion cards, and some other cards have memory on them, complete with parity checking for error detection. Turn off the computer, remove the covers, and take out all cards except the video card. If you still have the error when the power is turned back on, the problem must be with the video card. If the error is not displayed, turn off the computer and then reinstall and test the other cards one by one until you find the culprit.

Check 2 indicates a problem with one or more of the memory chips on the motherboard. You can remove the memory chips and take them to a computer shop for testing, or you can bring the entire unit to the shop. In some cases, the memory is okay, but the motherboard has failed and must be replaced.

POINTER DEVICE FAILURE

Your mouse, trackball, pen, or other device attached to the PS/2-style mouse port on the motherboard is not responding properly to the queries of the computer. Check to see whether it is properly attached. If the error continues, run the test program that comes with many peripheral devices.

PROBABLE NON-DOS DISK. CONTINUE (Y/N)?

The boot track on the disk has been erased or corrupted. This can happen as the result of an electrical spike, a misbehaving disk controller, and occasionally, a poorly designed piece of software. And sometimes the culprit is a computer virus.

First check for viruses by using an antivirus program on a floppy disk. Then try reinstalling the system tracks with the SYS command from DOS. Finally, you can try a disk-repair utility, such as SpinRite or Norton Disk Doctor. When all else fails, you may have to back up your data and reformat the disk. If you are unable to perform a backup, you can send the disk to a data-recovery service.

PROCESSING CANNOT CONTINUE

You receive this error when you try to run CHKDSK or other DOS utilities without enough memory. Add more RAM.

RAM BAD

The RAM failed the POST. You will have to test the RAM and replace the bad chips. You can remove chips and bring them to a computer repair shop for testing or take the entire unit in for testing. This error is usually generated by the failure of one or two chips. Sometimes, though, the circuitry on the motherboard itself has failed, and the motherboard must be replaced.

READ FAULT ERROR READING DRIVE *X*:, or SECTOR NOT FOUND ERROR READING (OR WRITING) DRIVE *X*:, or SEEK ERROR READING (OR WRITING) DRIVE *X*:, or UNRECOVERABLE READ (OR WRITE) ERROR ON DRIVE *X*:

Double-check your floppy disk. Is it installed in the drive correctly? It could be upside down or not fully installed. Press **R** for retry.

If the error recurs, at least one bad spot exists on the floppy or hard disk. Run a disk repair utility.

This is not necessarily a significant error. All drives eventually go out of alignment and produce this error. Luckily, DOS gives early warning. Disk utilities will cause the drive to rewrite the data, often moving it to a better-quality spot on the disk. Once rewritten, the data is in alignment with the aging drive's alignment, so you should have no more trouble with this particular disk until a bit further down the road.

REAL TIME CLOCK FAILURE

The real-time clock or the battery that supports it has failed. See "Time-Of-Day Clock Stopped."

RESUME = 'F1' KEY

An error has occurred; press F1 to continue processing.

ROM

If you're using an XT, this message means that the system ROM BIOS located on the motherboard has been damaged, and you will have to replace it, if possible.

ROM BAD CHECKSUM =, or ROM ERROR, or ROM BAD SUM =

This message from XT systems indicates that the BIOS ROM on the motherboard could not be read and must be replaced, if possible. In some cases, the motherboard itself is damaged and must be replaced.

XX = SCANCODE, CHECK KEYBOARD

An erroneous scancode was received from the keyboard. A stuck key or a bad keyboard connector can send a bad scancode from the keyboard to the CPU. Try swapping in a working keyboard. If the keyboard has an XT/AT switch (check the bottom of the keyboard), be sure the switch is properly set.

SHARING VIOLATION READING DRIVE X:

This is a software error; check your DOS manual.

*nnn*K STANDARD MEMORY

This is an informational message indicating that your computer has successfully tested *nnn* kilobytes of standard memory.

STRIKE THE F1 KEY TO CONTINUE

This message indicates that an error was found during the POST. The computer will display an error message describing the problem. You can try to boot the system despite this error. Correct the problem (for example, removing a nonbooting disk in drive A:) and then press F1 to try booting the system.

STUCK KEY SCANCODE = *XX*

A key is stuck on the keyboard. Locate and repair the stuck key. If the location of the stuck key is not obvious, try pressing each key individually. The stuck key will feel different than the others when you press it.

TARGET DISK IS WRITE PROTECTED

This error message should appear only if you are attempting to DISKCOPY to a write-protected floppy disk. Occasionally, the part of the floppy drive responsible for detecting the write-enable notch (on a 5.25-inch disk) or the covered write-enable slide (on a 3.5-inch disk) is broken. If so, the disk will assume all disks are write-protected. It is not easy and rarely cost-effective to repair a floppy disk drive, which retails for about $25.

TIMER CHIP COUNTER 2 FAILED, or
TIMER OR INTERRUPT CONTROLLER BAD

Either the timer chip or the interrupt controller chip has failed. Both are soldered to the motherboard and, therefore, the motherboard must be replaced.

TIME-OF-DAY CLOCK STOPPED, or
TIME-OF-DAY NOT SET UP — PLEASE RUN SETUP PROGRAM

Run the setup program that came with your computer or that resides in the ROM BIOS. If this error persists, try replacing the batteries that power the CMOS chip whenever the computer is turned off and then run the setup program again.

If the error message still appears, the error is probably caused by the power supply. Replace the power supply and run the setup program again. In rare situations, the error may be caused by a failing motherboard.

TRACK 0 BAD — DISK UNUSABLE

You may receive this error when you try to format a 1.2MB floppy disk in a 360K drive, or the other way around.
Another possibility is that the floppy disk actually has a damaged track 0; throw away the floppy disk and use another one.

If you get this error on a hard drive, the news is worse: It means that the hard drive has gone bad and must be replaced. Use a disk utility program, such as SpinRite or Norton Disk Doctor, to try to fix the problem.

If you don't have a backup for the data on the disk, you can send the disk to a data-recovery service.

UNEXPECTED HW INTERRUPT *XX*H AT *XXXX:XXXX*. TYPE (R)EBOOT, OTHER KEYS TO CONTINUE, or
TED SW INTERRUPT *XX*H AT *XXXX:XXXX*. TYPE (R)EBOOT, OTHER KEYS TO CONTINUE

This is a Phoenix BIOS error that can be caused by many hardware or software problems.

The message means an interrupt is being sent on an interrupt line that has not been properly initialized.

For example, a poorly designed card that is installed without its accompanying software driver or a card with malfunctioning driver software can cause this error message.

UNEXPECTED INTERRUPT IN PROTECTED MODE

A bad expansion card or a failed motherboard can cause this problem. Bad VGA or network cards can produce this error because both can use the NMI line to communicate with the CPU. In either case, though, the card is sending interrupts during boot, a time when it should not be using the NMI circuit.

Turn off the computer, pull out all cards except the video adapter, and reboot. If the error message does not reappear, reinstall the cards one at a time — turning the computer off as you install each card — and test until you find the bad card. If the error remains with only the video card installed, you will have to replace the video card, and then retest. The last possibility is to check for a bad motherboard. Before you do this, though, try installing a good, basic video card so that you can eliminate that device as the source of the problem.

UNLOCK SYSTEM UNIT KEYLOCK

This message appears when you lock the key on the front of the computer that grounds out the keyboard-to-motherboard circuit. Unlock the keylock and reboot the computer.

UNRECOVERABLE ERROR IN DIRECTORY. CONVERT DIRECTORY TO FILE (Y/N)?

Wait! Press **N** (No). If you press **Y** (Yes), you will lose everything in this directory and in all subdirectories within it. Sometimes a disk-repair utility can repair the error.

WRITE FAULT ERROR WRITING DRIVE *X:*, or CT ERROR WRITING DRIVE *X:*

The disk drive door may be open.

Occasionally, the part of the floppy drive responsible for detecting the write-enable notch (on a 5.25-inch disk) or the covered write-enable slide (on a 3.5-inch disk) is broken. If so, the disk will assume that all disks are write-protected. It is not easy and rarely cost-effective to repair a floppy disk drive, which retails for less than $25.

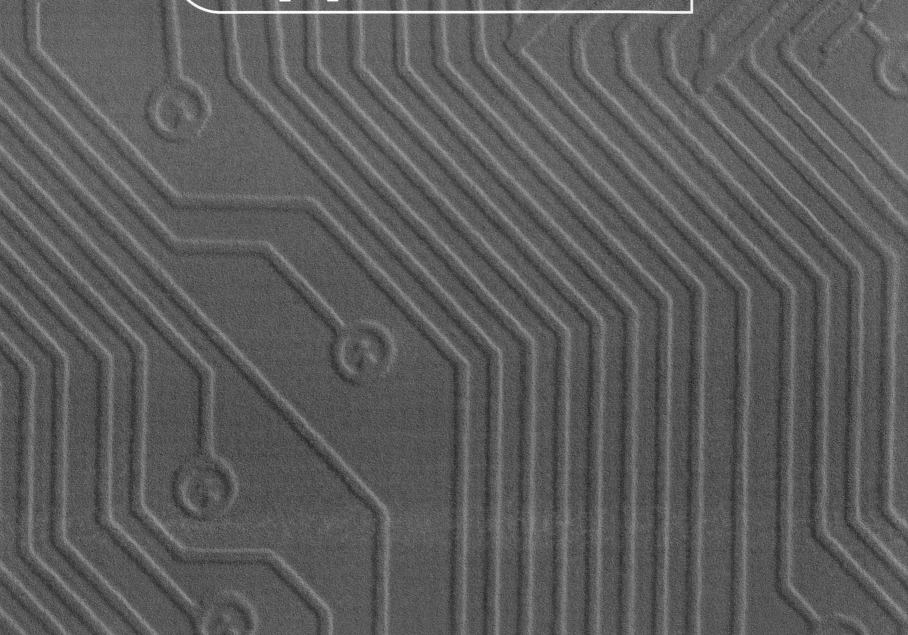

Appendix C

Beep Error Codes

How do you know what's going on inside your computer if the video monitor can't display error codes or messages? One answer is a series of sound codes that are built into the ROM BIOS of many PCs.

No official standard exists for the use of the codes, but over the years, the dominance of two BIOS makers — Phoenix and American Megatrends, Inc. (AMI) — has created a common group of codes for PC clones. IBM's own BIOS is also widely used and is close to AMI and Phoenix in its structure and syntax.

If you don't know the brand of your BIOS and can't see the brand name credit that flashes on the screen during bootup, check your computer's instruction manual, call the manufacturer, or take off the covers and examine the motherboard. The ROM BIOS consists of one or several chips near the CPU, usually marked with AMI or Phoenix; you may also see other chips identified as BIOS. (Ignore other ROMs on video cards, disk controllers, or other devices.)

AMI Codes

Computers using the AMIBIOS use an uninterrupted series of beeps to signal a fatal error (an error that halts the boot process before the video screen is usable). These AMIBIOS codes are listed here in numeric order. Count the number of beeps you hear — turn the machine off and on again to recount the beeps if necessary — and then look up the error code in the following list.

One beep: DRAM REFRESH FAILURE

Many XT- and some AT-class computers beep once or twice when booting up normally. If your computer shows standard information on the screen, you don't have a problem; if anything is wrong, the computer will display a screen-error message.

If you have no video display, check the simple things first. Is the video monitor plugged in and turned on? Did the video cable from monitor to computer become disconnected?

This single beep tells you that faulty memory refresh circuitry exists on your motherboard. The timer chip told the DMA chip to go into RAM and refresh the memory. The DMA chip did this, but the refresh process failed. The possible causes of this malfunction are the following:

- Bad memory chips
- A bad DMA chip
- Bad memory addressing chips on the motherboard

Turn off the computer. Reseat the memory chips or the SIMMs, and then retest the computer. Because the DMA chip is almost always soldered to the motherboard—as are the memory address logic chips—any problems with these chips almost always require replacement of the motherboard.

Two beeps: PARITY ERROR/PARITY CIRCUIT FAILURE

Many XT- and some AT-class computers beep once or twice when booting up normally. If your computer shows standard information on the screen, then you don't have a problem; if anything is wrong, the computer will display a screen-error message.

If you have no video display, check first that your monitor is turned on and plugged in properly. The double beep may occur to tell you of a parity error in the first 64K of memory. (This is the same as the Phoenix BIOS error 1-4-2, described later in this appendix.)

If you're lucky, a memory chip has simply worked itself loose on the motherboard. Reseat the chips or the SIMM memory strips; if this doesn't work, follow the directions for Phoenix error 1-3-3, given later in this appendix.

Three beeps: BASE 64K MEMORY FAILURE

This error can be caused by bad memory chips or by a bad motherboard. Try reseating the memory chips or SIMM memory strips. If this doesn't work, follow the directions for Phoenix error 1-3-3, given later in this appendix.

Four beeps: SYSTEM TIMER NOT OPERATIONAL

This code may indicate a malfunctioning timer 1 or failure in the first 64K of RAM memory. Turn off the computer, reseat any loose memory chips, and retest. If the beep error persists, you can try testing the motherboard with memory that you know to be good

from a comparable computer. Replace the first 64K of memory (the single row of chips in an XT clone, two rows of chips in a 286-based computer, and from one to four rows of chips in a 386 or 486 computer). If you still receive the four-beep error message, replace the motherboard. This error is not applicable to modern machines using SIMMs, DIMMs, and other multi-chip modules.

Five beeps: PROCESSOR FAILURE

The CPU chip appears to be dead. Turn off the computer, reseat the memory chips, and then retest. If the error continues, you can consider replacing the CPU, although doing so may not be cost-efficient—it may make more sense to replace the motherboard. If you transplant a CPU from another machine, it should ideally be the same speed as your old chip.

Six beeps: 8042 KEYBOARD CONTROLLER/GATE A20 FAILURE

This error, like Phoenix 4-2-3, can be caused either by keyboard problems or a bad motherboard. A rare handful of keyboards have a fuse; check whether it needs replacement or resetting. Try a different keyboard that you know to be good to see whether it solves the problem.

If the keyboard seems okay, AMI recommends reseating the keyboard controller chip if it is not soldered to the motherboard. If it still beeps, replace the keyboard controller if possible. The last resort is a new motherboard.

Seven beeps: PROCESSOR EXCEPTION INTERRUPT ERROR/VIRTUAL MODE EXCEPTION ERROR

The CPU is dead. Turn off the computer, reseat the memory chips, and then retest. This probably won't help, but if it does, it's a lot cheaper than replacing the whole motherboard. If the error continues, you can consider replacing the CPU, although that may not be cost-efficient—it may make more sense to replace the motherboard. If you transplant a CPU from another machine, it should ideally be the same speed as your old chip.

Eight beeps: DISPLAY MEMORY READ/WRITE ERROR

The video card is missing or bad. Check to make sure it is properly seated in the bus. Install a new video card or unit you know to be good to see whether it solves the problem. Another possibility is the failure of the memory on the video card itself, which may or may not be efficiently replaced.

Nine beeps: ROM BIOS CHECKSUM ERROR

This error indicates a damaged ROM BIOS. It is not likely that this error can be corrected by reseating the chips. If it persists, the BIOS chips have to be replaced.

Ten beeps: CMOS SHUTDOWN REGISTER READ/WRITE ERROR

When an AT or later CPU chip boots up, it transfers into protected mode and then transfers back to real mode (the mode it uses to run DOS). The chip has to reboot to transfer to real mode. Before it reboots, the CPU posts a note to itself in CMOS RAM saying, "I've just booted. I'm trying to get into real mode to do some work. Don't send me back into protected mode to initialize everything—I've just done that." The likely problem is that the CMOS shutdown register on the computer is broken, and the CMOS memory and associated chips will have to be replaced; it may be more cost-effective to replace the motherboard itself.

Eleven beeps: CACHE MEMORY BAD— DO NOT ENABLE CACHE

This is an indicator that the cache memory test has failed and has been disabled. On many AMI systems, you *could* press Ctrl + Alt + Shift ++ to enable cache memory, but AMI recommends against this. Instead, try reseating the cache memory on the motherboard and retesting. If the error persists, replace the cache memory.

One long beep, three short: MEMORY FAILURE

This indicates a conventional or extended memory failure on the motherboard.

One long beep, eight short: VIDEO DISPLAY ADAPTER FAILURE

This indicates a video card failure; try reinstalling in a different slot.

No beeps

If all you hear is silence and no image appears on the screen, check the power supply with a voltmeter. Next, inspect the motherboard for loose components. A loose or missing CPU, BIOS chip, clock crystal, or ASIC chip will cause the motherboard not to function.

Next, eliminate the possibility of interference by a failed or improperly set up I/O card by removing all cards except the video adapter. At the least, the system should power up and wait for a drive timeout. Insert the cards back into the system one at a time until the problem occurs again. When the system hangs up again, you can assume the problem is related to the last expansion card that you added.

If you can't determine the problem in this way, the motherboard will have to be replaced.

IBM Beep Codes

Many BIOS manufacturers have adapted and extended IBM's set of codes, which date back in their original form to the dinosaur IBM PC. They use a group of three or four sets of beeps separated by pauses. These codes are listed as a sequence of three numbers. For example, Beep <pause> Beep <pause> Beep Beep Beep is listed as 1-1-3.

1-1-3 CMOS WRITE/READ FAILURE

The computer is unable to read the configuration that should be stored in CMOS. If the error persists, replace the motherboard.

1-1-4 ROM BIOS CHECKSUM ERROR

The ROM BIOS has been damaged and will have to be replaced if possible.

1-2-1 PROGRAMMABLE INTERVAL TIMER FAILURE

A bad timer chip exists on the motherboard, and the motherboard will have to be replaced.

1-2-2 DMA INITIALIZATION FAILURE or 1-2-3 DMA PAGE REGISTER WRITE/READ FAILURE

The DMA chip is probably bad. Because this chip is usually permanently soldered onto the motherboard, you'll likely have to replace the whole motherboard.

A remote possibility exists that a bad expansion card is grabbing hold of one of the DMA lines and not letting go; you could try removing all cards except for the video card to see whether the error persists. If it doesn't persist, continue with the other cards to try to determine the very rare culprit.

1-3-1 RAM REFRESH VERIFICATION FAILURE

The timer chip told the DMA chip to go into RAM and refresh the memory. The DMA chip did this, but the refresh process failed. The possible causes of this malfunction include the following:

- Bad memory chips
- A bad DMA chip
- Bad memory addressing chips on the motherboard

Turn off the computer, remove all the memory chips, and test them. Replace any bad chips and retest the computer. Because the DMA chip and the memory address logic chips are almost always soldered to the motherboard, you will almost certainly have to replace the motherboard.

1-3-3 FIRST 64K RAM CHIP OR DATA LINE FAILURE, MULTI-BIT

For some reason, the first 64K of RAM is not responding to the CPU. The memory chips may be bad; you can try switching the high and low memory on your motherboard to see whether the problem goes away.

In 8086 and 8088 machines, the first bank of memory contains the first 64K (or the first 256K if the computer is using 256K chips), so switching the first and second banks (or the third and fourth banks) may solve the problem. Read your PC's instruction manual to find out which is the first bank on your particular motherboard.

A bad motherboard can also cause this problem. If the memory chips all test good, you will have to replace the motherboard itself.

1-3-4 FIRST 64K ODD/EVEN LOGIC FAILURE or 1-4-1 ADDRESS LINE FAILURE 64K OF RAM

These errors indicate a failure of address or logic chips on the motherboard, which will have to be replaced.

1-4-2 PARITY FAILURE FIRST 64K OF RAM

You have a bad memory chip, either a data-story chip or one of the chips dedicated to parity error checking. Read the directions for code 1-3-3.

Chips also exist on the motherboard that are responsible for calculating the memory parity. If these chips go bad, the motherboard will need to be replaced. Test the memory chips thoroughly first, though, before replacing the motherboard.

1-4-3 FAIL SAFE TIMER FAILURE

The fail-safe timer on your EISA motherboard has failed, and the motherboard will have to be replaced.

1-4-4 SOFTWARE NMI PORT FAILURE

The software port enables the EISA software to talk to EISA expansion boards; the motherboard will have to be replaced.

2-X-X FIRST 64K RAM FAILURE

The beep codes in the following list indicate that a bad memory chip exists in the first 64K of RAM. Each word of data on an AT-class computer has 16 bits. Because each bit in a particular word is stored in a different memory chip, there are 16 chips for each word. (386 and 486 computers also boot up as 16-bit computers, not as 32-bit machines, and the BIOS codes also apply for Phoenix ROMs.)

2-1-1	Bit 0	2-2-3	Bit 6	2-4-1	Bit 12
2-1-2	Bit 1	2-2-4	Bit 7	2-4-2	Bit 13
2-1-3	Bit 2	2-3-1	Bit 8	2-4-3	Bit 14
2-1-4	Bit 3	2-3-2	Bit 9	2-4-4	Bit 15
2-2-1	Bit 4	2-3-3	Bit 10		
2-2-2	Bit 5	2-3-4	Bit 11		

Unfortunately, when you look at the motherboard, it is not obvious which particular memory chip holds the indicated bit. Your computer's instruction manual may have memory chip location diagrams; some motherboards have the bit number printed alongside the chip sockets. The letter P stands for parity chip, 1 for bit 1, and so on. You may also have to call the manufacturer for help. The last and most time-consuming resort involves a trial-and-error search for the bad chip.

3-1-1 SLAVE DMA REGISTER FAILURE
3-1-2 MASTER DMA REGISTER FAILURE
3-1-3 MASTER INTERRUPT MASK REGISTER FAILURE
3-1-4 SLAVE INTERRUPT MASK REGISTER FAILURE

You have a bad DMA chip or interrupt controller chip. Because both of these chips are almost always soldered onto the motherboard, you will likely have to replace the motherboard.

3-2-4 KEYBOARD CONTROLLER TEST FAILURE

The keyboard controller chip is not sending the right replies to the controller's POST signals when it tests the keyboard at bootup. This is an indication that the keyboard cable or the keyboard itself has gone bad. Check the AT/XT switch on the bottom of the keyboard to make certain it is set properly. Check also for a stuck key. Also, try swapping a keyboard that you know to be good before you purchase and install a new keyboard.

3-3-4 SCREEN INITIALIZATION FAILURE

The computer can't find a video card. Is one installed? Is it properly seated in the bus? If you can't bring it to life, try swapping with a video card that you know to be good.

3-4-1 SCREEN RETRACE TEST FAILURE

The video chip on the video card is failing; the card will have to be replaced.

3-4-2 SCREEN RETRACE TEST FAILURE

A problem exists with your video card; it won't reset the retrace bit in the allotted time. The card will have to be replaced.

4-2-1 TIMER TICK FAILURE

The timer chip can't get the interrupt controller chip to send interrupt 0 (the timer interrupt). You have a bad motherboard and will have to replace it.

4-2-2 SHUTDOWN TEST FAILURE

This code applies only to AT-class machines. The computer must switch into protected mode to count and check the extended memory in an AT, even if no extended memory exists (it must check that there are zero kilobytes of extended memory). After the computer performs this check, it shuts down and reboots itself in real mode.

A bad motherboard can cause a failure to switch into protected mode, as can a failed keyboard controller chip on the motherboard; a bad keyboard is the easiest to check and replace.

4-2-3 GATE A20 FAILURE

This error message can be generated by an AT clone machine. The computer must switch into protected mode to count and check for extended memory in an AT clone (whether or not such memory is actually present). A bad motherboard or keyboard can cause a failure to switch into protected mode.

A faulty keyboard can cause the 8042 keyboard controller chip to keep sending signals to the processor on address line 20. Check the keyboard's switches to make certain that they are properly set, and then try a keyboard that you know to be good. If this does not solve the problem, you will have to replace the motherboard.

4-2-4 UNEXPECTED INTERRUPT IN PROTECTED MODE

Either a bad expansion card or a bad motherboard can cause this error. Bad VGA or network cards, for example, can produce this error because both can use the nonmaskable interrupt (NMI) line to communicate with the CPU. In either case, though, the card is sending interrupts during bootup, a time when it should not be using the NMI circuit.

Turn off the computer, pull out all the cards except the video card, and reboot. If the error disappears, reinstall the cards one at a time (turning the computer off as you install each card) and test each card in turn until you find the bad card. If the error remains with only the video card installed, you will have to replace the video card and then retest. The last possibility is a bad motherboard. Before you install a new motherboard, though, try installing a basic video card from another computer to make sure that the problem is not in the original video card.

4-3-1 RAM TEST ADDRESS FAILURE

The chips that are responsible for memory address logic have failed. Because these chips are almost always soldered to the motherboard, you will likely have to replace the motherboard.

4-3-2 PROGRAMMABLE INTERVAL TIMER CHANNEL 2 TEST FAILURE or 4-3-3 INTERVAL TIMER CHANNEL 2 FAILURE

The interval timer is used to refresh memory; the motherboard will have to be replaced.

4-3-4 TIME OF DAY CLOCK FAILURE

Run the setup program that came with the computer; if the error persists, replace the batteries that power the CMOS memory whenever the computer is turned off. Run the setup program again.

If the error still exists, the error is probably caused by the power supply. Replace the power supply with a unit that you know to be good and run the setup program again.

In some very rare instances, you will have to replace the motherboard to fix this problem.

4-4-1 SERIAL PORT TEST FAILURE or 4-4-2 PARALLEL PORT TEST FAILURE

The serial or parallel ports have failed the POST tests. Run a system diagnostic program to check them. Ports on an expansion card can be replaced by installing a new card. If the ports are located on the motherboard, placing a jumper can disable them; new ports can then be added with an add-in card.

4-4-3 MATH COPROCESSOR FAILURE

The math coprocessor chip used in some 8088, 286, and 386 systems may have failed. Use a coprocessor testing diagnostic program to double-check it. If the coprocessor is bad, it can be disabled (only a few software programs require its presence) or replaced.

Phoenix BIOS 3.x and Earlier

Computers using a Phoenix BIOS use a group of three or four sets of beeps separated by pauses, such as 1-1-3 for Beep < pause > Beep < pause > Beep Beep Beep. A few special codes, however, use short and long tones, as listed here.

One beep

This is ordinarily not an indication of a problem; the beep comes at the completion of the self-test just before DOS is loaded.

Two beeps

This indicates a possible configuration error. The BIOS may be detecting that the video card does not match its settings or that some other configuration is invalid. This could indicate a video card failure, monitor failure, or the loose monitor cable connection.

One long beep, one short beep

This indicates a video failure. Check the jumpers and DIP switches on the video card if present or the motherboard if any changes have been made lately.

One long beep, one short beep, one long beep, one short beep

This is a report of a double video failure, meaning that the BIOS attempted to initialize both a color and monochrome video adapter, and both failed or were not present.

Phoenix BIOS 4.0 Error Beep Codes

More recent modern machines may use an enhanced version of the Phoenix BIOS. Beep codes are presented as long, short, long, short; for example, 1-2-2-3 means one long, two short, two long, and three short beeps.

Phoenix also displays a message onscreen unless the video subsystem is not working properly. The warning for video problems is one long beep followed by two short beeps.

Beep Code	Indication
1	Test beep before boot
1-2	Checksum failure on option ROMs
1-2-2-3	BIOS ROM checksum
1-3-1-1	Test DRAM refresh
1-3-1-3	Test 8742 Keyboard Controller
1-3-4-1	RAM failure on address line *xxxx*
1-3-4-3	RAM failure on data bits *xxxx* of low byte of memory bus
1-4-1-1	RAM failure on data bits *xxxx* of high byte of memory bus
2-1-2-3	Check ROM copyright notice
2-2-3-1	Unexpected interrupts
2-2-3-1	Test for unexpected interrupts

Award BIOS Beep Codes

Award is another BIOS vendor with a lot of machines in the field. Award is now part of Phoenix, but there remain branded BIOS systems under the Award name. The Award BIOS beep code scheme is much simpler than some; you only have one beep condition to look for with this BIOS. If yours is an Award BIOS machine and you hear a single long beep followed by two short beeps, it indicates a video (display adapter) error. Any other beeps with an Award BIOS probably indicate a problem with RAM. Use the RAM troubleshooting suggestions in Chapter 8 to help solve this problem.

Getting BIOS Support

Most current BIOS manufacturers offer Web pages with information, troubleshooting help, and upgrades for their BIOS. You may start at the BIOS manufacturer's Web site instead of the motherboard manufacturer if you suspect BIOS problems, if you need a BIOS upgrade, or if you need help finding out which BIOS or BIOS version you have.

The following sites can help you to get the support you need:

- **IBM:** www.pc.ibm.com/support
- **Multiple vendors (AMI, Award, MR BIOS, Phoenix, and others):**
  - **Micro Firmware:** www.firmware.com
  - **Unicore:** www.unicore.com

CROSS-REFERENCE

For more details about BIOS upgrade and replacement, see Chapter 3.

Notes

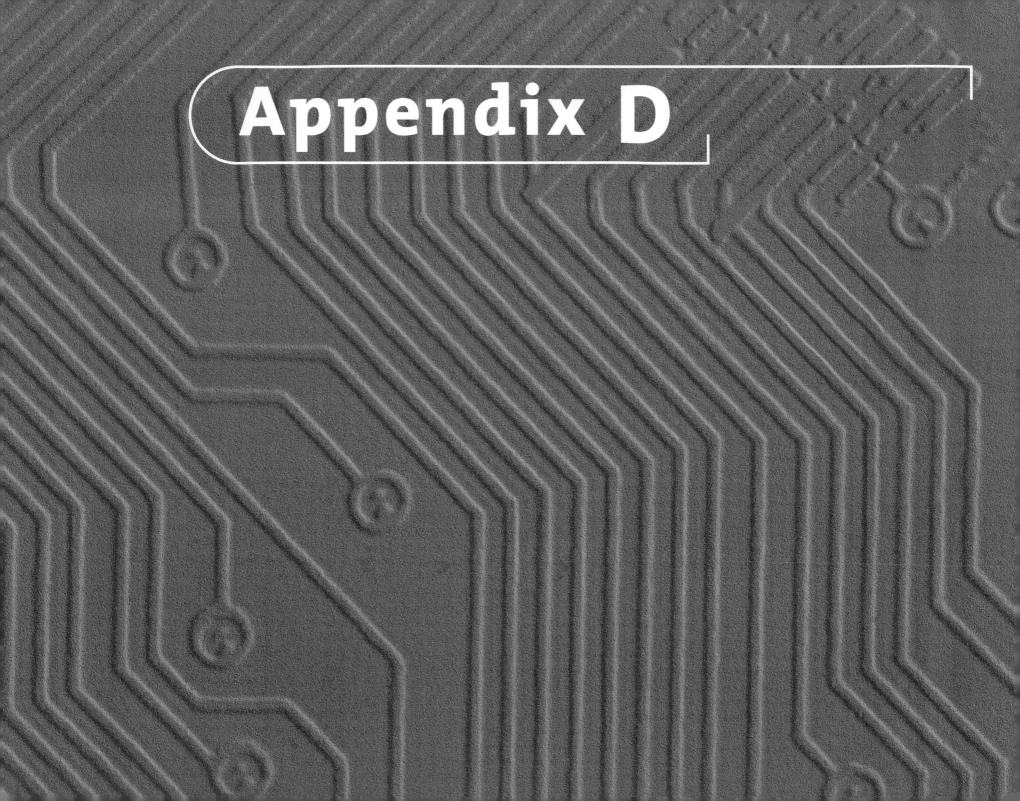

Appendix D

IRQ, DMA, and Memory Assignments

May I have your attention? Hardware needs a way to grab the attention of the CPU when it has to move information or ask for work to be done. Hardware can do this in two principal ways: by sending a signal to request an interruption of whatever the CPU is doing (called an *interrupt request* or IRQ), and through the use of a direct memory access channel (DMA) that enables the transfer of data directly without intervention by the microprocessor. The third piece of the equation is an input/output (I/O) address, a location in system memory assigned to a particular device.

Standard IRQ Assignments

Dinosaur XT-class fossils had eight available interrupts, numbered from 0 to 7. AT-class machines and all subsequent modern machines have eight additional IRQs, numbered from 8 to 15.

8-bit ISA bus default IRQ assignments

IRQ	Device	Slot/Motherboard
0	System timer	Motherboard resource
1	Keyboard controller	Motherboard resource
2	Available	8-bit slot
3	Serial port 2 (COM2)	8-bit slot
4	Serial port 1 (COM1)	8-bit slot
5	Hard disk controller	8-bit slot
6	Floppy disk controller	8-bit slot
7	Parallel port 1 (LPT1)	8-bit slot

Modern machine ISA/PCI bus default IRQ assignments

Here are the typical uses for interrupts for 16-bit buses, presented in the priority in which the computer is set to deal with them. To add a second tier of interrupts, designers used IRQ 2 as the gateway to a second interrupt controller; IRQ 2, then, is not available to be reassigned.

IRQ	Device	Slot/Motherboard
0	System timer	Motherboard resource
1	Keyboard controller	Motherboard resource
2	IRQ cascade 8–15 (programmable interrupt controller)	Motherboard resource
3	Serial port 2 (COM2)	8- or 16-bit card
4	Serial port 1 (COM1)	8- or 16-bit card
5	Sound card or parallel port 2 (LPT2)	8- or 16-bit card
6	Floppy disk controller	8- or 16-bit card
7	Parallel port 1 (LPT1)	8- or 16-bit card
8	Real-time clock	Motherboard resource
9	Available (default for network); redirected to IRQ 2	8- or 16-bit card
10	Available (default for USB root)	16-bit card
11	Available (default for SCSI adapter)	16-bit card
12	Available (default for motherboard mouse port)	16-bit card
13	Math coprocessor	Motherboard resource
14	Primary IDE controller	16-bit card
15	Available or secondary IDE controller	16-bit card

I've already mentioned that modern machines and modern devices can sometimes share IRQ assignments as well, so multiple devices can be assigned to some of these IRQ ports. The preceding table shows standards, or defaults. In Windows 98 and later, you can check the IRQs assigned in your system by clicking Start ➪ Programs ➪ Accessories ➪ System Tools ➪ System Information. Click the plus sign beside Hardware Resources on the left side of the System Information dialog box and choose IRQs. Note that where

I have listed the hardware resource (LPT1 for IRQ 7, for example), this list will show the printer or other device you have assigned to this port (see Chapter 4 for more information).

Standard DMA Assignments

XT-class machines have four DMA channels, while AT-class and all modern systems have eight (see Chapter 4 for more information).

8-bit ISA bus default DMA channel assignments

DMA	Device	Slot/Motherboard
0	Memory refresh	Motherboard resource
1	Available	8-bit slot
2	Floppy disk controller	8-bit slot
3	Hard disk controller or available	8-bit slot

16-bit modern machine default DMA-channel assignments

DMA	Device	Slot/Motherboard
0	Available	16-bit (8-bit data transfer)
1	Available (default for sound card)	8/16-bit (8-bit data transfer)
2	Floppy disk controller	8/16-bit (8-bit data transfer)
3	ECP parallel port or available	8/16-bit (8-bit data transfer)

DMA	Device	Slot/Motherboard
4	First DMA controller	Motherboard (16-bit data transfer)
5	Available (default for sound card)	16-bit (16-bit data transfer)
6	Available (default for SCSI card)	16-bit (16-bit data transfer)
7	Available	16-bit (16-bit data transfer)

Standard I/O Addresses

The I/O addresses in the following table are address ranges. Every device may not use all of this range, but the specified devices will likely fall within this range for the machine class noted. For example, I list the floppy controller with a range of 3F0 to 3F7. If you view system information for your particular machine, you may see 3F2-3F5 or another value, but this still falls within the range noted in the table.

In addition, this table provides basic information. Modern machines and later operating systems may assign these same devices to multiple locations as aliases; and your system may contain devices that don't show up on the table at all. Use this table as a basic guideline to locate items, but supplement this data with information from your System Information dialog box in Windows.

I/O Port Addresses by Bus Device	I/O Address (Hexadecimal)
Adaptec SCSI adapter and compatibles	0330-0333
CGA card	03D0-0EDF
COM1	03F8-03FF
COM2	02F8-02FF
COM3	3E8-3EF
COM4	2E8-2EF
COM5	2F0-2F7
COM6	2E8-2EF

I/O Port Addresses by Bus Device	I/O Address (Hexadecimal)
COM7	2E0-2E7
COM8	260-267
DMA controller 1	000-01F
DMA controller 2	0C0-0DF
EGA card	02B0-02DF, 03C0-03CF
Ethernet adapter (common alternates)	02A0-02AF, 02C0-02CF, 02E0-02EF
Ethernet adapter (typical)	0240-024F
Floppy	03F0-03F7
Game port or joystick adapter	0200-0207
Hard disk-AT	01F0-01F8
Hard disk-XT	0320-032F
IDE fourth interface	0168-016F
IDE primary interface	0170-0177
IDE secondary interface	01F0-01F7
IDE third interface	01E8-01EF
Interrupt controller 1	020-03F
Interrupt controller 2	0A0-0BF
Key press	060-06F
LPT1	0378-037F
LPT2	0278-027F
LPT1 ECP mode	0678-067F
LPT2 ECP mode	0778-077F
Math coprocessor	0F0-0FF
Real-time clock	070-07F
Sound Blaster 16 and compatible sound cards	0220-0233
Sound card FM synthesizer	0388-038B
USB root	FF80-FF9F
VGA and other video cards	03B0-03BB, 03C0-03CF, 03D0-03DF
Windows sound system	0530-0537

The following table contains a report from a typical modern machine, based on a Pentium 4 and running Windows XP Professional. (You can check assignments within Windows by going to the Device Manager and selecting View ➪ Resources by connection.)

Example of Memory Usage and I/O Ports Usage on Modern Machine

Memory Usage Summary:

[00000000-0009FFFF]	System board
[000A0000-000BFFFF]	PCI bus
[000A0000-000BFFFF]	Intel Processor to AGP Controller
[000A0000-000BFFFF]	NVIDIA GeForce2 MX/MX 400
[000C8000-000DFFFF]	PCI bus
[000F0000-000FFFFF]	System board
[00100000-00FFFFFF]	System board
[01000000-0FF76FFF]	System board
[C0000000-FFDFFFFF]	PCI bus
[E8000000-EFFFFFFF]	Intel Processor to AGP Controller
[F0000000-F7FFFFFF]	Intel Processor to AGP Controller
[F0000000-F7FFFFFF]	NVIDIA GeForce2 MX/MX 400
[FC000000-FDFFFFFF]	Intel Processor to AGP Controller
[FC000000-FCFFFFFF]	NVIDIA GeForce2 MX/MX 400
[FE1FFC00-FE1FFCFF]	CNet PRO200WL PCI Fast Ethernet Adapter
[FEC00000-FEC0FFFF]	System board
[FEE00000-FEE0FFFF]	System board

Memory Usage Summary:

[FFB00000-FFBFFFFF]	System board
[FFC00000-FFFFFFFF]	System board

I/O Ports Usage Summary:

[00000000-00000CF7]	PCI bus
[00000000-0000001F]	Direct memory access controller
[00000020-0000003F]	Programmable interrupt controller
[00000040-0000005F]	System timer
[00000060-00000060]	Enhanced keyboard
[00000061-00000061]	System speaker
[00000062-00000063]	System board
[00000064-00000064]	Enhanced keyboard
[00000065-0000006F]	System board
[00000070-0000007F]	System CMOS/real-time clock
[00000080-0000009F]	Direct memory access controller
[000000A0-000000BF]	Programmable interrupt controller
[000000C0-000000DF]	Direct memory access controller
[000000E0-000000EF]	System board
[000000F0-000000FF]	Numeric data processor
[00000170-00000177]	Secondary IDE Channel
[000001F0-000001F7]	Primary IDE Channel
[00000274-00000277]	ISAPNP Read Data Port
[00000279-00000279]	ISAPNP Read Data Port
[00000376-00000376]	Secondary IDE Channel
[00000378-0000037F]	ECP Printer Port (LPT1)

I/O Ports Usage Summary:

[000003B0-000003BB]	Intel Processor to AGP Controller
[000003B0-000003BB]	NVIDIA GeForce2 MX/MX 400
[000003C0-000003DF]	Intel Processor to AGP Controller
[000003C0-000003DF]	NVIDIA GeForce2 MX/MX 400
[000003F0-000003F5]	Standard floppy disk controller
[000003F6-000003F6]	Primary IDE Channel
[000003F7-000003F7]	Standard floppy disk controller
[000003F8-000003FF]	Communications Port (COM1)
[000004D0-000004D1]	Programmable interrupt controller
[00000778-0000077F]	ECP Printer Port (LPT1)
[00000800-0000085F]	System board
[00000860-000008FF]	System board

I/O Ports Usage Summary:

[00000A79-00000A79]	ISAPNP Read Data Port
[00000C00-00000C7F]	System board
[00000D00-0000FFFF]	PCI bus
[0000DCD0-0000DCDF]	Intel(R) 82801BA/BAM SMBus Controller-2443
[0000E800-0000E8FF]	CNet PRO200WL PCI Fast Ethernet Adapter
[0000ECD8-0000ECDF]	Creative SBLive! Gameport
[0000ECE0-0000ECFF]	Creative SB Live! Value (WDM)
[0000FF60-0000FF7F]	Intel(r) 82801BA/BAM USB Universal Host Controller
[0000FF80-0000FF9F]	Intel(r) 82801BA/BAM USB Universal Host Controller
[0000FFA0-0000FFAF]	Intel(r) 82801BA Bus Master IDE Controller

Appendix E

Hardware and Software Toolkit

I f you've read this far, then you know that *Fix Your Own PC* is a hands-on project. Through the book's many editions, I've worked with hundreds of pieces of hardware, dozens of SIMMs and DIMMs, and other pieces of expensive silicon and plastic. I've assembled and disassembled several dozen machines. I've put machines old and new through torturous tests. When it was over, the workroom of my office looked like the aftermath of a tornado at a computer swap meet.

But after all these years and all these editions of *Fix Your Own PC*, I now know what I like: good quality, good value, and good communication between the techies and the consumer who must make it work at home or in an office.

This appendix lists the best suppliers and manufacturers I worked with in creating this book. None of these companies paid for this honor; all are worthy of your consideration when you make buying decisions.

Hardware

Here are some of the hardware makers who helped with the research for this edition of *Fix Your Own PC*.

Belkin Components

Belkin offers a line of solid peripherals with a touch of style. The company's line of hubs, routers, and switches look a bit like the facades of Art Deco hotels in Miami Beach, an attractive, whimsical style. Among the Belkin products I worked with were:

- Hubs and Routers
  - **4-Port Cable/DSL Gateway Router.** A built-in switch permits file- and peripheral-sharing for as many as four computers, as well as circuitry to share an Internet connection among attached devices. The router includes a NAT firewall to block unauthorized intrusion.
  - **5-Port Network Switch.** A high-speed switch for as many as five devices on a 10/100Base-T Ethernet. The switch can also be attached to a gateway router to expand the number of devices and to connect to a broadband modem to share Internet access.
  - **FireWire 6-Port Hub.** Splits off a single FireWire connection to add six 400Mb/second FireWork ports.
- Network Interface Cards and I/O
  - **CardBus Network Card.** A 32-bit PC Card to connect a laptop or PC Card-equipped desktop to a 10/100Base-T Ethernet or a broadband modem.

- **Desktop Network PCI Card.** A 10/100Base-T Ethernet card.
- **USB 10/100 Ethernet Adapter.** A plug-in 10/100 Ethernet adapter for a USB port.
- **FireWire PCI Card.** Adds three FireWire ports to a modern machine.

Belkin Components
501 West Walnut Street
Compton, CA 90220
Phone: (800) 223-5546, (310) 898-1100
Web site: www.belkin.com

Evergreen Technologies

Performa 766MHz Processor Upgrade. An upgrade to Slot 1 Pentium II motherboards that boosts 233 MHz and faster Pentium II CPUs to an Intel Celeron running at 766MHz. Installation requires no software or operating system reinstallation.

Evergreen Technologies
808 NW Buchanan Avenue
Corvallis, OR 97330-6218
Phone: (541) 757-0934, (888) 888-5886
Web site: www.evergreennow.com

Keyspan

Keyspan specializes in neat solutions to expansion and enhancement needs:

- **Digital Media Remote.** A wireless infrared remote controller for PowerPoint, QuickTime, DVD, CD, and MP3 software. The receiver plugs into a USB port.

- **USB 2.0 PCI.** An adapter that adds four high-speed USB ports, capable of transfer speeds of as much as 480 megabits per second. The card will coexist with existing USB 1.1 hubs on modern machines.
- **USB 4-Port Mini Hub.** A tiny hub not much larger than a matchbook, well suited for a road trip with your laptop.
- **USB Serial Adapter.** Plugs into a USB port on a PC to add a high-speed (230 kilobits per second) serial adapter, adding functionality to a "legacy-free" PC or upgrading a modern machine.

Keyspan
InnoSys Incorporated
3095 Richmond Parkway, Suite 207
Richmond, CA 94806
Phone: (510) 222-0131
Web site: www.keyspan.com

Linksys

Linksys is the hub of the home and small-office universe, the leading manufacturer of consumer-level hubs, switches, routers, and gateways. It is also at the forefront of wireless networking.

EtherFast Cable/DSL Router with QoS. An eight-port 10/100Base-T Ethernet switch combined with a router. The PCs connected to each other through the hub can communicate with each other and share resources; an output of the router connects to a cable or DSL modem permitting an entire network to access the Internet with only one IP address — and only one subscription to an Internet Service Provider (ISP). A key feature of the router is a hardware firewall that protects devices on the switch from unwanted intrusion. The device is configured by commands from a Web browser on the PC that is registered with the ISP and, once configured, additional machines can be easily added. And, the Linksys router can be connected to additional switches or hubs to connect as many as 253 PCs together and to the Internet.

Linksys
17401 Armstrong Avenue
Irvine, CA 92614
Phone: (800) 546-5797
Web site: www.linksys.com

Maxtor Corporation

Maxtor is at the leading edge among manufacturers of hard drives.

Maxtor Personal Storage 3000LE. A Plug-and-Play external hard drive that connects to a USB port. Connected to a standard USB 1.1 port, it offers poky data transfer at 12Mbits/second; if you upgrade your system to include USB 2.0, the same drive becomes a hot rod with 480Mbits/second performance. In its first release, it included a 40GB hard drive; larger drives, and a FireWire version will also be offered.

Maxtor 544GX Ultra ATA/133 Hard Drive and **Maxtor Ultra ATA/133 PCI Adapter Card.** The state of the art in capacity and speed for consumer PCs in early 2002, this combination mates a 160GB hard drive with Maxtor's new Ultra ATA/133 interface card.

Maxtor Corporation
500 McCarthy Boulevard
Milpitas, CA 95035
Phone: (408) 894-5000
Web site: www.maxtor.com or www.maxtordirect.com

SIIG

SIIG distributes a line of quality adapters and peripherals. The products are sold in computer stores and by many direct-mail companies.

SIIG, Inc.
6708 Stewart Avenue
Fremont, CA 94538-3152
Phone: (510) 657-8688
Web site: www.siig.com

Unicomp

Unicomp designs and manufactures standard and custom keyboards that bear the same relation to mass market keyboards as does a Mack truck to a Beetle.

EnduraPro Keyboard. A heavy-duty keyboard derived from the original bulletproof, clicky IBM keyboard for the first PC. This modern version, which weighs in at nearly six pounds, includes an integrated pressure-sensitive pointing stick on the keyboard that can substitute for a mouse as well as a port for an external PS/2 mouse.

Unicomp, Inc.
510 Henry Clay Boulevard
Lexington, KY 40505
Phone: (800) 777-4886, (859) 233-2130
Web site: www.pckeyboard.com

Software

The following are some of the most valuable pieces of software I used in research for the seventh edition of *Fix Your Own PC*, listed with each manufacturer's address and contact information.

AMIDiag

American Megatrends, maker of the AMI BIOS as well as a range of utilities and special-purpose hardware, offers one of the more complete sets of generic hardware diagnostics for consumers.

AMIDiag detects and checks CPUs from Intel, AMD, Cyrix, SGS Thompson, and Texas Instruments. Component tests examine the processor, memory, floppy and hard drives, CD and DVD drives, video, USB, serial and parallel ports, sound cards, network interfaces, and more.

American Megatrends, Inc.
6145-F Northbelt Parkway
Norcross, GA 30071-2976
Phone: (770) 246-8600
Sales: (800) 828-9264
Technical support: (770) 246-8645
Web site: www.ami.com

CheckIt Utilities

Another well-regarded set of generic diagnostic programs is offered by Smith Micro Software. **CheckIt** Utilities also includes the Clean & Zip File Management Utility and InoculateIT Antivirus from Computer Associates.

Smith Micro Software, Inc.
51 Columbia
Aliso Viejo, CA 92656
Phone: (949) 362-5800
Web site: www.smithmicro.com/checkit

Diskeeper

Defragmenting your disk drive is an essential step in maintaining the health of your PC. It can also be one of the more annoying, time-consuming tasks for users. Defragmentation is the process of restructuring a drive so that the discontinuous fragments of long files are brought together; this increases the speed of access and frees up wasted space. Windows includes its own defragmentation utility that does an adequate job; however, performing the operation on a large hard drive can require hours of time. Norton SystemWorks includes an enhanced utility.

Diskeeper 7, from Executive Software, is a highly specialized, highly efficient tool that can accomplish the task in one-half or one-third the time required by Microsoft's utility. It also offers some advanced features including the ability to defragment multiple disks at the same time.

Executive Software International, Inc.
7590 North Glenoaks Boulevard
Burbank, CA 91504
Phone: (818) 771-1600, (800) 829-6468
Web site: www.diskeeper.com

DisplayMate for Windows

DisplayMate offers a suite of specialized diagnostics and adjustment tools for monitors. It presents a series of specialized test pattern images and step-by-step advice on adjustments for optimum quality.

DisplayMate Technologies Corp.
PO Box 550
Amherst, NH 03031
Phone: (800) 932-6323 or (603) 672-8500
Fax: (603) 672-8640
E-mail: info@displaymate.com
Web site: www.displaymate.com

Easy CD Creator, GoBack Deluxe

Easy CD Creator 5 Platinum is the most polished and dependable suite of utilities for owners of a wide range of CD-R and CD-RW drives. The product is offered by Roxio, a spinoff of Adaptec. Microsoft licensed the CD-R burning engine from Roxio for inclusion in Windows XP, and many CD manufacturers include the basic version of the software with their systems.

But the Easy CD Creator product in its Platinum package goes way beyond. Components include facilities to record music and data CD-Rs and CD-RWs, plus the ability to create MP3 discs, edit WAV files, and remove unwanted noise from recordings made from analog sources such as cassette decks or turntables. The Platinum edition also includes software to create self-running slide shows of digital photos, and to make video postcards on disc.

Another worthy product is **GoBack 3 Deluxe,** a power tool to turn back the hands of time when your computer fails to compute or files are damaged by accident, system crashes, or a virus. The product works continuously in the background to track every move you make that affects your hard drive. You can retrieve specific files, or restore the entire hard drive, from recent history.

Microsoft includes a System Recovery utility in Windows XP, but that product is limited only to system settings and preferences; it works by taking an electronic snapshot of the system at regular intervals and when directed by the user. It leaves untouched all data files and applications.

Roxio, Inc.
461 South Milpitas Boulevard
Milpitas, CA 95035
Phone: (303) 684-3850 or (866) 280-7694
E-mail: sales@roxio.com
Web site: www.roxio.com

Norton Internet Security, Norton SystemWorks, Norton Utilities

The various components of the Norton utilities, from Symantec Corporation, are the most common security features of modern PCs. Individual programs from other manufacturers may offer better features, but as a whole, the various Norton packages are the best on the market.

For most users, Norton SystemWorks has a lot of value: it includes Norton AntiVirus to protect from virus threats, Norton Utilities to optimize PC performance, Norton CleanSweep to clean up Internet and Windows clutter, and a version of GoBack by Roxio to allow system recovery to an earlier state. The package also includes WinFax Basic to send and receive faxes over an attached modem, and Norton Ghost to clone a PC's system to other drives.

An important next step for users connected to the Internet — especially if you have a broadband cable or DSL — is Norton Internet Security. The package includes Norton Personal Firewall to block unwanted intrusion, Norton Privacy Control to lock away personal data from intruders, and Norton Parental Control to place certain Web sites off limits to children. The package also includes Norton AntiVirus.

Symantec Corporation
20330 Stevens Creek Blvd.
Cupertino, CA 95014
Phone: (408) 253-9600
Customer service: (800) 441-7234
Web site: www.symantec.com

DriveWorks, Partition Commander, PC Upgrade Commander, System Commander

The set of "Commander" software and the DriveWorks suite from V Communications are a power toolkit for users faced with new hard drives and new operating systems on existing systems. Elements of the company's utilities allow you to change the size, type, and number of partitions on an existing drive; install and run multiple operating systems on one drive; and transfer applications, preferences, settings, files, and folders from one drive or system to another.

System Commander automatically prepares your hard drive to accept a new operating system while protecting everything already on your computer. The existing operating system can be left in place, and you can choose which one to use at bootup.

Partition Commander allows the resizing, moving, copying, and creating of partitions under Windows and Linux. You can also convert partitions from FAT16 to FAT32, or FAT32 to FAT16, or NTFS (including compressed volumes) to FAT. The BackStep Wizard allows you undo changes and return to a prior configuration.

The DriveWorks suite includes Partition Manager as well as Image Commander to back up and restore entire drives or partitions and Copy Commander to copy and expand one drive to another.

PC Upgrade Commander packs up applications, data, and settings on one machine and ships them to another.

V Communications, Inc.
2290 North First Street, Suite 101
San Jose, CA 95131
Phone: (800) 648-8266
Web site: `www.v-com.com`

Notes

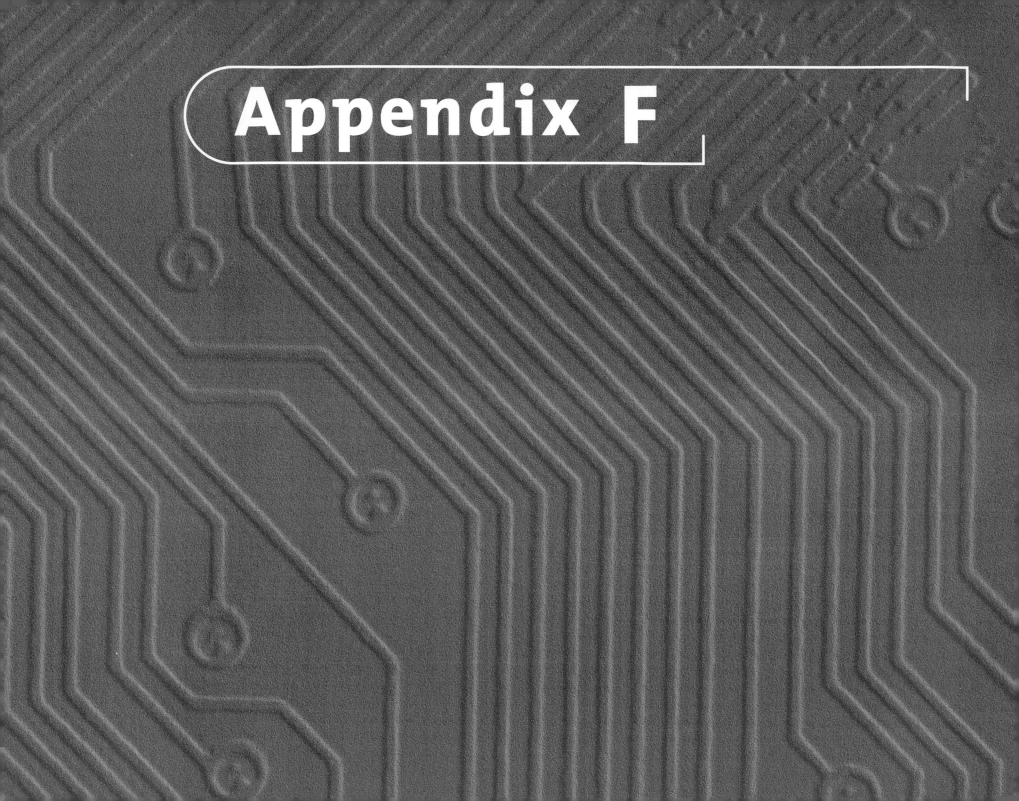

Appendix F

Encyclopedia of Cables and Connectors

The cables in this appendix are divided into two main categories: common PC cable connectors and special-purpose cable connectors. The listings are organized by the number of holes or pins in each connector. In many cases, you'll also find a description of standard uses for the connector.

Be aware, though, that the standard basically is intended to specify the design for the connector or cable and not for the type of data transmitted. Across time, for example, half a dozen different keyboard connectors have existed for PCs, and serial signals have been carried over DB-9, DB-25, and DIN cables, among others.

Common PC Cable Connectors

The following are common PC cable connectors. Virtually every machine, dinosaur to modern, includes one or more of the following cables:

Mini DIN 3 Female

Mini DIN 3 Male. Uses: Special purposes

Mini DIN 4 Female

Mini DIN 4 Male. Uses: Keyboards, SVHS video

DIN 5 Female

DIN 5 Male. Uses: Keyboards

Mini DIN 6 Female

Mini DIN 6 Male. Uses: Keyboards

Mini DIN 8 Female

Mini DIN 8 Male. Uses: Keyboards, Macintosh printers

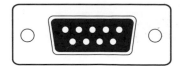

DB-9 Female

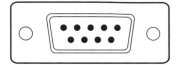

DB-9 Male. Uses: Multipurpose, including PC serial, mouse, keyboard, joysticks, monitor

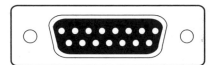

DB-15 Female

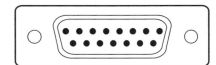

DB-15 Male. Uses: Multipurpose, including PC game port

High-Density DB-15 Female

High-Density DB-15 Male. Uses: VGA monitor, keyboard

DB-25 Female

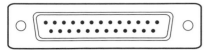

DB-25 Male. Uses: PC serial, PC parallel, SCSI controller cards, and Macintosh desktop external SCSI

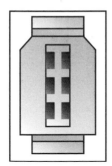

FireWire 6-wire connector

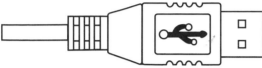

Universal Serial Bus USB-A external cable

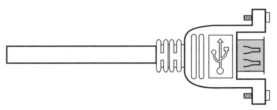

Universal Serial Bus USB-B external cable

IDC 34S Floppy Drive Connector. Uses: 34-pin internal floppy drive connector

Centronics 36 Female

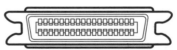

Centronics 36 Male. Uses: PC parallel devices

DB-37 Female

DB-37 Male

IDE Hard Drive Cable. Uses: IDC40S 40-pin internal drive connector

Centronics 50 Female

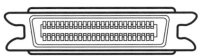

Centronics 50 Male. Uses: External cable used on SCSI and SCSI-2 controllers and devices

DB-50 Female

DB-50 Male. Uses: Multipurpose connector, SCSI, serial, parallel devices

IDC 50 Socket Header

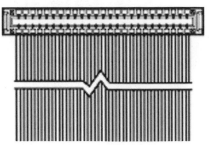

IDC 50 Card Edge. Uses: Internal cable connectors for SCSI and SCSI-2 controllers and devices

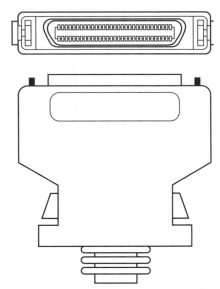

Mini Centronics SCSI-2, 0.050-inch, 50-pin Male. Uses: SCSI-2 controllers and peripherals

Mini D50M SCSI-2, 0.050-inch 50-pin. Uses: External SCSI connector for SCSI-2 devices originally used on Hewlett-Packard systems

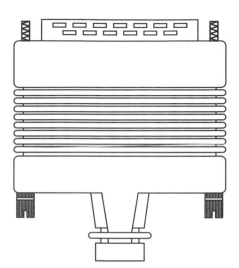

Centronics 60 Male. Uses: External SCSI connector for IBM PC and workstations

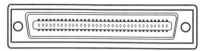

SCSI 8mm 68-pin Male. Uses: External SCSI connector for Ultra-2 and RAID controllers

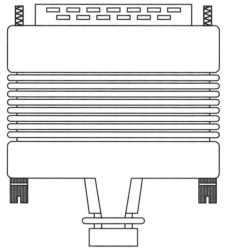

Centronics 68 Male. Uses: Special purposes

Mini D68M SCSI-3. Uses: External 0.050-inch, 68-pin SCSI connector for SCSI-2 and SCSI-3 controllers and devices

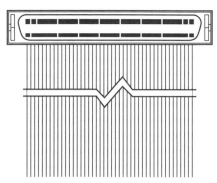

SCSI-3 IDC68M 0.025-inch, 68-pin Ribbon Style Connector. Uses: Internal cable connector for SCSI-2 and SCSI-3 controllers and devices

Special-Purpose Connectors

The following are special-purpose connectors found on advanced machines with nonstandard adapters, or are used for multiple purposes.

Twinaxial. Uses: Special-purpose video and other applications

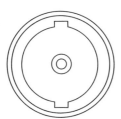

BNC Coaxial Male. Uses: Networking, audio, video applications

RJ11. Uses: 4-wire telephone twisted pair, networks

RJ12. Uses: 6-wire telephone twisted pair

RJ45. Uses: 8-wire Ethernet

Notes

Appendix G

Troubleshooting Charts

If-then-else. That's the way many computer programs analyze a problem. If this is the situation, then I am supposed to do the following; otherwise, I should move on to the point where I make the next logical decision.

Well, if it's good enough for a machine, it's good enough for you and me. It's called branching logic, and IBM and other computer makers understood its value as a technical tool right from the start. Computer repair staff was equipped with huge binders of troubleshooting if-then-else charts; the technical reference manuals for the original IBM PC followed the same form.

And so, welcome to the *Fix Your Own PC* troubleshooting charts. These 11 charts don't attempt to solve every possible problem with a personal computer, but they should be more than enough to get you started on setting a course to solution.

An important step in troubleshooting a Windows-based machine is to understand how to display and use the Device Manager to locate and fix most resource and device driver problems. You'll find a guide to its facilities in Chapter 23.

Among the steps in many of the charts is a suggestion that you substitute a known-good replacement for whatever part is in question. What does that mean? If you are questioning whether a printer cable has failed, one way to test is to find a cable that works on another machine and put it in place of the suspect cable. If the replacement works, you know the original doesn't; if the replacement cable does not solve the problem you can eliminate the cable as a suspect.

If your PC is a critical part of your business or personal life, I'd suggest you consider investing in a reasonable cache of extra parts. My electronic first aid closet includes a few extra keyboards and mice, a hard drive, a retired but still functional monitor, a basic video adapter, a network interface card, and every conceivable cable and connector I've worked with in twenty years of tinkering.

I also keep in touch with other knowledgeable computer users to borrow — and loan — equipment for troubleshooting purposes. And I've bartered some of my time and equipment with a local electronics repair shop in return for access to some specialized tools and testing devices.

Let's review some basic precautions I've explored in the book:

1. Back up the data files on your hard drive before performing any work under the covers. I recommend you make copies to a CD, an external hard drive, or another machine on a local area network.
2. Turn off and unplug the computer before removing the covers and touching any internal components.

3. Solve problems one at a time and keep notes of what you have done to make the repair. Work on the major problems first and then the lesser ones.

4. Respond to self-test error messages, codes, and beeps before working on other problems. These are generated by the BIOS before the system even begins to boot up and usually indicate a pure hardware problem — from a failed or improperly installed adapter card or block of memory to a failed component of the motherboard itself.

5. Follow the instructions in the chapters of this book about how to proceed under the covers. Among important recommendations: Ground yourself before touching sensitive parts; tag and label cables and connectors before you disconnect them; and make notes on any changes you make to switches, jumpers, or settings.

6. Wherever possible, test suspect hardware by substituting a known-good replacement in the computer you are troubleshooting. Or, take the suspect hardware and install it in a PC you know to be working properly.

7. Keep an eye on the bottom line. As I've explored in this book, prices for computer equipment and complete systems have continued to drop even as their speed and capability has improved. Before attempting a major repair such as replacing a failed motherboard or installing a more modern microprocessor, consider the cost of replacing the entire computer.

Now, go forth and troubleshoot . . .

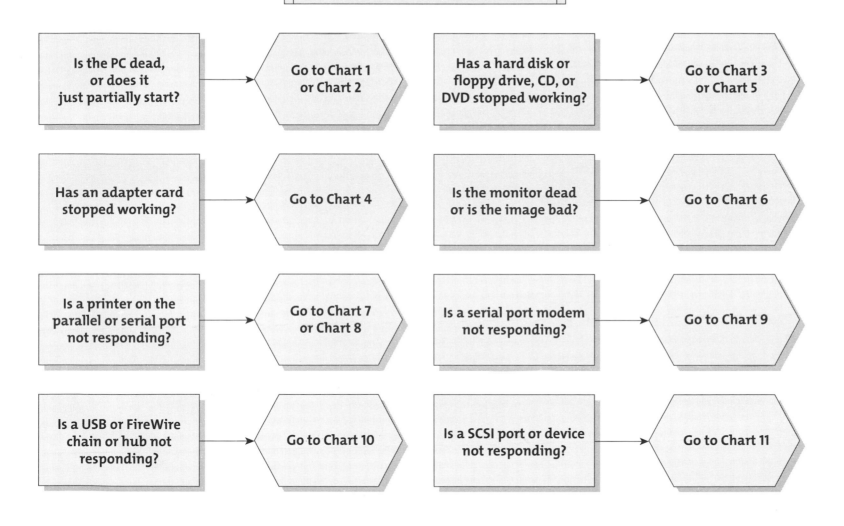

A GUIDE TO THE FLOWCHARTS

Is the PC dead, or does it just partially start? → Go to Chart 1 or Chart 2

Has a hard disk or floppy drive, CD, or DVD stopped working? → Go to Chart 3 or Chart 5

Has an adapter card stopped working? → Go to Chart 4

Is the monitor dead or is the image bad? → Go to Chart 6

Is a printer on the parallel or serial port not responding? → Go to Chart 7 or Chart 8

Is a serial port modem not responding? → Go to Chart 9

Is a USB or FireWire chain or hub not responding? → Go to Chart 10

Is a SCSI port or device not responding? → Go to Chart 11

CHART 1: BACK FROM THE DEAD

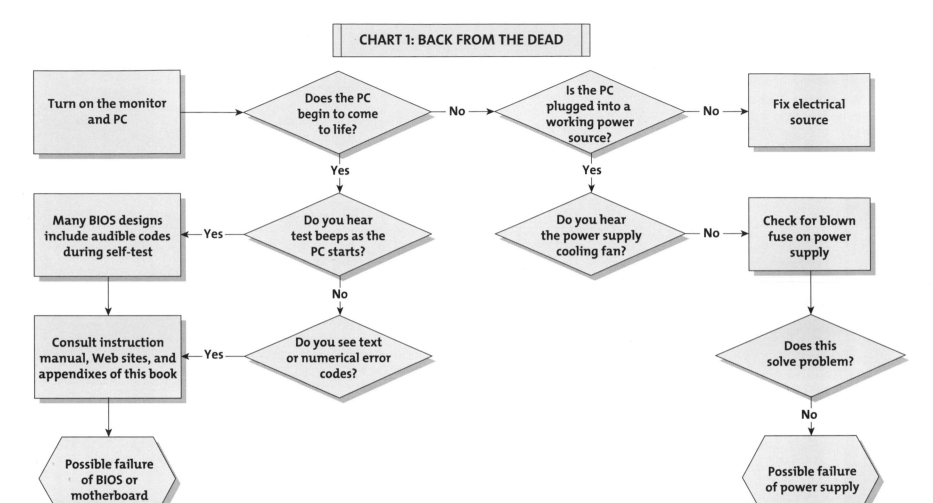

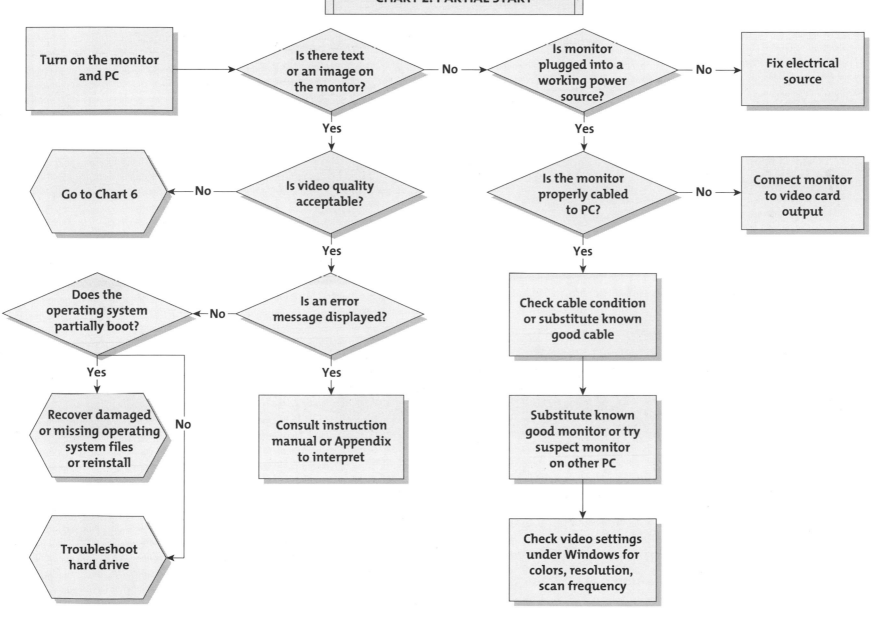

CHART 2: PARTIAL START

Turn on the monitor and PC → Is there text or an image on the montor? —No→ Is monitor plugged into a working power source? —No→ Fix electrical source

Is there text or an image on the montor? —Yes↓

Is monitor plugged into a working power source? —Yes↓

Go to Chart 6 ←No— Is video quality acceptable?

Is the monitor properly cabled to PC? —No→ Connect monitor to video card output

Is video quality acceptable? —Yes↓

Is the monitor properly cabled to PC? —Yes↓

Does the operating system partially boot? ←No— Is an error message displayed?

Check cable condition or substitute known good cable

Does the operating system partially boot? —Yes↓ ... —No→

Recover damaged or missing operating system files or reinstall

Is an error message displayed? —Yes↓

Consult instruction manual or Appendix to interpret

Substitute known good monitor or try suspect monitor on other PC

Troubleshoot hard drive

Check video settings under Windows for colors, resolution, scan frequency

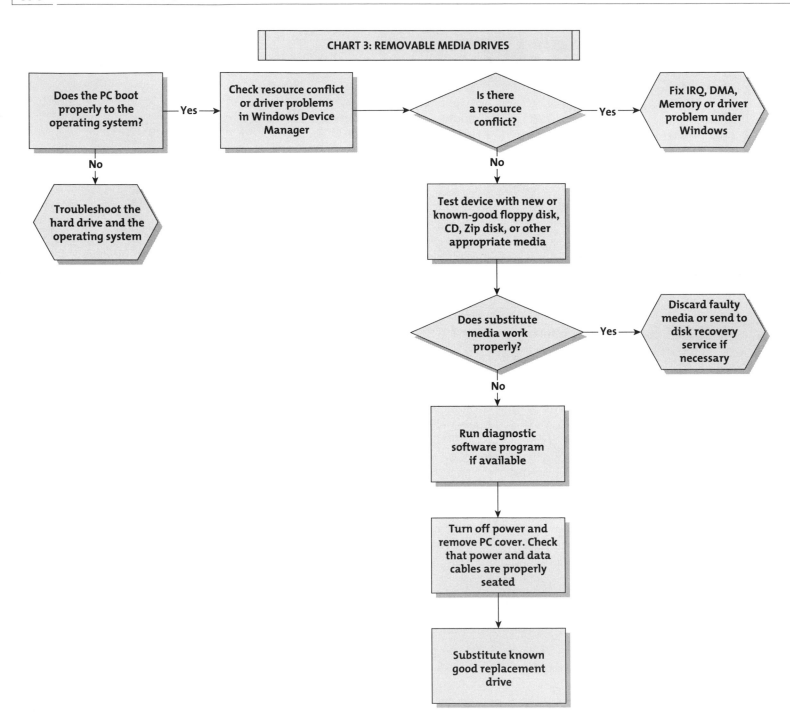

CHART 3: REMOVABLE MEDIA DRIVES

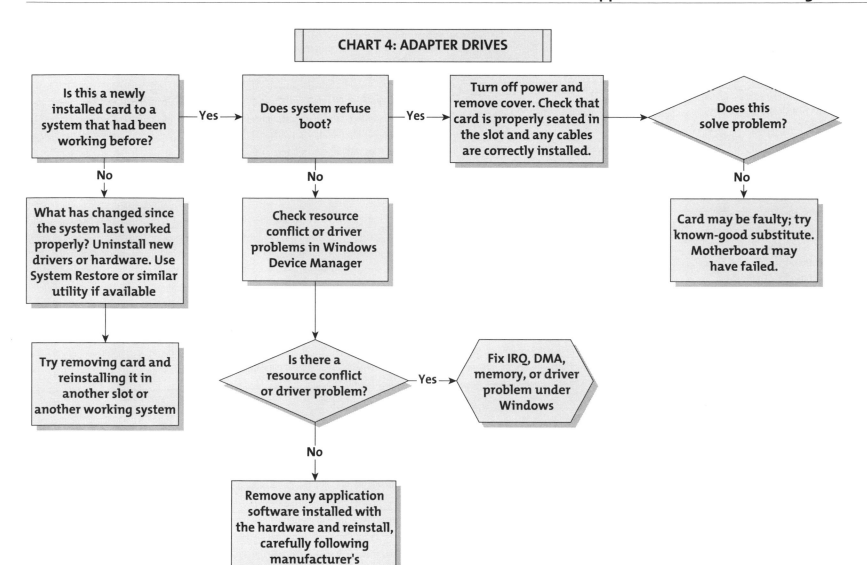

CHART 4: ADAPTER DRIVES

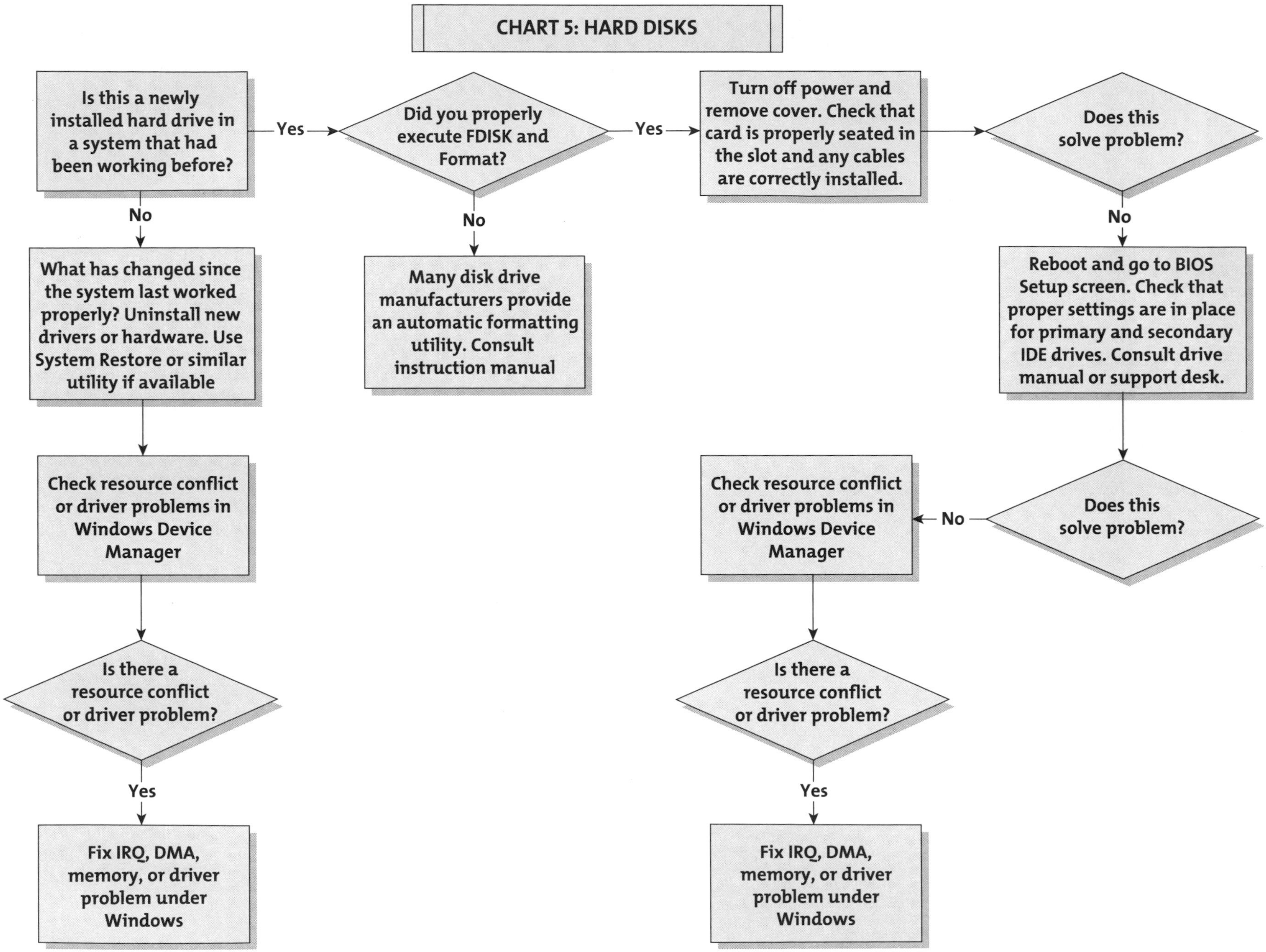

CHART 5: HARD DISKS

Is this a newly installed hard drive in a system that had been working before? —Yes→ Did you properly execute FDISK and Format? —Yes→ Turn off power and remove cover. Check that card is properly seated in the slot and any cables are correctly installed. → Does this solve problem?

No ↓

What has changed since the system last worked properly? Uninstall new drivers or hardware. Use System Restore or similar utility if available

↓

Check resource conflict or driver problems in Windows Device Manager

↓

Is there a resource conflict or driver problem?

Yes ↓

Fix IRQ, DMA, memory, or driver problem under Windows

No ↓ (FDISK)

Many disk drive manufacturers provide an automatic formatting utility. Consult instruction manual

No ↓ (Does this solve problem?)

Reboot and go to BIOS Setup screen. Check that proper settings are in place for primary and secondary IDE drives. Consult drive manual or support desk.

↓

Does this solve problem? —No→ Check resource conflict or driver problems in Windows Device Manager

↓

Is there a resource conflict or driver problem?

Yes ↓

Fix IRQ, DMA, memory, or driver problem under Windows

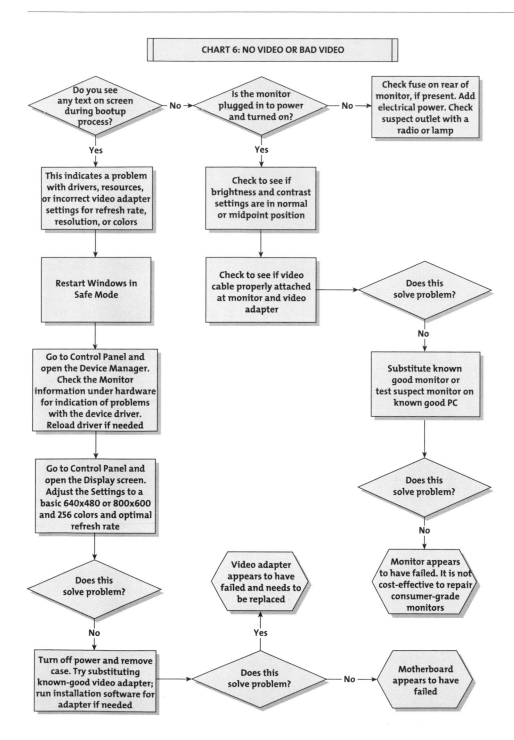

CHART 6: NO VIDEO OR BAD VIDEO

Do you see any text on screen during bootup process? — No → Is the monitor plugged in to power and turned on? — No → Check fuse on rear of monitor, if present. Add electrical power. Check suspect outlet with a radio or lamp

Yes ↓

This indicates a problem with drivers, resources, or incorrect video adapter settings for refresh rate, resolution, or colors

↓

Restart Windows in Safe Mode

↓

Go to Control Panel and open the Device Manager. Check the Monitor information under hardware for indication of problems with the device driver. Reload driver if needed

↓

Go to Control Panel and open the Display screen. Adjust the Settings to a basic 640x480 or 800x600 and 256 colors and optimal refresh rate

↓

Does this solve problem?

No ↓

Turn off power and remove case. Try substituting known-good video adapter; run installation software for adapter if needed →

Does this solve problem? — No → Motherboard appears to have failed

Yes ↑ Video adapter appears to have failed and needs to be replaced

Yes ↓ (from "Is the monitor plugged in to power and turned on?")

Check to see if brightness and contrast settings are in normal or midpoint position

↓

Check to see if video cable properly attached at monitor and video adapter → Does this solve problem?

No ↓

Substitute known good monitor or test suspect monitor on known good PC

↓

Does this solve problem?

No ↓

Monitor appears to have failed. It is not cost-effective to repair consumer-grade monitors

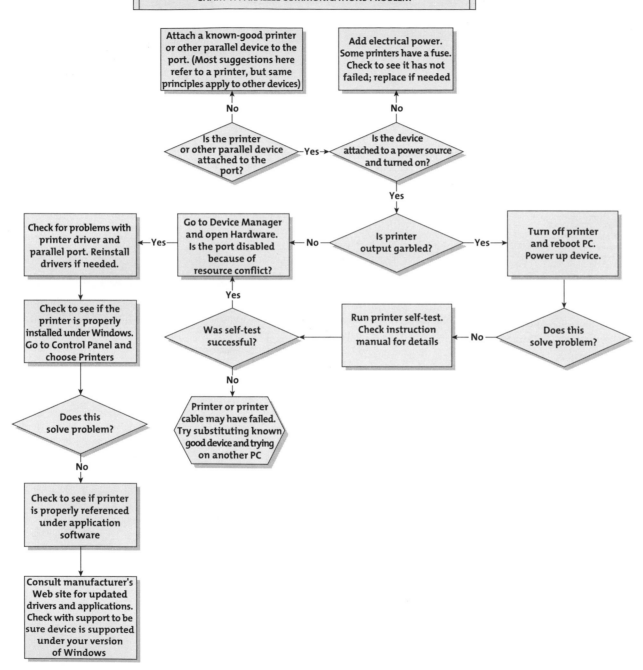

CHART 7: PARALLEL COMMUNICATIONS PROBLEM

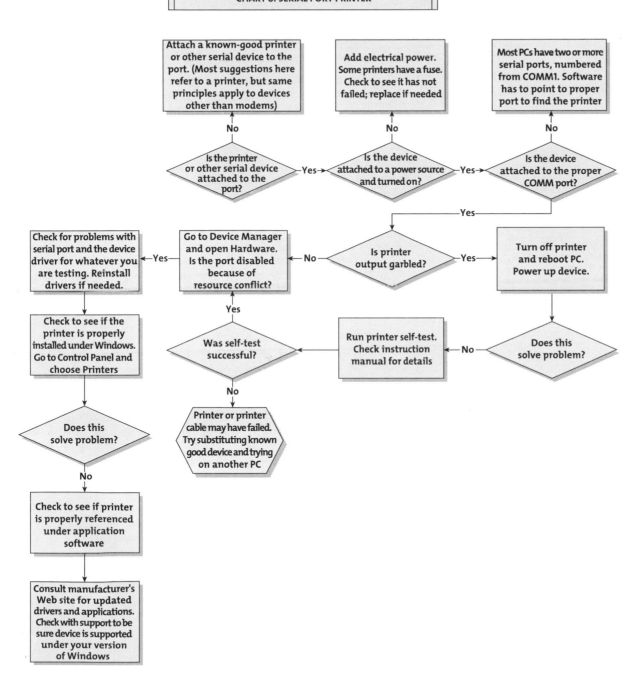

CHART 8: SERIAL PORT PRINTER

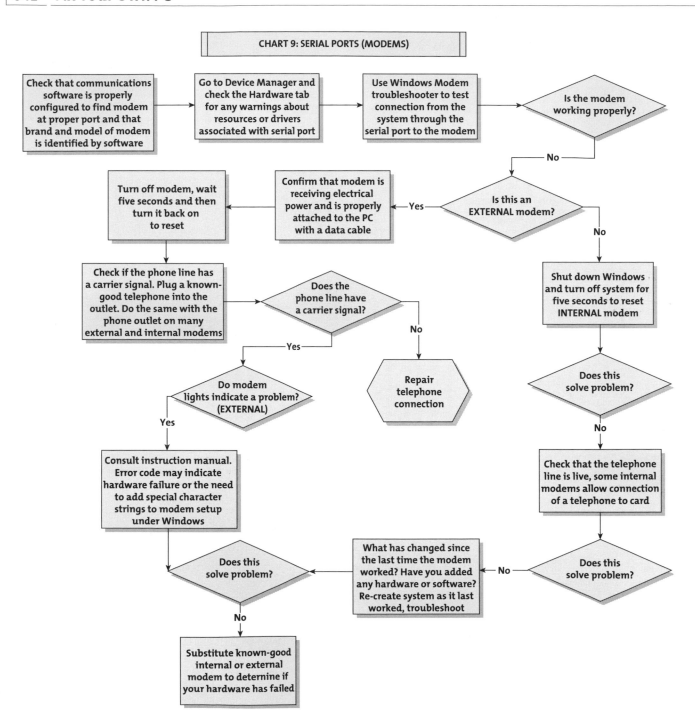

CHART 9: SERIAL PORTS (MODEMS)

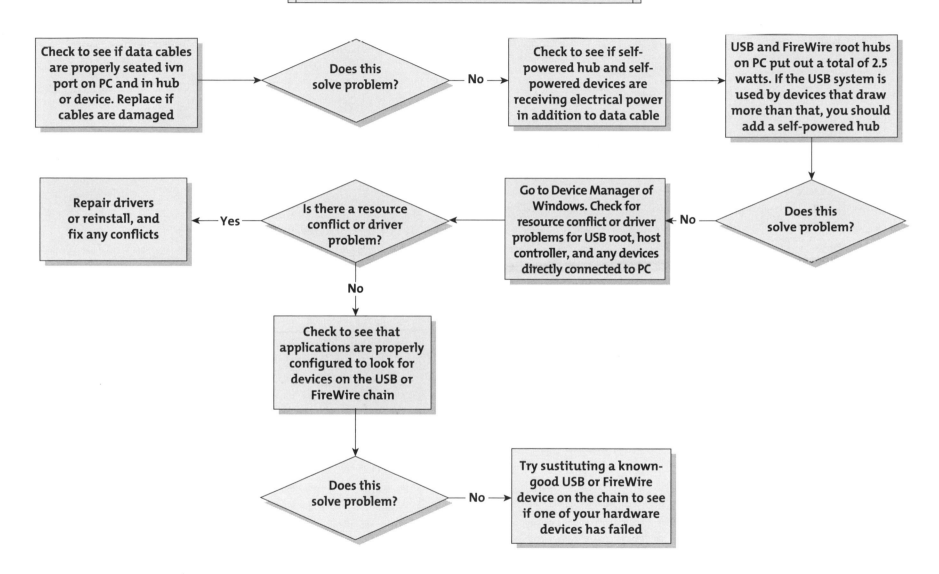

CHART 10: USB or FIREWIRE SYSTEMS

Check to see if data cables are properly seated ivn port on PC and in hub or device. Replace if cables are damaged

Does this solve problem? — No →

Check to see if self-powered hub and self-powered devices are receiving electrical power in addition to data cable

USB and FireWire root hubs on PC put out a total of 2.5 watts. If the USB system is used by devices that draw more than that, you should add a self-powered hub

Repair drivers or reinstall, and fix any conflicts

← Yes — Is there a resource conflict or driver problem?

Go to Device Manager of Windows. Check for resource conflict or driver problems for USB root, host controller, and any devices directly connected to PC

← No — Does this solve problem?

No

Check to see that applications are properly configured to look for devices on the USB or FireWire chain

Does this solve problem? — No →

Try sustituting a known-good USB or FireWire device on the chain to see if one of your hardware devices has failed

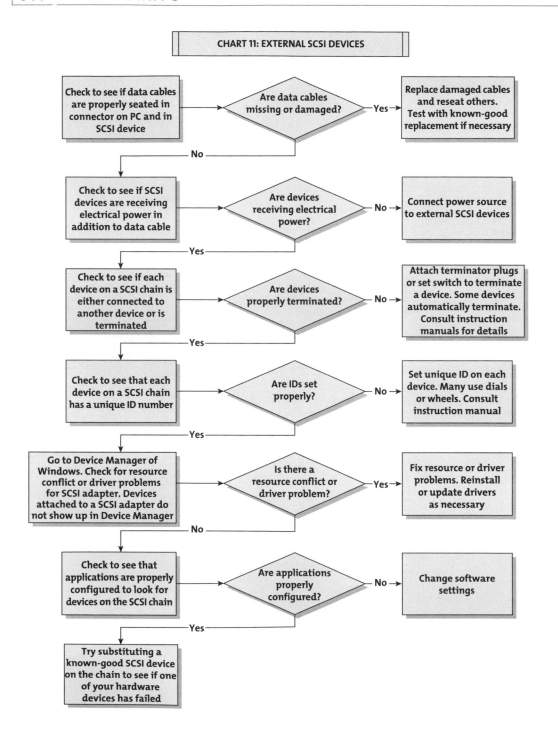

CHART 11: EXTERNAL SCSI DEVICES

Check to see if data cables are properly seated in connector on PC and in SCSI device → Are data cables missing or damaged? → Yes → Replace damaged cables and reseat others. Test with known-good replacement if necessary

No ↓

Check to see if SCSI devices are receiving electrical power in addition to data cable → Are devices receiving electrical power? → No → Connect power source to external SCSI devices

Yes ↓

Check to see if each device on a SCSI chain is either connected to another device or is terminated → Are devices properly terminated? → No → Attach terminator plugs or set switch to terminate a device. Some devices automatically terminate. Consult instruction manuals for details

Yes ↓

Check to see that each device on a SCSI chain has a unique ID number → Are IDs set properly? → No → Set unique ID on each device. Many use dials or wheels. Consult instruction manual

Yes ↓

Go to Device Manager of Windows. Check for resource conflict or driver problems for SCSI adapter. Devices attached to a SCSI adapter do not show up in Device Manager → Is there a resource conflict or driver problem? → Yes → Fix resource or driver problems. Reinstall or update drivers as necessary

No ↓

Check to see that applications are properly configured to look for devices on the SCSI chain → Are applications properly configured? → No → Change software settings

Yes ↓

Try substituting a known-good SCSI device on the chain to see if one of your hardware devices has failed

Notes

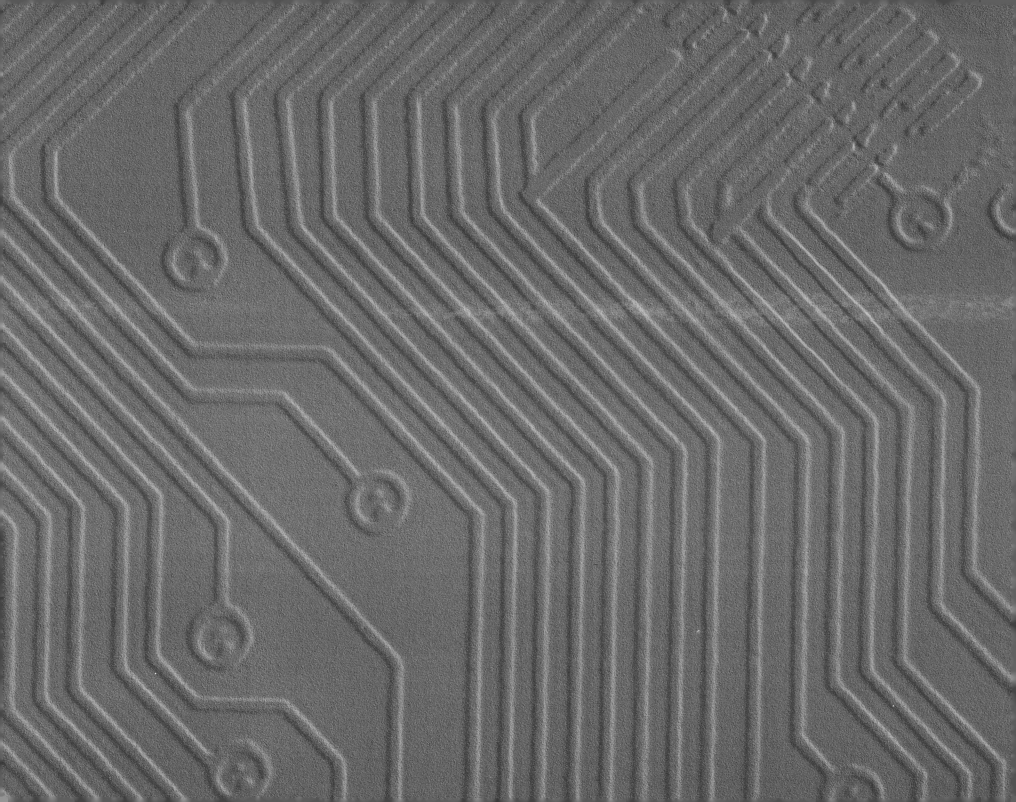

Glossary

10Base-T The standard for a local area network that uses simple twisted-pair cable and operates at a maximum of 10 Mbps. Also called *Twisted-pair Ethernet*.

100Base-T A current local area network standard that expands on 10Base-T to work at speeds of up to 100Mbps. Also called *Fast Ethernet*.

accelerated graphics port See *AGP*.

access time The time required to read or write data to a storage device, including RAM or a disk drive. The nature of the device, as well as the operating system settings, can affect the time.

adapter ROM Read-only memory on an adapter card installed in the computer's bus. The ROM contains code to control the adapter device, such as a disk drive adapter, a video card, or a memory card.

ADC On a sound card, an Analog-to-Digital Converter that takes in analog signals from a microphone or other nondigital source, and then outputs digital signals (computer bits) that can be held in computer memory or recorded on a storage device, such as a hard drive, for playback or manipulation.

address A specific location in memory.

address bus The lines from the microprocessor to other parts of the system that are used to specify a location in memory.

AGP Accelerated Graphics Port. A high-speed graphics expansion bus on certain modern motherboards that directly connects the display adapter and system memory. AGP operates independent of the PCI bus and normally runs at 66 MHz, which is twice that of PCI at 33 MHz. The original AGP standard makes a single transfer per cycle for a maximum data-transfer rate of 266 megabytes per second. AGP 2X makes two transfers per cycle (533MB/sec), and AGP 4X makes four transfers per second (1.06GB/sec).

allocation unit See *cluster*.

amplitude The height of a wave. This can represent the loudness of sound, brightness, or other measures.

analog A means of recording values by use of the fall and rise of a continuously variable signal. Analog signals are used, for example, to carry signals over standard phone lines. Contrast with digital, which represents values with discrete numbers.

analog loopback A modem test in which data is sent to the modem's transmitter, where it is modulated into analog form and then looped back to the receiver and demodulated into digital form.

anti-aliasing Despite how it appears from a short distance, your computer screen is made up of a straight vertical and horizontal alignment of tiny, identically sized rectangles. There are no real circles or diagonals. Instead, the graphics adapter draws shapes by stair stepping up and over, or down and across. The stair-stepping "Etch-a-Sketch"-like effect is called aliasing or jaggies. Advanced graphics cards deliver something called anti-aliasing, which makes these jagged edges appear smoother by reducing the intensity of pixels on the edges of the shapes.

API (application program interface) A set of subprograms and tools used to build software applications; APIs are behind the common look and feel of operating systems like Windows.

application software The program your computer uses to do work, such as a word processing or a spreadsheet program.

arbitration A technique that permits devices to compete for possession of the bus. Devices are assigned levels of priority and can seize control from a lower-valued unit.

ARQ Automatic Repeat Request. A form of error control protocols that use error detection to trigger automatic retransmission of defective blocks of data.

ASCII code American Standard Code for Information Interchange. A definition for numerical codes that represent controls and characters used by many computers.

ASIC Application-Specific Integrated Circuit. A chip designed to perform a specific function. The chip starts out as a nonspecific collection, or array, of logic gates. In the manufacturing process, a layer is added to connect specific gates so that the final product will perform a specific function. By changing the design of the connection layer, the chipmaker produces ASICs for different purposes.

ASL Adaptive Speed Leveling. A protocol for modems that enables the devices to monitor line conditions and adjust transmission

speed up or down if conditions affecting veracity change while connected.

ASPI Advanced SCSI Programming Interface defines a common language between SCSI host adapters and peripheral devices. It enables SCSI peripherals from many vendors to be easily used on a single SCSI chain.

asynchronous Not tied to a particular time frame or clockbeat. Asynchronous communication uses start and stop bits to mark computer words in the stream of data. Synchronous communication, mostly used in specialized terminal applications, uses time to separate the words.

ATA Advanced Technology Attachment, also known as IDE. A bus interface commonly used to connect to storage devices.

ATA/33, ATA/66, ATA/100, ATA133 (Ultra ATA/33) A set of current transfer protocols for hard disks and other devices, with a potential top transfer rate of 33MB, 66MB, 100MB, or 133MB per second. Also known as *Ultra ATA*.

AT bus The 16-bit data bus first used in IBM's PC AT computer, which was based on the Intel 80286 processor. The basic AT bus was adopted by other PC manufacturers, and it is now called the ISA (Industry Standard Architecture) bus.

AT command set A set of commands to control modems, originally developed by Hayes Microcomputer Products. Commands begin with the letters AT, which stand for attention.

Athlon A microprocessor family from AMD that is roughly comparable, in its various versions, to the Intel Pentium family.

ATX motherboard A specification for a motherboard, I/O connectors, and power supply widely used in modern machines, with sub-classes including MicroATX for small-footprint PCs.

autodetection A process that enables an IDE device to inform a system BIOS about proper settings for hard disks and other devices.

backside bus A dedicated bus that connects a microprocessor to a Level 2 (L2) cache to eliminate performance bottlenecks. No other system device shares the backside bus.

bandwidth The amount of data that can be transmitted over an electronic line in a fixed amount of time. For digital devices, bandwidth is usually expressed in bits per second or bytes per second. For analog devices, bandwidth is expressed in cycles per second, or Hertz (Hz).

bank A set of memory chips divided into segments for easy access. Most modern-machine motherboards have two banks for memory.

bank switching A technology to expand available system memory by switching between banks of memory as needed. The off bank retains its memory when not in use but is not immediately available.

base memory The amount of available memory for programs in the first megabyte of memory in a PC. A holdover from the original design of the IBM PC, which held the top 384KB of memory (called *high memory*) for system use, leaving 640KB of base, or *conventional* memory. Modern machines can work with huge amounts of memory, but technically everything above 1MB is considered *extended* or *expanded* memory.

baud A measure of the number of voltage transitions in one second in a communications link. Each of the transitions can transmit several bits of information. It is often incorrectly interchanged with bits per second.

BBS Bulletin Board System. A computer equipped with a modem and attached to a phone line that can be contacted by other computers for the exchange of information. BBS systems have been mostly supplanted by chat rooms and user groups on the Internet.

benchmark A utility program that calculates the speed of completion of a particular task. It can be used to compare the performance of systems or system components.

bezel A frame that holds a device in place or covers an opening on a PC. Also used by monitor manufacturers to describe the frame around the glass tube that makes up the screen.

binary A base-two numbering system used by computers. All numbers are composed of 0s and 1s.

BIOS Basic Input/Output System. Code that controls the lowest, most basic functions of a PC: get a keystroke, read a sector of a floppy disk, how to boot, and so on. The BIOS generally acts as the interface between hardware and the operating system. The system BIOS is stored in ROM, so it does not need to be loaded every time the PC is turned on. This ROM also contains a power-on self-test (POST) routine and the capability to search for other ROMs. Most modern video cards, hard disk controllers, and other internal devices have ROMs that contain code (firmware) for controlling their functions.

bit The smallest piece of information in a computer—a 1 or a 0. A bit can represent a number or a state, such as ON or OFF, or TRUE or FALSE.

bit depth The number of bits that lie behind the description of a color on a display. The more bits, the more gradations of color. A 1-bit pixel is monochrome; 24-bit or true-color allows for as many as 16.7 million shades for each pixel.

bitmap A representation of an image or font as a binary file. For two-color images (such as black and white), each bit in the map indicates whether the corresponding screen pixel is on or off. For images of more colors, every so many bits (depending on the number of colors) corresponds to each successive pixel in the image.

bits per second (BPS) The number of binary digits that can be transmitted in one second. A more accurate means of measuring the potential speed of a modem.

boot The process the computer goes through to set itself up and load its operating system. Two kinds of boot exist: hard (or cold) and soft (or warm). When you turn on the computer or press the reset button, the system performs a hard boot. A hard boot forces the PC to set itself up from scratch. It performs a check of all hardware and creates a table of devices on the machine (such as number and type of floppy drives, the presence and size of the hard disk, and so on) before it loads the operating system. If you press Ctrl + Alt + Del, the computer performs a soft boot and only reloads the operating system.

boot drive The disk drive from where the operating system is loaded.

boot sector The first sector of the active (bootable) partition. It contains code for loading the operating system. When the computer starts, the BIOS looks for the first hard drive and loads the hard drive's first sector, the Master Boot Record (MBR). The MBR contains a table describing the hard drive's partitions and code for loading the boot sector. Reviewing the table, the boot sector loader determines the location of the active partition and loads the boot sector.

bps See *bits per second.*

buffer An area of system memory or other memory used to facilitate I/O (input/output) transfers, allowing a constant stream of data even when data transfer to the I/O port is coming in discontinuous chunks.

burst mode A scheme for data transfer that permits a device to remain inactive, as far as the bus is concerned, and then send large amounts of data in a rapid burst. This design is used for DMA transfers on the EISA bus.

bus A parallel set of wires on which multiple devices can reside and use to communicate. Many buses exist inside a PC, including several within the CPU itself. When used generically, bus usually refers to a PC's expansion bus, the place in a PC where devices on printed circuit cards are added. The structure of the expansion bus determines what sort of devices can be added to a computer and how fast the PC can perform certain types of functions. PCs using ISA (the original AT bus), EISA (the extended ISA bus), or Micro Channel (IBM's proprietary PS/2 bus) run slower than the microprocessor and offer narrower data paths than modern CPUs can handle. Intel's PCI (peripheral component interconnect) bus, used in Pentium-class systems, is capable of operating at full processor speed. See also *bus board* and *bus connector.*

bus board Also called a *backplane.* Some manufacturers of older modern machines chose to put the bus and bus connectors on one board and the rest of the motherboard chips on a separate processor board. In theory, this configuration enables easier upgrades, although proprietary designs sometimes make this unrealistic.

bus connector Expansion cards are connected to the bus through bus connectors on the motherboard. Modern machines use a PCI bus, which branches off the IBM AT-style industry standard architecture (ISA) bus.

bus mastering An architecture introduced to the PC world with EISA and Micro Channel buses. The design permits add-in boards to perform complex tasks, including managing the bus independent of the CPU. Among devices that take advantage of this facility are some graphics accelerator cards and network adapters. The Micro Channel design permits multiple bus masters. The CPU arbitrates among contending bus master applicants.

byte Eight bits, the smallest unit of data moved about in a personal computer.

cache Memory used to store multiple pieces of data that the computer can reasonably guess it will need soon. It is a bridge between a slow device and a fast device—for example, a hard disk (slow) and main memory (fast). When data is needed from a slow device, nearby data is also retrieved and stored in the cache on the assumption it is likely to be needed soon. When a sector of data from a hard disk is requested, for example, a hard disk controller with cache memory will read and store the sector's entire track in the cache (reading a whole track is faster than reading multiple sectors one at a time). If the PC then soon needs data from that track, it can get it from the cache, which is far faster than reading data from the disk. In the same way, main memory, which is slow by comparison to the CPU (microprocessor chip), can benefit from a memory cache. Cache performance (how much it speeds up your work) depends on several factors, including the speed of the cache chips, the size of the cache, and most importantly, the intelligence of the cache controller.

CAS Column Address Strobe. A signal sent by the memory controller that tells the memory that it can read the column address signal.

CAS Latency The amount of time it takes memory to respond to a command. Specifically, the time between receiving a command to read data and the first piece of data being output from memory. Latency is measured in clock cycles, as in CL2 (two clock cycles) or CL3 (three clock cycles). If you mix memory of differing CAS Latency, your system will run at the speed of the slowest module.

CAV (constant angular velocity) A mechanism for disk storage in which the drive rotates at a constant speed, resulting in variations in data transfer rates between the inner and outer tracks. Compare to *CLV (constant linear velocity)*.

CCITT An international organization that defined standards for telegraphic and telephone equipment, part of the International Telecommunication Union, which draws its acronym from the French title International Telephone and Telegraph Consultative Committee.

CD-Audio, Compact Disc-Audio, or Compact Disc-Digital Audio (CD-DA) The original format for music CDs, established in 1980.

CD-Bridge A CD with additional information on the CD-ROM/XA track that enables the CD to play on a CD-I player used with a television or a PC. An example is the Photo CD.

CD-R Compact Disc-Recordable. A family of devices that can write a permanent record to a special type of CD, which can then be read on a standard CD-ROM drive or another CD-R device. Also known as *Compact Disc-Writable*.

CD-ROM Compact Disc Read-Only Memory. An adaptation of music CD technology that stores large amounts of data. A CD-ROM is fairly slow in transferring information, but can hold as much as 700MB of data.

CD-ROM/XA, CD-ROM/extended architecture An extended CD-ROM format that improves synchronization of data and audio, and adds hardware for the compression and decompression of audio information. Once a separate feature, it is now included as part of the capabilities of most modern CD drives.

CD-RW Compact Disc-Rewritable. A family of devices that can write a record to a special type of CD; the information can later be erased or changed. Although early CD-RW discs could only be read in a CD-RW device, newer CD-RW drives can create disks that can be read in newer CD-ROM players.

Celeron Intel's "value" version of the Pentium II or III, equipped with a smaller amount of L2 cache. See also *Duron*.

Centronics interface A link between a printer (or a few other devices including some scanners) and a PC's parallel port, using a 36-pin connector. A 50-pin version is used for SCSI devices. It provides eight parallel data lines, plus additional lines for control and status information.

CGA Color Graphics Adapter. A dinosaur display standard, introduced soon after the arrival of the IBM PC. By modern standards, it is extremely limited in number of colors and resolution.

checksum An algorithm for error checking. The CPU mathematically manipulates the bits in a block of data to create a checksum value. The value is compared with a checksum computed by another device or by a computer that has received the block of data.

chip A casual name for an integrated circuit. A chip is a silicon wafer that has layers of circuits photoetched into its silicon surface. Chip also refers to the ceramic or plastic packages in which chips come.

chipset An integrated set of chips that performs the functions of a larger number of discrete logical devices on a PC.

CISC Complex Instruction Set Computing. One design for a microprocessor. CISC uses complex assembly language instructions that usually require many clock cycles to execute. Compare to *RISC*.

clock multiplier A CPU design that improves processor performance by running internal processing at a multiple of the speed at which it communicates to the rest of the system outside of the chip. Intel's DX2 series of chips include the popular 486DX2/66, which runs at an internal speed of 66 MHz while it communicates with the system bus and memory at 33 MHz. Intel's DX4 series triples the processor's internal throughput; for example, the 486DX4/100 runs at 100 MHz internally and 33 MHz externally. Also referred to as *clock doubling* or *clock tripling*.

clock speed The rate at which a computer's clock oscillates, usually stated in MHz (one million cycles per second). A motherboard uses the ticks of the clock to synchronize the movement of information in the CPU and the rest of the system.

clone A generic equivalent to an original design. By definition, all AT-class machines other than IBM's are clones of the original Big Blue PC.

cluster A group of sectors treated by the operating system as a unit. The operating system controls the number of sectors in a cluster. Also called *allocation unit*.

CLV (constant linear velocity) A design for storage on a rotating disk that spaces data in equal sized physical blocks. Because there is more space available at the outside of the disk than near its center, a CLV drive varies the speed of rotation so that data flows evenly. The disk spins faster for tracks near the center and slower in the more densely packed outer tracks. CLV is used on most CD drives and in Macintosh floppy disk drives. Hard disk drives and some newer CD drives use a scheme called *CAV (constant angular velocity)* in which the drive rotational speed does not vary. CAV CD drives thus yield differing transfer rates depending on the location of blocks of data; these drives usually advertise their speed as a range or list a "maximum" transfer rate.

CMOS Complementary Metal Oxide Semiconductor chips require little electricity and, therefore, are used to store information using battery power. On most modern PCs, a block of CMOS memory is used to store critical system setup information, including drive type (a number that refers to a table listing its characteristics), memory settings, date, and time. CMOS memory must be edited when drives or memory, and certain other elements of the system, are added or changed.

CMYK The four-color process used in printers. See *RGB*.

CODEC COmpression/DECompression hardware or software used to compress or decompress digitized audio or video information.

cold boot Starting or restarting a computer by removing all power to the system or pressing the reset button. Compare to *warm boot*. In certain situations, a cold boot is necessary to reset some hardware devices.

COM port A serial communications port, as defined by the RS-232C standard. PCs usually have two serial ports and can support as many as four. The ports are numbered COM1, COM2, COM3, and COM4.

COMMAND.COM The command processor program of DOS, a basic element of the operating system.

Command overhead In a storage device interface, such as ATA, the time devoted to sending commands to a device instead of moving actual data.

command prompt A screen symbol from the operating system that indicates the system is awaiting input from the user — for example, C:>.

CompactFlash A form of flash memory used in many digital cameras and audio devices. They include circuitry that mimics an IDE disk controller, allowing them to appear to the system as if they were a disk driver. CompactFlash cards can be installed in readers attached to PCs for the download of information and can also be mounted in special PC Cards for the same purpose. See also *SmartMedia card*.

compression See *CODEC* and *disk compression*.

CONFIG.SYS The DOS configuration file that is part of the boot sector of a disk. It is used to instruct the operating system about device drivers to be loaded, and it provides settings for system variables, such as memory. It is an element of operating systems from DOS through Windows ME.

configuration The group of parameters and settings that controls communication between the system, major system components, adapter cards, and peripheral devices. Configurations are established from the setup screen on a modern machine and through choices made in some shells, such as Windows.

conventional memory Memory located between 0 and 640K, separated by IBM PC convention from addresses above 640K to 1MB, and intended for use by the OS (operating system) and applications. See also *base memory, expanded memory,* and *extended memory*.

coprocessor A chip that performs a function in parallel with the processor. It has no responsibility for control of the machine. The usual example is the x87 (8087, 80287, and so forth) math coprocessor that handles floating-point calculations for the microprocessor at a faster speed than the general-purpose CPU. The 80486 DX and Pentium CPUs contain an integrated math coprocessor. See also *floating-point unit*.

CPU The *Central Processing Unit* is the part of the computer that executes instructions and manipulates information. PCs are based on Intel or compatible CPUs, including the original 8088 and later chips, such as the 80286, 80386, 486, Pentium, Pentium MMX, Pentium II, Celeron, Pentium III, and Pentium 4.

cycle time The amount of time it takes to read from or write to a memory cell. Cycle time includes the precharge, when the cell is prepared to accept information, and the actual access, when data is moved between the memory and the bus or directly to the CPU.

cyclic redundancy check (CRC) A form of error checking that uses checksums.

cylinder Part of the computer's addressing scheme, used to locate data on a high-capacity hard disk. Data on a hard disk is stored on both sides of the disk in concentric circles, called tracks.

Large hard drives have multiple platters with separate read/write heads for each surface of each platter. A cylinder is composed of all of the tracks that are located in the same place, and on both sides, on their respective platters. Each track on one surface of a platter belongs to a different cylinder. (If you were to center a cylindrical cookie cutter over a hard disk and cut all the platters of the hard disk, you would cut through the tracks of one cylinder.) Large files are recorded on consecutive tracks of one cylinder, one file at a time (instead of consecutive tracks on one platter) to minimize the amount of movement and, therefore, minimize the time the heads need to read/write data.

DAC Digital-to-Analog Converter. On a modern video adapter, this circuitry is used to convert digital information into an analog signal that can be used by an analog monitor.

Data pre-fetch A scheme that instructs some advanced processors to "look-ahead" and fetch data from memory before it is needed by the processor. Modern systems using an L2 data cache usually employ a form of data pre-fetch.

data separation circuit The circuit in the path between the controller and the heads on the hard disk that extracts data from signals that were read from the media surface. See *encoding scheme.*

DDR SDRAM (Double Data Rate Synchronous Dynamic Random Access Memory) An advanced version of SDRAM that doubles the memory bandwidth. Normal SDRAM provides data bandwidth up to 1.1 gigabytes per second (GB/sec) while DDR SDRAM doubles the rate to 2.1GB/sec. DDR SDRAM was developed for graphics cards but has been adapted for use as a faster alternative to SDRAM in desktops.

Debug The process of finding and removing bugs, or errors, in a piece of software. From the very first PC through modern machines, the operating system has included a utility called *DEBUG* that allows advanced users to directly alter bytes of data in memory or in storage.

default A value, setting, or option that is preassigned by a program or system. Most configuration programs permit the user to drop back to the default settings, which are usually a good place to start when the user-selected configuration seems to be causing problems.

density The number of bits or characters that can be recorded in a specified space.

device driver A set of instructions to the computer that explains the commands a particular device understands. An extension of the BIOS, a device driver enables the operating system to access specific hardware in a hardware-blind fashion. The operating system doesn't need to know about the hardware details of a device to access the device driver that controls it.

DIMM Dual In-Line Memory Module. A high-capacity, high-speed memory carrier used in many current modern machines. The printed circuit board within the model allows dual channels to be used in a single interface. DIMM modules for desktops use 168 pins providing a pair of 32-bit memory paths forming a single 64-bit memory path. Laptops and printers commonly use 144-pin or 100-pin DIMMs. The predecessor to DIMMs was SIMM technology. (Direct Rambus DRAM uses a proprietary module, called a RIMM, for the same purpose as a DIMM.)

DIN connector A European-developed round plug and socket system, used on many PCs to connect keyboards and mice.

DIP switch Dual Inline Package switch. A little module containing several tiny switches. It is designed as a dual inline package (two rows of little legs) so that it can be mounted on a circuit board exactly like a DIP chip.

Direct memory access See *DMA.*

disk cache A segment of RAM set aside to temporarily hold data read from disks, which helps speed the movement of information

disk compression A system that reduces the size of data files stored on disks by applying an algorithm that substitutes codes for repeated characters. The efficiency is measured by the compression ratio, which compares the original size of the file to its compressed size. For example, a 2:1 ratio means the original file was twice as large as its compressed version.

display adapter Hardware, on an adapter card or in circuitry on the motherboard, that controls the display of images on a monitor.

DLL Dynamic Link Library programs are executable elements of many Windows applications.

DMA Direct Memory Access Data is transferred inside a computer through the DMA chip, not through the microprocessor, thus freeing the CPU to perform other tasks. For example, the hard disk controller uses DMA to read data from the hard disk and store it directly into RAM. PCs have eight available DMA channels.

DMF Distribution Media Format A special format developed by Microsoft for installation disks. It enables the disk to hold 1.8MB of data rather than the standard 1.4MB. DMF formatted disks cannot be copied with DOS or Windows disk-copy commands. Today, most applications are distributed on CDs.

dongle Specialized hardware used to prevent unauthorized use of a piece of software. The device (named after its inventor, Don Gill) includes an embedded serial number and typically attaches to a computer's parallel port. The software only works if it finds the dongle in place. Dongles are not commonly used anymore, except for certain expensive or custom software packages.

DOS Disk Operating System. The operating system originally provided by Microsoft to IBM in 1979, it has also underlaid all versions of Windows through Windows ME. Like all operating systems, it is an extension of the BIOS. It enables simple access to peripherals by higher (hardware-blind) programs. See also *COMMAND.COM*.

double buffering A scheme used by 3-D graphics cards that uses separate blocks of memory for the finished image and for another image that is in the process of being rendered. This enables smooth transitions from one scene to another or film-like animation.

DRAM Dynamic Random Access Memory. Memory chips that need to be refreshed regularly. DRAM temporarily stores data in a cell made up of a tiny capacitor and transistor. Cells are accessed by row addresses and column addresses. While being refreshed, a DRAM chip cannot be read by the microprocessor. Therefore, slow DRAM read and write accesses often require CPU wait states. See also *SRAM*.

DRDRAM. Direct Rambus DRAM. See *RDRAM*.

driver See *device driver*.

DS/DD Double-sided/double-density. The most common disk form for older PCs. It includes 5.25-inch 360K and 3.5-inch 720K disks. The original IBM PC was shipped with single-sided, double-density, 160K floppy disk drives (that later read 180K disks), but these dinosaurs with only one read/write head quickly became extinct.

DS/HD Double-sided/high-density. A floppy disk form used in most modern PCs. Currently, 3.5-inch 1.44MB disks are in common use.

DSP An element of a sound card, a modem, and other devices, the Digital Signal Processor chip is used to compress, filter, regenerate, and otherwise process signals and images.

dual boot A configuration that enables a computer to be loaded with more than one operating system, with the user able to choose between them at boot.

duplex A communications channel capable of carrying signals in both directions.

Duron A "value" version of AMD's Athlon processor, equipped with a smaller amount of L2 cache. See also *Celeron*.

DVD Digital Video Disc or Digital Versatile Disc. A developing standard for high-density data, audio, and video. DVD is stored on a media the size of a compact disc.

DX2, DX4 See clock doubling and clock tripling.

ECC Memory Error Checking and Correcting Memory A form of memory that uses algorithms to detect errors. When data is stored in memory, the systematic code creates a check bit that is stored along with the data byte; when the data is later retrieved, the chip consults a reference table to check the validity of the data. ECC memory can detect single and double bit errors, and correct single bit errors.

ECP (enhanced capabilities port) A form of improved, bidirectional parallel port interface.

EDO RAM Extended Data-Out RAM. A faster form of DRAM that improved memory access time by allowing two blocks of data to be accessed at the same time. One block of data is sent to the CPU while another is prepared for access. Modern machines use even-faster SDRAM, which uses a similar scheme.

EEPROM Electrically Erasable Programmable Read-Only Memory. A special type of integrated circuit that can be used to store BIOS and other programming; it can be erased and reprogrammed by a special device. Flash memory is a form of EEPROM that can be updated in place within a PC by using special programs.

EGA The Enhanced Graphics Adapter was a relatively short-lived display standard that was used between the CGA and VGA eras. It can display resolutions as high as 640 X 350 pixels with 16 colors from a palette of 64. EGA uses a digital (TTL) signal.

EISA Extended Industry Standard Architecture. An improvement over the 16-bit AT (ISA) bus, it includes a 32-bit path and bus mastering. It still runs at a slow 8 MHz, and it has been surpassed by local bus and PCI designs.

embedded controller Circuitry built into an IDE or SCSI driver that handles the management of the drive, as opposed to earlier designs that had a hard disk controller in the bus of the motherboard.

EMI On a power supply, electromagnetic interference is noise generated by switching action. Conducted EMI is interference reflected back into the power line; it can usually be cleaned up by a line filter. Radiated EMI, interference radiated into the air, can be blocked by proper shielding, including a metal case.

EMS Expanded Memory Specification. Also known as Lotus/Intel/Microsoft (LIM) EMS, named after the vendors that defined that standard in response to Quarterdeck's Expanded Memory Manager. Known as bank-switched memory, as well. See *expanded memory* for a complete definition.

encoding scheme Used to process data before it is stored on floppy disks, hard disks, tape, or other media. The encoding scheme massages raw data and turns it into a stream of signals, which makes error detection easier. Encoding schemes are also used to compress data.

Energy Star A specification for power-saving designs.

enhanced IDE An improvement to the IDE specification for disk drives and other devices, permitting data transfer rates up to 13MB per second.

EPP The Enhanced Parallel Port is an improved standard that permits data transfers of as much as 500K per second, more than triple the 150K speed of the original PC parallel interface.

EPROM Erasable Programmable Read-Only Memory. ROMs that are erased by a burst of ultraviolet light. See *EEPROM*.

ESDI The Enhanced Small Device Interface is an interface for hard drives in which the data separation circuit is in the hard drive, supporting a maximum transfer rate of 3MB per second. The cabling scheme is the same as the ST412/ST506 interface, but in ST412/ST506 the data separation circuits are on the hard drive controller. ESDI enables the manufacturer of the hard drive to use any encoding scheme it wishes, so the manufacturer can pack more data onto the physical drive surface.

Ethernet A local area network specification that uses a bus or star topology. In its basic design, sometimes referred to as *10Base-T*, it permits data transfer rates of 10 Mbps. *Fast Ethernet*, or 100Base-T allows transfer rates of 100 Mbps.

exabyte 1,000,000,000,000,000,000 bytes, or 1,024 petabytes. Abbreviated as EB.

expanded memory The memory used by an Expanded Memory Manager (see EMS) or bank-switched memory. This memory management scheme was designed to get around the 1MB memory barrier in 8088 CPU chips. It enables specially written applications to address as much as 32MB of memory, originally on a special memory board, by switching multiple 64K banks. EMS exploits a window of available address space above 640K, but below the 1MB barrier. Banks of memory are switched into and out of up to four consecutive 16K windows as needed, which provides effective access to as much as 8MB of additional memory. Many application programs have been written to use expanded memory to store data or to store programs until they are needed.

expansion slot A connector on the motherboard that allows an *expansion card* to electrically become part of the bus.

extended memory The memory in a modern machine with an address above 1MB. It can be used under DOS by programs that throw the 286, 386, or 486 CPU chip — and advanced CPUs that emulate earlier microprocessors — into protected mode, where the CPU and associated programs can take advantage of this memory. Can be used to provide *expanded memory*.

external drive A storage device that exists outside of the case of the PC, connected to it by a cable. Common interfaces for external devices include FireWire, parallel, SCSI, and USB.

fan rating Airflow measured in cubic feet per minute. Designers say a 100 percent increase in airflow reduces system operating temperatures by 50 percent relative to the ambient.

Fast Page Mode DRAM A DRAM that speeds data access by identifying sections of memory as pages once they have been accessed; subsequent requests for the same block of memory can be retrieved by a single row address.

FAT The File Allocation Table is a listing created by DOS that tracks the use of hard disk space, noting which cluster(s) a file occupies and in what order the clusters should be read. The FAT also notes which clusters are available (unused) and unavailable (currently in use or bad).

FAT16 A variation of the File Allocation Table that uses a 16-bit field to address clusters in a logical partition. FAT16 is limited to approximately 2.1GB and 65,000 clusters. FAT16 is compatible with DOS, Windows 3.1, Windows 95A, Windows NT 3.5 and 4.0, and OS/2.

FAT32 An advanced version of the File Allocation Table based on a 32-bit field, allowing partitions larger than 2.1GB with millions of clusters. FAT32 is compatible with Windows 95 SR2, Windows 98, Windows 2000, and Windows XP.

fax mode On a modem, the mode used to send and receive files in a facsimile format.

FCB File Control Block. The operating system maintains information about the status of every open file in this section of memory.

FDISK An operating system utility program used to partition a hard disk drive.

feature connector A means to add capabilities to certain adapters including display adapters and sound cards.

firewall A piece of software or a hardware device intended to block intruders from accessing computers attached to a local area network or the Internet.

FireWire A fast and flexible external bus standard originally developed as the IEEE 1394 specification and later renamed by Apple as FireWire. In its current version it permits data transfer rates of as much as 400 Mbps, with faster versions expected.

fixed-frequency monitor A display monitor that is designed to work with only one signal frequency and that must be matched to the proper display adapter. Compare to *multifrequency monitor*.

flash disk A storage device using *flash memory*. Examples include PC Card memory, *CompactFlash*, and *Smart Media* cards.

flash memory Special memory chips that can hold their contents without power and can be erased and reprogrammed.

floating-point unit The technical term for *math coprocessor*, used in parallel with some dinosaur and senior citizen microprocessors.

Floppy 3 Mode In Japan, the original standard for high-density floppy disks stored 1.2MB on a 3.5-inch diskette, instead of 1.44MB as is used elsewhere. In most systems, Floppy 3 Mode Support should be disabled in the BIOS to avoid problems.

floppy disk A storage device that uses flexible, Mylar disks coated with a medium that can hold a magnetic charge (similar to audio tape). The most commonly used disk on modern machines is the 3.5-inch disk, which adds a semirigid carrier and is capable of storing 1.44MB of data. Older machines used 5.25-inch floppy disks, with a top capacity of 1.2MB.

FM synthesis A technology of mixing sine waves that was used by older and lower-cost sound cards to simulate musical instruments, voice, and other sounds. A more advanced technology is wave table synthesis, which stores actual samples of musical instruments.

format (high-level) The process of preparing the media (disk or tape) for addressing by the operating system. Before formatting, the operating system checks the media for defects and creates certain tables. These tables enable the system to find the stored data.

format (low-level) The process of placing marks on the media so that data stored on the media can be found again.

FPU See *floating-point unit* and *coprocessor*.

frame In data communications, a block of data with header and trailer bits before and after the information. The added information is used for error-checking codes and start/end indicators.

Front-side Bus (FSB) Another name for the processor bus, the high-speed main highway that connects a microprocessor to other system devices.

FTP (file transfer protocal) A mechanism for transferring files over the Internet.

full-duplex A communications protocol permitting the sending and receiving of data signals at the same time. See also *duplex* and *half-duplex*.

function keys The set of extra keys on a computer keyboard, usually labeled F1 through F12, that can be programmed to perform special functions.

gas plasma display A specialized form of flat-screen display that uses a glass envelope filled with an excitable gas; application of electrical current to a particular point where horizontal and vertical electrodes intersect causes the gas to glow.

gender A description of the form of a connector, specifically whether it has protruding pins (male) or corresponding receptacles (female). To convert a connector from one form to another you can use a *gender bender*.

general MIDI A set of 128 standard sounds used in MIDI sound cards and output devices. See *MIDI*.

GIF Graphics Interchange Format. A compressed digital image format defined by CompuServe, commonly used on CompuServe and the Internet for transferring images. See *JPEG* and *PNG*.

giga One billion.

gigabyte Used informally to mean one billion bytes of storage in hard drives and other storage media. For RAM, the actual size of a gigabyte is 1,024 megabytes, or 1,073,741,824 bytes. Abbreviated as GB.

Gouraud shading An advanced method for shading colors within a shape that works by averaging the color values at the edges of a shape and then adjusting the color values to evenly blend them across the shape. Without Gouraud shading, most graphics schemes fill shapes with flat shading — a color or gray scale that does not vary within polygonal elements of an image.

GPF General Protection Fault. A system crash in some versions of Windows.

graphics adapter See *display adapter.*

GUI (graphical user interface) An operating system or program that allows the user to execute commands and move objects by pointing to icons, links, and pictures with the use of a keyboard or a pointing device such as a mouse. Microsoft Windows is the best-known example of a GUI. Technical types pronounce the term as "gooey."

half-duplex A communications protocol that permits only sending or receiving at one time. See also duplex and full-duplex.

hard disk A large-capacity storage medium that uses spinning platters coated with magnetic material.

hard reset Instructing a running system to reboot by pressing a reset button on the hardware. Also known as a *cold boot.* Compare to *warm boot.*

head The electromagnetic component of a floppy or hard disk drive that reads or writes data.

head actuator The mechanism the moves a read/write head to the center or back to the edge of a rotating disk.

head crash A disastrous failure of a hard disk that occurs when the read/write head that ordinarily hovers a few millionths of an inch above the platter comes to rest on the disk. In most cases, the hard disk is damaged beyond repair, although some data recovery services are able to extract data from the disk.

head load time On a floppy disk drive, the amount of time required for the drive head to settle after it is lowered onto the drive surface.

head settle time On a floppy disk drive, the amount of time required for the heads to settle after a seek operation.

head unload time On a floppy disk drive, the amount of time required for the drive head to settle after it is lifted from the drive surface.

heat sink A metallic (usually aluminum) structure with vanes that radiate heat away from a hot component, helping to prevent failure of electronic devices. Modern microprocessors require a heat sink, cooling fan, or both because of the amount of heat they produced.

helical scan A technique to record more data on a moving tape storage device. A rotating read/write head is mounted at an angle to the moving tape, writing bands of data on the tape.

Hercules standard A dinosaur monochrome text and graphics display standard that produced a 720-x-348-pixel screen.

hertz A measurement of the frequency of information; one hertz is one cycle per second. Abbreviated as *Hz*. A MHz (megahertz) is equal to one million cycles per second. The term is named after physicist Heinrich Hertz.

hexadecimal A base-16 numbering system. Digits are represented by the numbers 0 through 9 and the characters A through F.

high memory Memory of a DOS-based computer between 1MB plus 16 bytes to 1MB plus 65,536 bytes, or basically, the first 64K of extended memory. See *conventional memory, upper memory, expanded memory,* and *extended memory*.

HIMEM.SYS A device driver that manages extended memory. Current versions of DOS and Windows include it.

HMA High memory area. See *high memory*.

host In a SCSI system, the computer in which a host adapter is installed. The host adapter card permits connection of SCSI devices to the bus.

HTML Hypertext Markup Language. The authoring language behind the pages of a Web site on the Internet. It is up to the browser on the PC to interpret the generic HTML language for the needs of a specific computer and its display.

HTTP Hypertext Transfer Protocol. The mechanism behind the transfer of messages and Web pages over the Internet.

hub A common connection point for components attached to a network or an expandable subsystem. An Ethernet hub brings together the cables from PCs in a hub-and-spoke topology. A USB or FireWire hub expands the number of connectors and amplifies available electrical power for devices on the chain.

hypertext A means to link objects and files to one another. On a Web page, hypertext links allow you to jump to other pages or documents.

Hz See *hertz*.

IBM clone A computer that is functionally the same as an IBM PC, XT, or AT. After the Phoenix and AMIBIOSs came on the market, the terms clone and compatible came to mean the same thing. Some earlier IBM-compatible machines were unable to run standard software unless the software was modified.

IDE Integrated Device Electronics. A disk drive interface in which the electronic circuitry for the controller resides on the drive itself, eliminating the need for a separate controller card. The extended IDE (EIDE) interface is also used for some CD-ROM drives and other devices. See also *ATA*.

IEEE 1394 The technical standard behind FireWire. See *FireWire*.

INF file Windows drivers and information files use the .INF file description in their name.

initiator On a SCSI system, the device that requests an operation be performed by another SCSI device (the target).

inkjet printer A printing device that creates text or images by spraying tiny dots onto a page.

interleave Data is loaded onto the hard disk one sector at a time, but not necessarily in physically contiguous sectors. An interleave of two uses every other sector. An interleave of three uses one sector, skips two, loads one, skips two, and so on. Slow CPUs require higher interleave numbers to read from and write to a hard disk as quickly as possible. Some hard disk diagnostics find your computer's ideal interleave number and set up the hard disk for maximum access speed.

interleaved memory A method to reduce CPU wait states for slower RAM chips by placing odd-numbered and even-numbered bytes of memory in separate chips. Because the processor alternates the chips it accesses, each chip has more time to prepare for its next access. Therefore, slower RAM can be used.

internal drive A storage device that mounts within the case of a PC. A floppy disk, CD-ROM, Zip drive, and other forms of removable media require access to the outside of the case, while internal hard drives can be mounted anywhere in the case that is within reach of data and power cables. Compare to *external drive.*

interrupt For hardware, a call for the attention of a CPU. A PC is called an interrupt-driven system because every keystroke from the keyboard and every other event generates an interrupt to the processor. Unless two devices are designed to cooperate, they cannot share the same interrupt request line (IRQ). Current PCs have 16 IRQ channels. Hardware interrupts break in on a CPU's internal meditations and ask for attention from the CPU. Nonmaskable interrupts (NMIs) are hardware interrupts that demand immediate attention. The CPU must suspend operations for a NMI. Most hardware interrupts are maskable, though. They are mediated by an interrupt controller chip, which queues up the interrupts and asks the CPU to service each interrupt in its order of priority. Software interrupts are a jump to a subroutine. The subroutine locations and the interrupt numbers assigned to each subroutine are stored in the interrupt vector table.

Interrupt 13 and Interrupt 13 Extensions The BIOS routine that handles hard disk commands and data. The original routine, Interrupt 13, supported capacities up to 8.4GB. Extensions on newer BIOS chip sets add support for larger drives.

interrupt vector table A table of 256 interrupts, located in the first kilobyte of memory, that contains the subroutine address assigned to each interrupt.

I/O Input/output. The name for the process by which a computer communicates with the external world. Input comes from keyboards, mice, scanners, modems, and digital tablets. Output goes to printers, monitors, modems, and so forth. The term I/O is context-dependent. For example, data that is output from one program may become input for another program.

I/O port address A number assigned to a particular device (such as a disk drive, port, mouse, or other component) that is used to tell the device that data about to be sent down the bus is meant for that device. No two devices can be assigned the same I/O port address.

IO.SYS An element of MSDOS.SYS. See *MSDOS.SYS.*

IP address An identifying number for devices on a TCP/IP network.

IRQ Interrupt ReQuest Line. Hardware lines over which devices can send interrupts to the CPU. IRQs are assigned different priority levels to enable the processor to determine the comparative importance of requests for service. See also *interrupt.*

ISA The Industry Standard Architecture is the original IBM PC-AT bus architecture adopted by compatible-PC manufacturers.

ISO International Standards Organization. An international association of standard-setting organizations.

Itanium Intel's advanced 64-bit CPU aimed at servers and workstations.

joystick A pointing or controlling device based on an upright lever. Used in many arcade games and some specialty applications.

JPEG A graphics storage protocol developed by the Joint Photographic Experts Group that uses a compression scheme, which reduces the size of an image while preserving image quality. See GIF and PNG.

jumper A small metal clip within a plastic block that is placed on metal pins to turn on or off a specific function or to make a particular setting.

K Kilo, as in 1,000. In reference to memory, K means one kilobyte (1,024 bytes), because memory — and other computer values — are based on the binary number system (2 to a power). Therefore, one kilobyte of memory is actually 2^{10}, or 1,024.

Kb Kilobit; 1,024 bits.

KB Kilobyte; 1,024 bytes.

Kbps Kilobits per second.

KBps Kilobytes per second.

kernel The most basic, essential element of the operating system, loaded first and kept in memory.

keyboard buffer A block of memory that can store a particular number of keystrokes that have not yet been processed by the computer.

keyboard controller A special-purpose microprocessor in the keyboard that interprets keyboard presses, relieving the PC's main processor from this task. The keyboard controller BIOS, located on the motherboard, manages the interface between the keyboard and the system.

KHz Kilohertz stands for 1,000 hertz (Hz), used to measure the sampling rate of audio.

kilo One thousand.

L1 cache Level one cache is a small amount of SRAM memory integrated or packaged within the same module as the processor and used as a cache. L1 cache runs at the same clock speed as the processor. L1 cache is used to temporarily store instructions and data, keeping the processor supplied with data even if memory lags behind.

L2 cache Level two cache is SRAM memory near the processor or integrated into a processor. Also known as secondary cache, this is the second-fastest memory available to a microprocessor, second only to L1 cache.

landing zone On a hard disk drive, a particular cylinder where the read/write heads can safely park after power is shut off. Data is not stored in the landing zone.

laser printer A printer that produces pages based on electronic signals from a computer. The dots of an image are converted into a laser beam that imparts a charge to paper that attracts dry ink that is later fused in place by heat.

latency Generally, the amount of time a device has to wait to be served data from another. In terms of storage, latency is the average amount of time the drive has to wait for a particular sector to rotate into place beneath a read/write head. In networking, latency is the time it takes for a packet of information to travel from sender to destination. *See also CAS Latency.*

LBA (Logical Block Addressing) A mode of accessing a location of a hard drive based on sequential numbering for the sectors of a disk, eliminating a slower and more complex calculation of cylinder, head, and sector coordinates.

LCD Liquid Crystal Display. A display, used on most laptop PCs, that produces images by changing the polarity of light passing through individual pixels of a polarized filter in response to an electrical signal.

LED Light-Emitting Diode. A highly efficient semiconductor that converts electrical energy into light.

LIM Lotus-Intel-Microsoft (named for the vendors who developed the standard). A technique for expanding the amount of memory that a computer can use for data. This method only works with special LIM or EMS cards and programs designed to use this memory. See expanded memory.

local bus A data bus that connects directly to the microprocessor, capable of operating at the transfer speed of the CPU.

logic Name for the internal parts of a computer that perform functions defined by the rules of logic, as in philosophy.

logical unit In a SCSI system, a physical or virtual device addressed through a target. Each logical unit of a device has a logical unit number (LUN) by which it is addressed.

low level format The electronic markings placed on a hard drive that mark the start of each sector. The operating system further refines the indexing of a disk when it formats a drive's sectors.

LPT1 A computer's name for its first parallel port. The term comes from the days of mainframes, when LPT was an abbreviation for line printer.

magneto-optical disk drive A data storage device that combines a laser and a magnetic medium for storing information.

mainframe A large computer intended to serve the needs of dozens or hundreds of users at the same time. The definition of a mainframe has changed considerably over the course of the history of computers; today's PCs have more power than early mainframes.

main memory Another term for conventional memory.

master The first addressed drive (device 0) on an ATA/IDE chain.

master boot record An essential element of the operating system, it contains the information needed to identify the location of the boot components for the PC. By definition, it is located within the first sector of the hard disk. If the MBR is corrupted or lost, the system will not operate until it is repaired or re-created. One of the most damaging types of viruses infects the MBR, taking control of the system before any other program — including antivirus software — can protect it.

math coprocessor See *coprocessor.*

Mb See *megabit.*

MB See *megabyte.*

Mbps Megabits per second. The number of bits, in millions, moved in one second.

MBps Megabytes per second. The number of bytes, in millions, moved in one second.

MBR See *Master Boot Record.*

MCA Micro Channel Architecture. The name of the bus in the IBM PS/2 Model 50s and up. MCA buses are not compatible with ISA cards. The MCA bus supports multiple bus masters. On any bus, only one processor at a time can have control, but the MCA design enables any one of the processors in the machine to be in control. By comparison, ISA enables only the CPU to have control of the computer; all other processors are slaves to the CPU. EISA is a 32-bit bus and, like Micro Channel, enables other processors to control the bus. See also EISA, ISA, and PS/2.

MDA Monochrome Display Adapter. The original display standard for the IBM PC, it can produce only text at a screen resolution of 720 x 350 pixels.

media A physical device that stores computer-generated data. Floppy disks and hard disks are magnetic media. CD-ROMs are optical media.

mega A million. In reference to memory, equals 1,048,576 bytes, or 1,020.

megabit (Mb) A million bits. In reference to memory, equals 1,048,576 bits.

megabyte (MB) A million bytes. In reference to memory, equals 1,048,576 bytes.

megaflops A measure, in millions, of the number of floating-point operations per second of a CPU.

megahertz One million cycles per second, abbreviated as MHz.

memory The part of a computer that remembers 0s and 1s. Unlike human memory, it cannot remember any context. See also expanded memory, extended memory, RAM, refresh, ROM, and system memory.

memory management unit Hardware that supports the mapping of virtual memory addresses to physical memory addresses.

memory refresh See *refresh*.

MFM Modified Frequency Modulation. One of many possible encoding schemes. MFM uses clock bits interspersed with data. The ST412/ST506 standard for MFM was the most common hard disk controller-encoding scheme for years. See also ESDI, RLL, and SCSI, all of which are competing hard disk controller designs.

MGA Monochrome Graphics Array. A dinosaur video display standard.

MHz See *megahertz*.

micro One millionth. Sometimes represented by the Greek character μ.

Micro Channel Architecture See *MCA*.

micron One millionth of a meter (one-thousandth of a millimeter).

microprocessor The part of the computer that processes. In microcomputers, the chip that actually executes instructions and manipulates information. Also called the CPU or the processor.

MIDI The Musical Instrument Digital Interface protocol is a specification for the interchange of music data. MIDI consists of a set of instructions to be executed by a MIDI output device. Because MIDI devices do not store the sound itself, MIDI files are small.

milli One thousandth.

minicomputer A computer smaller than a mainframe in both power and cost. Minicomputers were widely used as servers for groups of terminals and then groups of PCs in the early years of the PC. They have been largely supplanted by high-end PCs.

MIPS Million Instructions Per Second. A measure of the speed at which a computer executes instructions.

MMX A set of multimedia extensions added to the Pentium instruction set and introduced in new Intel Pentium chips in 1997 and incorporated within later CPUs.

modem Modulator/demodulator. A device that converts digital data from a computer into analog data for transmission over telephone lines by modulating it into waves. At the other end, a modem converts the analog data back into digital form by demodulating it.

modified frequency modulation See *MFM*. An older method for recording data on a hard disk drive by varying the amplitude and frequency of a signal.

monitor A video display.

motherboard The main board of the PC, holding the microprocessor, system BIOS, expansion slots, and other critical components.

mouse A device used to control the location of an onscreen pointer that identifies data or issues commands to the processor.

MPC The Multimedia PC specifications were set by a consortium of hardware manufacturers and identify the minimum requirements for hardware that support multimedia applications.

MPEG A video image-compression scheme developed by the Motion Picture Expert Group.

MSCDEX The Microsoft CD-ROM Extensions is a device driver that controls management of CD-ROM drives that are attached to DOS and most Windows machines.

MSDOS.SYS A file that is the essential element of the boot files for Microsoft operating systems from DOS through Windows 98. (In IBM's version of DOS, a similar file is called IBMDOS.COM.)

MTBF Mean Time Between Failure is a measure by hardware manufacturers that purports to show the average time a component can be expected to work before it fails.

multifrequency monitor A display that is capable of adapting itself to different display adapters' output frequencies, also called a multisynchronous monitor.

multitasking Performing multiple jobs simultaneously.

multiuser An operating system that enables many users to perform different tasks on the same computer.

nano (n) One billionth. A nanosecond is abbreviated as ns.

NLX form factor A specification for motherboards and power supplies used in low-profile cases.

NMI Nonmaskable Interrupt. An interrupt generated by hardware that cannot be turned off. An error message usually indicates a serious memory or I/O problem.

node A device attached to a network, such as a computer, printer, or gateway.

noise Engineers measure the acoustical noise of a fan or other system devices in dB(A) at 1 meter. dB is expressed on a logarithmic scale, with each reduction of 3dB representing 50 percent less noise.

noise interference Noise from any source that interferes with your computer. Examples include erratic electric, magnetic, or radio waves. Likely causes are an electric clock (magnetic), a thunderstorm (electric), or a local radio station (radio waves).

nonvolatile memory Memory that does not need to be refreshed. Therefore, it doesn't require much power. CMOS RAM is a form of nonvolatile memory.

North Bridge A memory controller hub that is part of a modern PC's chipset. The processor communicates through the north bridge to close-in cache memory, main memory, and on to the peripheral bus (including PCI on a modern machine) and special-purpose buses such as AGP for a modern class of graphics cards. Some north bridge chipsets also include some integrated functions such as video and audio controllers. See also *South Bridge*.

NTSC The television standard used in the United States and some other countries, developed by the National Television Standards Committee. The format specifies a frame rate of 30 frames per second and a resolution of 485 visible lines.

null modem cable A specialized serial cable used to connect two serial devices directly, without the use of a modem.

numeric coprocessor For the PC, originally a special chip (8087, 80287, and 80387) designed to perform floating-point calculations, logarithms, and trigonometry. Today, numeric coprocessor circuitry is usually incorporated within a CPU.

OCR (optical character recognition) Software that converts scanned images of text back into files that can be edited with a word processor.

OEM An Original Equipment Manufacturer is a company that produces equipment that is sold by another company under the other company's brand name. For example, Intel and Micron are OEMs of motherboards to many PC manufacturers.

offset A way to address memory, using a numbering system that indicates the relative distance (offset) from the beginning of a memory segment.

operating range On a power supply, the minimum and maximum input voltage sufficient to allow the device to deliver proper DC voltage to the system. The more uneven your local electrical service, the more you need a power supply with a wide operating range.

operating system (OS) A program that enables a computer to load programs and that controls the screen, the drives, and other devices. Microsoft's DOS was used in early systems through Windows 95/98 and ME; Windows 2000 and Windows XP use new code that performs the same functions.

operating temperature The range of ambient temperatures within which a device can be safely operated.

OS/2 Operating System 2, by IBM/Microsoft. (Operating System 1 is DOS.) IBM originally intended this operating system for the 80286, but released it for PS/2s.

output current In a power supply, the maximum current that can be continuously drawn.

overclocking Running a processor at a speed faster than its manufacturer certifies as its top speed. Usually accomplished by adjusting the *clock multiplier*. The processor may work fine, or it may crash and burn.

OverDrive CPU An add-on chip from Intel for upgrading a PC with a faster and/or more powerful CPU.

overvoltage protection In a power supply, a circuit that shuts down the device if the output voltage exceeds a specified limit.

paged memory See expanded memory and LIM.

page frame A range of physical memory addresses in which a page of virtual memory can be mapped.

page mode memory access A means by which the computer accesses data in RAM. In an ordinary scheme, the CPU activates a RAS (row address strobe) and a CAS (column address strobe) signal in order to specify the row and column of the data. In page mode memory access, the CPU assumes the data is located in the same page as the initial data and, therefore, the CPU can obtain information more rapidly.

PAL The television standard used in Europe and other locations. The Phase Alternate Line format specifies a frame rate of 50 frames per second and a resolution of 575 visible lines. Compare to *NTSC*.

parallel A means of transmitting data with the bits that make up a computer word traveling alongside each other on adjacent wires, like the lanes of a superhighway. Compare to *serial*.

parallel port The I/O channel to a parallel device, such as a printer.

parity A system used to check each byte of data for errors. The parity bit plus the 8 bits in the byte must add up correctly. For even parity, the number of 1s in the byte plus the parity bit must add up to an even number. If they don't, the computer knows there has been an error in transmitting the signal. For odd parity, they must add up to an odd number.

partition A disk can be divided into several partitions, each of which can act as if it were a separate disk. Using multiple partitions is one way to deal with a hard drive that is larger than DOS will recognize, a problem more common with earlier versions of the operating system. Some users prefer to divide their disks into separate partitions for organizational reasons.

password check option A feature of some ROM BIOS systems, it can be used to prevent unauthorized use of the system or alterations to the setup.

PC100 SDRAM An Intel specification for SDRAM memory devices and modules that can operate at a 100 MHz Front Side Bus (FSB) frequency. PC-100 SDRAM memory is backward compatible with systems that use PC-66 SDRAM memory.

PC133 SDRAM An Intel Specification for SDRAM memory devices and modules that can operate at a 133 MHz Front Side Bus (FSB) frequency. PC-133 SDRAM memory is backward compatible with systems that use either PC-100 or PC-66 SDRAM memory.

PC1600 DDR A form of DDR SDRAM memory that provides 1.6GBps throughput.

PC2100 DDR A form of DDR SDRAM memory that provides 2.1GB/second throughput of data.

PC Card The Personal Computer Memory Card International Association specification for a credit-card-sized addition to PCs, most often used in portable computers. In 1995, the group dropped the forgettable acronym of PCMCIA in favor of PC Card. The original Type I card is primarily used in handheld personal assistants. Type II cards are principally used for memory, network adapters, and modems. Type III cards are thick enough to hold miniaturized disk drives and other devices.

PCI The Peripheral Component Interconnect is a high-performance peripheral bus designed by Intel that runs at 33 MHz and supports 32-bit and 64-bit-wide data paths and bus mastering capability.

PCMCIA See *PC Card*.

peer-to-peer A networking design in which any node on the network can be the source (server) of information or the client. A basic Ethernet using a hub-and-spoke design is a peer-to-peer network.

Pentium The fifth major generation of Intel CPUs used in PCs. Intel has gone on to produce the Pentium II, Pentium III, and Pentium 4 microprocessor families.

peripheral A hardware device connected to a computer. Typical peripherals include keyboards, monitors, printers, disk drives, and more.

petabyte 1,000,000,000,000,000 bytes, or 1,024 terabytes. Abbreviated as PB.

PGA Pin Grid Array. One method of mounting chips on a circuit board, used by devices with a large number of lines to connect. Pins stick out of the bottom of the chip and are meant to mate with holes in a socket. PGAs are used for most microprocessors, for example.

Photo CD A technology, developed by Eastman Kodak, that permits the storage and retrieval of photographs on a CD-ROM for display on home TVs or a personal computer.

physical address An actual memory address.

picosecond One-trillionth of a second.

PIF A Program Information File is an element of Windows that contains instructions on how to run non-Windows DOS applications.

pinout A drawing or table that lists the nature of the signals that use particular pins of a chip or connector.

pixel A picture element is the smallest addressable area of a computer image. Screen resolutions are expressed as pixels, such as the 640-X-480-pixel VGA specification.

platter The rotating disk within a hard disk drive used to hold data.

Plug and Play A component for a PC's BIOS jointly developed by Intel and Microsoft, with support incorporated within Windows 95/98 and subsequent versions, intended to make peripherals self-configuring. A new device plugged into such a system would be able to set its own IRQ, DMA channel, I/O port setting, and memory addresses while avoiding conflicts with other peripherals' settings.

PNG Portable Network Graphics. A compressed digital-image format designed as a patent-free alternative to CompuServe's GIF format for the transfer of images on the Web. See *JPEG* and *GIF*.

POST Power-On Self-Test. The BIOS ROM contains a series of hardware tests that runs each time a computer is turned on. If hardware errors are found, POST either beeps or displays error messages.

PostScript A page description language for printing documents and producing images on other devices; it was developed by Adobe Systems.

power good signal In a power supply, a delay circuit used to initialize the computer and provide a logic signal.

power supply A critical element of the PC that converts AC wall current to DC current. Electronic circuits run at 3.5 or 5 volts, while most disk drive and CD or DVD motors draw 12 volts.

primary The first ATA/IDE channel of a computer. Each channel supports a chain of one or two devices, configured as master and slave. See also *secondary*.

processor The part of the computer that executes instructions and manipulates information. In microcomputers, this is a single chip. It is also called a CPU or a microprocessor.

processor interrupt An interrupt generated by the microprocessor, also known as a logical interrupt. One example is a divide-by-zero logical error.

PROM Programmable Read-Only Memory. A special type of memory that can be custom-produced to hold information or programming. A PROM cannot be rewritten. See also *EEPROM* and *EPROM*.

protected mode The mode of an 80286 or later microprocessor in which the processor can address extended memory and protect OS memory from direct manipulation by applications. 80286 and later CPUs are capable of operating either in real mode (basically, no extended memory) or in protected mode. The 80386 and later CPUs also have a virtual mode, which lets them run multiple virtual real-mode segments. See also *virtual memory*.

PS/2 Personal System 2. This 1987 IBM family of microcomputers originally incorporated a patented bus called MCA (Micro Channel Architecture). Classic-bus partisans feel that IBM designed this line to thwart cloning. As sales declined, later PS/2s reverted to the ISA bus. See also *MCA*.

RAM Random Access Memory. Any part of this memory can be used by the microprocessor. Each storage location in RAM has a unique address, and each address can be either written to or read by the processor. In DOS, conventional memory, maximum 640K, is the area used to hold DOS, applications, and data. Expanded memory and extended memory (see both entries) are also RAM. When people use the term RAM casually (as in "How much RAM does your computer have?"), they're usually talking about conventional memory, plus expanded and extended memory. Windows, unlike DOS, uses both conventional memory and extended memory. See also *DRAM, ROM, refresh,* and *SRAM*.

RDRAM A type of memory, developed by Rambus, used to support some Intel CPUs beginning with the Pentium 4. Like DDR SDRAM, it transfers data on the rising and falling edges of the clock cycle. The memory device uses two data channels to improve transfer rates. Also known as *DRDRAM*.

read/write head The component of a storage device that reads recorded data and writes new information. Hard drives, floppy drives, and tape backup devices use magnetism to read and write; CD-Rs, CD-RWs, and DVD-RAMs use a laser to melt meaningful pits on a plastic disc.

real mode The 80286 and later microprocessors can operate in two memory addressing modes: real mode, which basically means no extended memory (such as an 8088 or 8086); and protected mode, which includes extended memory. The 80386 and later microprocessors also have a virtual mode that runs multiple virtual real-mode segments. These processors operate in real mode when running DOS. They operate in protected mode when running Windows.

reboot To restart the computer. See *boot, cold boot,* and *warm boot.*

refresh Dynamic memory (DRAM) forgets the information it holds unless it is rewritten regularly. Memory with a faster *refresh rate* responds quicker. Refresh rate also is another term for the vertical scan frequency of a monitor.

register One of several cells in a processor that is used to manipulate data. For example, a CPU can load a value from memory into a register, load another value into another register, add the two values together and put the result in a third register, and then copy the third register's value to a location in memory. The width of the register is measured by the number of bits it can hold, which, in turn, determines the range of values it can hold. The larger the register width, the more powerful the computer. Therefore, register width is used to describe CPUs. The 8088 is an 8-bit CPU, the 80286 and 386SX are 16-bit CPUs, and the 486 and Pentium CPUs are 32-bit CPUs. Numeric coprocessors usually have 80-bit registers. Many popular high-end graphics cards have dedicated 128-bit processors, meaning the processors use 128-bit registers to manipulate graphics data.

registry An essential component of Windows 95/98 and later versions holding the system configuration files including settings, preferences, and information about installed hardware and software. Microsoft includes a registry editor called `regedit.exe`, but recommends that mere users not touch it. If you are instructed to make changes to the registry by a support technician, be sure to make a backup of the file before you make changes to it.

resolution A measure of the sharpness or granularity of an image or monitor, usually expressed as a number of horizontal pixels multiplied by a number of vertical pixels.

RF interference Most electrical devices produce high frequency radio signals that can interfere with other devices, from your monitor to your neighbor's garage door opener. PC designers seek to shield cases so that RF does not escape.

RGB The red-green-blue specification describes one way in which colors are displayed on a monitor. This is an additive scheme; if all three colors are displayed at full intensity, the screen is white. *CMYK* (cyan, magenta, yellow, black) is a subtractive technology used in many color printers, which mixes colors to produce other hues.

ribbon cable A flat multiconductor cable used primarily under the covers of the computer to connect peripheral devices, such as disk drives to controllers.

RISC Reduced Instruction Set Computing. A design for microprocessor logic that concentrates on rapid and efficient processing of a relatively small and simple set of instructions that can be executed in a minimum number of instruction cycles. See also *CISC*.

RLL Run Length Limited. This is a method of encoding data on hard disk surfaces that can record more data in the same amount of space than MFM can record. It is similar to MFM, but does not require clock bits. Instead, it uses a rule about the number of consecutive zeroes written in any data stream. IBM developed the method for use in mainframes. It is as reliable as MFM for recording data, but the recording surface must be very good. If the hard disk is not RLL-certified by the manufacturer of the drive, don't use an RLL controller on the drive. See also *ESDI, MFM,* and *SCSI*.

ROM Read Only Memory. Recorded once, at the factory, ROM is the ideal way to hold instructions that should never change, such as the instructions your computer requires to access the disk drive. See also *BIOS* and *RAM*.

ROM address The memory address location within a ROM chip, often used to mean the first address. When a computer boots, its BIOS ROM searches for any additional ROM chips in its system, reading the setup information from each ROM chip that it finds. A typical ROM is 8K, 16K, or 32K long. Therefore, it uses an 8K, 16K, or 32K block of memory addresses, beginning at the ROM address (the starting address). No two ROMs can be at the same starting address, and their blocks of memory cannot overlap. ROMs are on your video card (EGA and above), hard drive controller and/or SCSI host adapter, and many other expansion cards. No ROMs exist for parallel or serial ports, game ports, or ordinary floppy controllers because the computer already knows how to use these simple devices; the instructions are stored in the computer's BIOS ROM.

ROM BIOS See *BIOS*.

ROM shadow A technique — used in systems with CPUs that can virtualize memory addresses — in which BIOS code is copied from slower ROM to faster RAM at boot. The RAM addresses are virtualized to impersonate the ROM addresses, and the BIOS is then executed from RAM.

router A device that connects network hubs together. A valuable modern router includes a firewall to prevent unwanted intrusion by hackers.

RS-232C One recommended standard set by the electronics industry for serial data transmission. See *COM port*.

sampling rate The number of times per second a sound card grabs a sample of an analog sound in order to create a digitized version or image of the sound. The higher the sampling rate, the better the sound.

scanner A device that converts printed or written text or illustrations into a digital file that can be manipulated by the computer. A modern *optical character recognition* application can convert text in the digital image into characters than can be worked with by a word processor.

SCSI Small Computer System Interface. An intelligent interface that exchanges data. A 50-pin connector is used in SCSI devices. Up to seven devices, including the SCSI controller itself, can be attached to the SCSI bus via a single SCSI connection. The interface lets the drive manufacturer use any encoding scheme it chooses. However, SCSI is not supported in a standard way by the BIOS in PCs, often posing interesting installation problems.

SDRAM Synchronous Dynamic Random Access Memory. An advanced form of dynamic RAM memory that can be synchronized with the processor's clock, eliminating wait states and latency. Unlike DRAM, SDRAM uses flowing current instead of a stored charge, eliminating the need for continual refreshing. SDRAM permits up to 1.1GBps data transfer while DDR SDRAM (Double Data Rate SDRAM) doubles the rate to 2.1GB/sec.

secondary The second ATA/IDE channel of a computer. Each channel supports a chain of one or two devices, configured as master and slave. See also *primary*.

sector The smallest unit of storage that can be allocated by a hard disk — usually 512 bytes.

seek time The length of time for a hard disk head to find a track, expressed in milliseconds (ms). Although fast seek times are often touted as an indication of a fast hard disk, seek time alone is rather useless as an expression of hard disk speed. Transfer rate is more meaningful. See also *settle time*.

segment An element of the processor's addressing scheme. A segment is a unit of contiguous, position-independent space.

serial Connector on a computer to which a serial device is attached. Serial devices include modems, mice, and certain printers.

Serial ATA (SATA) An emerging standard for interfacing computers to storage devices such as hard drives and DVD drives. SATA version 1 is capable of 1.5 Gbps, however the standard is scalable to 2x (3 Gbps) and 4x (6 Gbps). Current ATA interfaces transfer data in parallel, requiring wide, flat cables. SATA will use thinner cables and smaller connectors, which ultimately may improve air circulation inside computer cases and potentially allow the use of smaller cases.

serial communications The transmission of information between devices one bit at a time over a single line. Serial communications can be synchronous (controlled by a clock or timing device) or asynchronous (managed by control signals that accompany the information). For modern machines, nearly all serial communication is asynchronous.

server A computer or other device that manages a component of a network. A *file server* holds shared files; a *print server* manages printers, and a *network server* controls communication functions of the network.

settle time A measurement of how long it takes the heads to begin reading the hard disk once the specified track is found. See also *seek time*.

setup A program used to store hardware configuration information in the CMOS chip of a modern machine.

SGRAM Synchronous Graphics RAM. A variant of SDRAM optimized for video processing. SGRAM is single-ported, so the processor cannot write to memory while an image is being refreshed.

signal-to-noise ratio The relationship of a meaningful audio or video signal to background noise or interference; the greater the difference (the higher the ratio) the better the quality of the resulting output.

SIMM Single Inline Memory Modules are units that can hold a group of individual memory chips — typically eight or nine — in a single unit that plugs into a socket. A common current design is the 72-pin SIMM, which can hold from 1 to 64MB, delivered in a single 32-bit data path.

single user An operating system that allows only one user to use the computer at a time.

single user, multitask A version of single user (see preceding glossary definition) that allows only one user to perform multiple tasks simultaneously. Examples include OS/2, Windows 3.1, and VM/386.

single user, single task A version of single user that allows only one user at a time to do one task at a time. DOS is an example.

SIP Single Inline Package. A design for holding an electronic component in which all connectors emerge from one side of the package. See also *DIP*.

Smart Media A form of flash memory used in digital cameras and audio devices; it appears to the operating system as if it were a hard drive. Smart Media was first known as *SSFDC (solid state floppy disk card)*. Smart Media cards can be installed in readers attached to PCs for the download of information and can also be mounted in special PC Cards for the same purpose. See also *CompactFlash*.

software interrupt A request for service generated by a program.

South Bridge An I/O controller hub that is part of a modern PC's chipset. The processor bus connects through the PCI bus to the south bridge, which controls the IDE bus that transports data to and from storage devices. Other elements of the south bridge include the USB serial subsystem, a bridge from PCI to the older ISA bus still used by some devices, the keyboard/mouse controller, power management, and various other features, including support for plug-and-play technology. See also *North Bridge*.

SRAM Static Random Access Memory chips that do not require refresh as long as they are powered. They are quick, but expensive, and, therefore, are usually not made to hold as much information as a DRAM chip. SRAMs are often used as cache memory.

stack A scratch pad for the microprocessor. When the microprocessor is interrupted in the middle of a task by a more urgent task, it saves notes to itself about the contents of registers, and so on. These notes are essential if the microprocessor is to resume the first task where it left off.

start/stop bits Signaling bits that are part of a communications frame, attached to the beginning and end of a character before it is transmitted by a modem.

state Condition, as in On-Off, High-Low, or Zero-One. In computers, this means the particular way that all memory locations, registers, and logic gates are set. State is also used casually to indicate the particular condition and status of the computer.

step rate On a floppy disk drive, the amount of time required for the read/write head to move from one track to another.

ST412/ST506 The names of the original hard drives in microcomputers. The drives are no longer made, but the interface Seagate developed for them is still used. This interface is used on inexpensive XT and AT drives and controllers. See also MFM and RLL.

surface mount A circuit-board design in which chips are directly attached to the board instead of being soldered in pin holes or attached through sockets. In theory, a surface mount design is less susceptible to problems caused by bad connections. However, a failed chip often requires replacement of the entire circuit board.

surge protector A device to protect electrical components from damage caused by overvoltage (surges). A more sophisticated *uninterruptible power supply (UPS)* also protects against undervoltage (brownouts) and a short power outage.

SVGA (Super VGA) The most common graphics standard for modern machines, an enhancement of *VGA*.

system The memory in the computer that DOS (or the chosen operating system) can use for the OS, applications, and data. On most DOS computers, this is also called conventional memory, and it has a maximum memory of 640K. DOS 5.0 and later versions, and DR DOS 6.0 can also use high memory (the first 64K of extended memory), so these operating systems have an effective system memory of 704K.

system boot parameters Many BIOS chips permit the user to specify a number of options at boot. These include bus speed, whether the Num Lock function is on or off, and boot sequence, which establishes whether the PC boots from the A: or B: floppy drive, or from the C: drive.

system files The hidden files necessary to boot the operating system.

SYSTEM.INI A Windows file that contains information about the hardware environment. See *WIN.INI*.

tape drive A data storage device that records data on a moving tape, like an audio tape recorder in concept. Tape drives are used for data backup.

target A SCSI device — including both peripherals and the SCSI host adapter — that performs an operation requested by an initiator.

task The job (usually an application program) that the computer does. A task is not the same as what the computer is doing. One person can simultaneously perform multiple tasks on a single computer. See *multitasking*.

terabyte A trillion bytes; for RAM, 1,024 gigabytes — or more precisely, 1,099,511,627,776 bytes. Abbreviated as TB.

termination The first and last device on a SCSI bus must have a resistor pack that indicates it is the end of the line.

texels Pixels with a third layer of information defining the pixel's texture.

text mode A display mode in which the adapter converts ASCII character data directly into display information.

timeout The operating system or BIOS is usually instructed to end a process when a predetermined amount of time passes without response.

token ring A configuration for a network that places each device at a point on a continuous circle. The network carries tokens — special sequences of bits — and devices attach blocks of data to them for a circuit around the circle to the intended recipient.

tower An upright case for a computer.

tpi Tracks per inch, a measurement of the *track density* of recorded data on a rotating media such as a hard disk drive or CD.

track A magnetic ring of information on a disk drive, somewhat like a groove on an old vinyl record. On a sequential data storage device, such as a tape drive, tracks run parallel to the edge of the medium. See also *sector*.

track density See *tpi*.

track skew factor When a read/write head reaches the end of a track, and if information is sequential from one track to the next, the head must move to the next track in order to continue. If the next track starts at the sector where the preceding track ends, the disk drive must wait until the disk nearly completes spinning around before it can begin reading new information. Instead, most disk drives skew the starting point of each track

from the other track by a few sectors so that information can be read and written in a nearly continuous stream.

track-to-track access time How long it takes for the heads of a drive to move from one track to another. This number determines much of the speed with which data is read from a drive.

transfer rate The amount of data, measured in bytes per second, that a computer can read from or write to a device, such as a hard disk, a modem, or a network.

transient response In a power supply, this is the time needed for the output voltage to return to the normal range following a major change load. The faster the transient response the lower the risk of read/write errors during access.

true color A term applied to display adapters or monitors capable of displaying 24-bit color, which is about 16.8 million (technically, 16,777,216) colors.

TSR Terminate and Stay Resident. A DOS program that pops back into use when a hot key sequence is pressed. Sidekick is an example. TSRs sometimes present problems when they clash with each other or programs loaded after them, and they cause symptoms that you might think are hardware related.

TWAIN An industry interface that works between image-editing software and scanners or other capture devices. The acronym stands for Technology Without An Interesting Name.

twisted pair A cabling design that uses two thin unshielded wires twisted around each other to somewhat reduce interference. Twisted pair cables are used for telephones and basic Ethernet local area networks. More sophisticated systems use coaxial or fiber optic cables, which are more expensive and difficult to install.

UART The Universal Asynchronous Receiver Transmitter chip set manages communications through a serial port. The original PC used an 8250A UART, which proved incapable of handling high-speed data transfer. Modern machines use the 16550 UART. Many older machines can be upgraded to use the new chip either through a direct swap of chips or by disabling the existing serial port and installing a new serial card in the expansion bus.

Ultra ATA See *ATA/33, ATA/66, ATA/100, and ATA/133.*

Ultra DMA See *ATA/33, ATA/66, ATA/100, and ATA/133.*

UMA The Upper Memory Area is PC memory with addresses between 640K and 1,024K (1MB).

UMB Upper Memory Blocks are ranges of memory located within the UMA.

uninterruptible power supply A device that combines a surge protector, a large battery, and electronic circuitry to shield a PC or other system from surges, undervoltages, and short power outages.

Unix An operating system developed by AT&T in the early 1970s to run its computerized phone switching system on PDP-11s. This operating system is known for low overhead with easy connecting of different tasks. Unlike DOS, Unix is a true multiuser, multitasking system.

upper memory Memory located between 640K and 1,024K (1MB). Divided into blocks (upper memory blocks), modern machines can use upper memory for the system BIOS, video BIOS, video memory, shadowing, adapter ROM, additional device drivers, and TSRs. It is sometimes also called reserved memory or high DOS memory. This usage disappeared when programmers discovered they could address the first 64K of extended memory and Microsoft created a driver called HIMEM.SYS.

URL (Uniform Resource Locator) The global address system for files and resources attached to the World Wide Web, otherwise known as the Internet.

USRT Universal Synchronous Receiver-Transmitter. A synchronous equivalent of the UART, it is only used on PCs that have been adapted for use in synchronous communication applications.

VBI vertical blanking interval A short piece of a video field originally intended to account for the time an old television required to return the electron beam from the lower right corner to the upper right to trace a new frame. Today, the VBI is used to carry information including frame numbers and captions.

VGA Video Graphics Array. An advanced analog display standard capable of displaying as many as 256K colors at 640-×-480-pixel resolution. The Super VGA standard has superseded it in the market.

virtual address An alias address used to reference memory locations. In shadowing, it enables calls to a particular BIOS address to instead call the shadowed copy that resides in faster RAM at a different physical address. When using expanded memory, the memory management unit translates the virtual address to a physical address.

virtual memory A means to enable a system to work with a larger memory than it is permitted to use or with a memory that is larger than the memory that actually exists. Paged memory is one type of virtual memory. See *EMS.*

virtual mode A special protected mode of the 80386 and later CPUs that enables them to run multiple virtual real-mode segments. This is the mode Windows 3.1 uses for DOS windows.

virus A piece of code that corrupts your PC without your permission or knowledge.

VL-bus The VL-bus or VESA local bus is a high-speed data connection between the CPU and peripheral devices, developed by the Video Electronics Standards Association. It has been largely replaced in modern machines by the PCI bus.

voltage spike An electrical geyser.

voltage surge A big electrical wave.

VRAM A special type of display adapter memory that enables simultaneous read and write operations.

Vx Modem communications standard.

wait state A pause programmed into the operations of a micro-processor so that the CPU will wait for memory to catch up with it. The faster the memory, the fewer wait states necessary.

warm boot Restarting a computer without turning off the power or pressing the hardware reset button; that is, using the Ctrl + Alt + Delete combination. See also *cold boot*.

Weitek processor A non-Intel math coprocessor that can be used with some systems by some applications.

WIN.INI A file containing configuration information about Windows applications and the user environment, such as fonts, colors, and general appearance. Used in versions through Windows 3.1.

word Depending on the processor design, the standard size for a chunk of data manipulated by the CPU. For 16-bit computers, a word is made up of two bytes. For 32-bit computers, a word is made up of four bytes.

WORM drive Write Once, Read Many times. A data storage device that can be written to once and then read from as needed; the definition is now part of CD-R.

write precompensation As the head on a hard disk starts to write on the smaller inner tracks, data errors can occur if the data is recorded exactly as it was on the larger, outer tracks. Write precompensation boosts write current on the innermost tracks, providing clean, clear data storage.

Xenix A version of Unix developed for microcomputers that is not commonly used today.

XMS Extended Memory Specification. See *EMS*.

XT class A relic PC based on the 8088 or 8086 processor.

yottabyte 1,000,000,000,000,000,000,000,000 bytes, or 1,024 zetta-bytes. Abbreviated as YB.

z-buffering Z-buffering is used by advanced graphics cards to speed up the display of 3-D scenes. Z-buffering keeps track of each pixel's depth so that the graphics card can replace the color of that pixel if a 3-D object of less depth moves into that screen position. Hidden surface removal also helps speed up 3-D scenes because it minimizes the object pixels whose depths must be compared for z-buffering.

Zettabyte 1,000,000,000,000,000,000,000 bytes, or 1,024 exabytes. Abbreviated as ZB.

ZIF socket A Zero Insertion Force socket is used on many modern motherboards to enable easy removal and replacement of certain computer chips, including the CPU.

Zip drive A popular design for a large-capacity removable storage device, holding 100 or 250MB on a platter about the size of a floppy disk.

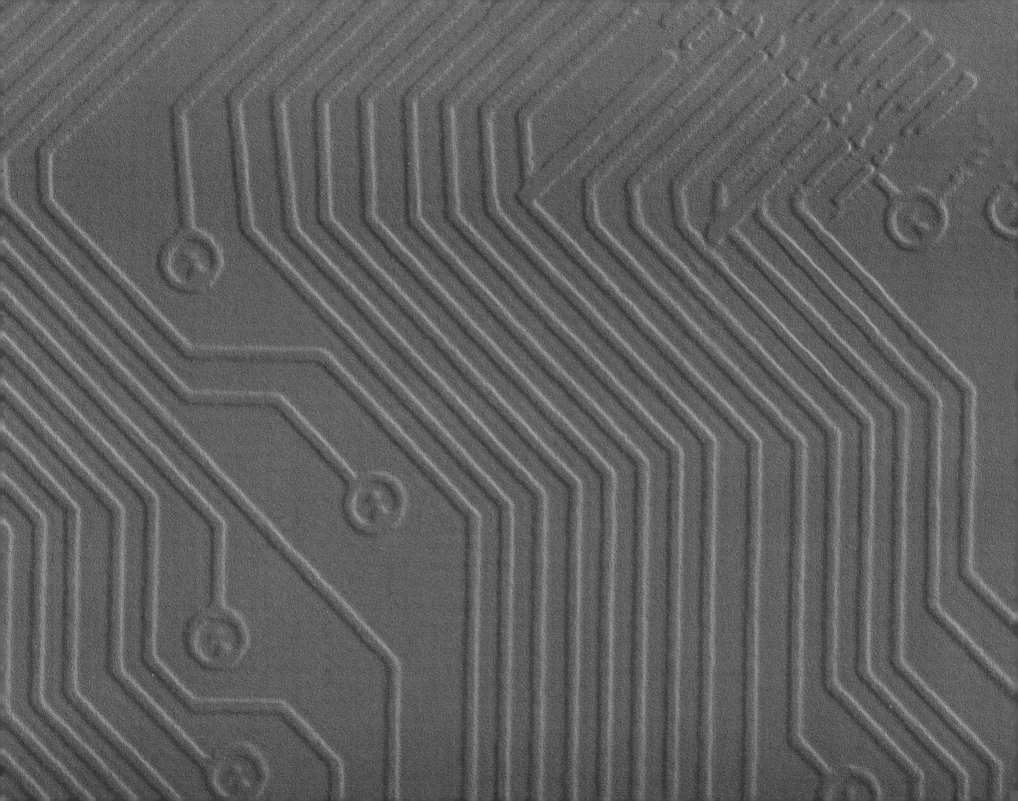

Index

NUMERICS

A

Continued

Continued

Continued

CPUs *(continued)*
determining, 17–18
dinosaur, 74–77, 124
functioning of, 23–24
high-speed, 57
installing, 143
instructions, 23, 24
Intel, 15–16, 26–40, 45–46, 53–60
list of, 124
location of, 12
measures, 24–26
mobile, 35–38
modern, 124
non-Intel, 16–17, 60–67
OverDrive, 77–79
P-Rating Specification, 61
processor clock speed, 25–26
registers, 23
senior citizen, 67–74, 124
sequence example, 23–24
sockets and slots, 51–53
testing, 139
CRT (cathode ray tube), 383
Crusoe processor, 59–60
CyberPro Quad I/O, 414–415
cyclic redundancy checking, 261
Cyrix processors
6x86, 77
486SL, 75
defined, 17, 60
MII chip, 66

D

daisywheel printers, 455
data bus, 24–25
data numbering scheme, 262
data protection strategy, 515–518
data recovery utilities, 526–527
dataflow analysis, 69
daughtercards, 365
DDR SDRAM (Double Data Rate SDRAM)
defined, 213, 223
DIMMs, 223
memory bus, 223
defragmenting utilities, 528–529
degaussing coil, 384
Device Driver Roll Back utility, 538
device drivers
disabling, 536
missing, 544–545
verification, 576
virtual, 235–236
Device Manager
accessing, 532, 533
defined, 532
expanding, 533, 534
functions, 532
General tab, 533, 535
Resources tab, 535
troubleshooting and, 631
devices. *See also specific devices*
conflicts, 532, 533

Continued

Continued

Continued

Continued

S

Continued

Continued